Irish Literature 1750–1900

Blackwell Anthologies
Editorial Advisers

Rosemary Ashton, University of London; Gillian Beer, University of Cambridge; Gordon Campbell, University of Leicester; Terry Castle, Stanford University; Margaret Ann Doody, Vanderbilt University; Richard Gray, University of Essex; Joseph Harris, Harvard University; Karen L. Kilcup, University of North Carolina, Greensboro; Jerome J. McGann, University of Virginia; David Norbrook, University of Oxford; Tom Paulin, University of Oxford; Michael Payne, Bucknell University; Elaine Showalter, Princeton University; John Sutherland, University of London.

Blackwell Anthologies are a series of extensive and comprehensive volumes designed to address the numerous issues raised by recent debates regarding the literary canon, value, text, context, gender, genre, and period. While providing the reader with key canonical writings in their entirety, the series is also ambitious in its coverage of hitherto marginalized texts, and flexible in the overall variety of its approaches to periods and movements. Each volume has been thoroughly researched to meet the current needs of teachers and students.

Old and Middle English c.890–c.1400:
An Anthology. Second edition
edited by Elaine Treharne

Medieval Drama: An Anthology
edited by Greg Walker

Chaucer to Spenser: An Anthology of English
Writing 1375–1575
edited by Derek Pearsall

Renaissance Drama: An Anthology of
Plays and Entertainments.
Second edition
edited by Arthur F. Kinney

Renaissance Literature: An Anthology
edited by Michael Payne and John Hunter

Restoration Drama: An Anthology
edited by David Womersley

British Literature 1640–1789: An Anthology.
Third edition
edited by Robert DeMaria, Jr.

Romanticism: An Anthology. Third edition
edited by Duncan Wu

Irish Literature 1750–1900: An Anthology
edited by Julia M. Wright

Children's Literature: An Anthology
1801–1902
edited by Peter Hunt

Victorian Women Poets: An Anthology
edited by Angela Leighton and Margaret Reynolds

Modernism: An Anthology
edited by Lawrence Rainey

American Gothic: An Anthology 1787–1916
edited by Charles L. Crow

The Literatures of Colonial America:
An Anthology
edited by Susan Castillo and Ivy T. Schweitzer

Postcolonial Discourses: An Anthology
edited by Gregory Castle

Nineteenth-century American Women Writers:
An Anthology
edited by Karen L. Kilcup

Nineteenth-century American Women Poets:
An Anthology
edited by Paula Bernat Bennett

Native American Women's Writing:
An Anthology of Works c.1800–1924
edited by Karen L. Kilcup

Irish Literature
1750–1900

AN ANTHOLOGY

EDITED BY JULIA M. WRIGHT

Blackwell
Publishing

Editorial material and organization © 2008 by Blackwell Publishing Ltd

BLACKWELL PUBLISHING
350 Main Street, Malden, MA 02148-5020, USA
9600 Garsington Road, Oxford OX4 2DQ, UK
550 Swanston Street, Carlton, Victoria 3053, Australia

First published 2008 by Blackwell Publishing Ltd

1   2008

Library of Congress Cataloging-in-Publication Data

Irish literature, 1750–1900 : an anthology / edited by Julia M. Wright.
    p. cm.—(Blackwell anthologies)
Includes bibliographical references and index.
ISBN 978-1-4051-4519-0 (hardcover : alk. paper)—ISBN 978-1-4051-4520-6 (pbk. : alk. paper)
1. English literature—Irish authors. 2. English literature—19th century. 3. English literature—18th century.
    4. Ireland—Literary collections. I. Wright, Julia M.

PR8843.I75 2008
820.8'09417—dc22
2007019833

A catalogue record for this title is available from the British Library.

Set in 10.5/12pt DanteMT
by SPi Publisher Services, Pondicherry, India

For further information on
Blackwell Publishing, visit our website at
www.blackwellpublishing.com

Contents

Selected Contents by Theme and Genre

Diaspora, Exile, Migration

The Gothic and the Supernatural

Outlaws, Prisoners, and Slaves

Poetry of Place: Landscape, Famine, Empire

Pre-colonial Ireland: Heroes, Saints, and Bards

Religion and Faith

Satire, Parody, and Social Critique

Translations from Irish

United Irishmen Uprising (1798) and the Act of Union (1800)

Introduction

The study of Irish literature in English from 1750 to 1900 is a relatively new field. There has always been some attention to this era. But, over the past thirty years or so, dozens of scholars working on the recovery and critical analysis of nearly forgotten authors have collectively made it an academic field in the best sense of the term.[1] Once a blank space on the map of Irish literary history, except for the occasional aside on James Joyce's references to Thomas Moore or W. B. Yeats's interest in William Allingham, this body of literature is now taking canonical shape and is emerging as a major area of enquiry in Irish studies and literary scholarship. Modern editions of novels by Frances Sheridan, Maria Edgeworth, Sydney Owenson (Lady Morgan), J. Sheridan LeFanu, and Bram Stoker have been published in recent years, supplementing reprint editions of John and Michael Banim, William Carleton, and others. Some novels from this era have remained in print for decades – particularly the gothic canon of Charles Robert Maturin's *Melmoth the Wanderer* (1820), Oscar Wilde's *Picture of Dorian Gray* (1891), and Bram Stoker's *Dracula* (1897) – but the recovery of realist and sentimental novels, as well as national tales, has led to an understanding of the Irish novel that goes beyond the remarkable success of the gothic. Poetry, short fiction, and drama, however, have been slow to follow novels into print,[2] even though they are not only worthy in their own right but also do much to contextualize Irish fiction.[3] The *Field Day Anthology of Irish Writing* created a watershed with its comprehensive survey of Irish writing from the seventh century onward, particularly with the two new supplementary volumes to the original three-volume set, but the breadth of its mandate necessitated slight selections from even significant authors. Further research, moreover, continues to bring more authors to light.[4] Scholars are thus still in the process of responding to the situation summed up by Margaret

Notes

[1] For much of this scholarship, see Further Reading listed in each section of the anthology, and the supplementary Selected Further Reading in the Bibliography.

[2] There was, however, a brief resurgence in pre-1900 Irish drama in the early years of this recovery work. See, for instance, *The Dolmen Boucicault*, ed. David Krause (Dublin: Dolmen Press, 1964); *The Plays of Frances Sheridan*, ed. Robert Hogan and Jerry C. Beasley (Newark: University of Delaware Press, 1984); and the edition of Thomas Sheridan's *Captain O'Blunder* in *Ten English Farces*, ed. Leo Hughes and A. H. Scouten (New York: University of Texas Press, 1970). R. B. Sheridan has, of course, remained in print.

[3] Morgan's satirical edge, for instance, is much less surprising in a woman writer if she is placed in a genealogy of eighteenth-century Irish women satirists such as Elizabeth Ryves and Mary O'Brien.

[4] Authors in this anthology whose texts do not appear in *Field Day* include John Leslie, John Corry, and Julia Kavanagh; other authors in *Field Day* represented by a single text or brief excerpt, but more substantively represented here, include Ryves and Denis Florence MacCarthy. See *The Field Day Anthology of Irish Writing*, 3 vols., gen. ed. Seamus Deane (Derry: Field Day, 1991); and *The Field Day Anthology of Irish Writing*, vols. 4–5, ed. Angela Bourke, Siobhán Kilfeather, Maria Luddy, et al. (Cork: Cork University Press, 2002).

Kelleher and Philip O'Leary: "The *Field Day Anthology* has created the anomalous situation in which Ireland now has a chronologically organised literary canon but no comprehensive literary history in light of which to think about it."[5]

This anthology contributes to a more detailed view of the writing from 1750 to 1900 as a body of literature that is both influential, in Ireland and abroad, and richly diverse in genre, mode, subject, and perspective. Circulating within a newly emergent transatlantic sphere and European print cultures, Irish literature participates in pan-English developments in literary form and convention, from innovations in versification to the rise of the gothic. Moreover, this larger geographical circulation of print involves Irish literature of this period in necessarily international discussions of empire, slavery, and migration, in addition to related domestic debates about national identity, politics, and the diasporic experience. Moreover, the rise in literacy across the West in this era contributes to an increasing interplay between "popular" and "high" culture.

Irish Literature and Irishness

British literature does not always represent Britain, and Irish literature does not always represent Ireland. This might seem an obvious statement, but it is an important starting-point for engaging the full range of Irish literature from 1750 to 1900. The cultural nationalism of the Gaelic Revival[6] and the attendant nationalist movements of the late nineteenth and early twentieth centuries stressed the "Irishness" of Irish literature, and Irish Modernist texts are typically set in Ireland. But such national themes are part of a specific nationalist project that is firmly located in a particular historical moment, worthy of analysis but proposing a limiting view of Irish literature. Indeed, to argue that Irish literature must thematize Ireland in some way is to ask of Irish literature what is not asked of other significant national literatures in English, such as American or British literatures. Moreover, there is a price to accepting this view of Irish literary history. Nineteenth-century British claims to cultural superiority, as David Lloyd has shown, are reflected in the idea of British literature as universal in its capacity to speak to a fundamental human condition that transcends particulars such as nationality.[7] Practically speaking, this has meant that Irish writers who do not obviously display "Irishness" can be read as sufficiently "universal" to be transmuted into "British" writers, and absorbed into British anthologies over the past century. This, along with cultural nationalism, has historically led to an implicit pattern of identification that can be broadly summed up as follows: good Irish literature is Irish when it is about Ireland and British when it is not. Such identifications export Irish cultural capital, at no charge, to Britain, and bolster the assumption that "minor" literature is bound by the particularities of nation but British literature is universal.[8] It is one of the aims of this anthology to offer a more inclusive Irish canon, one that pays due attention to the considerable importance of Ireland as setting and theme, while recognizing that Irish literature is

Notes

[5] Margaret Kelleher and Philip O'Leary, "Introduction," *The Cambridge History of Irish Literature* (Cambridge: Cambridge University Press, 2006), 2: 1.

[6] The Gaelic Revival is variously defined, temporally speaking. It is not unusual to confine it to the same period as the Irish Literary Renaissance, c.1880–1920, while some studies have pushed it back to 1840 (thus making it possible to include James Clarence Mangan and early Samuel Ferguson). Seamus Deane argues, more broadly, for a "Celtic Revival" from 1780 to 1880 that builds upon the work of

Scottish and Welsh Celtic scholars in the mid-1700s, and begins with Joseph Cooper Walker and Charlotte Brooke. See Seamus Deane, *A Short History of Irish Literature* (Notre Dame, IN: University of Notre Dame Press, 1986).

[7] See David Lloyd, *Nationalism and Minor Literature: James Clarence Mangan and the Emergence of Irish Cultural Nationalism* (Berkeley, CA: University of California Press, 1987), esp. the Introduction.

[8] See ibid., Introduction.

diverse in subject and that some of the best Irish literature is either not obviously, or not at all, about Ireland.

This anthology does not, therefore, posit some essential Irishness that unites Irish literature, as in a cultural nationalism that veers toward the ethnographic. An article in *Blackwood's* reveals the limits of such views, creating a close correlation between people and literature that virtually negates the possibility of debate, diversity, or individuality:

> It would appear, that the pleasure we receive from making ourselves acquainted with the literature of a people, and more especially with their literature of imagination, is intimately connected with an impression, that in their literature we see the picture of their minds . . . Every one who has applied himself with interest to the theory of a nation's literature . . . will most probably remember, that in the works he read, there seemed opening up to him, not the mind of a new author, but the mind of another nation.[9]

Cultural nationalism informs Modernist nationalist assessments of Irish literature and thus the early formation of the Irish literary canon. Katharine Tynan and Yeats, for instance, arrive at different conclusions about whether Jonathan Swift was "Irish," but they both single out Moore as if he only wrote the *Irish Melodies* (1807–34), and they complain, with a whiff of jealousy, that Moore's *Melodies* governs the popular taste, while their elder contemporary, Lady Jane Wilde, praises Moore's larger corpus at length.[10] More recently, politics has, in a sense, become the new Irishness, at least for the nineteenth century. As James H. Murphy notes in his essay on the resurgence of interest in Irish literature of this period, "the focus of all of this interest is social and cultural and not directly literary in an aesthetic sense. But, then, this was always true of nineteenth-century Irish literature, where politics and history lie so close to the surface of the ostensibly artistic."[11] But it is also arguable that current academic interests in coloniality, nationalism, gender, and class have sought out Irish literature from before 1900 that is compatible with those interests. This generative confluence of theoretical interests and literary themes has fueled the recovery of this body of literature as well as yielded a great deal of important scholarship, but it has also obscured, or again left to British literature scholarship, other compelling works of Irish literature.

Other notions of the coherence of Irish literature before 1900 are required if Irish studies is to grasp the diversity of literary trends within Irish letters. Instead of continuity of subject, for instance, it is possible to consider continuities of literary tradition. To take one example: for much of the twentieth century, Oliver Goldsmith's nationality was either quickly passed over or ignored. One 1963 anthology of "the major English and Scottish poets" includes Goldsmith as "an Anglo-Irish curiosity among Englishmen," focusing on his writing while in England.[12] However, his status as an Irish writer is not simply a matter of his place of birth, but also rooted in the recognition of him as an Irish writer in his lifetime and after by other Irish writers. Goldsmith is invoked, for instance, by two nationalist poets from the north of Ireland: James Orr uses Goldsmith's *Deserted Village* (1770) as the epigraph to a lengthy Ulster Scots poem about Irish emigration, "The Passengers" (1804), and John Corry uses the title of Goldsmith's *Citizen of the World* (1762) as his pseudonym for the British publication of his nationalist epic about pre-colonial Ireland, *The Patriot* (1797). Goldsmith's influence can also be traced more broadly from

Notes

[9] Anon., "Of a National Character in Literature," *Blackwood's* 3 (1818): 707.

[10] See excerpts from Tynan and Yeats and Wilde's "Thomas Moore" (1891) included below.

[11] James H. Murphy, "Canonicity: The Literature of Nineteenth-century Ireland," *New Hibernia Review* 7 (2003): 49.

[12] *English Poetry of the Mid and Late Eighteenth Century*, ed. Ricardo Quintana and Alvin Whitley (New York: Knopf, 1963), v: 187.

Morgan's *The Wild Irish Girl* (1806) to the poetry of Thomas Dermody and Moore. Irish literature is thus defined for the purposes of this anthology not simply in terms of an author's place of birth or residence, or compliance with the mandate of cultural nationalism that writers express their nationality in their writing, although all of the writers included here meet the first requirement and many meet the second in at least some of their literary works. It is also one of the key criteria for this anthology that writers participate in literary traditions that impacted Irish print culture in this era.

An emphasis on literary traditions allows us to trace, in addition to overtly political texts, a strong satiric tradition for the generations after Swift, a rich history of translation which includes Irish-language translation but also speaks to the cosmopolitanism of Irish print culture and education, and myriad other strata of a complex literary culture. It also necessitates some flexibility in the traditional focus of anthologies on "major authors" to allow attention to the various collaborations, affiliations, and literary networks that inform many individual authors' work. Hence this anthology includes sections that focus on collaborative pairs – the Edgeworths, the Banims, the Kavanaghs – and collaborative publications, particularly the populist *Paddy's Resource* and *The Nation*. Key collaborative periodicals, from *The Northern Star* to the *Dublin University Magazine*, are given weight in the selections from individual authors.

In order to organize and make selections from this rich and diverse array of literary works, two organizing rubrics have been followed here, as reflected in the two tables of Contents. The first rubric is traditionally canonical, gathering together the work of the more influential writers of the period who worked in literary forms that can be anthologized as complete texts. The other is broadly thematic, but with due deference to both traditional literary subjects, such as genre, and more recent critical concerns with the political work of literature. The author-based rubric facilitates the study of leading writers in some depth, while the topical rubric sketches out some of the ways in which we can start to understand Irish literature in English in terms of continuing threads of concern, convention, and debate.

Hence, this anthology makes selections from Irish literature (1750–1900) across an array of subjects and literary forms. There are some exceptions made for substantial selections from works too lengthy for an anthology of this size and scope, but in general this anthology is guided by the premise that full texts are more readable, teachable, and comprehensible. Irish-language literature is not included, except via translation, for reasons of space and focus. This anthology does not in any way suggest that English-language writing has priority within "Irish literature." Rather, the aim here is to explore in as much depth as possible in the allowable space the "school" of English-language writing in Ireland. Nevertheless, readers will find translations and the incorporation of non-English material throughout this anthology, from Ulster Scots verse to the use of Irish in works from Thomas Sheridan to Dion Boucicault. What sometimes appears as evidence of an "English" literary tradition in Ireland emerges, on closer inspection, less as evidence of submission to the dominance of English than as part of a polyglot erosion of English dominance and even of the idea of a monolingual nation. Irish, English, Ulster Scots, and continental European languages run through much of this body of literature, and the prevalence of translators among canonical Irish writers serves to emphasize what may be one key feature of Irish literature in this era – an engagement with a variety of different languages and literatures.

There are two notable exclusions in this anthology which must be acknowledged. First, as a broad generalization, eighteenth-century Irish writers were particularly successful as playwrights and nineteenth-century Irish writers as novelists. Because of the guiding principle of providing full texts of literary works, this rich tradition of drama- and fiction-writing can only be reflected here partially, in mostly short plays (with an exception made for Boucicault) and in a few tales selected from novelists' successful forays into short fiction. Fortunately, many of these plays and novels are available in modern editions and so will be readily available to readers. Secondly, although Irish Modernism and the latter part of the Gaelic Revival overlaps with the final years covered by this anthology, the literature traditionally associated with these movements is largely excluded here, in part because it is already so widely available and in part because the works selected from these decades were chosen to round out the threads and continuities from the preceding decades. Late Victorian literature rather than early Modernist literature is to the fore in the final pages of this anthology, and readers will find ample compensation for the absence of the Modernist canon in Dora Sigerson's stunning verse, Tynan's trenchant critique of women's mistreatment of women, and other valuable texts not otherwise readily available.

From 1750 to 1900: Historical Contexts

One of the central problems for Irish studies in this period is the cultural and economic interconnectedness, and geographical separateness, of Ireland and Britain.[13] Authors and texts often moved fluidly from one country to another, even as political thinkers sought to define individual identity in terms of nationality. Irish writers sent their work to be published in London, read British authors, and were materially (if not always willingly) governed by British subjects. Many lived in England for significant periods of time, and few did not travel abroad at some point. At the same time, Irish writers had considerable access to Irish-language material (both written and oral), though they did not always take advantage of it, as well as continental European and North American literatures. Variously positioned by writers within a transatlantic sphere (which allied Ireland especially with the post-revolutionary United States), the British Isles (Britain, Ireland, and the smaller islands of the archipelago), and Europe, Ireland's complicated political status is reflected in geography as well as the overlapping of different linguistic cultures.

Irish literature in this period is significantly, though not entirely, shaped by the history of colonialism in Ireland, a history that reaches back to Viking invasions and the arrival of Christian missionaries in the first millennium. Indeed, authors such as William Drennan, Corry, and MacCarthy refer to this longer history of political and cultural intervention in their verse.[14] English colonization, however, was at the forefront of political debate in the eighteenth and nineteenth centuries. The Norman-English first invaded Ireland in 1169–70, with the sanction of the Pope and Dermot MacMurrough, a deposed king of Leinster who was trying to regain his lands with English military support. One of the leaders of the invasion, Strongbow, was offered Aífe, the king of Leinster's daughter, as part of his reward and, on the reinstated king's death, became himself king of Leinster, the first Norman ruler in Ireland.[15] After Strongbow's death, the crown of Leinster passed to Henry II, king of England, who made his son, John, "Lord of Ireland." And so began English claims to rule Ireland.

Notes ——————————————————————————

[13] For a useful discussion of Ireland's geographical ambivalence, see Andrew Murphy, "Revising Criticism: Ireland and the British Model," in *British Identities and English Renaissance Literature*, ed. David J. Baker and Willy Maley (Cambridge: Cambridge University Press, 2002), 24–33. On the corollary difficulty of identifying an "England" or "Britain" in a complex British Isles, see Jim Smyth's succinct "Introduction: The British Problem," in *The Making of the United*

Kingdom, 1660–1800: State, Religion and Identity in Britain and Ireland (New York: Longman, 2001), xi–xiii.

[14] See Drennan's "Glendalloch" (1815), Corry's *The Patriot*, and MacCarthy's "A Walk by the Bay of Dublin" (1850) below.

[15] One of Daniel Maclise's best-known paintings deals with the subject; its longer title is often abbreviated as *The Marriage of Strongbow and Aoife* (1854).

Over the next century, the Norman-English expanded their territory, built fortifications, and mixed culturally and socially with their Irish neighbors. For much of this period, the core of English power was around Dublin, its perimeter marked by a fence that was called, in Norman-French, a "pale" – the origin of the phrase "beyond the pale" is in disparaging references to Irish territory beyond English control. By the middle of the thirteenth century, the English dominated nearly half of Ireland, with most of the north and parts of the south still under native Irish rule. Then the pendulum began to swing the other way and, in the fourteenth and early fifteenth centuries, the Irish reclaimed some of what they had lost. Still relying on feudal practices, English power was often driven by personality, local resources, and complex and rapidly shifting military alliances between aristocrats.[16] Irish resistance was similarly fragmented. Parts of Ireland not under English rule were still governed by a loose federation of kings with various alliances and sometimes divided by internecine conflict, while popular resistance was generally local and sporadic. From the 1560s to the 1580s, Elizabeth I of England, for instance, fought with local rulers in Tyrone, Cork, and Kerry, and Anglo-Irish relations were still largely understood feudally, in terms of aristocrats who both owed fealty to the queen and commanded those who lived under their protection. At a political level, the idea of a nation as a geographical space and a coherent people was not yet in place: politics and war were largely a matter of squabbling among the powerful, and sometimes the squabbling was within a nation rather than between nations. With the increasing centralization of state power and the religious motivation spurred by the Protestant Reformation in England in the 1540s, the conceptualization of nationhood in relation to politics began to shift. The colonization (or plantation) of Ulster in the late sixteenth century by Protestants, largely of Scottish extraction, was arguably the first organized, state-controlled attempt to dominate Ireland in modern ways – through local administration and the settlement of land rather than power struggles within a ruling class.

Oliver Cromwell expanded on this Ulster plantation with devastating consequences. Cromwell, spurred by a sense of religious mission, led an English parliament that had wrested power from the British monarchy and, in 1649, executed King Charles I. The same year, Cromwell invaded Ireland with a large military force in order to establish Protestantism coercively as the religion of the land and to colonize the country with English landholders. Bringing the entire island under English control, transferring estates from dispossessed Irish Catholic families to Protestants, massacring thousands of Irish men and women and shipping thousands more to the West Indies to serve the British empire as slave labor, Cromwell's invasion had an impact on Irish culture and politics that cannot be underestimated. From forcibly launching the Irish diaspora in North America to defining Protestant–Catholic relations in nearly genocidal terms, Cromwell's invasion did much to change Anglo-Irish relations from local tensions and a changing patchwork of negotiated arrangements to a conflict between nations – one people unified in their fight against another, with religion to authorize the claims of each side.

In 1660, the Cromwellian Protectorate was overthrown and Charles II returned to Britain as king, but his successor, his brother James II, a Catholic, was removed from the throne by James's daughter Mary and her husband, William of Orange. The Irish Battle of the Boyne (1690), in which the Catholic James II and his Irish allies fought against Protestants Mary II and William III, ended in defeat for the Irish Catholic side. Among its myriad consequences were the exile of the Irish military (thereafter known as the "Wild Geese"), the establishment of "Orange" as a symbol of militant Protestantism, and the

Notes ──

[16] Robert Kee, in *The Green Flag: A History of Irish Nationalism* (New York: Penguin, 1972), 9–10, notes that neither English nor Irish aristocrats were pursuing national interests but were primarily working to protect their individual power and autonomy.

institution of the Penal Statutes, a byzantine patchwork of laws that sought to limit or entirely prevent Catholic access to social and economic power. By the mid-eighteenth century, under the Penal Statutes (or Penal Laws), Catholics could not hold government office or vote, and had limited property rights and access to education. They could not take university degrees or send their children to Catholic schools in Ireland, creating a need for unofficial Catholic schools, known as "hedge schools" because they were often held outdoors. Wealthier families could send their children to the Continent for their education, but the only other option was renouncing Catholicism to enter a Protestant school.

This is not to say, however, that Ireland was divided neatly into Catholics and Protestants. Religion has not been systematically used to identify writers in this anthology primarily because an approach to literature based on the assumption of the priority of sectarianism in Ireland has limited use for this era of Irish literature. While the distinction between the Church of Ireland (the state-sanctioned branch of Protestantism, termed Anglicanism in England) and Catholicism was a key religious and community division, the line in practice was often blurred. Moreover, the increasing importance of Presbyterianism in the north and the presence of Methodists and Quakers throughout Ireland in this era complicate any simple grouping of Protestants versus Catholics. Like Catholics, the Presbyterians, Methodists, Quakers, and other Protestants outside the Church of Ireland were disenfranchised. For over half of the period covered by this anthology, they were subject to many of the same disabilities as Catholics. This shared disenfranchisement was mirrored in nationalist political movements. The United Irishmen of the 1790s had significant Presbyterian membership, and at the highest levels, but nevertheless included Catholic Emancipation in their political platform. Half a century later, Young Ireland sought a non-sectarian nationalist alternative to O'Connell's Catholic-centered movement to repeal the Act of Union (1800). There was considerable sectarian violence, organized through rural insurgency groups in particular, throughout the eighteenth and nineteenth centuries. But from roughly 1791 to 1848 there were also significant political movements which explicitly set aside sectarian differences. With Catholic Emancipation in 1829 and a general liberalizing of Britain's laws on religion, these few ties across sectarian divides began to dissolve, arguably contributing to the modern view of Ireland as divided by two religiously defined communities.

Apart from religious tensions and colonization, a more general imperial history helped to shape British–Irish relations and conflicts. The Seven Years' War (1756–63), in some regards the first world war, began with competition between the French and the British in North America, which led to the so-called French and Indian War that began in 1754. Involving a number of European nations and their North American settlements, the conflict was bloody, prolonged, and expensive. It decided British imperial supremacy in North America, particularly when British forces defeated the French on the Plains of Abraham in Quebec. But British debts incurred by the war created tensions in the American colonies where colonists were being asked to help pay for those debts through taxes. As tensions in these colonies rose, the British looked to pacify the French Catholic population just north of the colonies in what is now Canada. The Quebec Act of 1774 recognized religious rights for French Catholics in British North America, rights still denied to Catholics in Ireland – a point of contention from the 1770s until Catholic Emancipation in 1829.[17] In 1776, the American Revolution both offered a model for Irish

Notes _____

[17] For instance, Thomas Moore, in *Memoirs of Captain Rock* (1824), repeatedly praises the better treatment of Catholics in British North America.

anti-colonial agitation and led to some conciliatory measures by the British administration in Ireland. It also indirectly facilitated Irish nationalism. The Irish Volunteers, an informal militia, were first raised in 1778 to compensate for troops taken out of Ireland to fight the War of Independence with what would become the United States, and the Volunteers quickly became a focus for national pride, particularly among Protestants. In the early 1780s, nationalists pressed their advantage and argued for parliamentary reform. In the Irish parliament itself, in 1782, Henry Grattan gave a powerful speech contending that Ireland would go the way of the United States if not given some concessions. The period following is often called "Grattan's parliament" to mark a time when the Irish parliament had more autonomy than it would before or after.

The French Revolution began in 1789. As Jim Smyth vividly puts it, "The shock-wave known as the French Revolution transformed Irish and British politics by awakening radicals and reformers to new senses of change and possibility,"[18] and conservatives in both nations responded through a wide variety of repressive measures. In 1791, reacting partly to both the French Revolution and increased repression by the British, the Society of United Irishmen was founded. The United Irishmen, after some early heated debates, were explicitly pan-sectarian and counted among their number members of a variety of different religious denominations, including members of the Catholic Committee. Across the 1790s, United-men forged alliances with other nationalist groups and circulated political materials to the population at large through newspapers such as *The Northern Star* and single volumes such as *Paddy's Resource*, while reaching out at leadership levels to France and radical groups in Britain. The government reacted with prosecutions and arrests, including a sweep of United-men leaders in the weeks leading up to the United Irishmen Uprising of 1798. The Uprising took months to suppress, and required a significant number of British troops at a time when British resources were already stretched by the continuing military conflict with Napoleonic France. The Act of Union (1800) abolished the Irish parliament and brought Ireland under the direct rule of the British parliament. Ireland was given a block of seats in the parliament but, after years of argument that the British and Irish parliaments were both equal under the monarch, Union was a huge blow to nationalist aspirations and ended all semblance of Irish political autonomy. In 1803 there was a small, abortive uprising by Robert Emmett, the brother of a United-men leader. Emmett had more impact as a patriotic ideal in the wake of the defeat of the 1798 Uprising, especially because of a famous speech from the dock during his trial for treason. In his speech, knowing he would be executed, he asked that his grave be left unmarked until Ireland was free.

There is a lull in nationalist activity after 1803, but it was renewed, as it had been in the late 1770s, by continuing resistance to the Penal Statutes. This time, Catholic Emancipation was not simply part of a nationalist platform – it was the flag under which popular support rallied. The Catholic Association was founded in 1823 by Daniel O'Connell, a former member of the Catholic Committee affiliated with the United Irishmen. With rallies and protests, matters reached a head in 1828: O'Connell, a Catholic, was elected as a member of parliament for Clare, even though no Catholic could take a seat in parliament under existing legislation. This precipitated a crisis which led to the passage of Catholic Emancipation in 1829, and O'Connell became "The Liberator." Matters improved as well with the Irish Reform Bill (1832), the companion of the 1832 British Reform Bill, which extended the vote to more adult men of property. The "Tithe War" of the early 1830s preceded the settlement of another outstanding grievance: Catholics

Notes

[18] Smyth, *The Making of the United Kingdom*, 192.

were required to pay tithes (a portion of income) to the Church of Ireland, but tithes were reformed in various stages in the late 1830s to end this practice. In 1834, O'Connell brought the Repeal Movement to revoke the Act of Union to the British parliament. Repeal would dominate Irish nationalist politics for the next twenty years, spawning the Young Ireland movement as a secular alternative to O'Connell's Catholic movement: for instance, Thomas Davis, a leader of Young Ireland in the early 1840s, argued for non-denominational state education, while O'Connell argued for Catholic state education. Davis and Charles Gavan Duffy, along with others, founded *The Nation*, a weekly newspaper, in 1842 to argue for the nationalist cause on non-sectarian terms. R. F. Foster suggests that "The strength of this alternative tradition is indicated by the runaway success of the *Nation*: the readership was possibly 250,000 by 1843."[19] Throughout the mid-1840s, agitation for repeal continued on a variety of fronts: O'Connell in parliament, the Young Irelanders through *The Nation*, myriad others through speeches and print.

In 1845, the potato blight appeared and with it the worst famine of Irish history. Ireland had been no stranger to famines, dealing with a number in the eighteenth and early nineteenth centuries, and as recently as 1829–31.[20] The blight was not the sole cause. Ireland's agricultural output arguably over-emphasized a single crop, the potato; indus-trialization was slow to spread in comparison to Britain; and mismanagement through absentee landlords and other colonial practices also affected agricultural production and contributed materially to the first two causes listed here. And famine was simply part of European reality in this era when production barely met needs at the best of times; radical agitation in England in the late 1830s, for instance, was in part a response to food shortages. But the Irish Famine of 1845–9, reaching its nadir in 1847, was devastating. Estimates vary on the number of dead, and a lack of records makes any precise count impossible, but half a million is a minimum figure with some scholarly consensus.[21] Hundreds of thousands fled Ireland, beginning in earnest the Irish transatlantic diaspora, but hunger and crowded conditions on ships fueled disease and thousands more died in transit or soon after arriving in North America. Between 1841 and 1851 the population of Ireland dropped by about 20 percent, and it continued to decline throughout the nineteenth century, a decline from which the country has not yet recovered. The 2006 population of the island was still less than Ireland's population in 1851.

Potato blights occasionally recurred in the late nineteenth century but with less dramatic consequences as food importation and economic changes reduced their impact. Against this backdrop, the nationalist debate shifted more toward land issues. There had been agrarian insurgency for some time related to land rights – making famous such groups as the Whiteboys, the Ribbonmen, and the Rockites – but now land largely replaced religion as the central issue for nationalists. In 1850, the Irish Tenant League was founded and later a number of land leagues were established, including the Irish National Land League (1879) and the Ladies Land League (1881). Fenianism also arose across the Irish community at home and abroad, first as the Irish Republican Brotherhood in Ireland (1858) and the Fenian Brotherhood in the US (1859).[22] A secret society that attempted US invasions of Canada in 1866 and 1870 and an uprising in Ireland in 1867,

Notes

[19] R. F. Foster, *Modern Ireland, 1600–1972* (New York: Penguin, 1989), 311.

[20] Galen Broeker, *Rural Disorder and Police Reform in Ireland, 1812–1836* (Toronto: University of Toronto Press, 1970), 204; James H. Murphy, *Ireland: A Social, Cultural, and Literary History, 1791–1891* (Dublin: Four Courts Press, 2003), 97.

[21] On the difficulties of precisely dating and establishing mortality figures for the famine, see Christopher Morash, *Writing the Irish Famine* (Oxford: Clarendon Press, 1995), 1–3.

[22] The Fenians took their name from the Fianna, Irish warriors celebrated in the Fenian Cycle, a body of Irish-language texts about third-century Irish heroes.

the Fenian movement tended to view politics in more absolute terms than its predecessors: "its central motivation revolved around the view of England as a satanic power upon earth, a mystic commitment to Ireland, and a belief that an independent Irish republic, 'virtually' established in the hearts of men, possessed a superior moral authority."[23] Thomas D'Arcy McGee, contributor to *The Nation* and, in the 1860s, a member of Canada's parliament, argued strenuously in a number of published essays against the Fenians' oversimplification of political realities and their general position that the Irish were as oppressed in British North America as in Ireland. He was assassinated, and blame was placed on the Fenians. The group also became known for some striking rescues of prisoners from police custody and prison – a device echoed by Boucicault in *Arrah-na-Pogue* (1864) – including a deadly attack in Manchester in September 1867 on a police van that was carrying two Fenians to prison.

Suppressed through a series of legal measures, including arrests of members, Fenianism was soon sharing the nationalist stage with the new Home Rule movement which, like O'Connell's earlier political action, was geared toward parliamentary reform. Founded in 1870 by Isaac Butt, and then pursued by such luminaries as Charles Stewart Parnell, with strong interconnections with the various land leagues, the Home Rule movement dominated public politics in Ireland for the latter decades of the nineteenth century. Home Rule bills were brought before, and defeated by, the British parliament in 1874, 1886, and 1893, achieving only limited success in the 1910s, the years leading up to the Easter Rising of 1916. While Home Rule failed in the late nineteenth century, small advances were made on land issues throughout the same period, particularly after the Land War of 1879–82.

While this historical context is crucial to much of the literature in this anthology, from famine poems to political ballads and antiquarian texts that invoke cultural nationalism, aligning individual writers with particular positions is a fraught proposition. Writers changed their minds – on politics, on aesthetics, on morals, and even on religion – or joined groups without being completely aligned with them ideologically. Writers, in short, often crossed boundaries rather than helped to define them. Moreover, the sectarian divisions that are now so strongly associated with political conflict in Ireland were more fluid for much of the period covered by the anthology. Writers in this anthology who joined (or nearly joined) the United Irishmen included a Catholic (Moore) and Presbyterians (Drennan, Orr, James Porter), and, half a century later, prominent contributors to the Young Ireland newspaper, *The Nation*, included Catholics (Duffy, Mangan, MacCarthy, McGee) and mainstream Protestants (Wilde, Davis). Translators of Irish-language material in this anthology include Catholics (Jeremiah John Callanan, Mangan), Church of Ireland members (Morgan, Brooke), and writers from Dissenting backgrounds (Ferguson). Moreover, writers themselves moved across religious boundaries: Edmund Burke was professedly Protestant but Catholic in background and perhaps privately in faith as well, and he was educated at a Quaker school; Morgan had one Catholic and one Protestant parent, and her mother reportedly liked to have ministers of different faiths debate theology over her tea table; Ferguson migrated from Presbyterianism to the Church of Ireland; Oscar Wilde was raised in the Church of Ireland and converted to Catholicism in his final days. Even within families there are political differences despite a consistency of faith. The Sheridan Lefanu family, with Church of Ireland ministers in every generation for over a century, was vocally nationalist in the eighteenth and early nineteenth centuries; in the mid-1800s, though, Joseph

Notes ────────────────────────────────

[23] Foster, *Modern Ireland*, 391.

Sheridan LeFanu had a complex position on Ireland that was broadly conservative. In short, the positions of nationalists, conservatives, and other organized groups are fairly coherent and can be traced in the historical record, but writers, like most individuals, are not so easily pigeon-holed.

Literary Schools, Movements, and Periods

Irish literature of this period is not only partly shaped by politics, historical events, and religious distinctions, but also by literary movements that are both national and international. Irish writers' references to their own reading makes it clear that they were often well versed in British literature and philosophy, and that many, fluent in two languages or more, were also familiar with continental European literature. As classical literature was the cornerstone of advanced education for men in the eighteenth century and for much of the nineteenth century, classical references also pepper much of the literature in this anthology, from the works of Thomas Sheridan and John Leslie forward to Moore. Morgan was fluent in English, Irish, French, and Italian, and her fiction in particular is marked by references to a range of national literatures, as is the verse of the even more polyglot Mangan. Women writers, from Frances Sheridan and Ryves to Mary Leadbeater and Mary Tighe, made a point of establishing their credentials as classicists and thus cementing their participation in the neoclassical tradition that was supposedly limited to male poets.

Writers also engaged other recent European cultural developments. As Luke Gibbons has demonstrated, there was an Irish Enlightenment that responded to the Scottish Enlightenment of the early eighteenth century – an Enlightenment in which Edmund Burke is a central figure.[24] Burke's influential work on the sublime and his pamphlet on the Wilkes riots, excerpted in this anthology, both deal with the moral accompaniment of Enlightenment reason: the "social affections," the emotional ties that bind together members of a community through sympathy, particularly concern for each other's welfare. Such theories of "sensibility" or "moral sentiments" were put forward by a number of Enlightenment thinkers from across the British Isles, including Lord Shaftesbury (English), Frances Hutcheson and Burke (Irish), and David Hume and Adam Smith (Scottish). Generally, they viewed the moral improvement of individuals as a key social objective, and morality as ethical rather than rules-based. Enlightenment individuals were to sympathize with those who suffer, and act rationally in response to that suffering. Such models of communal feeling become crystallized as the foundation of national feeling in the Enlightenment-inspired work of such United-men as Drennan and Porter as well as the next generation of nationalist writers, including Morgan and Moore. Patriotism becomes understood as a moral feeling for the national community rather than unthinking tribalism.[25]

Likewise, eighteenth-century writers such as Thomas and Frances Sheridan, Burke, and Goldsmith, and later writers such as Drennan, Leadbeater, and the Edgeworths, arise from a related Enlightenment concern with education as the means of both individual improvement and social progress. Goldsmith's ideal rural community, its passing lamented in *The Deserted Village*, combines natural harmony and local education, while Leadbeater and the Edgeworths seek to educate a rural community that they view as

---

Notes

[24] Luke Gibbons, *Edmund Burke and Ireland: Aesthetics, Politics, and the Colonial Sublime* (Cambridge: Cambridge University Press, 2003).

[25] For further discussion of this, see Julia M. Wright, *Ireland, India, and Nationalism in the Nineteenth Century* (Cambridge: Cambridge University Press, 2007).

needing reform. Thomas Sheridan and his son, Richard Brinsley Sheridan, target prejudice, mocking English bias against Irish people on terms that would echo through
nineteenth-century Irish literature as well.[26] Other writers of the Sheridans' era followed
the neoclassicism of their contemporaries, valuing classical literature and its machinery
(particularly mythology and classical history) as the basis for literature of taste and
quality. Leslie, for instance, praises the Irish landscape in literary terms through a range
of classical references and comparisons, and Mangan and MacCarthy would later revise
this approach by referring to neoclassical landscape painters.

Neoclassicism also informs the growth of satire in the late eighteenth century.
A tradition that is traced back to the Roman poets Juvenal and Horace, satire was the
leading genre for political and social critique in the eighteenth century. That Swift's
corpus was largely satirical reinforced the eminence of satire in eighteenth-century
Ireland, while the political debates of the late eighteenth century gave satirists ample
material for their pens. The translation of satire from neoclassical verse to such populist
forms as the ballad produced a new generation of satirists that included Ryves, O'Brien,
the contributors to *Paddy's Resource*, and James Porter. After the failure of the United
Irishmen Uprising, satirists deflected their attention from colonial rule and turned to
broader targets, as in Corry's wide-ranging assault on English gullibility and moral
weakness, *The Detector of Quackery* (1802). Moore and Morgan also continued in this
vein, from Moore's *Intercepted Letters* (1813) to Morgan's long poem, *The Mohawks: A
Satirical Poem* (1822), co-written with her husband, Charles.

At the same time, what Seamus Deane in *A Short History of Irish Literature* terms
the "Celtic Revival" began to take place, with Joseph Cooper Walker and Charlotte
Brooke in the 1780s providing translations of Irish-language material and substantial
scholarly essays on Irish history and Irish-language literature. Corry's *The Patriot*
draws extensively on such materials, offering a legend of heroic Ireland to inspire
nationalists in the months leading up to the 1798 Irish Uprising. This recovery work
went hand in hand with attempts to inspire national pride, countering English claims
of Irish barbarity with evidence of a long history of literary sophistication, heroism
and military prowess, and advanced education. Translations and historical material not
only furthered Irish-language scholarship in English, and fostered a readership for such
poet-translators as Morgan, Callanan, Mangan, and Ferguson. They also impacted
English-language literature, from Drennan's "Glendalloch" and Moore's *Irish Melodies*
to novels by Morgan, paving the way for the nativist writing heralded in the 1830s and
1840s. This early part of the Revival, emerging at the same time as cultural nationalism,
made Irish-language literature a further basis for Irish national pride. Thus, the United
Irishmen published a small volume in 1795 which aimed to teach conversational and
literary Irish to anglophones, while phrases in Irish were included in nationalist ballads.
Sentimental writing extended the antiquarian project into affection not only for the Irish
past but also for contemporary heroes, martyrs, and cultural successes, creating a two-
pronged method of valuing the Irish people and Irish culture – that is, through the
recovery of the past and the depiction of the present. The use of both satire and nativist
material in nationalist writing from roughly 1790 to 1830, from United-men writers
to Morgan, Moore, and Callanan, speaks to another double strategy of nationalism in
the period, both critiquing English power and heralding Irish cultural and moral
strength.

Notes ———————————————————————————————

[26] See, for instance, Carleton's "Auto-biographical Introduction" (1843) and Boucicault's *Arrah-na-Pogue*, both included
here.

Satire waned after the 1820s, but was supplanted, in broad terms, by a cosmopolitan and diasporic view in which Irish writers located Ireland within a larger European or transatlantic frame. The seeds of the transatlantic perspective lie in United-men literature that connects Irish revolutionary sentiment to the American Revolution, but it was also energized by the Irish diaspora which escalated dramatically in the nineteenth century. At the same time, a pan-European view emerged from various other cultural exchanges: the Irish educational diaspora on the Continent (where Irish Catholics could get an advanced education before Emancipation in 1829); the tradition of Irishmen, after the Wild Geese, joining continental militaries; and, after Emancipation, the rise of "Young Europe," a pan-continental nationalist movement which placed various cultural-national groups in opposition to the European empires that dominated Europe at this time. Much of the material in *The Nation* in its early years is focused on this larger arena, with reports from Irish emigrants in Britain and the US, extensive reports on international events, and poetry that both continues the antiquarian project and addresses the diaspora within a global framework.

Against this cosmopolitan view was a new kind of nativism that was focused not on the remote past itself but on rural life as the remainder of that past. Prose fiction by Carleton, the Banims, Samuel Lover, and others, as well as poetry by Callanan and drama by Boucicault, focused on rural Irish people as the collective repository of Irish history, the Irish language, and a national character that could be both sentimentalized and eulogized as it disappeared under the pressure of modernization, emigration and, most devastatingly, famine. While it would be easy to view this material as ethnographic, as credible representations of an Irish oral and rural culture that was already disappearing in the 1840s, it is important to note that this group of authors and their writing are diverse. Take three male writers who spoke Irish, were born in the mid-1790s to Catholic families, and published in both Britain and Ireland: Callanan, Carleton, and Michael Banim. All three are deemed by many Victorian and modern critics to speak for rural, Catholic Ireland. But Carleton, likely the only one of the three who learned Irish at home and participated actively in insurgency, converted to the Church of Ireland as a young man and wrote anti-Catholic fiction in the 1830s. Callanan reputedly refused to marry a Methodist woman unless she converted to Catholicism but rarely refers to religion in his extant verse. Banim wrote fiction and verse that positively represented, and even advocated the claims of, the Catholic Irish. Beyond the broad similarities noted above, they are also a diverse group: Callanan was from Cork, and his family was probably moderately well off; Carleton was from Tyrone, and his family comprised poor tenant farmers; Banim was from Kilkenny, and inherited his father's shop. Religion and language appear to unite them, but class and region – and their different literary stances on Catholicism – widely separate them. Such writers do not fit easily into Romantic assumptions that idealize authors as geniuses who can transcend the particularities of their communities and so speak a less-biased truth, nor into nationalist assumptions in which authors are "native voices" speaking authentically *for* their shared community as the *Blackwood's* author quoted above would have them do. This is not a choice between two positions, but rather a warning not to oversimplify either communities or their authors. Class, gender, region, and education complicate religion-defined communities, and writers from within the same narrow demographic can still vary widely in literary taste, skills, and thematic preferences – not to mention personal politics.

Moreover, this body of nativist writing easily veered into caricature and condescension. The pages of *The Nation* included a critique of such material in the satiric "How to Make an Irish Story" (1843), while printing, in one form or another, pleas for the Irish to become better educated, support national culture through new art as well as literature, and exhibit a forward-looking national pride. Davis applauded:

how much have the Irish People gained and done! They have received, and grown rich under torrents of thought. Song, and sermon, and music, speech and pamphlet, novel and history, essay, and map, and picture, have made the dull thoughtful, and the thoughtful studious, and will make the studious wise and powerful. They have begun a system of self-teaching in their Reading-rooms. If they carry it, we shall, before two years, have in every parish men able to manufacture, to trade, and to farm – men acquainted with all that Ireland was, is, and should be – men able to serve The Irish Nation in peace and war.[27]

The poets and essayists associated with Young Ireland – Davis, Mangan, MacCarthy, Lady Wilde, McGee, Duffy, and others – offered a different view of Ireland from that lauded by the nativist novelists who dominated the 1830s and 1840s. In the pages of *The Nation* in its early years, Irishness resided not in contemporary rural culture where the Irish language was still a living language, but in a people proud of their past and educating themselves for a prosperous future.

After 1845, the Young Ireland poets continued to exhibit interest in international politics and Irish immigration but fell to grieving, first for Thomas Davis and then for the devastating effects of the Great Famine. Irish poetry of the late 1840s is not always bleak, but it is often shadowed by death and despair. Wasted landscapes, failing hope, regret, and frustration are the keynotes, even as poets experimented with complex versification. While their predecessors relied heavily on heroic couplets and ballad forms, MacCarthy, Lady Wilde, and especially Mangan used complex metrical forms that speak to their wide reading in the literatures of languages other than English (all three were published, influential translators). At the same time, there was a shift in prose fiction. Against the nativist realism of Carleton, the Banims, and others, J. Sheridan LeFanu returned to the gothic traditions of the early nineteenth century, traditions exemplified by such writers as Charles Robert Maturin, whose *Melmoth the Wanderer* has long been considered a gothic masterpiece. Whether LeFanu is responding to an Anglo-Irish anxiety about rural Irish insurgency, the Famine, an appetite for gothic tales of terror, or a continuing interest in Irish folklore, he made major contributions both to Irish gothic literature and to the mid-Victorian genre of sensation fiction. From ghosts and vampires to murderous uncles and tea-induced hallucinations, LeFanu's landscapes are populated by terror, mystery, and the supernatural.

Irish folklore was a topic of interest from Thomas Crofton Croker's *Fairy Legends and Traditions of the South of Ireland* (1825) onward. Lover's "King O'Toole and St. Kevin: A Legend of Glendalough" (1832) is among the early body of work on rural Ireland as a repository for tales of the fantastic rather than the site of poverty and the residues of Irish-language culture. The attachment to place reinforces the folkloric elements: titles set such tales in specific locations such as Glendalough (Lover), Tyrone (LeFanu), or "the South of Ireland" (Croker). Out of this mystification of rural Ireland arose the popular sub-genre of the fairytale in both prose and verse, from William Allingham's famous poems "The Fairies" and "The Maids of Elfen-Mere" (1855) to Bridget and Julia Kavanagh's "The Pearl Fountain" (1876) and Oscar Wilde's *The Happy Prince and Other Tales* (1888), and even a late-century return to Croker's model of folkloric collection in Lady Wilde's *Ancient Legends, Mystic Charms, and Superstitions of Ireland* (1887) and Yeats's *Fairy and Folk Tales of the Irish Peasantry* of the following year.

Other traditions cut across the period, from concerns with the status of women from Frances Sheridan to Dora Sigerson, to the regional tradition of Ulster Scots verse. Writers from Ulster in this anthology reflect the diversity of Ulster writing in the period, from

Notes ──────────────────────────────────────

[27] Thomas Davis, "The History of To-day," *Literary and Historical Essays* (Dublin: James Duffy, 1846), 111.

United-men poets Porter, Drennan, Corry, and Orr to Carleton and Ferguson. Orr and Ferguson are notable, however, for their key contributions to Ulster Scots verse. Both poets usually write in standard English, but occasionally draw on the Ulster Scots dialect and Scottish symbols – Scottish poet Robert Burns, Scottish history – to articulate a unique Irish cultural and linguistic milieu. Here, Scotland does not represent integration with Britain, as twentieth-century history might suggest, but rather a pan-Celtic history of oppression, so that the working-class Orr praises Robert Burns as a regional poet "wha baith amus'd / The man o' taste, an' taught the rude" ("Elegy, On the Death of Mr. Robert Burns" [1804]), appealing to readers across class divisions, while Ferguson's "Willy Gilliland: An Ulster Ballad" (1865) commemorates the English suppression of a Presbyterian movement for religious toleration in seventeenth-century Scotland. Orr's "The Passengers" reveals the transatlantic currency of Ulster Scots, representing Irish exiles after the 1798 Uprising speaking in Ulster Scots dialect as they migrate to the United States.[28]

Another thread in the literature of this period is translation. The focus in this anthology is Irish-language translations, though some of Mangan's important German translations have been included. These translations give a sense of the larger history of translation in Ireland during this period, a history that includes late eighteenth-century translations of French works by such authors as Philip Lefanu and Ryves, Moore's award-winning translations of Anacreon at the turn of the century, Lady Wilde's translations from German, and MacCarthy's translation of Spanish dramas. Seamus Deane suggests that Mangan's emphasis on translation is the effect of a national failure: "Ireland's history usurped Mangan's imagination."[29] But Mangan needs to be placed within a larger history of translation that contributes to efforts to place Ireland within a larger (often Catholic) Europe through translation, travel writing, fiction, poetry, and non-fiction engaging continental settings and issues. Translation could re-orient Irish writers, demonstrating mastery of English while establishing non-English affiliations, either with unanglicized Ireland through the Irish language or with European modernity through other continental languages. The evocations of migration, translation, non-English phrasing, and a larger global history that appear repeatedly in this anthology speak to this attempt to think through ways of defining identity outside the colonial frame, as well as interests and sympathies that reach beyond the polarizations of sect, nation, and empire. Irish literature does not always represent Ireland, just as British literature does not always represent Britain. The diversity of, and the continuities among, the texts in this anthology sketch a rich and complex literary tradition in which there is much that is critically interesting, more that is aesthetically compelling, and little that is easily forgotten.

Notes

[28] All three poems mentioned here are included in this anthology.

[29] Deane, *Short History of Irish Literature*, 81.

Editorial Note

Obvious typographical errors have been silently corrected and some punctuation modernized to avoid confusion, such as between "its" and "it's," but generally the spelling and punctuation of the copy-texts have been retained. The line between a vivid representation of colloquial speech and a misspelling is often indiscernible, and texts would lose that vividness if orthodoxy were imposed. Moreover, eighteenth-century printers were not as concerned with consistency as their successors, and a cleaned-up, modernized text provides a very different reading experience from originals that move fluidly between different acceptable spellings and often quote inaccurately.

Technical stage directions for Boucicault's *Arrah-na-Pogue* and some notes in other works have been reluctantly trimmed, especially in the case of verbosely annotated works. Notes have largely been retained, however. Notes in the original copy-text by the author are marked as such; where the authorship of the notes is uncertain, they are marked as "original." All other notes are mine and identify nationality only for those authors who were not born in Ireland, except where there might be some confusion. Apart from these elisions, Oliver Goldsmith's *Citizen of the World* (1762), James Porter's *Billy Bluff* (1796), and Thomas Moore's *Lalla Rookh* (1817), all of the prose fiction, drama, and poems in this anthology are complete texts.

A list of the copy-texts is provided in the Bibliography, but other editions from the period were also consulted. In cases where there were multiple early editions with disparities that may be of interest, further information has been provided in the editorial apparatus for the work in question. Where there were both early Irish and British editions, Irish editions have typically been selected for copy-texts, for a number of reasons, including the greater likelihood that the other writers in the anthology had access to that version. Book publications have, for similar reasons, been preferred, although occasionally the first periodical publication has been selected instead as the copy-text – as in, for instance, the cases of Joseph Sheridan LeFanu's "A Chapter in the History of a Tyrone Family," which predates the book publication of the story by decades, and James Clarence Mangan's verse, which appeared in a range of periodicals that inform the diversity of his work in a way that is often obscured in the first book publications of his poetry.

My general editorial aim is not to take sides in the various compelling and interesting debates about different models for constructing a meaningful edited text out of myriad possible copy-texts and associated documents. The concern of this anthology with literary traditions makes each text important not only as an authored work but also as a *read* work. The edition of Goldsmith that James Orr, Thomas Dermody, and their readers might have read is therefore more relevant than the complex array of textual variants among editions published during Goldsmith's lifetime. Moreover, for many of the authors in this anthology, there simply is little or no documentary survival of intentions, debates with publishers, proof corrections, and other apparatus so crucial to editors' research on intentionality or the tracing of others' participation in the production of the printed work. To treat authors differently based on the availability of papers would risk suggesting a hierarchy of authors in which some writers have a discernible, evolving intent while most do not. Given the biases that determine archival survival,[1] this would tacitly grant intentionality and authorial agency largely to wealthy, urban men, and implicitly deny it to nearly everyone else.

Biographical information has been culled from a variety of sources (see the Bibliography), but these sources have been corrected on occasion on the basis of archival evidence and recent scholarship. As many scholars in the field know, biographies are both scarce for many of these authors and sometimes contradictory, a point vividly made in the still-unresolved debate over whether Thomas Sheridan was born in Dublin or Co. Cavan and the continuing speculation on when and where Morgan was born. If there are such problems for well-published authors with famous parents, such as these, it is perhaps not surprising that we do not know when Leslie was born or what Callanan's father did for a living, and often have to rely on authors' sometimes unreliable autobiographical statements.

Notes

[1] There are always exceptions, but the papers of men famous in their lifetimes have generally been better preserved by families and later archivists than women famous in their lifetimes, and authors who died in relative obscurity are often the most woefully neglected. Authors from well-to-do, extended families are also more likely to benefit from the resources to preserve papers until transferred to archives.

Acknowledgments

I would like to thank the many research assistants who worked on this project over the years: James Allard, Holly Crumpton, Jeremy DeVito, Heather Doody, Melissa Holt, and Meagan Timney. I am also thankful to A. P. Watt Ltd. on behalf of Gráinne Yeats for permission to include an excerpt from W. B. Yeats, and gratefully acknowledge the generous research support of the Canada Foundation for Innovation, the Canada Research Chairs Program, and the Social Sciences and Humanities Research Council of Canada. Without their support, this anthology would have been the work of a lifetime rather than six years.

Dalhousie University, through its library resources and its ubiquitously generous spirit of collegiality, helped me daily on this project in myriad ways, particularly with the energy that comes from working at an institution in which intellectual enquiry thrives. This project would not have been possible at all without the British Library and the special collections at Dalhousie University, the University of Western Ontario, Concordia University, and the University of Waterloo, all of which provided invaluable access to literary texts and historical resources. At a time when we are expected to believe that electronic collections are comprehensive, these archives provide valuable reminders both of the durability of print and the limits of scanners and digital catalogues.

I am also grateful to Blackwell for its commitment to this project and for all its assistance along the way, with special thanks to editor Emma Bennett for her support and advice, and to Sue Ashton for her sharp attention to detail during production.

Finally, I would like to thank Jason Haslam, for many helpful conversations, as well as his unwavering support and relentless encouragement, without which this anthology would not have been begun, much less finished.

Chronology of Selected Historical Events and Irish Novels

1154	Pope Adrian IV (English) issues a papal bull granting Henry II, king of England, sovereignty over Ireland.
1169–71	The English (Anglo-Normans) invade Ireland, first taking Wexford (1169). They return in 1170, under the leadership of Strongbow (Richard de Clare, earl of Pembroke) who is acting under the invitation of the deposed king of Leinster. Strongbow becomes king of Leinster in 1171; Henry II lands with a large force to bolster the English crown's claims to Ireland.
1495	Poynings Law is passed, requiring that the English monarch's representatives in Ireland and in England approve of Irish parliamentary actions, including meeting. (The parliament dates back to the thirteenth century.)
1517	Martin Luther nails his "ninety-five theses" to the doors of a church, launching the Protestant Reformation. Anglicanism and Presbyterianism both emerge in the mid-1500s, the latter instituting key changes in the 1630s and 1640s; the Society of Friends (Quakers) developed in the 1650s and Methodism in the 1730s.
1534	The Act of Supremacy formalizes the English crown's breach with Catholicism, and makes the English monarch the head of the church in England (rather than the Pope).
1569–73	First Desmond Rebellion in Munster.
1572	St. Bartholomew's Day Massacre of Protestants (Huguenots) in France, part of the Wars of Religion (1562–98). Subsequently, some Huguenots migrate to Ireland, including ancestors of Charles Robert Maturin and J. Sheridan LeFanu.
1579–83	Second Desmond Rebellion in Munster.
1594–1603	Tyrone's Rebellion (or Nine Years' War) in Ireland between Irish leaders and the English government in Ireland under Elizabeth I. Ulster Famine, 1602–3.
1606–20	Plantation of Ulster as well as other regions of Ireland with English and Scottish Protestants.
1607	After the failure of Tyrone's Rebellion, the "Flight of the Earls": Irish leaders and many of their troops leave Ireland for continental Europe, beginning the tradition of exiled Irish men serving in the military of continental European nations.

1641–52	Irish Uprising begins in 1641 in Ulster, leading to further unrest in Ireland that overlaps with the English Civil War (1642–51). Soon there are conflicts across the British Isles in various religiously inflected struggles for power known collectively as the War of the Three Kingdoms. In Ireland, the conflict is ended by Oliver Cromwell's bloody invasion (1649–52).
1689	James II of Britain lands in Ireland because of conflict between him and his daughter, Mary, and her husband William of Orange over the British crown. James II is Catholic, and Mary and William are Protestant.
1690	William of Orange lands in Ireland, and weeks later defeats James II and his Irish troops at the Battle of the Boyne. This secures William III and Mary II's claims to the British throne, and launches Jacobite uprisings in Ireland and Scotland for the next decades in support of James II and later his descendants.
1690–1	Fighting continues in Ireland between Jacobite and Williamite forces until the Treaty of Limerick is signed in 1691. Among other provisions, including promises of religious toleration in Ireland, it offers Irish soldiers the option of emigrating to France – the exodus of soldiers and their families that ensued is termed "The Flight of the Wild Geese."
1695	Despite the Treaty of Limerick, the government institutes the first of the Penal Statutes which disenfranchise and disadvantage Catholics in Ireland.
1707	Act of Union between Scotland and England (and Wales), dissolving the Scottish Parliament.
1726	Jonathan Swift, *Gulliver's Travels*, arguably the first Irish novel.
1729	Irish parliament moves to a new building in Dublin, where it meets until its dissolution by the Act of Union (1800).
1731	Royal Dublin Society founded to promote agriculture, industry, science, and the arts.
1745	Jacobite Rebellion in Scotland seeks to place James II's grandson, "Bonny Prince Charlie," on the British throne.
1756–63	Seven Years' War, including the French and Indian War, with conflicts in what is now the United States and Canada as well as in Europe. The leading countries in the war are Britain and France.
1759–67	Novels responding to the new culture of sentiment: Laurence Sterne, *The Life and Opinions of Tristram Shandy, Gentleman* (in various parts, 1760–7); Frances Sheridan, *The Memoirs of Miss Sidney Bidulph* (1761); Oliver Goldsmith, *The Vicar of Wakefield* (1766).
1775–83	War of American Independence against Britain (American Revolution). United States Declaration of Independence (1776).
1778	Irish Volunteers founded. Catholic Relief Act passed eliminating some of the restrictions on Catholic rights to inheriting and leasing land.
1785	Royal Irish Academy founded to promote the study of science, literature, and antiquities.
1789	French Revolution begins.
1791	Society of United Irishmen founded.
1792	United-man Wolfe Tone becomes Secretary to the Catholic Committee, which sought to represent Catholic interests.
1792–3	Various alleviations of the Penal Statutes, affecting, for instance, Catholic access to education, the right to practice law, and other civil rights.
1793–4	French Revolution turns into "The Reign of Terror," including widespread executions of opponents of the Revolution via the newly invented guillotine.
1793–1802	French Revolutionary War: France declares war against Britain in 1793, and fighting continues until the Peace of Amiens in 1802.

1794–7	United Irishmen suppressed, including arrests of leaders such as William Drennan and the editors of *The Northern Star*. In England, naval mutinies at Spithead and the Nore in 1797 leave large sections of the English coast undefended.
1798	United Irishmen Uprising, with fighting involving tens of thousands across Ireland, including Wexford, Antrim, and Mayo. Leaders are captured early in the year, including Wolfe Tone and Lord Edward Fitzgerald.
1800	Act of Union abolishes the Irish parliament and brings Ireland under the direct political control of the British parliament. Maria Edgeworth, *Castle Rackrent*.
1803	Emmett Uprising. The leader, Robert Emmett, is executed after a famous speech from the dock.
1803–15	Despite the Peace of Amiens (1802), war resumes between Britain and France, continuing until Napoleon's defeat at Waterloo (1815).
1806	Sydney Owenson (later Lady Morgan) founds the "national tale": *The Wild Irish Girl: A National Tale*.
1809	Maria Edgeworth, *Ennui*.
1813	Catholic Relief Bill proposed (but not passed) following the Veto Controversy over altering the administration of the Catholic Church in Ireland in exchange for the lessening of strictures against Catholics.
1815	Congress of Vienna. In this meeting of major European powers after Napoleon's defeat to redraw the map of Europe, Britain is represented by two Dubliners: the Duke of Wellington and Viscount Castlereagh. The Congress consolidates British naval power.
1817	Maria Edgeworth, *Harrington*.
1820	Charles Robert Maturin, *Melmoth the Wanderer*.
1823	Catholic Association founded.
1827–8	Novels about the 1798 Irish Uprising: Lady Morgan (formerly Sydney Owenson), *The O'Briens and the O'Flahertys* (1827); Michael Banim, *The Croppy* (1828).
1828	Daniel O'Connell (the Liberator) is elected member of parliament for Clare, bringing the debate over Emancipation to a crisis because he is Catholic and cannot legally take his seat.
1829	Catholic Emancipation passed. Gerald Griffin, *The Collegians*.
c.1830–8	Tithe War, referring to largely local (rather than concerted national) violence related to Catholic resistance to being required to pay tithes to the Church of Ireland. The tithe system is eased somewhat in the 1830s, but not abolished for decades. Irish Reform Bill (1832) extends the franchise and increases the number of Irish seats in the British parliament.
1839	Charles James Lever, *Confessions of Harry Lorrequer*.
1840	Repeal Association founded to repeal the Act of Union (1800).
1842	*The Nation* founded, and with it Young Ireland, out of the Repeal Movement.
1845–9	The Great Famine, precipitated by a potato blight. Fatalities are due to hunger and disease which ravages the weakened population, including a cholera outbreak (1848–9). Between deaths and emigration, the Irish population drops from over eight million in 1841 to barely six and a half million in 1851. Contemporary famine novels include William Carleton, *The Black Prophet, A Tale of Irish Famine* (1847). A number of important historical novels also appear: Anna Maria Fielding, *The Whiteboy: A Story of Ireland in 1822* (1845); J. Sheridan LeFanu, *The Fortunes of Colonel Turlogh O'Brien* (1847); Charles James Lever, *The Knight of Gwynne: A Tale of the Time of Union* (1847); William Carleton, *The Tithe Proctor, a Novel: Being a Tale of the Tithe Rebellion in Ireland* (1849).

1848	Revolutions across Europe, and some revolutionary agitation in Ireland led by William Smith O'Brien of Young Ireland, but only a few dozen people are involved.
1853–8	British forces are engaged in two major military conflicts: the Crimean War (1853–6), involving an alliance of France, Britain, and the Ottoman empire against the Russian empire; the "Indian Mutiny" (1857–8) against British imperial rule in India.
1858–9	Founding of the Fenians in Ireland and the United States.
1863	Julia Kavanagh, *Queen Mab*.
1864	J. Sheridan LeFanu, *Uncle Silas*.
1866–7	US Fenians invade Canada; further Fenian action in the British Isles, including the attempted release of prisoners from Clerkenwell gaol in which gunpowder was fatally used to blow up a wall. Second Reform Bill (Britain) extends voting rights further (1867).
1868	Thomas D'Arcy McGee, then a member of the Canadian parliament, is assassinated in Ottawa; a supposed Fenian is blamed and executed.
1870	Irish Home Rule movement founded by Isaac Butt.
1872	Charles James Lever, *Lord Kilgobbin: A Tale of Ireland in Our Own Time*.
1873	Organization of Home rule movement into two groups: Home Rule Confederation of Great Britain and the Home Rule League.
1877	Charles Stewart Parnell becomes President of the Home Rule Confederation of Great Britain.
1879–82	Land War, largely consisting of boycotts and organized protests in defense of land rights for tenants. The Irish National Land League is founded in 1879 and the Ladies Land League in 1881; in late 1881, Parnell and others were arrested and the National Land League suppressed. Gladstone's Second Land Act passed (1881). First Boer War between Britain and Boer Republics in southern Africa (1880–1). Charles Kickham, *Knocknagow: Or, the Homes of Tipperary* (1879).
1882	"Phoenix Park murders," the assassination of the Irish Chief Secretary and his deputy. Foundation of Irish National League.
1884–5	Third Reform Bill and Redistribution Act (Britain); among other reforms, it extends voting rights to the agricultural laboring classes.
1885	Land Purchase Act (Ashbourne Act), followed by a series of other Acts in subsequent years which contribute to the reform of land ownership in Ireland.
1886	First Home Rule bill, from English Prime Minister Gladstone, defeated in the British parliament. Land War novels: George Moore, *A Drama in Muslin*; Marcella Grace, *Rosa Mulholland*.
1887–91	Parnell is caught up in a series of controversies: first allegations that he was involved in the Phoenix Park murders, and then he is named in a divorce action, undermining his political credibility and ultimately leading to divisions within the Irish Parliamentary Party he led. Alice Milligan, *A Royal Democrat* (1890); Bram Stoker, *The Snake's Pass* (1890) (his first novel, and set in Ireland).
1891	Oscar Wilde, *Picture of Dorian Gray*.
1893	Gladstone's second Home Rule bill defeated (the third Home Rule bill would not be put forward until 1912). Gaelic League founded.
1894	Creation of Irish Trades Union Congress. Somerville and Ross (the pseudonym of Edith Somerville and Violet Florence Martin), *The Real Charlotte*.
1897	Bram Stoker, *Dracula*.
1900	Renewal of the Irish Parliamentary Party. Canon (Patrick Augustine) Sheehan, *My New Curate*.

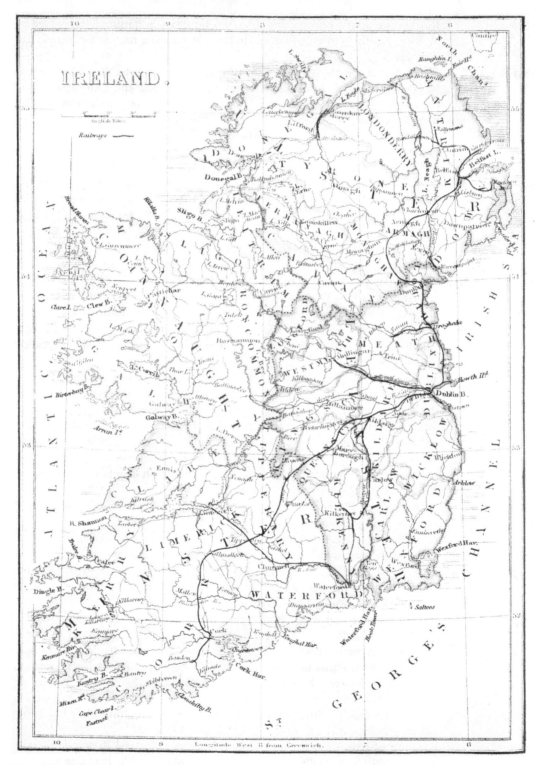

Map of Ireland From *Ireland: Its Scenery, Character, &c.* By Mr. & Mrs. S. C. Hall (Samuel Carter Hall and Anna Maria Fielding Hall), new edn., 3 vols. (Philadelphia: Gebbie and Barrie, 1860), 3: x.

Irish Literature 1750–1900

Thomas Sheridan (1719–1788)

Thomas Sheridan, probably born in Dublin but possibly in Co. Cavan, was the son of another Thomas Sheridan (clergyman and author) and the godson of Jonathan Swift (a close friend of the family). He may have been a descendant of Denis Sheridan (c.1610–83), a native Irish speaker who assisted in the translation of the Old Testament into Irish as part of Bishop Bedell's efforts to make the Church of Ireland accessible to Irish speakers. The younger Thomas Sheridan worked primarily in the theater, as actor, manager, playwright, and author of various tracts related to theater reform, but also published on other subjects, including *British Education: Or the Source of Disorders in Great Britain* (1755), *A Course of Lectures on Elocution* (1762), a dictionary (1780), and an edition of Swift's works (1784). Sheridan married Frances Chamberlaine in 1747, and they had a number of children. All those who survived into adulthood became published authors: playwrights Richard Brinsley Sheridan and Alicia Sheridan Lefanu, novelist (Anne) Elizabeth Lefanu, and essayist Charles Francis Sheridan (the sisters married Lefanu brothers).

Sheridan's career as a theater-manager in Dublin was generally successful, though notoriously marred by two riots spurred by political tensions. In 1747, Sheridan expelled a man named Kelly for assaulting an actress during a performance; Kelly's supporters rioted at Sheridan's theater two nights later on the grounds that Sheridan had exceeded his authority in disciplining a man of a higher social class. Another riot in 1754, after an actor failed to repeat a speech with political resonances, destroyed Sheridan's theater and left him financially ruined, a subject he deals with in his pamphlet, *An Humble Appeal to the Publick* (1758). His *Humble Appeal* also included a proposal for a national theater in Dublin that would be publicly administered and ensure fair treatment of theater workers.

As a dramatist, Sheridan mostly adapted other authors' works, as was common in his day; he adapted, for instance, *Coriolanus* (1755) from texts by English authors William Shakespeare and James Thomson. His enduringly popular farce *The Brave Irishman: Or, Captain O'Blunder* was published and staged throughout the second half of the eighteenth century and compactly abbreviated in three double-columned pages for the *Cabinet of Irish Literature* a century later. Based on the English play *Squire Trelooby* (1704), itself an adaptation of Molière's *Monsieur de Pourceaugnac* (1669), Sheridan's play differs from its predecessors in being concerned with challenging the pejorative theatrical figure of the "stage Irishman." The farce was reputedly written while Sheridan attended Trinity College Dublin in the mid-1730s, but it remained unpublished for some time. It also demonstrates Sheridan's continuing interest in language and dialect differences in the British Isles. Generally, O'Blunder's accent is represented by replacing "s" sounds with "sh," "wh" sounds with "ph," and sometimes by dropping "h"s or lengthening vowels: "shoul" for "soul," "phat" for "what," and "plaash" for "place." Sheridan detailed such variations in Irish pronunciation in his *Complete Dictionary of the English Language*, where he laments in general the lack of connection between spelling and sound in English.

Two distinct versions of the play appeared in print in the 1750s, reflecting regional adaptations of Sheridan's play: "as it is acted at the Theatre in Edinburgh" and "as it is acted at the Theatre-Royal in Smock-Alley" in Dublin.

The 1759 Dublin edition of the latter is the copy-text here; the Edinburgh version is available in *Ten English Farces* (Hughes and Scouten 1970). Among the significant differences are the inclusion of a prologue as well as a closing moral and epilogue in the Dublin version; the Edinburgh version ends on O'Blunder's song. In the Dublin version, Lucy has a more substantial and well-rounded role, and there is less emphasis on O'Blunder's Irish accent and idiom. The 1759 edition also corrects mistranscriptions of Irish in earlier editions, while contemporary British editions retain the error; a Belfast edition at the end of the century further improved the Irish-language content.

Further reading

Burke, Helen M., *Riotous Performances: The Struggle for Hegemony in the Irish Theatre, 1712–1784*. Notre Dame, IN: University of Notre Dame Press, 2003.

Hughes, Leo and Scouten, A. H. eds., *Ten English Farces*. New York: University of Texas Press, 1970.

Schneller, Beverly E., "No 'Brave Irishman' Need Apply: Thomas Sheridan, Shakespeare and the Smock-Alley Theater," in *Shakespeare and Ireland: History, Politics, Culture*, ed. Mark Thornton Burnett and Ramona Wray, 175–91. New York: Macmillan/St. Martin's Press, 1997.

Sheldon, Esther, *Thomas Sheridan of Smock-Alley*. Princeton, NJ: Princeton University Press, 1967.

A Proposal

From An Humble Appeal to the Publick (1758)

For saving the Stage in *Dublin* from the Ruin with which it is threatened, and establishing it on such a footing as may make it the Source of great Benefits to the Public.

N. B. Mr. Sheridan *intended to have offered this Proposal to the Consideration of Parliament this Winter, but from his want of Knowledge of the Rules of the House, and thro' Hurry of Business, he delayed it till the Time was elapsed that any Money could be granted, but he makes no doubt of meeting with Success in his Application next Sessions.*

After much Thought on the Subject, as well as much Experience, Mr. *Sheridan* thinks that he can lay down this as a Maxim.

That the Dublin *Stage never will remain long in a flourishing Condition whilst it is the Property of a private Person.*

The Constitution of the Stage of *Paris*, where the Theatre is the Property of the Public, and gives a certain Portion of the Profits to charitable Uses, seems to him the only one that would place that of *Dublin* on a good or durable Foundation.

The Actors there are divided into several Classes, according to their several Degrees of Merit. The Government is a kind of Commonwealth. And the Receipts are divided amongst the several Classes, according to their different Rates of Merit.

Upon a Vacancy in one Class, the best Actor in the next is elected to supply the Place.

Thus each Individual is interested in the Success of the Entertainment; their Incomes are larger or smaller in Proportion to the exerting or slackening of their united Endeavours to please. And their Advancement is the Reward of Merit, not Caprice.

In order to establish such a Theatre here, the following PROPOSAL was intended:

That Mr. *Sheridan*'s Interest in the Theatres, during the Remainder of the Lease, be purchased by Parliamentary Bounty, upon such Terms as shall be judged reasonable; together with the Wardrobe, Scenes, and all other Properties whatsoever belonging to him, for the Use of the *Dublin Society*, whose Property they shall become.

That, in Consideration of such Purchase, Mr. *Sheridan* shall undertake, that the Sum of three Pounds *per* Night for every Play, or publick Representation whatsoever, that shall be exhibited in the said Theatres, until the Expiration of said Lease, shall be paid in for the sole Use of the *Dublin Society*, to be by them employed in Premiums, for the Encouragement of the Liberal Arts, or for such other Purposes as they shall think meet. Which Sums of three Pounds *per* Night, according to the usual Number of times of performing, will probably produce an Income of near four hundred Pounds *per Annum*. He will farther undertake, that the Sum of one Pound *per* Night shall be laid aside for supplying the Wardrobe, whenever there may be any Deficiencies, and keeping the Scenery in repair, which, at a moderate Computation, may amount to one hundred and thirty Pounds *per Annum*: And considering the present State of the Scenery and Cloaths, that they are for the most Part new, will be a sufficient Provision to keep them to the Expiration of the Lease, in as good a Condition as they are at present.

Mr. *Sheridan* will farther undertake, that during that Term there shall be four Nights in each Season allotted for the sole Benefits and Advantage of four Publick Charities, *viz.* the Hospital of Incurables, the Lying-in Hospital, the Hospital in *Meath-Street*, and the Infirmary on the *Inns-quay*, without any Cost or Charge to them for the said Benefits. The Receipts of those four Nights will probably not fall short of five hundred Pounds; and thus the Theatre will yield a Fund of one thousand Pounds *per Annum*, to publick and charitable Uses.

If this Proposal is accepted, Mr. *Sheridan* will use his utmost Endeavours, and makes no doubt, but that he shall be able to execute some long-concerted Plans, whereby the Theatre of *Dublin* may be put upon a better footing than any in *Europe*; which may make it a pleasing School of Manners and Instruction to Youth; and a most rational Amusement to the Adult: Which may not only carry the Entertainments exhibited there to a much higher pitch of Perfection, than they can be brought to under the present Circumstances of the Stage, but also fix them upon a solid and durable Foundation.

The Brave Irishman: Or, Captain O'Blunder. A Farce (1759)

Prologue

Spoken by Capt. O'BLUNDER

Oagh, brilliant Shircle, shease to vend your Spleen
On ush, poor Irish, 'till our Faults are sheen;
My Business here, I'd swear, you ne'er would guesh;
But come, – my Duty 'tish, first to confesh;
To keep you then no longer in Suspince,
To wed a fair One ish my whole Pretince.

Phoo, now d'ye hear – the Titter ne'er will shease,
I plainly see the Curl in each merry Faash.

Well then, 'tish strange phat 'Fronts we her reshave,
Ven tish by us the English *Spalpeens¹ live.*
Have we not fought your Battles – bravely too;
And yet, ungrateful Boors, all that wont do.

Notes

THE BRAVE IRISHMAN

¹ *Spalpeen* (spailpín, Irish), rascal.

Oagh, would the Heroes of Hibernia's *Blood,*
Who lately in her Caush uprightly stood,
But shay with me, they'll mix their noble Breed
With Britain's *Daughters! then we should be freed.*
Hark, the Bell rings – I therefore must obey,
So smooth your Brows, and calmly hear the Play.

Dramatis Personae

Men	Women
Capt. *O'Blunder*	*Lucy,* Daughter to *Trader*
Mr. *Trader,* a Merchant	*Maid*
Cheatwell	
Sconce	
Jerry, Captain's Sergeant	
Dr. *Clyster*	
Dr. *Gallypot*	
Mons. *Ragou*	

SCENE LONDON
Mob, Keepers, &c.

ACT I, SCENE I

A Chamber

LUCY *repeating*

'Tis not the Marriage, but the Man we hate;
'Tis there we reason and debate:
For give us but the Man we love,
We're sure the Marriage to approve.

Well, this same barbarous Marriage-Act is a great Draw-back on the Inclinations of young People.[2]

MAID. Indeed and so it is, Mem; for my part I'm no Heiress, and therefore at my own Proposal! and if I was under the Restraint of the Act, and kept from Men, I wou'd run to Seed, so I wou'd – but, la! Mem, I had forgot to acquaint you, I verily believes that I saw your *Irish* Lover the Captain; and I conceits it was he and no other, so I do – and I saw him go into the Blue Postices,[3] so I did.

LUCY. My *Irish* Lover, Miss Pert;[4] I never so much as saw his Potato Face in all my born Days; but I hear he's a strange Animal of a Brute – Pray had he his Wings on? I suppose they saved him his Passage.

Notes ───────────────────────────────

[2] The Marriage Act of 1753 required parental consent for marriage; it aimed to prevent elopements and secret marriages, particularly with heiresses. This reference was a late addition to the play.

[3] The Blue Posts, a pub.
[4] impertinent

MAID. Oh! Mem, you mistakes the *Irishmen*; they deny that they've *Wings*, but they all confess and boast of their *Tails*.

LUCY. Oh Tawdry! but see who's at the Door. [*Exit, and return with*

CHEATWELL.

Miss! Your most humble and obedient – I came to acquaint you of our Danger: Our common Enemy is just imported hither, and is enquiring for your Father's House thro' every Street – The *Irish* Captain, in short, is come to *London*; such a Figure! and so attended by the Rabble –

LUCY. I long to see him – we love Variety; and *Irishmen*, I hear, are not so despicable; besides, the Captain may be misrepresented. [*Aside.*] Mr. *Cheatwell*, you know my Father's Design is to have as many Suitors as he can, in order to have a Choice of them all.

CHEAT. I have nothing but your Professions and Sincerity to depend on – Oh, here's my trusty Mercury.

Enter SCONCE.

So – Well, have you dogg'd the Captain?

SCONCE. Yes, yes, I left him snug at the *Blue Posts*; he's just pat for our Purpose, easily humm'd: as simple and as undesigning as we would have him. Well, and what do you propose?

CHEAT. Propose! why, to drive him back to his native Bogs as fast as possible.

LUCY. Oh! Mr. *Cheatwell* – pray let's have a Sight of the *Creture* –

CHEAT. Oh! Female Curiosity – Why, Child, he'd frighten thee – he's above six Feet high –

LUCY. A fine Size – I like a tall Man. [*Aside.*

SCONCE. A great huge Back and Shoulders.

LUCY. We Women love Length and Breadth in Proportion. [*Aside.*

SCONCE. Wears a great long Sword, which he calls his *Andreferara*. –

LUCY. I hear the *Irish* are naturally brave –

SCONCE. And carries a large oaken Cudgel, which he calls his *Shillela*.

LUCY. Which he can make use of on Occasions, I suppose. [*Aside.*

SCONCE. Add to this a great Pair of Jackboots, a *Cumberland* Pinch to his Hat, an old red Coat, and a damn'd Potato Face.

LUCY. He must be worth seeing truly –

CHEAT. Well, my dear Girl, be constant, wish me Success; for I shall so hum, so roast, and so banter this same *Irish* Captain, that he'll scarce wish himself in *London* again these seven Years to come.

LUCY. About it – Adieu – I hear my Father. [*Exeunt severally.*

SCENE II

A Street

Enter CAPTAIN O'BLUNDER *and* JERRY.

CAPT. And so you tells me, Chergeant, that *Terence M'Gloodtery* keeps a Goon?

SERJ. Yes, Sir.

CAPT. Monomundioul! but if I catches any of these Spalpeen Brats keeping a Goon to destroy the Game, but I will have 'em chot first, and phipt thorrough the Regiment afterwards.[5]

SERJ. One wou'd think that they should be whipp'd first, and then shot.

CAPT. Well, ishn't it the same Thing? Fat the Devil magnifies[6] that? – 'Tis but phipping and shooting all the time – 'Tis the same Thing in the End, sure, after all your Cunning, but still you'll be a Wiseacre: But that *Terence M'Gloodtery* is an old Pocher, he shoots all the Rabbits in the Country to stock his own Burrough with 'em.

Enter a MOB *who stare at him.*

1ST MOB. Twig his Boots.

2D MOB. Smoke his Sword, *&c. &c.*

CAPT. Well, you Scoundrels, did you never see an *Irish* Shentleman before?

Enter SCONCE.

SCONCE. O! fie! Gentlemen, are you not asham'd to mock a Stranger after this rude Manner.

CAPT. This is a shivil Short of a little Fellow enough. [*Aside.*

SCONCE. If he is an *Irishman*; you may see by his Dress and Behaviour, that he is a Gentleman.

CAPT. Yesh, you Shons of Whores, don't you see by my Dress and Behaviour that I'm a Shentleman-Stranger – By my Shoul if I take *Shillela* to you, I'll make you all smoke. [*Mob runs off.*

[*To Sconce*] Shir, your humble Sharvant; you seem to be a shivil mannerly Shentleman, and I shall be glad to be gratify'd with your nearer Acquaintance. [*Salute.*

Enter CHEATWELL.

CHEAT. Captain *O'Blunder*; Sir, you're extremely welcome to *London* – Sir, I'm your most sincere Friend and devoted humble Servant. –

CAPT. Yara! then how well every body knows me in *London* – to be sure they read of my Name in the Papers, and they know my Faash ever since. – Shir, your affected humble Sharvant. [*Salute.*

CHEAT. Well, and Captain, tell us, how long are you arrived; I hope you had a good Passage?

CAPT. By my Shoul, my own Bones are shore after it – We were on the Devil's own Turnpike for eight and forty Hours – to be sure, we were all in a comical Pickle. – 'Twas Old Nick's Race Horse we rode: and tho' I bid the Landlord of the Ferry-boat to stop it, he took no more Notice of me, than if I was one of the Spalpeens that was going over to reap the Harvest.

CHEAT. No, Captain! – The unmannerly Fellow; and what brought you to *London*?

CAPT. Faith, my dear Jewel, I came in the Stage-Coach from *Chester*.

CHEAT. I mean, what Business?

Notes —————————————————————

[5] *Monomundioul,* monumental; *goon,* gun.

[6] signifies; see R. B. Sheridan's Malaprop in *The Rivals* (1775) for similar wordplay.

CAPT. How damn'd inquisitive they are here! [*Aside.*] but I'll be as cunning as no Man alive. By my Shoul, my Jewel, I am going over to *Whirginny*[7] to beat the *Frinch* – They say they have driven our Countrymen out of their Plantaations; by my Shoul, my Jewel, if our Troops get vonse among them, we'll cut them all in Pieces, and then bring 'em over Prisoners of War besides.

CHEAT. Indeed, Captain, you are come upon an honourable Expedition – but pray, how is the old Gentleman your Father? I hope you left him in good Health?

CAPT. Oh! by my Shoul, he's very well, my Jewel; for he's dead these four Years.

CHEAT. And the old Gentleman, your Uncle.

CAPT. My Uncle! – You 'mean my Shister's Husband, you Fool you, that's my Brother-in-law –

CHEAT. Ay, a handsome Man –

CAPT. Ha, ha, a handsome Man? ay, for he's a damn'd crooked Fellow; he's crooked shoulder'd, and has a Hump upon his Nose, and a Pair of Huckle Backs upon his Shins, if you call that handsome – Ha, ha, ha.

CHEAT. And pray is that merry, joking Gentleman alive still – He that used to make us laugh so – Mr. – Mr. – a

CAPT. Phoo, I'll tell you who you mean – You mean *Sheela Shaghnassy*'s Husband the Exshiseman.

CHEAT. The very same.

CAPT. Oh! my dear Jewel, he's as merry as my Lord Chief Joker in *Dublin*; tho' he's not very wise phin I'm by; for I took him down – Ara, my Jewel, I'll tell you the whole Story – We took a Walk together, and the Wind was very high, considering 'twas a fine calm Morning –'Twas in our Back going, but, by my Shoul, as we return'd, it was in our Faash coming home – and yet I cou'd never persuade him that the Wind was turn'd.

CHEAT. Oh the Fool –

CAPT. Ara, so I told him, my Jewel; you great Oaf, says I – If the Wind blows in your Back going, and blows in your Faash coming, sure the Wind is turn'd – No, if I was to preach, and to preach, till last Year come Twelvemonth, I cou'd not dissuade him that the Wind was turn'd.

CHEAT. He had not common Sense – Well, and does the old Church stand where it did?

CAPT. The old Church – the Devil a Church within ten Mile of us. –

CHEAT. I'm sure there was a kind of an old Building like a Church or a Castle. –

CAPT. Phoo, my Jewel, I know what you call a Church – by my Shoul 'tis old lame *Will. Hurley*'s Mill you mean. [*Talk aside.*

Enter SCONCE *with* MONSIEUR RAGOU.

SCONCE. Consider, Monsieur, he's your Rival, and is come purely, and with an Intent to rob you of your Mistress.

MONS. Is he – Le Fripon – Le grand Fripon![8] Parblieu, me no indure dat! icy l'Epée[9] – vat you call – my Sword – Est bien assuré[10] – he may take my Vord for dat. –

SCONCE. And he's the greatest of all Cowards – tho' he carries that great swaggering broad Sword – believe me, Monsieur, he wou'd not fight a Cat – he'd run away if you drew upon him. –

Notes

[7] Virginia. Likely to be a reference to King George's War (1744–8), part of a series of conflicts between Britain and France that reached the American colonies in the 1740s and extended into the Seven Years' War.

[8] The rogue – the great rogue.

[9] Here is my sword.

[10] Be well assured.

MONS. You be bien assuré that he be de grand Coward – Mon Ami – Eh bien – vel den – I'll have his Blood – my heart dancé de pit a-pat. [*Aside.*] Je n'avois pas le Courage. I have not de good Courage.[11]

SCONCE. Tut, Man, only affront him – go up to him.

MONS. Me sal shew him de bon Addresse – Helas – [*goes up to the Captain*] Monsieur le Capitaine vous êtes le grand Fripon.[12] –

CAPT. *Wel gelun a gud*, have you any *Irish*?[13]

MONS. *Irelande*! me be no such outlandish Country: – You smell of de Potatoe. –

CAPT. Do I – by my Shoul I did not taasht a Praty since I left *Ireland*; may be he has a mind to put the Front upon me. [*To* Cheatwell.

CHEAT. It looks like it, very like it, Captain.

CAPT. Faith, my Jewel, I don't know a more peaceable Companion than *Andreferara* here – [*shewing his Sword.*] but if he's provok'd – he's no Slouch at it – do you mean to front me, you *French* Boogre – Eh –

MONS. Affront – you be de Teague, de vild *Irishman* – de Potato Face – me no think it vorth my while to notice you. Otez-vous, je dis – go about your Business. –

CAPT. Oh, ho, are you there? – come out, my trusty *Andreferara* – here take *Shillela* – [*Gives his Cudgel to* Cheatwell.]

SCONCE. Draw, for he won't fight. [*To the* Frenchman.

MONS. He be de terrible Countenance – he be fort enragé, dev'lish angry.

CAPT. Come on, you Soup Maigre.[14] [*They fight – Monsieur falls.*

CAPT. After that *you're* easy – who smells of Pratys now? you Refugee Son of a Whore – Affront an *Irish* Shentleman!

SCONCE. The Man's dead.

CAPT. Is he? – what magnifies that; I kill'd him in the fair duelling Way.

CHEAT. But, Captain, 'tis Death by the Law to duel in *England* – and this Place is not so safe a Place for you – I'm heartily sorry for this Accident.

CAPT. Ara, my Jewel, they don't mind it in *Ireland* one Trawneen.

CHEAT. Come, come, Captain, safe's the Word – the Street will be soon alarmed – you can come to my House till the Danger's over – and I will get you Bail.

CAPT. By my Shoul, I believe 'tis the best Way, for fear of the Boners.

CHEAT. Here's my Friend will shew you the Way to my House; I'll be with you in a Minute. [*Exit* Captain *with* Sconce.

CHEAT. Are you dead, Monsieur? Eveillez-vois – get up Man. [*Monsieur rises.*

MONS. Parblieu – ille avoit de long Rapier[15] – he be de terrible *Irishman* – 'tis well me fall in time, or he make me fall so dat me never resusciter[16] – never get up again.

CHEAT. Well, I'm glad there's no more Mischief done –
   Come, never mind the *Irishman* a Rush,
   You and the Captain shall have t'other Brush.

MONS. Parblieu – me kiss de Book – me just have swore,
   Never to fight an *Irishman*, no more. [*Exeunt.*

Notes ─────────────────────────────────────

[11] Ragou translates himself.

[12] Alas … Captain, you are a great rogue.

[13] O'Blunder translates himself. Eighteenth-century English and Scottish editions, as well as pre-1759 Dublin editions, print this as "Well, gelun a gud," but "wel" is the Irish verb "bhfuil" not the English word "Well." Christopher Murray gives O'Blunder's phrase in modern Irish spelling: "an bhfuil Gaelainn agat?" See Christopher Murray (ed.), "Drama, 1690–1800," in *The Field Day Anthology of Irish Writing* (Derry: Field Day, 1991), I: 535n.

[14] weak soup

[15] Of course! He has a long sword.

[16] revive

SCENE III

A Mad-house

Enter CAPTAIN *and* SCONCE.

SCONCE. Captain, this is your Cousin's House: I'll go and get proper Things for your Accommodation – Sir, your humble Servant for a Moment or so – give me your Things. [*Takes his Sword and Cudgel.*

CAPT. Shir, your most humble Sharvant. [*Looks about*] Faith my Cousin's House is a brave large Place – tho' it is not so very well furnished – but I suppose the Maid was cleaning out the Rooms: So – who are these now – Some Acquaintance of my Cousin's, to be sure.

Enter DR. CLYSTER *and* DR. GALLYPOT.[17]

[*Both salute the* Captain.]

CAPT. Shentlemen, your most humble Sharvant – but where's my Cousin?

CLYST. His Cousin – what does he mean? [*To Dr.* Gallypot.

GALLY. What shou'd a Madman mean? Sir, we come to treat you in a regular Manner.

CAPT. O, dear Shentlemen, 'tis too much Trouble – you need not be over regular, a single joint of Meat, and a good Glass of Ale, will be a very good Treat without any needless Expences.

CLYST. Do you mind that Symptom – the canine Appetite.

CAPT. Nine Appetites – no, my Jewel; I have an Appetite like other People; a Couple of Pounds will serve me if I was ever so hungry – phat the Devil do they talk of nine Appetites; do they think I'm a Cat, that have as many Stomachs as Lives.

GALLY. He looks a little wild, Brother.

CAPT. Fat! are you Brothers?

BOTH. Pray, Sir, be seated; we shall examine methodically into the Nature of your Case.

[*They sit –* Captain *in the Middle – they feel his Pulse – he stares at them.*

CAPT. Fat de devil do they mean by taking me by the Wrists – may-be 'tis the Fashion of Compliment in *London.*

CLYST. Brother, you plainly perceive that the Systole and Diastole are obstructed.

CAPT. My Piss-hole and Arse-hole – Fat the Devil ails them? Eh! sure dey're mad.

GALLY. First, Brother, let us examine the Symptoms.

CAPT. By my Shoul, the Fellows are Fools.

CLYST. Pray, Sir, how do you rest?

CAPT. In a good Feather-bed, my Jewel – and sometimes I take a Nap in an Arm-chair.

CLYST. But do you sleep sound?

CAPT. Faith I sleep and snore all Night; and when I awake in the Morning, I find myself fast asleep.

GALLY. The *Cerebrum* or *Cerebellum* is affected.

CAPT. The Devil a Sir Abram, or Bell either, I mind.

GALLY. How do you eat, Sir?

Notes

[17] *Clyster* means enema, and *gallypot* (or *gallipot*) is a pot for medicines.

CAPT. Width my Mouth – how the Devil shou'd I eat, d'ye think.

CLYST. Pray, Sir, have you a good Stomach, d'ye eat heartily?

CAPT. Oh, my Jewel, I'm no Slouch at that, tho' a clumsy Beef-stake, or the Leg and Arm of a Turkey, with a Griskin under the Oxter wou'd sharve my Turn.[18]

GALLY. Do you generally drink much?

CAPT. Oh, my Jewel, a Couple of Quarts of Ale and Porter wou'd not choke me; but fat the Devil magnifies so many Questions about eating and drinking – if you have a mind to order any thing, do it as soon as you can, for I am almost famish'd.

CLYST. I am for treating him regularly, methodically, and secundum Artem.[19]

CAPT. Secundum Fartem – I don't see any Sign of treating at all – Ara, my Jewels, send for a Mutton Chop, and don't trouble yourselves about my Stomach.

CLYST. I shall give you my Opinion, concerning this Case, Brother – *Galen* says.[20]

CAPT. *Wel gelun a gud?*

CLYST. I say that *Galen* is of Opinion, that in all adust Complexions.[21]

CAPT. Well, and who has a dusty Complexion?

CLYST. A little Patience, Sir.

CAPT. I think I have a great deal of Patience; that People can't eat a Morsel without so many impertinent Questions.

CLYST. *Qui habet vultum Adustum,*
      Habet caninum Gustum.[22]

CAPT. I'm sure 'tis an ugly Custom to keep a Man fasting so long after pretending to treat him.

GALLY. Ay, Brother, but *Hippocrates* differs from *Galen* in this Case.[23]

CAPT. Well, but my Jewels, let there be no Difference, nor falling out between Brodthers about me, for a small Matter will sharve my Turn.

CLYST. Sir, you break the Thread of our Discourse; I was observing that in gloomy opaque Habits, the Rigidity of the Solids causes a continual Friction in the Fluids, which, by being constantly impeded, grow thick and glutinous, by which Means they cannot enter the capillary Vessels, nor the other finer Ramifications of the Nerves.

GALLY. Then, Brother, from your Position, it will be deducible that the *Primae Viae* are first to be cleared, which must be effected by frequent Emeticks.[24]

CLYST. Sudorificks.

GALLY. Catharticks.

CLYST. Pneumaticks.

GALLY. Restoratives.

CLYST. Corrosives.

GALLY. Narcoticks.

CLYST. Cephalicks.

Notes

[18] *Clumsy* means cold, *griskin* is a cut of pork, and *oxter* is the underside of an arm.

[19] "According to the rules of art," here the skilled work of preparing medicines.

[20] Galen, second-century Greek physician whose ideas influenced European medicine until the Enlightenment. In this model, the human body is governed by humors – in Galen, they are choleric, melancholic, phlegmatic, and sanguine – which in excess cause disease. Cures purge excesses to restore balance, as in phlebotomy, the surgical opening of a vein to draw blood.

[21] An *adust complexion* refers to a patient who is sick because of dryness, in Galenic terms.

[22] These Latin lines suggest that someone with an *adust* humor will also have a dog's appetite, perhaps implying that the Captain's stomach is growling.

[23] Hippocrates (460–380 BCE), physician and early thinker on medical ethics.

[24] *Primae Viae* are "primary pathways." The doctors then list a series of medicines, beginning with purgatives – *emeticks* and *sudorificks*.

GALLY. Pectorals.

CLYST. Stypticks.

GALLY. Specificks.

CLYST. Causticks.

CAPT. How naturally they answer one another, like the Parish Minister and the Clerk – by my Shoul, Jewels, this Gibberish will never fill a Man's Belly.

CLYST. And thus to speak *Summatim*, and *Articulatim*, or categorically, to recapitulate the several Remedies in the Aggregate, the Emeticks will clear the first Passages, and restore the Viscera to their pristine Tone, and regulate their lost peristaltick or vermicular Motion; so that from the Oesephagus to the Rectum I am for potent Emeticks.

GALLY. And next for Sudorificks, as they open the Pores, or rather the porous Continuity of the cutaneous Dermis and Epidermis: thence to convey the noxious and melancholy Humours of the Blood.

CLYST. With Catharticks to purge him.

GALLY. Pneumaticks to scourge him.

CLYST. Narcoticks to doze him.

GALLY. Cephalicks to poze him.

CAPT. These are some of the Dishes they are to treat me with – Why, my Jewels, there's no need for all this Cookery – upon my Shoul this is to be a grand Entertainment. Well, they'll have their own Way.

CLYST. Suppose we use Phlebotomy, and take from him thirty Ounces of Blood.

CAPT. Flea my Bottom, d'ye say?

GALLY. His Eyes roll – call in the Keepers. [*Enter Keepers.*

CAPT. Flea my Bottom – Oh, my *Andreferara* and *Shillela*, I want ye now – but here's a Chair – Flea my Bottom – Ye Sons of Whores – ye Giberish Scoundrels. [*Drives them out.*

Oh! this Son of a Whore of a Cousin of mine, to bring me to these Thieves to flea my Bottom – If I meet him, I'll flea his Bottom. [*Exit.*

SCENE IV

The Street

Enter SERJEANT.

I have been seeking my Master every where, and cannot find him; I hope nothing has happened to him – I think that was one of the Gentlemen I saw with him.

Enter SCONCE.

Sir, Sir, pray did you see the Captain, my Master, Captain *O'Blunder*, the *Irish* Gentleman?

SCONCE. Not I, indeed, my Friend – I left him last with Mr. *Cheatwell* – I suppose they're taking a Bottle together – Oh, No! here's the Captain.

Enter CAPTAIN.

CAPT. Oh! my dear Friend, I had like to be lost, to be ruinated by that Scoundrel my Coushin – Well, I'm so out of Breath, I ran away with my Life from the

Thieves – You know you left me at my Coushin's House – Well, I walk'd about for some Time, to be sure I thought it an odd sort of a House, when I saw no Furniture – There I expected my Coushin every Moment; and, dear Honey, there came in two Bird-lime Sons of Whores, with great Whigs – they look'd like Conjurors and Fortune-tellers – one takes hold of one of my Wrists, and the other catches hold of my other Wrist; I thought by way of Complement. I sat down betwixt them; did they chatter such Gibberish, like a Couple of old Baboons; and all this Discourse was conchaarning me – they talk'd at first of treating me, and ask'd me, Had I a good Stomach? – one of 'em said, I had nine Appetites; but at length, my Jewels, what shou'd come of the Treat, but they agreed before my Face to flea my Bottom – Oh! if I tell you a Word of Lie, I'm not here – My Dear, they calls in the Keepers to tie me; I up with the Chair; for I gave you my *Shillela* and *Andreferara*, and drove them out, and made my Escape.

SCONCE. I am sorry to see that your Cousin has behaved so rudely towards you; but any thing that lies in my Power –

CAPT. Oh! Sir, you're a very worthy Shentleman; but, Cherjeant, I must go to see Mr. *Trader* the Merchant, and his fair Daughter. – Has the Taylor brought home my Clothes?

SERJ. Yes, Sir, and the old Gentleman expects you immediately, and sent a Man in Livery for you. –

CAPT. Come, my good Friend, I won't part with you – I'll step to my Lodgings, and just slip on my Clothes, that I may pay my due Regards to my Mishtress. [*Exeunt.*

SCENE V

The Madhouse

CHEATWELL, CLYSTER, *and* GALLYPOT.

CHEAT. I'm sorry for this Accident.

CLYST. In troth, Mr. *Cheatwell*, he was the most furious Madman that ever I met with during the whole Course of my Practice.

GALLY. I am now surpris'd how he sat so long quiet.

CHEAT. He'll run riot about the Streets; but I hope he'll be taken – Oh! here's *Sconce*.

Enter SCONCE.

Well, what News of the Captain?

SCONCE. I just ran to let you know of his Motions; he is preparing to dress, in order to pay a Visit to Miss *Lucy*, and to pay his Respects to *Trader*; and worse News for you, 'tis whisper'd on *Change*,[25] that *Trader* is broke.

CHEAT. If that shou'd fall out so, I shall easily resign my Pretensions to the Captain. 'Twas *Lucy*'s Purse, and not her Beauty, that I courted.

SCONCE. I must run back to the Captain, and keep in with him, to serve a Turn; do you at a Distance watch us, and proceed accordingly. [*Exit.*

CHEAT. Well, Gentlemen, I shall take care to acknowledge your Trouble the first Time I see you again; so adieu. [*Exeunt.*

Notes
_____

[25] The stock exchange.

Scene VI

The CAPTAIN's Lodgings

CAPT. Arrah but who the Divil do you think I met Yesterday full but in the Street but *Theady Shaghnassy?*

SERJ. Well, and how is he?

CAPT. Arrah staay till I tell you; he wash at todther Side of the Way, and when I came up, it wash not him. Tell me, dosh my new Regimentals become me?

SERJ. Yes indeed, Sir, I think they do.

CAPT. This Pocket is too high; I must be forced to stoop for my Snuff-box.

Enter SCONCE.

Ha! upon my Word, Captain, you look as spruce as a young Bridegroom.

CAPT. All in good Time – and does it fit easy?

SCONCE. Easy! Sir, it fits like your Shirt.

CAPT. I think it's a little too wide here in the Sleeve: I'm afraid the Fellow hasn't left Cloth enough to take it in; tho' I can't blame the Fellow neither; for I was not by when he took Measure of me – Cherjeant, here, go, take this Sixpence Halfpenny, and buy me a Pair of phite Gloves.

SCONCE. I don't think you can get a Pair for Sixpence.

CAPT. Why, how much will the Leatherman have?

SCONCE. Two Shillings.

CAPT. Two Thirteens!

SERJ. Indeed, Sir, you won't get them less in *London.*

CAPT. Not less than Two Thirteens! *Monomondioul!* but I'd rather my Hands shou'd go barefoot all the Days of their Lives, than give Two Thirteens for a Pair of Gloves – Come, come along, I'll go without 'em; my Mishtress must excuse me. [*Exeunt.*

Scene *changes to* TRADER's House

Enter TRADER *and* LUCY.

TRA. Well, Daughter, I have been examining into the Circumstances of *Cheatwell,* and find he is not worth a Six-pence; and, as for your *French* Lover, he is some run-away Dancing-master or Hair-cutter from *Paris;* so that really, among them all, I cannot find any one to come up to your *Irish* Lover, either for Birth, Fortune, or Character.

LUCY. Sir, you're the best Judge in the disposing of me; and indeed I have no real Tendre for any one of them – As to the *Irish* Captain, I have not seen him as yet.

TRA. You'll see him presently; I sent to his Lodgings, and expect him every Moment – Oh! here's Monsieur.

Enter MONSIEUR RAGOU.

TRA. Well, Monsieur, I have been trying my Daughter's Affections in Regard to you, and as she is willing to be guided by me in this Affair, I wou'd willingly know by what visible Means you intend to maintain her like a Gentlewoman, as she is both by Birth and Education?

MONS. Me have de grand Acquaintance with the Beau Monde;[26] and, si vous plais,[27] to do me the Honour of making me your Son-in-Law, me transact your Negotiations with all possible Care and Belle Air.[28]

Enter CAPTAIN O'BLUNDER, *&c.*

TRA. You're welcome to my House – Sir, this is my Daughter – this, Child, is Captain *O'Blunder*, whom I hope you will receive as he deserves.

CAPT. Fairest of Creatures, will you gratify me with a Taste of your sweet delicate Lips. [*Kisses.*] By my Shoul a neat Creature, and a good Bagooragh Girl – Oh, oh! I see my *Frenchman!* and, Faith, I have a Praty ready for him now.

MONS. Oh! Le Diable[29] – he espy me – me better go off while I am well.

CAPT. [*goes up to* Monsieur.] I thought, Monsieur *Ragou*, that you were dead – Do I smell of the Praty now, you Soupe Maigre Son of a *French* Boogre.

TRA. The Captain has a Mind to be merry with the *Frenchman.*

CAPT. By my Shoul, my Jewel, I have got a Praty for you now – here – eat it. Eat this – Oh oh, come forth. [*Draws.*] Eat that Praty this Minute. I'm sure 'tis better nor your Garlick nor Ingyons[30] in *France.* [*Frenchman eats it.*

Enter a SERVANT *to* TRADER.

SERV. Oh! Sir – there are certain Accounts come – but these Letters will better inform you.

TRA. [*reads*] Oh, Captain, I am ruin'd, undone – broke –

CAPT. Broke! what have you broke?

TRA. Oh! Sir, my Fortune's broke; I am not a Penny above a Beggar.

MONS. Oh! den me be off de Amour – me have no Dealings with Beggars; me have too many of de Beggar in my own Country; so me better slip away in good Time. [*Exit.*

TRA. So now, Captain, I have not concealed my Misfortunes from you; you are at Liberty to choose a happier Wife, for my poor Child is miserable.

CAPT. I thought your Ribs was broke; I am no Surgeon; but if 'tis only a little Money that broke you, give me this sweet Lady's Lilly-white Hand, and, as far as a good Estate in Land and Stock will go, I'll share it with her, and with yourself – Ara, never mind the Thieves, my Jewel, I'll break their Necks before they shall break your little Finger. Come, I'll give you a Song of my own Composition.

> *Wherever I'm going, and all the Day long,*
> *Abroad and at Home, or alone in a Throng,*
> *I find that my Passion's so lively and strong,*
> *That your Name, when I'm silent, runs still in my Song,*
> *Sing* Balinamone oro, Balinamone oro, Balinamone oro,
> *A Kiss of your sweet Lips for me.*

Notes ──

[26] fashionable society

[27] if you please

[28] good grace

[29] Oh, the devil!

[30] onions

Since the first time I saw you, I take no Repose,
I sleep all the Day to forget half my Woes;
So strong is the Flame in my Bosom which glows,
By St. Patrick I'm afraid it would burn thro' my Cloaths:
 Sing Ballinamone oro, &c.
  Your pretty black Hair for me.

On that happy Day, when I make you my Bride,
With a swinging long Sword, how I'll strut and I'll stride,
In a Coach and six Horses with Honey I'll ride,
As before you I walk to the Church by your Side,
 Sing Balinamone oro, &c.
  Your little white Fist for me.

Enter CHEATWELL.

Gentlemen, I beg Pardon for this Intrusion.

CAPT. Oh, by my Shoul, this is my friendly Coushin that bid the old Conjurors flea my Bottom.

CHEAT. Sir, I beg your Pardon in particular, and hope you'll grant me it; nothing but Necessity was the Cause of my ungenteel Behaviour – This Lady I had an Esteem for; but since Things have turn'd out as they have, my Pretensions are without Foundation; and therefore rais'd the Report of your Ships being lost at Sea, in hopes that this Gentleman would decline his Addresses to your Daughter, when he found she had no Fortune.

CAPT. Oagh, my Dear, we play no such dirty Tricks in our *Country*.

CHEAT. And now, Captain, I hope you'll grant me your Pardon, and look upon me in the Light of an unfortunate Man, rather than of a bad Man.

CAPT. Faath, my dear Coushin, since Love is the Cause of your Mourning, I shall forgive you with all my Heart. [*Shakes hands.*

CHEAT. Sir, I shall always look upon your Friendship as an Honour; and hope you'll look upon me as a poor unfortunate young Fellow, that has not a Shilling, nor the Means of getting one upon the Face of the Earth.

CAPT. Oh, upon my Shoul, then, cousin *Cheatwell*, I pitty your Condition with all my Heart; and since Things are so bad with you, if you'll take a Trip to my *Irish* Plantations with me and my dear Creature here, I'll give you 500 *l.* to stock a Farm upon my own Eshtate, at *Ballymascushlane*, in the County of *Monaghan*, and the Barony of *Coogafighy* – Fait, and here's *Betty*, a tight Girl; and since you cou'd not get the Mistress, if you'll take up with the Maid, my Dear here, shall give her a Couple of Hundred to fortune her off.

BETTY. Captain, I'm very much obliged to you, for getting me a Husband; if Mr. *Cheatwell* has any Tendre for me, I have a thousand Pound at his Service of my own saving.

CAPT. Oagh, dear Joy, a Servant-maid with a thousand Pound! Phy, in my Country, there is many a fine Lady has not half the Money, and goes to the Plays, and the Balls, and the Reddottos, and won't make her own Smock.

CHEAT. I should be blind to my own Interest not to accept of such valuable Proposals, and with Gratitude take your Hand, promising, for the future, to lead a Life which shall be a Credit both to myself and my Benefactor.

CAPT. Well then, without Compliments, I am glad to have made one poor Man happy; and since we have made a double Match of it, hey for *Ireland*, where we will all live like the Sons of *Irish* Kings.

LUCY. This Generosity amazes me, and greatly prejudices me in the Honesty and Goodness of the *Irish*.

CAPT. Oagh, my dear little Charmer, I've anodther Song just *à propos*.

> *Of all the Husbands living an* Irishman's *the best,*
> With my fal, lal, &c.
> *No Nation on the Globe, oagh like him can stand the Test,*
> With my fal, lal, &c.
> *The* English *are all Drones, as you may plainly see,*
> *But we're all brisk and airy, and lively as a Bee.*
> With my fal, lal, &c.

LUCY. Sir, your generous Behaviour so frankly shewn on so melancholy an Accident, has entirely gained my Heart, nor do I value your Estate, when set in Composition with your noble Soul.

> *Thus, let all Women judge and thus decide,*
> *Be Beauty still to noble Worth ally'd;*
> *Nor glittering Wealth shou'd blind the Fair-one's Eyes,*
> *Which, not with Honour join'd, we shou'd despise.* [*Exeunt.*
> FINIS

EPILOGUE

> *Tut! tut! I was mistaken – ne'er believe me,*
> *If any Scandal shall again deceive me:*
> *For now I find, they made me but a Child,*
> *To tell me that the* Irish *all were wild:*
> *My* Captain *is as gentle as a Dove,*
> *As innocent, and quite as full of Love –*
> *Ye British Fair, if ye wou'd wed* THE TRUTH,
> *You'll only find it in the* IRISH *Youth:*
> *The* Irish *to our Hearts have found the Way,*
> *I ne'er believ'd it till I saw – the Key.*
> *Our dearest Secret best such Youth rewards,*
> *Who find the Key-hole quick, and hit so* true *the Wards.*

Frances Sheridan (1724–1766)

Born Frances Chamberlaine in Dublin, Sheridan grew up in a household divided on the subject of women's education. Her father, a clergyman in the Church of Ireland, opposed women's education but her brothers thought differently. They helped her become not only literate but also knowledgeable in such traditionally masculine subjects as Latin and botany. A prolific author, she wrote her first novel, *Eugenie and Adelaide*, at the age of fifteen. She married Thomas Sheridan in 1747 (see above), and helped to educate her sons and daughters, all of whom became authors.

It was in the 1760s, however, after she and her husband fled Ireland for debt, that her own literary career began in earnest. Her novel *Memoirs of Miss Sidney Bidulph* (1761) was an enormous critical success and was repeatedly republished. She also published two plays, *The Discovery* (1763) and *The Dupe* (1763), and began a third, *A Journey to Bath*. These were followed, posthumously, by a sequel to her first novel, *Continuation of the Memoirs* (1767), and an oriental romance, *The History of Nourjahad* (1767). Sheridan's granddaughter, novelist and poet Alicia Lefanu, wrote a biography of her that was published in 1824 and remains the primary source on her life. Whyte's *Miscellany* (1799), however, includes a number of Frances Sheridan's letters to Samuel Whyte, along with other family materials that were not included in Lefanu's biography.

Of Sheridan's plays, *The Discovery* was the most successful. It ran for seventeen nights on its introduction to the stage and was subsequently published; it enjoyed a number of reprints as well as revivals on the stage in subsequent decades. As late as 1924, Aldous Huxley adapted it for the modern stage. In *The Discovery*, as in *Memoirs*, Sheridan not only deals with the conventional subject of marriage comedies, namely children who wish to marry those they love instead of those their parents have selected for them, but also frankly with extra-marital affairs and acceptingly of the children that result from such affairs.

While Sheridan's literary energies were directed primarily at lengthy works such as five-act dramas and novels, she also wrote a few short lyrics. One, "Ode to Patience," was included in Whyte's *Miscellany* (1799) as part of her letter to Samuel Whyte, dated May 12, 1764; the poem also appeared, with minor variations, in Lefanu's *Memoirs* (1824). Samuel Whyte was a family friend and ran a much-admired Dublin school that counted two of Sheridan's children, the future playwrights Richard and Alicia, among its students. After apologizing for not writing more frequently (a recurring theme in her letters to Whyte), Sheridan introduces her poem: "And now, Sam, by way of compensation, for that is not in my power to make you; but as a sort of little regale in your own way, for want of other matter, I will send you the result of a morning's meditation." The Whytes and Sheridan's granddaughter-biographer read the poem as a lament for trying difficulties in Sheridan's life, but Sheridan's introduction of the poem suggests a note of rebuke to Whyte as well for his apparently regular demands for more prompt replies to his letters.

Further reading

Doody, Margaret Anne, "Frances Sheridan: Morality and Annihilated Time," in *Fetter'd or Free? British Women Novelists, 1670–1815*, ed. Mary Anne Schofield and Cecilia Macheski, 324–58. Athens, OH: Ohio University Press, 1986.
Kuti, Elizabeth, "Rewriting Frances Sheridan," *Eighteenth-century Ireland* 11 (1996): 120–8.
Sheridan, Frances, *Plays of Frances Sheridan*, ed. Robert Hogan and Jerry C. Beasley. Newark: University of Delaware Press, 1984.

Prologue

From The Discovery (1763)

A Female culprit at your bar appears,
Not destitute of hope, nor free from fears.
Her utmost crime she's ready to confess,
A simple trespass – neither more nor less;
For, truant like, she rambled out of bounds,
And dar'd to venture on poetic grounds.

    The fault is deem'd high-treason by the men,
Those lordly tyrants, who usurp the pen;
Then try the vile monopoly to hide

5

With flattering Arts, "You ladies have beside   10
So many ways to conquer – Sure 'tis fit
You leave to us that dangerous weapon, wit!"
For women, like state criminals, they think,
Should be debarr'd the use of pen and ink.

    Our author, who disclaims such partial laws,   15
To her own sex appeals to judge her cause:
She pleads old MAGNA CHARTA on her side,
That BRITISH subjects by their peers be try'd.

    Ladies, to you she dedicates her lays,
Assert your right to censure or to praise;   20
Nor doubt a sentence by such lips decreed,
Firm as the laws of Persian or of Mede:[1]
Boldly your will in open court declare,
And let the men dispute it if they dare.

    Our humble scenes no charms of art can boast,   25
But simple nature, and plain sense at most:
Perhaps some character – a moral too –
And what is stranger still – the story's new:
No borrow'd thoughts throughout the piece are shown,
But what our author writes is ALL HER OWN.   30

    By no sly hint, or incident she tries
To bid on modest cheeks the blush arise:
The loosest thoughts our decent scenes suggest,
Virtue herself might harbour in her breast;
And where our harmless satyr vents its spleen,   35
The soberest prude may laugh without a screen.
But not to mirth alone we claim your ear,
Some tender scenes demand the melting tear;
The comic dame, her different powers to prove,
Gives you the dear variety you love;   40
Sometimes assumes her graver sister's art,
Borrows her form, and tries to touch the heart.
But fancy's pictures float upon the brain,
And short-liv'd o'er the heart is passion's reign,
Till judgement stamp her sanction on the whole,   45
And sink th'impression deep into the soul.

Ode to Patience (wr. 1764)

Unaw'd by threats, unmov'd by force,
My steady Soul pursues her course,
    Collected, calm, resign'd;
Say, you who search with curious eyes

Notes ——————————————————————————————

PROLOGUE
[1] Deioces the Mede, a judge of note and later king of the
Medes around 700 BCE.

The source whence human actions rise,   5
   Say, whence this turn of mind?

'Tis Patience ... Lenient Goddess, hail!
Oh! let thy votary's vows prevail,
   Thy threaten'd flight to stay;
Long hast thou been a welcome guest,   10
Long reign'd an inmate in this breast,
   And rul'd with gentle sway.

Thro' all the various turns of fate,
Ordain'd me in each several state,
   My wayward lot has known;   15
What taught me silently to bear,
To curb the sigh, to check the tear,
   When sorrow weigh'd me down?

'Twas Patience ... Temperate Goddess, stay!
For still thy dictates I obey,   20
   Nor yield to Passion's Power;
Tho' by injurious foes borne down,
My fame, my toil, my hopes o'erthrown,
   In one ill-fated hour.

When robb'd of what I held most dear,   25
My hands adorn'd the mournful bier
   Of her I lov'd so well;
What, when mute sorrow chain'd my tongue,
As o'er the sable hearse I hung,
   Forbade the tide to swell?   30

'Twas Patience! ... Goddess ever calm!
Oh! pour into my breast thy balm,
   That antidote to pain;
Which flowing from thy nectar'd urn,
By chymistry divine can turn   35
   Our losses into gain.

When sick and languishing in bed,
Sleep from my restless couch had fled,
   (Sleep, which even pain beguiles,)
What taught me calmly to sustain   40
A feverish being rack'd with pain,
   And dress'd my looks in smiles?

'Twas Patience! ... Heaven-descended Maid!
Implor'd, flew swiftly to my aid,
   And lent her fostering breast;   45
Watch'd my sad hours with parent care,
Repell'd the approaches of despair,
   And sooth'd my soul to rest.

Say, when dissever'd from his side,
My friend, protector, and my guide,   50
   When my prophetic soul,

Anticipating all the storm,
Saw danger in its direst form,
    What could my fears controul?

'Twas Patience! ... Gentle goddess, hear!   55
Be ever to thy suppliant near,
    Nor let one murmur rise;
Since still some mighty joys are given,
Dear to her soul, the gifts of Heaven,
    The sweet domestic ties.   60

Oliver Goldsmith (1728–1774)

Oliver Goldsmith was born in Co. Longford; his father was a Church of Ireland clergyman and a farmer. He completed a degree at Trinity College Dublin in the late 1740s and began medical studies at the University of Edinburgh in 1752, but did not complete them, spending much of the early 1750s touring Europe. In 1756, he arrived in London and, while trying his hand at various jobs, he began to work as a writer, starting with a position writing for the *Monthly Review*; among the books he reviewed was Edmund Burke's *Enquiry*. He continued to contribute to various periodicals, serially publishing some of his early works, such as a life of Voltaire and the letters later collected as *The Citizen of the World* (1762). He also briefly edited a periodical called *The Bee*. He socialized with many of the leading literary lights of his day, including Edmund Burke and English writers from Thomas Percy to Samuel Johnson.

In the *Citizen of the World*, originally a series of letters in *The Public Ledger* (1760–1) that drew heavily on earlier orientalist materials, Goldsmith depicts London from the perspective of "a Chinese Philosopher," Lien Chi Altangi. Goldsmith satirizes both English society and the misunderstandings of the traveler who is new to the vagaries of that society, while weaving in a larger narrative of the protagonist's social group in London. Using the letters of a foreign visitor

was an increasingly popular device for representing cultural difference, and intersects with the genre of the travelogue which was becoming increasingly important. Goldsmith's satire is also topical, dealing with the Seven Years' War and the fashion for orientalist literature. Over the next decade, he published *An History of England in a Series of Letters from a Nobleman to his Son* (1764); the poems *The Traveller* (1764) and *The Deserted Village* (1770); the important sentimental novel, *The Vicar of Wakefield* (1766); and two plays, *The Good-Natur'd Man* (1767) and, more famously, *She Stoops to Conquer* (1773). He was also commissioned to write a number of histories and wrote on Irish subjects, including an essay on O'Carolan.

The Deserted Village is his best-known poetic work. It was republished frequently after its original appearance in 1770 and remains a canonical example of pastoral even as it blends satire and elements of the Graveyard School in viewing the countryside as the site of loss and social decline. Whether Goldsmith was nostalgically depicting his early life and locale in Ireland has been much debated. But Goldsmith's haunted view of an emptied landscape where the speaker's memory is the only surviving record of a vibrant community also anticipates much of the best topographical verse produced by Irish writers over the next century, including poems in this anthology by Drennan, Mangan, and MacCarthy. "Retaliation" (1775) is in a quite different vein, following the conventions of Augustan verse satire to caricature famous friends, including the Burkes.

The copy-texts here are Irish editions. The 1770 Dublin edition of *The Deserted Village* used as a copy-text is one of two Dublin editions, and the one closest in many details, such as variant punctuation, to the 1770 London edition which Goldsmith may have proofread. The Dublin printer, however, uses apostrophes in place of letters more liberally. The 1775 Belfast edition of "Retaliation" is also substantially the same as the first London edition except for the notes, which varied somewhat from edition to edition.

Further reading

Cole, Richard C., "Oliver Goldsmith's Reputation in Ireland, 1762–74," *Modern Philology* 68 (1970): 65–70.

Deane, Seamus, "Goldsmith's *The Citizen of the World*," in *The Art of Oliver Goldsmith*, ed. Andrew Swarbrick, 33–50. London: Vision Press, 1984.

Griffin, Michael, "Delicate Allegories, Deceitful Mazes: Goldsmith's Landscapes," *Eighteenth-century Ireland* 16 (2001): 104–17.

Watt, James, "Goldsmith's Cosmopolitanism," *Eighteenth-century Life* 30 (2006): 56–76.

Letter XVII[1]

From The Citizen of the World (1762)

[*From Lien Chi Altangi ... to Fum Hoam, first president of the ceremonial academy at Pekin in China*]

Were an Asiatic politician to read the treaties of peace and friendship that have been annually making for more than an hundred years among the inhabitants of Europe, he would probably be surpriz'd how it should ever happen that christian princes could quarrel among each other. Their compacts for peace are drawn up with the utmost precision, and ratified with the greatest solemnity; to these each party promises a sincere and inviolable obedience, and all wears the appearance of open friendship and unreserved reconciliation.

Yet, notwithstanding those treaties, the people of Europe are almost continually at war. There is nothing more easy than to break a treaty ratified in all the usual forms, and yet neither party be the aggressor. One side, for instance, breaks a trifling article by mistake; the opposite party upon this makes a small but premeditated reprisal; this brings on a return of greater from the other; both sides complain of injuries and infractions; war is declar'd; they beat, are beaten; some two or three hundred thousand men are killed, they grow tired, leave off just where they began; and so sit cooly down to make new treaties.

The English and French seem to place themselves foremost among the champion states of Europe. Though parted by a narrow sea, yet are they entirely of opposite characters; and from their vicinity are taught to fear and admire each other. They are at present engaged in a very destructive war, have already spilled much blood, are excessively irritated; and all upon account of one side's desiring to wear greater quantities of *furs* than the other.

Notes ───────────────────────────────

LETTER XVII

[1] This letter deals with the Seven Years' War (1756–63), still being fought as Goldsmith was writing and publishing this work.

The pretext of the war is about some lands a thousand leagues off; a country cold, desolate, and hideous; a country belonging to a people who were in possession for time immemorial. The savages of Canada claim a property in the country in dispute; they have all the pretensions which long possession can confer. Here they had reigned for ages without rivals in dominion, and knew no enemies but the prowling bear or insidious tyger; their native forests produced all the necessaries of life, and they found ample luxury in the enjoyment. In this manner they might have continued to live to eternity, had not the English been informed that those countries produced furs in great abundance. From that moment the country became an object of desire; it was found that furs were things very much wanted in England; the ladies edged some of their cloaths with furs, and muffs were worn both by gentlemen and ladies. In short, furs were found indispensably necessary for the happiness of the state: and the king was consequently petitioned to grant not only the country of Canada, but all the savages belonging to it to the subjects of England, in order to have the people supplied with proper quantities of this necessary commodity.

So very reasonable a request was immediately complied with, and large colonies were sent abroad to procure furs, and take possession. The French who were equally in want of furs (for they were as fond of muffs and tippets as the English) made the very same request to their monarch, and met with the same gracious reception from their king, who generously granted what was not his to give. Wherever the French landed, they called the country their own; and the English took possession wherever they came upon the same equitable pretensions. The harmless savages made no opposition; and could the intruders have agreed together, they might peaceably have shared this desolate country between them. But they quarrelled about the boundaries of their settlements, about grounds and rivers to which neither side could shew any other right than that of power, and which neither could occupy but by usurpation. Such is the contest, that no honest man can heartily wish success to either party.

The war has continued for some time with various success. At first the French seemed victorious; but the English have of late dispossessed them of the whole country in dispute.[2] Think not, however, that success on one side is the harbinger of peace: on the contrary, both parties must be heartily tired to effect even a temporary reconciliation. It should seem the business of the victorious party to offer terms of peace; but there are many in England, who, encouraged by success, are still for protracting the war.

The best English politicians, however, are sensible, that to keep their present conquests, would be rather a burthen than an advantage to them, rather a diminution of their strength than an encrease of power. It is in the politic as in the human constitution; if the limbs grow too large for the body, their size, instead of improving, will diminish the vigour of the whole. The colonies should always bear an exact proportion to the mother country; when they grow populous, they grow powerful, and by becoming powerful, they become independent also; thus subordination is destroyed, and a country swallowed up in the extent of its own dominions. The Turkish empire would be more formidable, were it less extensive. Were it not for those countries, which it can neither command, nor give entirely away, which it is obliged to protect, but from which it has no power to exact obedience.

Yet, obvious as these truths are, there are many Englishmen who are for trans-planting new colonies into this late acquisition, for peopling the desarts of America

Notes

[2] British forces defeated the French in Canada on the Plains of Abraham, near the city of Quebec, in September 1759; the next year they captured Montreal, effectively wresting "New France" from French control.

with the refuse of their countrymen, and (as they express it) with the waste of an exuberant nation. But who are those unhappy creatures who are to be thus drained away? Not the sickly, for they are unwelcome guests abroad as well as at home; nor the idle, for they would starve as well behind the Appalachian mountains as in the streets of London. This refuse is composed of the laborious and enterprising, of such men as can be serviceable to their country at home, of men who ought to be regarded as the sinews of the people, and cherished with every degree of political indulgence. And what are the commodities which this colony, when established, are to produce in return? Why raw silk, hemp, and tobacco. England, therefore, must make an exchange of her best and bravest subjects for raw silk, hemp, and tobacco; her hardy veterans and honest tradesmen, must be truck'd for a box of snuff or a silk petticoat. Strange absurdity! Sure the politics of the Daures are not more strange, who sell their religion, their wives, and their liberty for a glass bead, or a paltry penknife. Farewell.

From *Letter XXXII*

From **The Citizen of the World** (1762)

From the Same

I am disgusted, O Fum Hoam, even to sickness disgusted. Is it possible to bear the presumption of those islanders, when they pretend to instruct me in the ceremonies of China! They lay it down as a maxim, that every person who comes from thence must express himself in metaphor; swear by Alla, rail against wine, and behave, and talk and write like a Turk or Persian. They make no distinction between our elegant manners, and the voluptuous barbarities of our eastern neighbours. Where-ever I come, I raise either diffidence or astonishment; some fancy me no Chinese, because I am formed more like a man than a monster; and others wonder to find one born five thousand miles from England endued with common sense. Strange, say they, that a man who has received his education at such a distance from London, should have common sense; to be born out of England and yet have common sense! impossible! He must be some Englishman in disguise; his very visage has nothing of the true exotic barbarity.

I yesterday received an invitation from a lady of distinction, who it seems had collected all her knowledge of eastern manners from fictions every day propagated here, under the titles of eastern tales, and oriental histories: she received me very politely, but seemed to wonder that I neglected bringing opium and a tobacco-box; when chairs were drawn for the rest of the company, I was assigned my place on a cushion on the floor. It was in vain that I protested the Chinese used chairs as in Europe; she understood decorums too well to entertain me with the ordinary civilities ...

I had no sooner begun to eat what was laid before me, than I found the whole company as much astonished as before; it seems I made no use of my chop-sticks. A grave gentleman, whom I take to be an author, harangued very learnedly (as the company seemed to think) upon the use which was made of them in China: he entered into a long argument with himself about their first introduction, without once appealing to me, who might be supposed best capable of silencing the enquiry. As the gentleman therefore took my silence for a mark of his own superior sagacity, he was resolved to pursue the triumph: he talked of our cities, mountains, and animals, as familiarly as if he had been born in Quamsi, but as erroneously as if a native of the moon; he attempted to prove that I had nothing of the true Chinese cut in my visage; shewed that my cheek bones should have been higher, and my forehead broader; in short, he almost reasoned me out of my country, and effectually persuaded the rest of the company to be of his opinion.

I was going to expose his mistakes, when it was insisted that I had nothing of the true eastern manner in my delivery. This gentleman's conversation (says one of the ladies, who was a great reader) is like our own mere chit chat and common sense; there is nothing like sense in the true eastern style, where nothing more is required but sublimity ... I have written many a sheet of eastern tale myself, interrupts the author, and I defy the severest critic to say but that I have stuck close to the true manner ... I have used *thee* and *thou* upon all occasions, I have described fallen stars, and splitting mountains, not forgetting the little Houries who make a very pretty figure in every description. But you shall hear how I generally begin. "Eben-ben-bolo, who was the son of Ban, was born on the foggy summits of Benderabassi. His beard was whiter than the feathers which veil the breast of the Penguin; his eyes were like the eyes of doves, when washed by the dews of the morning; his hair, which hung like the willow weeping over the glassy stream, was so beautiful that it seemed to reflect its own brightness; and his feet were as the feet of a wild deer which fleeth to the tops of the mountains." There, there is the true eastern taste for you; every advance made towards sense, is only a deviation from sound. Eastern tales should always be sonorous, lofty, musical and unmeaning.

I could not avoid smiling to hear a native of England attempt to instruct me in the true eastern idiom, and after he had looked round some time for applause, I presumed to ask him whether he had ever travelled into the east; to which he replied in the negative: I demanded whether he understood Chinese or Arabic, to which also he answered as before. Then how, Sir, said I, can you pretend to determine upon the eastern stile, who are intirely unacquainted with the eastern writings? Take, Sir, the word of one who is *professedly* a Chinese, and who is actually acquainted with the Arabian writers, that what is palm'd upon you daily for an imitation of eastern writing, no ways resembles their manner, either in sentiment or diction. In the east, similes are seldom used, and metaphors almost wholly unknown; but in China particularly, the very reverse of what you allude to, takes place; a cool phlegmatic method of writing prevails there ...

I was proceeding in my discourse, when, looking round, I perceived the company no way attentive to what I attempted, with so much earnestness to enforce. One lady was whispering her that sat next, another was studying the merits of a fan, a third began to yawn, and the author himself fell fast asleep: I thought it, therefore, high time to make a retreat, nor did the company seem to shew any regret at my preparations for departure; even the lady who had invited me, with the most mortifying insensibility, saw me seize my hat and rise from my cushion; nor was I invited to repeat my visit, because it was found that I aimed at appearing rather a reasonable creature, than an outlandish ideot. Adieu.

The Deserted Village (1770)

Sweet Auburn, loveliest village of the plain,
Where health and plenty chear'd the lab'ring swain,
Where smiling spring its earliest visit paid,
And parting summer's lingering blooms delay'd,
Dear lovely bowers of innocence and ease,
Seats of my youth, when every sport could please,

How often have I loiter'd o'er thy green,
Where humble happiness endear'd each scene;
How often have I paus'd on every charm,
The shelter'd cot, the cultivated farm,   10
The never-failing brook, the busy mill,
The decent church that topt the neighb'ring hill,
The hawthorn bush, with seats beneath the shade,
For talking age and whisp'ring lovers made.
How often have I blest the coming day,   15
When toil remitting lent its turn to play,
And all the village train, from labour free,
Led up their sports beneath the spreading tree,
While many a pastime circled in the shade,
The young contending as the old survey'd;   20
And many a gambol frolick'd o'er the ground,
And flights of art and feats of strength went round.
And still as each repeated pleasure tir'd,
Succeeding sports the mirthful band inspir'd;
The dancing pair that simply sought renown,   25
By holding out, to tire each other down,
The swain mistrustless of his smutted face,
While secret laughter titter'd round the place,
The bashful virgin's side-long looks of love,
The matron's glance that would those looks reprove.   30
These were thy charms, sweet village! sports like these,
With sweet succession, taught even toil to please;
These round thy bowers their chearful influence shed,
These were thy charms – But all these charms are fled.

    Sweet smiling village, loveliest of the lawn,   35
Thy sports are fled, and all thy charms withdrawn;
Amidst thy bow'rs the tyrant's hand is seen,
And desolation saddens all thy green:
One only master grasps the whole domain,
And half a tillage stints thy smiling plain;   40
No more thy glassy brook reflects the day,
But, choak'd with sedges, works its weedy way;
Along thy glades, a solitary guest,
The hollow sounding bittern guards its nest;
Amidst thy desert walks the lapwing flies,   45
And tires their echoes with unvary'd cries.
Sunk are thy bow'rs in shapeless ruin all,
And the long grass o'ertops the mould'ring wall,
And, trembling, shrinking from the spoiler's hand,
Far, far away thy children leave the land.   50

    Ill fares the land, to hast'ning ills a prey,
Where wealth accumulates, and men decay;
Princes and lords may flourish, or may fade;
A breath can make them, as a breath has made:
But a bold peasantry, their country's pride,   55
When once destroy'd, can never be supply'd.

A time there was, ere England's griefs began,
When every rood of ground maintain'd its man;
For him light labour spread her wholesome store,
Just gave what life requir'd but gave no more.   60
His best companions, innocence and health;
And his best riches, ignorance of wealth.

But times are alter'd; trade's unfeeling train
Usurp the land and dispossess the swain;
Along the lawn, where scatter'd hamlets rose,   65
Unwieldy wealth, and cumb'rous pomp repose;
And ev'ry want to luxury ally'd,
And ev'ry pang that folly pays to pride.
These gentle hours that plenty bade to bloom,
Those calm desires that ask'd but little room,   70
Those healthful sports that grac'd the peaceful scene,
Liv'd in each look, and brighten'd all the green;
These, far departing, seek a kinder shore,
And rural mirth and manners are no more.

Sweet AUBURN! parent of the blissful hour,   75
Thy glades forlorn confess the tyrant's power.
Here, as I take my solitary rounds,
Amidst thy tangling walks, and ruin'd grounds,
And, many a year elaps'd, return to view
Where once the cottage stood, the hawthorn grew,   80
Here, as with doubtful, pensive steps I range,
Trace ev'ry scene, and wonder at the change,
Remembrance wakes with all her busy train,
Swells at my breast, and turns the past to pain.

In all my wand'rings round this world of care,   85
In all my griefs – and GOD has giv'n my share –
I still had hopes my latest hours to crown,
Amidst these humble bow'rs to lay me down;
My anxious day to husband near the close,
And keep life's flame from wasting by repose.   90
I still had hopes, for pride attends us still,
Amidst the swains to shew my book learn'd skill,
Around my fire an ev'ning groupe to draw,
And tell of all I felt, and all I saw;
And, as an hare whom hounds and horns pursue,   95
Pants to the place from whence at first she flew,
I still had hopes, my long vexations past,
Here to return – and die at home at last.

O blest retirement, friend to life's decline,
Retreats from care, that never must be mine,   100
How blest is he who crowns in shades like these,
A youth of labour with an age of ease;
Who quits a world where strong temptations try,
And, since 'tis hard to combat, learns to fly.
For him no wretches, born to work and weep,   105

Explore the mine, or tempt the dang'rous deep;
No surly porter stands in guilty state,
To spurn imploring famine from his gate;
But on he moves to meet his latter end,
Angels around befriending virtue's friend;   110
Sinks to the grave with unperceiv'd decay,
While resignation gently slopes the way;
And, all his prospects bright'ning to the last,
His Heav'n commences ere the world be past!

Sweet was the sound, when oft at ev'ning's close,   115
Up yonder hill the village murmur rose;
There, as I past with careless steps and slow,
The mingling notes came soften'd from below;
The swain responsive as the milk-maid sung,
The sober herd that low'd to meet their young;   120
The noisy geese that gabbled o'er the pool,
The playful children just let loose from school;
The watch-dog's voice that bay'd the whisp'ring wind,
And the loud laugh that spoke the vacant mind;
These all in soft confusion sought the shade,   125
And fill'd each pause the nightingale had made.
But now the sounds of population fail,
No chearful murmurs fluctuate in the gale,
No busy steps the grass-grown foot-way tread,
But all the bloomy flush of life is fled.   130
All but yon widow'd, solitary thing
That feebly bends beside the plashy spring;
She, wretched matron, forc'd, in age, for bread,
To strip the brook with mantling cresses spread,
To pick her wintry faggot from the thorn,   135
To seek her nightly shed, and weep till morn;
She only left of all the harmless train,
The sad historian of the pensive plain.

Near yonder copse, where once the garden smil'd,
And still where many a garden flow'r grows wild;   140
There, where a few torn shrubs the place disclose,
The village preacher's modest mansion rose.
A man he was, to all the country dear,
And passing rich with forty pounds a year;
Remote from towns he ran his godly race,   145
Nor ere had chang'd, nor wish'd to change his place;
Unskilful he to fawn, or seek for power,
By doctrines fashion'd to the varying hour;
Far other aims his heart had learn'd to prize,
More bent to raise the wretched than to rise.   150
His house was known to all the vagrant train,
He chid their wand'rings, but reliev'd their pain;
The long-remember'd beggar was his guest,
Whose beard descending swept his aged breast;
The ruin'd spendthrift, now no longer proud,   155

Claim'd kindred there, and had his claims allow'd;
The broken soldier, kindly bade to stay,
Sate by his fire, and talk'd the night away;
Wept o'er his wounds, or tales of sorrow done,
Shoulder'd his crutch, and shew'd how fields were won.　　160
Pleas'd with his guests, the good man learn'd to glow,
And quite forgot their vices in their woe;
Careless their merits, or their faults to scan,
His pity gave ere charity began.

Thus to relieve the wretched was his pride,　　165
And even his failings lean'd to Virtue's side;
But in his duty prompt at every call,
He watched and wept, he pray'd and felt, for all.
And, as a bird each fond endearment tries,
To tempt its new fledged offspring to the skies;　　170
He tried each art, reprov'd each dull delay,
Allur'd to brighter worlds, and led the way.

Beside the bed where parting life was lay'd,
And sorrow, guilt, and pain, by turns dismay'd,
The reverend champion stood. At his control,　　175
Despair and anguish fled the struggling soul;
Comfort came down the trembling wretch to raise,
And his last fault'ring accents whisper'd praise.

At church, with meek and unaffected grace,
His looks adorn'd the venerable place;　　180
Truth from his lips prevail'd with double sway,
And fools, who came to scoff, remain'd to pray.
The service past, around the pious man,
With ready zeal, each honest rustic ran;
Ev'n children follow'd with endearing wile,　　185
And pluck'd his gown, to share the good man's smile.
His ready smile a parent's warmth exprest,
Their welfare pleas'd him, and their cares distrest;
To them his heart, his love, his griefs were giv'n,
But all his serious thoughts had rest in Heav'n.　　190
As some tall cliff that lifts its awful form,
Swells from the vale, and midway leaves the storm,
Tho' round its breast the rolling clouds are spread,
Eternal sunshine settles on its head.

Beside yon straggling fence that skirts the way,　　195
With blossom'd furze unprofitably gay,
There, in his noisy mansion, skill'd to rule,
The village master taught his little school;
A man severe he was, and stern to view,
I knew him well, and ev'ry truant knew;　　200
Well had the boding tremblers learn'd to trace
The day's disasters in his morning face;
Full well they laugh'd with counterfeited glee,
At all his jokes, for many a joke had he;
Full well the busy whisper circling round,　　205

Convey'd the dismal tidings when he frown'd;
Yet he was kind, or if severe in aught,
The love he bore to learning was in fault;
The village all declar'd how much he knew;
'Twas certain he could write, and cypher too;   210
Lands he could measure, terms and tides presage,
And ev'n the story ran that he could gauge:
In arguing too, the parson own'd his skill,
For e'en tho' vanquish'd, he could argue still;
While words of learn'd length, and thund'ring sound,   215
Amaz'd the gazing rustics rang'd around,
And still they gaz'd, and still the wonder grew,
That one small head could carry all he knew.

But past is all his fame. The very spot
Where many a time he triumph'd, is forgot.   220
Near yonder thorn, that lifts its head on high,
Where once the sign-post caught the passing eye,
Low lies that house where nut-brown draughts inspir'd,
Where grey-beard mirth and smiling toil retir'd,
Where village statesmen talk'd with looks profound,   225
And news much older than their ale went round.
Imagination fondly stoops to trace
The parlour splendours of that festive place;
The white-wash'd wall, the nicely sanded floor,
The varnish'd clock that click'd behind the door;   230
The chest contriv'd a double debt to pay,
A bed by night, a chest of drawers by day;
The pictures plac'd for ornament and use,
The twelve good rules, the royal game of goose;
The hearth, except when winter chill'd the day,   235
With aspen boughs, and flow'rs and fennel gay,
While broken tea-cups, wisely kept for shew,
Rang'd o'er the chimney, glisten'd in a row.

Vain transitory splendour! Cou'd not all
Reprieve the tott'ring mansion from its fall!   240
Obscure it sinks, nor shall it more impart
An hour's importance to the poor man's heart;
Thither no more the peasant shall repair,
To sweet oblivion of his daily care;
No more the farmer's news, the barber's tale,   245
No more the wood-man's ballad shall prevail;
No more the smith his dusky brow shall clear,
Relax his pond'rous strength, and lean to hear;
The host himself no longer shall be found
Careful to see the mantling bliss go round;   250
Nor the coy maid, half willing to be prest,
Shall kiss the cup to pass it to the rest.

Yes! let the rich deride, the proud disdain,
These simple blessings of the lowly train,
To me more dear, congenial to my heart,   255
One native charm, than all the gloss of art;

Spontaneous joys, where Nature has its play,
The soul adopts, and owns their first-born sway;
Lightly they frolic o'er the vacant mind,
Unenvy'd, unmolested, unconfin'd.   260
But the long pomp, the midnight masquerade,
With all the freaks of wanton wealth array'd,
In these, ere triflers half their wish obtain,
The toiling pleasure sickens into pain;
And, even while fashion's brightest arts decoy,   265
The heart distrusting asks, if this be joy.

   Ye friends to truth, ye statesmen who survey
The rich man's joys encrease, the poor's decay,
'Tis yours to judge, how wide the limits stand
Between a splendid and an happy land.   270
Proud swells the tide with loads of freighted ore,
And shouting Folly hails them from her shore;
Hoards, even beyond the miser's wish abound,
And rich men flock from all the world around.
Yet count our gains. This wealth is but a name   275
That leaves our useful product still the same.
Not so the loss. The man of wealth and pride,
Takes up a space that many poor supply'd;
Space for his lake, his park's extended bounds,
Space for his horses, equipage and hounds;   280
The robe that wraps his limbs in silken sloth,
Has robb'd the neighb'ring fields of half their growth,
His seat, where solitary sports are seen,
Indignant spurns the cottage from the green;
Around the world each needful product flies,   285
For all the luxuries the world supplies.
While thus the land adorn'd for pleasure all
In barren splendour feebly waits the fall.

   As some fair female unadorn'd and plain,
Secure to please while youth confirms her reign,   290
Slights ev'ry borrow'd charm that dress supplies,
Nor shares with art the triumph of her eyes.
But when those charms are past, for charms are frail,
When time advances, and when lovers fail,
She then shines forth, sollicitous to bless,   295
In all the glaring impotence of dress.
Thus fares the land, by luxury betray'd,
In nature's simplest charms at first array'd,
But verging to decline, its splendours rise,
Its vistas strike, its palaces surprize;   300
While, scourged by famine from the smiling land,
The mournful peasant leads his humble band;
And while he sinks, without one arm to save,
The country blooms – a garden, and a grave.

   Where then, ah, where shall poverty reside,   305
To 'scape the pressure of contiguous pride?

If to some common's fenceless limits stray'd,
He drives his flock to pick the scanty blade,
Those fenceless fields the sons of wealth divide,
And even the bare-worn common is deny'd.   310

    If to the city sped – What waits him there?
To see profusion that he must not share;
To see ten thousand baneful arts combin'd
To pamper luxury, and thin mankind;
To see each joy the sons of pleasure know,   315
Extorted from his fellow-creature's woe.
Here, while the courtier glitters in brocade,
There the pale artist plies the sickly trade;
Here, while the proud their long-drawn pomps display,
There the black gibbet glooms beside the way.   320
The dome where pleasure holds her midnight reign,
Here, richly deckt, admits the gorgeous train,
Tumultuous grandeur crowds the blazing square,
The rattling chariots clash, the torches glare;
Sure scenes like these no troubles ere annoy!   325
Sure these denote one universal joy!
Are these thy serious thoughts – Ah, turn thine eyes
Where the poor houseless shivering female lies.
She once, perhaps, in village plenty blest,
Has wept at tales of innocence distrest;   330
Her modest looks the cottage might adorn,
Sweet as the primrose peeps beneath the thorn;
Now lost to all; her friends, her virtue fled,
Near her betrayer's door she lays her head,
And, pinch'd with cold, and shrinking from the show'r,   335
With heavy heart deplores that luckless hour,
When idly first, ambitious of the town,
She left her wheel and robes of country brown.

    Do thine, sweet AUBURN, thine, the loveliest train,
Do thy fair tribes participate her pain?   340
Even now, perhaps, by cold and hunger led,
At proud men's doors they ask a little bread!

    Ah, no. To distant climes, a dreary scene,
Where half the convex world intrudes between,
To torrid tracts with fainting steps they go,   345
Where wild Altama[1] murmurs to their woe.
Far different there from all that charm'd before,
The various terrors of that horrid shore.
Those blazing suns that dart a downward ray,
And fiercely shed intolerable day;   350
Those matted woods where birds forget to sing,
But silent bats in drowsy clusters cling,

Notes ——————————————————————————————

THE DESERTED VILLAGE
[1] Altamaha, a US river.

Those poisonous fields with rank luxuriance crown'd
Where the dark scorpion gathers death around;
Where at each step the stranger fears to wake 355
The rattling terrors of the 'vengeful snake;
Where crouching tigers wait their hapless prey,
And savage men more murd'rous still than they;
While oft in whirls the mad tornado flies,
Mingling the ravag'd landscape with the skies. 360
Far different these from every former scene,
The cooling brook, the grassy vested green,
The breezy covert of the warbling grove,
That only shelter'd thefts of harmless love.
Good Heaven! what sorrows gloom'd that parting day, 365
That call'd them from their native walks away;
When the poor exiles, ev'ry pleasure past,
Hung round their bow'rs, and fondly look'd their last,
And took a long farewel, and wish'd in vain
For seats like these beyond the western main; 370
And shudd'ring still to face the distant deep,
Return'd and wept, and still return'd to weep.
The good old sire, the first prepar'd to go
To new found worlds, and wept for other's woe;
But for himself, in conscious virtue brave, 375
He only wish'd for worlds beyond the grave.
His lovely daughter, lovelier in her tears,
The fond companion of his helpless years,
Silent went next, neglectful of her charms,
And left a lover's for her father's arms. 380
With louder plaints the mother spoke her woes,
And blest the cot where ev'ry pleasure rose;
And kist her thoughtless babes with many a tear,
And claspt them close in sorrow doubly dear;
Whilst her fond husband strove to lend relief 385
In all the decent manliness of grief.

O luxury! Thou curst by heaven's decree,
How ill exchang'd are things like these for thee!
How do thy potions with insidious joy,
Diffuse their pleasures only to destroy! 390
Kingdoms by thee, to sickly greatness grown,
Boast of a florid vigour not their own.
At every draught more large and large they grow,
A bloated mass of rank unwieldy woe;
Till sapp'd their strength, and every part unsound, 395
Down, down they sink, and spread a ruin round.

Even now the devastation is begun,
And half the business of destruction done;
Ev'n now, methinks, as pond'ring here I stand,
I see the rural virtues leave the land. 400
Down where yon anch'ring vessel spreads the sail
That idly waiting flaps with ev'ry gale,

Downward they move, a melancholy band,
Pass from the shore, and darken all the strand.
Contented toil, and hospitable care,   405
And kind connubial tenderness, are there;
And piety with wishes plac'd above,
And steady loyalty, and faithful love.
And, thou, sweet Poetry, thou loveliest maid,
Still first to fly where sensual joys invade;   410
Unfit in these degen'rate times of shame,
To catch the heart, or strike for honest fame;
Dear charming nymph, neglected and decry'd,
My shame in crowds, my solitary pride.
Thou source of all my bliss, and all my woe,   415
That found'st me poor at first, and keep'st me so;
Thou guide by which the nobler arts excel,
Thou nurse of every virtue, fare thee well.
Farewell, and O, where'er thy voice be try'd,
On Torno's cliffs, or Pambamarca's side,²   420
Whether where equinoctial fervours glow,
Or winter wraps the polar world in snow,
Still let thy voice, prevailing over time,
Redress the rigours of th' inclement clime;
Aid slighted truth, with thy persuasive strain;   425
Teach erring man to spurn the rage of gain;
Teach him that states of native strength possest,
Tho' very poor, may still be very blest;
That trade's proud empire hastes to swift decay,
As ocean sweeps the labour'd mole away;   430
While self-dependent power can time defy,
As rocks resist the billows and the sky.

Retaliation

From Poems (1775)

Of old, when Scarron¹ his companions invited,
Each guest brought his dish, and the feast was united;
If our landlord supplies us with beef, and with fish,
Let each guest bring himself, and he brings the best dish:
Our Dean² shall be venison, just fresh from the plains;   5
Our Burke³ shall be tongue, with a garnish of brains;
Our Will⁴ shall be wild fowl, of excellent flavour,

Notes
───

² In Italy and the Andes respectively.

RETALIATION
¹ Paul Scarron, seventeenth-century French writer.
² Dean of Derry (original). English-born clergyman
Thomas Barnard (1727–1806), educated at Trinity College
Dublin, like Goldsmith, in the 1740s.

³ Edmund Burke, Esq. (original).
⁴ William Burke, Esq. (original). English political writer
(1728/30–98), claimed as a distant relation by Edmund Burke.

And Dick[5] with his pepper shall heighten their savour:
Our Cumberland's[6] sweet-bread, its place shall obtain,
And Douglas's[7] pudding, substantial and plain: 10
Our Garrick's[8] a sallad, for in him we see
Oil, vinegar, sugar, and saltness agree:
To make out the dinner, full certain I am,
That Ridge[9] is anchovy, and Reynolds[10] is lamb;
That Hickey's[11] a capon, and by the same rule,   15
Magnanimous Goldsmith, a goosberry fool:
At a dinner so various, at such a repast,
Who'd not be a glutton, and stick to the last:
Here, waiter, more wine, let me sit while I'm able,
'Till all my companions sink under the table;   20
Then with chaos and blunders encircling my head,
Let me ponder, and tell what I think of the dead.

    Here lies the good Dean, re-united to earth,
Who mixt reason with pleasure, and wisdom with mirth:
If he had any faults, he has left us in doubt,   25
At least, in six weeks, I could not find 'em out;
Yet some have declar'd, and it can't be denied 'em,
That Sly-boots was cursedly cunning to hide 'em.

    Here lies our good Edmund, whose genius was such,
We scarcely can praise it, or blame it too much;   30
Who, born for the universe, narrow'd his mind,
And to party gave up, what was meant for mankind.
Tho' fraught with all learning, kept straining his throat,
To persuade Tommy Townsend[12] to lend him a vote;
Who, too deep for his hearers, still went on refining,   35
And thought of convincing, while they thought of dining;
Tho' equal to all things, for all things unfit,
Too nice for a statesman, too proud for a wit:
For a patriot too cool; for a drudge, disobedient,
And too fond of the *right* to pursue the *expedient*.   40
In short, 'twas his fate, unemploy'd, or in play, Sir,
To eat mutton cold, and cut blocks with a razor.

    Here lies honest William, whose heart was a mint,
While the owner ne'er knew half the good that was in't;
The pupil of impulse, it forc'd him along,   45
His conduct still right, with his argument wrong;
Still aiming at honour, yet fearing to roam,
The coachman was tipsy, the chariot drove home;

Notes ──

[5] Richard Burke, Esq. (original). Edmund Burke's brother, lawyer, and political author (1733–94).

[6] Author of the West Indian (original). English playwright Richard Cumberland (1732–1811).

[7] John Douglas (1721–1807), Scottish clergyman and literary critic.

[8] David Garrick (1717–79), English actor and playwright.

[9] A later edition identifies Ridge as John Ridge, Irish lawyer.

[10] Sir Joshua Reynolds (original). English artist (1723–92).

[11] Probably a lawyer, nationality unknown.

[12] Thomas Townshend (1733–1800), first Viscount Sydney, English politician.

Would you ask for his merits, alas! he had none,
What was good was spontaneous, his faults were his own.   50

  Here lies honest Richard, whose fate I must sigh at,
Alas, that such frolic should now be so quiet!
What spirits were his, what wit and what whim,
Now breaking a jest, and now breaking a limb;
Now wrangling and grumbling to keep up the ball,   55
Now teazing and vexing, yet laughing at all?
In short so provoking a devil was Dick,
That we wish'd him full ten times a day at Old Nick.
But missing his mirth and agreeable vain,
As often we wish'd to have Dick back again.   60

  Here Cumberland lies having acted his parts,
The Terence[13] of England, the mender of hearts;
A flattering painter, who made it his care
To draw men as they ought to be, not as they are.
His gallants are all faultless, his women divine,   65
And comedy wonders at being so fine;
Like a tragedy queen he has dizen'd her out,
Or rather like tragedy giving a rout.
His fools have their follies so lost in a croud
Of virtues and feelings, that folly grows proud,   70
And coxcombs alike in their failings alone,
Adopting his portraits are pleas'd with their own.
Say, when has our poet this malady caught,
Or wherefore his characters thus without fault?
Say was it that vainly directing his view,   75
To find out men's virtues and finding them few,
Quite sick of pursuing each troublesome elf,
He grew lazy at last, and drew from himself?

  Here Douglas retires from his toils to relax,
The scourge of impostors, the terror of quacks: 80
Come all ye quack bards, and ye quacking divines,
Come and dance on the spot where your tyrant reclines,
When satire and censure encircl'd his throne,
I fear'd for your safety, I fear'd for my own;
But now he is gone, and we want a detector,   85
Our Dodds shall be pious, our Kenricks shall lecture;
Macpherson write bombast, and call it a style,
Our Townshend make speeches, and I shall compile;
New Landers and Bowers the Tweed shall cross over,
No countryman living their tricks to discover;   90
Detection her taper shall quench to a spark,
And Scotchman meet Scotchman and cheat in the dark.[14]

Notes

[13] Roman playwright (c.190–158 BCE).
[14] Goldsmith here lists various minor British authors, including satirist William Kenrick (1729/30–79) and antiquarian James "Ossian" Macpherson (1736–96). Douglas may be William Douglas (c.1710–?), a Scottish physician and satirist who published attacks on other medical men.

Here lies David Garrick, describe me who can,
An abridgement of all that was pleasant in man;
As an actor, confest without rival to shine, 95
As a wit, if not first, in the very first line,
Yet with talents like these, and an excellent heart,
The man had his failings, a dupe to his art;
Like an ill judge in beauty, his colours he spread,
And beplaister'd, with rouge, his own natural red. 100
On the stage he was natural, simple, affecting,
'Twas only that, when he was off, he was acting:
With no reason on earth to go out of his way,
He turn'd and he varied full ten times a day;
Tho' secure of our hearts, yet confoundedly sick, 105
If they were not his own by finessing and trick,
He cast off his friends, as a huntsman his pack;
For he knew when he pleased he could whistle them back.
Of praise, a mere glutton, he swallowed what came,
And the puff of a dunce, he mistook it for fame; 110
'Till his relish grown callous, almost to disease,
Who pepper'd the highest, was surest to please.
But let us be candid, and speak out our mind,
If dunces applauded, he paid them in kind.
Ye Kenricks, ye Kellys, and Woodfalls[15] so grave, 115
What a commerce was yours, while you got and you gave?
How did Grub-street re-echo the shouts that you rais'd,
While he was berossia'd, and you were be prais'd?
But peace to his spirit, wherever it flies,
To act as an angel, and mix with the skies: 120
Those poets, who owe their best fame to his skill,
Shall still be his flatterers, go where he will.
Old Shakespeare, receive him, with praise and with love,
And Beaumonts and Bens[16] be his Kellys above.

Here Hickey reclines a most blunt, pleasant creature, 125
And Slander itself must allow him good-nature:
He cherish'd his friend, and he relish'd a bumper;
Yet one fault he had, and that one was a thumper:
Perhaps you may ask if the man was a miser?
I answer, no, no, for he always was wiser; 130
Too courteous, perhaps, or obligingly flat;
His very worst foe can't accuse him of that.
Perhaps he confided in men as they go,
And so was too foolishly honest; ah, no.
Then what was his failing? come tell it, and burn ye, 135
He was, could he help it? a special attorney.

Here Reynolds is laid, and to tell you my mind,
He has not left a better or wiser behind;

Notes ───────────────────────────────────────

[15] Playwright Hugh Kelly (1739–77) and English printer
Henry Sampson Woodfall (1739–1805).

[16] English playwrights William Shakespeare (1564–1616),
Francis Beaumont (1584/5–1616), and perhaps Ben Jonson
(1572–1637).

His pencil was striking, resistless and grand,
His manners were gentle, complying and bland;   140
Still born to improve us in every part,
His pencil our faces, his manners our heart:
To coxcombs averse, yet most civilly staring,
When they judged without skill he was still hard of hearing:
When they talk'd of their Raphaels, Corregios[17] and stuff,   145
He shifted his trumpet, and only took snuff.

Edmund Burke (1729–1797)

Edmund Burke was born in Dublin, and spent parts of his childhood with his mother's family in Cork and at the Quaker school in Kildare run by Mary Shackleton Leadbeater's family. He then studied at Trinity College Dublin and, in 1750, moved to London to study law. His family illustrates the degree to which Catholic and various Protestant communities could mix in eighteenth-century Ireland, and shows the greater pressure on Irish men to accept the state-sanctioned religion: Burke's mother, sister, and wife were Catholic; Burke and his father, a solicitor, were officially Anglican.

Burke's publishing career began in 1756 with *A Vindication of Natural Society*, which was quickly followed the next year by *An Account of the European Settlements in North America* and one of his most enduring and influential essays, *A Philosophical Enquiry Into the Origin of Our Ideas of the Sublime and Beautiful*. In 1758, he became editor of the *Annual Register*, and in 1759 became private secretary to a member of parliament, William Gerard Hamilton. When Hamilton entered the office of the chief secretary of Ireland in 1761, Burke went with him to Dublin, but, after moving together through other government appointments, they quarreled in 1764 and Burke ended their working

relationship. In 1765, he became secretary to the new prime minister, Lord Rockingham, and was elected as a member of parliament in 1766, beginning an influential political career.

In his parliamentary speeches, Burke was often vivid, eloquent, and tireless, addressing the House for hours at a time. On two subjects, his speeches were particularly significant: tensions with the American colonists around the time of the American Revolution; and the impeachment of Warren Hastings (1787–95), which he inaugurated, which charged Hastings with abusing his power and authority in India. Burke's "Opening Speech" on Hastings' trial in parliament took place over four days in 1788, and attempted to argue for a moral imperial project that would respect the indigenous aristocracy. His position on the American colonies was generally in favor of "conciliation" as he termed it in *Speech on Conciliation with America* (1775). Among his political writings, however, the best known is his anti-revolutionary tract, *Reflections on the Revolution in France* (1790). In *Reflections*, Burke's argument was conservative in the originary sense of the term, seeking to preserve the traditional forms of government, including aristocracy and monarchy, and was later deemed prescient for anticipating the violence of the

Notes

[17] Raphael Sanzio (1483–1520) and Antonio Allegri (Il Correggio, c.1489–1534), Italian painters.

French Terror (1793–4). Burke continued to condemn the French Revolution in a number of works, including *Thoughts on French Affairs* (1791) and *Two Letters on a Regicide Peace* (1796).

Burke's *Philosophical Enquiry* influenced literature and aesthetic theory for decades throughout the English-speaking world, and is particularly important for the development of the gothic as a literary mode. Burke extends Longinus' work on the sublime through recent work on sensibility by such Scottish Enlightenment thinkers as David Hume and Adam Smith. Sensibility framed the capacity for sympathy as an imaginative reproduction of another's feelings, modified by the moral judgment of that person. Sympathy is more keenly aroused when the virtuous suffer than when the malicious suffer. Sublimity and accompanying concepts are thus defined in relation to social as well as aesthetic categories, allowing Burke to draw distinctions between real and fictional suffering as well as moral and immoral victims.

Burke's pamphlet on popular political protest, *Thoughts on the Cause of the Present Discontents* (1770), similarly extends absolute categories to more complex social dynamics. Burke's *Thoughts* responded to the crisis over popular radical politician John Wilkes (1725–97). A member of parliament, Wilkes was prosecuted for seditious libel in 1763 because of his printed criticisms of the government. He fled to France to avoid arrest, returned in 1768, and stood again for parliament but was quickly arrested; thousands protested his incarceration, shouting "Wilkes and Liberty." Fearing a rescue attempt, troops opened fire on the protesters, killing seven. In spring 1769, Wilkes was elected to parliament three times, and denied his seat by parliament on each occasion; parliament instead declared the candidate he defeated to be elected. Wilkes was released in April 1770, the same month that Burke published his *Thoughts*. While his *Reflections* famously condemned the masses as a "swinish multitude," Burke's earlier *Thoughts* show some regard for popular political protest and the respect for individual choice that shaped much of his thought on religious toleration and other matters.

Further reading

Boulton, James T., *The Language of Politics in the Age of Wilkes and Burke*. London: Routledge and Kegan Paul, 1963.

Furniss, Tom, *Edmund Burke's Aesthetic Ideology: Language, Gender, and Political Economy in Revolution*. Cambridge: Cambridge University Press, 1993.

Gibbons, Luke, *Edmund Burke and Ireland: Aesthetics, Politics, and the Colonial Sublime*. Cambridge: Cambridge University Press, 2003.

From *A Philosophical Enquiry Into the Origin of Our Ideas of the Sublime and Beautiful* (1757)

From Part I

XI.   SOCIETY and SOLITUDE

The second branch of the social passions, is that which administers to *society in general*.[1] With regard to this, I observe, that society, merely as society, without any particular heightnings, gives us no positive pleasure in the enjoyment; but absolute and entire *solitude*, that is, the total and perpetual exclusion from all society, is as

Notes ——————————————————————————————

FROM A PHILOSOPHICAL ENQUIRY
[1] The first is sexual, creating what Burke terms "the society of the *sexes*, which answers the purposes of propagation" (part I, section VIII).

great a positive pain as can almost be conceived. Therefore in the balance between the pleasure of general *society,* and the pain of absolute solitude, *pain* is the predominant idea. But the pleasure of any particular social enjoyment, outweighs very considerably the uneasiness caused by the want of that particular enjoyment; so that the strongest sensations relative to the habitudes of *particular society,* are sensations of pleasure. Good company, lively conversation, and the endearments of friendship, fill the mind with great pleasure; a temporary solitude, on the other hand, is itself agreeable. This may perhaps prove, that we are creatures designed for contemplation as well as action; since solitude as well as society has its pleasures; as from the former observation we may discern, that an entire life of solitude contradicts the purposes of our being, since death itself is scarcely an idea of more terror.

XIII.   SYMPATHY

It is by the first of these passions that we enter into the concerns of others; that we are moved as they are moved, and are never suffered to be indifferent spectators of almost any thing which men can do or suffer. For sympathy must be considered as a sort of substitution, by which we are put into the place of another man, and affected in a good measure as he is affected; so that this passion may either partake of the nature of those which regard self-preservation, and turning upon pain may be a source of the sublime; or it may turn upon ideas of pleasure, and then, whatever has been said of the social affections, whether they regard society in general, or only some particular modes of it, may be applicable here. It is by this principle chiefly that poetry, painting, and other affecting arts, transfuse their passions from one breast to another, and are often capable of grafting a delight on wretchedness, misery, and death itself. It is a common observation, that objects which in the reality would shock, are in tragical and such like representations the source of a very high species of pleasure. This taken as a fact, has been the cause of much reasoning. This satisfaction has been commonly attributed, first, to the comfort we receive in considering that so melancholy a story is no more than a fiction; and next, to the contemplation of our own freedom from the evils which we see represented. I am afraid it is a practice much too common in inquiries of this nature, to attribute the cause of feelings which merely arise from the mechanical structure of our bodies, or from the natural frame and constitution of our minds, to certain conclusions of the reasoning faculty on the objects presented to us; for I have some reason to apprehend, that the influence of reason in producing our passions is nothing near so extensive as is commonly believed.

XIV.   The effects of SYMPATHY in the distresses of others

To examine this point concerning the effect of tragedy in a proper manner, we must previously consider, how we are affected by the feelings of our fellow creatures in circumstances of real distress. I am convinced we have a degree of delight, and that no small one, in the real misfortunes and pains of others; for let the affection be what it will in appearance, if it does not make us shun such objects, if on the contrary it induces us to approach them, if it makes us dwell upon them, in this case I conceive we must have a delight or pleasure of some species or other in contemplating objects of this kind. Do we not read the authentic histories of scenes of this nature with as much pleasure as romances or poems, where the incidents are fictitious? The prosperity of no empire, nor the grandeur of no king, can so agreeably affect in the reading, as the ruin of the state of Macedon, and the distress of its unhappy prince.

Such a catastrophe touches us in history as much as the destruction of Troy does in fable. Our delight in cases of this kind, is very greatly heightened, if the sufferer be some excellent person who sinks under an unworthy fortune. Scipio and Cato are both virtuous characters; but we are more deeply affected by the violent death of the one, and the ruin of the great cause he adhered to, than with the deserved triumphs and uninterrupted prosperity of the other; for terror is a passion which always produces delight when it does not press too close, and pity is a passion accompanied with pleasure, because it arises from love and social affection. Whenever we are formed by nature to any active purpose, the passion which animates us to it, is attended with delight, or a pleasure of some kind, let the subject matter be what it will; and as our Creator has designed we should be united together by so strong a bond as that of sympathy, he has therefore twisted along with it a proportionable quantity of this ingredient; and always in the greatest proportion where our sympathy is most wanted, in the distresses of others. If this passion was simply painful, we would shun with the greatest care all persons and places that could excite such a passion; as, some who are so far gone in indolence as not to endure any strong impression actually do. But the case is widely different with the greater part of mankind; there is no spectacle we so eagerly pursue, as that of some uncommon and grievous calamity; so that whether the misfortune is before our eyes, or whether they are turned back to it in history, it always touches with delight; but it is not an unmixed delight, but blended with no small uneasiness. The delight we have in such things, hinders us from shunning scenes of misery; and the pain we feel, prompts us to relieve ourselves in relieving those who suffer; and all this antecedent to any reasoning, by an instinct that works us to its own purposes, without our concurrence.

XV.   Of the effects of TRAGEDY

It is thus in real calamities. In imitated distresses the only difference is the pleasure resulting from the effects of imitation; for it is never so perfect, but we can perceive it is an imitation, and on that principle are somewhat pleased with it. And indeed in some cases we derive as much or more pleasure from that source than from the thing itself. But then I imagine we shall be much mistaken if we attribute any considerable part of our satisfaction in tragedy to a consideration that tragedy is a deceit, and its representations no realities. The nearer it approaches the reality, and the further it removes us from all idea of fiction, the more perfect is its power. But be its power of what kind it will, it never approaches to what it represents. Chuse a day on which to represent the most sublime and affecting tragedy which we have; appoint the most favourite actors; spare no cost upon the scenes and decorations; unite the greatest efforts of poetry, painting and music; and when you have collected your audience, just at the moment when their minds are erect with expectation, let it be reported that a state criminal of high rank is on the point of being executed in the adjoining square; in a moment the emptiness of the theatre would demonstrate the comparative weakness of the imitative arts, and proclaim the triumph of the real sympathy. I believe that this notion of our having a simple pain in the reality, yet a delight in the representation arises from hence, that we do not sufficiently distinguish what we would by no means chuse to do, from what we should be eager enough to see if it was once done. We delight in seeing things, which so far from doing, our heartiest wishes would be to see redressed. This noble capital, the pride of England and of Europe, I believe no man is so strangely wicked as to desire to see destroyed by a conflagration or an earthquake, though he should be removed himself to the greatest distance from the danger. But suppose such a fatal accident to have happened, what numbers from all parts would croud to behold the ruins, and amongst them many who would have been content never to have seen London in its glory? Nor is it either in real or fictitious distresses, our immunity from them which produces our delight; in my own mind I can discover nothing like it. I apprehend that this mistake is owing to a sort of sophism, by which we are frequently imposed upon; it arises from our not distinguishing between what is indeed a necessary condition to our doing or suffering any thing, and what is the *cause* of some particular act. If a man kills me with a sword; it is a necessary condition to this that we should have been both of us alive before the fact; and yet it would be absurd to say, that our being both living creatures was the cause of his crime and of my death. So it is certain, that it is absolutely necessary my life should be out of any imminent hazard before I can take a delight in the sufferings of others, real or imaginary, or indeed in any thing else from any cause whatsoever. But then it is a sophism to argue from thence, that this immunity is the cause of my delight either on these or on any occasions. No one can distinguish such a cause of satisfaction in his own mind I believe; nay when we do not suffer any very acute pain, nor are exposed to any imminent danger of our lives, we can feel for others, whilst we suffer ourselves; and often then most when we are softened by affliction; we see with pity even distresses which we would accept in the place of our own.

From Part II

I.   Of the passion caused by the SUBLIME

The passion caused by the great and sublime in *nature*, when those causes operate most powerfully, is Astonishment; and astonishment is that state of the soul, in which all its motions are suspended, with some degree of horror. In this case the mind is so entirely filled with its object, that it cannot entertain any other, nor by consequence reason on that object which employs it. Hence arises the great power of the sublime, that far from being produced by them, it anticipates our reasonings, and hurries us on by an irresistible force. Astonishment, as I have said, is the effect of the sublime in its highest degree; the inferior effects are admiration, reverence and respect.

II.   TERROR

No passion so effectually robs the mind of all its powers of acting and reasoning as fear. For fear being an apprehension of pain or death, it operates in a manner that resembles actual pain. Whatever therefore is terrible, with regard to sight, is sublime too, whether this cause of terror, be endued with greatness of dimensions or not; for it is impossible to look on any thing as trifling, or contemptible, that may be dangerous. There are many animals, who though far from being large, are yet capable of raising ideas of the sublime, because they are considered as objects of terror. As serpents and poisonous animals of almost all kinds. Even to things of great dimensions, if we annex any adventitious idea of terror, they become without comparison greater. An even plain of a vast extent on land, is certainly no mean idea; the prospect of such a plain may be as extensive as a prospect of the ocean; but can it ever fill the mind with any thing so great as the ocean itself? This is owing to several causes, but it is owing to none more than to this, that the ocean is an object of no small terror.

III. OBSCURITY

To make any thing very terrible, obscurity seems in general to be necessary. When we know the full extent of any danger, when we can accustom our eyes to it, a great deal of the apprehension vanishes. Every one will be sensible of this, who considers how greatly night adds to our dread, in all cases of danger, and how much the notions of ghosts and goblins, of which none can form clear ideas, affect minds, which give credit to the popular tales concerning such sorts of beings. Those despotic governments, which are founded on the passions of men, and principally upon the passion of fear, keep their chief as much as may be from the public eye. The policy has been the same in many cases of religion. Almost all the heathen temples were dark. Even in the barbarous temples of the Americans at this day, they keep their idol in a dark part of the hut, which is consecrated to his worship. For this purpose too the druids performed all their ceremonies in the bosom of the darkest woods, and in the shade of the oldest and most spreading oaks. No person seems [better] to have understood the secret of heightening, or of setting terrible things, if I may use the expression, in their strongest light by the force of a judicious obscurity, than Milton. His description of Death in the second book is admirably studied; it is astonishing with what a gloomy pomp, with what a significant and expressive uncertainty of strokes and colouring he has finished the portrait of the king of terrors.

> The other shape,
> If shape it might be called that shape had none
> Distinguishable, in member, joint, or limb;
> Or substance might be called that shadow seemed,
> For each seemed either; black he stood as night;
> Fierce as ten furies; terrible as hell;
> And shook a deadly dart. What seemed his head
> The likeness of a kingly crown had on.[2]

In this description all is dark, uncertain, confused, terrible, and sublime to the last degree.

From Part III

I. Of BEAUTY

It is my design to consider beauty as distinguished from the sublime; and in the course of the enquiry, to examine how far it is consistent with it. But previous to this, we must take a short review of the opinions already entertained of this quality; which I think are hardly to be reduced to any fixed principles; because men are used to talk of beauty in a figurative manner, that is to say, in a manner extremely uncertain, and indeterminate. By beauty I mean, that quality or those qualities in bodies by which they cause love, or some passion similar to it.

Notes ———————————————————————————————

[2] *Paradise Lost* (1674), II: 666–73, by English author John Milton.

XXVIII.   The Sublime and Beautiful compared

On closing this general view of beauty, it naturally occurs, that we should compare it with the sublime; and in this comparison there appears a remarkable contrast. For sublime objects are vast in their dimensions, beautiful ones comparatively small; beauty should be smooth, and polished; the great, rugged and negligent; beauty should shun the right line, yet deviate from it insensibly; the great in many cases loves the right line, and when it deviates, it often makes a strong deviation; beauty should not be obscure; the great ought to be dark and gloomy; beauty should be light and delicate; the great ought to be solid, and even massive. They are indeed ideas of a very different nature, one being founded on pain, the other on pleasure; and however they may vary afterwards from the direct nature of their causes, yet these causes keep up an eternal distinction between them, a distinction never to be forgotten by any whose business it is to affect the passions.

From *Thoughts on the Cause of the Present Discontents* (1770)

It is an undertaking of some degree of delicacy to examine into the cause of public disorders. If a man happens not to succeed in such an enquiry, he will be thought weak and visionary; if he touches the true grievance, there is a danger that he may come near to persons of weight and consequence, who will rather be exasperated at the discovery of their errors, than thankful for the occasion of correcting them. If he should be obliged to blame the favourites of the people, he will be considered as the tool of power; if he censures those in power, he will be looked on as an instrument of faction. But in all exertions of duty something is to be hazarded. In cases of tumult and disorder, our law has invested every man, in some sort, with the authority of a magistrate. When the affairs of the nation are distracted, private people are, by the spirit of that law, justified in stepping a little out of their ordinary sphere. They enjoy a privilege, of somewhat more dignity and effect, than that of idle lamentation over the calamities of their country. They may look into them narrowly; they may reason upon them liberally; and if they should be so fortunate as to discover the true source of the mischief, and to suggest any probable method of removing it, though they may displease the rulers for the day, they are certainly of service to the cause of Government. Government is deeply interested in every thing which, even through the medium of some temporary uneasiness, may tend finally to compose the minds of the subject, and to conciliate their affections. I have nothing to do here with the abstract value of the voice of the people. But as long as reputation, the most precious possession of every individual, and as long as opinion, the great support of the State, depend entirely upon that voice, it can never be considered as a thing of little consequence either to individuals or to Government. Nations are not primarily ruled by laws; less by violence. Whatever original energy may be supposed either in force or regulation; the operation of both is, in truth, merely instrumental. Nations are governed by the same methods, and on the same principles, by which an individual without authority is often able to govern those who are his equals or his superiors; by a knowledge of their temper, and by a judicious management of it; I mean when ever publick affairs are steadily and quietly con-ducted; not when Government is nothing but a continued scuffle between the magistrate and the multitude; in which sometimes the one and some times the other is uppermost; in which they alternately yield and prevail in a series of contemptible victories and scandalous submissions. The temper of the people amongst whom he presides ought therefore to be the first study of a Statesman. And the knowledge of this temper it is by no means impossible for him to attain, if he has not an interest in being ignorant of what it is his duty to learn.

To complain of the age we live in, to murmur at the present possessors of power, to lament the past, to conceive extravagant hopes of the future, are the common dispositions of the greatest part of mankind; indeed the necessary effects of the ignorance and levity of the vulgar. Such complaints and humours have existed in all times; yet as all times have *not* been alike, true political sagacity manifests itself, in distinguishing that complaint, which only characterizes the general infirmity of human nature, from those which are symptoms of the particular distemperature of our own air and season.

Nobody, I believe, will consider it merely as the language of spleen or disappointment, if I say, that there is something particularly alarming in the present conjuncture. There is hardly a man in or out of power who holds any other language. That Government is at once dreaded and contemned; that the laws are despoiled of all their respected and salutary terrors; that their inaction is a subject of ridicule, and their exertion of abhorrence; that rank, and office, and title, and all the solemn plausibilities of the world, have lost their reverence and effect; that our foreign politicks are as much deranged as our domestic oeconomy; that our dependencies are slackened in their affection, and loosened from their obedience; that we know neither how to yield nor how to inforce; that hardly any thing above or below, abroad or at home, is sound and entire; but that disconnection and confusion, in offices, in parties, in families, in Parliament, in the nation, prevail beyond the disorders of any former time: these are facts universally admitted and lamented.

This state of things is the more extraordinary, because the great parties which formerly divided and agitated the kingdom are known to be in a manner entirely dissolved. No great external calamity has visited the nation; no pestilence or famine. We do not labour at present under any scheme of taxation new or oppressive in the quantity or in the mode. Nor are we engaged in unsuccessful war; in which, our misfortunes might easily pervert our judgement; and our minds, sore from the loss of national glory, might feel every blow of Fortune as a crime in Government.

It is impossible that the cause of this strange distemper should not sometimes become a subject of discourse. It is a compliment due, and which I willingly pay, to those who administer our affairs, to take notice in the first place of their speculation. Our Ministers are of opinion, that the encrease of our trade and manufactures, that our growth by colonization and by conquest, have concurred to accumulate immense wealth in the hands of some individuals; and this again being dispersed amongst the people, has rendered them universally proud, ferocious, and ungovernable; that the insolence of some from their enormous wealth, and the boldness of others from a guilty poverty, have rendered them capable of the most atrocious attempts; so that they have trampled upon all subordination, and violently borne down the unarmed laws of a free Government; barriers too feeble against the fury of a populace so fierce and licentious as ours. They contend, that no adequate provocation has been given for so spreading a discontent; our affairs having been conducted throughout with remarkable temper and consummate wisdom. The wicked industry of some libellers, joined to the intrigues of a few disappointed politicians, have, in their opinion, been able to produce this unnatural ferment in the nation.

Nothing indeed can be more unnatural than the present convulsions of this country, if the above account be a true one. I confess I shall assent to it with great reluctance, and only on the compulsion of the clearest and firmest proofs; because their account resolves itself into this short, but discouraging proposition, "That we have a very good Ministry, but that we are a very bad people"; that we set ourselves to bite the hand that feeds us; that with a malignant insanity we oppose the measures, and ungratefully vilify the persons of those, whose sole object is our own peace and prosperity. If a few puny libellers, acting under a knot of factious politicians, without virtue, parts, or character (such they are constantly represented by these gentlemen), are sufficient to excite this disturbance, very perverse must be the disposition of that people, amongst whom such a disturbance can be excited by such means. It is besides no small aggravation of the public misfortune, that the disease, on this hypothesis, appears to be without remedy. If the wealth of the nation be the cause of its turbulence, I imagine, it is not proposed to introduce poverty, as a constable to keep the peace. If our dominions abroad are the roots which feed all this rank luxuriance of sedition, it is not intended to cut them off in order to famish the fruit. If our liberty has enfeebled the executive power, there is no design, I hope, to call in the aid of despotism, to fill up the deficiencies of law. Whatever may be intended, these things are not yet professed. We seem therefore to be driven to absolute despair; for we have no other materials to work upon, but those out of which God has been pleased to form the inhabitants of this island. If these be radically and essentially vitious,[1] all that can be said is, that those men are very unhappy, to whose fortune or duty it falls to administer the affairs of this untoward people. I hear it indeed sometimes asserted, that a steady perseverance in the present measures, and a rigorous punishment of those who oppose them, will in course of time infallibly put an end to these disorders. But this in my opinion is said without much observation of our present disposition, and without any knowledge at all of the general nature of mankind. If the matter of which this nation is composed be so very fermentable as these gentlemen describe it, leaven never will be wanting to work it up, as long as discontent, revenge, and ambition, have existence in the world. Particular punishments are the cure for accidental distempers in the State; they inflame rather than allay those heats which arise from the settled mismanagement of the Government, or from a natural ill disposition in the people. It is of the utmost moment not to make mistakes in the use of strong measures; and firmness is then only a virtue when it accompanies the most perfect wisdom. In truth, inconstancy is a sort of natural corrective of folly and ignorance.

I am not one of those who think that the people are never in the wrong. They have been so, frequently and outrageously, both in other countries and in this. But I do say, that in all disputes between them and their rulers, the presumption is at least upon a par in favour of the people. Experience may perhaps justify me in going further. Where popular discontents have been very prevalent; it may well be affirmed and supported, that there has been generally something found amiss in the constitution, or in the conduct of Government. The people have no interest in disorder. When they do wrong, it is their error, and not their crime. But with the governing part of the State, it is far otherwise. They certainly may act ill by design, as well as by mistake.

Notes

From Thoughts on the Cause
[1] vicious

Isaac Bickerstaffe (1733–c.1812)

Isaac Bickerstaffe (or Bickerstaff) was born in Dublin and, at the age of eleven, became page to the Lord Lieutenant of Ireland. He then spent a number of years in the military, roughly from 1745 to 1763. He began his literary career in 1756 and quickly became a prolific playwright and librettist. Well known for his comic operas and songs, he was a leading figure in the London theater for much of the 1760s. He penned over two dozen volumes, and his songs were often published independently of the plays and operas from which they were taken. Jonathan Swift used "Isaac Bickerstaff[e]" as a pen-name, but there is no known connection between Swift and the actual Isaac Bickerstaffe.

Love in a Village (1762) was the first opera to earn him significant notice. Like many of his contemporaries, Bickerstaffe primarily adapted other writers' work, but he was particularly successful at adapting material into his form of choice – comedies with musical elements which aimed to have wide appeal. His theatrical career ended abruptly in 1771 when he had to flee England to escape charges of homosexuality (then punishable by death) and hide in France

under an alias; it is not clear how long or where Bickerstaffe lived, or whether he continued to write in the second half of his life, and even the evidence that he lived as late as 1812 is rather slight.

Bickerstaffe's *The Captive* (1769) is based on English playwright John Dryden's *Don Sebastian* (1690). *The Captive* provides a number of elements of the comic opera: a couple whose love is thwarted by interfering parents, exotic locales and dramatic adventures, mixed with songs and comedy. *The Captive* also refers extensively to the longstanding problem of piracy along the Barbary Coast (the northern coast of Africa). Tens of thousands of Europeans were captured and enslaved by Barbary pirates in the seventeenth and eighteenth centuries, threatening eighteenth-century British claims to maritime power.

Further reading

Gleckner, Robert F., "Blake, Bickerstaff, and Eighteenth-century Theater," *Essays in Literature* 7 (1980): 247–53.
Tasch, Peter A., *The Dramatic Cobbler: The Life and Works of Isaac Bickerstaff*. Lewisburg, PA: Bucknell University Press, 1972.

The Captive: A Comic Opera (1769)

ADVERTISEMENT

Mr. Foote's[1] Situation rendering it impossible for him to perform the smaller Pieces of his own Writing as often as the Public would desire them, thought that a Singing Farce, though pretending to no other Merit than that of good Music, would be more acceptable to his Auditors than others destitute of that Ornament, which had been often performed at the Winter Theatres.

The Dialogue of this Trifle is taken, with some Alterations, from a Play of Dryden's: In that Part it is inoffensive; and the Songs, which have been selected with great Care, will, it is hoped, afford Entertainment.

Notes ───────────────────────────────

The Captive
[1] Samuel Foote (c.1721–77), English playwright.

PERSONS

MEN	WOMEN
The Cadi	Fatima
Ferdinand	Zorayda

SCENE, *a Garden belonging to the* CADI, *near* ALGIERS.

ACT I, SCENE I

A Garden belonging to the CADI'*s house. On the curtain's rising the* CADI *appears, seated cross-legg'd, in a sort of pavilion. He is smoking a long pipe. On either side of him sit his wife* FATIMA *and his daughter* ZORAYDA. *Some men and women slaves appear at work in the garden. After the chorus the* CADI *and* FATIMA *rise, and are met by* FERDINAND, *who presents a letter.*

CHORUS

Ah, how sweet the rural scene!
　　Circled by those charming groves,
　　Slavery its labour loves,
　　And the captive hugs his chain.

CADI. Come, Fatima, we'll rise and take a walk towards the house, honey-bird. You, daughter Zorayda, may stay in the garden longer if you like it.

FERD. Now love and fortune assist me! [*kneeling*] Most noble Cadi, your friend Uchali, admiral of the Dey's gallies at Algiers, commands me thus to prostrate myself –

CADI. What are you, Christian?

FERD. That letter will inform you.

FAT. A good personable fellow.

CADI. [*reading*] "The bearer, a Spaniard by birth, has been a slave of mine upwards of a year, during which time he has behaved himself well; yesterday he received money for his ransom; and being now free, only waits for a ship to carry him to his own country: 'till an opportunity offers he desires to remain among your slaves, many of whom are his countrymen. You may venture to trust him; and he will repay your kindness by discharging any office in your family you think proper to appoint him."

FAT. I like him prodigiously.

CADI. This letter is, indeed, from my friend Uchali. Well, Christian, I have no objection to your staying awhile among my slaves, if you will conduct yourself quietly, and be of use in my garden here.

FERD. I have been bred to gardening from my youth.

FAT. I'll bring him into that arbour, where a rose-tree and a myrtle are just falling for want of a prop; if they were bound together they would help to keep one another up.

CADI. Come into the house, I say; he does not want your help. To work, sirrah, if you'd
stay with me –

FAT. Take this little alms to buy you tobacco.

> Lord, my dear, why such ill-nature?
>   Heaven and earth at once demand
> Pity for a wretched creature,
>   Captive in a foreign land.

> Shall our mein of harshness favour?
>   No, 'twas never your intent:
> Yet I hope my kind behaviour
>   Will be construed as 'twas meant.

SCENE II

*During the former Scene a black slave brings a basket of flowers to ZORAYDA, from which
she culls a nosegay. When the CADI and FATIMA go off, FERDINAND advances, but
retires again, upon a motion from ZORAYDA, who rises afterwards, and comes forward.*

FERD. They're gone. Now might I venture to speak to my dear Zorayda! – She makes
signs to me with her hand to keep back. I must do so for a while, till her father has
got at a greater distance.

ZOR. Cease, ye fountains, cease to murmur;
   Leave, ye gentle gales, to blow;
      Softly flowing,
      Gently blowing,
   Ye but wake my tender woe.

FERD. They are quite out of sight.

ZOR. Come near then.

FERD. My life! my angel!

ZOR. Have a care. My father has been but three days here in the country. I perceive you
have disposed of the money I conveyed to you, in the manner I desired, to procure
your ransom.

FERD. It is true. Owing to your bounty, I am at length a free man, and procured that
letter from my former master, to be received among your father's slaves; which has
answered to my wish, and I now only wait for your farther commands.

ZOR. Tho' this is the first time of our speaking together, my letters have sufficiently
informed you who and what I am. You have not forgot the purport of my last?

FERD. No, sweet creature.

ZOR. You know my desire is to become of your religion, and to go with you from
hence to Spain. What have you done about the directions I gave you with regard
to that?

FERD. I have spoken to a fast friend of mine, a renegado, who has taken care to prepare
a vessel for our departure. To-morrow night the galley will come to the point, west
of your garden here, with a dozen Spaniards, all of them able-bodied rowers, and of
approved fidelity.

ZOR. To-morrow night?

FERD. The sooner we can put our design in execution the better, lest some adverse
accident should prevent us.

ZOR. 'Tis true: – stay hereabouts, and presently I will come down into the garden again and let you know whether I can be prepared against to-morrow night, or not.

> Poor panting heart, ah! wilt thou ever
> Throb within my troubled breast?
> Shall I see the moment never
> That is doom'd to give thee rest?

> Cruel stars, that thus torment me!
> Fortune smooths her front in vain;
> Pleasure's self cannot content me,
> But is turn'd with me to pain.

SCENE III

FERDINAND, *and then* FATIMA *in a veil.*

FERD. If this be captivity, who would not be a captive? What a lucky day was it for me when I was set to work upon my master's terras in Algiers, where I was seen from the windows of her father's house by this charming infidel, who singled me from the rest of my companions!

FAT. Thus far my love has carried me almost without my knowledge – Yonder he is – Shall I proceed – Shall I discover myself?

FERD. [*not seeing her*] Oh, sweet Zorayda!

FAT. What's that he says?

FERD. Where is my flute? I will sit down upon this stump of a tree, and whistle away the minutes till she comes back.

FAT. Zorayda!

FERD. What melancholy love-tune shall I play now? [*sits down and plays*]

FAT. I can hold no longer. [*slaps him upon the shoulder*]

FERD. My dear Zorayda! – so soon returned!

FAT. Again! – What's the meaning of this? Do you take me for the Cadi's daughter? [*unveiling*]

FERD. By all that's good, the nauseous wife!

FAT. You are confounded.

FERD. Somewhat nonplust, I confess, to hear you deny your name so positively. Why, are you not Zorayda, the Cadi's daughter? Did not I see you with him but just now? Nay, were you not so charitable as to give me money?

FAT. But I am neither Zorayda, nor the Cadi's daughter.

FERD. I know not that; but I am sure he is old enough to be your father.

FAT. But once again – How came you to name Zorayda?

FERD. Another mistake of mine; for asking one of your slaves, when I came into the garden, who were the chief ladies about the house, he answered me Zorayda and Fatima; but she, it seems, is his daughter, (with a plague to her) and you are his beloved wife.

FAT. Say your beloved mistress, if you please, for that's the title I desire.

FERD. Ay, but I have a qualm of conscience.

FAT. Your conscience was very quiet when you took me for Zorayda.

FERD. I must be plain with you – You are married to a reverend man, the head of your law. Go back to your chamber, madam; go back.

FAT. No, sirrah; but I'll teach you, to your cost, what vengeance is in store for refusing a lady who has offered you her love.

> For vengeance dire, thou wretch! prepare,
> Nought shall my resentment stay,
> To a lion, to a bear,
> My nature turns,
> While my bosom burns
> To seize my destin'd prey.

> Oh, object to my soul how sweet!
> To see you grovling at my feet,
> While I no pity shew;
> To spurn your tears,
> To mock your fears,
> And tread you to the shades below.

Scene IV

FERDINAND, FATIMA, and afterwards the CADI.

FERD. What do you mean, madam? For Heaven's sake, peace.

FAT. Ungrateful wretch! What do I mean! Help, help, husband! my lord Cadi! I shall be undone; the villain will be too strong for me. Help, for pity of a poor distress'd creature.

FERD. Then I have nothing but impudence to assist me. I must drown the clamour, whate'er comes on it. [he takes out his flute and plays as loud as he possibly can, and she continues crying out]

CADI. What's here! What's here!

FAT. Oh, sweetest! I'm glad you're come; this Christian slave was going to be rude with me.

CADI. Oh, horrid! abominable! the villain – the monster – take him away, flay and impale him, rid the world of such a viper.

FERD. First hear me, worthy sir. What have you seen to provoke you?

CADI. I have heard the outcries of my wife, the bleatings of the poor innocent lamb. What have I seen, quotha! If I see the lamb lie expiring, and the wolf by her, is not that evidence sufficient of the murder?

FERD. Pray think in reason, Sir. Is a man to be put to death for a similitude? No violence has been committed; none intended. The lamb's alive; and, if I durst tell you so, no more a lamb than I am a wolf.

FAT. How's that, villain!

FERD. Be patient, madam, and speak but truth, I'll do any thing to serve you.

FAT. Well. – Hear him speak, husband; perhaps he may say something for himself I know not.

CADI. But did he mean no mischief? Was he endeavouring nothing?

FAT. In my conscience I begin to doubt he did not.

CADI. Then what meant all those outcries?

FAT. I heard music in the garden, and I stole softly down, imagining it might be he.

CADI. How's that! Imagining it might be he?

FAT. Yes, to be sure, my lord. Am not I the mistress of the family; and is it not my place to see good order kept in it? I thought he might have allured some of the she slaves to him, and was resolved to prevent what might have been betwixt them; when on a sudden he rush'd out upon me, and caught me in his arms with such a fury –

CADI. I have heard enough, – away with him.

FAT. Mistaking me, no doubt, for one of the slaves that work in the garden. With that, affrighted as I was, I discovered myself, and cry'd aloud; but as soon as ever he knew me, the villain let me go; and, I must needs say, he started back as if I were a serpent, and was more afraid of me than I of him.

CADI. O, thou ungrateful villain! Did'st thou come to get footing in my family in order to corrupt it? That's cause enough of death. Once more, again, away with him.

FAT. Well, but, love –

CADI. Speak not for him.

FAT. I must speak, and you hear me.

CADI. Away with him, I say.

FAT. What! for an intended trespass? No harm has been done, whatever may be. Then consider he does not belong to you, and is recommended by a friend you would not chuse to disoblige.

CADI. Why that's true.

FERD. I see she'll bring me off if she can.

CADI. And are you sure, rascal, you meant no harm?

FERD. No harm, upon my reputation, – no more than the child unborn. I was playing here by myself, (such is my foolish custom) and took madam, as she says, for one of the female slaves employ'd in your garden.

CADI. Well, sirrah, to your kennel; mortify your flesh, and consider in whose family you are.

FERD. Yes, sir, I'll consider.

FAT. And learn another time to treat the Cadi's wife as she would have you.

CADI. What do you mean by that?

FAT. What do I mean! – I'll shew you what I mean – give the puppy a remembrancer. –

CADI. Come, come, – enough.

FAT. Do let me beat him a little, husband.

CADI. No wife – no: – Get in before me –

FAT. Why sure!

CADI. Get in I say.

FAT. I won't.

CADI. March. –

FAT. Well, I will march; – but if I am not revenged on you for this, you old tyrant, the Devil take me.

CADI.   For all her art,
       I see her heart;
    She counterfeits too grosly:
      And, Lady fair,
      I shall take care
    To watch your waters closely.

      I'm us'd to keep
      A rod in steep;
    For long I've had suspicion:
      And if I find
      She's ill inclin'd,
    I'll bring her to contrition.

Scene V

FERDINAND *and then* ZORAYDA *behind him.*

ZOR. Christian where are you?

FERD. 'Tis her voice – I can't be mistaken again.

ZOR. Ferdinand! –

FERD. Zorayda! –

ZOR. Yes 'tis I.

FERD. Come nearer that I may be sure.

ZOR. There, there. –

FERD. Do you know what has happened to me since you went away?

ZOR. Yes, yes, I know it all. – "Any thing to serve you, Madam." – Whose words were these, Gentleman?

FERD. Come don't make yourself worse natur'd than you are. – To save my life you would be content I should promise any thing.

ZOR. Yes, if I was sure you would perform nothing.

FERD. But is your mother-in-law such a virago?

ZOR. What do you think of her?

FERD. Hang me if I know what to think of her! but this I'm sure of, she had like to play the Devil with me.

ZOR. Well, I assure you these freaks are nothing with her. – I perceiv'd she took a fancy for you the moment she saw you: – However, beware of her. – You think that's her face you see; but 'tis only a dawb'd vizard: And for constancy, I can tell you for your comfort, she would love till death – I mean till yours; – for when she was tir'd of you, she would certainly dispatch you to another world, for fear of telling tales.

FERD. But why all this? – What's Fatima to me? – You cannot imagine I would exchange a diamond for a pebble stone.

ZOR. No; – But I think you might like to have the diamond and the pebble stone too by way of variety.

FERD. By this fair hand I swear –

ZOR. Well, come – What do you swear?

FERD. To resist temptation.

ZOR. To avoid it is better. And since you say your friends and your ship will be ready to-morrow night, to-morrow night I am determined to go off with you. – Meet me here about ten o'clock. – I'll slip down from my chamber, and bring my father in my hand.

FERD. Your father!

ZOR. I mean what he considers as the better part of him, – his pearls and jewels, – his whole contents, – his heart and soul – as much as ever I can carry.

FERD. I shall be gone this moment and inform my companions.

> Thus low for all your favours,
>   Behold your servant bends;
> Through life my best endeavours
>   Shall be to make amends.
> Though life's too short to prove
> My truth, my gratitude and love.

Dear liberty possessing,
   Can man more happy be?
But what endears the blessing,
   Is that it comes from thee.

Scene VII

ZORAYDA

Let me consider a little. – Am not I a mad wicked girl, going to forsake my father, and leave my country, to run into a strange one with a slave whose freedom I purchase, and I first saw, by accident, thro' a window in my father's house that look'd into the place where he work'd? – Why, on maturely weighing the matter, not so mad and wicked as I at first appear. I have long hated both our Mahometan laws and religion in my heart, and I have no means to get rid of them both but by putting myself in the hands of a Christian. – This is a handsome man I am sure, and I will believe him an honest one.

   The wretch condemn'd with life to part,
      Yet, yet on hope relies;
   And the last sigh that rends his heart,
      Bids expectation rise.

   Hope, like the glimm'ring taper light,
      Adorns and chears our way;
   And still, as darker grows the night,
      Emits a brighter ray.

Act II, Scene I

*Scene changes to another View of the Garden by Moonlight, with
a Balcony and Portico belonging to the CADI's House.*

FERDINAND *enters leading* ZORAYDA.

FERD. I have been waiting here I know not how long! – Why, thou sweet delicious creature, why torture me with thy delay? – And art thou come at last! – But where hast thou been? – I was almost in despair.

ZOR. Don't be angry; it was well I could come at all. There has been a strange bustle this evening within.

FERD. As how! What has been the matter?

ZOR. Some cause which my father has lately decided, and, to tell you the truth, I believe not with the strictest attention to justice; however, the party has carryed his complaint to the Dey, and he has been obliged to go to court about it; but he's come back again, and I fancy the storm is pretty well blown over.

FERD. And what are we to do now?

ZOR. Why, what we have already schemed; but, as I had outstay'd the time appointed, I just slipped down to see if you had patience to keep to your post.

FERD. Could you doubt it?

ZOR. Is the galley ready?

FERD. I'm but this moment come from it. It lies within a pistol shot of us, just without the little gate of your garden which leads to the sea.

ZOR. Well, I'll run up again and bring down what I told you; in the mean time, do you take another look towards the galley, and prepare the men for our reception.

FERD. I have entrusted a countryman of mine, one of your father's slaves, with our design. I left him on the watch; but I'll go myself.

ZOR. Heigho!

FERD. What's the matter!

ZOR. Something – I don't know what.

FERD. Nay my love –

ZOR. Let me lean upon your arm – It will away again – My courage is good for all this.

FERD. Zorayda! –

ZOR. Feel my heart.

FERD. Poor little thing how it throbs!

ZOR. Oh me!

Alas! 'tis in vain my distress to dissemble.
　I wish, yet, with fear, I my wishes pursue;
I fain would be gone, yet in going I tremble;
　No stay to support me, no pilot but you.

At once, friends, and father, and country, forsaking,
　New faith, new companions, new climates to try;
Each step that I tread tender thoughts are awaking,
　And still I look back, and withdraw with a sigh.

Scene II

The CADI *alone in a Slave's Habit like that of* FERDINAND'*s.*

CADI. This it is to have a sound head-piece. – I have mewed up my suspected spouse in her chamber. – No more embassies to that lusty young Christian. Next, by this habit of a slave, I have made myself as like him as I can. Now walking under the windows of my Seraglio, if Fatima should look out, she will certainly take me for Ferdinand, and call to me, and by that I shall know what concupiscence is working in her. She cannot come down to commit iniquity, there's my safety; but if she peep, if she put her nose abroad, there's demonstration of her pious will, and let me alone to work her for it.

In emblem I am like a cat
That's watching for a mouse.
Close by his hole behold her squat,
While her heart goes pit-a-pat.

If a squeaking she hears,
She pricks up her ears,
And when he appears,
Leaps on him souse.

And so will I do with my wife.
Just so will I watch her,
And so if I catch her,
I'll worry her out of her life.

SCENE III

The CADI, ZORAYDA *running to him with the Casket in her Hand.*

ZOR. Now I can embrace you with a good conscience. – Here are the pearls and jewels – here's my father.

CADI. I am indeed thy father; but how the Devil didst thou know me in this disguise! – and what pearls and jewels dost thou mean?

ZOR. What have I done! and what will now become of me!

CADI. Ar't thou mad, Zorayda?

ZOR. I think you will make me so.

CADI. Why? – What have I done to you? – Recollect thyself, and speak sense to me.

ZOR. Then give me leave to tell you, that you are the worst of fathers.

CADI. Did I think I had got such a monster! – Proceed, my dutiful child, proceed, proceed.

ZOR. You have been raking together a mass of wealth, by indirect and wicked means. The spoils of orphans are in these jewels, and the tears of widows are in these pearls.

CADI. You amaze me!

ZOR. I would do so. – This casket is loaded with your sins. 'Tis the cargo of rapine and extortion, the iniquity of thirty years cadiship converted into diamonds.

CADI. Would some rich railing rogue dare say as much to me, that I might squeeze his purse for scandal.

ZOR. Here, Sir, don't think I'll be the receiver of your thefts. – I discharge my conscience of them. – Here, take again your filthy mammon, and restore it, you had best, to the true owners.

CADI. I am finely documented by my own daughter.

ZOR. And a great credit to me to be so. – Do but think how decent a habit you have on, and how becoming your function to be disguised like a slave, and eaves-dropping under the women's windows.

CADI. Pr'ythee, child, reproach me no more of human failings. – I am better at bottom than thou thinkest. – I am not the man you take me for.

ZOR. No, to my sorrow, Sir, you are not.

CADI. It was a very bad beginning; tho' methought to see you come running upon me with such a warm embrace – Pr'ythee, what was meaning of that violent hot hug?

ZOR. I'm sure I meant nothing but the zeal and affection which I bear to the man in the world whom I love best.

CADI. Why this is as it should be. – Take the treasure again – It will never be put into better hands.

> But, pr'ythee, spare me, dearest daughter,
> If ought that's past my conscience stings;
> Down my old cheeks it forces water,
> To hear your cruel taunts and flings.

> You should consider, child, if I
> Have in my office grip'd too nigh,
> 'Twas to the end you might have
> My wealth when I was in the grave.
> My failings then no longer press;
> We all have errors, more or less.

Scene IV

The CADI, ZORAYDA, FERDINAND *in a rich habit.*

FERD. What do you mean, my dear, to stand talking in this suspicious place, just under Fatima's window? – You are well met, comrade; I know you are the friend of our flight.

CADI. Ferdinand in disguise! – Now I begin to smell a rat.

FERD. And I another that outstinks it.   False Zorayda! thus to betray me to your father.

ZOR. Alas! I was betrayed myself. – He was here in disguise like you; and I, poor innocent, ran into his hands.

CADI. In good time you did so. – I laid a trap for a she fox, and worse vermin has caught himself in it. You would fain break loose now, tho' you left a limb behind you; but I am yet in my territories, and in call of company, that's my comfort.

FERD. Know I have a trick yet to put you past your squeaking.

ZOR. What do you mean? – You will not throttle him! – Consider he's my father.

FERD. Pr'ythee let us provide first for our own safety. – If I do not consider him, he will consider us with a vengeance afterwards.

ZOR. You may threaten him from crying out; but, for my sake, give him back a little cranny of his windpipe, and some part of speech.

FERD. Not so much as one single interjection. – Come away, father-in-law; this is no place for dialogues. – When you are upon the bench you talk by hours, and there no man must interrupt you. – This is but like for like, good father-in-law. – Now I am on the bench, 'tis your turn to hold your tongue. [*He struggles.*] Nay, if you will be hanging back, I shall take care you shall hang forwards. [*Pulls him along the stage with a sword at his reins.*]

ZOR. T'other way to the arbour with him, and make haste before we are discovered.

FERD. If I only bind and gag him there, he may commend me hereafter for civil usage; he deserves not so much favour for any action of his life.

ZOR. Yes pray bate him one for begetting your mistress.

FERD. Once more, come along in silence my Pythagorian father-in-law.

ZOR. Oh! dear me! – dear me! – I wish it was well over – All I'm afraid of is that my courage or strength will fail me. – Well, is he safe?

FERD. Yes, yes – I have lodg'd him. – He won't trouble us within this half hour, I warrant you.

Now, now, my fairest, let us go;
   Fortune, Fate can frown no more:
A gentle gale begins to blow
   To waft us to a safer shore.

Let us the fav'ring minute seize,
   Give all our canvas to the wind,
Take with us freedom, love and ease,
   And leave remorse and pain behind.

Scene V

ZORAYDA, FERDINAND, FATIMA *in the Balcony, who afterwards comes down.*

FAT. Oh! Heavens! what will become of us all! – Who's in the garden? – Ferdinand I say! – Ferdinand! – Help – assistance – the Dey's officers are in the house breaking open the doors of the women's apartments.

FERD. Oh! that scriech-owl in the balcony! – We shall be pursued immediately! – Which way shall we take?

ZOR. She talks of the Emperor's officers! – It will be impossible to escape them, at least for me. – Here take these jewels – You may get off.

FERD. And what will become of thee then, poor kind soul?

ZOR. I must take my fortune. – When you have got safe into your own country, I hope you will sometime bestow a sigh to the memory of her who lov'd you.

FERD. No, take back your jewels – It's an empty casket without thee. – Thou and it had been a bargain.

ZOR. I hear them coming! – Shift for yourself at least.

FERD. No, confound me if I budge from you now.

FAT. Who's there? – Zorayda! – Ferdinand!

FERD. O are you there, Madam! – You have ferritted me out.

FAT. Come, come, this is no time for follies of any kind. The Cadi, her father, my husband, is undone, and we shall all be involved in his ruin. The court have had new informations of his extortion, and the wealth he has amassed by it. The last circumstance is enough to condemn him, and an order is issued to strangle him, and seize upon his effects. It is not a moment since the guards, thinking he was hid in my room, broke open the door where he had lock'd me up.

FERD. And where are they now?

FAT. I had the presence of mind to tell them that the Cadi was at a house he has twelve miles off, where they are gone to look for him, by which means we have an hour or two's respite to look about us.

ZOR. Alas! what good can we derive from that?

FERD. Hold! stay here – By Heaven I have a thought.

FAT. Dear Zorayda give me your hand; if there was ever any jealousies between us, I hope they are now at an end.

FAT.   Hence with anger, hence with chiding;
      From my breast the cause is gone.

ZOR.   Ev'ry harsher thought subsiding,
      Henceforth shall our souls be one.

FAT.   Females, mean and envious creatures,
      Seldom love for gen'rous ends:

ZOR.   But let us, of nobler natures,
      Shew that women can be friends.

A. 2.   Come then, friendship, here unite us
      In thy soft, thy sacred bands;
      At thy shrine, behold we offer
      Hearts conjoin'd as well as hands.
      Envy, vanity and malice
      Plague the bosoms where they reign:
      She, who would herself be happy,
      Ne'er will seek a sister's pain.

SCENE VI

ZORAYDA, FATIMA, FERDINAND, *the* CADI.

FERD. Come, Sir, come out. – I have told you your condition, and, if there is any thing to be done for you, you see there's no time to be lost.

CADI. O dear! – O dear! – O dear! –

FAT. Well, you know I always told you what would be the consequence of your bribery and corruption. I said it would bring you to the mutes and the bowstring at last.

CADI. What will become of me!

FAT. Why you'll be strangled as soon as the officers come back.

CADI. Oh! that cursed strangling. – I can't bear the thoughts of it. – No, good bye to you all. – I'll go and drown myself.

FERD. Stop: since you're for taking to the water, I have a proposal to make to you. The galley is now waiting in which your daughter and I designed to make our escape; what say you, will you accompany us? – We have already got the chief part of your effects, which I promise to share with you when we get to Spain.

ZOR. Do, dear father.

FAT. Indeed, husband, 'tis the only thing left for us.

CADI.   Well, dear wife, give me a kiss then.

> With pleasure I this land forego:
> My fame will sure be mangled;
> But what care I, let it be so
> If I escape being strangled.
> Nay, pr'ythee, let's make haste away;
> I really tremble while I stay.
> Oh! dreadful thing!
> In a bow string
> To have one's neck intangled.

CHO.   Nay, pr'ythee, &c.

FAT.   Here, Sir, receive your willing wife;
> Aboard you need but hand me:
> From henceforth I am yours for life,
> Confide in and command me.
> To ancient husband's girls be good;
> Remember jointer'd widowhood.
> That time may come,
> And then – but mum!
> He – hem – You understand me.

CHO.   To ancient husbands, &c.

ZOR.   I have been naughty, I confess;
> But now, you need not doubt it,
> I mean my conduct to redress,
> And straight will set about it.
> Forgive me only, dear papa,
> I'll be obedient as mama,
> Contented still,
> When I've my will,
> And who is pleas'd without it?

CHO.   Forgive me only, dear papa, &c.

FERD.   And now our scenic task is done,
> This comes of course, you know, Sirs,
> We drop the mask of every one,
> And stand in *statu quo*, Sirs;

Your ancient friends and servants we,
Who humbly wait for your decree,
One gracious smile,
To crown our toil,
And happy let us go, Sirs.
CHO.   Your ancient friends, &c.

John Leslie (fl. 1772)

Little is known of John Leslie. In *The Poets of Ireland* (1912), D. J. O'Donoghue suggests that he "was tutor to Lord Clanwilliam" and "Died September 5, 1778," but his source for this information is not clear and O'Donoghue can be unreliable. "John Leslie" is a common name in eighteenth-century Ireland, making attribution difficult. Leslie appears to have written two works, the topographical poems *Killarney* and *Phoenix Park*, both of which were published in 1772. *Killarney*, in particular, is a leading instance of Irish topographical poetry in the eighteenth century, in part because of the place of Killarney and its lakes in depictions of the Irish landscape. Leslie draws extensively on topographical conventions, including classical allusion, painterly reference, and the tension between nature and art. He also engages more contemporary concerns such as the picturesque and its touristic resonances, as well as recent historical events.

Killarney is implicitly organized into three sections. The first section details the lower lake and tells the story of Elizabethan wars and, in the more remote past, "Donoghoe, the great," a legendary Irish king who is praised for his virtues and who prophesies, in welcoming terms, English colonization. The second section, the shortest, offers a "Sylvan Tale," as the speaker crosses from the lower to the upper lake, in which the Maid of Killarney, Donoghoe's last descendant, meets and becomes betrothed to a tourist. The third section surveys the upper lake and engages

contemporary events. Much of this section deals with the Seven Years' War (1756–63), a conflict that included most of Europe and arose out of the French and Indian War (1754–63) in North America. Britain was eventually the military victor, and both wars were formally ended by the Treaty of Paris between Britain, Spain, and France in 1763; the treaty transferred both Spanish- and French-controlled territories in the American colonies and Canada to British control. When Leslie published *Killarney*, the British victory appeared to have established Britain as a major global power, and one with a firm grasp over the economically important transatlantic trade. In 1776, the American Revolution would contest this view, but in 1772 Britain's maritime power was nearly unchallenged.

Further reading

Foster, John Wilson, "The Topographical Tradition in Anglo-Irish Poetry," *Irish University Review* 4–5 (1974–5): 169–87. Reprinted in *Colonial Consequences: Essays in Irish Literature and Culture*. Dublin: Lilliput Press, 1991.

Gibbons, Luke, "Topographies of Terror: Killarney and the Politics of the Sublime," *South Atlantic Quarterly* 95 (1996): 23–44.

Waters, John, "Topographical Poetry and the Politics of Culture in Ireland, 1772–1820," in *Romantic Generations: Essays in Honor of Robert F. Gleckner*, ed. Ghislaine McDayter, Guinn Batten, and Barry Milligan, 221–44. Lewisburg: Bucknell University Press, 2001.

Killarney: A Poem (1772)

ADVERTISEMENT

There is a secret power in Nature, which captivates the heart of every attentive observer. Mankind in general seem to have an innate love of her charms; but this passion chiefly predominates in those of warm and susceptible minds. The Author having visited the celebrated scenes of KILLARNEY,[1] beheld them with wonder and delight, diversified, as they are, with all that can awaken the powers, and gratify the pleasures of imagination. Under these impressions, he was induced, as leisure permitted, and fancy prompted, to delineate, from a variety of the most picturesque and sublime objects, a landscape, representing select and distinct pieces of Imagery. For this purpose, he has taken a separate view of the two Lakes, and characterized each of them with its own peculiar beauties. The same method is observed with regard to the mountains, woods, shrubbery, and every other remarkable object. The description he has endeavoured to enliven with fable and episode. For the sentiment and moral, he makes no apology; having only to hope, that the Picture, drawn from his own feelings, may present some pleasing similitude of the great original.

The Author cannot conclude this short address to the Reader, without making his acknowledgments to the many respectable persons, who have interested themselves in the success of the following poem; and he takes this opportunity of expressing, how much he is indebted to the taste and friendship of the Reverend Doctor BOWDEN.

ARGUMENT

THE Introduction. – *A view of the Mountains.* – MANGERTON *described.* – *A prospect from its summit to the influx of the* SHANNON *into the* ATLANTICK. – *Growsing.* – *A view of the Woods, Arbutus, and Shrubbery.* – *Description of the Isle of* INNISFALLEN. – *Prospect from thence to the lower Lake, terminated by the castle of* DUNLO *on one hand, and by that of* ROSS ISLAND *on the other.* – *The mythology of* O DONAGHOE. – *A sudden storm.* – *View of* MUCRUS. – *Passage to the upper Lake.* – *A Sylvan Tale.* – *The principal objects of the Lake described; the Arbutus Island; the Oak Island; a Rock, representing the hull of a Man of War; a wild Landscape; a remarkable Waterfall.* – *The Stag Hunt.* – *Eagle's Aiery.* – *Echoes.* – *A late evening Scene, and other circumstances native to the subject.* – *The whole, the progress of a day.*

> Thy scenes, Killarney, scenes of pure delight,
> Call forth my verse, and wing my daring flight.
> O form'd to charm, new rapture to inspire,
> To feed the Painter's, and the Poet's fire!
> Far other pow'rs than mine, thy praises claim;   5
> Yet, strongly glowing with the sacred flame,
> May I, advent'rous, sing thy matchless pride,
> Fair Nature's boast? Be Nature thou my guide.

Notes

KILLARNEY

[1] Situate in the province of Munster, and county of Kerry, 30 miles N. W. of Cork, and 125 computed miles from Dublin (author).

Teach me to think, my feeble voice to raise,
Thou safest, best inspirer of my lays.   10
Where-e'er we rove, thro' forest, lake, or wild,
Bring with thee Fancy, thy creative child,
And gay associate; aptest she to tell
The haunt of Dryad, and the Echo's cell;
Where dwells the mountain's Genius, where the wood's,   15
And where the Naiads of the silver floods;
Where, seldom seen, the rural Pow'rs retreat,
The Friends and Guardians of thy sacred seat.

    But lo! in sylvan majesty arise
The green-wood Mountains, and salute the skies,   20
Circling the deep, or shelt'ring yonder plains,
Where Ceres smiles, and Kenmare chears the swains:[2]
No Alpine horrors on their summits frown,
Nor Pride, dark-low'ring, on the vale looks down:
No massy fragments, pendant from on high,   25
With hideous ruin strike the aching eye.
The swelling Hills, in vernant bloom elate,
Smile by their sides, th' attendants of their state.

    High o'er the rest, our steps aspiring tread
Exalted Mangerton's[3] cerulean head;   30
Parent of springs, where nurs'd the dews and rains
Timely descend, to glad the thirsty plains:
Where spreads the Lake diffusive o'er his crown,
And, like another Caspian,[4] all his own:
While down his bounteous side the Torrent roars;[5]   35
A richer tide than huge Olympus[6] pours:
Lodg'd in the blue serene, supreme he stands,
And all the region, far and wide, commands:
The less'ning Mountains now no more aspire,
Parnassus' rivals[7] modestly retire.   40
In guiltless times, perhaps, a Druid throng
There strung Ierne's lyre,[8] and wak'd the song;
And still, tho' rude the note, a learned strain,
The simple peasants of the West[9] retain:
The Lakes, the Isles, the Forests shrink below,   45
And, but in miniature, their glory shew.

    New objects rise from his stupendous height,
Nor can the tow'ring region[10] bound the sight.
Prospect immense! our eyes excursive roam,
To yon tall beach, where rushing surges foam;   50
Where, ebbing from their shores, the waves retreat;
One blue expanse of majesty sedate.

Notes

[2] Kenmare is the name of a river and a village near Killarney.
[3] One of the highest mountains in Ireland (author).
[4] A sea supposed not to communicate with any other (author).
[5] A waterfall in view of Mucrus (author).
[6] A mountain abounding with springs (author).
[7] A remarkable double-top'd mountain (author).
[8] Ierne is a poetic name for Ireland.
[9] In allusion to many of them, who speak Latin (author).
[10] A range of mountains, called the Reeks (author).

Now skirting wide, the happy plains are seen,
Where vanquish'd Desmond[11] bow'd to freedom's Queen,[12]
The first that gave them peace, in triumph led   55
Their tyrant Lords, and crush'd Rebellion's head.
Now Kenmare's[13] harbours spreading from the main,
Invite the passing mariner in vain.
Hard fate! shall thousands on Ierne's coast,
Be still to Commerce and to Britain lost?   60

Copious and calm, lo! Bantry's lordly tide,
For all Britannia's fleets a station wide;
A Port secure, long since well known to fame,
And signaliz'd with gallant Herbert's[14] name.
To Dingle[15] far we stretch, and o'er the main,[16]   65
Once fatal to the naval pride of Spain;
And where, in fruitless war, conflicting tides
Dash foamy round the Skellig's[17] marble sides;
On to the Capes,[18] where haughty Shannon roars,
And drives th' Atlantick backward from his shores.   70

Thou mighty Pharos of Ierne's isle,
Round whom recountless charms, and graces smile;
Whose ample breast the tempest's force restrains,
A gracious bulwark to the distant plains;
Th' astonish'd soul all fitted to inspire   75
With silent wonder, and with holy fire.
Let me, on wing'd devotion, ardent fly
Tow'rd Him, who rear'd thy awful head on high.

Descending, now, from Aether's pure domain,
By fancy borne to range the nether plain,   80
Behold all-winning Novelty display'd
Along the vale, the mountain, and the shade.
The scenes but late diminutive, resume
Their native grandeur, and their wonted bloom.
The woods expand their umbrage o'er the deep,   85
And with ambitious aim ascend the steep.
Stage above stage, their vig'rous arms invade
The tallest cliffs, and wrap them in the shade.
Each in its own pre-eminence regains,
The high dominion of the subject plains,   90
Smiling beneath; such smiles the people wear,
Happy in some paternal Monarch's care.

Notes

[11] An ancient lord of that country (author).
[12] Elizabeth (author). Elizabeth I, queen of England (1553–1603).
[13] The river (author).
[14] The bay of Bantry, memorable for the naval engagement between him and the French fleet, 1689 (author). Arthur Herbert (1648–1716), English admiral.
[15] The most westerly port of Europe (author).
[16] The Sound of the Blasquets, where some of the Spanish Armada were supposed to be lost, particularly, the Rosary of 1000 Tons (author).
[17] Three remarkable islands on the S. W. of Kerry (author).
[18] Loophead and Kerry-point (author).

Shall we the thicket, hill, or vale explore,
To cull the healing God's[19] salubrious store?
Or climb th' empurpled summit, there to breathe   95
Aethereal air, and view a world beneath;
While o'er the steep, the Zephyr's early gale,
And perfume wild, assist us to prevail.

Ye sportive Youth, it is your season now,
At blush of morn, to range the mountain's brow.   100
The russet cock,[20] forth from his heathy lawn,
Defiance crows, and challenges the dawn.
Behind, robust and proud, the well-plum'd pack,
Rambling, pursue their parents mazy track.
Here is the mark to win a sportsman's fame,   105
The Partridge is a poor, domestick game;
Here, train'd to distant toil, you learn to dare
The roughest deeds, and steel your nerves for war;
With thund'ring tube prepar'd, disdain to set
The gen'rous brood, you murder with the net.   110
Let nought insidious tempt your manly hearts;
To poachers leave the circumventive arts.
Now to the covert brown, all closely pent,
The Pointer draws, and stiffens in the scent;
Expectance beats, while each successive springs,   115
And trusts his safety to the strength of wings;
The well-aim'd gun arrests him as he flies,
He wheels, he falls, he flutters, bounds and dies.

Chear'd by the rural sport, the active Mind
Flies all abroad, and scorns to be confin'd,   120
Sweeps o'er the forest, up the mountain springs,
Where, to his pendant flock, the goat-herd sings;
List'ning the while, Content that never wants,
And rosy Health reclin'd on balmy plants.
Whitening the verdant steep, the fountains play,   125
In concert with the Sylvan warbler's lay.
Autumn and Spring their diff'ring seasons join,
And, social on the bough, together twine.

The Arbutus,[21] array'd in flow'rs and fruits,
The pride of all the shrubby natives shoots,   130
Various their tints; (not more the Prism displays
When show'ring on the eye light's parted rays)
An union rare; and such the pleasing sight,
When Youth and Manhood gracefully unite.
Emblem of Him, whose heav'n-attemper'd mind   135
Is form'd to profit, and delight mankind.
Some proudly upward tend, some lowly creep,

Notes

[19] Apollo (author). Greek god of medicine.   [21] A shrub.
[20] The Grouse (author).

And some, inverted, stoop to kiss the deep,
Narcissus-like;[22] and as the seasons glide,
Blossom, and bear with interchanging pride.   140
While other tribes, but transient charms assume,
These thro' Killarney's wilds perennial bloom.

    Child of Marsh-elder, next the Guilder-rose
Of humble origin, yet gayly blows;
Silver'd by happy chance, how strange to see   145
An offspring,[23] so unlike the parent tree!
The splendid native of the mountain's side,
Now in the garden lifts its snowy[24] pride.
Graceful and rich, the Juniper appears,
Like the Arabian-tree, distilling tears;   150
Here spreading wide, magnificently dress'd,
In purple rob'd, and by Apollo[25] bless'd.
Deep blushing near, the Service-fruit[26] repays
The woodland warblers wild, and grateful lays;
Allur'd from far, they flock with eager wing,   155
They feast luxurious, and more tuneful sing.

    From one kind stem,[27] behold with wond'ring eyes,
Curious and lordly proud, a forest rise.
No art instructs the various boughs to spread,
Nor from inoculation grows the shade;   160
The regal Oak, the hardy Ash ascend,
And their umbrageous arms together blend;
The gold-stain'd Holly lifts its prickly spears,
The Quicken-tree its sanguine cluster bears.
Their strength, their bloom, all grateful strive to shew,   165
And grace the parent stock, from whence they grow.
Rarely such ornament spontaneous springs,
Nor wave such honours on the heads of kings.
The stranger Vine a friendly mansion finds,
Lodg'd in the cliff, and o'er the summit winds   170
In purple pomp, while, like a bashful bride,
The Myrtle joins its fragrance and its pride.
Together twin'd, their native union prove
The God of vineyards, and the Queen of love.

    Can Flora's self recount the shrubs and flow'rs,   175
That scent the shade, that clasp the rocky bow'rs?
From the hard veins of sapless marble rise
The fragrant race, and shoot into the skies.
Wond'rous the cause! can human search explore,
What vegetation lurks in ev'ry pore?   180
What in the womb of diff'rent strata breeds?

Notes

[22] Narcissus, in classical myth, fell in love with his reflection in the water and attempted to kiss it.
[23] The difference supposed to be accidental (author).
[24] Commonly called the snowball tree (author).
[25] In allusion to its medicinal virtues (author).
[26] This tree is remarkable for its attraction of singing birds (author).
[27] A stem of yew, under the mountain Glena (author).

What fills the universe with genial feeds?
Wond'rous the cause! and fruitless to inquire,
Our wiser part is humbly to admire.
The fair expanse of yonder opening flood,   185
Now calls us from the summit and the wood.
The barks are trim'd, melodious musick waits,
Impatient joy in ev'ry bosom beats,
The Zephyrs lead, while new unfolding charms
Steal on our course, as fancy works and warms.   190
Some coyly, maiden-like, themselves reveal,
And boldly some, our gliding passage heal.
Isles, rocks, and shrubs, united now are seen,
And now disjoin'd, the waters play between.
Beauty, before in narrower circle pent,   195
Spreads o'er the deep, and triumphs in extent.
In mazy rounds of loveliest scenery lost,
Fair Innisfallen[28] courts us to her coast,
To climb her rocky barrier, and to stray
Along the path of Kenmare's spiry way.[29]   200
Vary'd with gentle mounts, descents, and plains,
Rich, yet the forest-wild, it still retains.
How green the carpet! while Sylvanus spreads
His venerable arms around our heads.
How proud the ruin![30] once the ruthless home   205
Of pale Austerity, and monkish gloom,
The seat of Woe, now by its princely lord,
To Mirth devoted, and the social board.

Forming a checker'd scene, the pendant wood,
By turns excludes, by turns admits the flood;   210
The Sylvan's covert, Naiad's kind repose,
When rude the Zephyr, or when Phoebus glows.
New scenes of grandeur open to our eyes,
Where graceful hills,[31] and distant ruins rise;
Where down the rugged steep of Tomes[32] break   215
The white cascades, and thund'ring seek the lake.
Now stretching far and wide, the wat'ry waste
Softly retires to Glena's bow'ry breast.

Nature and Art their diff'rent claims maintain,
Divide their empire, and alternate reign.   220
The hamlet, villa, and the mountain-range,
Water and wood, and islands interchange.
By turns emboss'd, enamel'd they appear,
And manly strength with female softness wear.
Here Claude[33] had fail'd, unable to command   225

Notes

28 An island toward the center of the lower lake (author).
29 Formed round the island by that nobleman (author).
30 Now a banquetting-house (author).
31 Those of Aghadoe (author).

32 A mountain contiguous to that of Glena (author).
33 Of Lorrain (author). French landscape painter, Claude Lorrain (1600–82).

His ravish'd fancy, and his trembling hand.
The eye all wonder, rests with rapture new,
Where lofty Dunlo[34] terminates the view;
His all-commanding aspect, rev'rend mien,
Speak him the ruler of the happy scene.   230
Fast by, the Laun's and Lo's[35] fair currents meet,
Circle the Plain, and murmur at his feet;
The rural Pow'rs rejoice, Pomona[36] laves
Her glowing bosom in their lucid waves.
Once more the charms of Paradise appear,   235
And all, but Eden's innocence, are here.

    In rival contrast, lo, th' expanded Isle
Of Ross[37] displays her military pile![38]
Long since illustrious, and the royal seat,
As Fame informs, of Donaghoe, the great.   240
Renown'd he was, and rank'd with earliest kings,
Nor disbelieve what hoar Tradition sings.
The tale no guise of partial story wears,
Strengthen'd by faith, and sanctify'd by years.
Killarney's Prince; his wife, his gentle sway,   245
Shall stand rever'd thro' Time's eternal day.
Religion taught his heart, that crowns are giv'n,
To serve mankind, and as a trust from heav'n.
Integrity his guide, he ne'er misus'd
His pow'r, and happiness to all diffus'd.   250
Impartial he dispens'd, (Law's surest guard)
Disgraceful punishment, and bright reward.
Lenient, yet just, he spar'd not even his own;
The Prison-isle[39] records his rebel Son.
There, during life, the factious were immur'd,   255
And peace and order, without blood, secur'd.
Plenty within his walls her table spread,
And Hecatombs upon the mountains bled.[40]
Pure, as the Sun's bright beams, his justice shew'd;
His bounty, like the lakes around him, flow'd.   260

    Nor the imperial art alone he knew;
He read, he search'd all Nature's volume thro',
Unlock'd her springs, disclos'd the latent pow'r
Of ev'ry medicinal herb, and flow'r.
No marks he bore of all-consuming time,   265
But, as immortal, ever held his prime.

    Once, on a day distinguish'd from the rest,
Surrounded by his subjects at the feast,

Notes

[34] The Seat of Mr. Crosbie (author).
[35] Two adjoining rivers (author).
[36] Alluding to the orchards (author).
[37] Anciently Russ (author).
[38] A barrack (author).

[39] Where, agreeable to O Donaghoe's polity, the disturbers of the State were confined, and particularly his rebellious Son (author).
[40] Alluding to his hospitality (author).

Chearful he sat, and in prophetic rhymes,
Darkling, rehears'd the fate of future times: 270
When more refin'd, the wide extended globe,
Should change her face, and wear a brighter robe:
When, freed from Gothick gloom, a star should rise[41]
To dissipate the mists in Western skies:
When curious Guests should travel far from home   275
To sail his lakes, and o'er his mountains roam:
When Ocean's vacant bosom should be spread,
With forests wing'd, and Commerce lift her head:
Child of the North, when Industry should shine,[42]
All rob'd in white, and ope her golden mine;   280
New charms diffusing o'er Ierne's face,
The joys of plenty, and the arts of peace:
When Freedom shou'd uprear her infant head,
And on Britannia's realms her blessings shed:
When, from a-far, shou'd come a mighty Friend[43]   285
Her cause to second, and her rights defend;
Thence, how transmitted to a kindred line
Of royal chiefs,[44] triumphant, shou'd she shine,
Immortal Queen; and find, whene'er distress'd,
A fort impregnable in Albion's breast.   290

While from his tongue divine prediction flow'd,
And firm belief, in ev'ry bosom glow'd,
Sudden he rose, and, to the gazing throng,
As some light vision, seem'd to skim along
The neighb'ring lake; wide op'd his willing wave,   295
And quick receiv'd him in a chrystal grave.
But O! what plaintive numbers can express
Their doubt, their wonder, and their wild distress?
Fears without hope, and sorrows without end,
At once bereav'd of Monarch, Father, Friend.   300
Some years were pass'd, when as the usual day
Of solemn mourning brought them forth to pay
The tribute of their tears; with streaming eyes,
They call'd on Donoghoe to hear their cries,
Implor'd the dire abyss in piteous strain,   305
To give them back their Donoghoe again;
Unceasing, till their wild, and sore lament
To silence shrunk, and grief itself was spent.

Soft, at the solemn interval, the sound
Of airs celestial fill'd the scene around.   310
The hills, the dales, the shores began to smile,

Notes

[41] Learning (author).

[42] The linen manufacture (author).

[43] K. William the Third (author). William III, also "William of Orange," was co-ruler of England with Mary II and defeated his father-in-law, the Catholic James II, at the Battle of the Boyne (1690).

[44] The Brunswick family (author). After the Stuart royal line died out in 1714, the British crown passed to the next Protestant in line: George I, the Elector of Hanover and Duke of Brunswick-Lüneburg.

And tenfold brighter shone the royal Isle.[45]
The sylvan songsters warbled from each spray,
The waters blush'd, as at the rising day.
Thunder, at length, the awful signal gave;   315
A Form all-glorious started from the wave,
On graceful courser, by a princely train
Of guards escorted o'er the glassy plain,
'Twas Donaghoe; his soul, tho' rais'd above
All earthly joy, yet glow'd with patriot-love,   320
With ardor to review his dear abode,
That felt, and own'd the presence of a God:
His radiant visage, ravish'd to behold,
His subjects bend their sovereign to enfold,
Restor'd, they fondly deem him, as their own,   325
Seated immortal on his native throne.
Expectance vain! a happiness so great,
So wish'd for, was deny'd by rigid Fate:
Lamented, hail'd in gratulative strain,
Sudden he fought the yawning deep again.   330
Too long an absence, still the natives mourn,
And annual supplicate his bless'd return.
Oft as he deigns a visit, they behold
Their flocks increase, their harvests wave with gold.

    Thus far all happy, we serenely glide   335
Along the windings of the glassy tide;
Above, the clust'ring Isles their verdure join,
Beneath, all lucid lies the pearly mine:[46]
A grateful, trembling variance wide display'd
Streams from the mingl'd tints of light and shade.   340
No breeze steals forth the mirror to deface;
The Zephyrs sleep profound, and all is peace.
Such the unruffled, the divine repose,
Wrapp'd in itself, that conscious virtue knows.

    But lo! the wary mariner descries   345
Presages of a tempest in the skies.
Blunted his beams, the King of day displays
A paler visage, and a fainter blaze.
Check'd in his course sublime, the eagle bends
A downward flight, and to the plain descends.   350
The prescient flocks their flow'ry herbage leave,
And fearful peasants hie them to the cave.
Rous'd by the brooding storm, we swiftly seek
The friendly bosom of a neighb'ring creek;
Such as the grateful port, that tempest-toss'd,   355
The shatter'd Trojan[47] found on Lybia's coast.[48]

Notes

[45] The seat of Donaghoe (author).
[46] Alluding to a pearl-fishery (author).
[47] Aeneas (author). See Virgil's *Aeneid*.

[48] Est in secessu longo. VIRG. (author). Roughly, "in a deep harbor" (Virgil, *Aeneid*, 1.159). In this part of the poem, Aeneas and his companions, weary from a rough sea voyage, land in a safe and quiet harbor on the African coast.

Darkness extends a deeper shade around;
The lab'ring mountains groan an hollow sound.
Burst from their narrow caves, the whirlwinds sweep
Thro' the wide concave of the airy deep;   360
Down thro' the vales, their headlong fury urge,
The forests rend, and lash the sounding surge.
Torn from the bough, the fragrant leaf and flow'r
Whirl in the blast, and mingle with the show'r.
Wide o'er the waves, the beauteous ruins lie,   365
And Desolation wounds the pitying eye.

But soon forgot, the short and sudden pain;
Lo! lovely Nature looks herself again.
The radiant Ruler of the world appears,
Dispels the clouds, and dissipates our fears.   370
Forth from the covert of the calm retreat,
Joyous, he leads us to the charming seat
Of Mucrus fair;[49] her elegance and dress,
The hand of some superior Pow'r confess.
From the pure azure of the brighter day,   375
Her native beauties higher charms display.
Like some selected treasure rarely seen,
Her vistas open, and her alleys green,
Her verdant terras, Meditation's bow'r,
The yew-topp'd ruin,[50] and the sainted tow'r.[51]   380

From her proud bourn, behold the distant Isles,
And the rude masonry of rocky piles.[52]
Grotesque and various, from the deep they rise,
And catch, by turns, new forms to mock our eyes.
Wide as her bay's cerulean barriers stretch,[53]   385
Naiads and Sylvans sport along the beach.
There, the bold cliff for ample prospect made;
Here, for repose the grotto and the shade.
Nature and Art, in kind assemblage, shew
The charms, that from their happy union flow.   390
Hence beauteous Imitation wisely blends
The borrow'd graces of her common friends,
With kindred touch, she makes them all her own,
Scarce is the offspring from the parent known.

As one lov'd Image parts with farewel sweet,   395
Another, and another still we meet,
At length the channel gain, which Lene[54] divides,
And, winding, to his upper region guides.
A-while resisted by the current's force,

Notes ───────────────────────────────────────

[49] The seat of Mr. Herbert (author).
[50] Mucrus Abbey (author). Muckross in current usage.
[51] St. Finian (author).
[52] One in particular represents a horse in the attitude of drinking (author).
[53] The bay of Mucrus (author).
[54] The name of the Lake (author).

We seek the shore, and intermit our course–.[55]   400
And here, ye Pow'rs, who range the silent grove,
Watch o'er the haunt, and wild recess of love;
Permit a rural Wand'rer to reveal
The tender secrets of the sylvan tale.

Haply, a gen'rous Youth, that pensive stray'd,   405
From gay Companions, thro' the winding shade,
Unmindful of the vulgar scenes of art,
The love of Nature pressing on his heart;
Was bless'd in solitude; when gliding by,
A beauteous female Figure drew his eye;   410
Her looks primeval innocence express'd,
The rural Loves sat smiling on her breast;
Her auburn tresses to the breeze incline,
Like the loose tendrils of the curling vine.
He gaz'd with transport, ev'ry sense on fire,   415
He felt the fierce extreme of wild desire.
But Honour's feelings soon the flame repress'd,
And check'd each ruder purpose of his breast.
Love, virtuous love, the tim'rous silence broke,
And thus restor'd, the Youth enamour'd spoke.   420

Say, fairest Maid, whose steps unguarded rove,
And tempt the dangers of the lonely grove;
Say, whence, and who thou art? thy form, thy grace,
Proclaim thee far above the vulgar race,
Above the glare of ornament, or art;   425
Thy beauty beams resistless on my heart.

Abash'd she stood; but soon her fears subside,
When, to his soft entreaty, she reply'd,
Adding new blushes to the rose of youth,
She breath'd the voice of purity, and truth.   430

Deep in these fav'rite woods I oft have been,
And walk'd their glades, unseeing, and unseen;
My chief delight, amidst their sweets to roam,
Or lead the fleecy, bleating wand'rer home.

In yonder vale, my aged Parent dwells,   435
Who, led by sad remembrance, often tells,
How long our noble ancestors maintain'd
Here regal sway, and o'er Killarney reign'd,
A region fair; and happy was the state,
The scepter borne by Donaghoe the great;   440
A name invok'd on ev'ry circling year,
For ever sacred, and for ever dear.

Notes ――――――――――――――――――――――――――――――――

[55] In passing to the upper Lake, it is necessary to land, in
order to force the boats against the stream, thro' the arches
of an old bridge (author).

But, dire reverse! that best of Princes gone,
A lawless, rebel Son usurp'd the throne,
From Prison-isle unchain'd a ruffian Band,   445
And scatter'd desolation thro' the land.
Hence civil broil, hence kindred blood was spilt,
And all involv'd in one promiscuous guilt.
Nor sex, nor age, nor sacred home was spar'd,
And Nature's beauties too, the havock shar'd.   450
These shades, these mountains, ev'ry Isle can tell,
What miseries our royal race befel.
Their fortunes now no more, and all forgot,
They left posterity an humbler lot.
From these our fair descent; and with it came   455
A small inheritance, and honest fame.
Retir'd we live, yet live with decent pride,
The sheep, and distaff for our wants provide.
'Tis vain for lost possessions to repine,
And with Content ev'n Poverty may shine.   460
Whoe'er to Heav'n, when in a fall'n estate,
Bravely submits, continues to be great.

Taught to resign, yet in these pleasing bow'rs,
A private sorrow steals upon mine hours.
When Nature feels, complaint is some relief,   465
And Wisdom's self may yield a-while to grief.
The feeble Friend, that watch'd my infant days,
Like the ripe falling fruit, a-pace decays;
Then aid me, Providence, or soon, or late
To bear the trial of an orphan's fate.   470

As one amaz'd, whose all bewilder'd sense
Delusion mocks, and holds in dumb suspence,
He stood; 'till wond'ring in the wild to find
Such native eloquence, and beauty join'd.
Bless'd be thine haunts, he cry'd, exalted Maid,   475
And bless'd the chance, that led me to the shade.
Thou all divine, whose suff'ring merit shews,
As thro' the rugged thorn, the bright'ning rose.
Let not a Stranger's vows alarm thine ear,
Vows lib'ral, earnest, open, and sincere.   480
With courtly phrase, their suit let others move,
Sincerity's my Advocate in love.
You will, you must be kind; my all is thine,
The holy hour awaits to make thee mine.

Silence can better paint the soft surprize,   485
That flush'd her o'er, and melted in her eyes.
Pride, duty, gratitude, perplexing, strove
To rule her thought, and gave a pause to love.
Won by his virtue, to the nuptial band,
She look'd consent, and pledg'd it with her hand.   490
All blushing from the shade, he led her forth,
To higher scenes more suited to her worth.

Launch'd on the smoother flood, and brushing thro'
The bow'ry Streight,[56] new objects strike our view;
A wild, a rich Elysium they impart,   495
Play on the fancy, and dilate the heart.

Thy Isle, gay Green,[57] of never-fading dye,
Spreads Nature's comeliest wardrobe to the eye;
And when the honours of the groves are shed,
Midst the pale ruin lifts its blooming head;   500
Now o'er the glassy, and pellucid stream,
Throws the mild lustre of the em'rald's beam;
One everlasting smile of joy it wears,
And Winter's sickly, drear dominion chears.

Dodona's rival,[58] tow'rs the Oaken-grove,[59]   505
Sacred to Britain's Genius, and to Jove.
But Jove no longer speaks; those awful woods
Pour only Britain's thunder on the floods:
And see, when Nature first to Britain gave
The green domain, and charter of the wave,   510
From yon rude coast, she took the marble block,
And sketch'd her future navy in the rock;[60]
Chisel'd the prow, and hull; then o'er the tide,
Reclin'd its sable, adamantine side,
Bade her black bulwarks distant Empires shake,   515
And fix'd their glorious model on her lake.

Queen of the ocean, favour'd high of Heav'n,
To whom of late, all victory was giv'n,[61]
Great, and secure, unless too mighty grown,
Thy own oppressive grandeur bears thee down.   520
What tho' commotions for a-while prevail?
They purge, they purify the common weal.
Tho' with her wanton children Freedom strives,
She ne'er can perish, while a Briton lives:
On her own pile, she, Phoenix-like, expires,   525
Then rises all new burnish'd from her fires.

Blameless may I thus touch thine honour'd name?
While thy fair Sister's glories lead my theme,
Where, far from Art, unrival'd, and alone,
Nature, in solitude, erects her throne.   530
Awful Inspirer! shall we take the round
Of her romantick, and enchanting ground;
And thro' the wilderness of mountains trace
The line of order, dignity, and grace?
Shall we, embosom'd in their lonely scenes,   535

Notes ————————————————————————————————————

[56] Covered with Arbutus (author).
[57] The Arbutus Island (author).
[58] Where the oracles of Jupiter were delivered (author).
[59] The oak Island (author).
[60] Representing the hull of a man of war (author).

[61] Alluding to the years 1758, and 59 (author). A reference to
the Seven Years' War, probably the British defeat of French
forces in Canada at Louisburg, Nova Scotia (1758) and the
Plains of Abraham, Quebec (1759).

Forget the noise, and riot of the plains?
And deep retir'd from busy man's abode,
With rapture view this wond'rous work of God?
Curious to mark, why so profusely strew'd,
Contrasted lie the beautiful and rude;   540
Why, midst the laughing Isles, and o'er the wave,
All placid, rugged rocks uncoothly heave?
Think not the seeming, inconsistent scene
Was thrown at random, or dispos'd in vain;
No, thou Instructress fair, in this we see,   545
The natural, and moral world agree;
Evil and good, pleasure and pain, at strife,
Thus variegate the stream of human life.

    High o'er the wild, and thro' the verdant bow'rs,
Fast on the eye, the gleaming Torrent pours,[62]   550
Awful, as if within some God were hid,
And all access to human step forbid.
Bold, and beyond the reach of skill, we see
Majestick Nature's artless symmetry,
The mansion of the Sister-Graces, where   555
Unite the Wonderful, Sublime, and Fair.

    Fast by, Retirement holds her peaceful seat,
And views the humble hermit at her gate.
All rapt in fervent piety, he feels
His Maker's presence, and adoring kneels.   560
Let Tybur[63] boast her hill, her olive shade,
Her Sybil's grot, her Annio's fam'd cascade.
Let the vain Traveller the praise resound
Of distant realms, and rave of Classick ground;
Let him o'er Continents delighted run,   565
Or search the Isles, the fav'rites of the Sun;[64]
Let him of foreign wonders take the round,
Unrival'd still Killarney will be found:
Here, brighter charms, superior blessings reign,
And Law and Liberty protect the scene.   570

    The restless Passions, which, like pilgrims, roam,
Here pause a-while, and find a pleasing home.
From the wild store, the tuneful and the sage
Catch the warm image to illume their page.
To the fond Lover's ravish'd eyes appear,   575
The lively transcripts of his Fair-one here.
Th' ambitious, happy in exalted views,
The glowing fervour of his breast renews.
On deep research, the friend of Nature feeds,

Notes

[62] A remarkable waterfall (author).
[63] The summer retreat of the old Roman Nobility (author).
[64] Those called the Fortunate (author). The Fortunate Isles of Roman mythology where diverse fruits grow plentifully and without agricultural work by the virtuous dead who reside there.

Each in his fav'rite wish, and want succeeds. 580
As the scene varies, varies ev'ry grace,
And heart-felt pleasure smiles in ev'ry face.
The Hunter's musick breaks upon the ear,
Rouzing the savage tenant from his lair.
The mellow horn, the deeper note of hound, 585
The Foresters proclaim, the Stag is found;
On Echo's wing, the joyful accents fly,
The mountains round reverberate the cry.

    Rejoicing in his strength and speed, he mocks
Opposing thickets, and projecting rocks; 590
The shatter'd oak, in vain, resists his force;
The distant hills are swallow'd in his course:
Dauntless as yet, he stops a-while to hear;
List'ning he doubts, and doubt fore-runs his fear;
His well known range he tries, now devious strays, 595
Clamour pursues, the gale behind betrays;
Unsafe the covert, all alarm'd he feels
His foes instinctive, winding at his heels;
He bounds the cavern's yawning jaws, and now,
Darting, he gains the cliff's tremendous brow, 600
There, like the haughty Persian, station'd high,[65]
Seems all approaching dangers to defy;
He gazes on the deep, he snuffs from far
The gath'ring tumult, and prepares for war.

    A patient, active Band, Milesian blood, 605
Long us'd to scale the steep, and hem the wood,
Such as the Lord's own Hunter, fam'd of old,
For mightiest chace, would glory to behold;
Or such, by Wolfe inspir'd, that fearless strain'd
Up Abram's heights, and Quebeck's ramparts gain'd;[66] 610
Steel'd to extremest toil, and fit to bear
Hunger and thirst, and Zembla's keenest air,
Nay, time itself; a Race of old renown,
And thro' successive ages handed down;
Their brawny shoulders from incumbrance freed, 615
Their nervous limbs, wing'd with Achilles' speed,
Hotly pursue, and, with unweary'd pace,
O'ertake the fugitive, and urge the chace.

    Divided now 'twixt courage and dismay,
To yield a captive, or to stand at bay; 620
Maintaining in the pass the glorious strife,
Like Sparta's King,[67] for liberty and life.

Notes

[65] Xerxes seated on Mount Athos (author). Xerxes I was a Persian king after c.485 BCE who invaded Greece.

[66] Another reference to the Battle of the Plains of Abraham (1759), where General James Wolfe led British forces in Canada to end the siege of Quebec in Britain's favor.

[67] Leonidas (author). Leonidas, king of Lacedaemon, died about 480 BCE leading his soldiers against the invading forces of Xerxes I, despite overwhelming odds.

With fury wild, he glares around, nor knows
A refuge near, on ev'ry side his foes;
Forc'd to a long adieu, his native wood,   625
Determin'd, he forsakes, and braves the flood,
Dash'd headlong down: his spirit what avails?
Arrang'd below, a hostile fleet assails
With wild uproar; he rides the liquid plain,
And strives th' Asylum of the isles to gain.   630
Bays far remote he tries, and lonely creeks,
Steals to the shades, and moss-grown ruins seeks:
His lab'ring foes his mazy course pursue,
Like wand'ring Delos,[68] now he shifts the view;
Now, as the smaller galliot, swift and light,   635
Veering he shuns, or meets th' unequal fight;
At length bewilder'd, all confus'd he roves,
Catching a farewell prospect of his groves;
All efforts vain, o'erwhelm'd, he now must yield,
To die inglorious, in the wat'ry field: 640
High o'er his back th' insulting billow rides,
The prow and oar furrow his panting sides;
Ungracious sport! His victors, yet in dread,
Beat down th' emerging honours of his head:
Ah! what resource the lordly prey to save?   645
Driv'n from the wood, and hunted o'er the wave.
Bleeding he fails, he floats, he faints, he dies;
Ungen'rous shouts of triumph rend the skies.
His hapless fate, the sighing forests tell,
And all the ridgy regions sound his knell;   650
The Naiads weep, Lene mourns his lucid flood,
By wanton man usurp'd, and stain'd with blood.

  Some pious rites the Rustick's pity move,
Due to the fall'n, he lops the verdant grove:
The Arbutus descends, the fav'rite shade   655
He rang'd when living, now adorns him dead.[69]

  The hoary Peak,[70] with Heav'ns bright azure crown'd,
And brow, with wreaths of ivy compass'd round,
Leans o'er the deep; the base, and shaggy side,
In sylvan beauty clad, and forest pride;   660
Its form, unhurt by tempests, or by years,
Still in fresh robes of majesty appears:
The pile superb, as Nature careless threw,
Grandeur and Order up the summit grew:
Their easy steps tend gradual to the skies,   665
And teach aspiring Genius how to rise.

Notes

[68] Supposed to have been a floating Island (author). Roman myth.

[69] Alluding to the ceremony of covering the carcass with green boughs (author).

[70] The Eagle's Aiery, and where the remarkable Echoes are produced (author).

Here his dread seat, the royal Bird hath made,
To awe th' inferior subjects of the shade,
Secure he built it for a length of days,
Impervious, but to Phoebus' piercing rays;   670
His young he trains to eye the solar light,
And soar beyond the fam'd Icarian flight.

On Nature's fabrick, Builder, turn thine eye,
Whose strength and beauty, storm and time defy.
Build as thou may'st, still ruin makes a part,   675
Creeps in unseen, and mixes with thine art:
The pompous pile insensibly descends,
And in the dust, thy boasted labour ends.

Awe-struck, and wrapt in meditation still,
The sound of echoing horns around us trill,   680
Divinely sweet; their melody like those
That charm'd the croud, when Donaghoe arose:
Various the notes, they warble thro' the woods,
Talk in the cliffs, and murmur in the floods,
While Harmony, unloos'd from all her chains,   685
Free, and at large, pours forth her inmost strains;
A deeper tone each promontory rings,
And ev'ry rock, a Memnon's statue, sings[71]
Enchanting airs, that rule, without controul,
The captive sense, and steal away the soul!   690

Haply to tune her woes, the vocal Dame,
For this retreat, had chang'd Cephisus' stream;[72]
Her slighted passion breathes pathetick strains,
And of the coy Narcissus still complains.[73]

Awake to bolder notes; the cannon's roar   695
Bursts from the bosom of the hollow shore;
The dire explosion the whole concave fills,
And shakes the firm foundations of the hills,
Now pausing deep, now bellowing from a-far,
Now rages near the elemental war: 700
Affrighted Echo opens all her cells,
With gather'd strength, the posting clamour swells,
Check'd, or impell'd, and varying in its course,
It slumbers, now awakes with double force,
Searching the strait, and crooked, hill and dale,   705
Sinks in the breeze, or rises in the gale:
Chorus of earth and sky! the mountains sing,
And Heaven's own thunders thro' the valleys ring.

Notes

[71] A Statue mentioned by Strabo, which, on being touched by the rays of the sun, emitted musical sounds (author). Roman historian and geographer, Strabo (c.64 BCE – AD 24).

[72] The native residence of Echo, according to the Poets (author). Cephisus is a river in Greece; Echo is a Nymph who fell in love with Narcissus.

[73] Alluding to her ill requited love (author). Various versions of the myth end with Echo becoming a disembodied voice after Narcissus' rejection of her love.

Our progress o'er – day fading on the sight,
Closes this scene of wonder and delight;   710
What time the lakes, the shades, the grots unfold,
And nightly Jubilee, the Genii hold.
New dress'd by Flora's hand, the Nymphs are seen,
Radiant with beaded pearl, and stoles of green,
Airy they frolick, o'er the woodland sweep,   715
They brush the flow'rs unhurt, and skim along the deep
To softest musick; while the bright'ning moon,
And all the starry host look smiling on.

The homeward Peasant stops, and hastes by turns,
And his rude heart with strange emotion burns;   720
His joyful, rosy offspring gather near,
The wonders of his magick tale to hear,
List'ning they glow; while each believes he sees
More than he tells, and clings about his knees,
'Till fir'd their little breasts, they break away,   725
And round their Sire, in mimick gambols play.

Ye thoughtless Sons of Affluence and Ease,
Bewilder'd oft in Pleasure's flow'ry maze;
And Ye, who beat the rounds of Folly's fields,
Try what Killarney's blissful region yields: 730
'Tis Her's with lenient comfort to impart
A balm congenial to the human heart;
To fill the mind with sentiments divine,
And all the social feelings to refine;
To make the grateful tongue proclaim aloud,   735
The praise of Nature, and of Nature's God.

Joseph Cooper Walker (1761–1810) and Turlough O'Carolan (1670–1738)

Antiquarian Joseph Cooper Walker was born into a Dublin family. He was educated and began his working life in Dublin, but traveled in Europe for health reasons, later returning to Wicklow where he lived until his death. His antiquarian scholarship began with "Anecdotes of Chess in Ireland" (1770) and he was a founding member of the Royal Irish Academy in 1785. He published volumes on Italian drama, *A Historical Essay on the Dress of the Ancient and Modern Irish* (1788), *An Essay on the Origin of Romantic Fabling in Ireland* (1806), and various works on Ireland. *Historical Memoirs of the Irish Bards* (1786) was one of his earliest and without question his most influential work, helping to launch English-language scholarship on Irish-language culture.

Of special interest in Walker's volume was the poet Turlough O'Carolan (or Toirdhealbhach Ó Cearbhalláin, and sometimes just "Carolan"). O'Carolan was born in Co. Meath in 1670, and was educated locally in Co. Roscommon. He was blinded by smallpox at the age of eighteen, and subsequently trained as a harper. He was celebrated in the late eighteenth and early nineteenth centuries as the last of the Irish bards, his poetry collected and translated in such volumes as Walker's *Historical Memoirs* and Charlotte Brooke's *Reliques of Irish Poetry* (1789). In ancient bardic tradition, he toured Ireland with his harp, in the same decades that Jonathan Swift was publishing, visiting the wealthy who fed and sheltered him in return for his performances.

Further reading

Davis, Leith, *Music, Postcolonialism, Gender: The Construction of Irish National Identity, 1724–1874*. Notre Dame, IN: University of Notre Dame Press, 2006.

Welch, Robert, *A History of Verse Translation from the Irish*. Gerrards Cross: Colin Smythe, 1988.

From Walker's *Historical Memoirs of the Irish Bards* (1786)

The feudal system which had prevailed from time immemorial in Ireland, received a severe stroke from Elizabeth, which was repeated by Cromwell, and fatally reiterated by William III. The pride of the Chieftains was humbled, and many of their castles razed. Some of those unfortunate men fled to the Continent; others patiently waited to receive the English yoke. In their halls which formerly resounded with the voice of Minstrelsey and Song, and glittered with barbarous magnificence, there reigned

A death-like silence and a dread repose:

naught, save the flapping of the drowsy Bat, or shrieking of the moping Owl, could now be heard within them. To the clumsy Dutch, or light Grecian, the gloomy style of Gothic Architecture gave place. The English Customs and Manners were universally adopted, Agriculture was introduced, and the face of the Country began to smile.

But these happy innovations came fraught with destruction to the Bards. Their properties were forfeited with the estates of which they composed a part. They were no longer entertained in the families of the Great, nor treated with wonted respect. They degenerated into itinerant Musicians, wandering from house to house, their Harp slung at their back, soliciting admission, and offering to play for hire. Sometimes they were to be found exciting the sprightly Dance at a Patron; sometimes raising the solemn Dirge at a Country Wake. The last of this Order of Men, whose Name deserves to be recorded, was Turlough O'Carolan, a fine natural Genius, who died in the year 1738. To this Man we owe several of our best airs. His melodies, though extremely simple, give pleasure even to the most refined taste; and his poetry is not always below mediocrity. The genial current of his soul, it is true, was not, like that of his brother Minstrels, "chill'd by penury:" like them, indeed, his life was erratic; but he neither played for hire, nor refused a reward when offered with delicacy.

Bumpers, 'Squire Jones (imitated from Carolan)[1]

From **Walker's Historical Memoirs of the Irish Bards (1786)**

Ye Good-fellows all,
Who love to be told where there's claret good store,
Attend to the call
Of one who's ne'er frighted,
But greatly delighted,   5
With six bottles more:
Be sure you don't pass
The good house Money-Glass,
Which the jolly red god so peculiarly owns;
'Twill well suit your humour,   10
For pray what would you more,
Than mirth, with good claret, and bumpers, 'Squire Jones.

Ye lovers who pine
For lasses that oft prove as cruel as fair;
Who whimper and whine   15
For lillies and roses,
With eyes, lips, and noses,
Or tip of an ear:
Come hither, I'll show you,
How Phillis and Chloe,   20
No more shall occasion such sighs and such groans;
For what mortal so stupid
As not to quit Cupid,
When call'd by good claret, and bumpers, 'Squire Jones.

Ye Poets who write,   25
And brag of your drinking fam'd Helicon's brook,
Though all you get by 't
Is a dinner oft-times,
In reward of your rhimes
With Humphry the duke: 30
Learn Bacchus to follow
And quit your Apollo,
Forsake all the Muses, those senseless old crones:
Our jingling of glasses
Your rhiming surpasses,   35
When crown'd with good claret, and bumpers, 'Squire Jones.

Notes ――――――――――――――――――――――――――――――――――

BUMPERS, 'SQUIRE JONES

[1] According to the Appendix in which this imitation appeared, O'Carolan enjoyed the hospitality of "— Jones, Esq.; of Money-Glass in the county of Leitrim ... [H]e has enshrined his convivial character in one of his best PLANXTIES. Yet of this Planxty the air only is now remembered; the poetry, though one of Carolan's most brilliant effusions, is lost in the splendour of the facetious Baron Dawson's paraphrase ... This paraphrase is so excellent, that I cannot in justice to my readers, with-hold it from them" (71).

Ye soldiers so stout,
With plenty of oaths, tho' no plenty of coin,
Who make such a rout
Of all your commanders 40
Who serv'd us in Flanders,
And eke at the Boyne:
Come leave off your rattling
Of sieging and battling,
And know you'd much better to sleep in whole bones; 45
Were you sent to Gibraltar,
Your notes you'd soon alter,
And wish for good claret, and bumpers, 'Squire Jones.

Ye clergy so wise,
Who myst'ries profound can demonstrate most clear, 50
How worthy to rise!
You preach once a week,
But your tithes never seek
Above once in a year:
Come here without failing, 55
And leave off your railing
'Gainst bishops providing for dull stupid drones;
Says the text so divine,
What is life without wine?
Then away with the claret, a bumper, 'Squire Jones. 60

Ye lawyers so just
Be the cause what it will, who so learnedly plead,
How worthy of trust!
You know black from white
Yet prefer wrong to right, 65
As you chanc'd to be fee'd:
Leave musty reports,
And forsake the king's courts,
Where dulness and discord have set up their thrones;
Burn Salkeld and Ventris, 70
With all your damn'd entries,
And away with the claret, a bumper, 'Squire Jones.

Ye physical tribe,
Whose knowledge consists in hard words and grimace,
Whene'er you prescribe 75
Have at your devotion,
Pills, bolus, or potion,
Be what will the case:
Pray where is the need
To purge, blister, and bleed? 80
When ailing yourselves the whole faculty owns,
That the forms of old Galen
Are not so prevailing
As mirth with good claret, and bumpers, 'Squire Jones.

Ye foxhunters eke,   85
That follow the call of the horn and the hound,
Who your ladies forsake,
Before they're awake
To beat up the brake
Where the vermin is found: 90
Leave Piper and Blueman,
Shrill Duchess and Trueman;
No music is found in such dissonant tones:
Would you ravish your ears
With the songs of the spheres,   95
Hark away to the claret, a bumper, 'Squire Jones.

Carolan's Monody on the Death of Mary Mac Guire
(translated by a Lady)[1]

From **Walker's Historical Memoirs of the Irish Bards (1786)**

Were mine the choice of intellectual fame,
    Of spelful song, and eloquence divine,
Painting's sweet power, Philosophy's pure flame,
    And Homer's lyre, and Ossian's harp were mine;
The splendid arts of Erin, Greece, and Rome,   5
    In MARY lost, would lose their wonted grace,
All wou'd I give to snatch her from the tomb,
    Again to fold her in my fond embrace.

Desponding, sick, exhausted with my grief,
    Awhile the founts of sorrow cease to flow,   10
In vain! – I rest not – sleep brings no relief; –
    Cheerless, companionless, I wake to woe.
Nor birth nor beauty shall again allure,
    Nor fortune win me to another Bride;
Alone I'll wander, and alone endure,   15
    Till death restore me to my dear-one's side.

Once every thought, and every scene was gay,
    Friends, mirth and music all my hours employ'd –
Now doom'd to mourn my last sad years away,
    My life a solitude! – my heart a void! –   20
Alas the change! – to change again no more!
    For every comfort is with MARY fled:

Notes

CAROLAN'S MONODY
[1] Mary MacGuire is identified in the editorial apparatus of *Historical Memoirs* as O'Carolan's wife; she died in 1733. The translator may be Charlotte Brooke, but she is only identified as "a young Lady, whose name I am enjoined to conceal: – with the modesty ever attendant on true merit, and with the sweet timidity natural to her sex, she shrinks from the public eye" (92).

And ceaseless anguish shall her loss deplore,
    Till age and sorrow join me with the dead.

Adieu each gift of nature and of art,   25
    That erst adorn'd me in life's early prime! –
The cloudless temper, and the social heart,
    The soul ethereal and the flights sublime!
Thy loss, my MARY, chac'd them from my breast!
    Thy sweetness cheers, thy judgment aids no more: –   30
The muse deserts an heart with grief opprest –
    And lost is every joy that charm'd before.

Charlotte Brooke (c.1740–1793)

Charlotte Brooke was born in Co. Cavan but lived in Kildare in her early years, one of the youngest children of author Henry Brooke. While her 1816 biographer paints her as a recluse devoted to her father and then her work, she socialized in Dublin literary circles in the late eighteenth century, particularly those that gathered around her distant relation, Alicia Sheridan Lefanu, daughter of Thomas and Frances Sheridan. Devoting most of her adult life to the care of her father, Brooke did not begin publishing until after his death in 1783.

Her most influential work remains *Reliques of Irish Poetry* (1789), a collection of translations of Irish verse, with transcriptions of the originals to verify their authenticity, intermixed with her essays on Irish-language poetry. She also included her own pseudo-antique poem, "Maön: An Irish Tale," written from the perspective of a bard on the margins of heroic action and the central love story. *Reliques* influenced generations of Irish poets and novelists and was often cited in their writing. She also had a larger impact on the study of the Irish language. *Bolg an Tsolair: Or, Gaelic Magazine* (1795), a nationalist publication produced by *The Northern Star* office in Belfast, provided an Irish grammar, dictionary, and parallel translations of conversational dialogue and biblical passages to educate English speakers about the Irish language; the small volume included "a collection of choice Irish songs, translated by Miss Brooke," all taken from her *Reliques*. Her name also appears in discussions of translation in the early 1800s, such as letters between Lady Morgan and Alicia Sheridan Lefanu when Morgan was working on her own Irish translations.

Brooke's corpus includes non-Irish-language material as well. She edited, for instance, the four-volume *Poetical Works of Henry Brooke* (1792), which included her short biography of her father. She also published a children's volume, *The School for Christians* (1791), and may have written a tragedy, *Belisarius*, though evidence of the play's existence is slight: it was never published and, though her 1816 biographer asserts the play's existence, his account of the manuscript's disappearance is marred by inconsistencies.

Further reading

Davis, Leith, "Birth of the Nation: Gender and Writing in the Work of Henry and Charlotte Brooke," *Eighteenth-century Life* 18 (1994): 27–47.
— *Music, Postcolonialism, Gender: The Construction of Irish National Identity, 1724–1874*. Notre Dame, IN: University of Notre Dame Press, 2006.
Welch, Robert, *A History of Verse Translation from the Irish*. Gerrards Cross: Colin Smythe, 1988.

From *Preface*

From Reliques of Irish Poetry (1789)

In a preface to a translation of ancient Irish poetry, the reader will naturally expect to see the subject elucidated and enlarged upon, with the pen of learning and antiquity. I lament that the limited circle of my knowledge does not include the power of answering so just an expectation; but my regret at this circumstance is considerably lessened, when I reflect, that had I been possessed of all the learning requisite for such an undertaking, it would only have qualified me for an unnecessary foil to the names of O'CONOR, O'HALLORAN and VALLANCEY.[1]

My comparatively feeble hand aspires only (like the ladies of ancient Rome) to strew flowers in the paths of these laureled champions of my country. The flowers of earth, the *terrestrial* offspring of Phoebus, were scattered before the steps of victorious WAR; but, for triumphant GENIUS are reserved the *coelestial* children of his beams, the unfading flowers of the Muse. To pluck, and thus to bestow them, is mine, and I hold myself honoured in the task.

"The esteem (says Mr. O'HALLORAN) which mankind conceive of nations in general, is always in proportion to the figure they have made in arts and in arms. It is on this account that all civilized countries are eager to display their heroes, legislators, poets and philosophers – and with justice, since every individual participates in the glory of his illustrious countrymen." – But where, alas, is this thirst for national glory? when a subject of such importance is permitted to a pen like mine! Why does not some *son of Anak*[2] in genius step forward, and boldly throw his gauntlet to Prejudice, the avowed and approved champion of his country's lovely muse?

It is impossible for imagination to conceive too highly of the pitch of excellence to which a science must have soared which was cherished with such enthusiastic regard and cultivation as that of poetry, in this country. It was absolutely, for ages, the vital soul of the nation;[3] and shall we then have no curiosity respecting the productions of genius once so celebrated, and so prized?

True it is, indeed, and much to be lamented, that few of the compositions of those ages that were famed, in Irish annals, for the *light of song*, are now to be obtained by the most diligent research. The greater number of the poetical remains of our Bards, yet extant, were written during the middle ages; periods when the genius of Ireland was in its wane,

"— Yet still, not lost
All its original brightness —."

On the contrary, many of the productions of those times breathe the true spirit of poetry, besides the merit they possess with the Historian and Antiquary, as so many faithful delineations of the manners and ideas of the periods in which they were composed.

Notes

FROM PREFACE
[1] Antiquarians Charles O'Conor (1710–91), Sylvester O'Halloran (1728–1807), and Charles Vallancey (1726–1812). Vallancey was not born in Ireland but lived there for most of his life.

[2] a giant

[3] See the elegant and faithful O'CONOR upon this subject (*Dissertations on the History of Ireland*, p. 66); and he is supported by the testimonies of the most authentic of antient and modern historians (author).

With a view to throw some light on the antiquities of this country, to vindicate, in part, its history, and prove its claim to scientific as well as to military fame, I have been induced to undertake the following work. Besides the four different species of composition which it contains, (the HEROIC POEM, the ODE, the ELEGY, and the SONG) others yet remain unattempted by translation: – the ROMANCE, in particular, which unites the fire of Homer with the enchanting wildness of Ariosto.[4] But the limits of my present plan have necessarily excluded many beautiful productions of genius, as little more can be done, within the compass of a single volume, than merely to give a few specimens, in the hope of awakening a just and useful curiosity, on the subject of our poetical compositions.

Unacquainted with the rules of translation, I know not how far those rules may censure, or acquit me. I do not profess to give a merely literal version of my originals, for that I should have found an impossible undertaking. – Besides the spirit which they breathe, and which lifts the imagination far above the tameness, let me say, the *injustice*, of such a task, – there are many complex words that could not be translated literally, without great injury to the original, – without being "false to its sense, and falser to its fame."

I am aware that in the following poems there will sometimes be found a sameness, and repetition of thought, appearing but too plainly in the English version, though scarcely perceivable in the original Irish, so great is the variety as well as beauty peculiar to that language. The number of synonima[5] in which it abounds, enables it, perhaps beyond any other, to repeat the same thought, without tiring the fancy or the ear.

It is really astonishing of what various and comprehensive powers this neglected language is possessed. In the pathetic, it breathes the most beautiful and affecting simplicity; and in the bolder species of composition, it is distinguished by a force of expression, a sublime dignity, and rapid energy, which it is scarcely possible for any translation fully to convey; as it sometimes fills the mind with ideas altogether new, and which, perhaps, no modern language is entirely prepared to express. One compound epithet must often be translated by two lines of English verse, and, on such occasions, much of the beauty is necessarily lost; the force and effect of the thought being weakened by too slow an introduction on the mind; just as that light which dazzles, when flashing swiftly on the eye, will be gazed at with indifference, if let in by degrees.

But, though I am conscious of having, in many instances, failed in my attempts to do all the justice I wished to my originals, yet still, some of their beauties are, I hope, preserved; and I trust I am doing an acceptable service to my country, while I endeavour to rescue from oblivion a few of the invaluable reliques of her ancient genius; and while I put it in the power of the public to form some idea of them, by clothing the thoughts of our Irish muse in a language with which they are familiar, at the same time that I give the originals, as vouchers for the fidelity of my translation, as far as two idioms so widely different would allow.

However deficient in the powers requisite to so important a task, I may yet be permitted to point out some of the good consequences which might result from it, if it were but performed to my wishes. The productions of our Irish Bards exhibit a glow of cultivated genius, – a spirit of elevated heroism, – sentiments of pure

Notes

[4] Ludovico Ariosto (1474–1533), Italian poet.

[5] There are upwards of forty names to express a *Ship* in the Irish language, and nearly an equal number for a *House*, &c. (author).

honor, – instances of disinterested patriotism, – and manners of a degree of refine-ment, totally astonishing, at a period when the rest of Europe was nearly sunk in barbarism: And is not all this very honorable to our countrymen? Will they not be benefited, – will they not be gratified, at the lustre reflected on them by ancestors so very different from what modern prejudice has been studious to represent them? But this is not all. –

As yet, we are too little known to our noble neighbour of Britain; were we better acquainted, we should be better friends. The British muse is not yet informed that she has an elder sister in this isle; let us then introduce them to each other! together let them walk abroad from their bowers, sweet ambassadresses of cordial union between two countries that seem formed by nature to be joined by every bond of interest, and of amity. Let them entreat of Britain to cultivate a nearer acquaintance with her neighbouring isle. Let them conciliate for us her esteem, and her affection will follow of course. Let them tell her, that the portion of her blood which flows in our veins is rather ennobled than disgraced by the mingling tides that descended from our heroic ancestors. Let them come – but will they answer to a voice like mine? Will they not rather depute some favoured pen, to chide me back to the shade whence I have been allured, and where, perhaps, I ought to have remained, in respect to the memory, and superior genius of a Father[6] – it avails not to say how dear! – But my feeble efforts presume not to emulate, – and they cannot injure his fame.

To guard against criticism I am no way prepared, nor do I suppose I shall escape it; nay, indeed, I do not wish to escape the pen of the *candid* critic: And I would willingly believe that an individual capable of no offence, and pretending to no pre-eminence, cannot possibly meet with any severity of criticism, but what the mistakes, or the deficiencies of this performance, may be justly deemed to merit; and what, indeed, could scarcely be avoided by one unskilled in composition, and now, with extreme diffidence, presenting, for the first time, her literary face to the world.

Elegy (by Edmond Ryan, or Edmond of the Hill)

From Reliques of Irish Poetry (1789)

Bright her locks of beauty grew,
    Curling fair, and sweetly flowing;
And her eyes of smiling blue,
    Oh how soft! how heav'nly glowing!

Ah! poor plunder'd heart of pain!   5
    When wilt thou have end of mourning? –
This long, long year, I look in vain
    To see my only hope returning.

Oh! would thy promise faithful prove,
    And to my fond, fond bosom give thee;   10

Notes ────────────────────────────────

[6] Henry Brooke (c.1703–83), author and Charlotte Brooke's father.

Lightly then my steps would move,
    Joyful should my arms receive thee.

Then, once more, at early morn,
    Hand in hand we should be straying,
Where the dew-drop decks the thorn,   15
    With its pearls the woods arraying.

Cold and scornful as thou art,
    Love's fond vows and faith belying,
Shame for thee now rends my heart,
    My pale cheek with blushes dying!   20

Why art thou false to me and Love?
    (While health and joy with thee are vanish'd)
Is it because forlorn I rove,
    Without a crime, unjustly banish'd?

Safe thy charms with me should rest,   25
    Hither did thy pity send thee,
Pure the love that fills my breast,
    From itself it would defend thee.

'Tis thy Edmond calls thee love,
    Come, O come and heal his anguish!   30
Driv'n from his home, behold him rove,
    Condemn'd in exile here to languish!

O thou dear cause of all my pains!
    With thy charms each heart subduing,
Come, – on Munster's lovely plains,   35
    Hear again fond passion suing.

Music, mirth, and sports are here,
    Chearful friends the hours beguiling;
Oh wouldst thou, my love! appear,
    To joy my bosom reconciling!   40

Sweet would seem the holly's shade,
    Bright the clust'ring berries glowing;
And, in scented bloom array'd,
    Apple-blossoms round us blowing.

Cresses waving in the stream,   45
    Flowers its gentle banks perfuming;
Sweet the verdant paths would seem,
    All in rich luxuriance blooming.

O bright in every grace of youth!
    Gentle charmer! – lovely wonder!   50
Break not fond vows and tender truth!
    O rend not ties so dear asunder!

For thee all dangers would I brave,
    Life with joy, with pride exposing;
Breast for thee the stormy wave,   55
    Winds and tides in vain opposing.

O might I call thee now my own!
  No added rapture joy could borrow:
'Twould be, like heav'n, when life is flown,
  To chear the soul and heal its sorrow.   60

See thy falsehood, cruel maid!
  See my cheek no longer glowing;
Strength departed, health decay'd;
  Life in tears of sorrow flowing!

Why do I thus my anguish tell? –   65
  Why pride in woe, and boast of ruin? –
O lost treasure! – fare thee well! –
  Lov'd to madness – to undoing.

Yet, O hear me fondly swear!
  Though thy heart to me is frozen,   70
Thou alone, of thousands fair,
  Thou alone should'st be my chosen.

Every scene with thee would please!
  Every care and fear would fly me!
Wintery storms, and raging seas,   75
  Would lose their gloom, if thou wert nigh me!

Speak in time, while yet I live;
  Leave not faithful love to languish!
O soft breath to pity give,
  Ere my heart quite break with anguish.   80

Pale, distracted, wild I rove,
  No soothing voice my woes allaying;
Sad and devious, through each grove,
  My lone steps are weary straying.

O sickness, past all med'cine's art!   85
  O sorrow, every grief exceeding!
O wound that, in my breaking heart,
  Cureless, deep, to death art bleeding!

Such, O Love! thy cruel power,
  Fond excess and fatal ruin!   90
Such – O Beauty's fairest flower!
  Such thy charms, and my undoing!

How the swan adorns that neck,
  There her down and whiteness growing;
How its snow those tresses deck,   95
  Bright in fair luxuriance flowing.

Mine, of right, are all those charms!
  Cease with coldness then to grieve me!
Take – O take me to thy arms,
  Or those of death will soon receive me.   100

Song (by Patrick Linden)

From Reliques of Irish Poetry (1789)

O fairer than the mountain snow,
When o'er it north's pure breezes blow!
In all its dazzling lustre drest,
But purer, softer is thy breast!

Colla[1] the Great, whose ample sway   5
Beheld two kingdoms homage pay,
Now gives the happy bard to see
Thy branch adorn the royal tree!

No foreign graft's inferior shoot
Has dar'd insult the mighty root!   10
Pure from its stem thy bloom ascends,
And from its height in fragrance bends!

Hadst thou been present, on the day
When beauty bore the prize away,
Thy charms had won the royal swain,   15
And Venus 'self had su'd in vain!

With soften'd fire, imperial blood
Pours through thy frame its generous flood;
Rich in thy azure veins it flows,
Bright in thy blushing cheek it glows!   20

That blood whence noble SAVAGE sprung,
And he whose deeds the bards have sung,
Great CONALL-CEARNACH, conquering name!
The champion of heroic fame!

Fair offspring of the royal race!   25
Mild fragrance! fascinating grace!
Whose touch with magic can inspire
The tender harp's melodious wire!

See how the swan presumptuous strives,
Where glowing Majesty revives,   30
With proud contention, to bespeak
The soft dominion of that cheek!

Beneath it, sure, with subtle heed,
Some rose by stealth its leaf convey'd;
To shed its bright and beauteous dye,   35
And still the varying bloom supply.

Notes

SONG (BY PATRICK LINDEN)
[1] He was monarch of Ireland in the beginning of the fourth
century. By the second kingdom, we must suppose the poet
means the Dal-Riadas of Scotland (author).

The tresses of thy silken hair
As curling mists are soft and fair,
Bright waving o'er thy graceful neck,
Its pure and tender snow to deck!   40

But O! to speak the rapture found!
In thy dear voice's magic sound!
Its powers could death itself controul,
And call back the expiring soul!

The tide that fill'd the veins of Kings,   45
From whom thy noble lineage springs;
The royal blood of Colla, see
Renew'd, O charming maid! in thee.

Nor in thy bosom slacks its pace,
Nor fades it in thy lovely face;   50
But there with soft enchantment glows,
And like the blossom's tint it shows.

How does thy needle's art pourtray
Each pictur'd form, in bright array!
With Nature's self maintaining strife,   55
It gives its own creation life!

O perfect, all-accomplish'd maid!
In beauty's every charm array'd:
Thee ever shall my numbers hail,
Fair lilly of the royal vale!   60

Elizabeth Ryves (1750–1797)

Elizabeth Ryves was born in Ireland, and little is known of her early life. If we take her poem "presented to the King, with a petition, in May 1775" as autobiographical, her father had a long military career and, with his death, she lost his friends' protection and fell into poverty. Isaac Disraeli's much-republished *Calamities of Authors* (1812) is a more conventional biographical source, though it is somewhat excessive in representing a sometimes-caustic political writer as a self-effacing paragon of feminine virtue. But it is clear that she lived in London for most of her adult life and that she did not have the financial security that most in her social class took for granted. She consequently made her living by the pen.

She published her poem to the king in her first volume of verse, *Poems on Several Occasions* (1777); *Poems* also included two dramatic works, *The Prude* and *The Triumph of Hymen*, which appear not to have been staged. She wrote a novel, *The Hermit of Snowden* (1789), and a devastating verse satire, *The Hastiniad* (1785), which mocked the British government and its imperial administration in India, depicting, for instance, the wife of a colonial administrator, Warren Hastings, wearing "Rich spoils of many a ransack'd clime." Other volumes include *Dialogue in the Elysian Fields, Between Caesar and Cato* (1784) and *Ode to the Right Honourable Lord Melton, Infant Son of Earl Fitzwilliam*

(1787). She often praises those who oppose tyranny, and warns those who would exercise it. Her *Dialogue in the Elysian Fields*, for instance, has an epigraph from French author François de Salignac de la Mothe Fénelon (1651–1715; also a favourite of Morgan's): "Despotic and tyrannic power is so far from securing the peace and authority of Princes, that, on the contrary, it makes them wretched, and draws inevitable destruction on them." Ryves also supplemented her income with other literary work, publishing translations and contributing political articles to the periodical press as well as working in an editorial capacity for the *Annual Register.*

Ryves participates in the literary culture of her time – neoclassicism, sensibility, and politics. Like Morgan a generation later, and Julia Kavanagh a generation after that, some of her writing celebrates prominent women in Western history. Two poems in her 1777 collection, for instance, focus on women monarchs – Elizabeth I of England (see "Ballad" below) and Christina of Sweden – and another, included here, addresses the classical Greek poet Sappho. Sappho, as a number of recent scholars have noted, is a key figure in women's writing from the Renaissance forward, offering classical precedent and authority for women to write important poetry. Ryves's "Ode to Sensibility" participates in a late eighteenth-century literary concern with sympathy as the basis for moral virtue: R. W. Babcock (see Bibliography) records that two works with the title "Ode to Sensibility" appeared in British periodicals in the early 1770s, and poems on sensibility continued to appear in periodicals and books throughout the rest of the eighteenth century.

Further reading

Johns-Putra, Adeline, "Satirising the Courtly Woman and Defending the Domestic Woman: Mock Epics and Women Poets in the Romantic Age," *Romanticism on the Net* 15 (August 1999; http://users.ox.ac.uk/~scat0385/courtly.html).

Rainbolt, Martha, "Their Ancient Claim: Sappho and Seventeenth- and Eighteenth-century British Women's Poetry," *Seventeenth Century* 12 (1997): 111–34.

Ode to Sensibility

From Poems on Several Occasions (1777)

I

The sordid wretch who ne'er has known,
To feel for miseries not his own;
Whose lazy pulse serenely beats,
While injur'd worth her wrongs repeats;
Dead to each sense of joy or pain,   5
A useless link in nature's chain,
May boast the calm which I disdain.

II

Give me a generous soul, that glows
With others' transports, others' woes;
Whose noble nature scorns to bend,   10
Tho' Fate her iron scourge extend:
But bravely bears the galling yoke,
And smiles superior to the stroke,
With spirit free and mind unbroke.

III

Yet, by compassion touch'd, not fear,   15
Sheds the soft sympathizing tear,
In tribute to Affliction's claim,
Or envy'd Merit's wounded fame.
Let Stoics scoff! I'd rather be
Thus curst with Sensibility,   20
Than share their boasted Apathy.

A Ballad, Written in June, 1775[1]

From Poems on Several Occasions (1777)

I

Ye subjects of Britain, attend to my song;
For, to you both the Muse and her numbers belong:
No courtier, no hireling, no pensioner she;
By int'rest unsway'd, and from prejudice free.

II

A subject I chuse for the theme of my lays,   5
Well known to this realm in Elizabeth's[2] days;
That period of glory, that age of renown,
When a female supported the rights of the crown.

III

A Cabal there was form'd by the foes of the state,
Who like —— and —— could in senate debate: 10
Foreign gold lin'd their pockets, and bulls from the Pope
Remov'd all restraint, and gave conscience full scope.

IV

With manners and morals adapted to please,
They flow'd with opinions, as waves with the breeze;
For Rome grants indulgence for aiding her cause,   15
And, to favour her int'rest, relaxes her laws.

V

Well vers'd in dissembling, 'midst Jesuits bred,
And deep in each lecture of Machiavel[3] read;
With a latitude Truth must for ever detest,
They censur'd the tenets their hearts still profess'd;   20

Notes

A BALLAD

[1] The Battle of Bunker Hill, an early skirmish in the War of American Independence, was fought in June 1775. In 1777, when this poem was published, the war was well underway.

[2] Elizabeth I, queen of England from 1558 to 1603.
[3] Niccolò Machiavelli (1469–1527), Italian writer on politics.

VI

And loudly exclaim'd, that the nation again
Wou'd sink to the level of Mary's[4] weak reign;
For that Burleigh,[5] and those at the head of affairs,
From the cries of her people, had turn'd the Queen's ears:

VII

That a debt justly due to the Spaniards (they said)   25
Thro' the basest mismanagement, still lay unpaid:
That Iberia was arming her right to demand,
And had mann'd a huge fleet,[6] which no pow'r cou'd withstand:

VIII

That myriads of treasure, and oceans of gore,
Was the int'rest we soon with the loan must restore;   30
And that nought cou'd avert it, or ward off the blow,
But the Ministry's ruin and swift overthrow.

IX

Thus, with idle chimeras the people amus'd,
Their judgment perverted, their reason abus'd,
Obnoxious alike ev'ry statesman appear'd: 35
They were censur'd, revil'd, and condemn'd tho' unheard.

X

For Prejudice suffers not Justice to sway;
Caprice is the law that her subjects obey;
And the culprit is either accus'd or commended,
Not for what he has done, but what party offended.   40

XI

This point once attain'd, and the popular name
Of Patriot assum'd, to establish their fame,
They laugh'd at those gudgeons who swallow'd the bait,
And plann'd (in its guardians) the fall of the state.

XII

For they knew them so firm, so attach'd to the laws,   45
To religion, to truth, and Elizabeth's cause,
That, ere they cou'd give these a final o'erthrow,
They first at their bosoms must level the blow.

XIII

So away to Whitehall[7] they determin'd to hie them,
And see if her Majesty dar'd to deny them,   50

Notes ——

[4] Mary I, queen of England from 1553 to 1558.
[5] William Cecil (1521–98), Baron Burghley, English royal adviser during Elizabeth I's reign.
[6] The Spanish Armada attempted an invasion of England in 1588.

[7] The Privy Council, which advised the English monarch, met at Whitehall. When Benjamin Franklin pleaded the American colonists' case in 1774, he met the Council there.

When they shou'd demand the immediate disgrace
Of friends, fav'rites, ministers – all those in place.

XIV

Arriv'd at the palace, they soon gain'd admission,
As due to their rank, not their vaunted commission;
And boldly advanc'd to the foot of the throne,   55
Pretended abuses and wrongs to make known.

XV

The Queen, with a placid but resolute eye,
Prepar'd for a kind or an angry reply,
As their stile might deserve; most attentively heard them,
And shew'd that she neither neglected nor fear'd them.   60

XVI

With eloquence fram'd, their deep arts to disguise,
To fascinate reason by sudden surprize,
To lull the sound judgment to drowsy repose,
And win and insinuate still as it flows;

XVII

They talk'd of abuses, of rights unprotected,   65
Of the wrongs we endur'd, and of those we expected;
And, swell'd with importance, began to arraign
A conduct too partial, which made them complain.

XVIII

Said, our freedom hung pois'd in a wavering scale;
That the opposite balance must shortly prevail: 70
For they knew by that charm they shou'd strengthen the spell,
Which alone cou'd the schemes they concerted conceal.

XIX

But the Queen's penetration detected the snare;
No soft flowing words cou'd impose on her ear:
Yet, wisely dissembling, she mildly desir'd   75
They'd freely declare all her people requir'd.

XX

Encourag'd by this, opportunely they thought
The ministry's fall might be easily wrought;
And began to complain of their overgrown pow'r,
Which our freedom, our wealth, and our laws wou'd devour.   80

XXI

Said, their measures were wrong, and their administration
Obnoxious alike to all ranks in the nation;
Their disgrace they must therefore most humbly advise,
Lest the chiefs should revolt and the populace rise.

XXII

Unmov'd by the menace, Elizabeth frown'd   85
So sternly, as might the most daring confound;
And, enrag'd at their pride, struck the globe with her hand,
That ensign of honour and regal command.

XXIII

"By the God that I worship (if rightly I ween)
They're my friends, and I've prov'd them," reply'd the fair Queen;   90
"As such I regard them, as such I'll defend;
So desist from complaining, and to me attend.

XXIV

"As long as the scepter of Britain I sway,
I'll rule like a Queen, and ye all shall obey:
No laws I'll infringe, and no insolent Peer   95
Shall presume to intrude on the Royal barrier.

XXV

"My servants I'll chuse, and my friends I'll reward;
To the good of my subjects shew proper regard:
But when traitors the peace of my crown would destroy,
Let Justice the sword of correction employ."   100

XXVI

Repuls'd and abash'd, from the throne they retir'd,
And ne'er, from that moment, 'gainst statesmen conspir'd,
Whose wisdom and virtue secur'd them esteem,
And still furnish the Muse with a favourite theme.

XXVII

Success crown'd the measures they wisely pursu'd;   105
Our friendship was courted, our treaties renew'd,
Our commerce extended; while peace reign'd at home,
And Britain shook off the last shackle of Rome.

Song

From Poems on Several Occasions (1777)

I

Tho' Love and each harmonious Maid
To gentle Sappho lent their aid,
Yet, deaf to her enchanting tongue,
Proud Phaon scorn'd her melting song.[1]

Notes

SONG
[1] The story that Sappho, a Greek poet of the sixth-century BCE, committed suicide after being spurned by the sailor Phaon was the subject of a number of poems, including a sonnet sequence, *Sappho and Phaon* (1796), by English poet Mary Robinson (1758–1800).

II

Mistaken nymph! hadst thou ador'd   5
Fair Fortune, and her smiles implor'd;
Had she indulgent own'd thy claim,
And given thee wealth instead of fame,

III

Tho' harsh thy voice, deform'd and old,
Yet such th'omnipotence of gold,   10
The youth had soon confess'd thy charms,
And flown impatient to thy arms.

Richard Brinsley Sheridan (1751–1816)

Richard Brinsley Sheridan was born in Dublin to authors Thomas Sheridan and Frances Sheridan, and spent his early years in that city, attending Samuel Whyte's school for a brief period with his sister Alicia. In 1759, however, his parents moved permanently to England, and Richard Brinsley Sheridan left Ireland with them. He was briefly educated by both of his parents while in England, but entered Harrow for more formal schooling in 1762. By 1770, he had left school and begun to publish. He co-wrote a farce and a verse translation of Aristaenetus with his school friend, Nathaniel Brassey Halhed, as well as publishing a couple of poems in the early 1770s.

Sheridan's theatrical career began in earnest soon after his marriage to professional singer Eliza Linley. *The Rivals* opened in mid-January 1775 and, after a quick rewriting to address the misinterpretation of Sir Lucius O'Trigger as a "stage Irishman" by the first actor to perform the part, was extremely successful. Thereafter followed *The Duenna* (1775), *St. Patrick's Day* (first performed in 1775), *A Trip to Scarborough* (1777), *The School for Scandal* (1777), *The Camp* (1779), and, much later, *Pizarro* (1799). In 1776, he followed in his father's footsteps and became a theater manager, running Drury Lane Theatre in London, although by 1782 he had largely left the theater to others' hands, mostly his wife and father, because of his developing political career. Drury Lane helped to catapult him into elite London circles, putting Sheridan into contact with such notable politicians as Charles James Fox and Edmund Burke in the late 1770s. When the theater burned down in 1809, however, he was left in severe financial straits that marred the final years of his life.

In 1780, Sheridan became a member of parliament as a Whig. During his years in parliament, Sheridan supported Burke on the impeachment of Warren Hastings for imperial abuses in India, and was a strong proponent of political reform. He joined the Society of Friends of the People, a group in favor of political reform which had some communication with the United Irishmen in the early 1790s. He was periodically under suspicion and even questioned about nationalist activities in Ireland, and testified at the trial of Arthur O'Connor, arrested in early 1798 for seeking French aid for an Irish uprising. In his speeches, Sheridan argued strenuously against the Act of Union which abolished the Irish parliament in 1800, in favor of the abolition of slavery, and for both Catholic Emancipation and reforms in Ireland that would alleviate poverty.

St. Patrick's Day, like his father's *Brave Irishman*, critiques the figure of the "stage Irishman" and mocks contemporary medicine. It was written for a benefit performance for Lawrence Clinch, the actor who recovered the figure of Sir Lucius O'Trigger from the stereotypical simplicities of the stage Irishman and so helped to launch the success of the revised *Rivals* in 1775 (benefit performances allowed the theater to direct a portion of ticket proceeds to particular individuals). Clinch played the part of Lieutenant O'Conner. In *St. Patrick's Day*, the rural English are depicted in terms that recall the stage Irishman, particularly in Sheridan's emphasis on their accent and idiom, anticipating Boucicault's stage Englishman in *Arrah-na-Pogue* (below).

Further reading

Donoghue, Frank, "Avoiding the 'Cooler Tribunal of the Study': Richard Brinsley Sheridan's Writer's Block and Late Eighteenth-century Print Culture," *English Literary History* 68 (2001): 831–56.

Jones, Robert W., "Sheridan and the Theatre of Patriotism: Staging Dissent during the War for America," *Eighteenth-century Life* 26 (2002): 24–45.

Morwood, James, ed., *Sheridan Studies*. Cambridge: Cambridge University Press, 1995.

St. Patrick's Day; Or, the Scheming Lieutenant. A Comic Opera (1788)

Dramatis Personae

MEN	WOMEN
JUSTICE,	BRIDGET,
DOCTOR ROSY,	LAURETTA.
SERJEANT TROUNCE,	
CORPORAL FLINT,	
LIEUTENANT.	

Soldiers, Countrymen, &c.

ACT I

Enter TROUNCE, FLINT, *and Four* SOLDIERS.

1st SOLDIER

I say you are wrong; we should all speak together, each for himself, and all at once, that we may be heard the better.

2D SOL. Right Jack, we'll argue in Platoons.

3D SOL. Ay, ay, let him have our grievances in a volly, and if we be to have a spokesman, there's the Corporal is the Lieutenant's countryman; and knows his humour.

COR. Let me alone for that, I serv'd three years within a bit, under his honour, in the Royal Inniskillions, and I never will see a sweeter tempered gentleman, nor one more free with his purse. I put a great shamrogue in his hat this morning, and I'll be bound for him, he'll wear it, was it as big as Steven's green.

4TH SOL. I say again then you talk like youngsters, like Militia striplings, there is a discipline, look'ee, in all things, whereof the serjeant must be our guide, he's a gentleman of words, he understands your foreign lingo, your figures, and such like auxiliaries in scoring. – Confess now for a reckoning, whether in chalk or writing, ben't he your only man.

COR. Why the serjeant is a scholar to be sure, and has the gift of reading.

SER. Good soldiers, and fellow gentlemen, if you make me your spokesman, you will shew the more judgment, and let me alone for the argument. I'll be as loud as a drum, and point blank from the purpose.

ALL. Agreed, agreed.

COR. O Fait here comes the Lieutenant, now Serjeant.

SER. So then, to order. – Put on your mutiny looks, every man grumble a little to himself, and some of you hum the deserter's march.

Enter LIEUTENANT.

LIEU. Well honest lads, what is it you have to complain of.

SOL. Ahem! hem!

SER. So please your honour, the very grievance of the matter is this; – ever since your honour differed with Justice Credulous, our Innkeepers use us most scurvily. – By my halbert, their treatment is such, that if your *spirit* was willing to put up with it, flesh and blood could by no means agree, so we humbly petition, that your honour would make an end of the matter at once, by running away with the Justice's daughter, or else get us fresh quarters, hem! hem!

LIEU. Indeed! – Pray which of the houses use you ill.

1ST SOL. There's the Red Lion ha'n't half the civility of the old Red Lion.

2D SOL. There's the White Horse, if he was'n't case hardened, ought to be ashamed to shew his face.

LIEU. Very well, the Horse and the Lion shall answer for it, at the quarter sessions.

SER. The two Magpies are civil enough, but the Angel uses us like devils, and the rising sun refuses us light to go to bed by.

LIEU. Then upon my word, I'll have the rising sun put down, and the Angel shall give security for his good behaviour, but are you sure you do nothing to quit scores with them.

COR. Nothing at all your honour, unless now and then we happen to fling a cartridge into the kitchen fire, or put a spatterdash or so into the soup – and sometimes Ned drums up and down stairs a little of a night.

LIEU. Oh all that's fair, but hark'ee lads I must have no grumbling on St Patrick's day; so here take this and divide it amongst you. But observe me now, show yourselves men of spirit, and don't spend six pence of it in drink.

SER. Nay hang it your honour, soldiers should never bear malice, we must drink St Patrick's and your honour's health.

ALL. Oh damn malice. St Patrick's and his honour by all means.

COR. Come away then lads, and first we'll parade round the Market Cross, for the honour of King George.

1ST SOL. Thank your honour. Come along; St Patrick's, his honour, and strong beer for ever. [*Exit* Soldiers.

LIEU. Get along you thoughtless vagabonds, yet upon my conscience, 'tis very hard these poor fellows should scarcely have bread from the soil they would die to defend.

Enter DOCTOR ROSY.

Ah, my little Doctor Rosy, my galen[1] a-bridge, what's the news?

DOC. All things are as they were, my Alexander,[2] the Justice is as violent as ever, I felt his pulse on the matter again, and thinking his rage began to intermit, I wanted to throw in the bark of good advice, but it would not do. He says you and your cutthroats have a plot upon his life, and swears he had rather see his daughter in a scarlet fever, than in the arms of a soldier.

LIEU. Upon my word the army is very much obliged to him, well then, I must marry the girl first, and ask his consent afterwards.

DOC. So then, the case of her fortune is desperate, hey!

LIEU. O hang fortune, let that take its chance, there is a beauty in Lauretta's simplicity, so pure a bloom upon her charms.

DOC. So there is, so there is. – You are for beauty as nature made her, hey! No artificial graces, no cosmetic varnish, no beauty in grain, hey!

LIEU. Upon my word Doctor, you are right, the London ladies were always too handsome for me; – then they are so defended, such a circumvaluation of hoop, with a breast work of whale bone, that would turn a pistol bullet, much less Cupid's arrows, then turret on turret on top, with stores of concealed weapons, under pretence of black pins, and above all, a standard of feathers, that would do honour to a knight of the Bath. Upon my conscience I could as soon embrace an Amosen[3] arm'd at all points.

DOC. Right, right my Alexander – my taste to a tittle.

LIEU. Then Doctor, though I admire modesty in women, I like to see their faces. I am for the changeable rose, but with one of these quality amazons, if their midnight dissipations had left them blood enough to raise a blush, they have not room enough in their cheeks to show it. – To be sure, bashfulness is a very pretty thing, but in my mind, there is nothing on earth, so impudent as an everlasting blush.

DOC. My taste, my taste – Well Lauretta is none of these – Ah! I never see her, but she puts me in mind of my poor dear wife.

LIEU. Ay faith, in my opinion she can't do a worse thing. – Now is he going to bother me about an old hag that has been dead these six years. [*Aside.*

DOC. Oh poor Dolly! I never shall see her like again, such an arm for a bandage – Veins that seem'd to invite the lancet. Then her skin, smooth and white as a gallipot – her mouth as round and not larger than the mouth of a penny phial. Her lips conserve of roses – and then her teeth – none of your sturdy fixtures – aik as they wou'd – it was but a small pull and out they came. I believe I have drawn half a score of her poor dear pearls, [*weeps*] but what avails her beauty. Death has no consideration – one must die as well as another.

LIEU. O! if he begins to moralize [*takes out his snuff box*].

DOC. Fair or ugly, crooked or straight, rich or poor, flesh as grass flowers fade!

LIEU. Here Doctor, take a pinch, and keep up your spirits.

DOC. True, true my friend, grief can't mend the matter – all's for the best, but such a woman was a great loss, Lieutenant.

LIEU. To be sure, for doubtless she had mental accomplishments equal to her beauty.

Notes ————————————————————————————

St. Patrick's Day

[1] Galen, second-century Greek physician (see *The Brave Irishman*, above, p. 12n).

[2] Alexander the Great (355–323 BCE), king of Macedonia, known for his accomplishments as a military leader.

[3] Amazon. In classical myth, the Amazons are women renowned for their skills as warriors.

DOC. Mental accomplishments! she would have stuffed an alligator, or pickled a lizard with any Apothecary's wife in the kingdom. Why she could decypher a prescription, and invent the ingredients, almost as well as myself; then she was such a hand at making foreign waters for Setzer, Pyrmont, Islington or Chaly beate she never had her equal – and her Bath and Bristol springs exceeded the originals – Ah! Poor Dolly, she fell a martyr to her own discoveries.

LIEU. How so, pray?

DOC. Poor soul, her illness was occasioned by her zeal in trying an improvement on the Spa water, by an infusion of rum and acid.

LIEU. Ay, ay, spirits never agree with water drinkers.

DOC. No, no, you mistake. – Rum agreed with her well enough, it was not the rum that killed the poor dear creature, for she died of a dropsy. Well, she is gone never to return, and has left no pledge of our loves behind – No little babe, to hang like a label round papa's neck: well, well, we are all mortal, – sooner or later flesh is grass – flowers fade.

LIEU. O the devil again!

DOC. Life's a shadow, the world a stage, – we strut an hour.[4]

LIEU. Here Doctor. [*Offers snuff*].

DOC. True, true my friend – well, high grief can't cure it. All's for the best, hey! my little Alexander.

LIEU. Right, right, an Apothecary should never be out of spirits. But come, faith 'tis time honest Humphrey should wait on the Justice, that must be our first scheme.

DOC. True, true, you should be ready, the cloaths are at my house, and I have given you such a character, that he is impatient to have you; he swears you shall be his body guard. Well I honour the army, or I should never do so much to serve you.

LIEU. Indeed I am bound to you for ever Doctor, and when once I'm possessed of my dear Lauretta, I will endeavour to make work for you as fast as possible.

DOC. Now you put me in mind of my poor wife again.

LIEU. Ah, pray forget her a little, we shall be too late.

DOC. Poor Dolly.

LIEU. 'Tis past twelve.

DOC. Inhuman dropsy.

LIEU. The Justice will wait.

DOC. Cropt in her prime.

LIEU. For heaven's sake come.

DOC. Well, flesh is grass.

LIEU. O the devil!

DOC. We must all die.

LIEU. Doctor.

DOC. Kings, Lords and common Whores. – [*Forces him off.*

SCENE

Enter LAURETTA *and* BRIDGET.

LAU. I repeat it again mama, officers are the prettiest men in the world, and Lieutenant O'Conner is the prettiest officer I ever saw.

Notes

[4] While the Doctor's earlier laments use biblical phrases ("flesh is grass"), here he alludes to the English plays *As You Like It* and *Macbeth*, both by William Shakespeare.

BRI. For shame Laura, how can you talk so – or if you must have a military man, there's Lieutenant Plow or Captain Haycock, or Major Dray the Brewer; are all your admirers, and though they are peaceable good kind, of men they have as large cockades, and become scarlet as well as the fighting folks.

LAU. Psha! you know mama I hate militia officers, a set of dunghill cocks, with spurs on heroes scratch'd off a church door. Clowns in military masquerade, wearing the dress without supporting the character. No, give me the bold upright youth, who makes love to-day and his head shot off to-morrow. Dear to think how the sweet fellows sleep on the ground, and fight in silk stockings and lace ruffles.

BRI. Oh barbarous! to want a husband that may wed you to-day, and be sent the Lord knows where before night; then in a twelve month perhaps to have him come like a Colossus with one leg at New York, and the other at Chelsea Hospital.[5]

LAU. Then I'll be his crutch mama.

BRI. No, give me a husband that knows where his limbs are, though he want the use of them – and if he should take you with him – to sleep in a baggage cart, and stroll about the camp like a gipsey, with a knapsack and two children at your back – then by way of entertainment in the evening, to make a party with the Serjeant's wife, to drink bohea tea, and play at all fours on a drumhead, 'tis a precious life to be sure.[6]

LAU. Nay mama, you shou'dn't be against my Lieutenant, for I heard him say, you were the best natured and best looking woman in the world.

BRI. Why child, I never said but that Lieutenant O'Conner, was a very well bred and discerning young man, 'tis your papa is so violent against him.

LAU. Why cousin Sophy married an officer.

BRI. Ay Laury, an officer in the militia.

LAU. No indeed, mama, a marching regiment.

BRI. No child, I tell you he was a Major of militia.

LAU. Indeed mama it wasn't.

Enter JUSTICE.

JUS. Bridget my love, I have had a message –

LAU. It was Cousin Sophy told me so.

JUS. I have had a message, love –

BRI. No child, she could say no such thing.

JUS. A message, I say.

LAU. How could he be in the militia, when he was ordered abroad.

BRI. Ay, girl hold your tongue – well my dear.

JUS. I have had a message from Doctor Rosy.

BRI. He ordered abroad! He went abroad for his health.

JUS. Why Bridget.

BRI. Well deare – Now hold your tongue miss.

JUS. A message from Dr Rosy, and Doctor Rosy says –

LAU. I'm sure mama his regimentals –

JUS. Damn his regimentals – Why don't you listen?

BRI. Ay girl, how durst you interrupt your papa?

LAU. Well papa.

[5] A military hospital.

[6] *Bohea* was one of the cheaper sorts of tea; *all fours* is a card game.

JUS. Doctor Rosy says he will bring –

LAU. Were blue turn'd up with red, mama.

JUS. Laury – says he will bring the young man.

BRI. Red! yellow if you please, miss.

JUS. Bridget – the young man that is to be hir'd.

BRI. Besides miss, it is very unbecoming in you to want to have the last word with your
mama, you should know –

JUS. Why zounds! will you hear me or no?

BRI. I am listening my love – I am listening – But what signifies my silence, what
good is my not speaking a word, if this girl will interrupt and let nobody speak
but herself – Ay, I don't wonder my life, at your impatience, your poor dear lips
quiver to speak – but I suppose she'll run on and not let you put in a word –
you may very well be angry – there is nothing sure so provoking, as a chattering,
talking –

LAU. Nay, I'm sure mama it is you will not let papa speak now.

BRI. Why, you little provoking minx –

JUS. Get out of the room directly, both of you, get out.

BRI. Ay, go girl.

JUS. Go Bridget, you are worse than she, you old hag, I wish you were both up to the
neck in the canal to argue there till I took you out.

Enter SERVANT.

SERV. Doctor Rosy, sir.

JUS. Shew him up. [*Exit* Servant.

LAU. Then you own mama, it was a marching regiment.

BRI. You're an obstinate fool, I tell you, for if that had been the case –

JUS. You won't go.

BRI. We are going, Mr Surly – If that had been the case, I say, how could –

LAU. Nay, mama, one proof.

BRI. How could major –

LAU. And a full proof. [Justice *drives them off.*

JUS. There they go, ding dong in for the day. – Good lack, a fluent tongue is the only
thing a mother don't like her daughter should resemble her in.

Enter DOCTOR ROSY.

Well Doctor, where's the lad, where's trusty?

DOC. At hand, he'll be here in a minute – I'll answer for't, he's such a one as you a'n't
met with – brave as a lion, gentle as a saline draught.

JUS. Ah, he comes in the place of a rogue – a dog that was corrupted by the Lieutenant.
But this is a sturdy fellow, is he Doctor?

DOC. As Hercules – and the best back sword in the country. Egad he'll make the red
coats keep their distance.

JUS. O the villains! this is St. Patrick's Day, and the rascals have been parading my
house all the morning. I know they have a design upon me, but I have taken all
precautions, I have magazines of arms, and if this fellow does but prove faithful,
I shall be more at ease.

DOC. Doubtless he'll be a comfort to you.

Enter a SERVANT.

SERV. There is a man below sir, enquires for Doctor Rosy.

DOC. Shew him up.

JUS. Hold – a little caution – how does he look?

SERV. A country looking fellow, your worship.

JUS. O, well well, for Doctor Rosy, these rascals try all ways to get in here.

SERV. Yes please your worship, there was one here this morning wanted to speak to you – he said his name was Corporal Breakbones.

JUS. Corporal Breakbones!

SERV. And Drummer Crackskull came again.

JUS. Ay! did you ever hear of such a damned confounded crew. Well, shew the lad in here! [*Exit* Serv.

DOC. Ay, he'll be your porter, he'll give the rogues an answer.

Enter LIEUTENANT *disguised as* HUMPHREY.

JUS. So a tall Efacks,[7] what! has lost an eye.

DOC. Only a bruise he got in taking seven or eight highwaymen.

JUS. He has a damned wicked leer somehow with the other.

DOC. O no, he's bashful – a sheepish look.

JUS. Well my lad, what's your name?

LIEU. Humphrey Hum.

JUS. Hum – I don't like Hum.[8]

LIEU. But I be mostly called honest Humphrey.

DOC. There, I told you so – of noted honesty.

JUS. Well honest Humphrey, the Doctor has told you my terms, and you are willing to serve, hey!

LIEU. And please your worship, I shall be well content.

JUS. Well then, hark'ye honest Humphrey, you are sure now you will never be a rogue – never take a bribe, hey! honest Humphrey.

LIEU. A bribe! What's that?

JUS. A very ignorant fellow indeed.

DOC. His worship hopes you will never part with your honesty for money, Humphrey.

LIEU. Noa, noa.

JUS. Well said Humphrey – my chief business with you is to watch the motions of a rake helly fellow here, one Lieutenant O'Conner.

DOC. Ay, you don't value the soldiers, do you Humphrey?

LIEU. Not I – they are but zwaggerers, and you'll see they'll be as much affraid of me, as they wou'd of their captain.

JUS. And I faith Humphrey, you have a pretty cudgel there.

LIEU. Aye, the zwitch is better than nothing, but I should be glad of a stouter, ha' you got such a thing in the house as an old coach-pole, or a spare bed post.

JUS. Oon's what a Dragon it is – well Humphrey, come with me, I'll just shew him to Bridget, Doctor, and we'll agree, come along honest Humphrey. [*Exit.*

Notes

[7] *Efacks* and variants were used on the eighteenth-century stage for mild oaths.

[8] To *hum* was eighteenth-century slang for to hoax.

LIEU. My dear Doctor, now remember to bring the Justice presently to the walk, I have a scheme to get into his confidence at once.

DOC. I will, I will. [*Shake hands,* Justice *enters and sees them.*

JUS. Why honest Humphrey, hey! what the devil are you at?

DOC. I was just giving him a little advice – well I must go for the present – good morning to your worship – you need not fear the Lieutenant, while he is in your house.

JUS. Well, get in Humphrey – good morning to you Doctor. [*Exit* Doctor] Come along Humphrey. Now I think I am a match for the Lieutenant and all his gang. [*Exit.*

ACT II

Enter TROUNCE, DRUMMER *and* SOLDIERS.

SERJEANT

Come, silence your drum – there is no valour stirring to-day – I thought St. Patrick would have given us a Recruit or two to-day.

SOL. Mark Serjeant.

Enter two COUNTRYMEN.

SER. Oh! these are the lads I was looking for, they have the looks of gentlemen. A'n't you single my lads.

1ST COUN. Yes, an please you, I be quite single, my relations be all dead, thank heavens more or less. I have but one poor mother left in the world, and she's an helpless woman.

SER. Indeed! a very extraordinary case – quite your own master then – the fitter to serve his Majesty – Can you read?

1ST COUN. Noa, I was always too lively to take to learning but John here, is main clever at it.

SER. So, what, you're a scholar friend.

2D COUN. I was born so, measter. Feyther kept grammar school.

SER. Lucky man, in a campaign or two put yourself down chaplain to the regiment. And I warrant, you have read of warriors and heroes.

2D COUN. Yes that I have, I have read of jack the Giant killer, and the Dragon of Wantly, and the – noa, I believe that's all in the hero way, except once about a Comet.

SER. Wonderful knowledge! well my heroes, I'll write word to the King of your good intentions, and meet me half an hour hence, at the two Magpies.

COUN. We will, your honour, we will.

SER. But stay, for fear I shou'dn't see you again in the croud, clap these little bits of ribbon into your hats.

1ST COUN. Our hats are none of the best.

SER. Well, meet me at the Magpies, and I'll give you money to buy new ones.

COUN. Bless your honour, thank your honour. [*Exit.*

SER. [*Winking at* Sol.] Jack. [*Exit* Soldiers.

Enter LIEUTENANT.

So, here comes one would make a grenadier. Stop friend, will you list?[9]

LIEU. Who shall I serve under?

SER. Under me to be sure.

LIEU. Isn't Lieutenant O'Conner your officer?

SER. He is, and I am Commander over him.

LIEU. What! be your Serjeants greater than your Captains?

SER. To be sure we are, 'tis our business to keep them in order. For instance now, the General writes to me, dear Serjeant, or dear Trounce, or dear Serjeant Trounce, according to his hurry, if your Lieutenant does not demean himself accordingly, let me know.

    Yours,

      GENERAL DELUGE.

LIEU. And do you complain of him often?

SER. No hang him, the lad is good-natur'd at bottom, so I pass over small things. But hark'ee, between ourselves, he is most confoundedly given to wenching.

Enter CORPORAL.

COR. Please your honour, the Doctor is coming this way with his worship – We are all ready and have our cues.

LIEU. Then my dear Trounce, or my dear Serjeant, or my dear Serjeant Trounce, take yourself away.

SER. Zounds! the Lieutenant, I smell of the black hole already.[10] [*Exit.*

Enter JUSTICE *and* DOCTOR.

JUS. I thought I saw some of the cutthroats.

DOC. I fancy not, there's no one but honest Humphrey, ha! ods life, here comes some of them, we'll stay by these trees, and let them pass.

JUS. Oh the bloody looking dogs. [*Walks aside.*

Enter CORPORAL *and two* SOLDIERS.

COR. Holloa, friend, do you serve Justice Credulous?

LIEU. I do.

COR. Are you rich?

LIEU. Noa.

COR. Nor ever will with that old stingy booby, look here, take it. [*Gives him a purse.*

LIEU. What must I do for this?

Notes

[9] enlist

[10] *Black hole* was the term for a room in which British soldiers were occasionally locked for minor punishments. After a British fort was surrendered to the Nawab of Bengal in 1756, over 140 men were crowded into a single *black hole* and held prisoner overnight. Fewer than twenty-five survived.

COR. Mark me, our Lieutenant is in love with the old rogue's daughter, help us to break his worship's bones, and carry off the girl, and you are a made man.

LIEU. I'll see you hang'd first, you pack of skurry villains. [*Throws away the purse.*

COR. What sirrah, do you mutiny, lay hold of him.

LIEU. Nay then, I'll try your armour for you. [*Beats them.*

ALL. Oh, oh! Quarter, quarter. [*Exit.*

JUS. Trim them, trounce them, break their bones, honest Humphrey. What a spirit he has!

DOC. Aquafortis.

LIEU. Betray my master!

DOC. What a miracle of fidelity!

JUS. Ay, and it shall not go unrewarded – I'll give him sixpence on the spot. Here honest Humphrey, there's for yourself, as for this bribe [*takes up the purse*] such trash is best in the hands of justice. Now then Doctor, I think I may trust him to guard the women, while he is with them I may go out with safety.

DOC. Doubtless you may, I'll answer for the Lieutenant's behaviour while honest Humphrey is with your daughter.

JUS. Ay, ay, she shall go no where without him. Come along honest Humphrey. How rare it is to meet with such a servant. [*Exit.*

SCENE, A Garden.

LAURETTA *discovered.*

Enter JUSTICE *and* LIEUTENANT.

JUS. Why you little Truant, how durst you wander so far from the house without my leave, do you want to invite that scoundrel Lieutenant to scale the walls and carry you off?

LAU. Lud papa, you are so apprehensive for nothing.

JUS. Why hussey –

LAU. Well then, I can't bear to be shut up all day so like a nun. I am sure it is enough to make one wish to be run away with – and I wish I was run away with – I do – and I wish the Lieutenant knew it.

JUS. You do, do you hussey? Well I think I'll take pretty good care of you. Here, Humphrey. I leave this lady in your care. Now you may walk about the garden Miss Pert, but Humphrey shall go with you wherever you go. So mind honest Humphrey, I am obliged to go abroad for a little while, let no one but yourself come near her, don't be shame faced you booby, but keep close to her. And now Miss, let your Lieutenant or any of his crew come near you if they can. [*Exit.*

LAU. How this booby stares after him. [*Sits down and sings.*

LIEU. Lauretta.

LAU. Not so free fellow. [*Sings.*

LIEU. Lauretta, look on me.

LAU. Not so free fellow.

LIEU. No recollection!

LAU. Honest Humphrey be quiet.

LIEU. Have you forgot your faithful soldier?

LAU. Ah! O preserve me.

LIEU. 'Tis my soul your truest slave, passing on your father in this disguise.

LAU. Well now I declare this is charming – you are so disguised my dear Lieutenant, and you do look so delightfully ugly, I am sure no one will find you out, ha! ha! ha! you know I am under your protection, papa charg'd you to keep close to me.

LIEU. True my angel, and thus let me fulfil.

LAU. O pray now dear Humphrey.

LIEU. Nay, 'tis but what old Mittimus commanded. [*Offers to kiss her, Enter* Justice.

JUS. Laury my – hey! what the devil's here?

LAU. Well, now one kiss and be quiet.

JUS. Your very humble servant, honest Humphrey – don't me – Pray don't let me interrupt you.

LAU. Lud papa – Now that's so good natur'd – Indeed there's no harm – you did not mean any rudeness, did you Humphrey?

LIEU. No indeed miss, his worship knows it is not in me.

JUS. I know that you are a lying canting hypocritical scoundrel and if you don't take yourself out of my sight.

LAU. Indeed papa now I'll tell you how it was, I was sometime taken with a sudden giddiness, and Humphrey seeing me begin to totter ran to my assistance quite frighten'd poor fellow, and took me in his arms.

JUS. Oh! was that all, nothing but a little giddiness, hey!

LIEU. That's all indeed your worship, for seeing miss change colour I ran up instantly.

JUS. O 'twas very kind in you.

LIEU. And luckily recovered her.

JUS. And who made you a doctor, you impudent rascal, hey! Get out of my sight I say this instant or by all the statutes.

LAU. O now papa you frighten me and I am giddy again – oh help.

LIEU. O dear lady – she'll fall. [*Takes her into his arms.*

JUS. Zounds! what before my face – why then thou miracle of impudence [*lays hold of him and discovers him*]. Mercy on me who have we here, Murder – Robbery – Fire – Rape – Gun-powder – Soldiers – John – Susan – Bridget –

LIEU. Good sir, don't be alarm'd, I mean you no harm.

JUS. Thieves, Robbers, Soldiers.

LIEU. You know my love for your daughter.

JUS. Fire, Cutthroats.

LIEU. And that alone.

JUS. Treason, Gunpowder. [*Enter* Servant *with a Blunderbuss.*] Now Scoundrel let her go this instant.

LAU. O papa, you'll kill me.

JUS. Honest Humphrey, be advised – Ay miss this way if you please.

LIEU. Nay sir, but hear me.

JUS. I'll shoot.

LIEU. And you'll be convinc'd.

JUS. I'll shoot.

LIEU. How injurious.

JUS. I'll shoot, and so your very humble servant, Honest Humphrey Hum. [*Exit separately.*

Scene, A Walk.

Enter DOCTOR ROSY.

Doc. Well I think my friend is now in a fair way of succeeding. Ah! I warrant he is full of hope and fear, doubt and anxiety; truly he has the fever of love strong upon him; faint, peevish, languishing all day with burning restless nights – Ah! just my case when I pin'd for my poor dear Dolly – When she used to have her daily cholics, that her little Doctor be sent for – Then wou'd I interpret the language of her pulse – Declare my own sufferings in my receipt[II] for her, send her a pearl necklace in a pill box – or a cordial draught, with an acrostic on the label. – Well those days are over – no happiness lasting – all is vanity – now sun-shine – now cloudy – we are as it were, king and beggar – then what avails –

Enter LIEUTENANT.

Lieu. O Doctor, ruin'd and undone.

Doc. The pride of beauty.

Lieu. I am discovered and –

Doc. The gaudy palace.

Lieu. The justice is –

Doc. The pompous wig.

Lieu. Is more enraged than ever.

Doc. The gilded cane.

Lieu. Why Doctor [*Slapping him on the Shoulder.*]

Doc. Hey!

Lieu. Confound your morals, I tell you I am discovered, discomfited, disappointed, ruin'd.

Doc. Indeed! good lack, good lack, to think of the instability of human affairs – Nothing certain in this world – most deceived when most confident – fools of fortune all.

Lieu. My dear Doctor, I want at present a little practical wisdom – I am resolv'd this instant to try the scheme, we were going to put in execution last week – I have the letter ready, and only want your assistance to recover my ground.

Doc. With all my heart – I'll warrant you I'll bear a part in it – but how the deuce were you discovered?

Lieu. I'll tell you as we go, there's not a moment to be lost.

Doc. Heaven send we succeed better, but there's no knowing.

Lieu. Very true.

Doc. We may, and we may not.

Lieu. Right.

Doc. Time must show.

Lieu. Certainly.

Doc. We are but blind guessers.

Lieu. Nothing more.

Doc. Thick sighted mortals.

Notes ───────────────────────────────────

II prescription

LIEU. Remarkably.

DOC. Wandering in error.

LIEU. Even so.

DOC. Futurity is dark.

LIEU. As a cellar.

DOC. Men are moles. [Lieut. *forcing him out.*

SCENE, JUSTICE's House.

Enter JUSTICE *and* BRIDGET.

JUS. Odds Life Bridget, you are enough to make one mad, I tell you he would have deceived a chief justice, the dog seem'd as ignorant as my clerk, and talk'd of honesty as if he had been a church Warden.

BRI. Po! Nonsense, honesty indeed! – What had you to do pray with honesty; – A fine business you have made of it with your Humphrey Hum, and Miss too, she must have been privy to it. – Lauretta, ay, you would have her called so, but for my part I never knew any good come of giving girls these heathen christian names; if you had called her Deborah, or Tabitha, or Ruth, or Rebecca, or Joan, nothing of this had ever happened; but I always knew Lauretta was a runaway name.

JUS. Psha, you're a fool.

BRI. No, Mr Credulous, it is you who are a fool, and no one but such a simpleton would be so imposed on.

JUS. Why zounds! Madam, how durst you talk so, if you have no respect for your husband, I should think unus quorum[12] might command a little deference.

BRI. Don't tell me – Unus fiddlestick, you ought to be asham'd to shew your face at the sessions, you'll be a laughing stock to the whole bench, and a byeword with all the pig-tail'd Lawyers, and bag-wig'd Attornies about town.

JUS. Is this language for his Majesty's Representative, by the statutes, it's high treason, and petty treason both at once.

Enter SERVANT.

SERV. A letter for your worship.

JUS. Who brought it?

SERV. A soldier.

JUS. Take it away and bury it.

BRI. Stay – Now you're in such a hurry – it is some canting scrawl from the Lieutenant, I suppose, let me see – Ay, 'tis signed O'Conner.

JUS. Well, come read it out.

BRI. "Revenge is sweet"

JUS. It begins so, does it? I'm glad of that, I'll let the dog know I'm of his opinion.

BRI. "And though disappointed of my designs upon your daughter, I have still the satisfaction of knowing I'm revenged on her unnatural father, for this morning, in your chocolate, I had the pleasure to administer to you a doze of poison." – Mercy on us!

Notes ───

[12] *unus quorum* refers to his status as a justice.

JUS. No tricks, Bridget, come you know it is not so, you know it is a lie.

BRI. Read it yourself.

JUS. "Pleasure to administer a doze of poison" – Oh horrible – Cutthroat villain – Bridget.

BRI. Lovee, stay here's a postscript. N.B. 'Tis not in the power of medicine to save you.

JUS. Odds my life Bridget, why don't you call for help? I've lost my voice – My brain is giddy – I shall burst and no assistance. – John – Laury – John.

BRI. You see lovee what you have brought on yourself.

Enter SERVANT.

SERV. Your worship!

JUS. Stay, John, did you perceive any thing in my chocolate cup this morning?

SERV. Nothing your worship, unless it was a little grounds.

JUS. What colour were they?

SERV. Blackish, your worship.

JUS. Ay, arsenac, black arsenac. Why don't you run for Doctor Rosy, you rascal?

SERV. Now sir.

BRI. O lovee, you may be sure it is in vain, let him run for the Lawyer to witness your will, my life.

JUS. Zounds! go for the Doctor, you scoundrel. You are all confederate murderers.

SERV. O, here he is your worship. [*Exit.*

JUS. Now Bridget, hold your tongue, and let me see if my horrid situation be apparent.

Enter DOCTOR.

DOC. I have but just called to inform – hey! bless me, what's the matter with your worship?

JUS. There he sees it already – Poison in my face, in capitals. Yes, yes, I'm a sure job for the undertakers indeed.

BRI. Oh! Oh! alas Doctor.

JUS. Peace Bridget. Why Doctor, my dear old friend, do you really see any change in me?

DOC. Change, Never was man so altered, how came these black spots on your nose?

JUS. Spots on my nose!

DOC. And that wild stare in your right eye.

JUS. In my right eye!

DOC. Aye, and alack, alack, how you are swelled!

JUS. Swelled!

DOC. Aye, don't you think he is, madam?

BRI. O, 'tis in vain to conceal it, indeed lovee, you are as big again as you was this morning.

JUS. Yes, I feel it now – I'm poison'd – Doctor help me for the love of justice – Give me life to see my murderer hang'd.

DOC. What!

JUS. I'm poison'd I say.

DOC. Speak out.

JUS. What! can't you hear me?

DOC. Your voice is so low and hollow as it were, I can't hear a word you say.

JUS. I'm gone then, hic jacet.[13] Many years one of his Majesty's Justices.

BRI. Read Doctor – Ah, lovee the will – Consider, my life, how soon you will be dead.

JUS. No Bridget, I shall die by inches.

DOC. I never heard such monstrous iniquity. Oh, you are gone indeed my friend, the mortgage of your little bit of clay is out, and the sexton has nothing to do but to close. We must all go sooner or later – High and low – Death's a debt, his mandamus binds all alike – No bail, no demurrer.

JUS. Silence Doctor Croaker, will you cure me or will you not?

DOC. Alas, my dear friend, it is not in my power, but I'll certainly see justice done on your murderer.

JUS. I thank you, my dear friend, but I had rather see it myself.

DOC. Ay, but if you recover the villain will escape.

BRI. Will he? then indeed it would be a pity you shou'd recover, I am so enraged against the villain, I can't bear the thought of his escaping the halter.

JUS. That's very kind in you, my dear, but if it's the same thing to you, my dear, I had as soon recover notwithstanding. What Doctor, no assistance!

DOC. Efacks I can do nothing, but there's the German Quack whom you wanted to send from town, I met him at the next door, and I know he has antidotes for all poisons.

JUS. Fetch him, my dear friend, fetch him, I'll get him a diploma if he cures me.

DOC. Well, there's no time to be lost, you continue to swell immensely. [Exit.

BRI. What, my dear, will you submit to be cured by a Quack Nostrum[14] monger? for my part as much as I love you, I had rather follow you to your grave, than see you owe your life to any but a regular bred physician.

JUS. I'm sensible of your affection, dearest, and be assured nothing consoles me more in my melancholy situation, so much as the thoughts of leaving you behind me.

Enter DOCTOR *and* LIEUTENANT *disguised.*

DOC. Great luck, met him passing by the door.

LIEU. Metto dowsei pulsum.[15]

DOC. He desires to feel your pulse.

JUS. Can't he speak English?

DOC. Not a word.

LIEU. Palio vivem mortem soonem.

DOC. He says you have not six hours to live.

JUS. O mercy! does he know my distemper?

DOC. I believe not.

JUS. Tell him 'tis black arsnick they have given me.

DOC. Geneable illi arsnecca.

LIEU. Pisonatus.

JUS. What does he say?

DOC. He says that you are poison'd.

JUS. We know that, but what will be the effect?

DOC. Quid effectum?

Notes

[13] *hic jacet* (here lies) conventionally begins Latin epitaphs.

[14] medicine

[15] The doctors speak a kind of mock-Latin.

LIEU. Diable tutellum.

DOC. He says you die presently.

JUS. Oh horrible! What no antedote.

LIEU. Curum benakeré bono fullum.

JUS. What does he say, I must row in a boat to Fulham.

DOC. He says he'll undertake to cure you for L. 3000.[16]

BRI. L. 3000! 3000 halters, no lovee you shall never submit to such impositions, die at once and be a customer to none of them.

JUS. I won't die Bridget – I don't like death.

BRI. Psha, there is nothing in it, a moment and it is over.

JUS. Ay, but it leaves a numbness behind that lasts for a plaguy long time.

BRI. O my dear, pray do consider the will.

Enter LAURETTA.

LAU. O my father, what is it I hear.

LIEU. Quiddam seomriam deos tollam rosam.

DOC. The doctor is astonish'd at the sight of your fair daughter.

JUS. How so?

LIEU. Damsellum livivum suvum rislibani.

DOC. He says that he has lost his heart to her, and that if you will give him leave to pay his addresses to the young lady, and promise your consent to the union if he should gain her affections, he will on those conditions cure you instantly, without fee or reward.

JUS. The devil! did he say all that in so few words – what a fine language it is. Well, I agree, if he can prevail on the girl – and that I am sure he never will. [*Aside.*

DOC. Greal.

LIEU. Writhum bothum.

DOC. He says you must give this under your hand, while he writes you a miraculous receipt. [*Both sit down to write.*

LAU. Do mama, tell me the meaning of this.

BRI. Don't speak to me girl. – Unnatural parent.

JUS. There doctor, there's what he requires.

DOC. And here's your receipt, read it yourself.

JUS. Hey! what's here! plain English.

DOC. Read it out, a wondrous nostrum, I'll answer for it.

JUS. "In reading this you are cured, by your affectionate son-in-law, O'Conner." Who in the name of Beelzebub sirrah, who are you?

LIEU. Your affectionate son-in-law O'Conner, and your very humble servant, Humphrey Hum.

JUS. 'Tis false you dog, you are not my son-in-law, for I'll be poison'd again, and you shall be hang'd – I'll die sirrah, and leave Bridget my Estate.

BRI. Ay, Pray do my dear, leave me your Estate, I'm sure he deserves to be hang'd.

JUS. He does you say – hark'ee Bridget, you shew'd such a tender concern for me when you thought me poison'd, that for the future I am resolv'd never to take your advice again in any thing. So, do you hear sir, you are an Irishman, and a soldier, ar'n't you?

LIEU. I am sir, and proud of both.

JUS. The two things on earth I most hate, so I'll tell you what, renounce your country, and sell your commission, and I'll forgive you.

LIEU. Hark'ee, Mr Justice, if you were not the father of my Lauretta, I would pull your nose for asking the first, and break your bones for desiring the second.

DOC. Aye, aye, you're right.

JUS. Is he, then I'm sure I must be wrong. Here sir, I give my daughter to you, who are the most impudent dog, I ever saw in my life.

LIEU. O sir, say what you please, with such a gift as Lauretta, every word is a compliment.

BRI. Well my lovee, I think this will be a good subject for us to quarrel about the rest of our lives.

JUS. Why truly, my dear, I think so, tho' we are seldom at a loss for that.

DOC. This is all as it should be. My Alexander, I give you joy, and you my little god-daughter; and now my sincere wish is, that you may make just such a wife as my poor dear Dolly.

From *Union of Ireland with Great Britain* (parliamentary speech, January 23, 1799)[1]

When I found it stated that it is the principal object of the message from the crown to invite the commons of Great Britain to the consideration of means of finally adjusting the interests in common between Great Britain and Ireland, I am naturally led to enquire how the terms of the final adjustment made and agreed to by the parliaments of the two countries, in 1782,[2] came to fail of their object. In that year there was an adjustment; and no man acquainted with the history of that period, no man whose study has not been confined to mere local occurrences, can have forgotten in what kind of circumstances that adjustment arose, and under what kind of auspices it was made final. Nothing can be more obvious than the propriety of inquiring at this time how that adjustment failed of its object ...

Before ministers recommend to the house of commons to take measures that lead inevitably to the discussion of some plan of union, it was incumbent upon them to have shewn us that the last pledge of the English parliament to the people of Ireland, by which their independence was recognized and their rights acknowledged, has not produced that unanimity, that concord of sentiment, and earnest exertion to promote their own welfare, while they cordially and sincerely manifested their zeal for the happiness and prosperity of this country, which that people were expected to display, and which the parliaments of the two countries sought to cherish. – But more than the effect immediately upon the people, it is fit to inquire whether the final adjustment led to the measures of mutual confidence, and produced that unanimity of sentiment and object in the two parliaments, which, for the happiness and honor of

Notes ————————————————————————————

FROM UNION OF IRELAND
[1] Sheridan is speaking to the impending Act of Union which would abolish the Irish parliament and include Irish representation in the British parliament.

[2] In 1782, the Declaratory Act of 1720 which gave the British parliament some legislative control over Ireland was repealed, under pressure from the Irish Volunteers and, in the Irish parliament, Henry Grattan (1746–1820).

both kingdoms, every man wished might be its permanent effect. Sir, I think it impossible for any man clearly to shew that there has been any want of this unanimity on any important occasion. I am the more strongly impressed with this belief, because a solemn declaration of the Irish parliament, sanctioned by all Ireland, is now on record, wherein we have it emphatically stated that the independence of Ireland will be asserted by the people of Ireland, and that their parliament is an independent legislature. The recollection of this declaration brings to my mind the strong apprehension of the danger, the peril of agitating anew the question of Irish independence. What has that declaration stated? Sir, it is a manly, firm, and honorable testimony to all time, of the proud, noble spirit of a nation rising into distinction and mounting up to freedom. They there say, that "there is no power whatever competent to make laws for Ireland but the parliament of Ireland;" and among other things equally strong and just, we find them assert this as their birthright, and which they are determined in every situation to defend and maintain against whatever kind of enemy. When I find this declaration of the Irish parliament, and acquiesced in by the English, that they did come to a final adjustment is obvious; yet the words "a solid, permanent basis," convey some reflections on the proceedings of the parliament since that period, and it might fairly be supposed, that only its delinquency would have instigated His Majesty's ministers to adopt a course of conduct, by which, if they succeed in the enterprize, they shall accomplish for ever the subjugation of Ireland, and the slavery of its inhabitants. But, Sir, I must think the people in that country, who really cherish a love of rational liberty, who have dwelt with delight on the recollection of that, till now, auspicious period, when independence came upon them as it were by surprize, when the Genius of Freedom rested upon their island – the whole people, in short, will come to this second adjustment with a temper which I am afraid, Sir, will augur not tranquillity but disquietude; not prosperity but calamity; not the suppression of treason but the extension and increase of plots to multiply and ensanguine its horrors ...

I feel that to be silent on the present occasion were to act from terror in a way unworthy of the majesty of truth; unbecoming a man enamored of free discussion; unlike the friend and supporter of general liberty, I cannot do this. My country has claims upon me which I am not more proud to acknowledge than ready to liquidate, to the full measure of my ability. Is there any man who can wish to do less – or have the whole system of human connection and the economy of human passions been changed and perverted with those changes in the political world, from which some derive rank and emolument by the prostitution of integrity and all the virtues? But, Sir, there was a time when I should have been told that to agitate any question in this house relative to the affairs of Ireland, were to retrench upon the rights of the Irish parliament. That the independence of one legislature was not to be infringed upon by the discussion of questions which belonged to it exclusively to discuss upon and decide. That we could not agitate the affairs of Ireland in any manner without grossly insulting the dignity, and making a question of the constitutional competence of the parliament of that country to legislate for themselves. That, in short, it would be to arouse and inflame that quick spirit of independence, which the sister kingdom knew how to express, and had ever appeared both able and ready to infuse into a system of ardent, intrepid opposition to every kind of ulterior domination ... Sir, I can see the possible danger of adding to the discontents of the people of Ireland. An intriguing, ambitious enemy, may take advantage of the crisis, and desperate factious spirits at home may seize upon it as an opportunity favorable to the success of their wild and visionary projects. But these dangers are only to be apprehended from the innovation of the rights of the people of Ireland, as forming an independent nation; and he who merely seeks to arrest the arm of the invader, to check his spirit of aggression and usurpation, so far from justly incurring reproach, is in fairness entitled to the praise of honorable and virtuous enterprize. I shall speak out manfully on an occasion which eminently invites every friend of constitutional liberty to the utmost exertion of his powers. The present moment is ours, the next may be the enemy's ...

I do not, Sir, at all doubt that France[3] now anxiously looks on, eager to come in for a share of the plunder of the liberties of Ireland. The enemy with whom we have to contend, is as vigilant as dextrous, and it is in the constitution of his system of universal pillage, and the indiscriminate abuse of every maxim of honorable policy, on all occasions to profit by the distresses or agitations of other powers. To invite and encourage France, it was enough that His Majesty's ministers should have brought forward the present measure. There have been nations, who after asserting by their arms their independence, have, by their improvident use of victory, sown the seeds of future degradation and ruin too deep and too diffusive ever to be able again to resist their enemies. So true is it, that external dangers will unite communities, while the moment of triumph ushers in all those recollections of jealousy, of distrust, of uneasiness at the measures of a government or a minister, which had laid dormant in the hour of united exertion ... Sir, I do say, it is the conduct of ministers towards the Irish nation from which only we can have any reason to apprehend danger. By dividing the native and constitutional defenders of Ireland, they sow among them the seeds of treason, and encourage the attempts of the enemy on that unfortunate country ... But I do not know how to admit, that not to adopt an Union, were to invite the separation of the two countries by a French force. Nay, my opinion is directly the reverse of this; and I must say, that situated as Ireland is, without having in one instance manifested a wish to unite, but, on the contrary, having unequivocally declared herself hostile to the proposition of a union, that if it be effected, it will be a union accomplished by surprise, fraud, and corruption; and which must place the people of Ireland in a worse situation than they were before. I think there are two propositions which I have now established: the first, that it is decidedly an infraction and violation of her acknowledged right of independent legislation; and second, that union cannot prevent the separation of Ireland from this country by France. The third proposition I have to offer to the consideration of the house is, that it is not possible that, in the present state of Ireland, the people can declare and act upon their genuine sentiments; and let any man who has a head to conceive, and a heart to feel for the miseries of Ireland, put this memorable question to himself – Is it possible that the free, fair, and unbiassed sense of the people of Ireland, can be collected at this time on this question? The English force in that country is at once an answer to this question. I am not to be told, that if even the people should be cheated and tricked into union, and out of independence, it is of no consequence, as the measure is intended solely for their good, and that we ought to adopt it now, and convince them afterwards. This will not be argued by any man; or if it is, let gentlemen look to union under all its circumstances, and strange indeed must be their mode of reasoning, if they do not agree with me, that in the present conjuncture of affairs, union will lead to separate and not to perpetuate the connection ...

With respect to the enemies of the British government, it had two enemies in Ireland, "Poverty and Ignorance;" and unless it can be shewn that the present

[3] Revolutionary France was a supporter of Irish nationalist aims, and attempted to help the United Irishmen during the 1798 Uprising; France was also at war with Britain (1793–1802).

measure will remove these – will prevent the repetition of those scenes of distress which passed in Ireland when there were in the city of Dublin alone 12,000 labourers, &c. out of employment, living on raspings of bread, or starving with their families – unless these evils can be ameliorated, if not wholly corrected by a Union, I must be unfriendly to the measure. If the people of Ireland be active and industrious in every country but their own, it must be the effect of their government. First remove the causes of their misery, and then invite them, if you will, to a closer union ...

Abolition of Slavery (parliamentary speech, March 17, 1807)[1]

Mr. SHERIDAN having anxiously expected that the bill passed the preceding night[2] was the preamble of the ultimate measure of emancipation, thought that he should be guilty of the grossest inconsistency in giving a silent vote on the present question. With these sentiments he need scarcely say, that the noble earl had his thanks for having directed the attention of the house to this important subject, even at that early period. The noble earl's statement had been misrepresented. He had never proposed to enfranchise the living negroes; his measure, as he understood him, was to commence with infants born after a period, which would remain a matter of future parliamentary discussion. The planters were entitled to fair dealing on this subject. If the house meant to say, that by abolishing the slave trade they had done all that duty demanded, and that they would leave the emancipation of the slaves to the hazard of fortuitous circumstances, let them be explicit, and say so; but if there lurked in any man's mind a secret desire to proceed in that business, a secret conviction that more ought to be done than had been done, it was unmanly, it was dishonorable, not to speak out. For one he would boldly declare that he had further views; he hoped that the young nobleman who had done his feelings so much credit, by the proposition which he had that evening made, would stand to his ground. If he persevered in the pursuit of his object with the same zeal as his right honorable friend opposite had done, he had no doubt that he would meet with the same success. An honorable baronet had talked of a cloven foot; he pleaded guilty to the cloven foot, but he would say that of the man who expressed pleasure at the hope of seeing so large a portion of the human race freed from the shackles of tyranny; it ought rather to be said, that he had displayed the pennon[3] of an angel than the cloven foot of a demon. It was true no immediate connection existed between the abolition of the slave trade and the abolition of slavery, but the same feelings must be roused by the consideration of both questions; and he who detested the one practice must also detest the other. He did not like to hear the term property applied to the subjects of a free country. Could man become the property of man? A colony emancipating from the free constitution of England must carry with it the principles of that constitution, and could no more shake off its well known allegiance to the constitution than it could shake off its allegiance to its sovereign. He trusted that the planters might be induced to lead the way on the subject of emancipation; but he cautioned the house against being too sanguine on the subject. Were the planters themselves always resident on the islands, he should have greater hopes; but it was not probable that because cargoes

Notes

ABOLITION OF SLAVERY

[1] This is the full text of the speech as it appears in an 1816 edition.

[2] According to Sheridan's 1816 editor, the bill proposed "the gradual abolition of slavery in the West Indies." Later in March, the slave trade became illegal under the Abolition Act, but slavery itself continued in British colonies.

[3] pinion or part of a wing.

of human misery were no longer to be landed on their shores, that because their eyes were to be no longer glutted with the sight of human suffering, or their ears pierced with the cries of human distraction in any further importation of negroes, that the slave-drivers would soon forget their fixed habits of brutality, and learn to treat the unhappy wretches in their charge with clemency and compassion. Slavery would not wear itself out; it would become more rigid, unless the legislature became more vigilant, and reminded the planters of the new duty that had fallen upon them, of rearing the young slaves in such a manner, that they might be worthy of freedom. Adverting to the quotation from Gibbon, he contended, that the slavery of the West Indies was unlike any other slavery; it was peculiarly unlike the slavery of antient days, when the slaves frequently attained to the highest dignities; Esop, Terence, and Seneca were slaves.[4] Was there a possibility that any of the unfortunate negroes now in the West Indies should emulate such men? It might be dangerous to give freedom to the slaves in a mass, but that it was not dangerous to give it to them in detail, was sufficiently proved by a little pamphlet that had been put into his hands the preceding night, in which it was stated, that a Mr. David Barclay, to his eternal honor be it spoken, who had himself been a slave-owner in Jamaica, and who, regretting that he had been so, on a bequest of slaves being made to him, emancipated them, caused them to be conveyed to Pennsylvania, where they were properly instructed, and where their subsequent exemplary conduct was the general theme of admiration. With this fact before him, should he be told that he must give up all hope of abolishing slavery! No, he would never give it up. He would exclaim with the poet, in the words of the motto of the pamphlet which he had mentioned,

> I would not have a slave to till my ground,
> To fan me while I sleep, and tremble when
> I wake, for all that human sinews bought
> And sold, have ever earn'd.[5]

Mary O'Brien (fl. 1790)

Mary O'Brien's biographical details, like John Leslie's, are lost. The title page to *The Political Monitor* identified her as married to Patrick O'Brien Esq., "author of CHARLES HENLEY." Mary O'Brien is the author of at least three volumes, all of them political and satiric: a seven-canto poem *The Pious Incendiaries: Or, Fanaticism Display'd* (1785), a five-act play entitled *The Fallen Patriot* (1790), and a collection of verse, *The Political Monitor* (1790). With her attacks on William Pitt, often familiarly called "Billy," and the English national stereotype of John Bull, her use of speakers based on the stock types of "Paddy" and "Teague," and occasional use of Irish idiom, O'Brien's *Political Monitor* provides some early instances of Irish

Notes ————————————————————————————————

[4] Edward Gibbon (1737–94), English historian and author of *The Decline and Fall of the Roman Empire* (1776–88), often cited for its discussion of slavery in Rome and elsewhere. Aesop, Terence, and Seneca are all classical authors.

[5] These lines are slightly altered from Book II of *The Task* (1784) by English poet William Cowper (1731–1800).

political verse satire in ballad form during this period; for further examples, see *Paddy's Resource* (below). Her "Ode, For the Prince of Wales's Birth Day" bears comparison to another address to the same Prince of Wales, Moore's "The Prince's Day" (1811, below). Both poems are plaintive rather than satiric, inviting the Prince, a friend of R. B. Sheridan's, to follow his better nature, and his liberal leanings, in order to lead reform.

Ode, For the Prince of Wales's Birth Day

From The Political Monitor (1790)

Now nature bears imperial sway,
O'er earth enrob'd profusely gay;
Her swelling fruits, her golden wheat,
The joyful rustic's wishes meet,
   Replete with harvest mirth.   5
Great prince, in midst of all her pride,
As th' bridegroom ushers in his bride,
   Pomona[1] hails thy birth.

Ambitious of the royal theme,
Now Fancy seems to rise supreme,   10
Soaring to heaven's majestic height,
Gains power prophetic in her flight:
   And now the fair descends
Freighted with celestial truth,
Addresses thus the royal youth   15
   While Liberty attends:

"In thee, O prince, we Britons own,
Those virtues that adorn a throne,
Bold, gen'rous, gracefully refin'd,
Mercy and truth united find   20
   A seat within thy breast;
Judgment superior to thy years
In wisdom's sable vest appears,
   To blazon round thy crest.

"As autumn gathers in her store   25
From all seasons gone before;
Her fruits to full perfection run
Ripen'd by meridian sun,
   Maturer sweets display,
So shall the rising hero smile,   30
In glory on his native isle
   And ripen into day.

Notes

ODE
[1] Roman goddess of gardens and orchards, and particularly fruit.

"Wisdom shall then assume her power,
And crop the weeds from virtue's flower,
While sweet benevolence shall shed   35
Her meek-ey'd splendor round his head
    Like rays of blushing morn.
Justice in her mildest sphere
Shall govern each succeeding year,
    And all his acts adorn."   40

Paddy's Opinion: An Irish Ballad

From The Political Monitor (1790)

Since your fame, my dear Billy,
    Is burn'd to a snuff,
And your wisdom looks silly,
    For want of a puff;

Now, instead of a better,   5
    Take me for your minion,
Without law or letter,
    I'll state my opinion:

And to strengthen my case too,
    Thro' the maze of my journey,   10
By my *shoul* I'll take Fraud
    To be my Attorney;

And just to a hair too,
    So keen is my wit,
Without study or reas'ning   15
    The subject I've hit.

Thus stands my brief now,
    Of ev'ry gay light,
That shines by the day,
    Or burns by the night,   20

From the bright fiery beam,
    That gilds up your windows,
To the fat greasy taper,
    That's burning within doors;

All receive without murmur,   25
    In humble devotion,
(Except the late titles
    Made by your promotion,)

Without any cavil,
    The *badge* of taxation;[1]   30

Notes ──

PADDY'S OPINION
[1] Candles were heavily taxed in this period.

In compliment civil
   It's worn thro' the nation.

Since then, haughty Sol,[2]
   But darts in his flashes
Thro' the casement, my jewel,   35
   Of your silver sashes:

Ergo, the argument
   Sure will hold good,
All light, my dear joy,
   Of coal, grease, or wood,   40

From hay or from straw,
   From rush or from thatch;
Or spark that rekindles
   The sulphur of match,

Or vapour that tends   45
   By its lights to illume
A crevice or cobweb,
   That hangs in a room.

For light is a Critic
   No Premier can shun;   50
Your wit shines the brighter
   By taxing the sun.

Arrah, who then can blame you,
   By way of a joke,
To tax, without scruple,   55
   Tobacco and smoke.

But beware now, dear *crature*,
   Since wisdom may fail ye,
To smoke out our brains,
   In the land of Shillelah;   60

Lest Hibernia's high notions
   To anger should rise,
And smoke out your taxes,
   And blast your excise.

Arrah, then, my dear Billy,   65
   It might prove in the pull,
Paddy's not quite so silly
   As your Jacky Bull.

Notes ──────────────────────────────────

[2] the sun

James Porter (1752–1798)

James Porter was born in Co. Donegal, the son of a farmer. After a few years as a schoolmaster in Co. Down, he went to Glasgow to study to become a Presbyterian minister. He began working as a minister in Greyabbey, Co. Down, in 1787. Porter was on the periphery of the nationalist movement in Ireland, joining the Irish Volunteers and then, as nationalist activity intensified in the early 1790s, becoming a regular contributor to the United Irishmen newspaper, *The Northern Star*, published in Belfast from 1792 to 1797. Porter's contributions included a number of songs and a series of satiric letters, *Billy Bluff and 'Squire Firebrand* (1796). He also published further public, political letters, addressed to the Marquess of Downshire, and a sermon, *Wind and Weather* (1797), on the storm that prevented the landing of the French fleet in support of Irish independence. Whether because of *Billy Bluff* or more personal conflicts, Porter clearly had powerful enemies among the ruling regime. After the Uprising began, orders for his arrest were promptly distributed, and he was subsequently convicted on the uncorroborated testimony of a paid informer who asserted that Porter had illegally taken and read aloud the contents of a military note. Porter was sentenced to be hanged and quartered, though apparently his wife managed to solicit some mercy for her husband and he was not quartered.

Billy Bluff was popular in its day and for decades after. It appeared first as a series of letters in *The Northern Star* between May and December 1796. Nancy Curtin (see Further reading below) notes that the United Irishmen collected the letters as a pamphlet and published "3,000 copies for free distribution among the peasantry" (185). The satire is a pointed response to the turmoil of the mid-1790s, mocking particular political figures of the day while disseminating the key principles of the United Irishmen. But it also aims its barbs more broadly at leaders who see, and strike out at, conspiracy everywhere, sowing distrust and perpetuating the very problems they fear. The old man's vision in Billy's dream, for instance, is straightforward national allegory which counters the Squire's paranoid fears of conspiracy. The satire also offers a detailed view of a standard villain in Irish literature of this period – the informer. See, for instance, Boucicault's *Arrah-na-Pogue* (below) for one of Billy's Victorian counterparts.

The first three letters are given here from the 1812 edition, as it has fewer typographical errors than the 1797 Belfast edition with which it is, apart from some punctuation changes, substantively identical.

Further reading

Curtin, Nancy, *The United Irishmen: Popular Politics in Ulster and Dublin, 1791–1798*. Oxford: Clarendon Press, 1994.

Thuente, Mary Helen, *The Harp Re-strung: The United Irishmen and the Rise of Literary Nationalism*. Syracuse: Syracuse University Press, 1994.

Wright, Julia M., "Courting Public Opinion: Handling Informers in the 1790s," *Éire–Ireland* 33 (1997–8): 144–69.

From *Billy Bluff and 'Squire Firebrand: Or, A Sample of the Times* (1796)

Northern Star, May 21, 1796

By your leave Mr. Editor – if you please, a corner in your paper for this my letter, the first that ever I wrote for print, and probably will be the last. I am in danger of being hanged or put in gaol, perhaps both. I want your advice like an honest man. God help us, what is the world coming to at last? I'll tell you the whole affair, and the cause of it. – Billy Bluff, my neighbour, was up yesterday at the 'Squire's, with his duty hens. "Well, Billy, what news," says the 'Squire. Troth, sir, plenty of news, but none very good, says Billy. "What's your neighbour R— (meaning me) about now?" Why, please your honour, he's at the old cut; railing against the war, against the tythes, and against game laws, and he's still reading at the newspapers. "He is a d—n'd villain, and must be laid fast, by G–d; but what more do you know of him, Billy?" Why, bad enough, an' please your honour. Him and the Popish Priest drank together last market-day, till all was blue again with them; they shaked hands, so they did, drank toasts and sung songs. "Pretty work, by h——ns! did you over-hear them?" Ah, that I did so, and listened like a pig. "What were the toasts?" First, the Priest drank, *Prosperity to old Ireland*, and – "Stop, Billy! the toast is infamous; the world *Old* never was, and never ought to be applied to any country but England; and he who would apply it to Ireland is a rebel, and ought to be hanged." He ought, an' please your honour, as round as a hoop. "Well, what toast did the villain R— drink?" He drank, *Union and Peace to the People of Ireland*. "Worse and worse, Billy; a d—n'd deal worse: he who wishes union, wishes ruin to the country; I say ruin to the government, and that is ruin to the country. Union, forsooth! that is what never was, and what never must prevail in this country; and as to peace, 'tis flying in the face of government to speak of it; the d—l send the ruffians peace, till their betters chuse to give it to them."

Then, Sir, the Priest drank, here's *Every man his own road to Heaven*. "That, Billy, is a toast that no man would drink, but a Republican and a Sinner; for it supposes all men to be on an equality before God, and supposes that a man may go to heaven, without being of the established church, which is impossible." God bless your honour, I know that, and that is the reason I turned to church.

Then the toast R— gave, was *Liberty to those who dare contend for it*. "Impudent scoundrel! the signal of rebellion, anarchy, and confusion: to contend implies opposition; opposition implies resistance; resistance implies war: war against the established orders; war against man and the godhead, as the great Grattan expressed it; but tell me, what other toasts did they drink?" Severals that I can't just mind now. "Did they drink success to the French?" No, an' please your honour, but they drank success to the righteous. "That's near as bad – did they drink *no more Kings*?" They did, and shook hands upon it: my neighbour R— gave that toast, no more Kings, said he, no more Kings – to France. "To France, Billy, the villains had another meaning; aye, aye, they had another meaning. I know what the hypocritical villains meant, I know it perfectly; d–mn—n to my s—l but they shall both be hanged." Certainly, please your honour, and the sooner the better. "What songs did they sing?" Why the Priest sang, *Patrick's Day in the Morning*, and then R— sang, *Paddy Thwack*, then the Priest sang, *Grawny Wail*, and then R— sang, *O for a Union of Parties*. "D—n Union, and d—n Grawny Wail, and Paddy Thwack, and Patrick's Day in the Morning; they are all impudent national seditious songs: what more did you hear?" Please your honour, after the songs they began to talk about religion, and so I came off and left them.

"You have done very well, Billy, very well; go to the kitchen, and I'll order you a drink of small beer: See and get me more news, and I'll give you a job at the roads next summer." G–d prosper your honour. "But, Billy, you'll take care and be ready to swear when called on." Egad a pretty story, an' please your honour, if I could not swear what I would say, or what your honour would please.

Now, Mr. Editor, all this I had from the Butler, who is an honest fellow, though a Catholic: he told me through friendship to the Priest, for fear of the worst, as he called it. And, although Bluff told some truth, he did not tell all the truth, for we drank several loyal toasts – we drank the *King, Mr. Pitt, the Lord of the Manor,* and many others, and we sung several good loyal songs. But the religious conversation is what I must tell you myself. When we got a glass I thought of touching the Priest upon points: We had a tolerable bout on't; he made use of several hard words, not one of them did I understand, nor do I remember any of them but two, because he came over those two more than twenty times. What is the best religion, said I, *Bonus Homo,* said he; – What is your creed, said I, *Bonus Homo* said he again; – What is it to be one of the *elect,* said I, *Bonus Homo,* said he, – What is your opinion of the Pope, said I, can he send any body he pleases to Heaven; he neither can nor will, said he, send any body to Heaven but a *Bonus Homo.* O! then, said I, *Bonus Homo* means Popery, I suppose. He smiled and said, it means just *Bonus Homo,* and neither more nor less!

Off went I next day to our Minister, told him all the conversation, and how much I was puzzled about *Bonus Homo.* He said that the Priest was right in every thing he said, except that the creed was too short, quite too short to be adopted in any Christian country. Well, but if you please, what is the plain meaning of *Bonus Homo?* "Why the literal meaning of *Bonus Homo,* is a *Good Man.*" Ma-sha, fol-de-lol, said I, with a caper, if that be the case, *we are all one in the Latin.* So, Mr. Editor, good bye to you, *Bonus Homo* is the creed for me.

A PRESBYTERIAN.

N.B. Tell me whether you think I will be prosecuted for the company I kept with the Priest.

P.S. The 'Squire observed to Bluff, that the SHAKING HANDS between me and the priest was worse than all the rest put together.

Northern Star, July 18, 1796

Billy Bluff has been at the 'SQUIRE again, Mr. Editor, of which I wish to give you notice as formerly.

"Well, Billy, where's the list of what I gave you to spy out for me?" Here it is, an' please your honour – "Let me see; aye, well: –

1st, *To find out all in the parish who have not registered their arms.*

2d, *To find out how many United Irishmen there are in Ireland.*

3d, *To find out what those people say who will not register their freeholds.*

4th, *To find out the United Irishmen's word and sign.*

5th, *To find out what songs the people sing.*

6th, *To watch if R— and the Priest drink together at any time.*

7th, *To put notices on the Chapel, Church, and Meeting-house.*

"Well, have you managed all completely?" Egad, your honour, gif I have not done all like an *honest* man, never employ me again.

"Let us go through in order, Billy: –

"How many have not registered their arms?" Does your honour wish for the truth fairly? "To be sure I do, and be d—n'd to you for a fool; what did I send you through the parish for, these four weeks?" Why, then, there are just 41. "What reason do they give?" They say it's all a piece of stuff, and only to make them and the Catholics fall out, and that they have been too long at that already, and that they are getting more wit, and that – "Stop, Billy, enough, enough; we'll set out the search on Saturday; I'll secure both the scoundrels and their arms, I'll warrant you, by H——ns I will. Do you know them all?" Your honour, here's the list. "Very good. Have you found out how many United Irishmen are in Ireland?" I have, your honour, to a fraction. "But how?" Ah! let me alone at a push. I went, d'you see, to little Diagram the School-master, he's the man, your honour knows, can tell things that nobody else can; I gave him half-a-pint, and promised him half-a-guinea; he instantly fell to work; he cast a horrid scope,[1] counted the Planets, and found the nativity of every man of them, to the number of, of, of; there it is, in black and white. "Let me see; units, tens, hundreds, thousands, millions, hundreds of millions. – Why he must be wrong, all wrong – this is 150,000,000." Aye, that's the very thing exactly. O! gif I could read figures, like your honour. "Why, you booby, he's a fool or a knave; there's not half that number of people in the whole world." For certain then he must be wrong, as your honour says. – O, what it is to have learning!

I Ie told me he saw two men in it as old as Mathusalem. "He saw two devils as old as Mathusalem. I can't like that fellow since I got old M. hanged by his surmises, especially when I learnt last assizes that the poor deveil was perfectly innocent. But 'tis no great matter, Billy, one life is no great thing now-a-days. Now let me hear all you have heard against registering freeholds?" Why, an' please your honour, R. is the worst in the parish about that, and is filling their head full of notions, and setting them all a thinking. "D—n thinking, Billy, 'tis putting the world mad: O! what a happy country we had before men turned their thoughts to thinking: Catholics thought of nothing but just getting leave to live, and working for their meat: Presbyterians thought of nothing but wrangling about religion, and grumbling about tythes; and Protestants thought of nothing but doing and saying what their betters bid them: and the Gentlemen thought of nothing but drinking, hunting, and the game laws. O! how times are changed, and all for the worse. Your Catholic College – your Catholic Schools – your Catholic Emancipation – your Sunday Schools – your Charter Schools – your Book Societies – your Pamphlets and your Books; and your one h—l or another, are all turning the people's heads, and setting them a thinking about this, that and t'other. O! in my father's days, there was none of this work. No, no. He would put a fellow in jail, or in the stocks, just when he pleased – nobody said it was wrong. He would horse-whip a tradesman when he presented his bill – nobody said it was wrong. He would fancy a tenant's daughter – nobody said it was wrong. He shot dogs for barking; imprisoned Catholics for keeping arms in their houses; fined Quakers for not paying tythes; got a Presbyterian assassinated for voting against him at the Vestry; and kept a Farmer's Son in prison till he died for shooting a Partridge – nobody said – nobody dared to say this was wrong. But now, the impudence and conceit of the world is not to be borne. They think, and talk, and grumble, and prate, whenever they are offended. Go to H—l, you scoundrel, said I, yesterday to the Taylor, when I had no money to give him. The fellow had the impudence to look me straight in the face. 'I am no scoundrel, said he, and H–ll is a place for my betters.' Now, can flesh and blood bear such audacity? By H——ns I saw the day that I could have had interest enough with the Judge and Jury for to have got him hanged for a less fault." E'dad, it was a great impudence to a man like your honour, to be sure. "That it was, Billy: but go on with their talk about registering their freeholds."[2] I can't tell your honour the half of it: One says, 'tis all nonsense and folly; another says, we have been too long dupes and fools, but we are getting more wit; another says, can't they great folks buy us from our landlords *by the lump*, and not drive us to the market like swine; another says, there is more sin committed at every general election, than seven years prayers would atone for; another says, how can the Gentlemen expect that the country would thrive, when they sell their tenants – sell

Notes

FROM BILLY BLUFF
[1] horoscope

[2] The registry of freeholds was a voters' list, and included those who owned land worth 40 shillings or more.

themselves – encourage perjury – and share in the spoils of corruption? But, your honour, my neighbour R— is worse than them all. "I don't doubt the villain. Let me hear what he says, Billy."

" 'Tis all humbug on the country, says he; there's no fair play, *in* the parliament nor *out* of it. Squabbling in counties may serve the ambition of private families, but can do nothing for the nation at large; boroughs can bear the sway at any rate, even if we had honest men. But, says he, we have very few of them; our professed patriots, when once in, are all knaves, and the old knaves are every year growing worse; they tell lies and are not ashamed of it; they laugh in your faces if you talk of honour or truth – they say nobody but fools would look for any such thing from parliament-men. Then what mockery are elections, said he, I'll never disgrace myself or my country by going near one of them. Then, your honour, he fell on Mr. Pitt, and railed for a quarter of an hour. Your namesake[3] on the other side of the water, deserves a halter, said he – for what, said I – for all the mischief he has done. He has nothing in his mind but corruption; nothing in his tongue, but hypocrisy, and nothing at his heart but blood. His eloquence has deceived himself and his adherents – his plans have all failed – his country is nearly ruined, and for my part, I would vote for the devil sooner than for any man that would support him in his projects of ambition and wickedness." Then he fell on the Empress of Russia, the King of Prussia, the Emperor of Germany,[4] the – "Stop, Billy, stop, I have heard too much: I have heard too much. O! what will the world come to, when such villains get leave to talk at this rate? But I'll form a plan to have him taken off, I'll warrant you." – Then your honour, some say, we have been twice registered already; others say, we have been three times registered; and others we have been four times. "The vagabonds! What is it to them how often they have registered; it is the last time only that is good in law. You have registered, Billy." Gif your honour would not take it ill I would just mention that I am four times registered already; I voted three different days for your honour's friend at the last election, and your honour knows that I have never got my lease yet.[5] "Now, what a booby you are, to talk of such things when I have so much on hand; what matters it when you get your lease; 'tis ready for signing. I'll deceive no man who does all I bid him." – Then, e'dad, I'll never be deceived.

"Well, go directly and register." Your honour knows I never stood your word, I'll do it to-morrow. "That's right. O! if my tenants were all like you I would be a happy man; if the King's subjects were all like you he would be a happy King; if the world were all like you, it would be a happy world. Now, Billy, we are come to the word and sign; that's the point, that's the secret; have you found out the real *word* and the real *sign* of the United Irishmen." That I have, your honour, to a shaving. – "Well, the word first, Billy, let's have the word first." – 'Tis a short word, an' please your honour, but has great meaning in it, as I do suppose. "Let's have it, man, quickly!"

The word is, UP. "UP, Billy! – Stop; now I'll make English of it, I would not turn my back on any man at riddles or connondrums; first, U. that means unit – that's one – P. people – that is, the People is one." E'gad, an' please your honour, I'll swear that is the very thing. "But let's try again, Billy: U. stands for Up – P. stands for Pretender – that is, up with the Pretender – Treason, Billy." That's it, your honour, I'll take my

Notes

[3] William Pitt, prime minister of Britain, sometimes called "Billy" in *Northern Star* publications.

[4] Catherine the Great (Russia), Frederick William II (Prussia), and Francis II, ruler of the Holy Roman Empire which then included much of Germany.

[5] Billy is registered as a freeholder even though he does not have the land; the Squire, in effect, has created Billy's vote for his own use. Since the property requirements kept voters' lists small and voting did not yet use secret ballots, such practices made it possible to control elections.

oath of it – "But, let's try again, Billy – the Pretender is dead, that won't do. U. stands for Union, P. stands for Power – no, for Presbyterian – no, for Protestant – no, for Papist, Papist – Union with the Papists – now, I have it, Billy, as clear as the Sun." Huzza, your honour – huzza, your honour – huzza, your honour!!

Northern Star, **August 15, 1796**

O, your honour for discovering every thing that no body else could understand. "Now, Billy, we clearly understand the United Irishmen's word, have you got the sign?" Providence threw that in my way, your honour, by mere chance: there it is, arms across, just like an X. "Arms across just like an X. Let me see, X stands for ten – ten, that is tythe; now X is a cross, that is cross out the tythes:[6] more wickedness, Billy: how could man's salvation be secured without tythes. Bend your right arm, that's V, that's five, bend your other arm, another five; now, five and five are ten, that's X, or two V's joined together – now, 5 is the five points of knavery: I never had a schoolfellow could play that game with me; then ten, or X, is a double game. What think you of that, Billy?" Lord, your honour's learning is far beyond me. "Aye, aye, 'tis ease getting at the bottom of things, if people would take pains and have penetration. But I still think, Billy, it must have some French meaning in it: let us try – I have it! Lord, man, I have it, ten means Decade, the French Decade." Heavens! your honour, is the French *decayed?* I'll go mad with joy: O, as I'll laugh at R.; O, I'll crow over all the parish, O! O! "Hold, Billy, you have no learning, you have no understanding; pay more respect to your betters before you go mad." Your honour's pleasure for me. "Then the word is Decade, and not decayed as you foolishly imagine." Then, your honour, what does Decade mean? "Some damn'd contrivance of the republican scoundrels the French, by which they squeeze ten days into seven, and instead of 52 weeks, have nothing but 36 weeks and a half in the year, so that a man is as near his latter end at 40 years of age in France, as at 60 in any other country. Lord, Billy, if I had lived in France, I would have been dead long ago." God forbid, your honour, I hope your honour has more compassion on the good of your country than to die this 100 years to come. Lord protect you from all your enemies. "Thank you, Billy, thank you, I'll reward you for your kindness."

"But tell me, man, how came you by so much knowledge?" Your honour, I made trial as you desired me, to have myself made a *United Irishman.* I applied to every body I could think of for 5 days running; some said one thing, and some said another, but nobody would give me the oath. Don't be afraid, said I, *I am as honest as steel; I never deceived any man; I can keep a secret; I would die by my word if ever I said it, to the last drop.* "Well said, Billy." But all would not do till I went to the boys of G— ; they bid me meet them last Wednesday night at T— R—'s big barn; when I went there, in comes four men, I never saw before, with a candle. They shaked my hand, and says, so you wish to be an *United Irishman?* Yes, says I. They then laid a long ladder to a beam that went across the barn: one of them went up and came down. UP, says one; UP, says another; UP, said they all; that's the way I learned the word. "Very well, Billy, very well, go on."

O! your honour, I tremble to tell you the rest. As I went up, one of them followed, and at the top he pulled a rope out of his pocket. Friend, says he, if you can – "Zounds, Billy, going to hang you." Down I jumped, your honour, dropped on my bended

Notes ──

[6] Tithes were required to be paid to the Church of Ireland, regardless of religion, creating resentment among Dissenters (such as Presbyterians and Quakers) as well as Catholics.

knees, screamed, and cried murder, murder – I am no spy, gentlemen, I will swear I am no spy, *but as honest as steel; never deceived any man; can keep a secret; I would die by my word, if ever I said it, to the last drop.* – "L—d, Billy, how did you escape." One of them gave me a kick on the backside. Out, says he, you scoundrel. Two of them put their arms across, clinched each other, and made a kind of carriage, over which I was thrown like a bag of bran. When they crossed their arms, I knew that it was their sign, for they understood each other directly. I was carried to the bottom of a garden – it was midnight, and as dark as pitch. Can you dig any, says one, putting a spade into my hand. A little, said I. Then said they all, fall to and dig a hole, the length and breadth of your own dear self. "H—v–nly G–d, Billy, going to bury you alive." O, your honour, my knees smote against each other – my hat stood seven inches above my head, on the top of my hair – the spade fell from my hand – my breeches went all wrong – my heart plumped down to the bottom of my belly, like a black pudding in a broth pot, and I tumbled down as dead as a door nail. "I hope matters are at the worst – Zounds, what became of you afterwards?" Then I fell into a trance for 4 hours, for it was just day light as I awoke; they were all fled, and I never saw them more: but O, your honour, if you knew all I heard in my trance, you would think it stranger than any thing in all the world. "Let's hear, Billy." O! no tongue could tell; but for an ignorant man, like me, who is no scholar, to begin to it would be an arrant sin. "Well, well, Billy, you must give it me as well as you can." I thought a man with grey hairs and pretty countenance, well dressed in fine clothes, took me by the arm and said, if I would harken to him, he would tell me wonderful things. I told him I would be glad to get news, and would listen with all my might. We sat down and he began. As I came hither, said he, I was taken up by some unknown being, and carried through the air a long way, till at length I was let down on the ground; it was dark, very dark: after some time, a light began gradually to appear, not from the *East*, but from the *West*.[7] O! said I to myself, but this is strange – as the light became stronger, I could perceive nothing but a wide, wide extended plain: when the light grew still something stronger, I could perceive a beautiful green hill in the middle of the plain, when it grew bright as day: crowds of people, from all parts, appeared to walk into the plain towards the hill – I conversed with severals – some of them could speak English only, others could speak only in the Irish dialect, but the greatest number could speak both English and Irish.[8] They told me that the town that I saw at a distance, to the left, was called Athlone, and that the spot on which the hill stood, was the centre of Ireland.

I was all at once almost struck blind with amazement. The sky seemed to open near the western side, out of which came sailing through the air, a beautiful Angel, clad in robes of white: In her left hand she held a large flag, on which I could see written in letters of gold:

"THE GENIUS OF IRELAND."

In her right hand she held a branch of olive, which she waved round and round, at which all the people seemed filled with joy and began to smile: After hovering a little, she rested on the hill, and sat down on the verdant top that was covered with nothing

Notes

[7] In *Northern Star* iconography, the east is often associated with Britain and abusive power, and the west with the post-revolutionary United States and political liberty; see William Drennan's "Erin" (below, p. 136) for another example.

[8] Bilingualism was part of the United Irishmen project; they published a guide to the Irish language in 1795 that included material from Brooke's *Reliques of Irish Poetry*.

but shamrocks. The crowds pressed forward, with their eyes fixed on the Genius; as they approached the base of the hill, the throng became greater; they took each other by the hand and began to ascend. The Genius beckoned with the olive branch, as if inviting them to come forward. They ascended but a little way, when they linked in each other's arms, and the circle narrowing as they proceeded, they pressed closer together and grasped each other around the waist. There seemed to be mixed all ranks, ages and professions. The old and infirm were assisted by the young and vigorous. The weak leaned upon the strong, and the rich smiled upon the poor! While this was going forward, I espied here and there, several stop at the verge of the plain, others in the middle, some halted at the foot of the hill, and several were thrown down who had been a good way up. A vast number of coaches, chariots, phaetons, &c. were driving in promiscuous confusion over the plain; some had lost their drivers, and others their owners, who had flown to join the multitudes that were ascending the hill. But the greater part still retained their ponderous load of the dignitaries of the church, the sages of the law, and the lords of the land; they were flying to the dark clouds that still hung over the East, which had now turned to the colour of clotted blood. Then I immediately saw, issuing from the opening of the sky, from whence the Angel came, a beautiful transparent azure cloud, bordered all round with alternate shades of crimson, white and yellow, which spreading round, involved the whole hill, and hid from my sight the vast multitudes which covered it, and left nothing to be seen, but the face, neck and breast of the beautiful Angel. At that instant the Genius spoke, with a voice exquisitely fine, that ravished my ears: "THERE, *said she,* ARE ALL MY CHILDREN – *This is the* HILL *of* UNION. *The result of this meeting will be —*" Then shewing the other side of the FLAG, I perceived in great letters of gold,

"LIBERTY AND PEACE."

The unknown being then carried me away. You are the first person, said he, I have seen, to whom I could tell these wonderful things. He then, your honour, after shewing me a fine painting which he carried along with him, disappeared. Immediately I thought a big black eagle lifted me up in his claws and held me over a deep pit, where a shocking monster with red eyes and long teeth was roaring like thunder, when – O! L—d, your honour, it dropt me into his very mouth! As I fell, I awoke, and saw a big mastiff dog barking within ten yards of me. – Home I ran, half dead with fear, and could hardly believe I was alive for two days afterwards.

"Zounds, Billy, that was a hell of an adventure all over; I don't like that damn'd trance. I'll swear that old grey-headed scoundrel you saw, was an impostor, and an impudent impostor, and told you nothing but a bundle of lies. By heavens, if he could be laid hold of, I would teach him how to circulate such stories, as all descriptions of people linking, and grasping, and uniting on shamrock hills, with the Genius of Ireland in shape of an Angel at their head; pretty stuff to sow sedition among the people. Then his damn'd bloody cloud hanging over the East, and his celestial cloud from the West, is a wicked contrivance. E'gad, 'tis well that part of the Vision is not easily understood. Then the dignitaries of the church, the sages of the law, and the lords of the land, driving there in chariots, coaches, and phaetons, looks as if they wished to hide themselves in darkness and in blood: O! Billy, it was a damnable dream! I should rather that you had slept for ever, than that you awoke to reveal such things." – Sure, your honour knows that the fault was not mine. – "I don't know who the Devil's fault it was, but I am sure he gave you a damn'd false account of the Genius of Ireland. – Had he told you that he saw an old haggard looking witch, with bristly hair and black eyes, spitting fire and brimstone, with a great scourge of snakes in one hand, and a bunch of worm-wood in the other, he would have told you something like truth; he would have told you what the Irish rabble have seen, and what they deserve. Aye, aye, then you would have seen the emblem of good old times. But the old wizzard was an impostor, Billy.

Paddy's Resource (c.1800)

Paddy's Resource was a popular collection of nationalist ballads, many originally published in United Irishmen newspapers, particularly *The Northern Star*. Published surreptitiously in the late 1790s and early 1800s, there is no standard edition of *Paddy's Resource*; some versions included more lyrics than others, and the selection and sequence of songs varied. Known contributors include John Corry, James Porter, and William Drennan, whose "Erin" also appeared in *Paddy's Resource*. There were strong reasons for the publishers and contributors to remain anonymous: as Gillian O'Brien notes (see Further reading below), the first editor of *The Northern Star* was arrested in September 1796, and his replacements in February 1797; *The Northern Star*'s printing presses were destroyed by pro-government militia in May 1797 (11–12, 21).

The ballads in *Paddy's Resource* were often set to traditional tunes and expected to circulate through oral as well as print culture. The lyrics drew on a richly hybridized vocabulary: "Erin"

as an anglicized form of the Irish-Gaelic word for "Ireland" appears along with Irish-language phrases that were translated for English-language readers; "Paddy" and "Teague" as Irish everyman figures appear in some lyrics, while others focus on historical personages; and key texts in radical politics, especially Thomas Paine's *The Rights of Man* (1791–2), are frequently invoked alongside specifically Irish geographical, political, and cultural references. Some lyrics, such as "The United Real Reformer," explicitly addressed regional and sectarian divisions.

Further reading

Curtin, Nancy, *The United Irishmen: Popular Politics in Ulster and Dublin, 1791–1798*. Oxford: Clarendon Press, 1994.
O'Brien, Gillian, " 'Spirit, Impartiality, Independence': *The Northern Star, 1792–1797*," *Eighteenth-century Ireland* 13 (1998): 7–23.
Thuente, Mary Helen, *The Harp Re-strung: The United Irishmen and the Rise of Literary Nationalism*. Syracuse: Syracuse University Press, 1994.

The Exiled Irishman's Lamentation

Tune: "Savourna Deelish"

GREEN were the fields where my forefathers dwelt, O;
  "Erin ma vourneen! slan leat go brah!"[1]
Altho' our farm was small yet comforts we felt O.
  "Erin ma vourneen! slan leat go brah!"
At length came the day when our lease did expire,   5

Notes ————————————————————————————————

THE EXILED IRISHMAN'S LAMENTATION
[1] *Ireland, my darling! for ever adieu!* (original).

And fain would I live where before lived my sire;
But ah! well-a-day! I was forced to retire.
   "Erin ma vourneen! slan leat go brah!"

Tho' the laws I obey'd no protection I found, O;
   "Erin ma vourneen! slan leat go brah!"   10
With what grief I beheld my Cot[2] burn'd to the ground, O!
   "Erin ma vourneen! slan leat go brah!"
Forc'd from my home; yea from where I was born,
To range the wide world – poor helpless forlorn;
I look back with regret – and my heart strings are torn.   15
   "Erin ma vourneen! slan leat go brah!"

With principles pure, patriotic and firm,
   "Erin ma vourneen! slan leat go brah!"
To my country attached and a friend to reform,
   "Erin ma vourneen! slan leat go brah!"   20
I supported old *Ireland* – was ready to die for it;
If her foes e'er prevail'd I was well known to sigh for it;
But my faith I preserv'd and am now forc'd to fly for it.
   "Erin ma vourneen! slan leat go brah!"

In the North I see friends – too long was I blind, O;   25
   "Erin ma vourneen! slan leat go brah!"
The cobwebs are broken and free is mind, O.
   "Erin ma vourneen! slan leat go brah!"
North and South here's my hand – East and West here's my heart, O;
Let's ne'er be divided by any base art, O,   30
But love one another and never more part, O.
   "Boie yudh ma vourneen! Erin go brah!"[3]

But hark! I hear sounds and my heart strong is beating,
   "Boie yudh ma vourneen! Erin go brah!"
Frenchmen advancing – tyrants retreating.[4]   35
   "Boie yudh ma vourneen! Erin go brah!"
We have numbers, and numbers do constitute pow'r.
Let's WILL TO BE FREE – and we're FREE from that hour:
Of *Hibernia*'s sons – yes – we'll then be the flower.
   "Boie yudh ma vourneen! Erin go brah!"   40

Too long have we suffer'd and too long lamented;
   "Boie yudh ma vourneen! Erin go brah!"
By courage undaunted it may be prevented.
   "Boie yudh ma vourneen! Erin go brah!"
No more by oppressors let us be affrighted,   45
But with heart and with hand be firmly UNITED:
For by ERIN GO BRAH! – 'tis thus we'll be righted!
   "Boie yudh ma vourneen! Erin go brah!"

Notes

[2] house
[3] *Victory to you my darling! Ireland for ever* (original).
[4] The French Revolution of 1789, as well as the American Revolution of 1776, were invoked as precedents for nationalist agitation in 1790s' Ireland. The United Irishmen cultivated an alliance with revolutionary France.

The United Real Reformer

Tune: "The Jolly Tinker"

I am a Patriotic Bard,
   That loves the constitution,
This long time I have labour'd hard,
   Against each persecution:
But still in Virtue's path I'll go,   5
   In spite of each alarmer,
By actions, I intend to shew,
   That I'm a real REFORMER.

The PRESS is my *Artillery,*
   No hireling can debar me,   10
To rouse each grand *Auxillary,*
   And thus arrange my *Army* –
I've Reason drawn up in the van,
   And LIBERTY the stormer,
My centre is the "Rights of Man,"[1]   15
   To prove I'm a REFORMER.

When th' Irish Roman Catholics
   (The Bulwark of the Nation,)
Were chous'd by ministerial tricks,
   And lost Emancipation:[2]   20
Belfast, that's fan'd by freedom's air,
   And soars above all clamours,
Espous'd their cause, like gay, sincere
   Enlightned real REFORMERS.

How can the Sons of Ireland   25
   Endure this degradation?
With England we in *Union* stand,
   By scheming machination;
Our money constantly they squeeze,
   From Artisans and Farmers,   30
With pain the pride of *Absentees*
   Is view'd by real REFORMERS.

Our rights are thus infring'd by Knaves,
   Who glory in oppression,
And you all know that to be slaves,   35
   Was always a transgression:
Ourselves we now should extricate,
   Pure Virtue is our armour,
Each maid will then aloud repeat –
   "Success to my REFORMER."   40

We should find a stimulation,
   In ev'ry glowing feature,

Notes

THE UNITED REAL REFORMER

[1] American Thomas Paine's *The Rights of Man* (1791–2).

[2] Catholic Emancipation was included in the United Irishmen platform early in the organization's development.

Of the amiable creation,
  The grandest work of nature:
And now to gain the sweet embrace   45
  Of my dear matchless charmer,
I'll ev'ry danger boldly face,
  And act a real REFORMER.

With every community,
  May HE who made – Unite us!   50
Thus UP in honest unity,
  No danger can affright us –
Our motto's *"Death"* – or – *"Liberty,"*[3]
  We'll free the Isle from swarmers,
Our rights we'll gain – or boldly die   55
  United real REFORMERS.

I'm an United Irishman,
  And ne'er will act contrary,
In Ninety-two, I join'd that plan,
  Of tyranny being weary;   60
Old Erin's rights I'll still defend,
  And never will surrender;
I am its persecuted friend,
  A dauntless bold DEFENDER.

Edward[1]

Tune: *"When bidden to the Wake or Fair"*

What plaintive sounds strike on my ear!
  They're Erin's deep ton'd piteous groans,
Her harp attun'd to sorrow drear,
  In broken numbers join her moans.
In doleful groups around her stand,   5
  Her manly sons (her greatest pride,)
In mourning deep, for by the hand
  Of ruthless villain, EDWARD died.

Th' assassin horde had him beset,
  As slumb'ring on a bed he lay,   10
Arise my Lord, *Swan* cries up get,
  My prisoner, you I make this day.
Unaw'd our gallant CHIEF up steps,
  And in his vengeful hand he takes
His dagger keen – quite hard it gripes,   15
  Then to the savage crew he speaks.

Notes

[3] This may be a reference to American Patrick Henry who declared in 1775, "Give me liberty or give me death."

EDWARD
[1] This poem offers an account of the capture of United Irishmen leader Lord Edward Fitzgerald (son of the duke of Leinster) by Henry Charles Sirr, Major Swan, and Captain Ryan in May 1798. Fitzgerald seriously wounded two of his captors and was himself injured; he died of his injuries in prison on June 4, 1798.

"Come on who dare – your courage shew,
 'Gainst Erin's steady children's CHIEF,
Your burthen'd soul at single blow,
 I'll from your body soon relieve."   20
Fear-stricken at his manly form,
 The blood-stain'd tribe, save *Swan*, back drew;
Who from our Chieftain's potent arm,
 Receiv'd a stroke that made him rue.

Aloud he shriek'd, then *Ryan* came   25
 Unto his aid with trembling step;
Mean Caitiff *Ryan*, lost to shame,
 With deeds most foul was full your cup.
Like vivid light'ning at him flew
 With well-aim'd point, our Hero sweet,   30
The dastard's blood he forthwith drew,
 And left his bowels at his feet.

So wide the gash, so great the gore,
 That tumbling out his entrails came:
Poor grov'ling wretch! you'll never more   35
 Attempt to blast unsullied fame;
A baser death should you await,
 The hangman's rope – not EDWARD's hand,
The gallows-tree should be your fate,
 Your life deserv'd a shameful end.   40

Next came on *Sirr*, half dead with fear,
 Deep stain'd with crimes his guilty mind,
He shook all through, (by EDWARD scared,)
 Like Aspin-leaf before the wind;
With coward step, he advanc'd slow,   45
 Dreading to feel our EDWARD's might,
Tho' eager for to strike a blow,
 Yet fearful to appear in sight.

Assassin-like, he took his stand,
 Behind the door – and there he stood,   50
With pistol charg'd, in either hand,
 So great his thirst for EDWARD's blood;
Upon his brows stood imp of hell,
 Within his heart a Devil foul,
Dire murder dire, and slaughter fell,   55
 Had full possession of his soul.

His bosom-fiend suggested then,
 A bloody deed – a Devil's act –
An hell-fram'd thought ****** ARISE YE MEN,
 Revenge, revenge the horrid fact.   60
Sound, sound aloud the trump of war,
 Proclaim that EDWARD's blood is spill'd!
By traitor's hand, by coward *Sirr*,
 Revenge! revenge! for EDWARD's kill'd.

William Drennan (1754–1820)

William Drennan was born in Belfast, the son of Presbyterian minister Thomas Drennan. He received his early education from his father and in the school of a local Anglican clergyman. He earned his medical degree in Edinburgh in the 1770s and began work as a physician, moving to Dublin in 1789 where he soon had a successful medical practice. A founding member of the Society of United Irishmen, he was charged with sedition in 1794 for his part in publishing the first proclamation of the Society. He was successfully defended by prominent lawyer and fellow-Unitedman John Philpot Curran and continued to be a leader in the Society but left before the 1798 Uprising. He returned to Belfast in 1807 and helped to found the Belfast Academical Institution as well as the short-lived *Belfast Monthly Magazine*. By way of preface to reprinting Drennan's "Wake" in 1843, *The Nation* declared, "Of the United Irishmen, none was so popular as William Drennan ... His song ["Erin"] is one of the finest in the language, and is known everywhere. The following verses ["Wake"] are full of passion – very condensed and terse – the language simple, the imagery sublime."

His first political writings were a series of letters, collected as *Letters of Orellana, an Irish Helot, to the Seven Northern Counties not represented in the National Assembly of Delegates, held at Dublin, October, 1784, for obtaining a more equal representation of the People in the Parliament of Ireland* (1785). He contributed "Erin" to the immensely popular *Paddy's Resource*, and wrote "Wake" to commemorate the death of William Orr, executed, after a dubious trial, for administering the oath of the United Irishmen. After the Uprising, Drennan turned his pen to the debate over the impending Act of Union which would abolish the Irish parliament. He published at least three pamphlets arguing against the Act, and later collected some of his political poetry and essays under his own name in *Fugitive Pieces in Verse and Prose* (1815). His translation of Sophocles' *Electra* appeared in 1817. Long after his death, many of his poems were republished in *Glendalloch, and Other Poems* (1859), a collection that included verse by his sons.

The importance of "Glendalloch" is signaled by the decision to name the 1859 volume after the poem. There is a substantial tradition of writing about the region, including Thomas Moore's "By That Lake Whose Gloomy Shore" (1811), Dion Boucicault's *Arrah-na-Pogue* (1864), and later works such as Dora Sigerson Shorter's *Legend of Glendalough* (1919). Drennan's poem also bears comparison to John Corry's *The Patriot* (1797) for the mingled associations of Irish history with repeated invasion, a landscape that has become a graveyard, and the ideals of the social affections, liberty, and progress. (Drennan was among Corry's subscribers and so had a copy of *The Patriot*.) Corry's poem, written before the failed 1798 Uprising, is optimistic, however, in imagining the successful defence of Irish liberty, while Drennan's "Glendalloch," which the poet dated 1802 and published as well in *The Poetical Register, and Repository of Fugitive Poetry, for 1804* (London, 1806), reveals a much bleaker perspective.

Further reading

Larkin, Frances, ed., *The Trial of William Drennan*. Dublin: Irish Academic Press, 1991.

Thuente, Mary Helen, *The Harp Re-strung: The United Irishmen and the Rise of Literary Nationalism*. Syracuse: Syracuse University Press, 1994.

Vance, Norman, *Irish Literature: A Social History; Tradition, Identity, and Difference*. Oxford: Blackwell, 1990.

William Drennan

Erin

From **Fugitive Pieces in Verse and Prose (1815)**

When Erin first rose from the dark-swelling flood,
God bless'd the green island, He saw it was good:
The Emerald of Europe, it sparkled, it shone,
In the ring of this world the most precious stone!

In her sun, in her soil, in her station, thrice blest,   5
With back turn'd to Britain, her face to the West,
Erin stands proudly insular, on her steep shore,
And strikes her high harp to the ocean's deep roar.

But when its soft tones seem to mourn and to weep,
The dark chain of silence is cast o'er the deep;   10
At the thought of the past, tears gush from her eyes,
And the pulse of the heart makes her white bosom rise. –

"O, sons of green Erin! lament o'er the time
When religion was – war, and our country – a crime;
When men, in God's image, inverted his plan,   15
And moulded their God in the image of man.

When the int'rest of state wrought the general woe;
The stranger – a friend, and the native – a foe;
While the mother rejoic'd o'er her children distress'd,
And clasp'd the invader more close to her breast.   20

When with pale for the body, and pale for the soul,[1]
Church and state join'd in compact to conquer the whole;
And while Shannon ran red with Milesian blood,
Ey'd each other askance, and pronounc'd it was good!

By the groans that ascend from your forefathers' grave,   25
For their country thus left to the brute and the slave,
Drive the Demon of Bigotry home to his den,
And where Britain made brutes, now let Erin make men!

Let my sons, like the leaves of their shamrock, unite,
A partition of sects from one footstalk of right;   30
Give each his full share of this earth, and yon sky,
Nor fatten the slave, where the serpent would die!

Alas, for poor Erin! that some still are seen,
Who would dye the grass red, in their hatred to green!
Yet, oh! when you're up, and they down, let them live,   35
Then, yield them that mercy which they did not give.

Notes ───────────────────────────────────

Erin
[1] The word *pale* is Norman-French for fence, and originally
referred to the portion of Ireland ruled by the English when
Norman-French was the language of the English elite.

Arm of Erin! prove strong; but be gentle as brave,
And, uplifted to strike, still be ready to save;
Nor one feeling of vengeance presume to defile
The cause, or the men, of the EMERALD ISLE.[2]   40

The cause it is good, and the men they are true;
And the green shall outlive both the orange and blue;
And the daughters of Erin her triumph shall share,
With their full-swelling chest, and their fair-flowing hair.

Their bosoms heave high for the worthy and brave,   45
But no coward shall rest on that soft swelling wave;
Men of Erin! awake, and make haste to be blest!
Rise, arch of the ocean! rise, queen of the West!"

Wake[1]

From Fugitive Pieces in Verse and Prose (1815)

1797

Here, our brother worthy lies,
Wake not him with women's cries;
Mourn the way that mankind ought;
Sit, in silent trance of thought.

Write his merits on your mind,   5
Morals pure, and manners kind;
On his head, as on a hill,
Virtue plac'd her citadel.

Why cut off in palmy youth?
Truth he spoke, and acted truth;   10
"Countrymen, Unite!" he cried,
And died, for what his Saviour died!

God of Peace, and God of Love,
Let it not thy vengeance move!
Let it not thy lightnings draw,   15
A nation guillotin'd by law!

Hapless nation! rent and torn,
Early wert thou taught to mourn!
Warfare of six hundred years!
Epochs mark'd by blood and tears.   20

Hunted thro' thy native grounds,
A flung reward to human hounds,

[2] In 1815, Drennan added a lengthy note that stakes his claim to coining the phrase *the emerald isle*: "in a party song, written without the rancour of party, in the year 1795. From the frequent use made of the term since that time, he fondly hopes that it will gradually become associated

with the name of his country, as descriptive of its prime natural beauty, and its inestimable value."

WAKE
[1] This poem was published under various titles, including "The Wake of William Orr."

Each one pull'd, and tore his share,
Emblem of thy deep despair!

Hapless nation, hapless land,   25
Heap of uncementing sand!
Crumbled by a foreign weight,
Or by worse, domestic hate!

God of Mercy, God of Peace,
Make the mad confusion cease!   30
O'er the mental chaos move,
Through it speak the light of love!

Monstrous and unhappy sight!
Brothers' blood will not unite.
Holy oil, and holy water,   35
Mix – and fill the earth with slaughter.

Who is she, with aspect wild? –
The widow'd Mother, with her child;
Child, new stirring in the womb,
Husband, waiting for the tomb.   40

Angel of this holy place!
Calm her soul, and whisper, Peace!
Cord, nor axe, nor guillotine,
Make the sentence, not the sin.

Here we watch our brother's sleep;   45
Watch with us, but do not weep:
Watch with us, thro' dead of night –
But expect the morning light.

Conquer Fortune – persevere –
Lo! it breaks – the morning clear!   50
The chearful cock awakes the skies;
The day is come – Arise, arise!

Lines, On Some Improvements in the Town of Belfast, Superintended by the Marchioness of D——

From Fugitive Pieces in Verse and Prose (1815)

Dire was the magic, tho' the art was vain,
When Birnam wood march'd forth to Dunsinane.[1]
But here delusion seems to cheat the view –
We look again, and find th' enchantment true.
With higher art our fair magician grac'd,   5
Wields at her will the potent spell of taste:
In the charm'd circle where she takes her stand,

Notes ──

LINES, ON SOME IMPROVEMENTS
[1] See Shakespeare's *Macbeth*, especially Act V, scene v.

Ev'n rooted trees obey her beck'ning hand;
Fast from their forest heights descend in file,
And, waving, wait the sanction of her smile!   10
Where the axe fell'd, nor slacken'd in its toil,
Here a new wood adopts the grateful soil,
Breathes health and fragrance through the ambient air,
And makes the town reflect the country fair.
Then wave again your branches, when you meet   15
The fair enchantress, with a whisper sweet:
Let ev'ry fibre strike a firmer root,
Let the green blood in swifter eddies shoot;
To shape her name strive ev'ry sportive spray,
Prepare for her, ye flow'rs, your best bouquet,   20
And ev'ry leaf announce the radiant MAY!

Glendalloch

From Fugitive Pieces in Verse and Prose (1815)

1802

Th' enchantment of the place has bound
All Nature in a sleep profound;
And silence of the ev'ning hour
Hangs o'er GLENDALLOCH's hallow'd tow'r;[1]
A mighty grave-stone, set by Time,   5
That, 'midst these ruins, stands sublime,
To point the else-forgotten heap,
Where princes and where prelates sleep;
Where Tuathal rests th' unnoted head,
And Keivin finds a softer bed:[2]   10
"Sods of the soil" that verdant springs
Within the sepulchre of kings.

      HERE – in the circling mountain's shade,
In this vast vault, by Nature made,

Notes

GLENDALLOCH
[1] GLENDALLOCH, or Glyn of the Double Lake, is situated in Wicklow, a County which presents an abridgement of all that is pleasing in Nature. This particular Glyn is surrounded on all sides, except to the East, by stupendous mountains, whose vast perpendicular height throws a gloom on the vale below, well suited to inspire religious dread and horror. It has, therefore, been, from the most distant times, haunted with those spectres of illusive fancy, which delight to hover in the gloom of ignorance and superstition. It is said to have been an asylum of the Druids, who fled from Roman tyranny. It was afterwards the refuge of the Monks, who established there a different religious rule, in which mind and body were bound to the same bondage of five years' silence, severe fasts, obedience unto death; and this lake became their dead sea. Here, however, was the school of the West, an ark that preserved the remains of literature from the deluge of barbarism which overspread the rest of Europe. Here, the ancient Britons took refuge from the Saxons, and the native Irish from the incursions of the Danes. On the round tower of Glendalloch was often blown the horn of war. Amidst a silent and melancholy waste, it still raises its head above the surrounding fragments, as if moralizing on the ruins of our country, and the wreck of its legislative independence. We think of MARIUS, when he said to his lictor, "Go, and tell that you have seen Marius sitting on the *ruins* of Carthage!" (author). Marius was a general and consul of Rome who, on the losing side of one of Rome's political conflicts, was sentenced to death. Those charged with his execution would not kill the elderly Marius, however, and Marius fled to Carthage, where he was refused entrance and made this remark.

[2] Tuathal, legendary Irish king; St. Kevin.

Whose tow'ring roof excludes the skies 15
With savage Kyle's stupendous size;
While Lugduff heaves his moory height,
And giant Broccagh bars the light;[3]
Here – when the British spirit, broke,
Had fled from Nero's iron yoke,[4] 20
And sought this dreary dark abode,
To save their altars and their God,
From cavern black, with mystic gloom,
(Cradle of Science, and its tomb,)
Where Magic had its early birth, 25
Which drew the Sun and Moon to earth,
From hollow'd rock, and devious cell,
Where Mystery was fond to dwell,
And, in the dark and deep profound,
To keep th' eternal secret bound, 30
(Recorded by no written art,
The deep memorial of the heart,)
In flowing robe, of spotless white,
Th' Arch-Druid issued forth to light;
Brow-bound with leaf of holy oak, 35
That never felt the woodman's stroke.
Behind his head a crescent shone,
Like to the new-discover'd moon;
While, flaming, from his snowy vest,
The plate of judgment clasp'd his breast. 40
Around him press'd the illumin'd throng,
Above him rose the light of song;
And from the rocks and woods around
Return'd the fleet-wing'd sons of sound.

"MAKER OF TIME! we mortals wait 45
To hail thee at thy Eastern gate;
Where, these huge mountains thrown aside,
Expands for thee a portal wide.
Descend upon this altar, plac'd
Amidst Glendalloch's awful waste: 50
So shall the paean of thy praise
Arise, to meet thy rising rays,
From Elephanta's sculptur'd cave,[5]
To Eiren, of the Western wave;
And the rejoicing earth prolong 55
The orbit of successive song:
For we by thy reflection shine –
Who knows our God, becomes divine.

Notes

[3] Kyle Hill is in Leinster; Lugduff is a mountain in Wicklow, and Brocagh is near Lough Neath in Antrim.

[4] Nero, first-century Roman emperor. Britain was conquered by Rome (under Claudius) in AD 43, and remained part of the Roman empire until 410.

[5] The Elephanta Caves are in India; Drennan is charting the movement of the sun (the "maker of time") from east (India) to west (Ireland).

"But ah! what dim and dismal shade
Casts this strange horror o'er the glade,   60
Causes e'en hearts of brutes to quake,
And shudders o'er the stagnant lake?
What demon, enemy of good,
Rolls back on earth this night of blood?
What dragon, of enormous size,   65
Devours thee in thy native skies?
O, save thy children from his breath,
From chaos, and eternal death!"

The Druid mark'd the destin'd hour –
He mounted slow yon sacred tow'r;   70
Then stood upon its cap sublime,
A hoary chronicler of time;
His head, amidst the deathful gloom,
Seem'd Hope, new-risen from the tomb;
And, while he rais'd to Heav'n his hand,   75
That minister of high command
The terrors of the croud repress'd,
And smooth'd their troubl'd wave to rest –
Then spoke – and round the pillar'd stone
Deep silence drank his silver tone.   80

"He, who, from elemental strife,
Spoke all these worlds to light and life,
Who guides them thro' th' abyss above
In circles of celestial love,
Has this vast panorame design'd   85
A mirror of th' eternal mind.
To view of superficial eyes,
In broken points this mirror lies:
And knowledge, to these points apply'd,
Are lucid specks of human pride.   90
From beams of truth distorted, cross'd,
The image of our God is lost.
Those, only those become divine,
Who can the fractur'd parts combine:
Nature to them, and them alone,   95
Reflects from ev'ry part but ONE;
Their eagle eye, around them cast,
Descries the future from the past.
Justice will not annihilate
What Goodness did at first create.   100
The mirror, sully'd with the breath,
Suffers slight change – it is not death
That shadows yon bright orb of day:
See! while I speak, the orient ray
Breaks, sudden, thro' the darksome scene,   105
And Heav'n regains its blue serene.
And soon the mild propitious pow'r
Which consecrates this ev'ning hour,
Shall bend again her silver bow,

Again her softer day shall throw, 110
Smooth the dark brow of savage Kyle,
And grim Glendalloch teach to smile.
Now, Druids, hail the joyous light;
Fear God – be bold – and do the right."

He ceas'd – their chorus, sweet and strong, 115
Roll'd its full stream of sainted song.

"O! fountain of our sacred fire,
To whom our kindred souls aspire,
(Struck from the vast chaotic dark,
As from these flints we strike the spark,) 120
Thou Lord of Life and Light and Joy,
Great to preserve, but not destroy,
On us, thy favor'd offspring, shine!
Who know their God must grow divine.
And when thy radiant course is done, 125
Thou, shadow of another sun,
Shalt fade into his brighter sky,
And time become eternity."

But past, long past, the DRUID reign;
The CROSS o'ertopt the Pagan fane. 130
To this remote asylum flew
A priesthood of another hue;
More like the raven than the dove,
Tho' murm'ring much of faith and love.

A lazy sullen virtue slept 135
O'er the dull lake: around it crept
The self-tormenting anchorite,
And shunn'd th' approach of cheerful light;
Yet darkly long'd to hoard a name,
And in the cavern grop'd for fame. 140
Where Nature reign'd, in solemn state,
There Superstition chose her seat;
Her vot'ries knew, with subtle art,
Thro' wond'ring eyes to chain the heart;
By terrors of the scene, to draw 145
And tame the savage to their law,
Then seat themselves on Nature's throne,
And make her mighty spell their own.
The charming sorc'ry of the place
Gave Miracle a local grace; 150
And, from the mountain-top sublime,
The Genius of our changeful clime
A sort of pleasing panic threw,
Which felt each passing phantom true.

E'en at a more enlighten'd hour 155
We feel this visionary pow'r;
And, when the meanest of his trade,
The ragged minstrel of the glade,

With air uncouth, and visage pale,
Pours forth the legendary tale,   160
The Genius, from his rock-built pile,
Awful, looks down, and checks our smile.
We listen – then a pleasing thrill
Creeps thro' our frame, and charms our will,
Till, fill'd with forms fantastic, wild,   165
We feign – and then become the child.

    We see the hooded fathers take
Their silent circuit round the lake:
Silent – except a wailful song,
Extorted by the leathern thong.   170

    Cronan, Cornloch, Lochaun, Doquain,
Superiors of the servile train,
Envelop'd in their cowls, they move,
And shun the God of Light and Love.

    Who leads the black procession on?   175
St. Keivin's living skeleton,
That travels through this vale of tears,
Beneath the yoke of six score years;
Sustains his step a crozier wand;
Extended stiff one wither'd hand,   180
To which the blackbird flew distress'd,
And found a kind protecting nest;
There dropt her eggs, while outstretch'd stood
The hand – till she had hatch'd her brood!

    Hark! what a peal, sonorous, clear,   185
Strikes, from yon tow'r, the tingling ear!
(No more of fire the worship'd tow'r;
The holy water quench'd its pow'r.)
And now, from every floor, a bell
Tolls Father Martin's funeral knell,   190
Who slipt his foot on holy ground,
And plung'd into the lake profound;
Or, by the load of life oppress'd,
Sought refuge in its peaceful breast.

    What! – Did not, peace-delighted, dwell   195
The hermit of the mountain cell?

    No – 'twas a cage of iron rule,
Of pride and selfishness the school,
Of dark desires, and doubts profane,
And harsh repentings, late, but vain;   200
To fast – to watch – to scourge – to praise
The golden legend of their days;
To idolize a stick or bone,
And turn the bread of life to stone;
Till, mock'd and marr'd by miracles,   205
Great Nature from her laws rebels,

And man becomes, by monkish art,
A prodigy – without a heart.
No friend sincere, no smiling wife,
The blessing and the balm of life;   210
And Knowledge, by a forg'd decree,
Still stands an interdicted tree.
– Majestic tree! that proudly waves
Thy branching words, thy letter leaves; –
Whether, with strength that time commands,   215
An oak of ages, Homer stands,
Or Milton, high-topt mountain pine,
Aspiring to the light divine;
Or laurel of perennial green,
The Shakespeare[6] of the living scene, –   220
Whate'er thy form – in prose sublime,
Or train'd by art, and prun'd by rhyme,
All hail, thou priest-forbidden tree!
For God had bless'd, and made thee free.
God did the foodful blessing give,   225
That man might eat of it, and live;
But they who have usurp'd his throne,
To keep his Paradise their own,
Have spread around a demon's breath,
And nam'd thee Upas, tree of death.   230
Thy root is Truth, thy stem is Pow'r,
And Virtue thy consummate flow'r.
Receive the circling nations' vows,
And the world's garland deck thy boughs.

From the bleak Scandinavian shore   235
The DANE his raven standard bore:
It rose amidst the whit'ning foam,
When the fierce robber hated home;
And, as he plough'd the wat'ry way,
The raven seem'd to scent its prey;   240
Outstretch'd the gloomy om'nous wing,
For feast of carnage war must bring.
'Twas HERE the Christian savage stood,
To seal his faith in flame and blood.
The sword of midnight murder fell   245
On the calm sleeper of the cell.
Flash'd thro' the trees with horrid glare
The flames – and poison'd all the air.
Her song the lark began to raise,
As she had seen the solar blaze;   250
But, smote with terrifying sound,
Forsook the death-polluted ground;
And never since, these limits near,
Was heard to hymn her vigil clear.

Notes ──────────────────────────────────

[6] Classical Greek epic poet, Homer, and English authors
John Milton (1608–74) and William Shakespeare (1564–1616).

This periodic ravage fell,   255
How oft our bloody annals tell!
But, ah! how much of woe untold,
How many groans of young and old,
Has Hist'ry, in this early age,
Sunk in the margin of her page,   260
Which, at the best, but stamps a name
On vice, and misery, and shame.

Thus flow'd in flames, and blood, and tears,
A lava of two hundred years;
And tho' some seeds of science seen,   265
Shot forth, in heart-enliv'ning green,
To clothe the gaps of civil strife,
And smooth a savage-temper'd life,
Yet soon new torrents black'ning came,
Wrapt the young growth in rolling flame,   270
And, as it blasted, left behind
Dark desolation of the mind.

But now no more the rugged North
Pours half its population forth;
Nor more that iron-girded coast   275
The sheath of many a sworded host,
That rush'd abroad for bloody spoil,
Still won on hapless Erin's soil,
Where Discord wav'd her flaming brand,
Sure guide to a devoted land;   280
A land, by fav'ring Nature nurs'd,
By human fraud and folly curs'd,
Which never foreign friend shall know,
While to herself the direst foe!

Is that a friend, who, sword in hand,   285
Leaps, pond'rous, on the sinking strand,
Full plum'd, with ANGLO-NORMAN pride –
The base adult'rer by his side
Pointing to Leinster's fertile plain,
Where (wretch!) he thinks once more to reign?   290
Yes, thou shalt reign, and live to know
Thy own, amid thy country's woe!
That country's curse upon thy head,
Torments thee living, haunts thee dead;
And, howling thro' the vaults of Time,   295
E'en now proclaims and damns thy crime:
Six cen'tries past, her curse still lives,
Nor yet forgets, nor yet forgives
DERMOD, who bade the Normans come
To sack and spoil his native home.[7]   300

Notes

[7] In this verse and those following, Drennan refers to Dermot Mac Murchada, king of Leinster, who was deposed amidst various territorial wranglings in Ireland; he went to a former ally, Henry II of England, for help. England invaded Ireland in support of Dermod in 1169, and then returned in 1171 with a papal bull from Pope Adrian IV (English by birth) granting Henry II sovereignty over Ireland, marking the beginning of English colonialism in Ireland.

Sown by this traitor's bloody hand,
Dissension rooted in the land;
Mix'd with the seed of springing years,
Their hopeful blossoms steep'd in tears –
And late posterity can tell   305
The fruitage rotted as it fell.

Then Destiny was heard to wail,
While on black stone of INISFAIL
She mark'd this nation's dreadful doom,
And character'd the woes to come.   310
Battle, and plague, and famine, plac'd
The epochs of th' historic waste;
And, crowning every ill of life,
Self-conquer'd by domestic strife.

Was this the scheme of mercy, plann'd   315
In ADRIEN's heart, thro' HENRY's hand,
To draw the savage from his den,
And train the IRISHRY to men,
To fertilize the human clay,
And turn the stubborn soil to day?   320
No – 'twas two Englishmen, who play'd
The mast'ry of their sep'rate trade:
Conquest was then, and ever since,
The real design of priest and prince;
And, while his flag the king unfurl'd,   325
The father of the Christian world
Bless'd it, and hail'd the hallow'd deed –
For none but SAVAGES would bleed;
Yet, when those savages began
To turn upon their hunter, man –   330
Rush'd from their forests, to assail
Th' encroaching circuit of the pale –
The cause of quarrel still was good;
The ENEMY must be subdued.

Subdued! The nation still was gor'd   335
By law more penal than the sword;
Till Vengeance, with a tiger start,
Sprang from the covert of the heart.
Resistance took a blacker name,
The scaffold's penalty and shame;   340
There was the wretched REBEL led,
Uplifted there the TRAITOR's head.

Still there was hope th' avenging hand
Of Heav'n would spare a hapless land;
That days of ruin, havoc, spoil,   345
Would cease to desolate the soil;
Justice, tho' late, begin her course,
– Subdued the lion law of force.
There was a hope, that, civil hate

No more a policy of state,   350
Religion not the tool of pow'r,
Her only office, to adore –
That Education, HERE, might stand,
The harp of Orpheus[8] in her hand,
Of power t'infuse the social charm,   355
With love of peace and order warm,
The ruder passions all repress'd,
And tam'd the tigers of the breast,
By love of country and of kind,
And magic of a master mind.   360

   As from yon dull and stagnant lake
The streams begin to live, and take
Their course thro' Clara's wooded vale,
Kiss'd by the health-inspiring gale,
Heedless of wealth their banks may hold,   365
They glide, neglectful of the gold,
Yet seem to hope a Shakespeare's name
To give *our* Avon deathless fame;
So, from the savage barren heart,
The streams of science and of art   370
May spread their soft refreshing green,
To vivify the moral scene.

   O, vanish'd hope! – O, transient boast!
O COUNTRY, gain'd but to be lost!
Gain'd by a nation, rais'd, inspir'd,   375
By eloquence and virtue fir'd,
By trans-atlantic glory stung,
By GRATTAN's energetic tongue,[9]
By Parliament that felt its trust,
By Britain – terrify'd, and just.   380
Lost – by thy chosen children sold;
And conquer'd – not by steel, but gold:
Lost – by a low and servile great,
Who smile upon their country's fate,
Crouching to gain the public choice,   385
And sell it by their venal voice.
Lost – to the world and future fame,
Remember'd only in a name,
Once in the courts of Europe known
To claim a self-dependent throne.   390
Thy ancient records torn, and tost
Upon the waves that beat thy coast;
The mock'ry of a mongrel race,
Sordid, illiterate, and base.

Notes ───────────────────────────────────────

[8] Mythical musician (Greek) who could tame animals with his music.

[9] Henry Grattan, member of the Irish parliament, whose oratory helped secure some restoration of power to the Irish parliament in 1782 (see R. B. Sheridan's "Union of Ireland with Great Britain" above, p. 114).

To science lost, and letter'd truth;   395
The genius of thy native youth,
To Cam or Isis glad to roam,[10]
Nor keep a heart or hope for home:
Thy spark of independence dead;
Thy life of life, thy freedom, fled.   400

    Where shall her sad remains be laid?
Where invocate her solemn shade?

    HERE be the mausoléum plac'd,
In this vast vault, this silent waste; –
Yon mould'ring pillar, 'midst the gloom,   405
Finger of Time! shall point her tomb;
While silence of the ev'ning hour
Hangs o'er Glendalloch's ruin'd tow'r.

Mary Leadbeater (1758–1826)

Mary Leadbeater was born in Co. Kildare to the Quaker Shackleton family who ran a school there; her father, Richard Shackleton, attended the school at the same time as Edmund Burke, and subsequently ran the school. She lived in Ballitore her whole life, marrying William Leadbeater, a local farmer, in 1791, but she was an active letter-writer, corresponding with many of the leading authors of her day, including Edmund Burke and Maria Edgeworth. Like Edgeworth, she often wrote didactic literature which promoted domestic and religious virtues.

She published *Extracts and Original Anecdotes; For the Improvement of Youth* anonymously in 1794; a mix of short poems and prose pieces, many on biblical subjects and moral themes, this volume also included material on the history of the Quaker community and a number of short pieces opposed to slavery. The authorship of the pieces is often uncertain; the "extracts" of the title as well as the wording of some of the pieces suggest that she is anthologizing edifying passages from other works. (There is no preface or editorial apparatus to identify her sources.) All of the selections here are from the final section, "Poetry," which appears to be her own work. Her next volume, *Poems* (1808), shares a number of themes with *Extracts*, but is more sophisticated in its versification than the earlier poems, although part of the difference may be due to the fact that *Extracts* was a book for young readers and *Poems* was not.

Leadbeater was also an early and significant contributor to what became a substantial nineteenth-century genre – writing on Irish rural life – though her aims were more pedagogical than ethnographic. Her writing in this vein began with the first and second series of *Cottage Dialogues among the Irish Peasantry* (1811, 1813), composed of brief dialogues, many on such moral themes as "Fidelity," "Cruelty (Wanton)," and "Snuff-taking." She then

[10] The universities of Cambridge (on the river Cam) and Oxford (on a section of the Thames known as the Isis).

published *The Landlord's Friend* (1813), *Tales for Cottagers* (with Elizabeth Shackleton, 1814), and *Cottage Biography* (1822). Her other works included *The Pedlars: A Tale* (1824) and the posthumous publication of her account of local Ballitore history from 1766 to 1823 as *The Leadbeater Papers* (1862), a crucial work of local history that includes accounts of the 1798 Uprising.

Further reading

Gandy, Clara, "The Condition and Character of the Irish Peasantry as Seen in the *Annals* and *Cottage Dialogues* of Mary Leadbeater," *Women and Literature* 3 (1975): 28–38.

Rodgers, Nini, "Two Quakers and a Utilitarian: The Reaction of Three Irish Women Writers to the Problem of Slavery, 1789–1807," *Proceedings of the Royal Irish Academy* 100 (2000): 137–57.

On Youth, Beauty, Wealth and Virtue
(Addrest to a Child)

From **Extracts and Original Anecdotes** (1794)

> Blossom of the opening spring,
> Gentle Fair, one, hear me sing.
> Youth's jocund, and blithe, and gay
> Youth is fleet, and melts away.
> Beauty's lovely, fragrant, fair: 5
> Beauty was, and is not there.
> Wealth's a glittering, pleasing toy:
> Wealth's a fleeting, fading joy.
> Virtue learn, be early wise;
> Virtue only mounts the skies.   10

Divine Odes

From **Extracts and Original Anecdotes** (1794)

1. Supplication

> When I survey the bright design
>   Of Heaven, in forming Man,
> My labouring thoughts revere the cause,
>   Whence all effects began.
>
> With silence oft and rising awe   5
>   I run the system o'er,
> Unfit to write, unfit to speak,
>   Unworthy to adore.
>
> Yet, Lord, to one that's weak and poor
>   A little light bestow,   10
> Then will my soul with humble joy
>   To thee in praises flow.
>
> And as the Sun diffuses light
>   Through blue immensity,

The love that now my bosom feels
    Must surely flow from thee.   15

Though we the steeps of science scale,
    To pleasure's fane descend,
All these and each terrestial walk
    With disappointments end.   20

But if according to thy will,
    To know ourselves we seek,
Ourselves *thus* known, is knowing thee
    Then knowledge is complete.

Thou by thy solemn, lasting word,   25
    Thyself for ever binds',
That these thoul't teach, who wait thy will,
    With pure and lowly minds.

Nor deem the attestation vain,
    If thus my tongue declare   30
In feeble, broken, tender'd plight,
    My God, I've felt thy care.

Then give me strength to carry on
    What's oft and oft begun,
Give me still more and more to know   35
    The mission of thy Son.

For oft with deep concern I fear
    In speculative light;
The lowly Lord I but behold –
    O help my feeble sight.   40

And oft I've thought with fervent mind
    To make a league with thee
Still to obey – but, ah! I fear
    My incapacity.

And he that violates his vows   45
    With God, or man, must fall –
Oh make thy grace arise in me
    Triumphant over all.

Thou knowest when pleasure oft has swell'd
    My high-elated heart,   50
A secret sigh has stole to thee
    Still to retain a part.

And well thou know'st, Supreme and Wise,
    In all the gloom of thought,
My soul in weak humility   55
    Thy comfort oft has sought.

Thus still when on the tide of joy,
    I roll with prosperous gales,
Give me a sense of human want,
    To curb the flowing sails.   60

And when amid the storm of life,
  My shatter'd bark is tost,
Give me the anchor of thy hope
  To gain the promis'd coast.

II.   Praise

How oft, my God, to sound thy praise   65
  The holy man of old,
Judea's scepter would resign,
  And string the harp of gold!

And fain would I, though in the dust
  My trembling lips are laid,   70
Once more resume the sacred theme
  I late in fear essay'd.

Lo from the dust 'tis thine to raise
  The pure mellifluent lay,
To bid the very rocks break forth   75
  And vocal homage pay.

Creation speaks thy wonderous skill,
  All own thy power supreme,
From yon bright orb, unto the mote
  That dances in its beam.   80

Through all thy works is heard a song,
  The beasts that graze the plain,
The tenants of the verdant bough,
  The natives of the main.

The waxing moon, the waning light,   85
  The sun with golden rays,
The starry thousands of the sky,
  All mingle in thy praise.

Then can the human mind alone,
  A particle of thee,   90
At due returns forbear to rise
  In hymns of extasy!

Beyond the bounds of night and day
  Extends thy sovereign power,
Tho' Time's to thee a point thou cares   95
  For beings of an hour.

Tho' at thy feet heaven's golden works,
  In all their splendours rise,
One humble act of good below,
  'Scapes not thy gracious eyes,   100

Tho' throngs of Angels round thee stand,
  And tune their harps aloud,
The feeble prayer that's scarce essay'd,
  Breaks through the warbling croud.

The sigh that bursts from virtue's breast   105
    Is heard before thy throne,
The pious tear in silence shed
    Falls not to thee unknown.

Even I a worm before thy sight
    Have felt thy mercy shine,   110
And, tho' a wanderer, oft had cause
    To bless the beam divine.

When through affliction's deepening vale,
    My feet thou hast convey'd,
Thy kind assistance would prevail,   115
    Thy wisdom cheer the shade.

When restless on the sickening couch
    My weary limbs have lain,
Thou through the dark and toilsome hours
    Would still the nerve of pain.   120

Thou bring'st me through the perils of day,
    Safe to my humble shed,
Thou smoothst my pillow, sweet with toil,
    Whereon to lay my head.

Oft as thy goodness to these eyes   125
    Renews the morning-light,
Oft as thou draws around my head
    The closing shades of night.

Oft as thou bathes my walk with tears
    Then bids the moments glow,   130
So oft O teach the willing theme
    Of gratitude to flow.

And when translated from these vales
    Where feeble mortals groan,
Retain me in thy choir of love,   135
    Though humblest of thy throne.

The Negro (Addressed to Edmund Burke)[1]

From Poems (1808)

O thou, this country's boast, this age's pride,
Freedom's firm friend, and Pity's gen'rous guide,
Great Burke! whose voice, when wretchedness complains,

Notes

THE NEGRO
[1] Leadbeater dated this poem 1789, soon after English politician William Wilberforce began his campaign in the British
parliament to abolish slavery; the Abolition Act, which
ended the slave trade only, would not be passed until 1807
(see R. B. Sheridan's "Abolition of Slavery" above, p. 117).

Humanity's invaded rights maintains.
Hark! Nature speaks in injur'd Africk's right,   5
And deeds of horror are disclos'd to light: –
Thou wert not silent that important day,
On such a theme thou couldst not silent stay.
When such a voice arose in such debate,
And Truth roll'd onward with impetuous weight,   10
Who dar'd to vindicate the impious deed,
And with unblushing front for slav'ry plead?

　　Britain, thy laws are gen'rous, wise and good,
Did not stern Justice stain her sword with blood:
Still prompt to curb the spoiler's cruel hand,   15
And chase oppression from thy favour'd land.
And shall these laws, to foster freedom made, –
Shall these defend oppression's guilty trade?
Shall rapine wild, shall murder, foul with gore,
Ravage, unblam'd, affrighted Africk's shore;   20
And vilest treach'ry basely bear away,
From the lov'd native land, the human prey;
And vent'rous man resolve, (more rash than brave)
Resolve to make his fellow-man a slave? –

　　But that hard heart, which could not here relent,   25
Soon finds the crime become the punishment:
The gen'rous boast of liberty is flown,
The seeds of vengeance, are by slav'ry sown;
Ruling dejected men with sov'reign sway,
The Tyrant looks that *all* mankind obey.   30
With disappointed pride his haughty breast
Burns, and tumultuous passions rack his rest:
Or, in their wretched huts while captives weep,
See keen remorse, rous'd by the wailings deep,
Stalk round his nightly couch, and murder sleep!   35
What though wealth on thee pour her golden flood,
(Ah, dearly purchas'd with thy brother's blood!)
Wealth buys not peace: – the poor man pities thee: –
Wouldst thou be happy? – set thy captives free.

　　How oft did Woolman's[2] tears these woes deplore,   40
When that pure spirit mortal clothing wore!
He stood a sign the wond'ring world among,
Nor touch'd the product of oppressive wrong:
He saw, he mourn'd the hapless Negro's fate,
Bound in the horrors of a captive state;   45
Saw torn asunder Nature's tend'rest ties,
To bid th' unfeeling master's heaps arise,
And deeds of deadly die and foulest shame
Affix dishonour to the Christian name;

Notes ─────────────────────────────────

[2] John Woolman (1720–72), English Quaker abolitionist.

Heard the deep groans the sable bosoms rend: 50
(Shall not these groans to pitying Heav'n ascend?)
"And these are they," he cried, "whose lab'ring hands
With ceaseless toil maintain these peopled lands;
To them the means of life are scarce supplied,
While their lords revel in luxurious pride: 55
And yet the right of liberty is theirs;
No duty dooms them to these servile carcs;
And though proud man has mercy's law denied,
These are the souls for which a Saviour died,
And how we act to these – we must reply   60
To Him, who views mankind with equal eye."

   So spoke the Sage; – and glad his heart had been,
Had he this dawning day of freedom seen.
O favour'd age! – the genial beams expand
The feeling bosom, and the lib'ral hand;   65
The poor are pitied, all are Nature's sons,
And soften'd man his abject brother owns;
The youth to learning and to labour trains,
And smooths the couch where pale disease complains.
E'en on the cell where guilt and mis'ry lie,   70
Streams the sweet ray from Mercy's gracious eye;
For, rank'd in Virtue's cause, her chiefs appear,
Illustrious names to future ages dear!
Not theirs the bloody pomp of martial meed,
But brighter honours crown the nobler deed.   75

   There princely Leopold[3] his sway maintains,
Mild as the breeze which fans his Tuscan plains;
Though strictest Justice guards the favour'd shore,
He bids the sword of Justice slay no more;
He deem'd that Nature's laws no right could have   80
To take that life the God of Nature gave.

   Where the deserted babes protection find,
Their little lives to strangers' hands consign'd,
There noble Arabella's[4] worth is tried,
Her sex's glory and her nation's pride: 85
While gen'rous Raikes[5] bids idle sport give way,
And useful lore defend the solemn day.

   Lo! Howard,[6] like a pitying angel, speeds
From clime to clime, while mis'ry's cause he pleads,
The dungeon's depth all resolute explores,   90
Though putrid steams bedew the iron doors.

Notes

[3] Likely to be Leopold I, grand duke of Tuscany from 1765 to 1790.

[4] Arabella was a common name, so this reference cannot be definitively identified.

[5] Robert Raikes (1736–1811), English member of the Sunday school movement which sought to educate the poor on Sundays, their only non-working day.

[6] John Howard (1726–90), English prison reformer.

The sable vail see dauntless Clarkson[7] rend,
And bold avow himself the captive's friend;
Invoking sacred Pity's heav'nly rain,
To wash the blood which rusts upon his chain.   95

   There, Burke, thy lov'd, thine honour'd name shall stand,
And add new splendour to the godlike band.
The gracious Father, universal Friend,
To whom the cries of guiltless blood ascend,
Has to thy charge superior gifts assign'd,   100
And bless'd thee with the love of human kind: –
O then continue still, thus doubly blest,
Thy gen'rous zeal to succour the distrest.
Let proud Oppression from thy voice retire,
While the rapt nations kindle at thy fire;   105
Let either India echo back thy name,
While conscious Virtue yields the dearest fame.

   And when thy noble soul shall wing its flight
To the pure realms of liberty and light;
There, where the wicked shall no more molest,   110
There, where the wounded, wearied spirits rest,
There, where the captives meet, their sorrows o'er,
And tremble at th' oppressor's voice no more;
Amid the holy bands who glorious shine,
For ever hymning forth their songs divine;   115
The Patriarchs just, by early Nature blest
With the first sweets of her maternal breast;
Th' Apostles, who the sacred mandates bore
Of universal love from shore to shore;
And the meek Martyrs, with their precious blood   120
Sealing those truths a blinded world withstood: –
Amid these holy bands, that peaceful fold,
Shalt thou the naked Negro-slave behold,
Whose manly limbs the servile chain confin'd,
While heathen darkness wrapp'd his fetter'd mind.   125
This work of God, the spirit and the frame,
His tyrant fellow-man depress'd with shame.
What though his ear no social lip inform'd! –
The heart He made, the gracious Maker warm'd:
Though small his knowledge, yet his guide was true;   130
He kept that guide, and practis'd what he knew.

The Triumph of Terror

From **Poems** (1808)

On the morning in which Ballitore was given up to the military, the life of an old man was attacked: he was rescued by his daughter: but epileptick fits were the consequence of the shock which she received, and which caused her untimely death.

Notes ————————————————————————

[7] Thomas Clarkson (1760–1846), English abolitionist.

The morning, unconscious of horrors, arose,
    The whispering Zephyr breath'd soft thro' the shade;
And Nature, awaken'd from balmy repose,
    Her charms all bespangled with dew-drops display'd.

But hark! in the vale so secluded and sweet,   5
    The cries of destruction and misery blend;
And 'mid the green boughs, once of peace the retreat,
    The pitiless flames, wing'd with vengeance, ascend.

Oh what wrought this change? 'twas a people misled
    In deeds of rebellion and strife to engage: –   10
Yet listen to mercy; – the guilty are fled;
    Oh let not the guiltless fall victims to rage!

"Oh stay thy hand, soldier, – Oh pity my sire,
    And from his hoar head turn thy weapon aside:
Or, if thou a sacrifice seek to thine ire,   15
    Then deep in my breast let thy weapon be died"!

Filial Piety pleaded; – the soldier withdrew;
    And Ferdinand rose, while his beating heart glow'd:
Then swift to his daughter's fond bosom he flew,
    For now to each other existence they ow'd.   20

But ah! that fond bosom had agony seiz'd,
    With a gripe too severe e'en for Hope to unbind;
And what though the tumults of war were appeas'd,
    The fatal impression still dwelt on her mind.

'Twas then that the triumph of Terror began,   25
    And youth's sprightly grace from that moment decay'd:
Her eyes lost their lustre; and wither'd and wan
    Was that cheek on which Health once in dimples had play'd.

Her delicate nerves by convulsions were strain'd,
    Her eye-balls all haggard so wildly would rove;   30
Yet Reason unshaken her empire maintain'd,
    Undiminish'd the duties of filial love.

To cheer the lone couch where her parent was laid,
    When sickness oppress'd him, each effort she tried;
To cheer his lone cot, and his labours to aid,   35
    His food and his raiment her cares would provide.

In this pious act to the streamlet she came,
    To prepare the coarse viands which nature requir'd;
When sudden distemper assail'd her worn frame,
    And 'mid stifling waters poor Polly expir'd!   40

Fair maids of the valley, ye mourn'd for her woes,
    To you may the wretched with confidence come:
Down your cheek the soft current of tenderness flows,
    And Pity your bosoms has claim'd for her home.

Dialogue XVIII: Chastisement

From Cottage Dialogues among the Irish Peasantry (1813)

Tim, Jem.

JEM. My good neighbour Tim, I am sure you won't be angry for what I am going to say to you.

TIM. You know, Jem, you may say what you please to poor Tim.

JEM. I am sorry, then, to hear that you beat your wife.

TIM. What, then, she complained to you too, I suppose. It is well I did not kill a man, or rob on the high road, for she'd tell on me, and have me hanged. O, Jem, you have no notion what sort of woman she is!

JEM. Try what quietness will do for her. Poor Nancy is not a bad natured body; she would hear reason, I'm sure.

TIM. Not she! she'll hear no reason. I came home slaved and tired, and thought to sit down to my supper, but not a potatoe was washed – the fire was out – the door was hasped, and nobody within. I strove to rake out a coal of fire, and was washing the potatoes myself, when in came Nancy, laughing and tittering, with Peggy Donoghoe: and she never said "Tim, I'm sorry for serving you this way," or took the potatoes from me, to put them on, but flounced about, as if she had a right to be angry, and not I. I said nothing till Peggy was gone, and then I told her a bit of my mind, but she was on her high horse, and it don't signify talking, but she *aggravated* me so, that I beat her sure enough.

JEM. Well. Tim, it's a woman's duty to be sure to have her place comfortable for her husband, let him come home in a good humour, or a bad one. And it is a man's duty, too, to consider his wife, and make allowances for her, if she don't always do as he'd have her, and to come home pleasant; and if both of them are pleasant, they will long for the time of seeing each other again. Indeed I have no right to talk, for often I was cross to poor Rose, after spending most of my week's hire at the ale-house. I was so angry with myself for spending it so badly, that I used to come home in a wicked humour indeed: and sure I would have been worse, only she was so quiet, for though I'd see her wiping her eyes with her apron, not a cross word would she say. But I hope that is all over now.

TIM. O, indeed, Jem, you have no excuse to behave bad to Rose; she is no gossiper, no idler, no lazy body, no tea drinker.

JEM. Why did you give Nancy so much of her way at the first, and promise her tea, when you knew in your heart you could not afford it?

TIM. Ay, Jem, there I was wrong; and, indeed, it was wrong to marry till I had something *to the fore*, especially when I had such bad help.

JEM. O, Tim, never get into the way of being sorry you are married. That once done, is for life; but strive to live together comfortably; and nothing makes poor people more comfortable than content, and good humour. You're a man, Tim, and should have more sense; when you are in a good humour together, then draw down these little things, and talk them over quietly.

TIM. Ah, Jem, when we are pleasant, I am loath to speak any thing that might unsettle us, though I know that is the best time; for I love Nancy, and she loves me; and I wonder we don't agree better.

JEM. Well, make a resolution never to both be angry at the same time, and then I'll give my word for it you will agree better.

John Corry (fl. 1797–1825)

Little is known of John Corry except that he was from the north of Ireland. He worked as a journalist in Dublin before moving to London in the 1790s, and later seems to have made his way north in England to become a member of the Philological Society of Manchester. He may have published his first volume of poetry in 1780, but the evidence for this is slight. He was, however, close to the United Irishmen movement: Corry contributed to the movement's publications and his early volume, *Odes and Elegies, Descriptive and Sentimental, with The Patriot* (1797), has a list of subscribers that includes a number of prominent United-men, including William Drennan, Lord Edward Fitzgerald, Henry Joy McCracken, and Thomas Russell.

Corry's corpus is extremely diverse, including verse, moral tales, memoirs of prominent figures, and local histories. *The Patriot* includes three of "the four different species of composition" listed by Brooke in her Preface to *Reliques of Irish Poetry*, namely "the HEROIC POEM, the ODE, the ELEGY, and the SONG" (see p. 86 above): the main narrative of *The Patriot* is written in the first genre, but it also frames two odes and a "dirge" in the elegaic tradition. *The Patriot* clearly invokes not only the remote past but also the heightening tensions of the 1790s, and should be read alongside other nationalist works out of the north at this time, including *Paddy's Resource* and James Porter's *Billy Bluff*. Like these other texts, Corry's poem repeats the leading principles of the United Irishmen, from freedom and liberty to "social virtues" (l. 147), as well as, more uniquely for the 1790s, drawing on an Irish heroic past to encourage heroic action in the present: rallying them to fight, Cormac tells the Irish warriors of the poem, "think ... Of our great ancestors, who Freedom lov'd" (ll. 357–9), and Corry implies that his readers should do the same. Corry's *Patriot* also owes much to the Scottish poet, James Macpherson, whose Ossianic fragments, including *Fingal* (1762), also feature an Irish hero named Cormac. In 1798, Corry published *The Patriot* with a London press, but not under his name – the author was named only (nodding to Goldsmith) "A Citizen of the World."

In the Preface to *Odes and Elegies*, Corry writes that he aimed "to inculcate Benevolence, Piety, and the Love of Country." After the Union, the latter aim largely dropped from his corpus, but he continued to pursue the others in satires and moral tales. He was particularly vocal on women's morality and education, beginning with *The Gardener's Daughter of Worcester; Or the Miseries of Seduction* (1800), which concludes with "The Prostitute: An Elegy." His *Detector of Quackery*, which may have been published as early as 1798 but appeared in a number of editions after 1800, surveys a range of frauds and threats to public order, and was reissued in abbreviated form as *Quack Doctors Dissected* in 1810.

Further reading

Pitcher, E. W., "The Miscellaneous Works of John Corry (1760?–1825?)," *Papers of the Bibliographical Society of America* 80 (1986): 83–90.

Thuente, Mary Helen, *The Harp Re-strung: The United Irishmen and the Rise of Literary Nationalism*. Syracuse: Syracuse University Press, 1994.

Death: An Ode

**From Odes and Elegies, Descriptive and Sentimental,
with The Patriot: A Poem** (1797)

How awful Death! yet Man, secure,
    Lives here as if immortal made;
Th' approach of Death, unseen, tho' sure,
    Doth seldom make his heart afraid.

Whence can this strange indiff'rence rise,   5
    This fondness to forget our end?
To bus'ness, pleasure, or the noise
    Of empty Fame, our wishes tend.

Hope lifts the lively spirit high,
    And health invigorates the heart;   10
Yet this majestic frame must die –
    This active soul must hence depart.

Unwelcome truth to Beauty's ear,
    Elate with praise, the lively mind
Employs its fondest wishes here,   15
    To gaity and love inclin'd.

Ah! since His will who being gave,
    Foredoom'd his creatures here to die,
Let us, ere buried in the grave,
    In virtuous acts our time employ.   20

Let us our appetites restrain,
    And crave Religion's pow'rful aid;
Then after Death, in Heav'n serene,
    Our souls shall live, in light array'd.

Peace: An Elegy

**From Odes and Elegies, Descriptive and Sentimental,
with The Patriot: A Poem** (1797)

From the pure regions of eternal joy,
    Thou friend of man, delightful Peace! descend;
Then shall ferocious War no more destroy,
    But, nations into lasting friendship blend.

Ah! hear afflicted Nature's plaintive cries,   5
    Who mourns the miseries her children feel;
Let thy lov'd presence chear her bright'ning eyes,
    And sheath, for ever, Death's destructive steel.

Suppress vindictive Wrath and tyrant Pride,
    Those worst of fiends that haunt the human mind;   10
O'er Europe, with thy olive wand, preside,
    And thy true blessings give to all mankind.

Then shall the drum unbrac'd and silent lie,
    And deathful arms, in sable rust, decay;
The bolt of war no more shall, hissing, fly –   15
    No more sulphureous smoke obscure the day.

No more shall bombs burst with explosive roar,
    And with fierce flames the wealthy towns devour; –
No more the hind his wasted farm deplore –
    Nor ghastly Famine o'er the landscape low'r.   20

Beneath thy guidance, shall the hand of Toil,
    With Agriculture's treasures fill the land;
Rapine no more shall Nature's bloom despoil,
    Nor Men expire at Tyranny's command.

The Arts and Sciences, O, gracious Peace!   25
    Shall flourish, blest with thy inspiring smile;
Wisdom and Wealth shall o'er the globe encrease,
    And Public Zeal take place of selfish Guile.

Then Justice shall her guardian arm extend,
    And equal laws preserve each social right;   30
And Piety, from highest Heav'n, descend,
    To guide the human race to endless light.

Come, blissful Peace, our wishes realise,
    And over harass'd Europe joy dispense: –
O, come! and with one glance of thy bright eyes,   35
    Chase all the demons of Destruction hence.

The Patriot: A Poem, Descriptive of an Invasion of Ireland by the Danes, and their Expulsion by the Irish

From Odes and Elegies, Descriptive and Sentimental, with The Patriot: A Poem (1797)

The ARGUMENT

Ireland described – amusements of the natives – Cormac – Ellen – Cormac ascends a mountain, and descries the Danish fleet – he descends – alarms the villagers, and dispatches couriers to the interior, to inform his countrymen of the invasion – terror and grief of the women – parting of Cormac and Ellen – speech of Brian to the warriors – they march to the shore – the fleet of the Danes – Orfar, their general – morning – the Danes land – speech of Orfar – the Irish troops hasten from different parts of the country, and are arrayed by their chiefs – the bards – Ode, in which Connal animates his countrymen – ardour of the Irish army – the battle – bravery of Orfar – patriotism of Cormac, who rallies the routed Irish, and leads them again to battle – Cormac and Orfar engage – Orfar slain – the Danes fly, and are pursued to their boats by the Irish – Cormac is carried wounded from the field – Brian, from a hill, sees Cormac lie wounded, and hastens down – Cormac dies – the Irish army carry the wounded off the field of battle – the bards celebrate the victory – the women descend from the mountains – grief of Ellen – she dies – the army repose during the night, and next morning bury the dead – dirge at the grave of Cormac and Ellen – the poem concludes with Connal's exhortation to the army.

Secure and happy, with the smiles of Peace,
The sons of Erin saw their wealth encrease:
The fertile fields gave plenteous crops of grain,
And num'rous herds and flocks enrich'd the swain –
Expansive lakes in wavy radiance flow'd,   5
And to the vales unfailing brooks bestow'd –
Extensive bogs, with heath and reeds o'erspread,
Oft sunk, unfaithful to the wand'rer's tread –
Along the shore vast mountains rear'd their forms,
By light'ning smote, and swept by roaring storms –   10
Here swell'd high summits, tap'ring like a cone,
There pond'rous cliffs, by Time's strong hand o'erthrown,
Hung o'er the precipice – the eagle there
Built her rude nest, and breath'd the purer air –
Green woods adorn'd the mountain's sloping side,   15
And sunny lawns were deck'd in Nature's pride;
There, harmless shepherds fed their useful flocks,
And nibbling goats oft climb'd the pendent rocks,
Where couchant wolves sprung on their help[less]-prey,
And nimbly bore the bleeding prize away.   20
Temp'rate, and tender as the guiltless dove,
The beauteous women warm'd the heart with love;
The men reliev'd, with hospitable hand,
The shipwreck'd stranger, cast upon their land.
But, if with hostile arms they sought the shore,   25
Free Erin's sand was moisten'd with their gore.
In manly sports, along the level green,
Each summer's eve, the hardy youth were seen –
They wrestle, leap, or throw the shining dart –
In sportive fight, they learn the martial art,   30
On their small shields receive the well-aim'd blow,
Whilst in their hearts heroic ardours glow;
Their swords, keen-edg'd, and pointed for the fight,
Which their bold fathers oft, with conq'ring might,
Aim'd, like descending light'ning, on the Dane,   35
Now glitter'd, harmless o'er the glassy plain.

    The chase the gen'rous CORMAC lov'd, whose art
Sent, with unerring aim, the pointed dart,
Oft on the plain he train'd the martial band –
The living bulwark of their native land –   40

Careless and fearless, thus he pass'd his days,
And from the hoary bards oft heard his praise.

 ELLEN, the sweetest of Ierne's maids,
Smil'd like the Genius of her native shades;
In perfect symmetry, her youthful form   45
All-beauteous shone, with vital spirits warm;
Her face, expressive of her blameless mind,
Display'd the fairest tints of health combin'd;
Her soft blue eyes where love and pity smil'd,
In purest light, express'd her temper mild;   50
Redundant flow'd her shining light-brown hair,
Adown her shoulders and her bosom fair,
And, thro' the veil, the living beauties rise.
Thro' parting clouds, the moon thus chears our eyes.
Young Cormac the delightful virgin lov'd,   55
And his fond vows her feeling heart approv'd;
Four genial moons their varying light had shed,
Since his fair consort grac'd the nuptial bed.

 One morn, with spirits lively as the breeze,
Bold Cormac climb'd the mountain, 'mid the trees, 60
Light-arm'd, his polish'd darts the wolves arrest,
And lively pleasure fills his throbbing breast,
'Till, panting with fatigue and noontide heat,
Beneath a cliff he finds a shady seat,
Then to the glitt'ring sea he turns his eyes,   65
And thinks he sees the air-borne clouds arise
Along the dim horizon; but, more near,
They soon a large approaching fleet appear;
He views with stedfast look the coming storm,
And gen'rous passions his bold bosom warm;   70
His wife – his kindred – and his native land,
His love and his solicitude demand.
The lofty precipice he now descends,
And, with commanding voice, collects his friends.
"My countrymen! the Danes approach our coast; 75
To arms! – repel the foe, or all is lost.
Let swiftest messengers the tidings bear,
To bid the distant villagers prepare;
With active zeal, my fellow soldiers, arm,
Whilst Erin's horns the villages alarm."   80
Quick, at his word, the nimble couriers fly;
His village brethren, with a martial cry,
Express their ardour, and their leader hail:
The women, with surprize and terror, pale,
Alarm'd and trembling, hear the boist'rous sound, 85
Which all the neigh'bring woods and hills rebound;
They clasp their children with a fond embrace,
And straight prepare to leave the dang'rous place.

The aged men, and striplings immature,
With eager haste, the flocks and herds secure;   90
Together driven to a lonely glen,
By mountains screen'd, and seldom trod by men;
Thither the women, with their children, hie,
With tearful eyes, and many a mournful sigh;
Yet, ere they go, they bid a fond adieu   95
To their defenders, who, arrang'd to view,
In order stood, with helmets, spears, and shields,
Whilst fading twilight glimmer'd o'er the fields;
Sons – husbands – lovers, form'd the little train,
Who heard, with sorrowing hearts, their friends complain;   100
'Till Cormac, leader of the noble band,
Repress'd their wailings, with a mild command,
"Forbear these sounds of woe, the hero said,
You know our brave forefathers often bled,
To keep the lovely vales of Erin free,   105
And guard our virtuous women's chastity:
Then, why unman my fellow-soldiers here,
With foolish sorrows, and the gushing tear?
No, rather rouze your countrymen to arms,
To guard from foreign violence your charms."   110
He paus'd – then upwards turn'd his sparkling eyes,
And thus address'd the Pow'r who rules the skies,
"Guardian of Erin! to thy creatures lend
Thy potent aid, by which we shall defend
Our native island from a foreign foe,   115
That comes our social comfort to o'erthrow."
He ceas'd – and, from the village, now appears
A mournful maiden, trembling with her fears:
"Oh! Cormac, haste, she cries, thy Ellen fair
Now tears, with frantic hand, her graceful hair;   120
Haste, haste to comfort her afflicted mind,
Nor leave thy wife in sad despair behind."
The youthful warrior to his Ellen flies;
The weeping women then renew their cries.

    Now Cormac at his native cot arrives,   125
His well-known voice his fainting spouse revives,
Prone at his feet the weeping fair one fell,
And clasp'd the knees of him she lov'd so well.
"Ah! whither would'st thou go? my guardian, stay,
Nor leave me here, to certain death a prey;   130
Soul of my life, thou dearer than my breath,
I never, never can survive thy death;
And well I know, the ardour of thy mind,
Intent on noble deeds, to danger blind,
Will overwhelm thee in the gulf of Fate,   135
And leave me here in a defenceless state."
Convulsive sobs her failing voice suppress'd,

And dropping tears impearl'd her beauteous breast;
In wild disorder flow'd her auburn hair,
And cloudy grief o'ercast her aspect fair.   140
Her husband slowly rais'd her in his arms,
And to his sighing bosom clasp'd those charms,
Which ne'er again shall bless his eager sight –
No more her dulcet voice his ears delight –
No more her eyes, mild-beaming purest love,   145
With extasy his thrilling bosom move –
No more her social virtues warm his heart;
The moment's come they must for ever part.
"My dearest Ellen, why this useless woe?
Thy Cormac must repel th' invading foe;   150
Our Island claims her sons' protecting care,
For her the iron mail of War I wear,
And, guarding her, my much-lov'd friends I free
From slavish fears, and Danish tyranny.
Remember, love! how, in our youthful state,   155
I snatch'd my Ellen from the jaws of Fate,
When the fell wolf my charming girl pursu'd,
With glaring eyes, and tusks defil'd with blood,
Whilst, on the wings of Fear, my darling fled,
My rapid dart transfix'd his horrid head.   160
Thus shall the cruel Danes before us fall,
Nor by their prowess Erin's isle enthral.
Adieu, my dearest love!" he sighing said;
At the afflicting word her spirits fled,
And fainting Life seem'd ready to depart,   165
So much conflicting passions rent her heart.
Recover'd by her kind attendant's care,
She for her quick departure must prepare.

    Now, Brian comes to view his native band,
Where, on a little hill, in arms they stand;   170
Oft had he labour'd in the fields of fight,
And deeds of glory were his chief delight;
Tho' Age had long relax'd his weaken'd arm,
His animating eloquence could warm.
And, whilst the moon ascends above the main,   175
He thus harangues the patriotic train:
"My countrymen! I hope you'll soon o'erthrow,
By brave exertions, Ireland's ancient foe;
Act like your fathers, and the Danes expel,
Then Liberty and Peace with you shall dwell.   180
This feeble arm of mine, once young and strong,
Achiev'd bold deeds, that live in sacred song;
The leader of your fathers I have been,
And toil'd with them in many a dreadful scene;
My Cormac's now your chief, by gen'ral choice;   185

In battles still obey his lofty voice.
The martial art I taught my only son –
In open field the ambuscade to shun,
With steady valour to attack the foe,
And strike a pow'rful and decisive blow.   190
Act so, and may kind Heav'n with conquest crown
Your arms, and sacred bards chaunt your renown."
With chearful shouts, the youth their zeal express,
Whilst Brian breathes a pray'r for their success.
He then retires – and tow'rds the hostile plain,   195
The warriors march, despising Death and Pain;
Beside the shore a spacious village rose,
Thither they march, and whilst in deep repose,
New spirits fill their hearts, two centries stand,
With eyes attentive to the neighb'ring strand.   200

    Two furlongs from the shore the fleet was moor'd,
By the safe bay from sudden storms secur'd;
Orfar, the leader of the hardy host,
In war was frozen Denmark's fav'rite boast,
Allur'd by Fame, to Erin's happy isle   205
He came, her sons to conquer and despoil,
And in the genial clime unrivall'd reign;
He warms his soldiers with the hope of gain;
The army soon embark'd, a fav'ring wind
Bears to the shore, where grizzly Fate they find.   210
Thirty large ships a dreadful line compose,
O'er which the moon her pleasing radiance throws,
In each one hundred chosen warriors lie
Asleep, till vivid Morn illumes the sky.

    Now rosy Dawn appears, cncreasing light,   215
Effulgent, rises o'er the mountain's height;
To their dark dens the howling wolves retire,
The glorious Morning's beams the birds inspire
With joy, sweet-warbled from the leafy grove,
And chearful larks, ascending, sing above,   220
No early footsteps marks the dewy green –
No playful lamb, or grazing ox, are seen;
The flowing tide rolls on, with hollow roar
The sparkling waves, that lash the rocky shore –
The screaming sea-fowl skim the swelling tide,   225
Where, near the land, the ships, at anchor, ride –
The bold invaders in their boats descend,
Row'd to the land where soon they must contend
With Erin's sons – along the shelly strand,
Form'd by the chiefs, in order'd ranks they stand.   230
Proud Orfar views the lines, and waves his hand,
The army's mute, attention to command:
"Brave Danes!" he cries "behold the beauteous scene,

See, ev'n the highest mountains rob'd in green;
Rich is the blissful isle, and mild the clime –   235
The earth bestows its fruits in perfect prime;
And shall yon timid bands the isle defend?
Your vet'ran valour will their force transcend.
Like a short blaze, their courage will expire –
Like fearful deer the dastards will retire: 240
Gain but this battle, and the Isle is ours,
Its cultivated fields, and rose-deck'd bow'rs.
We sail'd from Denmark's bleak and barren shore,
Thro' stormy seas, Ierne to explore;
And oft ye murmur'd at the kind decree   245
That sent ye hither, o'er the spacious sea.
Of all your toils behold the rich reward,
Nor think the painful task of conflict hard;
Ere yon bright sun bestows his noontide light,
I hope, you'll be victorious in the fight;   250
Then yon thin ranks shall, conquer'd vassals, bend,
And their fair women at our feasts attend.
Let the incautious foe attack, and then
Repel their sudden force, like valiant men;
They'll soon retreat, and Erin's fertile isle   255
Reward my soldiers for their martial toil."
With chearful shouts the Danes their gen'ral hail,
And the loud sounds fly on the morning gale.

The mountain warriors Cormac's voice obey,
He rouzes them to arms with rising day;   260
Whilst, from the distant hills, for many a mile,
Erin's brave youth descend, to guard their Isle;
Assembled near the shore, arrang'd they stand –
The bands obedient to their chief's command;
Two thousand men in arms, elate and brave,   265
Resolv'd to march to conquest, or the grave;
The chiefs, in silence on the bards await,
Who, rob'd in white, approach in solemn state;
In the left hand the tuneful harp they bear,
And wave the right, the warriors to prepare,   270
'Till Connal, chief of bards, prepares the strain,
To animate with zeal the warlike train;
He views the sparkling lustre of their eyes,
And thus his voice bids ardent Valour rise:

ODE

Erin's hope! my soul's delight,   275
    Now attack your country's foe;
Let them feel your conq'ring might –
    Lay the bold invaders low.

Oft your fathers met the Dane,
    With victorious grasp, in fight,   280
And along the crimson'd plain,
    Clos'd their eyes in endless night.

Firmly face the pointed lance,
    Broken on the guarding shield;
Like a torrent, still advance,   285
    And with slaughter fill the field.

If, like cowards, ye retreat,
    And your native Isle betray,
Infamy and chains await
    Erin's hapless sons this day.   290

Think how the rapacious foe
    Will your women violate,
And the happiness o'erthrow
    Of your peaceful social state.

Think of Liberty enjoy'd,   295
    Now in danger to be lost.
Rouze! O rouze your martial pride,
    As ye fight the Danish host.

Now! defend your children dear –
    Parents – brethren – native isle;   300
Banish ev'ry trembling fear,
    Then shall Conquest on you smile.

In firm ranks repel the Dane –
    Charge them in old Erin's name,
Where your sires have often slain   305
    Their selectest sons of Fame.

  With shouts the warriors interrupt his song,
And, dreadful, on the foe they pour along;
The Danes await them, eager to engage,
And the fierce ranks now close with cruel rage.   310
As some volcano, from its bursting side,
Emits a fiery torrent on the tide,
Down flames the burning flood, with horrid noise,
Impell'd by Storm, the adverse surges rise,
'Till, mix'd in conflict, on the quaking shore,   315
Those elements contend with awful roar,
Whilst o'er the dreadful scene dark vapours rise,
And, with their gloom, conceal the lucid skies.
So join the furious armies, fierce and loud,
And o'er their heads ascends a dusty cloud.   320

  The sons of Erin – ardent – valiant – fierce –
The thickest ranks of their opponents pierce;
The wary enemy, inur'd to fight,

Surround their scatter'd bands, gloomy as Night;
Imperious Orfar, gen'ral of their host,   325
Slays Erin's heroes on their native coast;
High on the gilded helm that guards his head,
Three sable plumes their waving beauty spread;
His well-tried shield repels each hostile dart,
And sanguine Vengeance fills his fearless heart.   330

    New to the fight, the gallant Cormac views,
Where War with mangled men the plain bestrews –
He sees his countrymen by danger press'd,
And all the PATRIOT rouzes in his breast;
Swift as a whirlwind on the foe he flies –   335
The hapless Dane who meets his weapon, dies.
His wife – his country, nerve his manly arm –
He life contemns, to guard them free from harm;
With ev'ry blow he strikes new ardours rise,
And warlike lustre fills his eager eyes.   340
The sons of Erin, weak with breathless toil,
Shrink, whilst their smoking blood distains the soil –
With frantic shouts they fly, and wild Dismay,
With tenfold horror fills their disarray;
The furious Danes their broken bands pursue,   345
And in their gushing lives their hands imbrue.

    Fierce Cormac, with indignant soul, retires,
And, rallied on a hill, the troops inspires
With love of Liberty – "Alas! my friends,
This fatal day our country's freedom ends;   350
Ne'er in our vales shall joyful sounds be heard,
By our ferocious conquerors deterr'd.
Tim'rous as deer, our youth their necks shall bend
Beneath their yoke, and Erin's glory end.
Now, rouze, my countrymen, your noble ire –   355
Let your dear country's love your souls inspire.
O! think how oft yon woody hills have rung,
When tuneful bards the great achievements sung
Of our great ancestors, who Freedom lov'd,
And in the field of War their valour prov'd.   360
And shall WE fly? Ah! shall we tamely yield
Our country's rights, nor our dear kindred shield
From Rapine, Violation, Death, and chains?
Shall our best friends be vassals to the Danes?
Grasp firmly, now, your swords – one effort try –   365
For our lov'd Isle we'll conquer or we'll die."
Encourag'd thus, the hardy ranks again,
Descend with rapid fury on the plain:
Like the red light'ning, Cormac's blood-stain'd sword
Destroy'd the Danes, and Erin's hopes restor'd;   370
Impulsive might the daring van o'erthrows,
Where, frantic with revenge, the armies close.

The Danish soldiers, long inur'd to fight,
Condense their ranks, and, gloomy as the Night,
Their sable shields before their ranks they bear,   375
Of the fierce Irish energy aware.
Ierne's sons impetuously assail
This formidable phalanx, and prevail:
The broken ranks before the victors fly,
Whilst mingled shouts and groans ascend the sky.   380
A forest, thus, resists a sudden blast,
But the encreasing storm prevails at last,
Uproots the strongest oaks, with dreadful noise,
And all the beauty of the scene destroys.

 Amid the carnage of the dreadful fight,   385
Unconquer'd Orfar, fill'd with martial might,
Repels the Irish, aided by his men,
And seeming Conquest chears their hearts again.
Young Cormac, breathless, with incessant toil,
Leans on a rock, and sees his native soil   390
With mangled carcasses of men bestrew'd –
Sees Orfar's hands in Irish blood embru'd –
Hears his majestic voice to Conquest call –
And sees his native youth before him fall:
Enrag'd, he rouzes all the ardent fire   395
That Freedom, and his country's cause, inspire.
He chears the leaders of Ierne's bands,
Who hear, with ready zeal, his wise commands.
"My friends," the patriotic hero cries,
"This hour brave Orfar or your gen'ral dies;   400
Unconquer'd, still your native land defend –
Destroy the Danes, and all your dangers end."
Ardent he spoke – and, with undaunted mien,
Seeks Orfar, glorious in the dreadful scene,
Who his approaching foe, with joy, espies,   405
And kindling vengeance sparkles in his eyes.
With blood-stain'd swords the rival chiefs engage,
Inspir'd with all the force of Valour's rage;
Active and strong, their keen-edg'd blades they wield,
And their warm blood flows plenteous on the field;   410
Their helmets and their shields in pieces hewn,
They fight, all-breathless, in the blaze of noon.
At length the Dane, with a resistless blow,
Lopt the left arm of his unconquer'd foe.
Brave Cormac, warm with life, despising pain,   415
Makes a last effort on his native plain –
With one swift blow, he cleft fierce Orfar's head,
And laid the pride of Denmark's army dead.
So the red light'ning from the cloud descends,
And the high cliff, with force tremendous, rends,   420
The smoking fragments on the summit lie,

And the loud crash ascends the echoing sky.
Thus died proud Orfar – and his broken host,
Impell'd by Terror, hasten to the coast;
The shouting Irish their retreat pursue,   425
And in the blood of Danes their hands imbrue.
The Danes their num'rous boats, in haste, prepare –
Their bravest troops defend the flying rear.
Like raging fire, the Irish bands assail
Their foes, and their resistless pow'rs prevail: 430
Plung'd in the tide, the mingled warriors fight –
Lost to the vanquish'd Danes the hope of flight;
Wounded, and fainting with the loss of blood,
They sink, expiring, in the rising flood.
The eager front of their pursuing foes   435
The rising waves in one dark grave enclose;
Together they descend, with hostile grasp,
And Hatred dies in their expiring gasp.
Meantime the half-fraught boats float on the tide,
To where the stately ships at anchor ride;   440
The Danes their anchors weigh, and leave the coast,
Where their best warriors lie, in battle lost.
There Erin's sons, victorious in the fight,
Their voices, in loud shouts of joy, unite.
Meantime, brave Cormac's friends their gen'ral bear   445
To where a hawthorn waves in Summer's air;
There, shaded from the sun, his wounds they bind;
He rests upon a mossy stone, reclin'd;
Reviv'd, a momentary joy pervades
His manly heart – he views the distant shades   450
Beside his cot, but sees not Ellen, there,
Walk graceful o'er the flow'ry summits fair.
The distant shelt'ring glen his spouse conceals,
And her fair breast the pang of Sorrow feels;
Beneath a flow'ry thorn, beside a spring,   455
Whilst o'er her head harmonious thrushes sing,
She sits among her maids, in sad suspense,
And ev'ry sudden sound affrights her sense.

   Meantime, old Brian, from a hill surveys
The field of battle, with attentive gaze;   460
With martial ardour fill'd, he sees, below,
His countrymen their enemies o'erthrow;
Joy swells his thrilling bosom, and, elate,
He sees bold Victory on Erin wait –
Sees her brave sons triumphant on the plain,   465
And Death, ev'n to their boats, pursue the Dane.
A nearer object next attracts his sight –
He views a wounded warrior, from the fight
Borne by his friends. Now sudden fears arrest
The rising transports of old Brian's breast;   470
He calls a youth, "Haste downward, and enquire

His name who seems just ready to expire.
Alas! I fear he is my noble son,
And that his morning race of glory's run."
The youth descends, the dying hero sees,   475
Whose ebbing spirits sink by slow degrees.
With frighted heart, the stripling climbs the hill,
Whilst from his eyes the tears of Grief distil.
"Your doubts, unhappy Brian, were too true,
'Tis dying Cormac yonder lies in view."   480
The venerable sire with speechless woe,
Descends to the afflicted train below;
The grateful soldiers, with respectful love,
To aid the tott'ring father quickly move.
The father's presence lights a gleam of joy   485
In that pale visage Death shall soon destroy;
And Cormac strives to rise, alas! in vain,
He faints, o'ercome by weakness and by pain.
Reviv'd – old Brian clasp'd his conq'ring hand,
"Oh! thou defender of our native land,"   490
He cries, "For Erin's weal my hero dies –
To guard her freedom, thou did'st Death despise."
"Yes, worthy sire," the dying son reply'd,
"To serve my country was my chiefest pride;
Kind Heav'n with conquest bless'd our patriot bands,   495
And Denmark's pride lies low, beneath their hands.
Thy presence, father, chears my fainting heart,
But where did'st thou with my dear Ellen part?"
"I left her safe," reply'd the mournful sire.
"O! Heaven for ever bless my soul's desire!   500
May my fair Ellen happiness enjoy,
And no invader Erin's peace destroy.
May Liberty, and Social Love, prevail
For ever here." – His dying spirits fail;
To scenes of peace and joy his spirit flies,   505
And on the gory grass his body lies.
Sad sounds of woe the woody hills resound,
Whilst his brave friends their leader's corse surround;
Of verdant branches soon they form a bier,
And bear him to his cot, with grief sincere.   510
Arriv'd, the customary rites, with care,
To grace the noble warrior, they prepare.

   Meantime, along the shore, Ierne's host
See their defeated foe forsake the coast;
The wounded to the villages they bear,   515
And ease their anguish, with fraternal care.
The wearied warriors lay their arms aside,
'Till Nature's craving wants are satisfy'd;
Nutritious food and drink their strength restore –
With joyful looks, they view the spacious shore,   520

And flying foe, whose ships, at distance, glide
O'er the soft swellings of the ev'ning tide.
Now, from their green recess, the bards appear,
Their presence the triumphant soldiers chear;
They rise respectfully, and loud acclaim   525
Salutes old Connal, whose sweet song was Fame;
In his bright eyes the light of Genius shone,
And now his lofty voice sings Glory won: –

ODE

How silently, along the shore,
    The gory foes of Erin lie;   530
Their threat'ning voices shall no more
    With foreign clamours fill the sky.

Lo! where the vanquish'd prowlers fly
    From happy Erin's dang'rous coast.
Daughters of Denmark! loudly cry,   535
    And weep your dearest lovers lost.

Around me stand the noble throng
    Who Erin's liberty secure;
Their valour claims my grateful song,
    Who for our Isle such toils endure.   540

Ye guardians of each peaceful joy,
    That rural Innocence bestows,
Your valiant efforts did destroy
    The pride of our invading foes.

Now may our spritely maids again   545
    Their native villages adorn,
And gracefully trip o'er the plain,
    With faces blooming as the Morn.

Yet, some there are that will deplore
    Their dearest friends, destroy'd in fight;   550
But, wailing never can restore
    The spirits, who ascend to Light.

Again, ye glorious heroes, hail!
    Your acts shall grace my daily song,
And the light pinions of the gale   555
    Shall bear your fame our vales along.

He ceas'd – the youthful bards, with pleasing skill,
The echoing groves with martial music fill;
Their harps they next attune to softer strains,
And sing fair Freedom's reign on Erin's plains.   560
The warriors hear the song, with silent joy,
And no intrusive fears their peace annoy.
The minstrels cease – and down the sloping dales,

The voice of Sorrow vibrates in the gales;
And, lo! descending from the woody height,   565
The wailing women haste, with pale affright;
The mountain villagers, with joyful love,
To meet their dearest friends, with ardour move.
Immingling with the bands, the fearful fair
Their sorrow, or their lively joy, declare –   570
Some clasp their heroes with a fond embrace,
And sudden happiness illumes the face –
Whilst others their dear kindred's fall bewail,
Who lie, beneath the hand of Slaughter, pale.

   Now Ellen comes, with her attendant maids,   575
Like a bright vision from the verdant shades,
Her raiment white, and her expressive face,
Tho' pale with grief, displays transcendent grace;
For Cormac she enquires – but, silent, all,
With grateful tears, weep his untimely fall.   580
At length, old Connal, with a secret sigh,
Began, "Fair Ellen, all mankind must die:
Some in the dang'rous path of Honour tread,
And early mingle with the peaceful dead;
Whilst others find the grave by slow degrees,   585
Oppress'd with Age, Misfortune, and Disease.
Thy Cormac, warm in Liberty's defence,
Repell'd our country's fell invaders hence;
By his brave arm, the Danish gen'ral, slain,
Lies, cold and pale, on Erin's glorious plain.   590
Victorious Cormac, then, by wounds oppress'd,
Like a tir'd labourer, sunk to silent Rest."
Dim Anguish veils the lustre of her eyes –
She faints, unconscious of her maidens' cries,
'Till Nature's vital pow'r her life restores,   595
Then thus impassion'd she her loss deplores:
"Life of my dearest hopes! and art thou dead!
Alas! my youthful happiness is fled.
Oh! Cormac! Cormac! never shall thy voice,
With sweetest sounds of love, my soul rejoice.   600
Ah! what to me my country, now he's lost?
Dear is the price our liberty hath cost.
Alas! my boding heart too plainly told
I ne'er again would my dear love behold;
Blooming in manly grace, by Death destroy'd,   605
Low lies my soul's desire, my bosom's pride,
My lost, lost husband." – Here convulsive sighs
Suppress'd her voice, and tears bedew'd her eyes,
Fast flowing down, the lucid drops of Grief
Afford her swelling heart a short relief.   610
Then starting up, with an impatient bound,
She darts her penetrating looks around,
And begs they'll lead her to where Cormac, dead,
Lies, with Spring's sweetest blossoms round him spread.

Arriv'd, she views him pale and mangled lie,   615
And not a rising tear swells in her eye;
Down sinks the tender Ellen, and her breath,
In sudden gasps, foretels approaching Death,
From her fond heart the warm arterial blood
Burst forth, with sudden suffocating flood.   620
She dies – her weeping maids behold her fall,
But no kind aid her spirit can recal.
Beside her husband plac'd her body lies,
And mournful friends attend their obsequies.

    Now, Ev'ning's solemn twilight ushers Night,   625
And Darkness overwhelms the fading light,
The martial bands, fatigu'd, retire to rest,
With Victory, and Peace, and Freedom blest.
The field of battle, strew'd with mangled slain,
Exhibits now a melancholy train;   630
In groups, the women search for slaughter'd friends,
The feeble star-light small assistance lends;
But soon fair Cynthia,[1] rising o'er the main,
Pours light o'er all the mountains, vales, and plain;
Then, some who find their friends, in sad despair,   635
Fill, with terrific cries, the gusty air.
The rising gales sigh in the waving grove,
And gliding clouds conceal the moon above;
Oft, thro' the parting gloom, the lunar light
Gives all the various objects to the sight,   640
And shews the women weeping o'er their dead,
Where the fresh verdure is with gore o'erspread;
All night they mourn, 'till chearful Morn removes
Dull Darkness, and displays the vernal groves;
The warriors, summon'd by the martial horn,   645
March to the field, where, wet with dews of Morn,
Cold, ghastly, pale, and horrid to the eye,
The slain, in wide promiscuous ruin, lie.
Commanded by their chiefs, the bands, with care,
Now to the grave the mangled bodies bear;   650
The Danes they bury in the gory plain,
And no memorials of their death remain.
In a deep trench they lay their native dead,
Who nobly for their country's freedom bled,
And o'er the grave a lofty trophy rear,   655
Which shall their fame to future times declare.
The bards attend, to grace their obsequies;
Meantime, their friends, with mingled tears and sighs,
Bear Cormac and his Ellen to the tomb,

Notes ——————————————————————————————————————

THE PATRIOT
[1] the moon

Where, on a hill, unfading laurels bloom; 660
There Connal goes, with sadly-solemn pace,
Whilst tears bedew his venerable face,
Descending o'er his hoary beard, they shine –
The offspring of his feeling heart benign;
With plaintive melody, above their grave 665
He stands, and mourns the beautiful and brave.

DIRGE

Together, in this earthy tomb,
In prime of Life, and Beauty's bloom,
Brave Cormac and his Ellen, dead,
Lie, with the grassy turf o'erspread. 670
Alas! no more his voice shall warm
Our youth to brave War's iron storm –
No more shall Ellen grace the grove,
Sacred to Friendship, Peace, and Love.

Below, in yonder trophied plain, 675
Lie Erin's sons, in battle slain;
With Life they purchas'd Victory,
And left their native Island free.
Dear, honour'd heroes! lost in fight,
Behold us from the climes of Light, 680
Our tutelary spirits be,
And shield Ierne's liberty.

Ambitious Denmark, scourge of Earth,
Thy soil gives cruel prowlers birth –
Where'er they come, destructive Death 685
Blast blooming Peace with baleful breath.
But lately, yonder summits rung
With strains of love, by Ellen sung;
Now, lost in silence – and her charms
No more her Cormac's bosom warms. 690

Alas! how many maids shall mourn
Their lovers, who shall ne'er return;
And widows shall, with tearful eyes,
Express their grief, with plaintive cries.
Ah! see where Brian, wrapt in woe, 695
Beneath yon oak, feels Sorrow's throe –
The hope and glory of his age
Was lost, amid the battle's rage.

Adieu! unconscious dust! adieu!
Our tears shall often fall for you; 700
And oft the sorrow-breathing strain
Shall of your sudden death complain;
Your lov'd remembrance ne'er shall die

Whilst yonder sun illumes the sky –
For you the bards, in future days, 705
Shall chaunt traditional lays.

Responsive to his voice, the bards around,
With their sweet harps, make woods and rocks resound,
On the soft breeze the mellow music flies,
And mingling sounds melt in the distant skies. 710

Now, venerable Connal, on a height,
Stands forth, conspicuous to the army's sight,
Who stand arrang'd in ranks, and all attend
To the wise counsel of their faithful friend:
"My countrymen," the hoary bard began, 715
"I see our fame ascend, like rising Dawn –
I see progressive arts our Island grace,
And Population, Wealth, and Love encrease.
Our liberty's secur'd by native might,
Which put our sanguine enemies to flight. 720
Now, in fraternal love our rising youth
Shall live, inspir'd by love of sacred Truth;
But, if Ambition prompts a brother's mind,
To violate the rights of human kind,
Let love of Liberty, and Public Zeal, 725
Doom growing Tyranny your wrath to feel;
But let the sapient sages, white with years,
Direct your councils – dry the widow's tears –
Preserve the orphan, to his country dear –
And, by wise laws, bid Justice flourish here. 730
Oft let our hardy youth their weapons wield –
To arms accustom'd in the peaceful field –
Then, when the stormy horns of War shall sound,
They'll pant to be, like you, with laurels crown'd;
And will preserve their native Island free, 735
Thus nurtur'd in the love of Liberty.
Now, to your homes, our Erin's guardians, go,
And pleasure to your pensive friends bestow;
Again ye shall behold your women's charms,
Preserv'd unblemish'd, by your conq'ring arms; 740
Your patrimony, by your risk, secur'd,
Shall yield you Earth's refreshing fruits matur'd;
Your flocks and kine the verdant hills shall graze,
And rip'ning corn reflect the solar rays.
Again the shepherd's pipe, with simple strain, 745
Shall, with the melody of Love, complain;
Or, breathing spritely airs, the heart rejoice,
Whilst blooming maids respond, with tuneful voice.
Adieu, ye chiefs – adieu, each noble band;
Ye brave defenders of our happy land: 750
Thus, join'd in love, our foreign foes, in vain,
Shall, with their hostile thousands, load the main.

'Tis Concord gives you pow'r – the torrent's force,
With feeble progress, murmurs near its source;
But, join'd by many streams, adown the steep,   755
It rolls impetuous, with resistless sweep.
Still, when your foes invade, like brethren join,
Then shall the light of Glory on you shine,
And Erin, blooming 'mid the wavy sea,
Shall be for ever safe – for ever free.   760

    He ceas'd – and joyful shouts of loud acclaim
Triumphant rise, and swell with Erin's name.
The joyful conquerors return'd again,
To cultivate the fertile hill and plain,
Where, chear'd by Health – of Social Love possess'd,   765
They flourish'd, with the smiles of Freedom bless'd.

From *Medical Empiricism*

From The Detector of Quackery; Or, Analyser of Medical, Philosophical, Political, Dramatic, and Literary Imposture (1802)

Credulity, which may be called the foible of a good heart, has in all ages rendered the worthy part of mankind dupes to the artifice of the knavish, who, unrestrained by principle, are ever eager to profit by the unsuspicious disposition of generous minds.

Among the various kinds of imposture practised in polished society, Quackery has been the most successful, in consequence of the extreme respect paid to the professors of the art of healing. Our ancestors, indeed, like the ancient Greeks, seem to have considered the knowledge of medicine as an immediate communication from Heaven; hence physicians were not accountable to man for any accident which might attend the administration of remedies.

Empirics profited by the superstition of mankind, and while the wretch who committed a robbery was condemned to an ignominious death, the dispensers of nostrums, which deprived many individuals of their property and their lives, were hailed as public benefactors!

Quack Doctors will ever be most successful in a wealthy commercial country like England; especially in the busy, populous, and luxurious capital, where the multitude have neither leisure nor inclination to detect imposture.[1] Accustomed to obtain every luxury and accommodation for money, most people imagine that gold can procure even health and longevity. Indeed, the principle of self-preservation is so strongly entwined with the fibres of the human heart, that cunning and unprincipled men, who assume the character of physicians, easily impose on the public credulity.

Even regular physicians often profit by the fears of mankind, and thus realize a fortune. Many persons, in other respects very sensible, are so much under the

---

Notes ————————————————————————————

From Medical Empiricism
[1] Corry is more pointed in the book's Dedication: "To that most liberal Patron, the British Public, whose

Munificence confers Riches on empirics and impostors of every Description."

influence of *medical superstition*, that, alarmed at the slightest qualm, they hastily send for the physician, who, of course, prescribes something to relieve that agony which might have been prevented by temperance. – Hence the constitution of the valetu-dinarian is gradually worn out; a premature old age overwhelms him, and he expires surrounded by boluses and physicians.

Opulent persons pay their physician annually for keeping their constitution *in repair*; and from the irregularity of the debauchee, he seems determined that the physician's engagement shall not be a *sinecure*. – On the other hand, Quack Doctors seem to consider the human frame merely as a *subject* for experiments, which, if successful, will ensure the reputation of the practitioner. The acquisition of fame and fortune is, in the estimation of these philosophers, cheaply purchased by sacrificing the lives of a few of *the vulgar*. To such they prescribe *gratis*[2]; in other words, they require no fee for making an experiment upon some credulous being, which may cost him his life!

Indeed the health of the people would soon be in a hopeful state were they all equally credulous. Between the *internal* use of the *Nervous Cordial*, or the *Balm of Gilead*, and the *external* application of *Perkins's Metallic Tractors*, our *inside* and our *outside* would be completely medicated. By the way, the phrase *inside* is very expres-sive, and used as a general term by the common people when speaking of disease. Whatever be their internal complaint, they simply say that their *inside* is disordered; and when they recover, their inside is quite well again. This comes to just the same conclusion as all the learned phrases adopted by the empiric. While Dr. Brodum, Dr. Solomon, or some other *graduate* of the same fraternity, is, with a grave air, employed in feeling the patient's pulse and investigating symptoms; while his active imagination is like the mole pervading all the dark intricacies of the *viscera*, penetrat-ing through every obstruction, to the *abdomen*, and eventually making its escape from the *anus* in a puff of *flatulency*, the patient contents himself with describing the sensations which he feels in his *inside*.

Notes

[2] Nothing can be more ridiculous than the slavish obedi-ence of some patients to the dictates of the doctor. A convalescent lately wrote from Bath to his physician in London, to know whether he might *eat sauce with his pork* (author).

Maria Edgeworth (1768–1849) and Richard Lovell Edgeworth (1744–1817)

Richard Lovell Edgeworth was born in England to an Irish father whose family was from Co. Longford. He visited Ireland on a number of occasions but only settled there after his father's death, taking control of the family estate at Edgeworthstown in 1769. Edgeworth was an unrelenting improver, considering in his life and writing the ways in which technology, estate management, and education could improve the quality of people's lives. An amateur engineer and inventor, he authored volumes on related subjects, including *A Letter to the Right Hon. the Earl of Charlemont, on the Tellograph, and on the Defence of Ireland* (1797) and *An Essay on the Construction of Roads and Carriages* (1813). He was interested in directly managing his own estate so as to avoid the social and economic ills that generally arose in estates where absentees left management to agents. His greatest interest, perhaps, was in education.

His collaboration with his eldest daughter, Maria Edgeworth, produced a number of works on education, including *Practical Education* (1788) and *Essays on Professional Education* (1809). Their *Essay on Irish Bulls* (1802) also has significant educational concerns, including the story of "Little Dominick" who has the misfortune to have a poorly prepared and abusive schoolmaster. Maria Edgeworth's many pedagogical publications arise from this context, including her volumes of short stories for children, such as *The Parent's Assistant* (1796, 1800), *Moral Tales for Young People* (1801), *Early Lessons* (1801–2), and *Continuation of Early Lessons* (1814). The Edgeworths corresponded with like-minded contemporaries, including Mary Leadbeater, and were acquainted with many of Britain's leading intellectuals, from radical publisher Joseph Johnson to the scientist Sir Humphrey Davy and novelist Sir Walter Scott. The collaboration of father and daughter was so close that Maria Edgeworth's autonomy as an author has long been a question of critical interest; Julia Kavanagh suggests in *English Women of Letters* (1862) that, on R. L. Edgeworth's death, "ceases his daughter's literary history. She was fifty, and can scarcely have been exhausted, but she had long relied on his guidance; too long, perhaps, for her own good" (209), and Elizabeth Kowaleski-Wallace (see Further reading) has more recently taken up the question of the Edgeworths' collaboration.

Maria Edgeworth was born in England but moved to Ireland in 1782 to live with her father. Apart from occasional travels in Britain and continental Europe, she lived in Ireland until her death in 1849. In addition to her work on children's education alone and with her father, she continued the educational project in such works as *Popular Tales* (1804), explicitly offered as reading to educate the lower classes, and *Ennui* (1809), a novel which focuses on the education of the protagonist. While much of her fiction for adults follows the novel of manners, and so bears comparison to novels by such English contemporaries as Jane Austen and Fanny Burney, Edgeworth also contributed to the representation of Ireland in national tales, from *Castle Rackrent* (1800) to *The Absentee* (1812).

Despite a continuing concern with representing the Irish people and regular statements against anti-Irish prejudice, Edgeworth pays scant attention to Irish culture. The lower-class Irish characters of her fiction speak non-standard English or display traits associated with national stereotypes (loyalty, for instance) and she occasionally touches on contemporary events in Ireland, but she rarely invokes Irish cultural practices, Irish-language literature, music, or pre-colonial history. Her ideal Irish characters are often hardworking businessmen or professionals who work within rather than against English culture.

Further reading

Kowaleski-Wallace, Elizabeth, *Their Father's Daughters: Hannah More, Maria Edgeworth, and Patriarchal Complicity*. Oxford: Oxford University Press, 1991.

Myers, Mitzi, "Goring John Bull: Maria Edgeworth's Hibernian High Jinks versus the Imperialist Imaginary," in *Cutting Edges: Postmodern Critical Essays on Eighteenth-century Satire*, ed. James E. Gill, 367–94. Knoxville, TN: University of Tennessee Press, 1995.

Ó Gallchoir, Clíona, *Maria Edgeworth: Women, Enlightenment, and Nation*. Dublin: University College Dublin Press, 2005.

Wohlgemut, Esther, "Maria Edgeworth and the Question of National Identity," *Studies in English Literature, 1500–1800* 39 (1999): 645–58.

From *Essay on Irish Bulls* (by Richard Lovell Edgeworth and Maria Edgeworth, 1802)

Chapter I. *Vulgar Errours*

It is much to be regretted, that the learned and judicious author[1] of *"An Enquiry into Vulgar Errors"* omitted to notice that propensity to blunder, which is commonly supposed to be characteristic of the irish nation. An essay on the nature and origin of irish bulls would, perhaps, have been almost as well worthy the attention of the public as some of the questions, which this celebrated antiquarian, and natural philosopher, has discussed; such as, Whether storks can live only in republics? Whether peacocks are ashamed when they look at their ugly legs? Why we are taught, from our childhood, to break an egg-shell after we have eaten the egg? Why candles burn blue before the apparition of a spirit, or how their wicks foretel the approach of strangers?

We have the more reason to lament sir Thomas Browne's omitting to treat of irish bulls, because, in speaking of one of the english popular notions with respect to Ireland, he evinces that admirable degree of philosophical scepticism which is necessary in judging a national cause with impartiality.

"Most men," says he, "affirm, and few here will believe the contrary, that there be no spiders in Ireland; but we *have* seen some in that country; and, though but few, some cobwebs we behold in irish wood[2] in England. Thus the crocodile from an egg growing up to an exceeding magnitude, common conceit, and divers writers deliver, it hath no period of increase, but groweth as long as it liveth; and thus, in brief, in most apprehensions the conceits of men extend the considerations of things, and dilate their notions beyond the propriety of their natures."

The received opinion, that there exists amongst the natives of Ireland an innate and irresistible propensity to blunder, cannot, however, be one of those notions which have been dilated by common conceit, because we have argument and evidence sufficient to establish our belief. English readers may smile at this grave preparation to prove what *nobody* doubts: but these apparent truisms are always suspicious in the

Notes ───────────────

From Essay on Irish Bulls
[1] Sir Thomas Browne, fl. 1660 (authors). English author (1605–82), better known for *Religio Medici* (1642) than *Enquiries into Vulgar and Common Errors* (1646).

[2] The person who shows Westminster Abbey assures the public, at this day, that there are no cobwebs in the oak there, because it is irish (authors).

eyes of accurate philosophers. In the first place it must be observed, that *nobody* is a word of very uncertain signification, varying according to time, place, and circumstance. Nobody in a physical and nobody in a fashionable sense, nobody in a moral and nobody in a political view, are obviously as different as possible; nobody at court may be somebody in the country; nobody in England may be somebody in Ireland. In short, nobody in argument usually implies, nobody of my nation, acquaintance, party, or way of thinking: hence the extreme difficulty of ascertaining what is meant by the phrase. Unless we know the style of life, connexions, birth, parentage, education, and understanding of the person who makes such an assertion, it is often impossible to perceive its full force or weakness. Hence also the frequent necessity of proving what *nobody* doubts: therefore let us soberly proceed with the proof, that the irish nation is prone to make those blunders, which are usually called bulls.

According to the common custom of able logicians, we must begin with an argument a priori. It seems but reasonable to suppose, that Irishmen were designed by providence to make bulls, because, in the universal distribution of things in this world, good is ever balanced by evil. Each country upon the face of this earth has peculiar advantages and disadvantages. Look round the globe: – here you find a mild climate with an oppressive government; there you see a profusion of the necessaries and luxuries of life, with an indolent, inept race of inhabitants: even the sparkling mines and fragrant spices of the east are blessings fully balanced by hurricanes and pestilence. Thus equality is preserved amongst nations as amongst individuals, and Hibernia cannot be exempted from this equitable law of nature. Amongst her various advantages, we must recollect one by which she is peculiarly distinguished: – as Alba and Gyraldus[3] have left upon ancient record, and as a modern farce, called "The Genius of Ireland" sufficiently confirms, no venomous animal can exist on the soil or in the air of Ireland. This enviable national immunity, although bestowed by the special favour of St. Patrick, must, according to the system that we have just established, be counterbalanced by some evil; probably by that vernacular defect in their mode of speech, for which the Irish are so justly ridiculed and reviled. As there are no toads, or serpents, or vipers in this favoured island, it must necessarily abound with irish bulls.

A priori arguments, though their use be justified by the highest authority, do not suit all tastes, or carry conviction to all understandings. Now, according to the prudent practise avowed by an experienced orator,[4] we should employ, not only the strongest, but the weakest arguments possible, that we may captivate both the nice judging few, and the numerous, and, consequently, respectable vulgar. Without relying entirely upon this one a priori argument to prove, that Irishmen ought to make bulls, I shall adduce another of an inferiour species, drawn simply from *existing circumstances*.

English is not the mother tongue of the natives of Ireland; to them it is a foreign language, and, consequently, it is scarcely within the limits of probability, that they should avoid making blunders both in speaking and writing. We most of us are aware of the difficulty of acquiring that accurate grammatical knowledge, that practical fluency, and all the idiomatic niceties of a foreign language, which could put us on a par with the natives themselves. It was not till after a seven years apprenticeship at Lausanne, that the great Gibbon[5] thought himself able to speak french like a Frenchman; and his writing a manifesto in elegant french was a matter of pride to him, and of

Notes ————————————————————————

[3] Geraldus Cambrensis (Gerald of Wales), Welsh historian (c.1146–1223); Alba is unidentified. *The Genius of Ireland* (1758) was written by John Macaulay (nationality unknown).

[4] Charles Fox (authors). English politician (1749–1806),

part of the same political circle as Edmund Burke and R. B. Sheridan.

[5] Edward Gibbon (1737–94), English historian.

admiration to the rest of the world. How then can it be expected, that the illiterate irish should instinctively possess that command of a foreign language, which is only to be acquired after long labour by the brightest, and most cultivated genius, assisted by all the advantages of books and society? Such an expectation would be extravagant. Thus by arguments both ad absurdum and a priori, we are compelled to the same conclusion, that the Irish must be blunderers. Indeed, so perfectly persuaded are Englishmen of the truth of this proposition, that the moment an unfortunate Hibernian opens his lips they expect a bull, and listen with that well known look of sober contempt and snug self-satisfaction, which sufficiently testifies their sense of safety and superiority. Not the half animated Bondstreet lounger, not the bawling native of Billingsgate, no inveterate cockney of high or low degree, between the vast extremes of St. James's and St. Mary Axe, no guttural man of Cumberland, or Zomerzetshire Zim, or ultimate Northumbrian, can forbear to join in the liberal laugh against the wild Irishman, or refrain from raising in their multifarious dialects the national hue and cry after an irish bull. Whether this cry be ever raised by mistake, when no irish bull has broken loose, may, perhaps, be questioned by those, who have observed, that every dog is not mad which falls a victim to the ignorance or malice of the populace: but let us avoid this inquiry; it might prove troublesome; for it would drive us at last to describe and define what we mean by an irish bull. Definitions are as much the bane of easy writing as of easy conversation.

Chapter VI. *Little Dominick*

We have laid down the general law of bulls and blunders; but as there is no rule without an exception, we may perhaps allow an exception in favour of little Dominick.

Little Dominick was born at Fort-Reilly, in Ireland, and bred no where until his tenth year, when he was sent to Wales to learn manners and grammar at the school of Mr. Owen ap Davies ap Jenkins ap Jones. This gentleman had reason to think himself the greatest of men; for he had over his chimney-piece a well-smoked genealogy, duly attested, tracing his ancestry in a direct line up to Noah; and moreover he was nearly related to the learned etymologist, who in the time of queen Elizabeth wrote a folio to prove that the language of Adam and Eve in paradise was pure Welsh. – With such causes to be proud, Mr. Owen ap Davies ap Jenkins ap Jones was excusable for sometimes seeming to forget that a schoolmaster is but a man. He however sometimes entirely forgot that a boy is but a boy; and this happened most frequently with respect to little Dominick.

This unlucky wight was flogged every morning by his master, not for his vices, but for his vicious constructions, and laughed at by his companions every evening for his idiomatic absurdities. They would probably have been inclined to sympathise in his misfortunes, but that he was the only irish boy at school; and as he was at a distance from all his relations, and without a friend to take his part, he was a just object of obloquy and derision. Every sentence he spoke was a bull; every two words he put together proved a false concord, and every sound he articulated betrayed the brogue. But as he possessed some of the characteristic boldness of those who have been dipped in the Shannon, though he was only little Dominick, he showed himself able and willing to fight his own battles with the host of foes by whom he was encompassed. Some of these, it was said, were of nearly twice his stature. This may be exaggerated; but it is certain that our hero sometimes ventured with sly irish humour to revenge himself upon his most powerful tyrant by mimicking the welsh accent, in which

Mr. Owen ap Jones said to him, "Cot pless me, you plockit, and shall I never *learn* you enclish crammer?"

It was whispered in the ear of his Dionysius, that our little hero was a mimick; and he was treated with increased severity.

The midsummer holydays approached; but he feared that they would shine no holydays for him. He had written to his mother to tell her, that school would break up the 21st, and to beg an answer, without fail, by return of post: but no answer came.

It was now nearly two months since he had heard from his dear mother or any of his friends in Ireland. His spirits began to sink under the pressure of these accumulated misfortunes; he slept little, ate less, and played not at all; indeed nobody would play with him upon equal terms, because he was nobody's equal: his schoolfellows continued to consider him as a being, if not of a different species, at least of a different *cast*[6] from themselves.

Mr. Owen ap Jones's triumph over the little irish plockit was nearly complete, for the boy's heart was almost broken, when there came to the school a new scholar – O, how unlike the others! – His name was Edwards; he was the son of a neighbouring welsh gentleman; and he had himself the spirit of a gentleman. When he saw how poor Dominick was persecuted, he took him under his protection, fought his battles with the welsh boys, and, instead of laughing at him for speaking Irish, he endeavoured to teach him to speak English. In his answers to the first questions Edwards ever asked him, little Dominick made two blunders, which set all his other companions in a roar; yet Edwards would not allow them to be genuine bulls.

In answer to the question, "Who is your father?" Dominick said, with a deep sigh, "I have no father – I am an orphan – I have only a mother."[7]

"Have you any brothers and sisters?"

"No; I wish I had; for perhaps they would love me, and not laugh at me," said Dominick with tears in his eyes; "but I have no brothers but myself."

One day Mr. Jones came into the school-room with an open letter in his hand, saying, "Here, you little irish plockit; here's a letter from your mother."

The little irish blockhead started from his form, and, throwing his grammar on the floor, leaped up higher than he or any boy in the school had ever been seen to leap before; and, clapping his hands, he exclaimed, "A letter from my mother! – And *will* I hear the letter? – And *will* I see her once more? – And *will* I go home these holydays? – O, then I will be too happy!"

"There's no tanger of that," said Mr. Owen ap Jones; "for your mother, like a wise ooman, writes me here, that, py the atvice of your cardian, to oom she is coing to be married, she will not pring you home to Ireland till I send her word you are perfect in your enclish crammer at least."

"I have my lesson perfect, sir," said Dominick, taking his grammar up from the floor; "*will* I say it now?"

"No, you plockit, you *will* not; and I will write your mother word, you have proke Priscian's head four times this tay, since her letter came."

Little Dominick, for the first time, was seen to burst into tears – "*Will* I hear the letter? – *Will* I see my mother? – *Will* I go home?"

"You irish plockit!" continued the relentless grammarian; "you irish plockit, will you never learn the difference between *shall* and *will*?"

The welsh boys all grinned, except Edwards, who hummed loud enough to be heard,

---

Notes

[6] caste or rank

[7] Illiad, 6th Book, l. 432, Andromache says to Hector, "You will make your son an orphan, and your wife a widow" (authors). Homer's classical Greek epic, *The Iliad*, a staple of boys' education in the era.

"And *will* I see him once again?
And *will* I hear him speak?"[8]

Many of the boys were fortunately too ignorant to feel the force of the quotation; but Mr. Owen ap Jones understood it, turned upon his heel, and walked off.

Soon afterward he summoned Dominick to his awful desk; and, pointing with his ruler to the following page in Harris's Hermes, bade him "reat it, and undertant it, if he could."

Little Dominick read, but could not understand.

"Then reat it loud, you plockit."

Dominick read aloud –

"There is *nothing appears so clearly* an object of the mind or intellect as *the future* does, since we can find no place for its existence any where else: not but the same, if we consider, *is equally true* of the past – ."

"Well, co on – What stops the plockit? – Can't you reat Enclish now?"

"Yes, sir; but I was trying to understand it – I was considering, that this is like what they would call an irish bull, if I had said it."

Little Dominick could not explain what he meant in English, that Mr. Owen ap Jones *would* understand; and, to punish him for his impertinent observation, the boy was doomed to learn all that Harris and Lowth have written to explain the nature of *shall* and *will*. – The reader, if he be desirous of knowing the full extent of the penance enjoined, may consult Lowth's Grammar, p. 52, ed. 1799, and Harris's Hermes, p. 10, 11, and 12, 4th edition.[9]

Undismayed at the length of his task, little Dominick only said, "I hope, if I say it all without missing a word, you will not give my mother a bad account of me and my grammar studies, sir."

"Say it all first, without missing a word, and then I shall see what I shall say," replied Mr. Owen ap Jones.

Even the encouragement of this oracular answer excited the boy's fond hopes so keenly, that he lent his little soul to the task, learned it perfectly, said it at night, without missing one word, to his friend Edwards, and said it the next morning, without missing one word, to his master.

"And now, sir," said the boy, looking up, "Will you write to my mother? And shall I see her? And shall I go home?"

"Tell me first, whether you understand all this that you have learnt so cliply,"[10] said Mr. Owen ap Jones.

That was more than his bond. Our hero's countenance fell; and he acknowledged, that he did not understand it perfectly.

"Then I cannot write a coot account of you and your crammer studies to your mother; my conscience coes against it," said the conscientious Mr. Owen ap Jones.

No intreaties could move him. Dominick never saw the letter that was written to his mother; but he felt the consequence. She wrote word this time punctually *by return of the post*, that she was sorry she could not send for him home these holidays, as she had heard so bad an account from Mr. Jones, &c., and as she thought it her duty not to interrupt the course of his education, especially his grammar studies.

Little Dominick heaved many a sigh when he saw the packings up of all his schoolfellows, and dropped a few tears as he looked out of the window, and saw

Notes ─────────────────────────────────────

[8] A slight misquotation of the Scottish song "The Mariner's Wife" (1776) by W. J. Mickle.

[9] Eighteenth-century grammar textbooks.

[10] glibly

them, one after another, get on their welsh ponies, and gallop off towards their homes.

"I have no home to go to," said he.

"Yes, you have," cried Edwards; "and *our* horses are at the door to carry us there."

"To Ireland? me! the horses!" said the poor boy, quite bewildered.

"No; the horses cannot carry you to Ireland," said Edwards, laughing good-naturedly, "but you have a home now in England. I asked my father to let me bring you home with me; and he says 'Yes,' like a dear good father, and has sent the horses – Come, let's away."

"But will Mr. Jones let me go?"

"Yes; he dare not refuse; for my father has a living in his gift, that Jones wants, and which he will not have, if he do not change his tune to you."

Little Dominick could not speak one word, his heart was so full. – No boy could be happier than he was, during these holydays: "the genial current of his soul," which had been frozen by unkindness, flowed with all its natural freedom and force.

Whatever his reasons might be, Mr. Owen ap Jones from this time forward was observed to change his manners towards his irish pupil. He never more complained unjustly of his preaking Priscian's head, seldom called him irish plockit, and once would have flogged a welsh boy for taking up this cast expression of the master's, but that the irish blockhead begged the culprit off.

Little Dominick sprang forward rapidly in his studies: he soon surpassed every boy in the school, his friend Edwards only excepted. In process of time his guardian removed him to a higher seminary of education. Edwards had a tutor at home. The friends separated. Afterward they followed different professions in distant parts of the world; and they neither saw nor heard any more of each other for many years.

Dominick, now no longer little Dominick, went over to India as private secretary to one of our commanders in chief. How he got into this situation, or by what gradations he rose in the world, we are not exactly informed: we know only, that he was the reputed author of a much-admired pamphlet on India affairs, that the dispatches of the general to whom he was secretary were remarkably well written, and that Dominick O'Reilly, esq., returned to England, after several years absence, not miraculously rich, but with a fortune equal to his wishes. His wishes were not extravagant: his utmost ambition was to return to his native country with a fortune that should enable him to live independently of all the world, especially of some of his relations, who had not used him well. His mother was no more.

Upon his arrival in London, one of the first things he did was to read the irish newspapers. – To his inexpressible joy, he saw the estate of Fort-Reilly advertised to be sold – the very estate which had formerly belonged to his own family. Away he posted directly to an attorney's in Cecil-street, who was empowered to dispose of the land.

When this attorney produced a map of the well-known demesne, and an elevation of that house, in which he had spent the happiest hours of his infancy, his heart was so touched, that he was on the point of paying down more for an old ruin than a good new house would cost. The attorney acted *honestly by his client*, and seized this moment to exhibit a plan of the stabling and offices, which, as sometimes is the case in Ireland, were in a style far superiour to the dwelling-house. Our hero surveyed these with transport. He rapidly planned various improvements in imagination, and planted certain favourite spots in the demesne. – During this time the attorney was giving directions to a clerk about some other business, suddenly the name of *Owen ap Jones* struck his ear – He started.

"Let him wait in the front parlour: his money is not forthcoming," said the attorney; "and if he keep Edwards in jail till he rots – ."

"Edwards! Good heavens! – in jail! – What Edwards?" exclaimed our hero.

It was his friend Edwards.

The attorney told him that Mr. Edwards had been involved in great distress by taking upon himself his father's debts, which had been incurred in exploring a mine in Wales; that of all the creditors none had refused to compound, except a welsh parson, who had been presented to his living by old Edwards; that this Mr. Owen ap Jones had thrown young Mr. Edwards into jail for the debt.

"What is the rascal's demand? He shall be paid off this instant," cried Dominick, throwing down the plan of Fort-Reilly; "send for him up, and let me pay him off upon the spot."

"Had not we best finish our business first, about the O'Reilly estate, sir," said the attorney.

"No, sir; damn the O'Reilly estate," cried he, huddling the maps together on the desk, and, taking up the bank notes, which he had begun to reckon for the purchase money – "I beg your pardon, sir – If you knew the facts, you would excuse me – Why does not this rascal come up to be paid?"

The attorney, thunderstruck by this hibernian impetuosity, had not yet found time to take his pen out of his mouth. As he sat transfixed in his arm-chair, O'Reilly ran to the head of the stairs, and called out, in a stentorian voice, "Here, you Mr. Owen ap Jones; come up and be paid off this instant, or you shall never be paid *at all*."

Up stairs hobbled the old schoolmaster, as fast as the gout and welsh ale would let him – "Cot pless me, that voice," he began. –

"Where's your bond, sir?" said the attorney.

"Safe here, Cot be praised," said the terrified Owen ap Jones, pulling out of his bosom, first a blue pocket-handkerchief, and then a tattered welsh grammar, which O'Reilly kicked to the farther end of the room.

"Here is my pond," said he, "in the crammer," which he gathered from the ground; there, fumbling over the leaves, he at length unfolded the precious deposit.

O'Reilly saw the bond, seized it, looked at the sum, paid it into the attorney's hands, tore the seal from the bond; then, without looking at old Jones, whom he dared not trust himself to speak to, he clapped his hat upon his head, and rushed out of the room. He was however obliged to come back again, to ask where Edwards was to be found.

"In the King's Bench prison, sir," said the attorney: "but am I to understand," cried he, holding up the map of the O'Reilly estate, "am I to understand, that you have no farther wish for this bargain?"

"Yes – No – I mean you are to understand that I am off," replied our hero, without looking back – "I'm off – That's plain English."

Arrived at the King's Bench prison, he hurried to the apartment, where Edwards was confined – The bolts flew back; for even the turnkeys seemed to catch our hero's enthusiasm.

"Edwards, my dear boy! how do you do? – Here's a bond debt, justly due to you for my education – O, never mind asking any unnecessary questions; only just make haste out of this undeserved abode – Our old rascal is paid off – Owen ap Jones, you know – Well, how the man stares! – Why now will you have the assurance to pretend to forget who I am? and must I *spake*," continued he, assuming the tone of his childhood – "and must I *spake* to you again in my old irish brogue, before you will ricollict your own *little Dominick?*"

When his friend Edwards was out of prison, and when our hero had leisure to look into business, he returned to the attorney, to see that Mr. Owen ap Jones had been legally satisfied.

"Sir," said the attorney, "I have paid the plaintiff in this suit; and he is satisfied; but I must say," added he with a contemptuous smile, "that you irish gentlemen are rather in too great a hurry in doing business: business, sir, is a thing that must be done slowly, to be well done."

"I am ready now to do business as slowly as you please; but when my friend was in prison, I thought the quicker I did his business the better – Now tell me what mistake I have made, and I will rectify it instantly."

"*Instantly!* – 'Tis well, sir, with your promptitude, that you have to deal with what prejudice thinks uncommon – an honest attorney. – Here are some bank notes of yours, sir, amounting to a good round sum – You made a little blunder in this business: you left me the penalty, instead of the principal, of the bond – just twice as much as you should have done."

"Just twice as much as was in the bond, but not twice as much as I should have done, nor half as much as I should have done, in my opinion," said O'Reilly; "but whatever I did, was with my eyes open: I was persuaded you were an honest man; in which you see I was not mistaken; and as a man of business, I knew you would pay Jones only his due. The remainder of the money I meant, and mean, should lie in your hands for my friend Edwards's use. I feared he would not have taken it from my hands: I therefore left it in yours. To have taken my friend out of prison merely to let him go back again to day, for want of money to keep himself clear with the world, would have been a blunder indeed, but not an irish blunder: our irish blunders are never blunders of the heart."

The Limerick Gloves (by Maria Edgeworth)

From **Popular Tales** (1804)

CHAPTER I
Surmise is often partly True and partly False.

It was Sunday morning, and a fine day in autumn; the bells of Hereford cathedral rang, and all the world smartly dressed were flocking to church.

"Mrs. Hill! Mrs. Hill! – Phoebe! Phoebe! There's the cathedral bell, I say, and neither of you ready for church, and I a churchwarden;" cried Mr. Hill, the tanner, as he stood at the bottom of his own staircase. "I'm ready, Papa," replied Phoebe; and down she came, looking so clean, so fresh, and so gay, that her stern father's brows unbent, and he could only say to her, as she was drawing on a new pair of gloves, "Child, you ought to have had those gloves on before this time of day."

"Before this time of day!" cried Mrs. Hill, who was now coming down stairs completely equipped, "Before this time of day! She should know better, I say, than to put on those gloves at all: more especially when going to the cathedral."

"The gloves are very good gloves, as far as I see," replied Mr. Hill. "But no matter now. It is more fitting that we should be in proper time in our pew, to set an example, as becomes us, than to stand here talking of gloves and nonsense."

He offered his wife and daughter each an arm, and set out for the cathedral; but Phoebe was too busy in drawing on her new gloves, and her mother was too angry at the sight of them, to accept of Mr. Hill's courtesy: "What I say is always nonsense,

I know, Mr. Hill," resumed the matron: "but I can see as far into a millstone as other folks. Was it not I that first gave you a hint of what became of the great dog, that we lost out of our tan-yard last winter? And was it not I who first took notice to you, Mr. Hill, churchwarden as you are, of the hole under the foundation of the cathedral? Was it not, I ask you, Mr. Hill?"

"But, my dear Mrs. Hill, what has all this to do with Phoebe's gloves?"

"Are you blind, Mr. Hill? Don't you see that they are Limerick gloves?"

"What of that?" said Mr. Hill; still preserving his composure, as it was his custom to do as long as he could, when he saw his wife was ruffled.

"What of that, Mr. Hill! why don't you know that Limerick is in Ireland, Mr. Hill?"

"With all my heart, my dear."

"Yes, and with all your heart, I suppose, Mr. Hill, you would see our cathedral blown up, some fair day or other, and your own daughter married to the person that did it; and you a churchwarden, Mr. Hill."

"God forbid!" cried Mr. Hill; and he stopped short and settled his wig. Presently recovering himself, he added, "But, Mrs. Hill, the cathedral is not yet blown up; and our Phoebe is not yet married."

"No; but what of that, Mr. Hill? Forewarned is forearmed, as I told you before your dog was gone: but you would not believe me, and you see how it turned out in that case; and so it will in this case, you'll see, Mr. Hill."

"But you puzzle and frighten me out of my wits, Mrs. Hill," said the churchwarden; again settling his wig. "*In that case and in this case!* I can't understand a syllable of what you've been saying to me this half hour. In plain English, what is there the matter about Phoebe's gloves?"

"In plain English then, Mr. Hill, since you can understand nothing else, please to ask your daughter Phoebe who gave her those gloves. Phoebe, who gave you those gloves?"

"I wish they were burnt," said the husband; whose patience could endure no longer. "Who gave you those cursed gloves, Phoebe?"

"Papa," answered Phoebe, in a low voice, "they were a present from Mr. Brian O'Neill."

"The Irish glover!" cried Mr. Hill, with a look of terror.

"Yes," resumed the mother; "very true, Mr. Hill, I assure you. Now, you see, I had my reasons."

"Take off the gloves directly: I order you, Phoebe," said her father, in his most peremptory tone. "I took a mortal dislike to that Mr. Brian O'Neill the first time I ever saw him. He's an Irishman, and that's enough, and too much for me. Off with the gloves, Phoebe! When I order a thing, it must be done."

Phoebe seemed to find some difficulty in getting off the gloves, and gently urged that she could not well go into the cathedral without them. This objection was immediately removed, by her mother's pulling from her pocket a pair of mittens, which had once been brown, and once been whole, but which were now rent in sundry places; and which, having been long stretched by one who was twice the size of Phoebe, now hung in huge wrinkles upon her well-turned arms.

"But, papa," said Phoebe, "why should we take a dislike to him because he is an Irishman? Cannot an Irishman be a good man?"

The churchwarden made no answer to this question; but, a few seconds after it was put to him, observed that the cathedral bell had just done ringing; and, as they were now got to the church door, Mrs. Hill, with a significant look at Phoebe, remarked that it was no proper time to talk or think of good men, or bad men, or Irishmen, or any men, especially for a churchwarden's daughter.

We pass over in silence the many conjectures that were made, by several of the congregation, concerning the reason why Miss Phoebe Hill should appear in such a shameful shabby pair of gloves on a Sunday. After service was ended the churchwarden went, with great mystery, to examine the hole under the foundation of the cathedral; and Mrs. Hill repaired, with the grocer's and the stationer's ladies, to take a walk in the Close; where she boasted to all her female acquaintance, whom she called her friends, of her maternal discretion in prevailing upon Mr. Hill to forbid her daughter Phoebe to wear the Limerick gloves.

Chapter II

Words ill understood are among our worst Misfortunes.

In the mean time, Phoebe walked pensively homewards; endeavouring to discover why her father should take a mortal dislike to a man, at first sight, merely because he was an Irishman; and why her mother had talked so much of the great dog, which had been lost last year out of the tan-yard; and of the hole under the foundation of the cathedral? What has all this to do with my Limerick gloves? thought she. The more she thought, the less connexion she could perceive between these things: for, as she had not taken a dislike to Mr. Brian O'Neill at first sight, because he was an Irishman, she could not think it quite reasonable to suspect him of making away with her father's dog; nor yet of a design to blow up Hereford cathedral. As she was pondering upon these matters, she came within sight of the ruins of a poor woman's house, which, a few months before this time, had been burnt down. She recollected that her first acquaintance with her lover began at the time of this fire; and she thought that the courage and humanity he shewed, in exerting himself to save this unfortunate woman and her children, justified her notion of the possibility that an Irishman might be a good man.

The name of the poor woman, whose house had been burnt down, was Smith: she was a widow, and she now lived at the extremity of a narrow lane in a wretched habitation. Why Phoebe thought of her with more concern than usual at this instant we need not examine, but she did; and, reproaching herself for having neglected it for some weeks past, she resolved to go directly to see the widow Smith, and to give her a crown which she had long had in her pocket, with which she had intended to have bought play tickets.

It happened that the first person she saw in the poor widow's kitchen was the identical Mr. O'Neill. "I did not expect to see any body here but you, Mrs. Smith," said Phoebe, blushing.

"So much the greater the pleasure of the meeting; to me, I mean, Miss Hill," said O'Neill rising, and putting down a little boy, with whom he had been playing. Phoebe went on talking to the poor woman; and, after slipping the crown into her hand, said she would call again. O'Neill, surprised at the change in her manner, followed her when she left the house, and said, "it would be a great misfortune to me to have done any thing to offend Miss Hill; especially if I could not conceive how or what it was, which is my case at this present speaking." And, as the spruce glover spoke, he fixed his eyes upon Phoebe's ragged gloves. She drew them up in vain; and then said, with her natural simplicity and gentleness, "You have not done any thing to offend me, Mr. O'Neill; but you are some way or other displeasing to my father and mother, and they have forbid me to wear the Limerick gloves."

"And sure Miss Hill would not be after changing her opinion of her humble servant for no reason in life, but because her father and mother, who have taken a prejudice against him, are a little contrary."

"No," replied Phoebe; "I should not change my opinion, without any reason; but I have not yet had time to fix my opinion of you, Mr. O'Neill."

"To let you know a piece of my mind then, my dear Miss Hill," resumed he, "the more contrary they are the more pride and joy it would give me to win and wear you, in spite of 'em all; and, if without a farthing in your pocket, so much the more I should rejoice in the opportunity of proving to your dear self, and all else whom it may consarn, that Brian O'Neill is no Irish fortune-hunter, and scorns them that are so narrow-minded as to think that no other kind of cattle but them there fortune-hunters can come out of all Ireland. So, my dear Phoebe, now we understand one another, I hope you will not be paining my eyes any longer with the sight of these odious brown bags, which are not fit to be worn by any Christian's arms, to say nothing of Miss Hill's, which are the handsomest, without any compliment, that ever I saw; and, to my mind, would become a pair of Limerick gloves beyond any thing; and I expect she'll show her generosity and proper spirit by putting them on immediately."

"You expect, Sir!" repeated Miss Hill, with a look of more indignation than her gentle countenance had ever before been seen to assume. Expect! If he had said hope, thought she, it would have been another thing: but expect! what right has he to expect?

Now Miss Hill, unfortunately, was not sufficiently acquainted with the Irish idiom to know that to expect, in Ireland, is the same thing as to hope in England; and, when her Irish admirer said I expect, he meant only in plain English I hope. But thus it is that a poor Irishman, often, for want of understanding the niceties of the English language, says the rudest when he means to say the civilest things imaginable.

Miss Hill's feelings were so much hurt by this unlucky "I expect," that the whole of his speech, which had before made some favourable impression upon her, now lost its effect; and she replied with proper spirit, as she thought, "You expect a great deal too much, Mr. O'Neill; and more than ever I gave you reason to do. It would be neither pleasure nor pride to me to be won and worn, as you were pleased to say, in spite of them all; and to be thrown, without a farthing in my pocket, upon the protection of one who expects so much at first setting out. – So I assure you, Sir, whatever you may expect, I shall not put on the Limerick gloves."

Mr. O'Neill was not without his share of pride, and proper spirit: nay, he had, it must be confessed, in common with some others of his countrymen, an improper share of pride and spirit. Fired by the lady's coldness, he poured forth a volley of reproaches; and ended by wishing, as he said, a good morning for ever and ever, to one who could change her opinion point blank, like the weathercock. "I am, Miss, your most obedient; and I expect you'll never think no more of poor Brian O'Neill, and the Limerick gloves."

If he had not been in too great a passion to observe any thing, poor Brian O'Neill would have found out that Phoebe was not a weathercock: but he left her abruptly, and hurried away, imagining all the while that it was Phoebe, and not himself, who was in a rage. Thus, to the horseman, who is galloping at full speed, the hedges, trees, and houses, seem rapidly to recede; whilst, in reality, they never move from their places. It is he that flies from them, and not they from him.

CHAPTER III

Endeavours to be consistent often lead to Obstinacy in Error.

On Monday morning Miss Jenny Brown, the perfumer's daughter, came to pay Phoebe a morning visit, with face of busy joy.

"So, my dear!" said she: "fine doings in Hereford! but what makes you look so downcast? To be sure you are invited, as well as the rest of us."

"Invited where?" cried Mrs. Hill, who was present, and who could never endure to hear of an invitation in which she was not included. "Invited where, pray, Miss Jenny?"

"La! have not you heard? Why, we all took it for granted that you, and Miss Phoebe, would have been the first and foremost to have been asked to Mr. O'Neill's ball."

"Ball!" cried Mrs. Hill; and luckily saved Phoebe, who was in some agitation, the trouble of speaking. "Why this is a mighty sudden thing: I never heard a tittle of it before."

"Well, this is really extraordinary! And, Phoebe, have you not received a pair of Limerick gloves?"

"Yes, I have," said Phoebe, "but what then? What has my Limerick gloves to do with the ball?"

"A great deal," replied Jenny. "Don't you know that a pair of Limerick gloves is, as one may say, a ticket to this ball? for every lady, that has been asked, has had a pair sent to her along with the card; and I believe as many as twenty, beside myself, have been asked this morning."

Jenny then produced her new pair of Limerick gloves; and, as she tried them on, and showed how well they fitted, she counted up the names of the ladies who, to her knowledge, were to be at this ball. When she had finished the catalogue, she expatiated upon the grand preparations which it was said the widow O'Neill, Mr. O'Neill's mother, was making for the supper; and concluded by condoling with Mrs. Hill, for her misfortune in not having been invited. Jenny took her leave, to get her dress in readiness: "for," added she, "Mr. O'Neill has engaged me to open the ball, in case Phoebe does not go: but I suppose she will cheer up and go, as she has a pair of Limerick gloves as well as the rest of us."

There was a silence for some minutes, after Jenny's departure, which was broken by Phoebe, who told her mother that, early in the morning, a note had been brought to her, which she had returned unopened: because she knew, from the hand-writing of the direction, that it came from Mr. O'Neill.

We must observe that Phoebe had already told her mother of her meeting with this gentleman at the poor widow's; and of all that had passed between them afterwards. This openness, on her part, had softened the heart of Mrs. Hill; who was really inclined to be good-natured, provided people would allow that she had more penetration than any one else in Hereford. She was moreover a good deal piqued and alarmed by the idea that the perfumer's daughter might rival and outshine her own. Whilst she had thought herself sure of Mr. O'Neill's attachment to Phoebe, she had looked higher; especially as she was persuaded, by the perfumer's lady, to think that an Irishman could not be a good match: but now she began to suspect that the perfumer's lady had changed her opinion of Irishmen, since she did not object to her own Jenny's leading up the ball at Mr. O'Neill's.

All these thoughts passed rapidly in the mother's mind; and, with her fear of losing an admirer for her Phoebe, the value of that admirer suddenly rose in her estimation. Thus, at an auction, if a lot is going to be knocked down to a lady, who is the only person that has bid for it, even she feels discontented, and despises that which nobody covets; but if, as the hammer is falling, many voices answer to the question, Who bids more? then her anxiety to secure the prize suddenly rises; and, rather than be outbid, she will give far beyond its value.

"Why, child," said Mrs. Hill, "since you have a pair of Limerick gloves; and since certainly that note was an invitation to us to this ball; and since it is much more fitting that you should open the ball than Jenny Brown; and since, after all, it was very handsome and genteel of the young man to say he would take you without a farthing in your pocket, which shows that those were misinformed who talked of him as an Irish adventurer; and since we are not certain t'was he made away with the dog, although he said its barking was a great nuisance, and since, he did not kill or entice away the dog, there is no great reason to suppose he was the person who made the hole under the foundation of the cathedral, or that he could have such a wicked thought as to blow it up, and since he must be in a very good way of business to be able to afford giving away four or five guineas worth of Limerick gloves, and balls and suppers, and since, after all, it is no fault of his to be an Irishman, I give it as my vote and opinion, my dear, that you put on your Limerick gloves and go to this ball; and I'll go and speak to your father, and bring him round to our opinion; and then I'll pay the morning visit I owe to the widow O'Neill, and make up your quarrel with Brian. Love quarrels are easy to make up, you know; and then we shall have things all upon velvet again; and Jenny Brown need not come, with her hypocritical condoling face, to us anymore."

After running this speech glibly off, Mrs. Hill, without waiting to hear a syllable from poor Phoebe, trotted off in search of her consort. It was not, however, quite so easy a task, as his wife expected it would be, to bring Mr. Hill round to her opinion. He was slow in declaring himself of any opinion; but, when once he had said a thing, there was but little chance of altering his notions. On this occasion, Mr. Hill was doubly bound to his prejudice against our unlucky Irishman; for he had mentioned, with great solemnity, at the club which he frequented, the grand affair of the hole under the foundation of the cathedral; and his suspicions that there was a design to blow it up. Several of the club had laughed at this idea; others, who supposed that Mr. O'Neill was a Roman Catholic, and who had a confused notion that a Roman Catholic *must* be a very wicked dangerous being, thought that there might be a great deal in the churchwarden's suggestions; and observed that a very watchful eye ought to be kept upon this Irish glover, who had come to settle at Hereford nobody knew why, and who seemed to have money at command nobody knew how.

The news of this ball sounded to Mr. Hill's prejudiced imagination like the news of a conspiracy. Aye! aye! thought he; the Irishman is cunning enough! But we shall be too many for him: he wants to throw all the good sober folks of Hereford off their guard, by feasting and dancing, and carousing, I take it; and so to perpetrate his evil designs when it is least suspected: but we shall be prepared for him! Fools as he takes us plain Englishmen to be, I warrant.

In consequence of these most shrewd coagitations, our churchwarden silenced his wife with a peremptory nod, when she came to persuade him to let Phoebe put on the Limerick gloves, and go to the ball. "To this ball she shall not go; and I charge her not to put on those Limerick gloves, as she values my blessing," said Mr. Hill. "Please to tell her so, Mrs. Hill, and trust to my judgment and discretion in all things, Mrs. Hill. Strange work may be in Hereford yet: but I'll say no more, I must go and consult with knowing men, who are of my opinion."

He sallied forth, and Mrs. Hill was left in a state which only those who are troubled with the disease of excessive curiosity can rightly comprehend or compassionate. She hied her back to Phoebe, to whom she announced her father's answer; and then went gossiping to all her female acquaintance in Hereford, to tell them all that she knew, and all that she did not know; and to endeavour to find out a secret where there was none to be found.

CHAPTER IV

The Certainties of Suspicion are always doubtful, and often ridiculous.

There are trials of temper in all conditions; and no lady, in high or low life, could endure them with a better grace than Phoebe. Whilst Mr. and Mrs. Hill were busied abroad, there came to see Phoebe one of the widow Smith's children. With artless expressions of gratitude to Phoebe, this little girl mixed the praises of O'Neill, who, she said, had been the constant friend of her mother, and had given her money every week since the fire happened. "Mammy loves him dearly, for being so good natured," continued the child; "and he has been good to other people as well as to us."

"To whom?" said Phoebe.

"To a poor man who has lodged for these few days past next door to us," replied the child; "I don't know his name rightly, but he is an Irishman; and he goes out a haymaking in the day-time, along with a number of others. He knew Mr. O'Neill in his own country, and he told mammy a great deal about his goodness."

As the child finished these words, Phoebe took out of a drawer some clothes, which she had made for the poor woman's children, and gave them to the little girl. It happened that the Limerick gloves had been thrown into this drawer; and Phoebe's favourable sentiments of the giver of those gloves were revived by what she had just heard, and by the confession Mrs. Hill had made, that she had no reasons, and but vague suspicions, for thinking ill of him. She laid the gloves perfectly smooth, and strewed over them, whilst the little girl went on talking of Mr. O'Neill, the leaves of a rose which she had worn on Sunday.

Mr. Hill was all this time in deep conference with those prudent men of Hereford, who were of his own opinion, about the perilous hole under the cathedral. The ominous circumstance of this ball was also considered, the great expence at which the Irish glover lived, and his giving away gloves; which was a sure sign he was not under any necessity to sell them, and consequently a proof that, though he pretended to be a glover, he was something wrong in disguise. Upon putting all these things together, it was resolved, by these overwise politicians, that the best thing that could be done for Hereford, and the only possible means of preventing the immediate destruction of its cathedral, would be to take Mr. O'Neill into custody. Upon recollection, however, it was perceived that there were no legal grounds on which he could be attacked. At length, after consulting an attorney, they devised what they thought an admirable mode of proceeding.

Our Irish hero had not that punctuality which English tradesmen usually observe in the payment of bills: he had, the preceding year, run up a long bill with a grocer in Hereford; and, as he had not at Christmas cash in hand to pay it, he had given a note, payable six months after date. The grocer, at Mr. Hill's request, made over the note to him; and it was determined that the money should be demanded, as it was now due, and that, if it was not paid directly, O'Neill should be that night arrested. How Mr. Hill made the discovery of this debt to the grocer agree with his former notion, that the Irish glover had always money at command, we cannot well conceive; but anger and prejudice will swallow down the grossest contradictions without difficulty.

When Mr. Hill's clerk went to demand payment of the note, O'Neill's head was full of the ball which he was to give that evening. He was much surprised at the unexpected appearance of the note: he had not ready money by him to pay it; and, after swearing a good deal at the clerk, and complaining of this ungenerous and ungentleman-like behaviour in the grocer and the tanner, he told the clerk to be gone, and not to be bothering him at such an unseasonable time; that he could not have the money then, and did not deserve to have it at all.

This language and conduct were rather new to the English clerk's mercantile ears: we cannot wonder that it should seem to him, as he said to his master, more the language of a madman than a man of business. This want of punctuality in money transactions, and this mode of treating contracts as matters of favour and affection, might not have damned the fame of our hero in his own country, where such conduct is, alas! too common; but he was now in a kingdom where the manners and customs are so directly opposite that he could meet with no allowance for his national faults. It would be well for his countrymen if they were made, even by a few mortifications, somewhat sensible of this important difference in the habits of Irish and English traders, before they come to settle in England.

But, to proceed with our story. On the night of Mr. O'Neill's grand ball, as he was seeing his fair partner, the perfumer's daughter, safe home, he felt himself tapped on the shoulder by no friendly hand. When he was told that he was the king's prisoner, he vociferated with sundry strange oaths, which we forbear to repeat, "No, I am not the king's prisoner! I am the prisoner of that shabby rascally tanner, Jonathan Hill. None but he would arrest a gentleman, in this way, for a trifle not worth mentioning."

Miss Jenny Brown screamed when she found herself under the protection of a man who was arrested; and, what between her screams and his oaths, there was such a disturbance that a mob gathered.

Among this mob there was a party of Irish haymakers; who, after returning late from a harvest-home, had been drinking in a neighbouring ale-house. With one accord, they took part with their countryman, and would have rescued him from the civil officers with all the pleasure in life, if he had not fortunately possessed just sufficient sense and command of himself to restrain their party-spirit, and to forbid them, as they valued his life and reputation, to interfere, by word or deed, in his defence.

He then dispatched one of the haymakers home to his mother, to inform her of what had happened; and to request that she would get somebody to be bail for him as soon as possible, as the officers said they could not let him out of their sight till he was bailed by substantial people, or till the debt was discharged.

The widow O'Neill was just putting out the candles in the ball-room when this news of her son's arrest was brought to her. We pass over Hibernian exclamations: she consoled her pride by reflecting that it would certainly be the most easy thing imaginable to procure bail for Mr. O'Neill in Hereford, where he had so many friends who had just been dancing at his house; but to dance at his house she found was one thing, and to be bail for him quite another. Each guest sent excuses; and the widow O'Neill was astonished at what never fails to astonish every body when it happens to themselves. "Rather than let my son be detained in this manner for a paultry debt," cried she, "I'd sell all I have within half an hour to a pawnbroker." It was well no pawn-broker heard this declaration: she was too warm to consider economy. She sent for a pawnbroker, who lived in the same street, and, after pledging goods to treble the amount of the debt, she obtained ready money for her son's release.

O'Neill, after being in custody for about an hour and a half, was set at liberty upon the payment of his debt. As he passed by the cathedral in his way home, he heard the clock strike; and he called to a man, who was walking backwards and forwards in the church-yard, to ask whether it was two or three that the clock struck. "Three," answered the man; "and, as yet, all is safe."

O'Neill, whose head was full of other things, did not stop to inquire the meaning of these last words. He little suspected that this man was a watchman, whom the over vigilant churchwarden had stationed there to guard the Hereford cathedral from his attacks. O'Neill little guessed that he had been arrested merely to keep him from blowing up the cathedral this night. The arrest had an excellent effect upon his mind, for he was a young man of good sense: it made him resolve to retrench his expences in time, to live more like a glover, and less like a gentleman; and to aim more at establishing credit, and less at gaining popularity. He found, from experience, that good friends will not pay bad debts.

Chapter V

Conjecture is an Ignis Fatuus,[1] that by seeming to light may dangerously mislead.

On Thursday morning, our churchwarden rose in unusually good spirits, congratulating himself upon the eminent service he had done to the city of Hereford, by his sagacity in discovering the foreign plot to blow up the cathedral, and by his dexterity in having the enemy held in custody, at the very hour when the dreadful deed was to have been perpetrated. Mr. Hill's knowing friends further agreed it would be necessary to have a guard that should sit up every night in the church-yard; and that, as soon as they could, by constantly watching the enemy's motions, procure any information which the attorney should deem sufficient grounds for a legal proceeding, they should lay the whole business before the mayor.

After arranging all this most judiciously and mysteriously with friends who were exactly of his own opinion, Mr. Hill laid aside his dignity of churchwarden; and, assuming his other character of a tanner, proceeded to his tan-yard. What was his surprise and consternation, when he beheld his great rick of oak bark levelled to the ground; the pieces of bark were scattered far and wide, some over the close, some over the fields, and some were seen swimming upon the water! No tongue, no pen, no muse can describe the feelings of our tanner at this spectacle! feelings which became the more violent from the absolute silence which he imposed on himself upon this occasion. He instantly decided, in his own mind, that this injury was perpetrated by O'Neill, in revenge for his arrest; and went privately to the attorney to enquire what was to be done, on his part, to secure legal vengeance.

The attorney unluckily, or at least as Mr. Hill thought unluckily, had been sent for, half an hour before, by a gentleman at some distance from Hereford, to draw up a will; so that our tanner was obliged to postpone his legal operations.

We forbear to recount his return, and how many times he walked up and down the close to view his scattered bark, and to estimate the damage that had been done to him. At length that hour came which usually suspends all passions by the more imperious power of appetite – the hour of dinner; an hour of which it was never needful to remind Mr. Hill by watch, clock, or dial; for he was blessed with a punctual appetite, and powerful as punctual: so powerful, indeed, that it often excited the spleen of his more genteel, or less hungry wife. – "Bless my stars, Mr. Hill," she would oftentimes say, "I am really downright ashamed to see you eat so much; and when company is to dine with us, I do wish you would take a snack by way of a damper before dinner, that you may not look so prodigious famishing and ungenteel."

Notes

THE LIMERICK GLOVES
[1] *Foolish fire*, lights that would sometimes appear over marshy ground and mislead travelers.

Upon this hint, Mr. Hill commenced a practice, to which he ever afterwards religiously adhered, of going, whether there was to be company or no company, into the kitchen regularly every day, half an hour before dinner, to take a slice from the roast or the boiled before it went up to table. As he was this day, according to his custom, in the kitchen, taking his snack by way of a damper, he heard the house-maid and the cook talking about some wonderful fortune-teller, whom the housemaid had been consulting. This fortune-teller was no less a personage than the successor to Bampfylde Moore Carew, king of the gipsies, whose life and adventures are probably in many, too many, of our readers' hands.[2] Bampfylde the second, king of the gipsies, assumed this title, in hopes of becoming as famous, or as infamous, as his predecessor: he was now holding his court in a wood near the town of Hereford, and numbers of servant-maids and 'prentices went to consult him – nay, it was whispered that he was resorted to, secretly, by some whose education might have taught them better sense.

Numberless were the instances which our churchwarden heard in his kitchen of the supernatural skill of this cunning man; and, whilst Mr. Hill ate his snack with his wonted gravity, he revolved great designs in his secret soul. Mrs. Hill was surprised, several times during dinner, to see her consort put down his knife and fork, and meditate. "Gracious me, Mr. Hill, what can have happened to you this day? What can you be thinking of, Mr. Hill, that can make you forget what you have upon your plate?"

"Mrs. Hill," replied the thoughtful churchwarden, "our grandmother Eve had too much curiosity; and we all know it did not lead to good. What I am thinking of will be known to you in due time; but not now, Mrs. Hill; therefore, pray no questions, or teizing, or pumping. What I think, I think; what I say, I say; what I know, I know; and that is enough for you to know at present: only this, Phoebe, you did very well not to put on the Limerick gloves, child. What I know, I know. Things will turn out just as I said from the first. What I say, I say; and what I think, I think; and this is enough for you to know at present."

Having finished dinner with this solemn speech, Mr. Hill settled himself in his arm-chair, to take his after-dinner's nap; and he dreamed of blowing up cathedrals, and of oak-bark floating upon the waters; and the cathedral was, he thought, blown up by a man dressed in a pair of woman's Limerick gloves, and the oak-bark turned into mutton-steaks, after which his great dog Jowler was swimming; when, all on a sudden, as he was going to beat Jowler for eating the bark transformed into mutton steaks, Jowler became Bampfylde the second king of the gipsies; and, putting a horsewhip with a silver handle into Hill's hand, commanded him three times, in a voice as loud as the town-crier's, to have O'Neill whipped through the market-place of Hereford: but, just as he was going to the window to see this whipping, his wig fell off and he awoke.

It was difficult, even for Mr. Hill's sagacity, to make sense of this dream: but he had the wise art of always finding in his dreams something that confirmed his waking determinations. Before he went to sleep, he had half resolved to consult the king of the gipsies, in the absence of the attorney; and his dream made him now wholly determine upon this prudent step. From Bampfylde the second, thought he, I shall learn for certain who made the hole under the cathedral, who pulled down my rick of bark, and who made away with my dog, Jowler; and then I shall swear examinations against O'Neill without waiting for attornies. I will follow my own way in this business: I have always found my own way best.

So, when the dusk of the evening increased, our wise man set out towards the wood to consult the cunning man. Bampfylde the second, king of the gipsies, resided in a sort

Notes ——————————————————————————————————

[2] *An Apology for the Life of Bampfylde Moore Carew* (1745) was republished a number of times in the eighteenth century.

of hut made of the branches of trees: the churchwarden stooped, but did not stoop low enough, as he entered this temporary palace; and, whilst his body was almost bent double, his peruke was caught upon a twig. From this aukward situation he was relieved by the consort of the king; and he now beheld, by the light of some embers, the person of his gipsey majesty, to whose sublime appearance this dim light was so favourable that it struck a secret awe into our wise man's soul; and, forgetting Hereford cathedral, and oak-bark, and Limerick gloves, he stood for some seconds speechless. During this time, the queen very dexterously disencumbered his pocket of all superfluous articles. When he recovered his recollection, he put, with great solemnity, the following queries to the king of the gipsies, and received the following answers:

"Do you know a dangerous Irishman, of the name of O'Neill; who has come, for purposes best known to himself, to settle at Hereford?"

"Yes, we know him well."

"Indeed! And what do you know of him?"

"That he is a dangerous Irishman."

"Right! And it was he, was it not, that made away with my dog Jowler, that used to guard the tan-yard?"

"It was."

"And who was it that pulled down, or caused to be pulled down, my rick of oak-bark?"

"It was the person that you suspect."

"And was it the person whom I suspect that made the hole under the foundation of our cathedral?"

"The same, and no other."

"And for what purpose did he make that hole?"

"For a purpose that must not be named," replied the king of the gipsies; nodding his head in a mysterious manner.

"But it may be named to me," cried the churchwarden, "for I have found it out, and I am one of the churchwardens; and is it not fit that a plot to blow up the Hereford cathedral should be known *to* me, and *through* me?"

> "Now, take my word,
> Wise man of Hereford,
> None in safety may be,
> Till the *bad man* doth flee."

These oracular verses, pronounced by Bampfylde with all the enthusiasm of one who was inspired, had the desired effect upon our wise man; and he left the presence of the king of the gipsies with a prodigiously high opinion of his majesty's judgment and of his own, fully resolved to impart, the next morning, to the mayor of Hereford, his important discoveries.

Chapter VI

Falsehood and Folly usually confute themselves.

Now it happened that, during the time Mr. Hill was putting the foregoing queries to Bampfylde the second, there came to the door, or entrance of the audience-chamber, an Irish haymaker, who wanted to consult the cunning man about a little leathern purse which he had lost, whilst he was making hay, in a field near Hereford. This hay-maker was the same person who, as we have related, spoke so advantageously of our hero, O'Neill, to the widow Smith. As this man, whose name was Paddy M'Cormack, stood at the entrance of the gipsies' hut, his attention was caught by the name of O'Neill; and he lost not a word of all that passed. He had reason to be somewhat surprised at hearing Bampfylde assert it was O'Neill who had pulled down the rick of bark. "By the holy poker," said he to himself, "the old fellow now is out there. I know more o' that matter than he does, no offence to his majesty: he knows no more of my purse, I'll engage now, than he does of this man's rick of bark and his dog: so I'll keep my tester in my pocket, and not be giving it to this king o' the gipsies, as they call him; who, as near as I can guess, is no better than a cheat. But there is one secret which I can be telling this conjuror himself, he shall not find it such an easy matter to do all what he thinks; he shall not be after ruining an innocent countryman of my own, whilst Paddy M'Cormack has a tongue and brains."

Now Paddy M'Cormack had the best reason possible for knowing that Mr. O'Neill did not pull down Mr. Hill's rick of bark; it was M'Cormack himself who, in the heat of his resentment for the insulting arrest of his countryman in the streets of Hereford, had instigated his fellow hay-makers to this mischief: he headed them, and thought he was doing a clever spirited action.

There is a strange mixture of virtue and vice in the minds of the lower class of Irish: or rather a strange confusion in their ideas of right and wrong, from want of proper education. As soon as poor Paddy found out that his spirited action of pulling down the rick of bark was likely to be the ruin of his countryman, he resolved to make all the amends in his power for his folly: he went to collect his fellow hay-makers and persuaded them to assist him this night in rebuilding what they had pulled down.

They went to this work when every body except themselves, as they thought, was asleep in Hereford. They had just completed the stack, and were all going away except Paddy, who was seated at the very top finishing the pile, when they heard a loud voice cry out, "Here they are; Watch! Watch!"

Immediately all the hay-makers, who could, ran off as fast as possible. It was the watch who had been sitting up at the cathedral who gave the alarm. Paddy was taken from the top of the rick, and lodged in the watch-house till morning. "Since I'm to be rewarded this way for doing a good action, sorrow take me," said he, "if they catch me doing another the longest day ever I live."

Happy they who have in their neighbourhood such a magistrate as Mr. Marshal. He was a man who, to an exact knowledge of the duties of his office, joined the power of discovering truth from the midst of contradictory evidence; and the happy art of soothing, or laughing, the angry passions into good humour. It was a common saying in Hereford – that no one ever came out of Justice Marshal's house as angry as he went into it.

Mr. Marshal had scarcely breakfasted when he was informed that Mr. Hill, the churchwarden, wanted to speak to him on business of the utmost importance. Mr. Hill, the churchwarden, was ushered in; and, with gloomy solemnity, took a seat opposite to Mr. Marshal.

"Sad doings in Hereford, Mr. Marshal! Sad doings, sir."

"Sad doings? Why, I was told we had merry doings in Hereford. A ball the night before last, as I heard."

"So much the worse, Mr. Marshal; so much the worse: as those think with reason that see as far into things as I do."

"So much the better, Mr. Hill," said Mr. Marshal laughing; "so much the better: as those think with reason that see no farther into things than I do."

"But, Sir," said the churchwarden, still more solemnly, "this is no laughing matter, nor time for laughing; begging your pardon, Mr. Mayor. Why, Sir, the night of that there diabolical ball, our Hereford cathedral, Sir, would have been blown up – blown up from the foundation, if it had not been for me, Sir!"

"Indeed, Mr. Churchwarden! And pray how, and by whom, was the cathedral to be blown up; and what was there diabolical in this ball?"

Here Mr. Hill let Mr. Marshal into the whole history of his early dislike to O'Neill, and his shrewd suspicions of him the first moment he saw him in Hereford; related in the most prolix manner all that the reader knows already, and concluded by saying that, as he was now certain of his facts, he was come to swear examinations against this villanous Irishman, who, he hoped, would be speedily brought to justice, as he deserved.

"To justice he shall be brought, as he deserves," said Mr. Marshal; "but, before I write, and before you swear, will you have the goodness to inform me how you have made yourself as certain as you evidently are, of what you call your facts?"

"Sir, that is a secret," replied our wise man, "which I shall trust to you alone;" and he whispered into Mr. Marshal's ear that his information came from Bampfylde the second, king of the gipsies.

Mr. Marshal instantly burst into laughter; then composing himself said, "My good Sir, I am really glad that you have proceeded no farther in this business; and that no one in Hereford, besides myself, knows that you were on the point of swearing examinations against a man on the evidence of Bampfylde the second, king of the gipsies.[3] My dear Sir, it would be a standing joke against you to the end of your days. A grave man, like Mr. Hill; and a churchwarden too! Why, you would be the laughing-stock of Hereford!"

Now Mr. Marshal well knew the character of the man to whom he was talking, who, above all things on earth, dreaded to be laughed at. Mr. Hill coloured all over his face, and, pushing back his wig by way of settling it, shewed that he blushed not only all over his face but all over his head.

"Why, Mr. Marshal, Sir," said he, "as to my being laughed at, it is what I did not look for, being as there are some men in Hereford, to whom I have mentioned that hole in the cathedral, who have thought it no laughing matter, and who have been precisely of my own opinion thereupon."

"But did you tell these gentlemen that you had been consulting the king of the gipsies?"

"No, Sir, no: I can't say that I did."

"Then, I advise you, keep your own counsel, as I will."

Mr. Hill, whose imagination wavered between the hole in the cathedral and his rick of bark on one side, and between his rick of bark and his dog Jowler on the other, now began to talk of the dog, and now of the rick of bark; and when he had exhausted all he had to say upon these subjects, Mr. Marshal gently pulled him towards the window, and putting a spy-glass into his hand, bid him look towards his own tan-yard, and tell him what he saw. To his great surprise, Mr. Hill saw his rick of bark rebuilt. "Why, it was not there last night," exclaimed he, rubbing his eyes. "Why some conjurer must have done this."

Notes

[3] The following passage is an extract from Colquhoun, On the Police of the Metropolis, page 69: – "An instance of mischievous credulity, occasioned by consulting this impostor," (*a man calling himself an astrologer, who practised long in the Curtain-road, Shoreditch, London; and who is said, in conjunction with his associates, to have made near 300l. a year by practising on the credulity of the lower order of the people,*) "fell lately under the review of a police magistrate. A person, having property stolen from him, went to consult the conjurer respecting the thief; who having described something like the person of a man whom he suspected, his credulity and folly so far got the better of his reason and reflection, as to induce him, upon the authority of this impostor, actually to charge his neighbour with a felony, and to cause him to be apprehended. The magistrate settled the matter by discharging the prisoner, reprimanding the accuser severely, and ordering the conjurer to be taken into custody, according to law, as a rogue and a vagabond" (author). Patrick Colquhoun's *Treatise on the Police of the Metropolis* (1796) was a key work in the early development of modern policing.

"No," replied Mr. Marshal, "no conjurer did it; but your friend Bampfylde the second, king of the gipsies, was the cause of its being rebuilt; and here is the man who actually pulled it down, and who actually rebuilt it."

As he said these words, Mr. Marshal opened the door of an adjoining room, and beckoned to the Irish hay-maker, who had been taken into custody about an hour before this time. The watch who took Paddy had called at Mr. Hill's house to tell him what had happened; but Mr. Hill was not then at home.

CHAPTER VII

Our Mistakes are our very selves; we therefore
combat for them to the last.

It was with much surprise that the churchwarden heard the simple truth from this poor fellow; but no sooner was he convinced that O'Neill was innocent, as to this affair, than he recurred to his other ground of suspicion, the loss of his dog.

The Irish hay-maker now stepped forward, and, with a peculiar twist of the hips and shoulders, which those only who have seen it can picture to themselves, said, "Please your honor's honor, I have a little word to say too about the dog."

"Say it then," said Mr. Marshal.

"Please your honor, if I might expect to be forgiven, and let off for pulling down the jontleman's stack, I might be able to tell him what I know about the dog."

"If you can tell me any thing about my dog," said the tanner, "I will freely forgive you for pulling down the rick; especially as you have built it up again. Speak the truth now: Did not O'Neill make away with the dog?"

"Not at-all at-all, plase your honor," replied the hay-maker: "and the truth of the matter is, I know nothing of the dog, good or bad; but I know something of his collar, if your name plase your honor is Hill, as I take it to be?"

"My name is Hill; proceed," said the tanner, with great eagerness. "You know something about the collar of my dog Jowler."

"Plase your honor, this much I know, any way, that it is now, or was the night before last, at the pawnbroker's there, below in town; for, plase your honor, I was sent late at night, (that night that Mr. O'Neill, long life to him! was arrested,) to the pawnbroker's for a Jew, by Mrs. O'Neill, poor cratur! she was in great trouble that same time."

"Very likely," interrupted Mr. Hill: "but go on to the collar; what of the collar?"

"She sent me, – I'll tell you the story, plase your honor, *out of the face* – she sent me to the pawnbroker's, for the Jew; and, it being so late at night, the shop was shut, and it was with all the trouble in life that I got into the house any way; and, when I got in, there was none but a slip of a boy up; and he set down the light that he had in his hand, and ran up the stairs to waken his master; and, whilst he was gone, I just made bold to look round at what sort of a place I was in, and at the old clothes, and rags, and scraps; and there was a sort of a frieze trusty."

"A trusty!" said Mr. Hill; "what is that, pray?"

"A big coat sure, plase your honor: there was a frieze big coat lying in a corner, which I had my eye upon, to trate myself to; I having, as I then thought, money in my little purse enough for it. Well, I won't trouble your honor's honor with telling of you now how I lost my purse in the field, as I found after: but about the big coat, as I was saying, I just lifted it off the ground, to see would it fit me; and, as I swung it round, something, plase your honor, hit me a great knock on the shins: it was in the pocket of the coat, whatever it was, I knew; so I looks into the pocket, to see what was it, plase your honor, and out I pulls a hammer, and a dog-collar; it was a wonder, both together, they did not break my shins entirely: but it's no matter for my shins now: so, before the boy came down, I just, out of idleness spelt out to myself the name that was upon the collar; there were two names, plase your honor; and out of the first there were so many letters hammered out I could make nothing of it, at-all at-all; but the other name was plain enough to read any way, and it was Hill, plase your honor's honor, as sure as life: Hill, now."

This story was related in tones, and with gestures, which were so new and strange, to English ears and eyes, that even the solemnity of our churchwarden gave way to laughter. – Mr. Marshal sent a summons for the pawnbroker, that he might learn from him how he came by the dog-collar. The pawnbroker, when he found from Mr. Marshal that he could by no other means save himself from being committed to prison, for receiving stolen goods, knowing them to be stolen, confessed that the collar had been sold to him by Bampfylde the second, king of the gipsies.

A warrant was immediately dispatched for his majesty; and Mr. Hill was a good deal alarmed, by the fear of its being known in Hereford, that he was on the point of swearing examinations against an innocent man, upon the evidence of a dog-stealer and a gipsy.

Bampfylde the second made no sublime appearance, when he was brought before Mr. Marshal: nor could all his astrology avail upon this occasion: the evidence of the pawnbroker was so positive, as to the fact of his having sold to him the dog-collar, that there was no resource left for Bampfylde but an appeal to Mr. Hill's mercy. He fell on his knees, and confessed that it was he who stole the dog; which used to bark at him at night so furiously that he could not commit certain petty depredations, by which, as much as by telling fortunes, he made his livelihood.

"And so," said Mr. Marshal, with a sternness of manner which till now he had never shewn, "to skreen yourself, you accused an innocent man; and by your vile arts would have driven him from Hereford, and have set two families for ever at variance, to conceal that you had stolen a dog."

The king of the gipsies was, without further ceremony, committed to the house of correction. We should not omit to mention, that, on searching his hut, the Irish haymaker's purse was found, which some of his majesty's train had emptied. The whole set of gipsies decamped, upon the news of the apprehension of their monarch.

CHAPTER VIII

Good Sense and good Humour are the best Peace-makers.

Mr. Hill stood in profound silence, leaning upon his walking-stick, whilst the committal was making out for Bampfylde the second. The fear of ridicule was struggling with the natural positiveness of his temper: he was dreadfully afraid that the story of his being taken in, by the king of the gipsies, would get abroad; and, at the same time, he was unwilling to give up his prejudice against the Irish glover.

"But, Mr. Marshal," cried he, after a long silence, "the hole under the foundation of the cathedral has never been accounted for: that is, was, and ever will be, an ugly mystery to me; and I never can have a good opinion of this Irishman, till it is cleared up; nor can I think the cathedral in safety."

"What," said Mr. Marshal, with an arch smile, "I suppose the verses of the oracle still work upon your imagination, Mr. Hill. They are excellent in their kind. I must have them by heart that, when I am asked the reason why Mr. Hill has taken an aversion to an Irish glover, I may be able to repeat them.

'Now, take my word,
Wise men of Hereford,
None in safety may be,
Till the bad man doth flee.' "

"You'll oblige me, Mr. Mayor," said the churchwarden, "if you would never repeat those verses, Sir; nor mention, in any company, the affair of the king of the gipsies."

"I will oblige you," replied Mr. Marshal, "if you will oblige me. Will you tell me honestly whether, now that you find this Mr. O'Neill is neither a dog-killer nor a puller down of bark-ricks, you feel that you could forgive him for being an Irishman, if the mystery, as you call it, of the hole under the cathedral was cleared up?"

"But that is not cleared up, I say, Sir," cried Mr. Hill; striking his walking-stick forcibly upon the ground, with both his hands. "As to the matter of his being an Irishman, I have nothing to say to it: I am not saying any thing about that, for I know we all are born where it pleases God; and an Irishman may be as good as another. I know that much, Mr. Marshal; and I am not one of those illiberal-minded ignorant people that cannot abide a man that was not born in England. Ireland is now in his majesty's dominions, I know very well, Mr. Mayor; and I have no manner of doubt, as I said before, that an Irishman born may be as good, almost, as an Englishman born."

"I am glad," said Mr. Marshal, "to hear you speak, almost, as reasonably as an Englishman born and every man ought to speak; and I am convinced that you have too much English hospitality to persecute an inoffensive stranger, who comes amongst us trusting to our justice and good-nature."

"I would not persecute a stranger, God forbid, Mr. Mayor," replied the churchwarden, "if he was, as you say, inoffensive."

"And if he was not only inoffensive but ready to do every service in his power, to those who are in want of his assistance, we should not return evil for good; should we?"

"That would be uncharitable, to be sure; and moreover a scandal," said the churchwarden.

"Then," said Mr. Marshal, "will you walk with me as far as the widow Smith's, the poor woman whose house was burnt last winter? This hay-maker, who lodged near her, can shew us the way to her present abode."

During his examination of Paddy M'Cormack, who would tell his whole history, as he called it, *out of the face*, Mr. Marshal heard several instances of the humanity and goodness of O'Neill, which Paddy related to excuse himself for that warmth of attachment, to his cause, that had been manifested so injudiciously by pulling down the rick of bark, in revenge for the arrest. Amongst other things, Paddy mentioned his countryman's goodness to the widow Smith: Mr. Marshal was determined, therefore, to see whether he had, in this instance, spoken the truth; and he took Mr. Hill with him, in hopes of being able to shew him the favourable side of O'Neill's character.

Things turned out just as Mr. Marshal expected. The poor widow and her family, in the most simple and affecting manner, described the distress from which they had been relieved by the good gentleman and lady; the lady was Phoebe Hill; and the praises that were bestowed upon Phoebe were delightful to her father's ear, whose angry passions had now all subsided.

The benevolent Mr. Marshal seized the moment when he saw Mr. Hill's heart was touched, and exclaimed, "I must be acquainted with this Mr. O'Neill. I am sure we people of Hereford ought to shew some hospitality to a stranger, who has so much humanity. Mr. Hill, will you dine with him to-morrow at my house?"

Mr. Hill was just going to accept of this invitation when the recollection of all he had said to his club, about the hole under the cathedral, came across him; and, drawing Mr. Marshal aside, he whispered, "But Sir, Sir, that affair of the hole under the cathedral has not been cleared up yet."

At this instant, the widow Smith exclaimed, "Oh! here comes my little Mary: (one of her children who came running in) "this is the little girl, Sir, to whom the lady has been so good. Make your curtsy, child. Where have you been all this while?"

"Mammy," said the child, "I've been showing the lady my rat."

"Lord bless her! Gentlemen, the child has been wanting me this many a day to go to see this tame rat of hers; but I could never get time, never: and I wondered too at the child's liking such a creature. Tell the gentlemen, dear, about your rat. All I know is that, let her have but never such a tiny bit of bread, for breakfast or supper, she saves a little of that little for this rat of hers: she and her brothers have found it out somewhere by the cathedral."

"It comes out of a hole under the wall of the cathedral," said one of the elder boys; "and we have diverted ourselves watching it, and sometimes we have put victuals for it, so it has grown, in a manner, tame like."

Mr. Hill and Mr. Marshal looked at one another, during this speech; and the dread of ridicule again seized on Mr. Hill, when he apprehended that, after all he had said, the mountain might, at last, bring forth – a rat. Mr. Marshal, who instantly saw what passed in the churchwarden's mind, relieved him from this fear, by refraining even from a smile on this occasion. He only said to the child, in a grave manner, "I am afraid, my dear, we shall be obliged to spoil your diversion. Mr. Churchwarden, here, cannot suffer rat-holes in the cathedral: but, to make you amends for the loss of your favourite, I will give you a very pretty little dog, if you have a mind."

The child was well pleased with this promise; and, at Mr. Marshal's desire, she then went along with him and Mr. Hill to the cathedral, and they placed themselves at a little distance from that hole which had created so much disturbance. The child soon brought the dreadful enemy to light; and Mr. Hill, with a faint laugh, said "I'm glad it's no worse: but there were many in our club who were of my opinion; and, if they had not suspected O'Neill too, I am sure I should never have given you so much trouble, Mr. Mayor, as I have done this morning. But, I hope, as the club know nothing about that vagabond, that king of the gipsies, you will not let any one know any thing about the prophecy, and all that? I am sure, I am very sorry to have given you so much trouble, Mr. Mayor."

Mr. Marshal assured him that he did not regret the time which he had spent in endeavouring to clear up all these mysteries and suspicions; and Mr. Hill gladly accepted his invitation to meet O'Neill at his house the next day. No sooner had Mr. Marshal brought one of the parties to reason and good humour, than he went to prepare the other for a reconciliation. O'Neill and his mother were both people of warm but forgiving tempers: the arrest was fresh in their minds; but when Mr. Marshal represented to them the whole affair, and the churchwarden's prejudices, in a humorous light, they joined in the good-natured laugh, and O'Neill declared that, for his part, he was ready to forgive and to forget every thing, if he could but see Miss Phoebe in the Limerick gloves.

Phoebe appeared the next day, at Mr. Marshal's, in the Limerick gloves; and no perfume ever was so delightful to her lover as the smell of the rose-leaves, in which they had been kept.

Mr. Marshal had the benevolent pleasure of reconciling the two families. The tanner and the glover of Hereford became, from bitter enemies, useful friends to each other; and they were convinced, by experience, that nothing could be more for their mutual advantage than to live in union.

James Orr (1770–1816)

James Orr was born in Co. Antrim. Educated at home, he showed an early aptitude as a poet but earned his living as a weaver like his father. When the United Irishmen began to publish *The North ern Star*, Orr became a contributor. His active involvement in the United Irishmen Uprising at the Battle of Antrim made him an outlaw, and he was an exile for a few years in the United States. He soon returned to Ireland, however, and settled back in Ballycarry. Apart from *Poems* (1804), he published in periodicals for most of his career, particularly Belfast papers. The full extent of his periodical writings has yet to be traced, despite his longstanding reputation as "the poet of Ballycarry" and "the Burns of Ulster." Orr remains the best remembered of the weaving poets of the period: working-class poets, associated with Presbyterianism and the United Irishmen, who used Ulster Scots in their verse.

The influence of Scottish poet Robert Burns on Ulster poetry is clear in Orr's verse. Orr's elegy on Burns celebrates the poet, who died in 1796, in the Scots dialect that Burns had so innovatively used himself. Orr's poetry also, as critics such as Baraniuk and Lunney (see Further reading) note, draws on Presbyterian traditions. Like other Irish poets of his day, including Thomas Dermody, he was also influenced by neoclassical traditions and the Graveyard School inaugurated by English poet Thomas Gray – an influence most obvious in Orr's "Elegy, Written in the Church-yard of Templecorran," but also more broadly in the prevalence of elegy in his poetry (about a fifth of the lyrics in *Poems* are explicitly marked as elegaic). "A Prayer" is more topical, addressing what was in 1804 still a sensitive political subject: the United Irishmen and the failed 1798 Uprising. "The Banks of Larne" not only celebrates, in Romantic terms, the speaker's attachment to a natural place but also, like "The Passengers," deals with a recurring theme of Irish poetry in this period – exile.

Further reading

Baraniuk, Carol, "James Orr: Ulster-Scot and Poet of the 1798 Rebellion," *Scottish Studies Review* 6 (2005): 22–32.

Hewitt, John, *Rhyming Weavers and Other Poets of Antrim and Down*. Belfast: Blackstaff Press, 1971.

Lunney, Linde Connolly, "Attitudes to Life and Death in the Poetry of James Orr," *Ulster Folklife* 31 (1985): 1–12.

Robinson, Philip, "The Historical Presence of Ulster-Scots in Ireland," in *The Languages of Ireland*, ed. Michael Cronin and Cormac Ó Cuilleanáin, 112–26. Dublin: Four Courts Press, 2005.

Elegy, On the Death of Mr. Robert Burns, the Ayrshire Poet

From Poems, On Various Subjects (1804)

A great man, solely of God Almighty's making such.
(HERON)[1]

The lift° begud° a storm to brew,	*sky / began*
The cloudy sun was vext, an' dark;	
A forket flash° cam sklentin'° thro'	*lightning bolt / slanting*

Notes

ELEGY

[1] Robert Heron, *Memoir of the Life of the Late Robert Burns* (1797).

Before a hawk, that chas'd a lark;
Then, as I ran to reach a booth,   5
I met a swain an' ax't° "what news?"   *asked*
When thus he mourned the far-famed youth
Wha fills the dark, an' narrow hoose.

Sad news! He's gane, wha baith amus'd
The man o' taste, an' taught the rude;   10
Whase warks hae been mair read an' roos'd°   *roused*
Than onie,° save the word o' Gude: *any*
Him genius foster'd on her lap,
An' for his fa' fand fancy mourns;
Dumfries might weel steek° ev'ry shap,°   *shut / shop* 15
An' sen' her tribes to bury Burns.

Oh Burns! oh Burns! the wale o' swains,
Wi' thee the Scottish music fell;
Till nature change, thy artless strains
Shall last, an' seem her second sel':   20
Was pain thy theme; or pastime daft?
Thou rais'dst the roar, or mov'dst the tear;
Thy "woodnotes wild" were sweet, an' saft,
As grace divine to sauls sincere.

Oh Scotia! Bards of note you've rear'd: 25
E'en kings were counted i' their train;
But lo! a barefoot moorlun' herd
Frae a' their pipes the praise has ta'en:
Wha e'er before sae finely felt?
Sae "strongly mark'd" your rustic rings?   30
What mopin' min' unapt to melt,
Was cauldrife° when he swept the strings?   *indifferent*

Nae mair wi' rash, repentant share,
He'll breeze the *Daisies* modest breast;
Nor thro' the fur claut° here-an'-there   *clutch* 35
The poor wee *Mousie's* motley nest;
Nae mair, at night, frae toil releas'd,
In "social key" *Scotch Drink* he swiggs;
Nor on a palpitating breast
Is blest amang the *Barley Rigs*.²   40

Nae mair in kirk he stan's tip-tae,
To see the Rooks *ordain* the Raven;
Nor hears his *Cotter* read an' pray,
An' tell the weans° the way to heav'n;   *children*
But till, unsair't° by ear an' e'e,   *unserved* 45
Auld mem'ry's types ilk° image tine,°   *each / lose*
Wi' a' I hear, and a' I see,
Instinctive thought shall BURNS combine.

Notes ──

² In this verse and below, Orr refers to various Burns poems,   Mouse," and "The Brigs of Ayr."
usually by title, including "The Rigs O' Barley," "To a

Death, wha delay'd, and doff'd his shaft,
An leugh,° langsine,° to hear his strain,   *laughed / long ago* 50
Has pent him in the cell, which aft
He wiss'd° to close him in frae pain: *wished*
An' now th' *aerial Wreath* he wears,
Adjudg'd him by the *Phantom Fair*,
An' comes wi' shadowy compeers°   *friends (Fr. compères)* 55
To warble on the *Brigs o' Ayr.*

But while the poet we applaud,
We manna° less approve the man;   *must not*
A heart to beauty ay he had,
An' to the brave a frienly han';   60
None felt the love o' country mair,
Nor wiss't the BRETHREN's peace an' health;
For Independence, firm, an' fair,
He strave as much as fools for wealth.

An' maun his fam'lie i' the slough   65
O' dreary poortith,° pining, lye?   *poverty*
The want o' him is hard enough,
Without the want o' ought forbye:°   *as well*
Monie fine chiels° hae set their hearts,   *children*
Like him, owre much on wine an' mirth;   70
The *failin's* o' a man o' parts
Are nobler than a numscull's *worth.*

In times to come, tho' now obscure,
His line may flourish for his sake;
An sons o' sang frae monie a shore   75
Cleave reliques frae his plough or braik:
Sublime, yet simple; wild, yet wise;
He ne'er was match'd wham Scotia mourns –
A noble peal convuls'd the skies,
'Twas Nature's sel' respectin BURNS.   80

A Prayer, Written on the eve of the unfortunate 7th of June, 1798[1]

From Poems, On Various Subjects (1804)

Almighty Lord of life and death!
    While men for strife prepare,
Let but this heart thy favour feel,
    And peace will still be there.

How oft I've err'd! at pleasure's shrine   5
    How fondly bent my knee!
But if I have not cruel been,
    Be clement, Lord! to me.

Notes ──

A PRAYER
[1] In a significant battle during the 1798 Uprising, United
Irishmen forces were defeated at Antrim on this date.

If pride in this aspiring breast
   Made poverty give pain,   10
Expel that pride; nor in its stead
   Let mean dishonour reign.

If e'er ill passions prompted me
   Off wisdom's path to go,
Let not revenge, the worst one, strive   15
   To hurt a private foe.

How dare I ask thy bolts to throw?
   Whose mandates "do not kill."
But, whilst as man I have to fight,
   As man O may I feel!   20

Let not this frame, whose fleshless bones
   These summer suns may bleach,
Lie writhing long; nor, while it stands,
   The hand of pillage stretch.

But in the vict'ry, or the rout,   25
   In glory, or in gall,
May moderation mark my power,
   And fortitude my fall.

Why dread to die? what griefs I've borne?
   What pains have pluck'd each nerve?   30
Yet why not wish to grow more wise,
   And live my friends to serve?

Resign'd I'll rest then, whether oft
   Yon silver curve to see;
Or hail the sun, and, ere he set,   35
   Beyond his system be.

Almighty Lord of life and death!
   Whilst men for strife prepare,
Let but this heart thy favour feel,
   And peace will still be there.   40

The Banks of Larne

From Poems, On Various Subjects (1804)

On Larne's sweet banks, in early years,
I careless stray'd, and void of art,
Attun'd a reed that pleas'd my peers,
To praise the maid that charmed my heart:
A blyther swain rang'd not the green,   5
And gaudy hills of hapless ERN,
Till spite and malice, chang'd the scene
To grief and care on gentle Larne.

Oft disappointed, oft deceiv'd,
With heart-achs there have marr'd my health!　　　　10
What humbling insults I've received
From worthless heirs of pride and wealth!
I strove to rise, yet sank the lower;
I sought esteem, and sad concern
From falsehood rose; yet all I bore,　　　　15
While blest with peace, on gentle Larne.

'Twas there, my heart! a priest-like sire
Impress'd thee with his precepts mild;
There nature's breath, my simple lyre,
Awoke thee soon to warble wild;　　　　20
There love was selfless and sincere,
There friendship joy'd to watch and warn;
Then is it strange I shed a tear
To leave the gentle banks of Larne?

Inchanting banks! how fair their charms!　　　　25
The mead adorns, the mountain shields,
On her smooth bosom, cots, flocks, farms,
Reflected, look like fairy-fields:
There villages, and villas rise,
There plenty fills each peasant's barn;　　　　30
For care, and culture, prompt the wise
To plant, and plow, on gentle Larne.

And must I cease, sweet lake, to view
Thee basking in the tepid ray;
Or tempest-toss'd, and darkly blue;　　　　35
Or closely veil'd in vapour grey!
Shall I no more, conceal'd by briars,
Eye bathing nymphs, might melt the stern?
Nor mark the meteor of the mires
That nightly glides on gentle Larne?　　　　40

And must I leave thee, natal cot?
And must thy roof the floor o'erspread?
Alas! my foes, ere long, may blot
My memory on thy ruin'd *stead*:
But welcome shame, and slander's sting,　　　　45
Th' endanger'd day, the bed of Fern,
Ev'n pain, and death; if these could bring
Repose and peace to gentle Larne.

My comrades kind, these long-lov'd shores,
No more we'll roam on Sundays fine:　　　　50
Prosperity and peace be yours!
To wander, and to wail, be mine:
You'll sometimes mind a friend, far hence,
Who shares the woes he did not earn,
And pray that fate may recompense　　　　55
The love he bears to gentle Larne.

Elegy, Written in the Church-yard of Templecorran

From Poems, On Various Subjects (1804)

Farewell ye cheerful fields! ye blooming plains!
Enough for me the church-yard's lonely mound;
Where melancholy with still silence reigns,
And the rank grass waves o'er the cheerless ground.[1]

(BRUCE)

Fatigu'd with toil, yet kept from rest,
    By contemplation, and by care,
I rise and woo the howling East,
    To spread the plaint of grief sincere:
The falling fragment, heard with fear,   5
    To silence awes the Owls that scream,
While round this long-fallen place of prayer
    I stalk, with spectre-seeming frame.

Hail, hoary structure! wrapt I trace
    The grass-crown'd wall, the weedy pew,   10
And arches tott'ring to their base,
    And doors on high, that none pass thro';
Craz'd are the cape-stones, once so true,
    Th' unglaz'd, dark holes appal my eye:
The loose pile nods o'er heaps that strew   15
    Their graves, perhaps, that pil'd them high.

The tile-borne roof, and ponderous beams,
    Dissolved, long since, have chang'd their mode;
Where virgins sung, the cat-club screams,
    And Ruin yawns where Rapture glow'd: 20
Awe-striking wrecks, where Time has gnaw'd
    Rude bites, and left his cank'rous mark,
On many a slave's long-wish'd abode,
    Your frigid shade lies long and dark.

Some soldier here may rest his head,   25
    Against the breast that brav'd his ball;
Some shepherd join the gentle maid,
    Who frown'd because his flocks were small:
Some never-resting heart of gall
    May melt with his who hated strife –   30
Oh what a trifle parted all!
    The brittle, frail barrier of life.

How still their hands! how mute their tongues!
    Nor hearts embrace, nor heads invent,
With party toasts, and party songs,   35
    These trampled roofs are never rent;

Notes

ELEGY, WRITTEN IN THE CHURCH-YARD
[1] From "Elegy, Written in Spring" by Scottish poet Michael
Bruce (1746–67).

No sceptic shocks the senseless saint,
    No fiend of faith stems truth by blows;
In vest of Green the breast is pent,
    Who once the badge of Orange chose.   40

Pale empress! burst thy sable veil,
    And let me trace thy grave-stones rude:
Why waste the time? what would they tell,
    But some were great – and all were good?
Unnotic'd worth, I know, induc'd   45
    The nameless dust o'er which I pause,
While to yon shark's sham'd life ensu'd
    The palm of posthumous applause.

Where'er I stray, my footsteps tread
    On some fair maid, and faithful wife;   50
Some STERNE,[2] whose mirth amusement spread,
    Or PENN,[3] who mourn'd when rage was rife.
Friends of my dawn, tho' low their life,
    Brave were the hearts whose fall I weep;
Soon shall I leave the scene of strife,   55
    And in some cell beside them sleep.

The storm shall rise my leaves to spread,
    No fost'ring sun shall raise me higher;
Borne down I droop my friendless head,
    Live on in scorn, and rest require: 60
So have I seen a trampled briar,
    Whose rustick form could find no prop,
Forbear to fruitlessly aspire,
    And root in earth its simple top.

Here, wallowing wild, the reptile hordes   65
    Shall share the heart whose griefs are vast –
Ah! hark, the harsh-ton'd bones and boards!
    Above my bier I hear them cast:
These ashes old, where bless'd with rest.
    The gale-rock'd ravens safely sleep,   70
Ne'er shed their foliage on a breast
    More pure than his who fills this heap.

His providence with watchful wing
    Screen'd my young life from danger's dart;
I sported in the hamlet's ring,   75
    While care was his my wants to thwart:
He strove to form my taste and heart,
    My hand he train'd without a rod,
And bade me, void of self and art,
    Befriend my race, and love my God.   80

Rise Retrospection! gild, re-tread,
    The glimm'ring cells of Mem'ry's cave;
For there stand pictur'd, ne'er to fade,

Notes ──────────────────────────────────

[2] Novelist Laurence Sterne (1713–68).   [3] Possibly James Penn (1727–1800), English religious author.

The scenes we join'd in, gay and grave:
And let him smile, as when, at eve,   85
   I chas'd the shower-succeeding arch;
And fire his eye to see the brave
   In self-rais'd ranks beside me march.

And paint his cheek, where care and ease,
   The wrinkle and the rose combine;   90
And let me hear him, resting raise
   The genial song of love and wine:
And to contrast his converse fine,
   Strike up the harsh and jarring loom:
Th' ennobling fife that leads the line,   95
   Soft mingling thus, endears the drum.

Yes, drench me, rain! and pierce me, wind!
   And doleful darkness shade me o'er!
Ye can't to me be more unkind,
   Than fate by him was felt before.   100
Why censure fate? how was he poor
   Whom nature stor'd with honour's pride?
Or how unschool'd, whose want of lore
   By intuition seem'd supply'd?

Tho' warm, not rash; (his manly mind   105
   Did adverse attributes contain)
Tho' placid, firm; tho' frugal, kind;
   Tho' deep, not dark; tho' prudent, plain. –
Elate with hope, 'midst friends in pain,
   He reach'd the solemn shore of life,   110
And in the world-dividing main,
   Bold, launching left the coasts of strife.

The "meek-eye'd morn" divinely wakes: –
   Wrecks, tombs, and trees, once more I mark;
The place of sculls my foot forsakes,   115
   Reclaim'd by toil, in shop or park;
But no fond Father's voice I'll hark,
   I had one Friend and here he lies:
His cold clay house is sad and dark,
   But blest repose seals up his eyes.   120

The Passengers

From Poems, On Various Subjects (1804)

Down where yon anch'ring vessel spreads the sail,
That, idly waiting, flaps with ev'ry gale;
Downward they move, a melancholy band,
Pass from the shore, and darken all the strand.
               (GOLDSMITH)[1]

Notes ────────────────────────────

THE PASSENGERS
[1] Goldsmith, *The Deserted Village* (1770).

James Orr

How calm an' cozie is the wight,°   person
  Frae cares an' conflicts clear ay,
Whase settled headpiece never made,
  His heels or han's be weary!
Perplex'd is he whase anxious schemes   5
  Pursue applause, or siller,°   silver (money)
Success nor sates, nor failure tames;
  Bandied frae post to pillar
                    Is he, ilk° day.   each

As we were, Comrades, at the time   10
  We mov't frae Ballycarry,
To wan'er thro' the woody clime
  Burgoyne gied° oure to harrie: gave
Wi' frien's consent we prie't° a gill,²   tasted
  An' monie a house did call at,   15
Shook han's, an' smil't; tho' ilk fareweel
  Strak,° like a weighty mallet,   struck
                    Our hearts, that day.

On shore, while ship-mates halt, tho' thrang't,°   crowded
  Wi' lasses hearts to barter;   20
Nybers,° an' frien's, in boatfu's pang't,°   neighbors / boatfuls packed
  Approach our larboard quarter;
Syne speel° the side, an' down the hatch   then climb
  To rest, an' crack,° an' gaze on   chat
The boles° o' births,° that monie a wratch   recesses / berths   25
  Maun° squeeze in, for a season,   must
                    By night, an' day.

"This is my locker, yon'ers Jock's,
  In that auld creel,° sea-store is,   basket
Thir births beside us are the *Lockes*,³   30
  My uncle's there before us;
Here hang my tins an' vitriol jug,
  Nae thief's at han' to meddle 'em" –
"L—d, man, I'm glad ye're a' sae snug;
  But och! 'tis owre° like Bedlam⁴   too much   35
                    Wi' a' this day.

"All boats ashore!" the mate cries stern,
  Wi' oaths wad fear a saunt° ay: saint
"Now Gude be wi' ye, Brice, my bairn°" –   child
  "An' Gude be wi' ye, Auntie."   40
What *keep-sakes*, an' what news are sent!
  What smacks,° an' what embraces!   kisses
The hurryin' sailors sleely sklent°   slyly glance sideways

Notes ————————————————————————————————————

² Unit of measure, usually for alcohol.   ⁴ English insane asylum.
³ A family who sailed for America in 1798 (author).

Droll leuks at lang wry faces,
  Fu'° pale that day.   *full* 45

While "Yo heave O!" wi' monie a yell
 The birkies° weigh the anchor;   *fine fellows*
Ilk mammies pet conceits° itsel'   *imagines*
 The makin' o' a Banker;
They'll soon, tho', wiss to lieve° at hame,   *live* 50
 An' dee° no worth a totam,°   *die / spinning top*[5]
Whan brustin'° breast, an' whamlin' wame,° *bursting / tossing*
 Mak' some wise men o' Gotham   *and turning belly*
   Cry halt! this day.

Some frae the stern, wi' thoughts o' grief   55
 Leuk back, their hearts to Airlan';°   *Ireland*
Some mettle't° bucks, to work ay brief,   *spirited*
 At en's o' rapes° are harlin';°   *ropes / pulling*
Some haud aback frae danger's brow
 Their toddlin o'er, no cautious;   60
An' some, wi' monie a twine° an' throe,   *twist*
 Do something wad be nauceous
   To name, this day.

Meanwhile, below, some count their beads,
 While prudes, auld-light sit cantin';° *singing or story-telling* 65
Some mak' their beds; some haud their heads,
 An' cry wi' spite, a' pantin'! –
"Ye brought us here ye luckless cauf!°   *calf*
 (Aye did he; whisht° my darlin'!)   *hush*
L—d sen' me hame! wi' poke° an' staff,   *sack* 70
 I'd beg my bread thro' Airlan',
   My lane,° that day."   *self (alone)*

In twathree° days the maist cam' to,   *two or three*
 Few heads were sair or dizzy;
An' chiel's° wha scarce a turn cud do,   *boys* 75
 Begoud° to be less lazy: *began*
At night (to tell amang oursel's)
 They crap,° wi' fandness fidgin',°   *creep / fidgeting*
To court – or maybe something else,
 Gif folk becam' obligin',   80
   Atween an' day.

Roun' the cambouse° what motley ban's   *ship's galley*
 At breakfast-time cam' swarmin'!
Tins, tankards, kettles, pots, an' pans,
 The braid flat fire was warmin':   85
The guid auld rule, "first come first ser't,"
 Was urg't by men o' mettle;

Notes

[5] For games of chance, specifically.

An' ay whan callens° grew mislear't,°   *young people / unmannerly*
    The arm o' flesh boost° settle   *drive off*
        Th' affray, that day.   90

A bonie sight I vow it was,
    To see on some lown° e'nin',   *calm*
Th' immense, smooth, smilin' sea o' glass,
    Whare porpoises were stenin':°   *leaping*
To see at night the surface fine   95
    That Cynthia[6] made her path on;
An' snove,° an' snore° thro' waves o' brine,   *glide / snort*
    That sparkle't like a heath on
        A bleaze° some day.   *blaze*

But now a gale besets our bark,°   *ship* 100
    Frae gulph to gulph we're tumble't;
Kists,° kits, an' fam'lies, i' the dark,   *trunks*
    Wi' ae side-jerk are jumble't:
Some stauchrin'° thro' a pitch lays laigh° –   *staggering / low*
    Some, drouket,° ban° the breaker;   *drenched / curse* 105
While surge, on surge, sae skelps° her – Hegh!   *splashes*
    Twa three like that will wreck her
        A while ere day.

Win's, wives, an' weans, rampage an' rave,
    Three score at ance are speakin';   110
While blacks wha a' before them drave,
    Lye cheepin' like a chicken –
"What gart° us play? or bouse° like beasts?   *makes / animal stalls*
    Or box in fairs wi' venom?"
Hear how the captain laughs an' jests,   115
    An' bit a bord between him
        An' death, this day.

'Tis calm again. While rightin' things,
    The heads o' births are bizziet,°   *bustling*
The seaman chews his quid,° an' sings,   *tobacco* 120
    An' peys his frien's a visit –
"Eh! dem my eyes! how is't, goodman?
    Got clear of *Davy's*[7] locker?
Lend me a facer till we lan',
    Till blind as Newgate's[8] knocker   125
        We'll swig,° that day."   *drink*

Here, gash° guidmen, wi' nightcaps on,   *talkative*
    At ance baith pray an' watch;
An', there, for light, sits monie a loun°   *rascal*
    At Cartes° beneath the hatch;   *playing cards* 130

Notes

[6] the moon

[7] Davy Jones's locker, the bottom of the sea.

[8] English prison.

Here, some sing sangs, or stories tell,
    To ithers bizzy knittin';
An', there some readin' to themsels,
    Nod owre asleep, while sittin'
              Twa fold that day.   135

Now Newfoun'lan's becalmin' banks
    Our ship supinely lies on;
An' monie a ane his lang line fanks,°   *tangles*
    Whase heuk° some captive dies on: *hook*
An' now, disguis't, a fore-mast-man   140
    Shaves dry, the churls unwillin'
To pay the poll-tax on deman' –
    A pint, or else a shillin'
              A piece that day.[9]

Aince mair luck lea's us (plain 'tis now   145
    A murd'rer in some mess is)
An English frigate heaves in view,
    I'll bail her board, an' press us:
Taupies° beneath their wives wha stole,   *fools*
    Or 'mang auld sails lay flat ay,   150
Like whitrats peepin' frae their hole,
    Cried, "is she British, wat ye,
              Or French, this day?"

'Twas but a brig frae Baltimore,
    To Larne wi' lintseed steerin';   155
Twa days ago she left the shore,
    Let's watch for lan' appearin':
Spies frae the shrouds, like laigh dark clouds,
    Descried domes, mountains, bushes;
The Exiles griev't – the sharpers thiev't –   160
    While cronies bous't like fishes,
              Conven't, that day.

Whan glidin' up the *Delaware*,
    We cam' forenent° Newcastle,   *in front of*
Gypes° co'ert the wharf to gove,° an' stare,   *fools / gawk* 165
    While out, in boats, we bustle:
Creatures wha ne'er had seen a black,
    Fu' scar't took to their shankies;°   *legs*
Sae, wi' our best rags on our back,
    We mix't amang the Yankies,   170
             An skail't,° that day.   *scattered*

Notes

[9] It has been a long established custom for the seamen, on reaching the banks of Newfoundland, to exact a shilling, or a shilling's worth of liquor, from every passenger; and to shave, without soap, those who refuse to contribute to their quota (author).

Mary Tighe (1772–1810)

Mary Tighe was born in Dublin. Her father, Reverend William Blachford, died when she was an infant, and she was raised by her mother, Theodosia Tighe Blachford, a supporter of the Methodist movement and women's education. After marrying her maternal cousin, Henry Tighe, in 1793, Mary Tighe spent much of the 1790s in London, but returned to Ireland periodically and settled permanently in Dublin in 1801. There, she moved in the same social circles as Alicia Sheridan Lefanu, Sydney Owenson (later Lady Morgan), and Thomas Moore, part of a Dublin literary scene that was striking for its support of women writers. She died of consumption, after many years' illness, in 1810.

She published only one volume during her lifetime, *Psyche* (1805), a long allegorical poem that influenced a number of Romantic poets, from Thomas Moore to English poet John Keats. The poem established Tighe's reputation as a poet, and was republished throughout the nineteenth century in English-speaking countries. *Psyche, With Other Poems* (1811) was published posthumously by her husband and includes a wide variety of poems in different forms and on different themes. Her sonnets on Killarney contribute to the large body of writing on the region, but innovate on those which preceded her. Instead of writing a long topographical poem, like Leslie's, she offers three sequential sonnets, and presents them as poetic effusions through the Romantic device of giving a poem a specific date. "Bryan Byrne, of Glenmalure" is nearly unique in Tighe's corpus for its representation of political violence and its use of the ballad form. While she generally used elite forms – blank verse, Spenserian stanzas, the sonnet – this tale of rural Ireland engages a very different literary tradition. In particular, it bears comparison to Leadbeater's "The Triumph of Terror" for its domestic perspective on political violence.

Further reading

Kucich, Greg, "Gender Crossings: Keats and Tighe," *Keats–Shelley Journal* 44 (1995): 29–39.

Linkin, Harriet Kramer, "More than *Psyche*: The Sonnets of Mary Tighe," *European Romantic Review* 13 (2002): 365–78.

— ed., *The Collected Poems and Journals of Mary Tighe*. Lexington, KY: University Press of Kentucky, 2005.

Written at the Eagle's Nest, Killarney (July 26, 1800)

From Psyche, With Other Poems (1811)

Here let us rest, while with meridian blaze
  The sun rides glorious 'mid the cloudless sky,
  While o'er the lake no cooling Zephyrs fly,
But on the liquid glass we dazzled gaze,
And fainting ask for shade: lo! where his nest   5
  The bird of Jove has fixed: the lofty brow,
With arbutus and fragrant wild shrubs drest,

Impendent frowns, nor will approach allow:
Here the soft turf invites; here magic sounds
 Celestially respondent shall enchant,   10
While Melody from yon steep wood rebounds
 In thrilling cadence sweet. Sure, life can grant
No brighter hours than this; and memory oft
Shall paint this happiest scene with pencil soft.

Written at Killarney (July 29, 1800)

From Psyche, With Other Poems (1811)

How soft the pause! the notes melodious cease,
 Which from each feeling could an echo call;
 Rest on your oars; that not a sound may fall
To interrupt the stillness of our peace:
The fanning west-wind breathes upon our cheeks   5
 Yet glowing with the sun's departed beams.
 Through the blue heavens the cloudless moon pours streams
Of pure resplendent light, in silver streaks
Reflected on the still, unruffled lake.
 The Alpine hills in solemn silence frown,   10
 While the dark woods night's deepest shades embrown.
And now once more that soothing strain awake!
Oh, ever to my heart, with magic power,
Shall those sweet sounds recal this rapturous hour!

On Leaving Killarney (August 5, 1800)

From Psyche, With Other Poems (1811)

Farewel, sweet scenes! pensive once more I turn
 Those pointed hills, and wood-fringed lakes to view
 With fond regret; while in this last adieu
A silent tear those brilliant hours shall mourn
For ever past. So from the pleasant shore,   5
 Borne with the struggling bark against the wind,
 The trembling pennant fluttering looks behind
With vain reluctance! 'Mid those woods no more
For me the voice of pleasure shall resound,
 Nor soft flutes warbling o'er the placid lake   10
 Aërial music shall for me awake,
And wrap my charmed soul in peace profound!
Though lost to me, here still may Taste delight
To dwell, nor the rude axe the trembling Dryads fright!

The Shawl's Petition, To Lady Asgill[1]

From Psyche, With Other Poems (1811)

Oh, fairer than the fairest forms
Which the bright sun of Persia warms,
Though nymphs of Cashmire[2] lead the dance
With pliant grace, and beamy glance;
And forms of beauty ever play   5
Around the bowers of Moselay;
Fairest! thine ear indulgent lend,
And to thy suppliant Shawl attend!

If, well content, I left for thee
Those bowers beyond the Indian sea,   10
And native, fragrant fields of rose
Exchanged for Hyperborean snows;
If, from those vales of soft perfume,
Pride of Tibet's far boasted loom,
I came, well pleased, thy form to deck,   15
And, from thy bending polished neck
Around thy graceful shoulders flung,
With many an untaught beauty clung,
Or added to thy brilliant zone
A charm that Venus well might own,   20
Or, fondly twined, in many a fold
To shield those lovely limbs from cold,
Fairest! thine ear indulgent lend,
And to thy suppliant Shawl attend.

Oh! by those all attractive charms   25
Thy slender foot, thine ivory arms;
By the quick glances of thine eyes,
By all that I have seen thee prize;
Oh! doom me not in dark disgrace,
An exile from Sophia's face,   30
To waste my elegance of bloom
In sick and melancholy gloom;
Condemned no more in Beauty's train
To hear the viol's sprightly strain,
Or woo the amorous zephyr's play   35
Beneath the sunbeam's vernal ray;
Banished alike from pleasure's scene,
And lovely nature's charms serene,
Oh, fairest! doom me not to know
How hard it is from thee to go!   40

Notes ———————————————————————————

THE SHAWL'S PETITION
[1] Sophia Jemima, Lady Asgill, was part of the same Dublin
social circle as Tighe; her husband, Sir Charles Asgill, helped
to suppress the 1798 Irish Uprising and commanded the
garrison at Dublin from 1800.

[2] Shawls in this period were, as luxury items, associated
with the "East" – here represented by India, Cashmire
(Kashmir), Persia, and Tibet.

But if my humble suit be vain,
If destined to attend on pain,
My joyless days in one dull round,
To one eternal sopha bound,
Shut from the breath of heaven most pure,   45
Must pass in solitude obscure;
At least to cheat these weary hours
Appear with all thy gladdening powers,
Restore thy sweet society,
And bless at once thy friend and me.   50

Bryan Byrne, of Glenmalure[1]

From Psyche, With Other Poems (1811)

Bright shines the morn o'er Carickmure,
    And silvers every mountain stream;
The autumnal woods on Glenmalure
    Look lovely in the slanting beam.

And hark! the cry, the cry of joy,   5
    The hounds spring o'er yon heathy brow! –
" 'Tis but the hunter's horn, my boy,
    No death-tongued bugle scares us now."

In vain the widowed mother smiled,
    And clasped her darling to her breast;   10
Horror and rage o'er all the child
    A manly beauty strange impressed.

Fierce rolled his eye, of heaven's own hue,
    And the quick blood strong passions told,
As fresh the breeze of morning blew   15
    From his clear brow the locks of gold.

'Tis not alone the horn so shrill; –
    Yon martial plume that waves on high,
Bids every infant nerve to thrill
    With more than infant agony.   20

Yet gentle was the soldier's heart,
    Whom 'mid the gallant troop he spied
Who let the gallant troop depart,
    And checked his eager courser's pride.

"What fears the child?" he wondering cried,   25
    With courteous air as near he drew.

Notes

BRYAN BYRNE
[1] The story of Bryan Byrne is founded upon facts which were related to the author in the autumn of 1798: though the circumstances may not have happened in the exact manner which is recorded in the poem, yet it gives but too faithful a picture of the sentiments and conduct of those days. It is certain that at that period, several unarmed persons, report says above twenty, were put to death by the troops near Wicklow, to retaliate the murder of many loyalists and particularly of the three brothers mentioned in this ballad (original).

"Soldier, away! my father died,
   Murdered by men of blood like you."

Even while the angry cherub speaks,
   He struggles from the stranger's grasp: 30
Kissing the tears that bathed her cheeks,
   His little arms his mother clasp.

"And who are these, – this startled pair,
   Who swift down Glenmalure are fled?
Behold the mother's maniac air,   35
   As seized with wild and sudden dread!"

"'Tis Ellen Byrne," an old man cried;
   "Poor Ellen, and her orphan boy!"
Then turned his silvered brow aside,
   To shun the youth's enquiring eye.   40

"And is there none to guard the child,
   Save that lone frenzied widow's hand?
These rocky heights, these steep woods wild,[2]
   Sure some more watchful eye demand."

"Ah, well he knows each rock, each wood,   45
   The mountain goat not more secure;
And he was born to hardships rude,
   The orphan Byrne of Carickmure.

"That boy had seen his father's blood,
   Had heard his father's murdered groan;   50
And never more in playful mood
   With smiles his infant beauty shone."

Sad was the pitying stranger's eye:
   "Too well," said he, "I guess the truth;
His father, sure, was doomed to die,   55
   Some poor deluded rebel youth."

"No rebel he," with eye inflamed,
   And cheek that glowed with transient fire,
Roused to a sudden warmth, exclaimed
   The hapless Ellen's aged sire.   60

"He did not fall in Tarah's fight,
   No blood of his the Curragh stains,
Where many a ghost that moans by night
   Of foully broken faith complains.

"He triumphed not that fatal day,   65
   When every loyal cheek looked pale,
But heard, like us, with sad dismay,
   Of fallen chiefs in Clough's dark vale.

Notes

[2] Clough, the place at which Colonel Walpole was killed,
and his detachment defeated by the rebels (original). The
battle took place in June 1798, part of the 1798 Uprising.

"For, wedded to our Ellen's love,
   One house was ours, one hope, one soul: 70
Though fierce malignant parties strove,
   No party rage could love control.

"Though we were sprung from British race,
   And his was Erin's early pride,
Yet matched in every loveliest grace,   75
   No priest could e'er their hearts divide.

"What though no yeoman's arms he bore;
   'Twas party hate that hope forbad:
What though no martial dress he wore,
   That dress no braver bosom clad.   80

"And had our gallant Bryan Byrne
   Been welcomed to their loyal band,
Home might I still in joy return
   The proudest father in the land.

"For, ah! when Brian Byrne was slain,   85
   With him my brave, my beauteous son
His precious life-blood shed in vain; –
   The savage work of death was done!" . . .

He ceased: for now, by memory stung,
   His heart's deep wounds all freshly bled,   90
While with a father's anguish wrung,
   He bowed to earth his aged head.

Yet soothing to his broken heart
   He felt the stranger's sympathy,
And age is ready to impart   95
   Its page of woe to pity's eye.

Yes! it seemed sweet once more to dwell
   On social joys and peaceful days,
And still his darling's virtues tell,
   And still his Ellen's beauty praise.   100

"But say," at length exclaimed the youth,
   "Did no one rash, rebellious deed
E'er cloud thy Bryan's loyal truth,
   And justice doom thy boy to bleed?"

"No; never rash, rebellious deed   105
   Was his, nor rash rebellious word;
That day of slaughter saw him bleed,
   Where blushing Justice dropped the sword.

"In Fury's hand it madly raged,
   As urged by fierce revenge she flew;   110
With unarmed Innocence she waged
   Such war as Justice never knew."

" 'Twas ours (the sorrowing father cried),
   'Twas ours to mourn the crimes of all:

Each night some loyal brother died;
   Each morn beheld some victim fall. 115

"Oh, 'twas a sad and fearful day
   That saw my gallant boys laid low;
The voice of anguish and dismay
   Proclaimed full many a widow's woe! 120

"But doubly o'er our fated house
   The accursed hand of murder fell,
And ere our Ellen wept her spouse,
   She had a dreadful tale to tell!

"For early on that guilty morn 125
   The voice of horror reached our ears;
That, from their thoughtless slumber torn,
   Before a helpless sister's tears,

"Beneath their very mother's sight
   Three youthful brothers butchered lie, 130
Three loyal yeomen brave in fight,
   Butchered by savage treachery.

"They were my nephews; boys I loved,
   My own brave boys alone more dear;
Their rashness oft my heart reproved, 135
   And marked their daring zeal with fear.

"They were my widowed sister's joy;
   Her hope in age and dark distress;
And Ellen loved each gallant boy
   Even with a sister's tenderness. 140

"It was from Ellen's lips I heard
   The tidings sadly, surely true:
To me, ere yet the dawn appeared,
   All pale with fear and grief she flew.

"Roused by her call, with her I sought 145
   The sad abode of misery:
But to the wretched mother brought
   No comfort, but our sympathy.

"On the cold earth, proud Sorrow's throne,
   In silent majesty of woe, 150
She sat, and felt herself alone,
   Though loud the increasing tumults grow.

"In throngs the assembled country came,
   And every hand was armed with death:
Revenge! revenge! (they all exclaim,) 155
   Spare no suspected traitor's breath:

"No; let not one escape who owns
   The faith of Rome, of treachery:
This loyal blood for vengeance groans,
   And signal vengeance let there be! 160

"What, shall we feel the coward blow,
    And tamely wait a late defence?
No; let us strike the secret foe,
    Even through the breast of innocence!

"Poor Ellen trembled as they raved;   165
    Her pallid cheek forgot its tears;
While from the hand of fury saved,
    Her infant darling scarce appears.

"I saw her earnest searching eye,
    In that dark moment of alarm,   170
Ask, in impatient agony,
    A brother's dear, protecting arm.

"Woe! bitter woe, to me and mine!
    Too well his brave, his feeling heart
Already could her fears divine,   175
    And more than bear a brother's part.

"When the first savage blast he knew
    Would bid each deadly bugle roar,
Back to our home of peace he flew:
    Ah, home of peace and love no more!   180

"Oh! would to God that I had died
    Beneath my wretched sister's roof!
Thus heaven in mercy had denied
    To my worst fears their utmost proof.

"So had these eyes been spared a sight   185
    That wrings my soul with anguish still,
Nor known how much of life, ere night,
    The blood-hounds of revenge could spill.

"Sinking at once with fear and age,
    Her father's steps my child upheld;   190
The mangled victims of their rage
    Each moment shuddering we beheld.

"Down yon steep side of Carickmure,
    Our rugged path we homeward wound;
And saw, at least, that home secure,   195
    'Mid many a smoking ruin round.

"Low in the Glen our cottage lies
    Behind yon dusky copse of oak:
On its white walls we fixed our eyes,
    But not one word poor Ellen spoke!   200

"We came ... the clamour scarce was o'er,
    The fiends scarce left their work of death: –
But never spoke our Bryan more,
    Nor Ellen caught his latest breath.

"Still to the corse by horror joined,   205
    The shrinking infant closely clung,

And fast his little arms intwined,
   As round the bleeding neck he hung.

"Oh, sight of horror, sight of woe!
   The dead and dying both were there: 210
Our dreadful moment served to show,
   For us was nothing but despair.

"Oh, God! even now methinks I see
   My dying boy, as there he stood,
And sought with fond anxiety   215
   To hide his gushing wounds of blood,

"Ere life yet left his noble breast,
   Gasping, again he tried to speak,
And twice my hand he feebly pressed,
   And feebly kissed poor Ellen's cheek.   220

"No word she spoke, no tear she shed,
   Ere at my feet convulsed she fell,
Still lay my children, cold and dead!
   And I yet live, the tale to tell!

"She too awoke to wild despair   225
   With frenzied eye each corse to see,
To rave, to smile with frantic air;
   But never more to smile for me!

"But hold! from yonder grassy slope
   Our orphan darling calls me hence: 230
Sweet child, last relic of our hope,
   Of love and injured innocence.

"Soldier, farewel! To thee should power
   Commit the fate of lives obscure,
Remember still in fury's hour   235
   The murdered youths of Glenmalure.

"And chief, if civil broils return,
   Though vengeance urge to waste, destroy;
Ah! pause! . . . think then on Bryan Byrne,
   Poor Ellen, and her orphan boy!"   240

Thomas Dermody (1775–1802)

Thomas Dermody was born in Co. Clare, the son of a schoolmaster. A child prodigy, he was fluent in Greek and Latin by a very young age and working at his father's school before he was ten. At the age of fifteen he ran away to Dublin, where the literati worked to protect him. Robert Owenson, Morgan's father, briefly took him into the Owenson home as a tutor, and Dermody taught Sydney and her sister Olivia to read and maintained a relationship with the girls after he left Dublin. He had other patrons and mentors as well, including such leading lights as Charlotte

Brooke and the politician Henry Grattan, but financial woes and alcoholism plagued him. He eventually enlisted in the army and was wounded, and soon thereafter died in poverty, but was still remembered decades later – he was dubbed "young and neglected" by *The Nation* in 1843.

In his short life, Dermody published a number of volumes, including *Poems* (1789), *Poems, Consisting of Essays, Lyric, Elegiac, &c.* (1792), *Poems, Moral and Descriptive* (1800), *Peace* (1801), *The Histrionade: Or, Theatric Tribunal* (1802), and *Poems, On Various Subjects* (1802). Clearly influenced by Jonathan Swift and Oliver Goldsmith, English poets Thomas Gray and Alexander Pope, and Scottish poet Robert Burns, Dermody was very much a poet of the late eighteenth century and moved fluidly between sentimental, elegiac, and satiric verse. His poem *Peace* is perhaps his most unconventional work, written after he enlisted in the army and detailing in compelling terms the physical and emotional damage that war inflicts on soldiers.

His satiric verse displays a biting wit, including his long satire on the theatrical scene in London, *The Histrionade*. "The Poet's Pen" is a more compact instance of satire, as well as an example of Dermody's recurring theme – poverty. His four volumes titled *Poems* include verse addressed to patrons and mentors, friends, and leading writers, as well as comic pieces and a number of works that bear comparison to the emerging modes of the gothic and the Graveyard School inaugurated by Gray, including "Contemplative Verses On the Tombs in Drumcondra Church-Yard," which owes much both to Gray's "Elegy Written in a Country Church-yard" (1751) and Goldsmith's *The Deserted Village* (1770). "The Days of Yore" is unusual in Dermody's corpus as a poem that invokes antiquity. Though dubbed "the minstrel boy" in Morgan's poem of that name, Dermody generally dealt with subjects of his own time – people he knew, contemporary events, and current literary trends.

Further reading

Dornan, Stephen, "Thomas Dermody, Robert Burns, and the Killeigh Cycle," *Scottish Studies Review* 6 (2005): 9–21.
Schirmer, Gregory A., *Out of What Began: A History of Irish Poetry in English*. Ithaca, NY: Cornell University Press, 1998.

Contemplative Verses On the Tombs in Drumcondra Church-Yard, in the Manner of Gray

From **Poems** (1789)

Now sober Ev'ning, clad in mantlet grey,
　In solemn pomp steals on to shadowy Night,
The twinkling Stars begin their lucid way,
　And bashful Cynthia[1] shews her silver light.

No noise is heard, save yonder hooting Owl,   5
　That shrieks his mournful dirge in scream of woe –
This is the time to cultivate the soul,
　And bid it spurn at vain terrestrial shew!

Here oft with me, my pensive Muse, retire,
　And o'er each hillock heave a sigh sincere;   10

Notes ———————————————————

CONTEMPLATIVE VERSES ON THE TOMBS
[1] the moon

Here let me softly string th' elegaic lyre,
    And pay the humble dead a tribute tear. –

Yon ghastly scull, at which my step recoils,
    Perhaps was once some lovely Sylvan maid;
Was once the seat of all the dimpled smiles,   15
    But ah! those winning charms are now decay'd.

Where is the front[2] where bashful meekness beam'd,
    Where is each charm that won th'enraptur'd swain,
Where now the eyes where heav'nly brightness flam'd,
    Oh! where is she, the Venus of the plain? –   20

Perhaps yon verdant turf, tho' humbly low,
    Contains the village Patriot's noisy head;
Who guess'd of tott'ring states the future woe,
    And mourn'd bright freedom from his country fled.

The rustic Punster here perhaps may rest,   25
    Possess'd of many a quibble, many a joke;
Each word he utter'd was esteem'd a jest,
    And Bumpkins gap'd, and titter'd as he spoke.

The Preacher's lowly stone deserves my tear,
    Who by example shew'd the good he taught,   30
His life was blameless, and his heart sincere,
    And if he gave not much, 'twas not his fault.

When at his door he saw the child of woe,
    The bursting tear stood trembling in his eye,
To give his little alms he ne'er was slow,   35
    And oft he wish'd for riches with a sigh. –

And tho' he long is dead, the silent clown
    Passes his humble tomb in rev'rend awe;
He thinks he sees the goodman's chiding frown
    Desire him follow Virtue's lovely law;   40

And as he reads the moral lesson rang'd
    In antique order, on the sculptur'd stone,
All in a trice, his vicious thoughts are chang'd,
    And sad, in honest grief, he heaves a groan.

Blest be thy name! and may thy peaceful shade   45
    For ever taste the bliss of heav'nly love!
And tho' beneath this earthly hillock laid,
    Yet soar triumphant to the plains above! –

Perchance, the Poet here reclines his head,
    No stone or slate to tell that once he sung;   50
His varying dreams, and self-made pomp are fled,
    And mute, alas! too mute, his tuneful tongue!

Notes —————————————————————————————
[2] forehead

The wonder of the village once was he,
    His witty song could jocund mirth diffuse,
He'd deify the Rustics for a fee,   55
    And all would ask, "What fairy is his Muse?"

How bless'd was he, his life in pleasure spent!
    He had no *Patron*, each one was his *Friend*,
He aim'd no high'r, with frugal praise content,
    And what he wrote, was but by *Nature* penn'd.   60

Oh! may I thus, his calm enjoyments share,
    Nor vainly mix amongst the giddy crowd!
Despising flattery's guile, and folly's snare,
    And if possess'd of riches, yet not proud.

And, when I die, beneath yon weeping yew,   65
    Oh! may I lie, by cypress hem'd around;
And with no epitaph, but what is true,
    Which only serves to shew the burial ground.

While oft the swain quick trudging o'er the tomb,
    Of worldly cares, and village business full,   70
Shall pass neglectful of his certain doom,
    And careless, kick the hallowed Poet's scull. –

But hark – methinks I hear the pealing knell, –
    The sound encreas'd comes swelling on the gale,
Kind Sexton, turn a while, and gently tell,   75
    Altho' I dread to hear the horrid tale.

'Tis he – my panting heart did sure forebode,
    The trickling tear did now unbidden flow,
Some friend I guess'd was near his last abode,
    My heart confess'd anticipated woe!   80

And lo! the herse in solemn grandeur comes,
    The torches flashing thro' the dusk of night,
Each chequer'd gleam reflects the murky tombs,
    And horror is encreas'd by glimm'ring light.

Those yonder weeping ministers of woe,   85
    Now near approach, in sable robes array'd,
Like messengers of fate, now moving slow,
    Solemn they walk, and pray o'er all the dead.

And now – but first oh! let me fondly weep,
    And clasp thy coffin to my panting breast;   90
Snatch one farewell – then lay Philander[3] deep,
    And sing his *requiem* to eternal rest.

Now the cold clay, thrice on his coffin cast,
    The greedy earth for ever hides my friend –
Alas! thy transitory life is past,   95
    And all thy earthly honors at an end.

Notes ─────────────────────────────────────

[3] Poetic term for a male beloved.

But tho' thy body I shall view no more,
   Thou e'er shalt gain a tablet of my heart;
Thy loss, my faithful friend, I'll e'er deplore,
   And never shall thy *memory* depart.   100

The Poet's Pen, A Fable

From Poems, Consisting of Essays, Lyric, Elegiac, &c. (1792)

As dry, and destitute of thought,
   One evening in Olympian[1] garret,
My head devoid of brain, my belly void of claret,
   I sat my nails in frenzy biting,
And with most odd emotions sought,   5
   The favourable jerk for writing.

   Sudden my pen, like any thistle,
Began to caper, shake and bristle,
And in a shower of ink so muddy,
Thus broke upon my study: –   10

   "Rash wight! who, better taught than fed,
With purse much emptier than head,
Art doom'd to earth, unlucky sinner!
To scrawl and flatter for a dinner;
Black was the hour, at Fate's command,   15
When first I flourish'd in thy hand,
When first my spotless plumes I gave,
To daub some good-for-nothing knave;
When first I left the rib of goose,
To deck the ink-stand of a Muse.   20

   "Ah! better with attorney's clerk,
To trace huge folios in the dark;
Or, vile, poetic alligator!
T'ave pleas'd some German commentator,
Whose Pindus[2] lies before the kitchen,   25
Bacon, and grease, and genius rich in;
Whose works as luscious as his cheese,
Could give the sleepless eye-lid ease;
Than with thee tag rude rhimes together,
Bending my supple snout like leather,   30
From morn till night – at last my stump
Is fairly nibbled to the rump;
I therefore think yours a hard case,
Inform you that within my carcase,
Performing penances, doth lye,   35
The evil sprite of POVERTY."

Notes ──────────────────────────────

THE POET'S PEN
[1] Like Mount Olympus.

[2] Greek mountains.

I started, and to end my tale,
Present this same curs'd pen for sale,
And without higgling much, or arguing,
  Any poor actor, author, curate,   40
  Or beau, whom footmen shut the door at,
Shall have it, at this moment, a fair bargain.

To Miss Sidney and Miss Olivia Owenson

From **Poems, Consisting of Essays, Lyric, Elegiac, &c. (1792)**

BLITHE, in the blooming morn of youth,
SINCERITY, my guide, and TRUTH,
Ere Pride my tranquil slumber broke,
Ere Praise in pomp unmeaning spoke,
To YOU I tun'd the fervent lay,   5
Tender, and innocently gay;
And while I sought your candid ear,
Listening, you lean'd, well pleas'd to hear
Numbers that could pure joy impart,
And melody that won the heart;   10
Twin-roses, now, in vernal prime;
Accept this fond, this grateful rhime!
And, 'stead of toiling up Parnassus,
Wooing, so warm, its tuneful lasses,
Let me, (now Wit his pow'r infuses,)   15
E'en make ye, ladies, serve as muses;
SYDNEY and LIVY, then, shall be
THALIA and MELPOMENE.[1]

The Days of Yore

From **Poems, Moral and Descriptive (1800)**

In knightly hall, or lady's bow'r,
Erewhile, the vocal wire was strung;
And many a laurel, many a flow'r,
Round the sweet Minstrel's harp was hung;

Graceful array'd in flowing stole   5
Of green, with tissued roses wove,
His ardor warm'd th' heroic soul,
His softness sooth'd disastrous love;

Notes

TO MISS SIDNEY
[1] Dermody is commenting on the sisters' characters through the sister muses: Thalia of pastoral and comic poetry (Sydney Owenson, later Lady Morgan), and Melpomene of tragedy (Olivia Owenson, later Lady Clarke).

Mid harmony's responsive hoard,
His cunning fingers featly¹ caught   10
Each sound, that rapture might afford,
Or lift sublime the towering thought.

Yet oft to shun the garish beam,
Mid the deep desert would he stray,
And following quick some haunted stream,   15
Oft wander from the world away:

Stretch'd, listless, on the headlong steep,
Oft would he gaze the scene below,
The painted cloud, the toiling deep,
The purple heath, with golden glow!   20

And oft, in silent transport laid,
'Till the shrill curfew struck his ear,
Has Twilight don'd her checquer'd shade,
And Darkness veil'd him, musing there.

But yet no fear, mid wild forlorn,   25
The Bard should seek a savage bed,
Some hermit, at his glad return,
The pillow blest that lap'd his head.

Of hateful penury no fear,
The Poet still a welcome sound: 30
The peasant prest his homely cheer,
And magic song the banquet crown'd.

Gay as the little birds, that fly,
All devious, thro' the tangled wood,
To whom boon Nature's stores supply   35
Their vernal couch, their simple food!

Ah me! those happy days are past,
And alter'd sore his heavy fate,
By each rude vassal's scoff disgrac'd,
And banish'd from the lordly gate;   40

Yet nought of Heav'n illumes that heart,
That deals its tuneful servant wrong,
Nor aught of bliss can wealth impart
To him, who slights the honied song;

For, sure, of Heav'n that purer flame,   45
That hath his polish'd mind possest,
And sure, from source coelestial, came
The sunshine that pervades his breast.

Then, nobles, deign, and barons bold,
To rear the glory of your land,   50
And when true genius you behold,
Confess th' Almighty Master's hand;

Notes ——————————————————————————

THE DAYS OF YORE
¹ fitly

Nor dazzling gem on Beauty's brow,
Nor titled Grandeur's garter'd shine,
Can aught so passing bright bestow
Oh, GENIUS, as thy splendid line!

55

Thomas Moore (1779–1852)

Thomas Moore was born in Dublin. Although he was remembered for much of the twentieth century as Byron's friend and biographer, he was Ireland's most successful living poet for the first half of the nineteenth century and widely cited in the second half. The Scottish poet Byron rated him one of the best three poets of the early nineteenth century, and his poetry was read widely in Ireland, Britain, and elsewhere, and not only in the English-speaking world. Many of his texts were translated into other European languages and published on the Continent, and in Irish literature his influence can be traced from J. J. Callanan through *The Nation* poets in the 1840s forward to James Joyce.

Like a number of other Dublin writers of the era, Moore attended Samuel Whyte's school for a time. He entered Trinity College, Dublin, in 1795, where he was close friends with Robert Emmet, who was later executed for leading the 1803 Uprising. Moore was moderately involved in nationalist activity and published some pieces in nationalist periodicals, but did not, on advice from friends, join the United Irishmen. At Trinity, Moore's studies emphasized the classics, and he translated Anacreon's odes, publishing them as a volume in 1800. He could not, however, take his degree because he was a Catholic and the Penal Statutes were still in force. *The Nation*, celebrating Moore in its third issue, notes that Moore had friends in the United Irishmen and praises his loyalty: "Moore was cross-questioned by Clare at the famous College visitation of '97, and he held his own manfully against the imperious inquisitor." Moore entered the Middle Temple to study law in 1799, but his social and literary success, including his pseudonymous *Poetical Works of the Late Thomas Little* (1801), led to an appointment in the naval prize court in Bermuda (1803–4). While he did not remain long in Bermuda, it did give him the opportunity to travel, both before and after his appointment, in the United States.

He then returned and published *Epistles, Odes, and Other Poems* (1806), his first original work under his own name. When *Epistles* was savagely reviewed by Francis Jeffrey – a critic lampooned as the intolerant Fadladeen in Moore's *Lalla Rookh* (1817) – Moore challenged Jeffrey to a duel, which Jeffrey accepted. There are different accounts of what transpired, but the duel did not take place and the two apparently became friends. Moore then wrote a number of satires, including the verse satires *Corruption and Intolerance* (1808), *The Sceptic* (1809), and *Intercepted Letters* (1813), and satirical works in prose from *Memoirs of Captain Rock* (1824) to *Travels of an Irish Gentleman in Search of Religion* (1833). While many of these works ran through multiple editions, none was as successful as Moore's *Irish Melodies*, lyrics set to music that were published in a series of ten numbers and a supplement. Moore began the project with Sir John Stevenson, who worked on the music, in early 1807, though the year of the first number's publication is disputed. No year of publication appears in the early numbers: 1807 is the traditional dating, but Percy Muir made a strong, though not conclusive, argument for 1808 in a 1933 article (see Bibliography). In its combination of English lyrics and traditional Irish music, the *Melodies* echo Morgan's *Twelve Original Hibernian Melodies* (1805), and Morgan perhaps intended to call attention to the debt by referring to her 1805 volume as her "collection of *Irish Melodies*" in her *Lay of an Irish Harp* (1807).

Lalla Rookh was nearly as great a success as *Irish Melodies*, earning Moore a record advance from the publisher. While sometimes dismissed as an attempt to capitalize on a fad for orientalist narratives, *Lalla Rookh* is one of the few such works to be republished across the nineteenth century. It also spawned illustrated editions and musical adaptations from the 1840s to the 1880s, and was translated into German, French, and Italian. Early editions of *Lalla Rookh* included both footnotes, which were largely relevant to the meaning of particular passages, and endnotes, which were more digressive; later editions combined all of the notes as footnotes, losing the distinction between them. For the excerpt here from *Lalla Rookh* – the first three-quarters of "The Fire-Worshippers," the third of four narratives in *Lalla Rookh* – the footnotes have largely been retained, but not the endnotes. Moore used dozens of now-obscure orientalist works for *Lalla Rookh*, but his leading sources are the English orientalists William Jones, Abraham Parsons, and John Richardson, and often French sources of Arabic and other non-European materials. In her essay on Moore, Lady Wilde cites the near-homonym Erin/Iran and the theme of persecution to connect Moore's narrative to Irish history (see her essay on Moore below). The relationship between Ireland and "fire-worshippers" is perhaps further explained by a poem republished about the time Moore began to compose *Lalla Rookh*, Drennan's "Glendalloch"; in Drennan's poem, the early Irish, like Moore's Iranians, are depicted worshipping the sun as a "sacred fire."

After *Lalla Rookh*, Moore turned most of his literary attention to non-fiction prose. He had already published a political pamphlet, *A Letter to the Roman Catholics of Dublin* (1810), but after 1820 he wrote biographies of Richard Brinsley Sheridan (1825), United Irishmen leader Lord Edward Fitzgerald (1831), and Byron (1831), as well as a four-volume *History of Ireland* (1835–46). He received a government pension, though he was in some danger of losing it: *The Nation* indicated, in an 1843 piece "Tom Moore's Treason," that "The *Belfast News-Letter* calls upon the Government to deprive MOORE of his pension for contributing to this journal," claiming that one of the poems was clearly Moore's because of its style (the identification was nevertheless wrong). Morgan was among those who agitated for a public monument to Moore in Dublin soon after his death, and Lady Wilde, nearly forty years after Moore's death, asked for the poet's remains to be returned to Ireland.

Further reading

Davis, Leith, *Music, Postcolonialism, and Gender: The Construction of Irish National Identity, 1724–1874*. Notre Dame, IN: University of Notre Dame Press, 2006.

Jones, Catherine A., "'Our Partial Attachments': Tom Moore and 1798," *Eighteenth-century Ireland* 13 (1998): 24–43.

Lennon, Joseph, *Irish Orientalism: A Literary and Intellectual History*. Syracuse: Syracuse University Press, 2004.

Wright, Julia M., *Ireland, India, and Nationalism in Nineteenth-century Literature*. Cambridge: Cambridge University Press, 2007.

Epistle II: To Miss M——e[1] (from Norfolk, in Virginia, November, 1803)

From **Epistles, Odes, and Other Poems (1806)**

In days, my KATE, when life was new,
When, lull'd with innocence and you,
I heard, in home's beloved shade,
The din the world at distance made;
When, every night my weary head   5
Sunk on its own unthorned bed,
And, mild as evening's matron hour
Looks on the faintly shutting flower,
A mother saw our eyelids close,
And bless'd them into pure repose!   10
Then, haply if a week, a day,
I linger'd from your arms away,
How long the little absence seem'd!
How bright the look of welcome beam'd,
As mute you heard, with eager smile,   15
My tales of all that pass'd the while!
Yet now, my Kate, a gloomy sea
Rolls wide between that home and me;
The moon may thrice be born and die,
Ere ev'n your seal can reach mine eye;   20
And oh! ev'n then, that darling seal,
(Upon whose print, I us'd to feel
The breath of home, the cordial air
Of loved lips, still freshly there!)
Must come, alas! through every fate   25
Of time and distance, cold and late,
When the dear hand, whose touches fill'd
The leaf with sweetness may be chill'd!
But hence, that gloomy thought! at last,
Beloved Kate! the waves are past: 30
I tread on earth securely now,
And the green cedar's living bough
Breathes more refreshment to my eyes
Than could a Claude's[2] divinest dies!
At length I touch the happy sphere   35
To liberty and virtue dear,
Where man looks up, and proud to claim
His rank within the social frame,
Sees a grand system round him roll,
Himself its centre, sun and soul!   40
Far from the shocks of Europe; far
From every wild, elliptic star

Notes

EPISTLE II
[1] Moore's sister, Catherine.

[2] Claude Lorrain (1600–82), French artist.

That, shooting with a devious fire,
Kindled by heaven's avenging ire,
So oft hath into chaos hurl'd   45
The systems of the ancient world!

The warrior here, in arms no more,
Thinks of the toil, the conflict o'er,
And glorying in the rights they won
For hearth and altar, sire and son,   50
Smiles on the dusky webs that hide
His sleeping sword's remember'd pride!
While peace, with sunny cheeks of toil,
Walks o'er the free, unlorded soil,
Effacing with her splendid share,   55
The drops that war had sprinkled there!
Thrice happy land! where he who flies
From the dark ills of other skies,
From scorn, or want's unnerving woes,
May shelter him in proud repose!   60
Hope sings along the yellow sand
His welcome to a patriot land;
At once, the mighty wood receives
The stranger in its world of leaves,
Which soon their barren glory yield   65
To the warm shed and cultur'd field;
And he, who came, of all bereft,
To whom malignant fate had left
Nor home nor friends nor country dear,
Finds home and friends and country here!   70

Such is the picture, warmly such,
That long the spell of fancy's touch
Hath painted to my sanguine eye
Of man's new world of liberty!
Oh! ask me not, if truth will seal   75
The reveries of fancy's zeal,
If yet, my charmed eyes behold
These features of an age of gold –
No – yet, alas! no gleaming trace!
Never did youth, who lov'd a face   80
From portrait's rosy, flattering art,
Recoil with more regret of heart,
To find an owlet eye of grey,
Where painting pour'd the sapphire's ray,
Than I have felt, indignant felt,   85
To think the glorious dreams should melt,
Which oft, in boyhood's witching time,
Have rapt me to this wond'rous clime!

But, courage! yet, my wavering heart,
Blame not the temple's meanest part,   90
Till you have trac'd the fabric o'er: –

As yet, we have beheld no more
Than just the porch to freedom's fane,
And, though a sable drop may stain
The vestibule, 'tis impious sin   95
To doubt there's holiness within!
So here I pause – and now, my Kate,
To you (whose simplest ringlet's fate
Can claim more interest in my soul
Than all the Powers from pole to pole)   100
One word at parting; in the tone
Most sweet to you, and most my own.
The simple notes I sent you here,[3]
Though rude, my love, would still be dear,
If you but knew the trance of thought,   105
In which my mind their murmurs caught.
'Twas one of those enchanting dreams,
That lull me oft, when music seems
To pour the soul in sound along,
And turn its every sigh to song!   110
I thought of home, the according lays
Respir'd the breath of happier days;
Warmly in every rising note
I felt a sweet remembrance float,
Till, led by music's fairy chain,   115
I wander'd back to home again!
Oh! love the song, and let it oft
Live on your lip, in warble soft!
Say that it tells you, simply well,
All I have bid its murmurs tell,   120
Of memory's glow, of dreams that shed
The tinge of joy when joy is fled,
And all the heart's illusive hoard
Of love renew'd and friends restor'd!
Now, sweet, adieu! – this artless air,   125
And a few rhymes, in transcript fair,
Are all the gifts I yet can boast
To send you from Columbia's coast;[4]
But when the sun, with warmer smile,
Shall light me to my destin'd isle,[5]   130
You shall have many a cowslip-bell
Where Ariel[6] slept, and many a shell,
In which the gentle spirit drew
From honey flowers the morning dew!

Notes

[3] A trifling attempt at musical composition accompanied this Epistle (author).

[4] In the general sense of the regions "discovered" by Christopher Columbus (1451–1506), Italian explorer.

[5] Bermuda (author). Moore traveled to North America to take up a post in Bermuda.

[6] A character in the English play *The Tempest* (1612) by Shakespeare, and thus associated with the Americas.

To Mrs. Henry T–ghe,[1] On Reading Her "Psyche"

From **Epistles, Odes, and Other Poems** (1806)

Tell me the witching tale again,
    For never has my heart or ear
Hung on so sweet, so pure a strain,
    So pure to feel, so sweet to hear!

Say, Love! in all thy spring of fame,   5
    When the high heaven itself was thine;
When piety confess'd the flame,
    And even thy errors were divine!

Did ever Muse's hand, so fair,
    A glory round thy temples spread?   10
Did ever lip's ambrosial air
    Such perfume o'er thy altars shed?

One maid there was, who round her lyre
    The mystic myrtle wildly wreath'd –
But all _her_ sighs were sighs of fire,   15
    The myrtle wither'd, as she breath'd!

Oh! you, that love's celestial dream,
    In all its purity, would know,
Let not the senses' ardent beam
    Too strongly through the vision glow!   20

Love sweetest lies, conceal'd in night,
    The night where heaven has bid him lie;
Oh! shed not there unhallow'd light,
    Or, Psyche knows, the boy will fly![2]

Dear Psyche! many a charmed hour,   25
    Through many a wild and magic waste,
To the fair fount and blissful bower[3]
    Thy mazy foot my soul hath trac'd!

Where'er thy joys are number'd now,
    Beneath whatever shades of rest,   30
The Genius of the starry brow[4]
    Has chain'd thee to thy Cupid's breast;

Whether above the horizon dim,
    Along whose verge our spirits stray,
(Half sunk within the shadowy brim,   35
    Half brighten'd by the eternal ray)[5]

Notes

To Mrs. Henry T–ghe

[1] Mary Tighe (see above).

[2] See the story in Apuleius (author). Lucius Apuleius, second-century north African author who included the story of Cupid and Psyche in his text, _The Golden Ass_ (or _The Metamorphoses_).

[3] Allusions to Mrs. T–ghe's poem (author).

[4] Constancy (author).

[5] By this image the Platonists expressed the middle state of the soul between sensible and intellectual existence (author).

Thou risest to a cloudless pole!
   Or, lingering here, dost love to mark
The twilight walk of many a soul
   Through sunny good and evil dark;   40

Still be the song to PSYCHE dear,
   The song, whose dulcet tide was given,
To keep her name as fadeless, here,
   As nectar keeps her soul, in heaven!

Preface

From Intercepted Letters; Or, the Two-Penny Post-Bag (1813)

The Bag, from which the following Letters are selected, was dropped by a Twopenny Postman about two months since, and picked up by an emissary of the Society for the S–pp—ss—n of V—e,[1] who, supposing it might materially assist the private researches of that Institution, immediately took it to his employers and was rewarded handsomely for his trouble. Such a treasury of secrets was worth a whole host of informers; and, accordingly, like the Cupids of the poet (if I may use so profane a simile) who "fell at odds about the sweet-bag of a bee,"[2] those venerable Suppressors almost fought with each other for the honour and delight of first ransacking the Post-Bag. Unluckily, however, it turned out upon examination, that the discoveries of profligacy which it enabled them to make, lay chiefly in those upper regions of society, which their well-bred regulations forbid them to molest or meddle with. – In consequence, they gained but very few victims by their prize, and, after lying for a week or two under Mr. H–TCH—D's counter,[3] the Bag, with its violated contents, was sold for a trifle to a friend of mine.

It happened that I had been just then seized with an ambition (having never tried the strength of my wing but in a Newspaper) to publish something or other in the shape of a Book; and it occurred to me that, the present being such a letter-writing era, a few of these Twopenny Post Epistles, turned into easy verse, would be as light and popular a task as I could possibly select for a commencement. I did not think it prudent, however, to give too many Letters at first, and, accordingly, have been obliged (in order to eke out a sufficient number of pages) to reprint some of those trifles, which had already appeared in the public journals.[4] As in the battles of ancient times, the shades of the departed were sometimes seen among the combatants, so I thought I might remedy the thinness of my ranks, by conjuring up a few dead and forgotten ephemerons to fill them.

Such are the motives and accidents, that led to the present publication; and as this is the first time my Muse has ever ventured out of the go-cart of a Newspaper, though I feel all a parent's delight at seeing little Miss go alone, I am also not without a parent's anxiety, lest an unlucky fall should be the consequence of the experiment; and I need

Notes

PREFACE

[1] The Society for the Suppression of Vice was established by abolitionist William Wilberforce (1759–1833) in 1802.

[2] Herrick (author). "The Bag of the Bee" by English poet Robert Herrick (1591–1674); Moore reverses the order of the first two lines.

[3] Likely to be John Hatchard (1768–1849), a bookseller with royal patrons who published the *Christian Observer*.

[4] It is but fair to mention that some of these reprinted jeux-d'esprit (as the Parody on the R–G—T's Letter, the Insurrection of the Papers, the New Costume of the Ministers, and the Sale of the Tools) are *not mine* – but they appeared to be so perfectly *in keeping* with my own, and were so very convenient in filling up my pages, that I trust their Author (whoever he may be) will excuse the liberty I have taken in making use of them (author). These are other letters in *Intercepted Letters*: Letter III purports to be from the Prince Regent, for instance.

not point out the many living instances there are, of Muses that have suffered severely in their heads, from taking too early and rashly to their feet. Besides, a Book is so very different a thing from a Newspaper! – in the former, your doggerel, without either company or shelter, must stand shivering in the middle of a bleak white page by itself; whereas, in the latter, it is comfortably backed by advertisements, and has sometimes even a Speech of Mr. St–ph–n's, or something equally warm, for a *chauffe-pié* – so that, in general, the very reverse of "laudatur et alget" is its destiny.[5]

Ambition, however, must run some risks, and I shall be very well satisfied if the reception of these few Letters, should have the effect of sending me to the Post-Bag for more.

LETTER I

From Intercepted Letters; Or, the Two-Penny Post-Bag (1813)

FROM THE PR–NC–SS CH———E OF W———S TO THE LADY B–RB—A A–SHL–Y[1]

My dear Lady BAB, you'll be shock'd, I'm afraid,
When you hear the sad rumpus your Ponies have made;
Since the time of horse-consuls (now long out of date,)
No nags ever made such a stir in the State!
Lord ELD–N[2] first heard – and as instantly pray'd he   5
To God and his King – that a Popish young Lady
(For though you've bright eyes and twelve thousand a year,
It is still but too true you're a Papist, my dear)
Had insidiously sent, by a tall Irish groom,
Two priest-ridden Ponies, just landed from Rome,   10
And so full, little rogues, of pontifical tricks,
That the dome of St. Paul's was scarce safe from their kicks!

Off at once to Papa, in a flurry, he flies –
For Papa always does what these statesmen advise,
On condition that they'll be, in turn, so polite   15
As, in no case whate'er, to advise him *too right* –
"Pretty doings are here, Sir, (he angrily cries,
While by dint of dark eyebrows he strives to look wise)
" 'Tis a scheme of the Romanists, so help me God!
To ride over your most Royal Highness roughshod –   20
Excuse, Sir, my tears – they're from loyalty's source –
Bad enough 'twas for Troy to be sack'd by a *Horse*,
But for us to be ruin'd by *Ponies* still worse!"
Quick a Council is call'd – the whole Cabinet sits –
The Archbishops declare, frighten'd out of their wits,   25

Notes ————

[5] *Chauffe-pié* means hot pie; *laudatur et alget* is from Roman satirist Juvenal's oft-cited Latin phrase *probitus laudatur et alget*, meaning roughly that virtue is praised but not rewarded.

LETTER I

[1] This young Lady, who is a Roman Catholic, has lately made a present of some beautiful Ponies to the Pr–nc–ss

(author). Princess Charlotte of Wales (1796–1817), the Prince Regent's daughter, and Lady Barbara Ashley.

[2] John Scott (1751–1838), Viscount Encombe and Earl of Eldon, Lord Chancellor from 1801 to 1806 and 1807 to 1827.

That if vile Popish Ponies should eat at my manger,
From that awful moment the Church is in danger!
As, give them but stabling, and shortly no stalls
Will suit their proud stomachs but those at St. Paul's.

The Doctor and he, the devout Man of Leather,   30
V–NS–TT—T,[3] now laying their Saint-heads together,
Declare that this skittish young *a*-bominations
Are clearly foretold in Chap. vi. Revelations –
Nay, they verily think they could point out the one
Which the Doctor's friend Death was to canter upon!   35

Lord H–RR—BY,[4] hoping that no one imputes
To the Court any fancy to persecute brutes,
Protests, on the word of himself and his cronies,
That had these said creatures been Asses, not Ponies,
The Court would have started no sort of objection,   40
As Asses were, *there*, always sure of protection.

"If the PR–NC–SS *will* keep them, (says Lord C–STL–R—GH –)[5]
To make them quite harmless the only true way,
Is (as certain Chief-Justices do with their wives)
To flog them within half an inch of their lives –   45
If they've any bad Irish blood lurking about,
This (he knew by experience) would soon draw it out."
Or – if this be thought cruel – his Lordship proposes
"The new *Veto* snaffle to bind down their noses –
A pretty contrivance, made out of old chains,   50
Which appears to indulge, while it doubly restrains;[6]
Which, however high-mettled, their gamesomeness checks,
(Adds his Lordship humanely) or else breaks their necks!"

This proposal receiv'd pretty general applause
From the Statesmen around – and the neck-breaking clause   55
Had a vigour about it, which soon reconcil'd
Even ELD–N himself to a measure so mild.
So the snaffles, my dear, were agreed to nem. con.[7]
And my Lord C–STL–R—GH, having so often shone
In the *fettering* line, is to buckle them on.   60

I shall drive to your door in these *Vetos* some day,
But, at present, adieu! – I must hurry away
To go see my Mamma, as I'm suffer'd to meet her
For just half an hour by the QU—N's best repeater.[8]
                                        C———E.

Notes

[3] Likely to be Nicholas Vansittart (1766–1851), first Baron Bexley, who became Chancellor of the Exchequer in 1812.

[4] Dudley Ryder (1762–1847), first Earl of Harrowby, was a key government minister for much of the early nineteenth century.

[5] Robert Stewart (1769–1822), Lord Castlereagh, was involved in the suppression of the 1798 Irish Uprising.

[6] A reference to the Veto Controversy, in which Irish Catholics debated a choice offered by the British: Catholic emancipation at the price of a British veto over the appointment of bishops, or the status quo. Moore published a pamphlet on the subject in 1810.

[7] *nemine contradicente*, without dissent (Latin).

[8] The queen's clock.

LETTER VII

From Intercepted Letters; Or, the Two-Penny Post-Bag (1813)

FROM MESSRS. L–CK—GT–N AND CO. TO ——— ———, ESQ.[1]

Per Post, Sir, we send your MS. – look'd it thro' –
Very sorry – but can't undertake – 'twouldn't do.
Clever work, Sir! – would *get up* prodigiously well –
Its only defect is – it never would sell!
And though *Statesmen* may glory in being *unbought*,   5
In an *Author*, we think, Sir, that's *rather* a fault.

Hard times, Sir, – most books are too dear to be read –
Though the *gold* of Good-sense and Wit's *small-change* are fled,
Yet the *paper* we Publishers pass, in their stead,[2]
Rises higher each day, and ('tis frightful to think it)   10
Not even such names as F–TZG–R—D's can sink it![3]

However, Sir – if you're for trying again,
And at somewhat that's vendible – we are your men.

Since the Chevalier C–RR[4] took to marrying lately,
The Trade is in want of a *Traveller* greatly –   15
No job, Sir, more easy – your *Country* once plann'd,
A month aboard ship and a fortnight on land
Puts your Quarto of Travels, Sir, clean out of hand.

An East-India pamphlet's a thing that would tell –
And a lick at the Papists is *sure* to sell well.   20
Or – supposing you've nothing *original* in you –
Write Parodies, Sir, and such fame it will win you,
You'll get to the Blue-stocking Routs of ALB–N–A[5]!
(Mind – *not* to her *dinners* – a *second-hand* Muse
Mustn't think of aspiring to *mess* with the *Blues*.)   25
Or – in case nothing else in the world you can do –
The deuce is in't, Sir, if you cannot *review*!

Should you feel any touch of *poetical* glow,
We've a Scheme to suggest – Mr. SC–TT,[6] you must know,
(Who, we're sorry to say it, now works for *the Row*[7])   30
Having quitted the Borders, to seek new renown,

Notes

LETTER VII

[1] From motives of delicacy, and, indeed, of *fellow-feeling*, I suppress the name of the Author, whose rejected manuscript was inclosed in this letter … (author).

[2] Paper currency was increasingly replacing coins.

[3] Perhaps William Thomas Fitzgerald (1759–1829), English hack writer invoked in *English Bards and Scotch Reviewers* by Moore's friend, the Scottish poet Byron (1788–1824).

[4] Sir John Carr (1772–1832), English travel writer, author of *The Stranger in Ireland* (1806); he married in 1811.

[5] This alludes, I believe, to a curious correspondence, which is said to have passed lately between ALB–N–A, Countess of B–CK—GH–MS—E, and a certain ingenious Parodist (author). Albinia Hobart (1737/8–1816), Countess of Buckinghamshire.

[6] Scottish novelist Sir Walter Scott (1771–1832) was in 1813 known for his poetry, including *Minstrelsy of the Scottish Border* (1802–3) and *Rokeby* (1813).

[7] Paternoster Row (author). A publishing district in London.

Is coming, by long Quarto stages, to Town;
And beginning with ROKEBY (the job's sure to pay)
Means to *do* all the Gentlemen's Seats on the way.
Now, the Scheme is (though none of our hackneys can beat him)   35
To start a fresh Poet through Highgate to *meet* him;
Who, by means of quick proofs – no revises – long coaches –
May do a few Villas, before SC–TT approaches –
Indeed, if our Pegasus be not curst shabby,
He'll reach, without found'ring, at least WOBURN-ABBEY.   40

Such, Sir, is our plan – if you're up to the freak,
'Tis a match! and we'll put you *in training* next week –
At present, no more – in reply to this Letter, a
Line will oblige very much
                    Yours, et cetera.   45
Temple of the Muses.

Oh! Breathe Not His Name[1] (1st number, 1807)

From Irish Melodies (1807–1834)

I

Oh! breathe not his name, let it sleep in the shade
Where cold and unhonor'd his relics are laid:
Sad, silent and dark, be the tears that we shed,
As the night-dew that falls on the grass o'er his head!

II

But the night-dew that falls, though in silence it weeps,   5
Shall brighten with verdure the grave where he sleeps,
And the tear that we shed, though in secret it rolls,
Shall long keep his memory green in our souls.

Take Back the Virgin Page (2nd number, 1807)

From Irish Melodies (1807–1834)

Written on returning a Blank Book

I

Take back the virgin page,
    White and unwritten still;
Some hand, more calm and sage,
    The leaf must fill.

Notes

OH! BREATHE NOT HIS NAME

[1] Robert Emmet, hanged for leading a brief uprising in 1803,
asked that his epitaph not be written until Ireland became a
sovereign nation.

Thoughts come, as pure as light,   5
   Pure as even *you* require;
But oh! each word I write
   Love turns to fire.

         II
Yet let me keep the book;
   Oft shall my heart renew,   10
When on its leaves I look,
   Dear thoughts of you!
Like you, 'tis fair and bright;
   Like you, too bright and fair
To let wild passion write   15
   One wrong wish there!

        III
Haply, when from those eyes
   Far, far away I roam,
Should calmer thoughts arise
   Tow'rds you and home;   20
Fancy may trace some line,
   Worthy those eyes to meet;
Thoughts that not burn, but shine
   Pure, calm and sweet!

        IV
And, as the records are,   25
   Which wandering seamen keep,
Led by their hidden star
   Through cold deep;
So may the words I write
   Tell thro' what storms I stray,   30
You still the unseen light,
   Guiding my way!

From *Letter to the Marchioness Dowager of Donegal*[1] (3rd number, 1810)

From **Irish Melodies** (1807–1834)

While the Publisher of these Melodies very properly inscribes them to the Nobility and Gentry of Ireland in general, I have much pleasure in selecting *one* from that number, to whom *my* share of the Work is particularly dedicated.[2] Though your Ladyship has been so long absent from Ireland, I know that you remember it well and warmly – that you have not allowed the charm of English society, like the taste of the

Notes ——————————————————————————————

FROM LETTER TO THE MARCHIONESS
[1] Sometimes titled "Prefatory Letter on Music."

[2] Moore only wrote the lyrics for the *Irish Melodies*; the musical arrangements were composed by Sir John Stevenson (1761–1833).

lotus, to produce oblivion of your country, but that even the humble tribute which I offer derives its chief claim upon your interest from the appeal which it makes to your patriotism. Indeed absence, however fatal to some affections of the heart, rather strengthens our love for the land where we were born; and Ireland is the country, of all others, which an exile must remember with enthusiasm. Those few darker and less amiable traits, with which bigotry and misrule have stained her character, and which are too apt to disgust us upon a nearer intercourse, become softened at a distance, or altogether invisible; and nothing is remembered but her virtues and her misfortunes – the zeal with which she has always loved liberty, and the barbarous policy which has always withheld it from her – the ease with which her generous spirit might be conciliated, and the cruel ingenuity which has been exerted to "wring her into undutifulness."[3]

It has often been remarked, and oftener felt, that our music is the truest of all comments on our history. The tone of defiance, succeeded by the languor of despondency – a burst of turbulence dying away into softness – the sorrows of one moment lost in the levity of the next – and all that romantic mixture of mirth and sadness, which is naturally produced by the efforts of a lively temperament, to shake off, or forget, the wrongs which lie upon it: – such are the features of our history and our character, which we find strongly and faithfully reflected in our music; and there are many airs, which, I think, it is difficult to listen to, without recalling some period or event to which their expression seems peculiarly applicable. Sometimes, when the strain is open and spirited, yet shaded here and there by a mournful recollection, we can fancy that we behold the brave allies of Montrose,[4] marching to the aid of the royal cause, notwithstanding all the perfidy of Charles and his ministers, and remembering just enough of past sufferings to enhance the generosity of their present sacrifice. The plaintive melodies of Carolan take us back to the times in which he lived, when our poor countrymen were driven to worship their God in caves, or to quit for ever the land of their birth (like the bird that abandons the nest, which human touch has violated); and in many a song do we hear the last farewell of the exile, mingling regret for the ties he leaves at home, with sanguine expectations of the honours that await him abroad – such honours as were won on the field of Fontenoy, where the valour of Irish Catholics turned the fortune of the day in favour of the French, and extorted from George the Second that memorable exclamation, "Cursed be the laws which deprive me of such subjects!" ...

I must again observe, that, in doubting the antiquity of our music, my scepticism extends but to those polished specimens of the art, which it is difficult to conceive anterior to the dawn of modern improvement; and that I would by no means invalidate the claims of Ireland, to as early a rank in the annals of minstrelsy, as the most zealous antiquary may be inclined to allow her. In addition, indeed, to the power, which music must always have possessed over the minds of a people so ardent and susceptible, the stimulus of persecution was not wanting, to quicken our taste into enthuasiasm; the charms of song were ennobled with the glories of martyrdom, and the acts against minstrels in the reigns of Henry VIII, and Elizabeth, were as successful, I doubt not, in making my countrymen musicians, as the penal laws have been in keeping them Catholics.

Notes ——————————————————————————————

[3] Moore identifies this as "A phrase which occurs in a letter from the Earl of Desmond to the Earl of Ormond, in Elizabeth's time" (Elizabeth I of England).

[4] There are some gratifying accounts of the gallantry of these Irish auxiliaries in "The Complete History of the Wars in Scotland, under Montrose" (1660) ... (author).

With respect to the verses which I have written for these Melodies, as they are intended rather to be sung than read, I can answer for their sound with somewhat more confidence than their sense; yet, it would be affectation to deny that I have given much attention to the task, and that it is not through want of zeal or industry, if I unfortunately disgrace the sweet airs of my country, by poetry altogether unworthy of their taste, their energy, and their tenderness.

Though the humble nature of my contributions to this work, may exempt them from the rigours of literary criticisms, it was not to be expected that those touches of political feeling, those tones of national complaint, in which the poetry sometimes sympathizes with the music, would be suffered to pass without censure or alarm. It has been accordingly said, that the tendency of this publication is mischievous, and that I have chosen these airs but as a vehicle of dangerous politics – as fair and precious vessels (to borrow an image of St. Augustin), from which the wine of error might be administered.[5] To those who identify nationality with treason, and who see, in every effort for Ireland, a system of hostility towards England, – to those too, who nursed in the gloom of prejudice, are alarmed by the faintest gleam of liberality, that threatens to disturb their darkness; like that Demophon of old who, when the sun shone upon him, shivered! – to such men I shall not deign to apologize, for the warmth of any political sentiment which may occur in the course of these pages. But, as there are many, among the more wise and tolerant, who, with feeling enough to mourn over the wrongs of their country, and sense enough to perceive all the danger of not redressing them, may yet think that allusions in the least degree bold or inflammatory, should be avoided in a publication of this popular description – I beg of these respected persons, to believe, that there is no one who deprecates, more sincerely than I do, any appeal to the passions of an ignorant and angry multitude; but, that it is not through that gross and inflammable region of society, a work of this nature could ever have been intended to circulate. It looks much higher for its audience and readers – it is found upon the piano-fortes of the rich, and the educated – of those, who can afford to have their national zeal a little stimulated, without exciting much dread of the excesses into which it may hurry them; and of many, whose nerves may be, now and then, alarmed with advantage, as much more is to be gained by their fears, than could ever be expected from their justice ...

Oh! Blame Not the Bard[1] (3rd number, 1810)

From Irish Melodies (1807–1834)

I

Oh! blame not the bard, if he fly to the bowers,
   Where pleasure lies, carelessly smiling at fame;
He was born for much more, and in happier hours,
   His soul might have burn'd with a holier flame.
The string, that now languishes loose o'er the lyre,   5

Notes ————————————————————————————

[5] St. Augustine's *Confessions* (bk. 1, ch. 16).

OH! BLAME NOT THE BARD

[1] We may suppose this apology to have been uttered by one of those wandering bards, whom Spencer so severely, and, perhaps, truly describes in his State of Ireland, and whose poems, he tells us, "Were sprinkled with some pretty flowers of their natural device, which gave good grace and comeliness unto them, the which it is great pity to see abused to the gracing of wickedness and vice, which, with good usage, would serve to adorn and beautify virtue" (author). *View of the Present State of Ireland* by English author Edmund Spenser (c.1552–99).

Might have bent a proud bow to the warrior's dart,
And the lip, which now breathes but the song of desire
   Might have pour'd the full tide of the patriot's heart!

II

But alas! for his country – her pride is gone by,
   And that spirit is broken, which never would bend;   10
O'er the ruin her children in secret must sigh,
   For 'tis treason to love her, and death to defend.
Unpriz'd are her sons, till they've learn'd to betray;
   Undistinguish'd they live, if they shame not their sires;
And the torch, that would light them thro' dignity's way,   15
   Must be caught from the pile, where their country expires!

III

Then blame not the bard, if, in pleasure's soft dream,
   He should try to forget, what he never can heal;
Oh! give but a hope – let a vista but gleam
   Through the gloom of his country, and mark how he'll feel!   20
That instant, his heart at her shrine would lay down
   Every passion it nurs'd, every bliss it ador'd,
While the myrtle, now idly entwin'd with his crown,
   Like the wreath of Harmodius, should cover his sword.[2]

IV

But tho' glory be gone, and tho' hope fade away,   25
   Thy name, loved Erin! shall live in his songs,
Not ev'n in the hour, when his heart is most gay,
   Will he lose the remembrance of thee and thy wrongs!
The stranger shall hear thy lament on his plains;
   The sigh of thy harp shall be sent o'er the deep,   30
Till thy masters themselves, as they rivet thy chains,
   Shall pause at the song of their captive and weep!

The Irish Peasant to His Mistress (3rd number, 1810)

From Irish Melodies (1807–1834)

I

Through grief and through danger, thy smile hath cheer'd my way,
Till hope seem'd to bud from each thorn, that round me lay;
The darker our fortune, the brighter our pure love burn'd,
Till shame into glory, till fear into zeal was turn'd;
Oh! slave as I was, in thy arms my spirit felt free,   5
And bless'd even the sorrows that made me more dear to thee.

Notes ——————————————————————————————

[2] See the Hymn, attributed to Alcaeus..."I will carry my sword, hidden in myrtles, like Harmodius and Aristogiton, &c." (author). Harmodius and Aristogiton tried to overthrow an Athenian tyrant.

II

Thy rival was honour'd, while thou wert wrong'd and scorn'd,
Thy crown was of briers, while gold her brows adorn'd;
She woo'd me to temples, while thou lay'st hid in caves,
Her friends were all masters, while thine, alas! were slaves;   10
Yet, cold in the earth, at thy feet I would rather be,
Then wed what I lov'd not, or turn one thought from thee.

III

They slander thee sorely, who say thy vows are frail –
Hadst thou been a false one, thy cheek had look'd less pale!
They say too, so long thou hast worn those lingering chains,   15
That deep in thy heart they have printed their servile stains –
Oh! do not believe them – no chain could that soul subdue –
Where shineth *thy* spirit, there liberty shineth too![1]

The Prince's Day[1] (4th number, 1811)

From Irish Melodies (1807–1834)

I

Tho' dark are our sorrows, to-day we'll forget them,
    And smile thro' our tears, like a sun-beam in showers;
There never were hearts, if our rulers would let them,
    More form'd to be grateful and blest than ours!
        But, just when the chain   5
        Has ceas'd to pain,
    And hope has enwreath'd it round with flowers,
        There comes a new link
        Our spirit to sink –
Oh! the joy that we taste, like the light of the poles,   10
    Is a flash amid darkness, too brilliant to stay;
But tho' 'twere the last little spark in our souls,
    We must light it up now, on our Prince's Day.

II

Contempt on the minion, who calls you disloyal!
    Tho' fierce to your foe, to your friends you are true;   15
And the tribute most high to a head that is royal,
    Is love from a heart, that loves liberty too.
        While cowards, who blight
        Your fame, your right,
    Would shrink from the blaze of the battle array,   20
        The Standard of Green

Notes ———————————————————————————

The Irish Peasant to His Mistress
[1] "Where the spirit of the Lord is, there is liberty." St. Paul,
2 Corinthians, iii.17 (author). Biblical reference.

The Prince's Day
[1] This song was written for a fête in honor of the Prince of Wales's Birth-Day, given by my friend, Major Bryan, at his seat in the county of Kilkenny (author).

In front would be seen –
Oh! my life on your faith! were you summon'd this minute,
   You'd cast every bitter remembrance away,
And shew what the arm of old ERIN has in it,   25
   When rous'd by the foe, on her Prince's Day.

III

He loves the Green Isle, and his love is recorded
   In hearts, which have suffered too much to forget;
And hope shall be crown'd, and attachment rewarded,
   And ERIN's gay jubilee shine out yet!   30
     The gem may be broke
     By many a stroke,
  But nothing can cloud its native ray;
     Each fragment will cast
     A light, to the last! –   35
And thus, ERIN, my country! tho' broken thou art,
   There's a lustre within thee, that ne'er will decay;
A spirit, which beams thro' each suffering part,
   And now smiles at their pain, on the Prince's Day.

By That Lake Whose Gloomy Shore[1] (4th number, 1811)

From Irish Melodies (1807–1834)

I

By that Lake, whose gloomy shore
Sky-lark never warbles o'er,
Where the cliff hangs high and steep,
Young Saint KEVIN stole to sleep.
"Here at last," he calmly said,   5
Woman ne'er shall find my bed."
Ah! the good Saint little knew
What that wily sex can do.

II

'Twas from KATHLEEN's eyes he flew,
Eyes of most unholy blue!   10
She had lov'd him well and long,
Wish'd him hers, nor thought it wrong.
Whereso'er the saint would fly,
Still he heard her light foot nigh;
East or west, where'er he turn'd,   15
Still her eyes before him burn'd.

Notes

BY THAT LAKE WHOSE GLOOMY SHORE
[1] This Ballad is founded upon one of the many stories related of St. Kevin, whose bed in the rock is to be seen at Glendalough, a most gloomy and romantic spot in the County of Wicklow (author).

III

On the bold cliff's bosom cast,
Tranquil now he sleeps at last;
Dreams of heav'n, nor thinks that e'er
Woman's smile can haunt him there.   20
But nor earth, nor heaven is free
From her power, if fond she be:
Even now, while calm he sleeps,
KATHLEEN o'er him leans and weeps.

IV

Fearless she had track'd his feet,   25
To this rocky, wild retreat;
And when morning met his view,
Her mild glances met it too.
Ah! your Saints have cruel hearts!
Sternly from his bed he starts,   30
And with rude, repulsive shock,
Hurls her from the beetling rock.

V

GLENDALOUGH! thy gloomy wave
Soon was gentle KATHLEEN's grave;
Soon the Saint, (yet ah! too late,)   35
Felt her love, and mourn'd her fate.
When he said, "Heav'n rest her soul!"
Round the Lake light music stole;
And her ghost was seen to glide,
Smiling, o'er the fatal tide!   40

She Is Far from the Land[1] (4th number, 1811)

From Irish Melodies (1807–1834)

I

She is far from the land, where her young hero sleeps,
    And lovers are round her, sighing;
But coldly she turns from their gaze, and weeps,
    For her heart in his grave is lying!

II

She sings the wild song of her dear native plains,   5
    Every note which he lov'd awaking. –
Ah! little they think, who delight in her strains,
    How the heart of the Minstrel is breaking!

Notes _____

SHE IS FAR FROM THE LAND
[1] This poem, like "Oh! Breathe Not His Name," reputedly refers to Robert Emmett. His parting letter to his fiancée Sarah Curran, daughter of United Irishmen lawyer John Philpot Curran, and his visit to her before his arrest were the stuff of romantic legend.

III

He had liv'd for his love, for his country he died,
    They were all that to life had entwin'd him, –   10
Nor soon shall the tears of his country be dried,
    Nor long will his love stay behind him!

IV

Oh! make her a grave, where the sun-beams rest,
    When they promise a glorious morrow;
They'll shine o'er her sleep, like a smile from the West,   15
    From her own lov'd Island of sorrow!

The Minstrel-Boy (5th number, 1813)

From Irish Melodies (1807–1834)

I

The Minstrel-Boy to the war is gone,
    In the ranks of death you'll find him,
His father's sword he has girded on,
    And his wild harp slung behind him. –
"Land of song!" said the warrior-bard,   5
    "Tho' all the world betrays thee,
One sword, at least, thy rights shall guard,
    One faithful harp shall praise thee!"

II

The Minstrel fell! – but the foeman's chain
    Could not bring his proud soul under;   10
The harp he lov'd ne'er spoke again,
    For he tore its chords asunder;
And said, "No chains shall sully thee,
    Thou soul of love and bravery!
Thy songs were made for the pure and free,   15
    They shall never sound in slavery!"

Shall the Harp Then Be Silent?[1] (8th number, 1821)

From Irish Melodies (1807–1834)

I

Shall the Harp then be silent, when he, who first gave
    To our country a name, is withdrawn from all eyes?
Shall a Minstrel of Erin stand mute by the grave,
    Where the first – where the last of her Patriots lies?

Notes ―――――――――――――――――――――――

SHALL THE HARP THEN BE SILENT?
[1] The subject of this poem is Henry Grattan (1746–1820),
orator and member of the Irish parliament.

II

No – faint tho' the death-song may fall from his lips,   5
    Tho' his Harp, like his soul, may with shadows be crost,
Yet, yet shall it sound, mid a nation's eclipse,
    And proclaim to the world what a star hath been lost![2]

III

What a union of all the affections and powers,
    By which life is exalted, embellish'd, refin'd,   10
Was embrac'd in that spirit – whose centre was ours,
    While its mighty circumference circled mankind.

IV

Oh, who that loves Erin – or who that can see,
    Through the waste of her annals, that epoch sublime –
Like a pyramid, rais'd in the desert – where he   15
    And his glory stand out to the eyes of all time! –

V

That *one* lucid interval, snatch'd from the gloom
    And the madness of ages, when, fill'd with his soul,
A Nation o'erleap'd the dark bounds of her doom,
    And, for *one* sacred instant, touch'd Liberty's goal!   20

VI

Who, that ever hath heard him – hath drunk at the source
    Of that wonderful eloquence, all Erin's own,
In whose high-thoughted daring, the fire, and the force,
    And the yet untam'd spring of her spirit are shewn.

VII

An eloquence, rich – wheresoever its wave   25
    Wander'd free and triumphant – with thoughts that shone through
As clear as the brook's "stone of lustre," and gave,
    With the flash of the gem, its solidity, too.

VIII

Who, that ever approach'd him, when, free from the crowd,
    In a home full of love, he delighted to tread   30
'Mong the trees which a nation had giv'n, and which bow'd,
    As if each brought a new civic crown for his head –

IX

That home, where – like him who, as fable hath told,[3]
    Put the rays from his brow, that his child might come near,
Every glory forgot, the most wise of the old   35
    Became all that the simplest and youngest hold dear.

Notes

[2] It is only these two verses, that are either fitted or intended to be sung (author).

[3] Apollo, in his interview with Phaëton, as described by Ovid. "*Deposuit radios propriùsque accedere jussit*" (author).

Moore's next line gives the import of this Latin quotation from Book II of *The Metamorphoses* by Ovid (c.43 BCE – AD 17), Roman poet.

X

Is there one, who hath thus, through his orbit of life,
    But at distance observ'd him – through glory, through blame,
In the calm of retreat, in the grandeur of strife
    Whether shining or clouded, still high and the same.   40

XI

Such a union of all that enriches life's hour,
    Of the sweetness we love and the greatness we praise,
As that type of simplicity blended with power,
    A child with a thunderbolt only portrays. –

XII

Oh no – not a heart, that e'er knew him, but mourns,   45
    Deep, deep, o'er the grave, where such glory is shrin'd –
O'er a monument Fame will preserve, 'mong the urns
    Of the wisest, the bravest, the best of mankind!

From [*The Fire-Worshippers*]

From Lalla Rookh (1817)

"And this," said the Great Chamberlain, "is poetry! this flimsy manufacture of the brain, which, in comparison with the lofty and durable monuments of genius, is as the gold filigree-work of Zamara beside the eternal architecture of Egypt!" After this gorgeous sentence, which, with a few more of the same kind, FADLADEEN kept by him for rare and important occasions, he proceeded to the anatomy of the short poem just recited. The lax and easy kind of metre in which it was written ought to be denounced, he said, as one of the leading causes of the alarming growth of poetry in our times. If some check were not given to this lawless facility, we should soon be overrun by a race of bards as numerous and as shallow as the hundred and twenty thousand Streams of Basra.[1] They who succeeded in this style deserved chastisement for their very success; – as warriors have been punished, even after gaining a victory, because they had taken the liberty of gaining it in an irregular or unestablished manner. What then was to be said to those who failed? to those who presumed, as in the present lamentable instance, to imitate the license and ease of the bolder sons of song, without any of that grace or vigour which gave a dignity even to negligence; – who, like them, flung the jereed[2] carelessly, but not, like them, to the mark; – "and who," said he, raising his voice, to excite a proper degree of wakefulness in his hearers, "contrive to appear heavy and constrained in the midst of all the latitude they allow themselves, like one of those young pagans that dance before the Princess, who has the ingenuity to move as if her limbs were fettered, in a pair of the lightest and loosest drawers of Masulipatam!"

Notes

FROM [THE FIRE-WORSHIPPERS]
[1] "It is said that the rivers or streams of Basra were reckoned in the time of Belal ben Abi Bordeh, and amounted to the number of 120 thousand streams" – *Ebn Haukal* (author).

[2] "The name of the javelin with which the Easterns exercise" (author).

It was but little suitable, he continued, to the grave march of criticism to follow this fantastical Peri, of whom they had just heard, through all her flights and adventures between earth and heaven; but he could not help adverting to the puerile conceitedness of the Three Gifts which she is supposed to carry to the skies, – a drop of blood, forsooth, a sigh, and a tear! How the first of these articles was delivered into the Angel's "radiant hand" he professed himself at a loss to discover; and as to the safe carriage of the sigh and the tear, such Peris and such poets were beings by far too incomprehensible for him even to guess how they managed such matters. "But, in short," said he, "it is a waste of time and patience to dwell longer upon a thing so incurably frivolous, – puny even among its own puny race, and such as only the Banyan Hospital for Sick Insects[3] should undertake."

In vain did LALLA ROOKH try to soften this inexorable critic; in vain did she resort to her most eloquent common-places, – reminding him that poets were a timid and sensitive race, whose sweetness was not to be drawn forth, like that of the fragrant grass near the Ganges, by crushing and trampling upon them; – that severity often destroyed every chance of the perfection which it demanded; and that, after all, perfection was like the Mountain of the Talisman, – no one had ever yet reached its summit.[4] Neither these gentle axioms, nor the still gentler looks with which they were inculcated, could lower for one instant the elevation of FADLADEEN's eyebrows, or charm him into any thing like encouragement or even toleration of her poet. Toleration, indeed, was not among the weaknesses of FADLADEEN; – he carried the same spirit into matters of poetry and of religion, and, though little versed in the beauties or sublimities of either, was a perfect master of the art of persecution in both. His zeal too was the same in either pursuit; whether the game before him was pagans or poetasters, – worshippers of cows or writers of epics.

They had now arrived at the splendid city of Lahore, whose mausoleums and shrines, magnificent and numberless, where Death seemed to share equal honours with Heaven, would have powerfully affected the heart and imagination of LALLA ROOKH, if feelings more of this earth had not taken entire possession of them already. She was here met by messengers, dispatched from Cashmere, who informed her that the King had arrived in the valley, and was himself superintending the sumptuous preparations that were making in the Saloons of the Shalimar for her reception. The chill she felt on receiving this intelligence, – which to a bride whose heart was free and light would have brought only images of affection and pleasure, – convinced her that her peace was gone forever, and that she was in love, irretrievably in love, with young FERAMORZ. The veil, which this passion wears at first, had fallen off, and to know that she loved was now as painful as to love *without* knowing it had been delicious. FERAMORZ, too, – what misery would be his, if the sweet hours of intercourse so imprudently allowed them should have stolen into his heart the same fatal fascination as into hers; – if, notwithstanding her rank, and the modest homage he always paid to it, even *he* should have yielded to the influence of those long and happy interviews, where music, poetry, the delightful scenes of nature, – all had tended to bring their hearts close together, and to waken by every means that too ready passion, which often, like the young of the desert-bird, is warmed into life by the eyes alone![5] She saw

Notes

[3] For a description of this Hospital of the Banyans, v. *Parsons's Travels*. (author). *v.* is an abbreviation for *vide* (see). Abraham Parsons (d. 1785), author of *Account of Travels in Asia and Africa*, first published in 1808.

[4] "Near this is a curious hill, called Koh Talism, the Mountain of the Talisman, because, according to the traditions of the country, no person ever succeeded in gaining its summit" – *Kinneir* (author).

[5] "The Arabians believe that the ostriches hatch their young by only looking at them" – P. *Vanslebe, Relat. D'Egypte* (author). Father Vansleb, French Dominican monk, and travel-writer on Egypt in the late seventeenth century.

but one way to preserve herself from being culpable as well as unhappy, and this, however painful, she was resolved to adopt. Feramorz must no more be admitted to her presence. To have strayed so far into the dangerous labyrinth was wrong, but to linger in it, while the clew was yet in her hand, would be criminal. Though the heart she had to offer to the King of Bucharia might be cold and broken, it should at least be pure; and she must only endeavour to forget the short dream of happiness she had enjoyed, – like that Arabian shepherd, who in wandering into the wilderness, caught a glimpse of the Gardens of Irim, and then lost them again forever!⁶

The arrival of the young Bride at Lahore was celebrated in the most enthusiastic manner. The Rajas and Omras in her train, who had kept at a certain distance during the journey, and never encamped nearer to the Princess than was strictly necessary for her safeguard, here rode in splendid cavalcade through the city, and distributed the most costly presents to the crowd. Engines were erected in all the squares, which cast forth showers of confectionary among the people; while the artisans, in chariots adorned with tinsel and flying streamers, exhibited the badges of their respective trades through the streets. Such brilliant displays of life and pageantry among the palaces, and domes, and gilded minarets of Lahore, made the city altogether like a place of enchantment; – particularly on the day when Lalla Rookh set out again upon her journey, when she was accompanied to the gate by all the fairest and richest of the nobility, and rode along between ranks of beautiful boys and girls, who waved plates of gold and silver flowers over their heads⁷ as they went, and then threw them to be gathered by the populace.

For many days after their departure from Lahore, a considerable degree of gloom hung over the whole party. Lalla Rookh, who had intended to make illness her excuse for not admitting the young minstrel, as usual, to the pavilion, soon found, that to feign indisposition was unnecessary; – Fadladeen felt the loss of the good road they had hitherto travelled, and was very near cursing Jehan-guire (of blessed memory!) for not having continued his delectable alley of trees,⁸ at least as far as the mountains of Cashmere; – while the Ladies, who had nothing now to do all day but to be fanned by peacocks' feathers and listen to Fadladeen, seemed heartily weary of the life they led, and, in spite of all the Great Chamberlain's criticisms, were tasteless enough to wish for the Poet again. One evening, as they were proceeding to their place of rest for the night, the Princess, who, for the freer enjoyment of the air, had mounted her favourite Arabian palfrey, in passing by a small grove, heard the notes of a lute from within its leaves, and a voice, which she but too well knew, singing the following words:—

> Tell me not of joys above,
>   If that world can give no bliss,
> Truer, happier than the Love
>   Which enslaves our souls in this!
>
> Tell me not of Houris' eyes; –   5
>   Far from me their dangerous glow,
> If those looks that light the skies
>   Wound like some that burn below!

Notes

⁶ See Sale's *Koran* (author). George Sale (c.1696–1736), English orientalist scholar known for his translation of the Qur'ān.

⁷ Ferishta (author). Mohammed Kasim Ferishta (c.1570–1611), Persian author of a history of India, available in English translation by 1768.

⁸ The fine road made by the Emperor Jehan-Guire from Agra to Lahore, planted with trees on each side (author).

Who, that feels what Love is here,
  All its falsehood – all its pain –   10
Would, for ev'n Elysium's sphere,
  Risk the fatal dream again?

Who, that midst a desert's heat
  Sees the waters fade away,
Would not rather die than meet   15
  Streams again as false as they?

The tone of melancholy defiance in which these words were uttered, went to LALLA ROOKH's heart; – and, as she reluctantly rode on, she could not help feeling it as a sad but sweet certainty, that Feramorz was to the full as enamored and miserable as herself.

The place where they encamped that evening was the first delightful spot they had come to since they left Lahore. On one side of them was a grove full of small Hindoo temples, and planted with the most graceful trees of the East; where the tamarind, the cassia, and the silken plantains of Ceylon were mingled in rich contrast with the high fan-like foliage of the Palmyra, – that favorite tree of the luxurious bird that lights up the chambers of its nest with fire-flies.[9] In the middle of the lawn where the pavilion stood there was a tank surrounded by small mangoe-trees, on the clear cold waters of which floated multitudes of the beautiful red lotus, while at a distance stood the ruins of a strange and awful-looking tower, which seemed old enough to have been the temple of some religion no longer known, and which spoke the voice of desolation in the midst of all that bloom and loveliness. This singular ruin excited the wonder and conjectures of all. LALLA ROOKH guessed in vain, and the all-pretending FADLADEEN, who had never till this journey been beyond the precincts of Delhi, was proceeding most learnedly to show that he knew nothing whatever about the matter, when one of the Ladies suggested, that perhaps FERAMORZ could satisfy their curiosity. They were now approaching his native mountains, and this tower might be a relic of some of those dark superstitions, which had prevailed in that country before the light of Islam dawned upon it. The Chamberlain, who usually preferred his own ignorance to the best knowledge that any one else could give him, was by no means pleased with this officious reference; and the Princess too was about to interpose a faint word of objection, but, before either of them could speak, a slave was despatched for FERAMORZ, who, in a very few minutes, appeared before them, – looking so pale and unhappy in LALLA ROOKH's eyes, that she already repented of her cruelty in having so long excluded him.

That venerable tower, he told them, was the remains of an ancient Fire-Temple, built by those Ghebers or Persians of the old religion, who, many hundred years since, had fled hither from their Arab conquerors, preferring liberty and their altars in a foreign land to the alternative of apostacy or persecution in their own. It was impossible, he added, not to feel interested in the many glorious but unsuccessful struggles, which had been made by these original natives of Persia to cast off the yoke of their bigoted conquerors. Like their own Fire in the Burning Field at Bakou,[10] when suppressed in one place, they had but broken out with fresh flame in another; and, as a

[9] The Baya, or Indian Gross-beak. – *Sir W. Jones* (author). Sir William Jones (1746–94), English orientalist scholar.
[10] The "Ager [g]ardens" described by *Kempfer, Amoenitat. Exot.* (author). Engelbert Kaempfer (1651–1716), German orientalist and author of *Amoenitatum exoticarum* (1716) about his travels in Persia.

native of Cashmere, of that fair and Holy Valley, which had in the same manner become the prey of strangers, and seen her ancient shrines and native princes swept away before the march of her intolerant invaders, he felt a sympathy, he owned, with the sufferings of the persecuted Ghebers, which every monument like this before them but tended more powerfully to awaken.

It was the first time that FERAMORZ had ever ventured upon so much *prose* before FADLADEEN, and it may easily be conceived what effect such prose as this must have produced upon that most orthodox and most pagan-hating personage. He sat for some minutes aghast, ejaculating only at intervals, "Bigoted conquerors! – sympathy with Fire-worshippers!" – while FERAMORZ, happy to take advantage of this almost speechless horror of the Chamberlain, proceeded to say that he knew a melancholy story, connected with the events of one of those struggles of the brave Fire-worshippers of Persia against their Arab masters, which, if the evening was not too far advanced, he should have much pleasure in being allowed to relate to the Princess. It was impossible for LALLA ROOKH to refuse; – he had never before looked half so animated, and when he spoke of the Holy Valley his eyes had sparkled, she thought, like the talismanic characters on the scimitar of Solomon. Her consent was therefore most readily granted, and while FADLADEEN sat in unspeakable dismay, expecting treason and abomination in every line, the poet thus began his story of the Fire-worshippers:—

'Tis moonlight over OMAN's Sea;[11]
   Her banks of pearl and palmy isles
Bask in the night-beam beauteously,
   And her blue waters sleep in smiles.
'Tis moonlight in HARMOZIA's[12] walls,   5
And through her EMIR's porphyry halls,
Where, some hours since, was heard the swell
Of trumpet and the clash of zel,[13]
Bidding the bright-eyed sun farewell; –
The peaceful sun, whom better suits   10
   The music of the bulbul's nest,
Or the light touch of lovers' lutes,
   To sing him to his golden rest.
All hush'd – there's not a breeze in motion;
The shore is silent as the ocean.   15
If zephyrs come, so light they come,
   Nor leaf is stirr'd nor wave is driven; –
The wind-tower on the EMIR's dome[14]
   Can hardly win a breath from heaven.

Ev'n he, that tyrant Arab, sleeps   20
Calm, while a nation round him weeps;
While curses load the air he breathes,
And falchions from unnumber'd sheaths
Are starting to avenge the shame

Notes

[11] The Persian Gulf, sometimes so called, which separates the shores of Persia and Arabia (author).

[12] The present Gombaroon, a town on the Persian side of the Gulf (author).

[13] A Moorish instrument of music (author).

[14] "At Gombaroon and other places in Persia, they have towers for the purpose of catching the wind, and cooling the houses" – *Le Bruyn* (author).

His race hath brought on IRAN's[15] name.　25
Hard, heartless Chief, unmov'd alike
Mid eyes that weep, and swords that strike; –
One of that saintly, murderous brood,
　To carnage and the Koran given,
Who think through unbelievers' blood　30
　Lies their directest path to heaven.
One, who will pause and kneel unshod
　In the warm blood his hand hath pour'd,
To mutter o'er some text of God
　Engraven on his reeking sword; – [16]　35
Nay, who can coolly note the line,
The letter of those words divine,
To which his blade, with searching art,
Had sunk into its victim's heart!

Just ALLA! what must be thy look,　40
　When such a wretch before thee stands
Unblushing, with thy Sacred Book, –
　Turning the leaves with blood-stain'd hands,
And wresting from its page sublime
His creed of lust and hate and crime! –　45
Ev'n as those bees of TREBIZOND, –
　Which, from the sunniest flowers that glad
With their pure smile the gardens round,
　Draw venom forth that drives men mad.[17]

Never did fierce ARABIA send　50
　A satrap forth more direly great;
Never was IRAN doom'd to bend
　Beneath a yoke of deadlier weight.
Her throne had fall'n – her pride was crush'd –
Her sons were willing slaves, nor blush'd,　55
In their own land, – no more their own, –
To crouch beneath a stranger's throne.
Her towers, where MITHRA once had burn'd,
To Moslem shrines – oh shame! – were turn'd;
Where slaves, converted by the sword,　60
Their mean, apostate worship pour'd,
And cursed the faith their sires ador'd.
Yet has she hearts, mid all this ill,
O'er all this wreck high buoyant still
With hope and vengeance; – hearts that yet, –　65
　Like gems, in darkness, issuing rays
They've treasured from the sun that's set, –
　Beam all the light of long-lost days!

Notes

[15] "Iran is the true general name for the empire of Persia" – *Asiat. Res. Disc.* 5 (author). *Asiatick Researches*, a periodical with contributions by members of the East India Company in Bengal.

[16] "On the blades of their scimitars some verse from the Koran is usually inscribed" – *Russel* (author).

[17] "There is a kind of Rhododendros about Trebizond, whose flowers the bee feeds upon, and the honey thence drives people mad" – *Tournefort* (author).

And swords she hath, nor weak nor slow
   To second all such hearts can dare;   70
As he shall know, well, dearly know,
   Who sleeps in moonlight luxury there,
Tranquil as if his spirit lay
Becalm'd in Heav'n's approving ray!
Sleep on – for purer eyes than thine   75
Those waves are hush'd, those planets shine.
Sleep on, and be thy rest unmov'd
   By the white moonbeam's dazzling power; –
None but the loving and the lov'd
   Should be awake at this sweet hour.   80

And see – where, high above those rocks
   That o'er the deep their shadows fling,
Yon turret stands; – where ebon locks,
   As glossy as a heron's wing
   Upon the turban of a king,[18]   85
Hang from the lattice, long and wild, –
'Tis she, that EMIR's blooming child,
All truth and tenderness and grace,
Though born of such ungentle race; –
An image of Youth's fairy Fountain   90
Springing in a desolate mountain![19]

Oh, what a pure and sacred thing
   Is Beauty, curtain'd from the sight
Of the gross world, illumining
   One only mansion with her light!   95
Unseen by man's disturbing eye, –
   The flower, that blooms beneath the sea,
Too deep for sunbeams, doth not lie
   Hid in more chaste obscurity!
So, HINDA, have thy face and mind,   100
Like holy mysteries, lain enshrin'd.
And oh what transport for a lover
   To lift the veil that shades them o'er! –
Like those who, all at once, discover
   In the lone deep some fairy shore,   105
   Where mortal never trod before,
And sleep and wake in scented airs
No lip had ever breath'd but theirs!

Beautiful are the maids that glide,
   On summer eves, through YEMEN's[20] dales,   110

Notes

[18] "Their kings wear plumes of black herons' feathers upon the right side, as a badge of sovereignty" – *Hanway* (author).
[19] "The Fountain of Youth, by a Mahometan tradition, is situated in some dark region of the East" – *Richardson* (author).

[20] Arabia Felix (author). Latin term for a region that corresponds roughly to what is now known as Yemen.

And bright the glancing looks they hide
    Behind their litters' roseate veils; –
And brides, as delicate and fair
As the white jasmine flowers they wear,
Hath YEMEN in her blissful clime,   115
    Who, lull'd in cool kiosk or bower,
Before their mirrors count the time,
    And grow still lovelier every hour.
But never yet hath bride or maid
    In ARABY's gay Haram smil'd,   120
Whose boasted brightness would not fade
    Before AL HASSAN's blooming child.

Light as the angel shapes that bless
An infant's dream, yet not the less
Rich in all woman's loveliness; –   125
With eyes so pure, that from their ray
Dark Vice would turn abash'd away,
Blinded like serpents, when they gaze
Upon the emerald's virgin blaze![21]
Yet, fill'd with all youth's sweet desires,   130
Mingling the meek and vestal fires
Of other worlds with all the bliss,
The fond, weak tenderness of this!
A soul too, more than half divine,
    Where, through some shades of earthly feeling,   135
Religion's soften'd glories shine,
    Like light through summer foliage stealing,
Shedding a glow of such mild hue,
So warm, and yet so shadowy too,
As makes the very darkness there   140
More beautiful than light elsewhere!

Such is the maid who, at this hour,
    Hath risen from her restless sleep,
And sits alone in that high bower,
    Watching the still and moonlight deep.   145
Ah ! 'twas not thus, – with tearful eyes
    And beating heart, – she used to gaze
On the magnificent earth and skies,
    In her own land, in happier days.
Why looks she now so anxious down   150
Among those rocks, whose rugged frown
    Blackens the mirror of the deep?
Whom waits she all this lonely night?
    Too rough the rocks, too bold the steep,
For man to scale that turret's height! –   155

Notes

[21] "They say that if a snake or serpent fix his eyes on the lustre of those stones (emeralds), he immediately becomes blind" – *Ahmed ben Abdalaziz*, Treatise on Jewels (author).

So deem'd at least her thoughtful sire,
    When high, to catch the cool night-air,
After the day-beam's withering fire,[22]
    He built her bower of freshness there,
And had it deck'd with costliest skill,   160
    And fondly thought it safe as fair: –
Think, reverend dreamer! think so still,
    Nor wake to learn what Love can dare –
Love, all-defying Love, who sees
No charm in trophies won with ease; –   165
Whose rarest, dearest fruits of bliss
Are pluck'd on Danger's precipice!
Bolder than they, who dare not dive
    For pearls, but when the sea's at rest,
Love, in the tempest most alive,   170
    Hath ever held that pearl the best
He finds beneath the stormiest water!
Yes – Araby's unrivall'd daughter,
Though high that tower, that rock-way rude,
    There's one who, but to kiss thy cheek,   175
Would climb th' untrodden solitude
    Of Ararat's tremendous peak,[23]
And think its steeps, though dark and dread,
Heaven's path-ways, if to thee they led!
Ev'n now thou seest the flashing spray,   180
That lights his oar's impatient way;
Ev'n now thou hear'st the sudden shock
Of his swift bark against the rock,
And stretchest down thy arms of snow,
As if to lift him from below!   185
Like her to whom, at dead of night,
The bridegroom, with his locks of light,[24]
Came, in the flush of love and pride,
And scal'd the terrace of his bride; –
When, as she saw him rashly spring,   190
And mid-way up in danger cling,
She flung him down her long black hair,
Exclaiming breathless, "There, love, there!"
And scarce did manlier nerve uphold
    The hero Zal in that fond hour,   195
Than wings the youth who, fleet and bold,
    Now climbs the rocks to Hinda's bower.
See – light as up their granite steeps
    The rock-goats of Arabia clamber,[25]

Notes

[22] At Gomboroon and the Isle of Ormus it is sometimes so hot, that the people are obliged to lie all day in the water – *Marco Polo* (author).

[23] This mountain is generally supposed to be inaccessible (author).

[24] In one of the books of Shâh Nâmeh, when Zal (a celebrated hero of Persia, remarkable for his white hair), comes to the terrace of his mistress Rodahver at night, she lets down her long tresses to assist him in his ascent; – he, however, manages it in a less romantic way by fixing his crook in a projecting beam. – v. *Champion's Ferdosi* (author). Joseph Champion, translator of *The Poems of Ferdosi* (1785); Ferdusi is an important Persian poet (c.940–1020).

[25] "On the lofty hills of Arabia Petraea are rock-goats" – *Niebuhr* (author).

Fearless from crag to crag he leaps,   200
 And now is in the maiden's chamber.

She loves – but knows not whom she loves,
 Nor what his race, nor whence he came; –
Like one who meets, in Indian groves,
 Some beauteous bird, without a name,   205
Brought by the last ambrosial breeze,
From isles in th' undiscover'd seas,
To show his plumage for a day
To wondering eyes, and wing away!
Will *he* thus fly – her nameless lover?   210
 Alla forbid! 'twas by a moon
As fair as this, while singing over
 Some ditty to her soft Kanoon,²⁶
Alone at this same witching hour,
 She first beheld his radiant eyes   215
Gleam through the lattice of the bower,
 Where nightly now they mix their sighs;
And thought some Spirit of the air
(For what could waft a mortal there?)
Was pausing on his moonlight way   220
To listen to her lonely lay!
This fancy ne'er hath left her mind:
 And – though, when terror's swoon had past,
She saw a youth, of mortal kind,
 Before her in obeisance cast, –   225
Yet often since, when he has spoken
Strange, awful words, – and gleams have broken
From his dark eyes, too bright to bear,
 Oh! she hath fear'd her soul was given
To some unhallow'd child of air,   230
 Some erring Spirit, cast from heaven,
Like those angelic youths of old,
Who burn'd for maids of mortal mould,
Bewilder'd left the glorious skies,
And lost their heaven for woman's eyes!   235
Fond girl! nor fiend nor angel he,
Who woos thy young simplicity;
But one of earth's impassion'd sons,
 As warm in love, as fierce in ire
As the best heart whose current runs   240
 Full of the Day-God's living fire!

But quench'd to-night that ardor seems,
 And pale his cheek, and sunk his brow; –
Never before, but in her dreams,
 Had she beheld him pale as now: 245

Notes

²⁶ Moore's note, from a French source, indicates that this is
a stringed instrument often played by women.

And those were dreams of troubled sleep,
From which 'twas joy to wake and weep;
Visions, that will not be forgot,
    But sadden every waking scene,
Like warning ghosts, that leave the spot   250
    All wither'd where they once have been!

"How sweetly," said the trembling maid,
Of her own gentle voice afraid,
So long had they in silence stood,
Looking upon that tranquil flood –   255
"How sweetly does the moonbeam smile
To-night upon yon leafy isle!
Oft, in my fancy's wanderings,
I've wish'd that little isle had wings,
And we, within its fairy bowers,   260
    Were wafted off to seas unknown,
Where not a pulse should beat but ours,
    And we might live, love, die alone!
Far from the cruel and the cold, –
    Where the bright eyes of angels only   265
Should come around us, to behold
    A paradise so pure and lonely!
Would this be world enough for thee?"
Playful she turn'd, that he might see
    The passing smile her cheek put on;   270
But when she mark'd how mournfully
    His eyes met hers, that smile was gone;
And, bursting into heart-felt tears,
"Yes, yes," she cried, "my hourly fears,
My dreams, have boded all too right –   275
We part – for ever part – to-night! –
I knew, I knew it *could* not last –
'Twas bright, 'twas heavenly, but 'tis past!
Oh! ever thus, from childhood's hour,
    I've seen my fondest hopes decay;   280
I never lov'd a tree or flower,
    But 'twas the first to fade away;
I never nurs'd a dear gazelle,
    To glad me with its soft black eye,
But when it came to know me well,   285
    And love me, it was sure to die!
Now too – the joy most like divine
    Of all I ever dreamt or knew,
To see thee, hear thee, call thee mine, –
    Oh misery! must I lose *that* too?   290
Yet go – on peril's brink we meet; –
    Those frightful rocks – that treacherous sea –
No, never come again – though sweet,
    Though heaven, it may be death to thee.
Farewell – and blessings on thy way,   295
    Where'er thou go'st, beloved stranger!

Better to sit and watch that ray,
And think thee safe, though far away,
   Than have thee near me, and in danger!"

"Danger! oh, tempt me not to boast" –   300
The youth exclaim'd – "thou little know'st
What he can brave, who, born and nurst
In Danger's paths, has dared her worst!
Upon whose ear the signal-word
   Of strife and death is hourly breaking;   305
Who sleeps with head upon the sword
   His fever'd hand must grasp in waking!
Danger! –"

     "Say on – thou fear'st not then,
And we may meet – oft meet again?"   310

"Oh! look not so, – beneath the skies
I now fear nothing but those eyes.
If aught on earth could charm or force
My spirit from its destin'd course, –
If aught could make this soul forget   315
The bond to which its seal is set,
'Twould be those eyes; – they, only they,
Could melt that sacred seal away!
But no – 'tis fix'd – *my* awful doom
Is fix'd – on this side of the tomb   320
We meet no more – why, why did heaven
Mingle two souls that earth has riven,
Has rent asunder, wide as ours?
Oh Arab maid! as soon the Powers
Of Light and Darkness may combine,   325
As I be link'd with thee or thine!
Thy Father –"

     "Holy ALLA save
   His grey head from that lightning glance!
Thou know'st him not – he loves the brave;   330
   Nor lives there under heaven's expanse
One who would prize, would worship thee,
And thy bold spirit, more than he.
Oft when, in childhood, I have play'd
   With the bright falchion by his side,   335
I've heard him swear his lisping maid
   In time should be a warrior's bride.
And still, whene'er, at Haram hours,
I take him cool sherbets and flowers,
He tells me, when in playful mood,   340
   A hero shall my bridegroom be,
Since maids are best in battle woo'd,
   And won mid shouts of victory!
Nay, turn not from me – thou alone
Art form'd to make both hearts thy own.   345

Go – join his sacred ranks – thou know'st
    Th' unholy strife these Persians wage: –
Good Heav'n, that frown! – even now thou glow'st
    With more than mortal warrior's rage.
Haste to the camp by morning's light,   350
And, when that sword is raised in fight,
Oh still remember, Love and I
Beneath its shadow trembling lie!
One victory o'er those Slaves of Fire,
Those impious Ghebers, whom my sire   355
Abhors –"

      "Hold, hold – thy words are death –"
The stranger cried, as wild he flung
His mantle back, and show'd beneath
    The Gheber belt that round him clung –.[27]   360
"Here, maiden, look – weep – blush to see
All that thy sire abhors in me!
Yes – *I* am of that impious race,
    Those Slaves of Fire, who, morn and even,
Hail their Creator's dwelling-place   365
    Among the living lights of heaven![28]
Yes – *I* am of that outcast few,
To IRAN and to vengeance true,
Who curse the hour your Arabs came
To desolate our shrines of flame,   370
And swear, before God's burning eye,
To break our country's chains, or die!
Thy bigot sire – nay, tremble not –
    He, who gave birth to those dear eyes,
With me is sacred as the spot   375
    From which our fires of worship rise!
But know – 'twas he I sought that night,
    When, from my watch-boat on the sea,
I caught this turret's glimmering light,
    And up the rude rocks desperately   380
Rush'd to my prey – thou know'st the rest –
I climb'd the gory vulture's nest,
And found a trembling dove within: –
Thine, thine the victory – thine the sin –
If Love has made one thought his own,   385
That Vengeance claims first – last – alone!
Oh! had we never, never met,
Or could this heart ev'n now forget
How link'd, how bless'd, we might have been,
Had fate not frown'd so dark between!   390
Hadst thou been born a Persian maid,

Notes

[27] "They (the Ghebers) lay so much stress on their cushee or girdle, as not to dare to be an instant without it" – *Grose's Voyage* (author).

[28] They suppose the Throne of the Almighty is seated in the sun, and hence their worship of that luminary – *Hanway* (author).

In neighboring valleys had we dwelt,
Through the same fields in childhood play'd,
　At the same kindling altar knelt, –
Then, then, while all those nameless ties, 395
In which the charm of Country lies,
Had round our hearts been hourly spun,
Till IRAN's cause and thine were one; –
While in thy lute's awakening sigh
I heard the voice of days gone by, 400
And saw in every smile of thine
Returning hours of glory shine! –
While the wrong'd Spirit of our Land
　Lived, look'd, and spoke her wrongs through thee, –
God! who could then this sword withstand? 405
　Its very flash were victory!
But now – estrang'd, divorced forever,
Far as the grasp of Fate can sever;
Our only ties what love has wove, –
　Faith, friends, and country, sunder'd wide; – 410
And then, then only, true to love,
　When false to all that's dear beside!
Thy father, IRAN's deadliest foe –
Thyself, perhaps, ev'n now – but no –
Hate never look'd so lovely yet! 415
　No – sacred to thy soul will be
The land of him who could forget
　All but that bleeding land for thee!
When other eyes shall see, unmov'd,
　Her widows mourn, her warriors fall, 420
Thou'lt think how well one Gheber lov'd,
　And for *his* sake thou'lt weep for all!
But look – "

　　　　With sudden start he turn'd
　And pointed to the distant wave, 425
Where lights, like charnel meteors, burn'd
　Bluely, as o'er some seaman's grave;
And fiery darts, at intervals,[29]
　Flew up all sparkling from the main,
As if each star that nightly falls, 430
　Were shooting back to heaven again.

"My signal-lights! – I must away –
Both, both are ruin'd, if I stay.
Farewell – sweet life! thou cling'st in vain –
Now – Vengeance! – I am thine again." 435
Fiercely he broke away, nor stopp'd
Nor look'd – but from the lattice dropp'd

Notes

29 "The Mameluks that were in the other boat, when it was dark used to shoot up a sort of fiery arrows into the air, which in some measure resembled lightning or falling stars" – *Baumgarten* (author).

Down mid the pointed crags beneath,
As if he fled from love to death.
While pale and mute young HINDA stood,   440
Nor mov'd, till in the silent flood
A momentary plunge below
Startled her from her trance of woe; –
Shrieking she to the lattice flew,
   "I come – I come – if in that tide   445
Thou sleep'st to-night – I'll sleep there too,
   In death's cold wedlock by thy side.
Oh! I would ask no happier bed
   Than the chill wave my love lies under; –
Sweeter to rest together dead,   450
   Far sweeter than to live asunder!"
But no – their hour is not yet come –
   Again she sees his pinnace fly,
Wafting him fleetly to his home,
   Where'er that ill-starr'd home may lie;   455
And calm and smooth it seem'd to win
   Its moonlight way before the wind,
As if it bore all peace within,
   Nor left one breaking heart behind!

The Princess, whose heart was sad enough already, could have wished that FERAMORZ had chosen a less melancholy story; as it is only to the happy that tears are a luxury. Her Ladies, however, were by no means sorry that love was once more the Poet's theme; for when he spoke of love, they said, his voice was as sweet as if he had chewed the leaves of that enchanted tree, which grows over the tomb of the musician, Tan Sein.

Their road all the morning had lain through a very dreary country; – through valleys, covered with a low bushy jungle, where, in more than one place, the awful signal of the bamboo staff, with the white flag at its top, reminded the traveller that in that very spot the tiger had made some human creature his victim. It was therefore with much pleasure that they arrived at sunset in a safe and lovely glen, and encamped under one of those holy trees, whose smooth columns and spreading roofs seem to destine them for natural temples of religion. Beneath the shade, some pious hands had erected pillars ornamented with the most beautiful porcelain, which now supplied the use of mirrors to the young maidens, as they adjusted their hair in descending from the palankeens. Here while, as usual, the Princess sat listening anxiously, with FADLADEEN in one of his loftiest moods of criticism by her side, the young Poet, leaning against a branch of the tree, thus continued his story: –

The morn hath risen clear and calm,   460
   And o'er the Green Sea[30] palely shines,
Revealing BAHREIN's[31] groves of palm,
   And lighting KISHMA's amber vines.
Fresh smell the shores of ARABY,
While breezes from the Indian sea   465

Notes

[30] The Persian Gulf – "To dive for pearls in the Green Sea, or Persian Gulf" – *Sir W. Jones* (author).

[31] Islands in the Gulf (author).

Blow round SELAMA's[32] sainted cape,
    And curl the shining flood beneath, –
Whose waves are rich with many a grape,
    And cocoa-nut and flowery wreath,
Which pious seamen, as they pass'd,   470
Have tow'rd that holy head-land cast –
Oblations to the Genii there
For gentle skies and breezes fair!
The nightingale now bends her flight
From the high trees, where all the night   475
    She sung so sweet, with none to listen;
And hides her from the morning star
    Where thickets of pomegranate glisten
In the clear dawn, – bespangled o'er
With dew, whose night-drops would not stain   480
The best and brightest scimitar[33]
That ever youthful Sultan wore
On the first morning of his reign!

And see – the Sun himself! – on wings
Of glory up the East he springs.   485
Angel of Light! who from the time
Those heavens began their march sublime,
Has first of all the starry choir
Trod in his Maker's steps of fire!
    Where are the days, thou wondrous sphere,   490
When IRAN, like a sun-flower, turn'd
To meet that eye, where'er it burn'd? –
    When, from the banks of BENDEMEER
To the nut-groves of SAMARCAND
Thy temples flam'd o'er all the land?   495
Where are they? ask the shades of them
    Who, on CADESSIA's[34] bloody plains,
Saw fierce invaders pluck the gem
From IRAN's broken diadem,
    And bind her ancient faith in chains: –   500
Ask the poor exile, cast alone
On foreign shores, unlov'd, unknown,
Beyond the Caspian's Iron Gates,[35]
    Or on the snowy Mossian mountains,
Far from his beauteous land of dates,   505
    Her jasmine bowers and sunny fountains!

Notes

[32] Or Selemeh, the genuine name of the headland at the entrance of the Gulf, commonly called Cape Musseldom. "The Indians, when they pass the promontory, throw cocoa-nuts, fruits, or flowers, into the sea, to secure a propitious voyage" – *Morier* (author).

[33] In speaking of the climate of Shiraz, Francklin says, "the dew is of such a pure nature, that, if the brightest scimitar should be exposed to it all night, it would not receive the least rust" (author).

[34] The place where the Persians were finally defeated by the Arabs, and their ancient monarchy destroyed (author).

[35] Derbend – "Les Turcs appellent cette ville Demir Capi, Porte de Fer; ce sont les Caspae Portae des anciens" – *D'Herbelot* (author). Roughly, "The Turks call this city Demir Capi, Iron Gate; these are the 'Caspiae Portae' of the ancients." The Iron Gates are a natural pass in Derbent, Russia, reportedly fortified by Alexander the Great to defend his territories along their northern edge.

Yet happier so than if he trod
His own belov'd but blighted sod,
Beneath a despot stranger's nod; –
Oh! he would rather houseless roam   510
    Where Freedom and his God may lead,
Than be the sleekest slave at home
    That crouches to the conqueror's creed!

Is IRAN's pride then gone for ever,
    Quench'd with the flame in MITHRA's caves? –   515
No – she has sons that never – never –
    Will stoop to be the Moslem's slaves,
    While heaven has light or earth has graves.
Spirits of fire, that brood not long,
But flash resentment back for wrong;   520
And hearts where, slow but deep, the seeds
Of vengeance ripen into deeds,
Till, in some treacherous hour of calm,
They burst, like ZEILAN's giant palm,[36]
Whose buds fly open with a sound   525
That shakes the pigmy forests round!

Yes, EMIR! he who scaled that tower,
    And, had he reach'd thy slumbering breast,
Would teach thee, in a Gheber's power
    How safe ev'n tyrant heads may rest –   530
Is one of many, brave as he,
Who loathe thy haughty race and thee;
Who, though they know the strife is vain,
Who, though they know the riven chain
Snaps but to enter in the heart   535
Of him who rends its links apart,
Yet dare the issue, – blest to be
Ev'n for one bleeding moment free,
And die in pangs of liberty!
Thou know'st them well – 'tis some moons since   540
    Thy turban'd troops and blood-red flags,
Thou satrap of a bigot Prince!
    Have swarm'd among these Green-Sea crags;
Yet here, ev'n here, a sacred band,
Ay, in the portal of that land   545
Thou, Arab, dar'st to call thy own,
Their spears across thy path have thrown.
Here – ere the winds half wing'd thee o'er –
Rebellion braved thee from the shore.

Notes

[36] The Talpot or Talipot tree. "This beautiful palm-tree, which grows in the heart of the forests, may be classed amongst the loftiest trees, and becomes still higher when on the point of bursting forth from its leafy summit. The sheath which then envelopes the flower is very large, and, when it bursts, makes an explosion like the report of a cannon" – *Thunberg* (author).

Rebellion! foul, dishonoring word,   550
    Whose wrongful blight so oft has stain'd
The holiest cause that tongue or sword
    Of mortal ever lost or gain'd.
How many a spirit, born to bless,
    Has sunk beneath that withering name,   555
Whom but a day's, an hour's success
    Had wafted to eternal fame!
As exhalations, when they burst
From the warm earth, if chill'd at first,
If check'd in soaring from the plain,   560
Darken to fogs and sink again; –
But, if they once triumphant spread
Their wings above the mountain-head,
Become enthron'd in upper air,
And turn to sun-bright glories there!   565

And who is he, that wields the might
    Of Freedom on the Green-Sea brink,
Before whose sabre's dazzling light
    The eyes of YEMEN's warriors wink?
Who comes embower'd in the spears   570
Of KERMAN's hardy mountaineers: –
Those mountaineers, that truest, last
    Cling to their country's ancient rites,
As if that God, whose eyelids cast
    Their closing gleams on IRAN's heights,   575
Among her snowy mountains threw
The last light of his worship too!

'Tis HAFED – name of fear, whose sound
    Chills like the muttering of a charm; –
Shout but that awful name around,   580
    And palsy shakes the manliest arm.
'Tis HAFED, most accurst and dire
(So rank'd by Moslem hate and ire)
Of all the rebel Sons of Fire!
Of whose malign, tremendous power   585
The Arabs, at their mid-watch hour,
Such tales of fearful wonder tell,
That each affrighted centinel
Pulls down his cowl upon his eyes,
Lest HAFED in the midst should rise!   590
A man, they say, of monstrous birth,
A mingled race of flame and earth,
Sprung from those old, enchanted kings,[37]
    Who, in their fairy helms, of yore,

Notes

[37] Tahmuras, and other ancient Kings of Persia; whose adventures in Fairy-Land among the Peris and Dives may be found in Richardson's curious Dissertation. The griffin Simoorgh, they say, took some feathers from her breast for Tahmuras, with which he adorned his helmet, and transmitted them afterwards to his descendants (author). See John Richardson's "Dissertation on the Languages, Literature, and Manners of Eastern Nations," appended to his *Dictionary, Persian, Arabic, and English* (1777).

A feather from the mystic wings   595
  Of the Simoorgh resistless wore;
And gifted by the Fiends of Fire,
Who groan'd to see their shrines expire,
With charms that, all in vain withstood,
Would drown the Koran's light in blood!   600

Such were the tales that won belief,
  And such the coloring fancy gave
To a young, warm and dauntless Chief, –
  One who, no more than mortal brave,
Fought for the land his soul ador'd,   605
  For happy homes and altars free,
His only talisman, the sword, –
  His only spell-word, Liberty!
One of that ancient hero line,
Along whose glorious current shine   610
Names, that have sanctified their blood;
As LEBANON's small mountain-flood
Is render'd holy by the ranks
Of sainted cedars on its banks![38]
'Twas not for him to crouch the knee   615
Tamely to Moslem tyranny; –
'Twas not for him, whose soul was cast
In the bright mould of ages past,
Whose melancholy spirit, fed
With all the glories of the dead,   620
Though fram'd for IRAN's happiest years,
Was born among her chains and tears! –
'Twas not for him to swell the crowd
Of slavish heads, that shrinking bowed
Before the Moslem, as he pass'd,   625
Like shrubs beneath the poison-blast –
No – far he fled – indignant fled
  The pageant of his country's shame;
While every tear her children shed
  Fell on his soul, like drops of flame;   630
And, as a lover hails the dawn
  Of a first smile, so welcom'd he
The sparkle of the first sword drawn
  For vengeance and for liberty!

But vain was valor – vain the flower   635
Of KERMAN, in that deathful hour,
Against AL HASSAN's whelming power. –
In vain they met him, helm to helm,
Upon the threshold of that realm
He came in bigot pomp to sway,   640
And with their corpses block'd his way –

Notes

[38] This rivulet, says Dandini, is called the Holy River from
the "cedar-saints" among which it rises (author).

In vain – for every lance they rais'd,
Thousands around the conqueror blaz'd;
For every arm that lin'd their shore,
Myriads of slaves were wafted o'er, –   645
A bloody, bold and countless crowd,
Before whose swarm as fast they bow'd
As dates beneath the locust-cloud!

There stood – but one short league away
From old HARMOZIA's sultry bay –   650
A rocky mountain, o'er the Sea
Of OMAN beetling awfully.
A last and solitary link
     Of those stupendous chains that reach
From the broad Caspian's reedy brink   655
     Down winding to the Green-Sea beach.
Around its base the bare rocks stood,
Like naked giants, in the flood,
     As if to guard the Gulf across; –
While, on its peak that brav'd the sky,   660
A ruin'd Temple tower'd, so high
     That oft the sleeping albatross[39]
Struck the wild ruins with her wing,
And from her cloud-rock'd slumbering
Started – to find man's dwelling there   665
In her own silent fields of air!
Beneath, terrific caverns gave
Dark welcome to each stormy wave
That dash'd, like midnight revellers, in; –
And such the strange, mysterious din   670
At times throughout those caverns roll'd, –
And such the fearful wonders told
Of restless sprites imprison'd there,
That bold were Moslem, who would dare,
At twilight hour, to steer his skiff   675
Beneath the Gheber's lonely cliff.

On the land side, those towers sublime,
That seem'd above the grasp of Time,
Were sever'd from the haunts of men
By a wide, deep and wizard glen,   680
So fathomless, so full of gloom,
     No eye could pierce the void between;
It seem'd a place where Gholes might come
With their foul banquets from the tombs,
     And in its caverns feed unseen.   685
Like distant thunder, from below,
     The sound of many torrents came;

Notes ──

[39] These birds sleep in the air. They are most common
about the Cape of Good Hope (author).

Too deep for eye or ear to know
If 'twere the sea's imprison'd flow,
   Or floods of ever-restless flame.   690
For each ravine, each rocky spire,
Of that vast mountain stood on fire;[40]
And, though forever past the days,
When God was worshipp'd in the blaze
That from its lofty altar shone, –   695
Though fled the priests, the votaries gone,
Still did the mighty flame burn on
Through chance and change, through good and ill,
Like its own God's eternal will,
Deep, constant, bright, unquenchable!   700

Thither the vanquish'd HAFED led
   His little army's last remains; –
"Welcome, terrific glen!" he said,
"Thy gloom, that Eblis' self might dread,
   Is heaven to him who flies from chains!"   705
O'er a dark, narrow bridge-way, known
To him and to his Chiefs alone,
They cross'd the chasm and gain'd the towers; –
"This home," he cried, "at least is ours –
Here we may bleed, unmock'd by hymns   710
   Of Moslem triumph o'er our head;
Here we may fall, nor leave our limbs
   To quiver to the Moslem's tread.
Stretch'd on this rock, while vultures' beaks
Are whetted on our yet warm cheeks,   715
Here, – happy that no tyrant's eye
Gloats on our torments – we may die!"

'Twas night when to those towers they came,
And gloomily the fitful flame,
That from the ruin'd altar broke,   720
Glar'd on his features, as he spoke: –
" 'Tis o'er – what men could do, we've done –
If Iran *will* look tamely on,
And see her priests, her warriors, driven
   Before a sensual bigot's nod,   725
A wretch, who takes his lusts to heaven,
   And makes a pander of his God!
If her proud sons, her high-born souls,
   Men, in whose veins – oh last disgrace!
The blood of ZAL and RUSTAM[41] rolls, –   730
   If they *will* court this upstart race,
And turn from MITHRA's ancient ray,
To kneel at shrines of yesterday! –

Notes

[40] The Ghebers generally built their temples over subterraneous fires (author).

[41] Ancient heroes of Persia. "Among the Guebres there are some, who boast their descent from Rustam" – *Stephen's Persia* (author).

If they *will* crouch to IRAN's foes,
    Why, let them – till the land's despair   735
Cries out to heav'n, and bondage grows
    Too vile for ev'n the vile to bear!
Till shame at last, long hidden, burns
Their inmost core, and conscience turns
Each coward tear the slave lets fall   740
Back on his heart in drops of gall!
But *here,* at least, are arms unchain'd,
And souls that thraldom never stain'd; –
    This spot, at least, no foot of slave
Or satrap ever yet profan'd;   745
    And, though but few – though fast the wave
Of life is ebbing from our veins,
Enough for vengeance still remains.
As panthers, after set of sun,
Rush from the roots of LEBANON,   750
Across the dark sea-robber's way,[42]
We'll bound upon our startled prey; –
And when some hearts that proudest swell
Have felt our falchion's last farewell;
When Hope's expiring throb is o'er,   755
And ev'n Despair can prompt no more,
This spot shall be the sacred grave
Of the last few who, vainly brave,
Die for the land they cannot save!"

His Chiefs stood round – each shining blade   760
Upon the broken altar laid –
And though so wild and desolate
Those courts, where once the Mighty sate;
Nor longer on those mouldering towers
Was seen the feast of fruits and flowers,   765
With which of old the Magi fed
The wandering Spirits of their Dead;[43]
Though neither priest nor rites were there,
    Nor charmed leaf of pure pomegranate;[44]
Nor hymn, nor censer's fragrant air,   770
    Nor symbol of their worshipp'd planet;[45]

Notes

[42] V[ide] Russell's account of the panthers attacking travellers in the night on the sea-shore about the roots of Lebanon (author).

[43] "Among other ceremonies the Magi used to place upon the tops of high towers various kinds of rich viands, upon which it was supposed the Peris and the spirits of their departed heroes regaled themselves " – *Richardson* (author).

[44] In the ceremonies of the Ghebers round their Fire, as described by Lord, "the Daroo," he says, "giveth them water to drink, and a pomegranate leaf to chew in the mouth, to cleanse them from inward uncleanness" (author).

[45] "Early in the morning, they (the Parsees or Ghebers at Oulam) go in crowds to pay their devotions to the Sun, to whom upon all the altars there are spheres consecrated, made by magic, resembling the circles of the sun, and when the sun rises, these orbs seem to be inflamed, and to turn round with a great noise. They have every one a censer in their hands, and offer incense to the sun" – *Rabbi Benjamin* (author).

Yet the same God that heard their sires
Heard *them*, while on that altar's fires
They swore the latest, holiest deed
Of the few hearts, still left to bleed,   775
Should be, in IRAN's injur'd name,
To die upon that Mount of Flame –
The last of all her patriot line,
Before her last untrampled Shrine!

Brave, suffering souls! they little knew   780
How many a tear their injuries drew
From one meek heart, one gentle foe,
Whom Love first touch'd with others' woe –
Whose life, as free from thought as sin,
Slept like a lake, till Love threw in   785
His talisman, and woke the tide,
And spread its trembling circles wide.
Once, EMIR! thy unheeding child,
Mid all this havoc, bloom'd and smil'd, –
Tranquil as on some battle-plain   790
    The Persian lily shines and towers,
Before the combat's reddening stain
    Has fall'n upon her golden flowers.
Light-hearted maid, unaw'd, unmov'd,
While heav'n but spar'd the sire she lov'd,   795
Once at thy evening tales of blood
Unlistening and aloof she stood –
And oft, when thou hast pac'd along
    Thy Haram halls with furious heat,
Hast thou not curs'd her cheerful song,   800
    That came across thee, calm and sweet,
Like lutes of angels, touch'd so near
Hell's confines, that the damn'd can hear!

Far other feelings Love has brought –
    Her soul all flame, her brow all sadness,   805
She now has but the one dear thought,
    And thinks that o'er, almost to madness!
Oft doth her sinking heart recal
His words – "for *my* sake weep for all;"
And bitterly, as day on day   810
    Of rebel carnage fast succeeds,
She weeps a lover snatch'd away
    In every Gheber wretch that bleeds.
There's not a sabre meets her eye,
    But with his life-blood seems to swim;   815
There's not an arrow wings the sky,
    But fancy turns its point to him.
No more she brings with footstep light
AL HASSAN's falchion for the fight;
And, – had he look'd with clearer sight,   820
Had not the mists, that ever rise

From a foul spirit, dimm'd his eyes, –
He would have mark'd her shuddering frame,
When from the field of blood he came,
The faltering speech – the look estrang'd –   825
Voice, step, and life, and beauty chang'd –
He would have mark'd all this, and known
Such change is wrought by Love alone!

Ah! not the Love that should have bless'd
So young, so innocent a breast;   830
Not the pure, open, prosperous Love,
That, pledg'd on earth and seal'd above,
Grows in the world's approving eyes,
    In friendship's smile and home's caress,
Collecting all the heart's sweet ties   835
    Into one knot of happiness!
No, HINDA, no – thy fatal flame
Is nurs'd in silence, sorrow, shame. –
    A passion, without hope or pleasure,
In thy soul's darkness buried deep,   840
    It lies, like some ill-gotten treasure, –
Some idol, without shrine or name,
O'er which its pale-ey'd votaries keep
Unholy watch, while others sleep!
Seven nights have darken'd OMAN's Sea,   845
    Since last, beneath the moonlight ray,
She saw his light oar rapidly
    Hurry her Gheber's bark away, –
And still she goes, at midnight hour,
To weep alone in that high bower,   850
And watch, and look along the deep
For him whose smiles first made her weep, –
But watching, weeping, all was vain,
She never saw that bark again.
The owlet's solitary cry,   855
The night-hawk, flitting darkly by,
    And oft the hateful carrion-bird,
Heavily flapping his clogg'd wing,
Which reek'd with that day's banquetting –
    Was all she saw, was all she heard.   860

'Tis the eighth morn – AL HASSAN's brow
    Is brighten'd with unusual joy –
What mighty mischief glads him now,
    Who never smiles but to destroy?
The sparkle upon HERKEND's Sea,   865
When tost at midnight furiously,[46]
Tells not of wreck and ruin nigh,

Notes ────────────────────────────────

[46] "It is observed, with respect to the Sea of Herkend, that
when it is tossed by tempestuous winds it sparkles like
fire" – *Travels of two Mohammedans* (author).

More surely than that smiling eye!
"Up, daughter, up – the Kerna's[47] breath
Has blown a blast would waken death,   870
And yet thou sleep'st – up, child, and see
This blessed day for heaven and me,
A day more rich in Pagan blood
Than ever flash'd o'er OMAN's flood.
Before another dawn shall shine,   875
His head – heart – limbs – will all be mine;
This very night his blood shall steep
These hands all over ere I sleep!" –

"*His* blood!" she faintly scream'd – her mind
Still singling *one* from all mankind –   880
"Yes – spite of his ravines and towers,
HAFED, my child, this night is ours.
Thanks to all-conquering treachery,
    Without whose aid the links accurst
That bind these impious slaves, would be   885
    Too strong for ALLA's self to burst!
That rebel fiend, whose blade has spread
My path with piles of Moslem dead,
Whose baffling spells had almost driven
Back from their course the Swords of Heaven,   890
This night, with all his band, shall know
How deep an Arab's steel can go,
When God and vengeance speed the blow.
And – Prophet! – by that holy wreath
Thou wor'st on OHOD's field of death,[48]   895
I swear, for every sob that parts
In anguish from these heathen hearts,
A gem from PERSIA's plunder'd mines
Shall glitter on thy Shrine of Shrines.
But ha! – she sinks – that look so wild –   900
Those livid lips – my child, my child,
This life of blood befits not thee,
And thou must back to ARABY.
    Ne'er had I risk'd thy timid sex
In scenes that man himself might dread,   905
Had I not hoped our every tread
    Would be on prostrate Persian necks –
Curst race, they offer swords instead!
But cheer thee, maid, – the wind, that now
Is blowing o'er thy feverish brow,   910

Notes

[47] A kind of trumpet; – it "was that used by Tamerlane, the sound of which is described as uncommonly dreadful, and so loud as to be heard at the distance of several miles" – *Richardson* (author).

[48] "Mohammed had two helmets, an interior and exterior one; the latter of which, called Al Mawashah, the fillet, or wreathed garland, he wore at the battle of Ohod" – *Universal History* (author).

To-day shall waft thee from the shore;
And, ere a drop of this night's gore
Have time to chill in yonder towers,
Thou'lt see thy own sweet Arab bowers!"

His bloody boast was all too true –   915
There lurk'd one wretch among the few
Whom HAFED's eagle eye could count
Around him on that Fiery Mount, –
One miscreant, who for gold betray'd
The pathway through the valley's shade   920
To those high towers, where Freedom stood
In her last hold of flame and blood.
Left on the field last dreadful night,
When, sallying from their Sacred Height,
The Ghebers fought hope's farewell fight,   925
He lay – but died not with the brave;
That sun, which should have gilt his grave,
Saw him a traitor and a slave; –
And, while the few, who thence return'd
To their high rocky fortress, mourn'd   930
For him among the matchless dead
They left behind on glory's bed,
He liv'd, and, in the face of morn,
Laugh'd them and Faith and Heaven to scorn!

Oh for a tongue to curse the slave,   935
    Whose treason, like a deadly blight,
Comes o'er the councils of the brave,
    And blasts them in their hour of might!
May life's unblessed cup for him
Be drugg'd with treacheries to the brim, –   940
With hopes, that but allure to fly,
    With joys, that vanish while he sips,
Like Dead-Sea fruits, that tempt the eye,
    But turn to ashes on the lips!
His country's curse, his children's shame,   945
Outcast of virtue, peace and fame,
May he, at last, with lips of flame
On the parch'd desert thirsting die, –
While lakes that shone in mockery nigh
Are fading off, untouched, untasted,   950
Like the once glorious hopes he blasted!
And, when from earth his spirit flies,
    Just Prophet, let the damn'd-one dwell
Full in the sight of Paradise,
    Beholding heaven, and feeling hell!   955

Lines on the Entry of the Austrians into Naples, 1821

From Fables for the Holy Alliance (1823)

Carbone notati[1]

Ay – down to the dust with them, slaves as they are,
    From this hour, let the blood in their dastardly veins,
That shrunk at the first touch of Liberty's war,
    Be suck'd out by tyrants, or stagnate in chains.

On, on like a cloud, through their beautiful vales,   5
    Ye locusts of tyranny, blasting them o'er –
Fill, fill up their wide sunny waters, ye sails
    From each slave-mart of Europe, and poison their shore!

Let their fate be a mock-word – let men of all lands
    Laugh out, with a scorn that shall ring to the poles,   10
When each sword, that the cowards let fall from their hands,
    Shall be forg'd into fetters to enter their souls.

And deep, and more deep, as the iron is driven,
    Base slaves! may the whet of their agony be,
To think – as the Damn'd haply think of that heav'n   15
    They had once in their reach – that they *might* have been free.

Shame, shame – when there was not a bosom, whose heat
    Ever rose o'er the *zero* of ———'s heart,
That did not, like echo, your war-hymn repeat,
    And send all its prayers with your Liberty's start –   20

When the world stood in hope – when a spirit, that breath'd
    The fresh air of the olden time, whisper'd about;
And the swords of all Italy, half-way unsheath'd,
    But waited one conquering cry, to flash out!

When around you the shades of your Mighty in fame,   25
    FILICAJAS and PETRARCHS,[2] seem'd bursting to view,
And their words, and their warnings – like tongues of bright flame
    Over Freedom's apostles – fell kindling on you!

Good God, that, in such a proud moment of life,
    Worth the hist'ry of ages – when, had you but hurl'd   30
One bolt at your bloody invader, that strife
    Between freemen and tyrants had spread through the world –

That then – oh! disgrace upon manhood – ev'n then,
    You should falter, should cling to your pitiful breath;

Notes

LINES ON THE ENTRY
[1] Loosely translated, "a black mark." Moore's source is Horace's *Satires* (II.3), but he is also alluding to a political organization, the Carbonari, key in the 1820 uprising in Naples that Austria sought to suppress in 1821.
[2] Italian poets Vicenzo da Filicaja (1642–1707) and Francesco Petrarch (1304–74).

Cow'r down into beasts, when you might have stood, men,   35
    And prefer the slave's life of damnation to death.

It is strange, it is dreadful – shout, Tyranny, shout
    Through your dungeons and palaces, "Freedom is o'er" –
If there lingers one spark of her light, tread it out,
    And return to your empire of darkness once more.   40

For, if *such* are the braggarts, that claim to be free,
    Come, Despot of Russia, thy feet let me kiss –
Far nobler to live the brute bond-man of thee,
    Than to sully ev'n chains by a struggle like this!

Sydney Owenson, Lady Morgan (c.1783–1859)

Sydney Owenson was the child of actor and theater manager Robert Owenson (formerly MacOwen) and the English Jane Mill, with nationalist poet Edward Lysaght as her godfather. Robert Owenson was Catholic, but Sydney and her sister Olivia were raised in their mother's Protestant faith. The sisters were tutored at home for awhile by Thomas Dermody, and later sent to school in Clontarf; after her formal schooling was over, about 1800, Owenson began working as a governess in Dublin. From 1803 to 1817, she benefited from the mentoring of Alicia Sheridan Lefanu, Frances and Thomas Sheridan's daughter. In 1812, already a successful author, she married Sir T. Charles Morgan, a medical doctor and author, becoming Lady Morgan – an arrangement of her aristocratic friends who picked Charles and then had him knighted so that the young author would have a title. (Morgan's sister Olivia, who published a play, *The Irishwoman* [1819], similarly became Lady Clarke after marrying a Dublin doctor.) The Morgans settled in Dublin, but eventually moved to London in 1837; that same year, Morgan received a government pension for her literary work, the first woman ever to do so.

Morgan was one of the most important and prolific women writers of her generation, remarkable in part for her engagement with the major political questions of the day. Julia Kavanagh's remark in *English Women of Letters* (1862) is typical: "The quiet, prudent Miss Edgeworth shunned Irish politics, but fearless Lady Morgan rushed into them, and into politics of every sort as well." Morgan's career falls roughly into three periods: first, her early work as a translator of Irish verse and sentimental poet; then a novelist; and finally a woman of letters who published memoirs, essays, and reviews. Her best-known novel remains *The Wild Irish Girl* (1806), a novel with a significant cultural and political impact. She published a number of novels afterwards, including her best, *The O'Briens and the O'Flahertys* (1827), which is set primarily in the months leading up to the 1798 Uprising. Most of her volumes went through multiple editions in London and many were also published in the United States as well as translated and published across Europe. As a woman of letters, Morgan contributed to *New Monthly Magazine* and the British *Athenaeum*, wrote controversial travelogues (one of which got her barred from entering the Austrian empire), and an important biography of the Italian painter Salvator Rosa.

In the first phase of her career, Morgan did important work on Irish translation, and the impact of Irish-language material is clear in her own English verse. The form of "Twilight" (below) bears comparison to the poetry of another translator of Irish verse, Mangan. More importantly, perhaps, her *Hibernian Melodies* (1805) paved the way for Moore's *Irish Melodies*, in pairing traditional Irish music with English-language lyrics in music-book form. *Hibernian Melodies* also emerges from an eighteenth-century tradition of translation and retaining ties to Irish popular music by matching English lyrics with Irish tunes, as in *Paddy's Resource* (above).

Further reading

Davis, Leith, *Music, Postcolonialism, and Gender: The Construction of Irish National Identity, 1724–1874.* Notre Dame, IN: University of Notre Dame Press, 2006.

Ferris, Ina, *The Romantic National Tale and the Question of Ireland.* Cambridge: Cambridge University Press, 2002.

Wright, Julia M., "'Sons of Song': Irish Literature in the Age of Nationalism," in *Romantic Poetry*, ed. Angela Esterhammer, 333–53. Amsterdam: John Benjamins, 2002.

From Preface

From Twelve Original Hibernian Melodies (1805)

Notwithstanding the celebrity which the bards of Ireland had obtained for their musical compositions from the remotest antiquity, we have the strongest reason to believe that no general collection of their works had ever been made previous to the year 1792, when a meeting was convened in the north of Ireland of the few lingering members of that once sacred order, which had spread "the light of song" over the gloom of unillumined ignorance, or softened the ferocity of uncivilized heroism. But while the broad field of Irish music, even in its autumnal decline, afforded a rich harvest to the successful exertions of national taste, some few blossoms of poesy and song were still left, "to waste their sweetness on the desart air:" It was reserved for the minute and enquiring glance of the humble gleaner, to discover the neglected charms, and to behold them like the rose, fragrant even in decay. With a timid hand I have endeavoured to snatch them from the chilling atmosphere of oblivion, and bound them in a wild and simple wreath, in the faint hope that public approbation would nourish and perpetuate their existence.

Many of the airs and poems which compose this little selection, were orally collected in what may be deemed the classic wilds of Ireland – where *Ossian* sung, where *Fingal* fought, and *Oscar* fell.

The singular and plaintive beauty of *Emant Acnuick*, or Ned of the Hills, which, replete with the characteristic wildness and melting pathos, of Irish music, may be deemed an epitome of the ancient Irish style of composition, induced me into the attempt of adapting an English translation to its melody; the task was difficult, though not wholly unsuccessful, for the music and poetry of the Irish are so closely analogous, and the sound so faithful an echo to the sense, that the former seems almost to bid defiance to the adapting any other language to its melodies; and the latter must always sustain an injury in its energetic and idiomatic delicacies, when its sentiments are given through the medium of a translation. The *Author*, and the *Hero* of *Emant Acnuick*, and many other popular ballads, was the chief or captain of one of those numerous banditti which infested Ireland, during that period when relegous animosity and civil discord, involved its unfortunate natives in all the horrors of anarchy and warfare. The accounts which are given of *Emant Acnuick*, are various and improbable – but that most current and consonant to truth, sketches him as an outlaw'd gentleman, whose confiscated lands and forfeited life, animated him to the resolution of heading a band of robbers, and committing many acts of desperation, which were frequently counteracted by a generosity almost romantic, or performed with a spirit truly heroic. – A warrior and a poet, his "soul was often brightened by the song;" and *Eva*, the daughter of a northern chieftain, was at once his *inspiration* and his *theme* . . .

"*Gracy Nugent*," is an air but little known beyond the interior parts of Ireland; its heroine was a *Miss Nugent*, of Clonlost, in the county of Westmeath: its composer, the celebrated CAROLAN. The last itinerant bard of any eminence in Ireland, "and so happy, so elevated was he in many of his compositions, that he excited the wonder and obtained the approbation of a great master who never saw him – I mean the celebrated Geminiani;"[1] though born blind, he never regretted the loss of his sight, but used to say – "his eyes were transplanted into his ears." His first poetic and musical effort was the effusion of an enamoured heart, elicited by the charms of *Bridget Cruise*; the high rank of his mistress proved an insurmountable barrier to his wishes, and like most other poetical enamoratos, his passion was as unsuccessful, as it was ardent. He, however, soon became an adept in the philosophy of love, and every song had for its theme a new mistress: – of a roving and unsettled disposition, with his harp flung over his shoulder, he wandered like the bards of old, celebrating with Pindaric boldness the charms of love, the joys of social life, and the virtues of cordial hospitality.[2] Considered as the Anacreon of his country, his arrival at the castle of the great, or the hut of the indigent, was ever hailed with a smile; he was every where received with delight, listened to with rapture, and relinquished with regret.

To the ear, which is alone made up to the delicacies of Italian music, or the refinements of scientific composition, the following melodies will probably sound wildly inelegant, or barbarously simple; but they are not offered as the correct effusions of musical talent, schooled into science, corrected by experience, and sanctioned by reigning modes; but as "*the native wood notes wild*" of those, whose genius, unimproved by art, unrestrained by rule, only vibrated, like the far famed statue of Memnon, to the genial beam of heaven's own light, – as specimens of a national music, strongly characterized by those idiomatic features, which to musical philosophy afford so wide a field for reflection . . . If the excellence of musical composition is to be estimated by the effect it produces on the human mind, by its power over the passions, or its influence over the heart, the Irish melodies, it must be allowed, graduate to a very high degree on the scale of musical excellence; always composed under the operation of the feelings, whether the warm inspirations of gratitude – whether the tender effusions of love, or the bold spirit of martial enthusiasm awakens the strain – it still breathes the truest intimation of the soul, and surrounded by a *compatriot auditory*, the rapt musician never fails to awaken in every bosom a corresponding emotion to that which animates his own. But there is in "*souls a sympathy with sound*," and much of musical enthusiasm depends upon an intimate association of ideas; those airs, which are connected with local incidents, or

Notes

FROM PREFACE

[1] He was born at NOBBER, county of Westmeath, in 1670, and died 1738, at KILRORIAN, in the county of ROSCOMMON (author).

[2] In the course of his rambles, he used frequently to spend some months at the house of the editor's great grandfather. –

It was then usual for him, during the act of composition, to applaud or revile any passage, as he liked or disapproved it. – He was fond of his national liquor, and used sportively to say in excuse for his excesses, that "it added *strength* to the flights of his genius" (author).

public events, whose national idiom is perfectly understood and deeply felt, will ever be heard with delight in that country where they were first breathed. But when these circumstances cease to operate, they must stand the test of dispassionate judgment: – when, however, it is considered, that the following airs were composed by *men*, ignorant of the rules of that art they practised, it is hoped that what a celebrated personage once said of the errors of illustrious characters, will be applied to *them*, and "that their faults will be thought to bring their excuses along with them."

Ah who is that; or Emunh a Cnuic, or Ned of the Hills

From Twelve Original Hibernian Melodies (1805)

Ah! Who is that whose thrilling tones
    Puts my tranquil sleep astray
More Plaintive than the wood Doves moans,
    And send my airy dreams away.
'Tis I Edmund of the Hill   5
Who puts thy tranquil sleep astray
Whose plaintive songs of sorrow thrill
And send thy airy dreams away.

Here nightly thro' the long long year
    My heart with many a love pang wrung;   10
Beneath thy casement Eva dear,
    My sorrows and thy charms I've sung.
Thine eye is like the moon's mild ray,
Its glance first stole my heart away,
    And gave its every wish to you.   15

Like a soft gloomy cloud's thine hair,
    Tinged with the setting sun's warm rays;
And lightly o'er thy forehead fair,
    In many a spiry ringlet plays,
Oh! come then rich in all thy charms;   20
    For Eva I'm as rich in love,
And panting in my circling arms;
    I'll bear thee to old Thuar's grove.

When floating o'er; or Cathleen Nolan

From Twelve Original Hibernian Melodies (1805)

When floating o'er th' impending steep
    My love appears in beauty's glow
She's like the golden clouds that sweep
    Light o'er the mountains lofty brow.

Nor does the tenderest blossoms heed,   5
    To her light footsteps her light footsteps yield,
Nor weeping flowers a dew drop shed,
    When like a breeze she skims the field.

Loose o'er her arm of snow is flung,
 Her mantle of old Erin's green;   10
And o'er her shoulder careless hung,
 Her fairy axe of gold is seen.

She hastes (the Forest's sweetest rose)
 To cull the forest's sweetest flowers;
To prune the branch that wildly grows,   15
 And shades the bud from nurturing showers.

Her hair like golden tendrils gleams,
 On the fresh gale's inconstant wing;
To me more splendidly she beams
 Then the proud Saxons' mighty king.   20

Oh! Gracy Once I Thought Thee Mine (by Carolan)

From Twelve Original Hibernian Melodies (1805)

Oh Gracy once I thought thee mine
How could'st thou love deceive me
And the dream was so divine
I dare not disbelieve thee.

For when thine eye of languid blue   5
Seem'd soft to say I love thee oh!
Tho' thy trait'rous wiles I knew
I dar'd not love reprove thee oh!

Come then Gracy come again
To bless and to deceive me   10
And tho' I know thou dost but feign
Yet I'll again believe thee.

Twilight (Fragment XXII)

From Lay of an Irish Harp (1807)

The pensive pleasures sweet
Prepare thy shadowy car.[1]
(COLLINS)

I
There is a mild, a solemn hour,
And oh! how soothing is its pow'r
To smile away Care's sombre low'r!
This hour I love!

Notes ———————————————————————

TWILIGHT
[1] "Ode to Evening," by English Poet William Collins (1721–59).

It follows last the feath'ry train   5
That hovers round *Time*'s rapid wain.
            'Tis then I rove.

II

'Tis when the day's last beam of light
Sleeps on the rude tow'r's mould'ring height,
With many an age's moss bedight,   10
      The dreary home
Of some sad victim of despair,
Who from the world finds shelter there;
            'Tis then I roam.

III

'Tis when the west clouds faintly blush,   15
And his last vesper sings the thrush,
And soft mists veil gay nature's flush,
      And not a ray
From the morn's cloud-embosom'd crest
Silvers the green wave's swelling breast;   20
            'Tis then I stray.

IV

'Tis the soft stilly dawn of night,
When many an elf and fairy sprite
Pursue the glow-worm's furtive light,
      Like me fonder   25
Of that soft, pale, mysterious beam
Which lures wild fancy's wizard dream,
            While I wander.

V

Day cannot claim this charming hour,
Nor night subdue it to its power,   30
Nor sunny smiles, nor gloomy low'r,
      Does it betray:
But blandly soothing, sweetly wild,
Soft, silent, stilly, fragrant, mild,
            It steals away.   35

From *Absenteeism, No. 1*

From **New Monthly Magazine (1824)**[1]

The phrase "Absentee," says Dr. Johnson,[2] is one "used *with regard to Irishmen* living
out of their country:" and as its origin is Irish, so its use and application are strictly

Notes

FROM ABSENTEEISM, NO. 1
[1] "Absenteeism" was published anonymously in three parts
(1824–5) and then collected and published under Morgan's
name in a volume, *Absenteeism* (1825). These are the opening

paragraphs of the first part.
[2] This definition is from the *Dictionary of the English
Language* by Samuel Johnson (1709–84), English author.

confined to the history of that unfortunate people. The inference to be drawn from this fact is plain: that there is something in the circumstances of the Irish, peculiar to themselves, – something which forces upon them a line of conduct contrary to the ordinary instincts of humanity, and compels them to fly from that land which all other nations regard with more or less of favour and affection, – from that land which youth quits with regret, and to which age clings with passion, when all other passions fade, – the land of their nativity.

In every history of Irish grievances, this cabalistical term "absentee" appears in the front of the array, and, like the terrible *"Il Bondocani"* of the Calif of Bagdat,[3] strikes down all before it: the apology for every abuse, the obstacle to every plan of amelioration, the bugbear of the timid, the stalking-horse of the designing.

"Absenteeism," observes the Secretary for the Home Department, "is an operative cause of tumult, but it is without remedy;" and thus dismissing all ministerial responsibility with a laconic aphorism, he launches an integral portion of the empire committed to his management, to revolve for ever in the turbulent whirlpool of cause and effect. Tumult expels the rich landowners, the absence of the rich landowners perpetuates tumult: this is a law of nature, which admits of "no remedy;" and the executive have nothing to do but to procure the passing of penal statutes according to the necessities of the moment, and to find the means of extorting four millions a year from English industry, to pay the expense of Irish misrule.

In political philosophy there are no evils without a remedy, save those which arise out of the common condition of humanity; – and the minister who confesses a political evil which he cannot remove, should remove himself; for he is himself the greatest evil with which the people have to contend . . .

To what physiological peculiarity of constitution this irremediable tendency to wander, inherited from their progenitors by the restless sons of the great Milesius, is to be attributed, the learned Secretary has not informed us; and it is certain Spurzheim, on his visit to the Irish capital, discovered no migratory inequality upon the surface of the Irish cranium, to account for the disposition. But in whatever particular of temperament or exuberance of cerebral development the cause of this effect defective lies latent, it is matter of historic fact, that though the native Irish were restless enough at home ("never," says Campion, "wanting drift to drive a tumult,") yet this activity, which induced them "to pick a quarrel, fall in love, or any other diverting accident of that kind," never found vent in absenteeism. Where, indeed, could Irishmen go to better their condition, when all in Ireland, who were no saints, were kings; and many were both, while none were martyrs . . . In those true church and state times of Ireland's prosperity, of which the Orangeman's Utopia is but a type, it is little wonderful that the people gave into no wanderings, but those *"du cœur et de l'esprit;"* and that a pilgrimage to St. Patrick's purgatory, a royal progress of some Toparck of the South to a Dynast in the North, or a morning visit from King Mac Turtell to his close neighbour King Gillemohalmoghe[4] (which occasionally ended in the broken heads of both parties), should include the recorded absenteeism of two thousand years.

It was reserved, however, for one of these royal heroes first to commit the patricidal crime: and the first Irish absentee of note, though a great king, was but a *mauvais sujet*, having pillaged his people, wasted his revenue, ran away with his neighbour's wife, and sold his country for a mess of pottage. It is almost unnecessary to add that

Notes ───

[3] The comic opera, *Il Bondocani, or the Caliph Robber* (1800), by Thomas Dibdin et al.

[4] King Mac Turtell was King of Dublin, and held his kingdom by tribute from the King of Leinster. "Not far from Dublin," says the admirable Maurice Regan, historiographer to Mac Murrogh, and who wrote in French, – "not far from Dublin there lived an Irish king named Gillemohalmoghe" . . . (author).

this royal founder of absenteeism is condemned to the contempt of posterity by the title of Dermot Mac Murrogh O'Kavenagh, King of Leinster; and that the result of his absenteeship was the successful invasion of Ireland by Henry II, the crusading grants of Pope Adrian IV, and, above all, the fearful forfeitures followed by rebellion on one part, and on the other by an effort of extermination, which have multiplied from age to age those possessors and deserters of the soil, who have drawn over "the profits raised out of Ireland, and refunded nothing."[5] . . .

But if the first barbarous English legislators for Ireland (and when has the epithet been inapplicable?) were, at an early period of their unfixed power, sensible of the injury which the state and the country suffered from absenteeism – if the Plantagenets[6] took cognizance of the evil, and endeavoured to provide against it by statute, the Tudors[7] (those sanguinary but sagacious despots) considered the absence of the Irish from their homes and country as a state engine; and wielded it with a policy which always advanced their own interests, and confirmed their power over that unhappy land. Sometimes they allured the Irish nobility to their splendid court for the purpose of dazzling their imagination and corrupting their patriotism. Sometimes they cited them as accused or criminals on shallow pretexts, to awe them by their array of power, or to intimidate them by their display of cruelty . . .

The English were accustomed to the presence of the Geraldines, the Butlers, the De Courceys, De Burgos, and other great Anglo-Irish lords of the pale who, though by "gossipry and alliance" they occasionally fell into Irish habits, and sported a glib or a mantle at home, were still sure to resume the English costume when at the English court. But the true aboriginal Irish gentlemen, the brave O's and Macs, who, driven to their woods and morasses with no other weapon of defence than their skein, their hatchet, or their pike, had for centuries resisted the well-armed force of England, – they were creatures of almost fabulous interest and existence; and the "anthropophagi and men whose heads do grow beneath their shoulders," were not more monstrous to English apprehensions as the "flying Irish," whose wings were supposed to grow beneath their heads. To the higher castes, however, they were known by the reputation of their prowess and their comeliness; and were noted by some of the poets of the day, alike for their invincible spirits and their lofty stature.[8]

William Carleton (1794–1869)

William Carleton was born in Co. Tyrone. It is difficult to tell how much of his life was reflected in his fiction and how much of his fiction has shaped the mythology of his life. He was raised in rural Catholic Ireland; his father was a farmer and his mother, fluently Irish, was the repository of a considerable body of Irish-language verse. He was educated first in hedge schools and then at a classical school before becoming a teacher himself at various institutions. There are also suggestions, largely if not entirely derived from his story "Wildgoose Lodge," that Carleton was

Notes

[5] Child's Discourse Upon Trade. – "No inconsiderable portion of the entire of Ireland has been confiscated twice, and perhaps thrice, in the course of a century" – *Lord Clare's Speech on the Union* . . . (author).

[6] English royal family, ruled from 1154 to 1485, beginning with Henry II (king of England 1154–89).

[7] The Tudors followed the Plantagenets on the English

throne, ruling England from 1485 to 1603, ending with Elizabeth I's death.

[8] "Then came the Irishmen of valiant hearts, And active limbs, and personages tall" – *Sir J. Harrington's Translation of Orlando Furioso* (author). *Orlando Furioso* (1516) by Italian poet Ludovico Ariosto (1474–1533).

briefly a member of a secret rural society related to insurgency. Carleton did not, however, conform to the usual assumptions about a bilingual Catholic from rural Ireland. He settled in Dublin and became a Protestant in the late 1810s and, in 1826, wrote to the British government claiming that Daniel O'Connell's Catholic Association was contributing to rural insurgency.

Soon thereafter, Carleton caught the eye of Caesar Otway who encouraged him to write for the *Christian Examiner,* a periodical which supported the Church of Ireland, and effectively launched Carleton's literary career in 1828. By 1831, however, Carleton had stopped contributing to the *Christian Examiner* in favor of the less partisan *Dublin University Magazine* and other Irish periodicals. He continued to draw on Irish oral traditions of story-telling and to write about the rural, Catholic Ireland he had left behind him. He published the first series of *Traits and Stories of the Irish Peasantry* in 1830 and a second series in 1833; this was followed by *Tales of Ireland* in 1834. A new edition of *Traits and Stories* appeared in 1843, along with his "Autobiographical Introduction," a key source for much Carleton biography. While the *Traits* remain at the heart of Carleton's enduring reputation, largely for their construction of an attractive rural Ireland, they were controversial in their day for their sour, anti-Catholic notes.

After a decade of writing short fiction, Carleton published his first novel, *Fardorougha the Miser; or, the Convicts of Lisnamona*, first serially (in the *Dublin University Magazine*, 1837–8) and then in book form (1839). He continued to publish tales and novels throughout his life, producing dozens of volumes over the next three decades. Some dealt with current political and religious tensions, such as *Rody the Rover or the Ribbonman* (1845) and *The Tithe Proctor* (1849); others addressed the devastation of the famine, including *The Black Prophet* (1847), first published serially (*Dublin University Magazine*, 1846). Throughout, Carleton's politics remain broadly Unionist, pro-anglicization, and anti-insurgency, though not simplistically so; Carleton in part blamed poor education and rural poverty for Irish unrest, and published in periodicals with a wide array of political affiliations.

"Wildgoose Lodge" complicates any easy sectarian view of rural violence: the Catholic rebels are not devout Catholics, their motives are personal rather than political, and the group depicted in the tale is far from coherent or united. Complex ties of community, fear, honor, and faith put the narrator in an untenable position, even as he simplistically renders the Captain and the other ringleaders as typical gothic villains – bestial, immoral, duplicitous, and manipulative. Carleton's "Auto-biographical Introduction" is similarly complex, praising his mother and the Irish oral traditions she knew, while sweepingly complaining of the "ignorance" of the community that sustained those traditions, looking forward to anglicization while condemning anti-Irish stereotypes and praising Irish writers.

Further reading

Kilfeather, Siobhán, "Terrific Register: The Gothicization of Atrocity in Irish Romanticism," *boundary 2* 31 (2004) 49–71.

Krause, David, *William Carleton the Novelist: His Carnival and Pastoral World of TragiComedy.* Washington: University Press of America, 2000.

Morash, Christopher, *Writing the Irish Famine.* Oxford: Clarendon Press, 1995.

O'Connell, Helen, "Improved English, and the Silence of Irish," *Canadian Journal of Irish Studies* 30 (2004): 13–20.

Wildgoose Lodge[1]

From Traits and Stories of the Irish Peasantry (second series, 1833)

I had read the anonymous summons, but from its general import, I believed it to be one of those special meetings convened for some purpose affecting the usual objects and proceedings of the body; – at least the terms in which it was conveyed to me had nothing extraordinary or mysterious in them, beyond the simple fact, that it was not to be a general, but a select meeting: this mark of confidence flattered me, and I determined to attend punctually. I was, it is true, desired to keep the circumstance entirely to myself, but there was nothing startling in this, for I had often received summonses of a similar nature. I therefore resolved to attend, according to the letter of my instructions, "on the next night, at the solemn hour of midnight, to deliberate and act upon such matters as should, then and there, be submitted to my consideration." The morning after I received this message, I arose and resumed my usual occupations; but, from whatever cause it may have proceeded, I felt a sense of approaching evil hang heavily upon me: the beats of my pulse were languid, and an undefinable feeling of anxiety pervaded my whole spirit; even my face was pale, and my eye so heavy, that my father and brothers concluded me to be ill; an opinion which I thought at the time to be correct, for I felt exactly that kind of depression which precedes a severe fever. I could not understand what I experienced, nor can I yet, except by supposing that there is in human nature some mysterious faculty, by which, in coming calamities, the dread of some fearful evil is anticipated, and that it is possible to catch a dark presentiment of the sensations which they subsequently produce. For my part I can neither analyze nor define it; but on that day I knew it by painful experience, and so have a thousand others in similar circumstances.

It was about the middle of winter. The day was gloomy and tempestuous, almost beyond any other I remember: dark clouds rolled over the hills about me, and a close sleet-like rain fell in slanting drifts that chased each other rapidly towards the earth on the course of the blast. The out-lying cattle sought the closest and calmest corners of the fields for shelter; the trees and young groves were tossed about, for the wind was so unusually high that it swept in hollow gusts through them, with that hoarse murmur which deepens so powerfully on the mind the sense of dreariness and desolation.

As the shades of night fell, the storm, if possible, increased. The moon was half gone, and only a few stars were visible by glimpses, as a rush of wind left a temporary opening in the sky. I had determined, if the storm should not abate, to incur any penalty rather than attend the meeting; but the appointed hour was distant, and I resolved to be decided by the future state of the night.

Ten o'clock came, but still there was no change; eleven passed, and on opening the door to observe if there were any likelihood of its clearing up, a blast of wind, mingled with rain, nearly blew me off my feet. At length it was approaching to the hour of midnight; and on examining a third time, I found it had calmed a little, and no longer rained.

William Carleton Wildgoose Lodge

Notes

WILDGOOSE LODGE

[1] The story was also published under the title "Confessions of a Reformed Ribbonman."

I instantly got my oak stick, muffled myself in my great coat, strapped my hat about my ears, and, as the place of meeting was only a quarter of a mile distant, I presently set out.

The appearance of the heavens was lowering and angry, particularly in that point where the light of the moon fell against the clouds, from a seeming chasm in them, through which alone she was visible. The edges of this chasm were faintly bronzed, but the dense body of the masses that hung piled on each side of her, was black and impenetrable to sight. In no other point of the heavens was there any part of the sky visible; a deep veil of clouds overhung the horizon, yet was the light sufficient to give occasional glimpses of the rapid shifting which took place in this dark canopy, and of the tempestuous agitation with which the midnight storm swept to and fro beneath it.

At length I arrived at a long slated house, situated in a solitary part of the neighborhood; a little below it ran a small stream, which was now swollen above its banks, and rushing with mimic roar over the flat meadows beside it. The appearance of the bare slated building in such a night was particularly sombre, and to those, like me, who knew the purpose to which it was usually devoted, it was, or ought to have been, peculiarly so. There it stood, silent and gloomy, without any appearance of human life or enjoyment about or within it. As I approached, the moon once more had broken out of the clouds, and shone dimly upon the wet, glittering slates and windows, with a death-like lustre, that gradually faded away as I left the point of observation, and entered the folding-door. It was the parish chapel.

The scene which presented itself here, was in keeping not only with the external appearance of the house, but with the darkness, the storm, and the hour, which was now a little after midnight. About eighty persons were sitting in dead silence upon the circular steps of the altar.[2] They did not seem to move; and as I entered and advanced, the echo of my footsteps rang through the building with a lonely distinctness, which added to the solemnity and mystery of the circumstances about me. The windows were secured with shutters on the inside, and on the altar a candle was lighted, which burned dimly amid the surrounding darkness, and lengthened the shadow of the altar itself, and those of six or seven persons who stood on its upper steps, until they mingled in the obscurity which shrouded the lower end of the chapel. The faces of the men who sat on the altar steps were not distinctly visible, yet their prominent and more characteristic features were in sufficient relief, and I observed, that some of the most malignant and reckless spirits in the parish were assembled. In the eyes of those who stood at the altar, and whom I knew to be invested with authority over the others, I could perceive gleams of some latent and ferocious purpose, kindled, as I soon observed, into a fiercer expression of vengeance, by the additional excitement of ardent spirits, with which they had stimulated themselves to a point of determination that mocked at the apprehension of all future responsibility, either in this world or the next.

The welcome which I received on joining them was far different from the boisterous good-humour that used to mark our greetings on other occasions: just a nod of the head from this or that person, on the part of those *who sat*, with a *ghud dhemur tha thu?*[3] in a suppressed voice, even below a common whisper: but from the standing group, who were evidently the projectors of the enterprise, I received a convulsive

Notes ───

[2] In later editions, among other minor changes, Carleton reduced the number of people involved to "forty persons" in the chapel and "eight or eleven" in the house.

[3] How are you? (author). As is common (see Thomas Sheridan above), Carleton has his characters speak Irish and then translate themselves into English.

grasp of the hand, accompanied by a fierce and desperate look, that seemed to search my eye and countenance, to try if I were a person not likely to shrink from whatever they had resolved to execute. It is surprising to think of the powerful expression which a moment of intense interest or great danger is capable of giving to the eye, the features, and the slightest actions, especially in those whose station in society does not require them to constrain nature, by the force of social courtesies, into habits that conceal their natural emotions. None of the standing group spoke; but as each of them wrung my hand in silence, his eye was fixed on mine, with an expression of drunken confidence and secrecy, and an insolent determination not to be gainsayed without peril. If looks could be translated with certainty, they seemed to say, "we are bound upon a project of vengeance, and if you do not join us, remember we *can* revenge." Along with this grasp, they did not forget to remind me of the common bond by which we were united, for each man gave me the secret grip of Ribbonism in a manner that made the joints of my fingers ache for some minutes afterwards.[4]

There was one present, however, – the highest in authority – whose actions and demeanour were calm and unexcited. He seemed to labour under no unusual influence whatever, but evinced a serenity so placid and philosophical, that I attributed the silence of the sitting group, and the restraint which curbed in the outbreaking passions of those who *stood*, entirely to his presence. He was a schoolmaster, who taught his daily school in that chapel, and acted also, on Sunday, in the capacity of clerk to the priest – an excellent and amiable old man, who knew little of his illegal connexions and atrocious conduct.

When the ceremonies of brotherly recognition and friendship were past, the Captain (by which title I shall designate the last-mentioned person) stooped, and, raising a jar of whiskey on the corner of the altar, held a wine-glass to its neck, which he filled, and with a calm nod, handed it to me to drink. I shrank back, with an instinctive horror, at the profaneness of such an act, in the house, and on the altar of God, and peremptorily refused to taste the proffered draught. He smiled mildly at what he considered my superstition, and added quietly, and in a low voice, "You'll be wantin' it, I'm thinkin', afther the wettin' you got."

"Wet or dry," said I, –

"Stop, man!" he replied, in the same tone; "spake low. But why wouldn't you take the whiskey? Sure there's as holy people to the fore as you: didn't they all take it? An' I wish we may never do worse nor dhrink a harmless glass o' whiskey, to keep the cowld out, any way."

"Well," said I, "I'll jist trust to God and the consequences, for the cowld, Paddy, ma bouchal; but a blessed dhrop of it won't be crossin' my lips, avick; so no more ghosther about it; dhrink it yourself if you like. Maybe you want it as much as I do; wherein I've the patthern of a good big-coat upon me, so thick, your sowl, that if it was rainin' bullocks, a dhrop wouldn't get undher the nap of it."

He gave me a calm, but keen glance, as I spoke.

"Well, Jim," said he, "it's a good comrade you've got for the weather that's in it; but, in the manetime, to set you a dacent patthern, I'll just take this myself," – saying which, with the jar still upon its side, and the fore-finger of his left hand in its neck, he swallowed the spirits – "It's the first I dhrank to-night," he added, "nor would I dhrink it now, only to show you that I've heart an' spirit to do the thing that we're all

Notes

[4] Ribbonism variously refers to agrarian insurgency in general and secret societies in particular among Catholic nationalists.

bound an' sworn to, when the proper time comes;" after which, he laid down the glass, and turned up the jar, with much coolness, upon the altar.

During our conversation, those who had been summoned to this mysterious meeting were pouring in fast; and as each person approached the altar, he received from one to two or three glasses of whiskey, according as he chose to limit himself; but, to do them justice, there were not a few of those present, who, in despite of their own desire, and the Captain's express invitation, refused to taste it in the house of God's worship. Such, however, as were scrupulous he afterwards recommended to take it on the outside of the chapel door, which they did, as, by that means, the sacrilege of the act was supposed to be evaded.

About one o'clock they were all assembled except six; at least so the Captain asserted, on looking at a written paper.

"Now, boys," said he, in the same low voice, "we are all present except the thraitors, whose names I am goin' to read to you; not that we are to count thim thraitors, till we know whether or not it was in their power to come. Any how, the night's terrible – but, boys, you're to know, that neither fire nor wather is to prevint yees, when duly summoned to attind a meeting – particularly whin the summons is widout a name, as you have been told that there is always something of consequence to be done *thin*."

He then read out the names of those who were absent, in order that the real cause of their absence might be ascertained, declaring that they would be dealt with accordingly. After this, with his usual caution, he shut and bolted the door, and having put the key in his pocket, ascended the steps of the altar, and for some time traversed the little platform from which the priest usually addresses the congregation.

Until this night I had never contemplated the man's countenance with any particular interest; but as he walked the platform, I had an opportunity of observing him more closely. He was slight in person, apparently not thirty; and, on a first view, appeared to have nothing remarkable in his dress or features. I, however, was not the only person whose eyes were fixed upon him at that moment; in fact, every one present observed him with equal interest, for hitherto he had kept the object of the meeting perfectly secret, and of course we all felt anxious to know it. It was while he traversed the platform that I scrutinized his features with a hope, if possible, to glean from them some evidence of what was passing within him. I could, however, mark but little, and that little was at first rather from the intelligence which seemed to subsist between him and those whom I have already mentioned as *standing* against the altar, than from any indication of his own. Their gleaming eyes were fixed upon him with an intensity of savage and demon-like hope, which blazed out in flashes of malignant triumph, as upon turning, he threw a cool but rapid glance at them, to intimate the progress he was making in the subject to which he devoted the undivided energies of his mind. But in the course of his meditation, I could observe, on one or two occasions, a dark shade come over his countenance, that contracted his brow into a deep furrow, and it was then, for the first time, that I saw the satanic expression of which his face, by a very slight motion of its muscles, was capable. His hands, during this silence, closed and opened convulsively; his eyes shot out two or three baleful glances, first to his confederates, and afterwards vacantly into the deep gloom of the lower part of the chapel; his teeth ground against each other, like those of a man whose revenge burns to reach a distant enemy, and finally, after having wound himself up to a certain determination, his features relapsed into their original calm and undisturbed expression.

At this moment a loud laugh, having something supernatural in it, rang out wildly from the darkness of the chapel; he stopped, and putting his open hand over his brows, peered down into the gloom, and said calmly in Irish, *"Bee dhu husth; ha nihl anam inh*: – hold your tongue, it is not yet the time."

Every eye was now directed to the same spot, but, in consequence of its distance from the dim light on the altar, none could perceive the person from whom the laugh proceeded. It was by this time, near two o'clock in the morning.

He now stood for a few moments on the platform, and his chest heaved with a depth of anxiety equal to the difficulty of the design he wished to accomplish:

"Brothers," said he – "for we are all brothers – sworn upon all that's blessed an' holy, to obey whatever them that's over us, *manin' among ourselves*,[5] wishes us to do – are you now ready, in the name of God, upon whose althar I stand, to fulfil yer oaths?"

The words were scarcely uttered, when those who had *stood* beside the altar during the night, sprang from their places, and descending its steps rapidly, turned round, and raising their arms, exclaimed, "By all that's sacred an' holy, we're willin'."

In the mean time, those who *sat* upon the steps of the altar, instantly rose, and following the example of those who had just spoken, exclaimed after them, "To be sure – by all that's sacred an' holy, we're willin'."

"Now, boys," said the Captain, "ar'n't yees big fools for your pains? an' one of yees doesn't know what I mane."

"You're our Captain," said one of those who had stood at the altar, "an' has yer ordhers from higher quarthers; of coorse, whatever ye command upon us we're bound to obey you in."

"Well," said he, smiling, "I only wanted to thry yees; an' by the oath yees tuck, there's not a captain in the county has as good a right to be proud of his min as I have. Well, yees won't rue it, maybe, when the right time comes; and for that same rason every one of yees must have a glass from the jar; thim that won't dhrink it *in* the chapel can dhrink it *widout*; an' here goes to open the door for them."

He then distributed another glass to every one who would accept it, and brought the jar afterwards to the chapel door, to satisfy the scruples of those who would not drink within. When this was performed, and all duly excited, he proceeded: –

"Now, brothers, you are solemnly sworn to obay me, and I'm sure there's no thraithur here that 'ud parjure himself for a thrifle; but *I'm* sworn to obey them that's above me, manin' still among ourselves; an' to show that I don't scruple to do it, here goes!"

He then turned round, and taking the Missal between his hands placed it upon the altar. Hitherto every word was uttered in a low precautionary tone; but on grasping the book, he again turned round, and looking upon his confederates with the same satanic expression which marked his countenance before, exclaimed, in a voice of deep determination:

"By this sacred an' holy book of God, I will perform the action which we have met this night to accomplish, be that what it may; an' this I swear upon God's book, an' God's althar!"

On concluding he struck the book violently with his open hand.

At this moment the candle which burned before him went suddenly out, and the chapel was wrapped in pitchy darkness; the sound as if of rushing wings fell upon our ears, and fifty voices dwelt upon the last words of his oath with wild and supernatural tones, that seemed to echo and to mock what he had sworn. There was a pause, and an exclamation of horror from all present: but the Captain was too

Notes

[5] In opposition to the constituted authorities (author).

cool and steady to be disconcerted. He immediately groped about until he got the candle, and proceeding calmly to a remote corner of the chapel, took up a half-burned turf which lay there, and after some trouble, succeeded in lighting it again. He then explained what had taken place; which indeed was easily done, as the candle happened to be extinguished by a pigeon which sat directly above it. The chapel, I should have observed, was at this time, like many country chapels, unfinished inside, and the pigeons of a neighbouring dove-cot had built nests among the rafters of the unceiled roof; which circumstance also explained the rushing of the wings, for the birds had been affrighted by the sudden loudness of the noise. The mocking voices were nothing but the echoes, rendered naturally more awful by the scene, the mysterious object of the meeting, and the solemn hour of the night.

When the candle was again lighted, and these startling circumstances accounted for, the persons whose vengeance had been deepening more and more during the night, rushed to the altar in a body, where each, in a voice trembling with passionate eagerness, repeated the oath, and as every word was pronounced, the same echoes heightened the wildness of the horrible ceremony, by their long and unearthly tones. The countenances of these human tigers were livid with suppressed rage; their knit brows, compressed lips, and kindled eyes, fell under the dim light of the taper, with an expression calculated to sicken any heart not absolutely diabolical.

As soon as this dreadful rite was completed, we were again startled by several loud bursts of laughter, which proceeded from the lower darkness of the chapel; and the captain, on hearing them, turned to the place, and reflecting for a moment, said in Irish, "*Gutsho nish, avohelhee* – come hither now, boys."

A rush immediately took place from the corner in which they had secreted themselves all the night; and seven men appeared, whom we instantly recognised as brothers and cousins of certain persons who had been convicted, some time before, for breaking into the house of an honest poor man in the neighborhood, from whom, after having treated him with barbarous violence, they took away such fire-arms as he kept for his own protection.

It was evidently not the captain's intention to have produced these persons until the oath should have been generally taken, but the exulting mirth with which they enjoyed the success of his scheme betrayed them, and put him to the necessity of bringing them forward somewhat before the concerted moment.

The scene which now took place was beyond all power of description; peals of wild, fiend-like yells rang through the chapel, as the party which *stood* on the altar, and that which had crouched in the darkness, met; wringing of hands, leaping in triumph, striking of sticks and fire-arms against the ground and the altar itself, dancing and cracking of fingers, marked the triumph of some hellish determination. Even the Captain for a time was unable to restrain their fury; but, at length, he mounted the platform before the altar once more, and with a stamp of his foot, recalled their attention to himself and the matter in hand.

"Boys," said he, "enough of this, and too much; an' well for us it is that the chapel is in a lonely place, or our foolish noise might do us no good. Let thim that swore so manfully jist now, stand a one side, till the rest kiss the book one by one."

The proceedings, however, had by this time taken too fearful a shape, for even the Captain to compel them to a blindfold oath; the first man he called, flatly refused to answer, until he should hear the nature of the service that was required. This was echoed by the remainder, who taking courage from the firmness of this person, declared generally, that until they first knew the business they were to execute, none of them would take the oath. The Captain's lip quivered slightly, and his brow again became knit with the same hellish expression, which I have remarked gave him so much the appearance of an embodied fiend; but this speedily passed away, and was succeeded by a malignant sneer, in which lurked, if there ever did in a sneer, "a laughing devil," calmly, determinedly atrocious.

"It wasn't worth yer whiles to refuse the oath," said he mildly, "for the truth is, I had next to nothing for yees to do. Not a hand, maybe, would have to *rise*, only jist to look on, an' if any resistance would be made, to show yourselves; yer numbers would soon make them see that resistance would be no use whatever in the present case. At all evints, the oath of *secrecy must* be taken, or woe be to him that will refuse *that*; he won't know the day, nor the hour, nor the minute, when he'll be made a spatch-cock of."[6]

He then turned round, and, placing his right hand on the Missal, swore, "In the presence of God, and before his holy altar, that whatever might take place that night, he would keep secret, from man or mortal, except the priest, and that neither bribery, nor imprisonment, nor death, would wring it from his heart."

Having done this, he again struck the book violently, as if to confirm the energy with which he swore, and then calmly descending the steps, stood with a serene countenance, like a man conscious of having performed a good action. As this oath did not pledge those who refused to take the other to the perpetration of any specific crime, it was readily taken by all present. Preparations were then made to execute what was intended: the half-burned turf was placed in a little pot; another glass of whiskey was distributed; and the door being locked by the Captain, who kept the key as parish clerk and master, the crowd departed silently from the chapel.

The moment those who lay in the darkness during the night, made their appearance at the altar, we knew at once the persons we were to visit; for, as I said before, they were related to the miscreants whom one of those persons had convicted, in consequence of their midnight attack upon himself and his family. The Captain's object in keeping them unseen was, that those present, not being aware of the duty about to be imposed on them, might have less hesitation about swearing to its fulfilment. Our conjectures were correct, for on leaving the chapel we directed our steps to the house in which this devoted man resided.

The night was still stormy, but without rain; it was rather dark too, though not so as to prevent us from seeing the clouds careering swiftly through the air. The dense curtain which had overhung and obscured the horizon, was now broken, and large sections of the sky were clear, and thinly studded with stars that looked dim and watery, as did indeed the whole firmament; for in some places black clouds were still visible, threatening a continuance of tempestuous weather. The road appeared washed and gravelly; every dike was full of yellow water; and every little rivulet and larger stream dashed its hoarse music in our ears; every blast, too, was cold, fierce, and wintry, sometimes driving us back to a stand still, and again, when a turn in the road would bring it in our backs, whirling us along for a few steps with involuntary rapidity. At length the fated dwelling became visible, and a short consultation was held in a sheltered place, between the Captain and the two parties who seemed so eager for its destruction. Their fire-arms were now loaded, and their bayonets and short pikes, the latter shod and pointed with iron, were also got ready. The live coal which was brought in the small pot had become extinguished; but to remedy this, two or three persons from a remote part of the county, entered a cabin on the

Notes

[6] *Spatch-cock* or *dispatch cock*, a hen killed and immediately cooked.

wayside, and under pretence of lighting their own and their comrades' pipes, pro-cured a coal of fire, for so they called a lighted turf. From the time we left the chapel until this moment a profound silence had been maintained, a circumstance which, when I considered the number of persons present, and the mysterious and dreaded object of their journey, had a most appalling effect upon my spirits.

At length we arrived within fifty perches[7] of the house, walking in a compact body, and with as little noise as possible; but it seemed as if the very elements had conspired to frustrate our design, for on advancing within the shade of the farm-hedge, two or three persons found themselves up to the middle in water, and on stooping to ascertain more accurately the state of the place, we could see nothing but one immense sheet of it – spread like a lake over the meadows which surrounded the spot we wished to reach.

Fatal night! The very recollection of it, when associated with the fearful tempests of elements, grows, if that were possible, yet more wild and revolting. Had we been engaged in any innocent or benevolent enterprise, there was something in our situation just then that had a touch of interest in it to a mind imbued with a relish for the savage beauties of nature. There we stood, about a hundred and thirty in number, our dark forms bent forward, peering into the dusky expanse of water, with its dim gleams of reflected light, broken by the weltering of the mimic waves into ten thousand fragments, whilst the few stars that overhung it in the firmament appeared to shoot through it in broken lines, and to be multiplied fifty-fold in the gloomy mirror on which we gazed.

Over us was a stormy sky, and around us a darkness through which we could only distinguish, in outline, the nearest objects, whilst the wild wind swept strongly and dismally upon us. When it was discovered that the common pathway to the house was inundated, we were about to abandon our object and return home. The Captain, however, stooped down low for a moment, and almost closing his eyes, looked along the surface of the waters, and then rising himself very calmly, said, in his usual quiet tone, "Yees needn't go back, boys, I've found a way; jist follow me."

He immediately took a more circuitous direction, by which we reached a causeway that had been raised for the purpose of giving a free passage to and from the house, during such inundations as the present. Along this we had advanced more than half way, when we discovered a breach in it, which, as afterwards appeared, had that night been made by the strength of the flood. This, by means of our sticks and pikes, we found to be about three feet deep, and eight yards broad. Again we were at a loss how to proceed, when the fertile brain of the Captain devised a method of crossing it.

"Boys," said he, "of coorse you've all played at leap-frog; very well, strip and go in, a dozen of you, lean one upon the back of another from this to the opposite bank, where one must stand facing the outside man, both their shoulders agin one another, that the outside man may be supported. Then *we* can creep over you, an' a dacent bridge you'll be, any way."

This was the work of only a few minutes, and in less than ten we were all safely over.

Merciful heaven! how I sicken at the recollection of what is to follow! On reaching the dry bank, we proceeded instantly, and in profound silence, to the house; the Captain divided us into companies, and then assigned to each division its proper station. The two parties who had been so vindictive all the night, he kept about himself; for of those who were present, they only were in his confidence, and knew his nefarious purpose; their number was about fifteen. Having made these dispositions, he, at the head of about five of them, approached the house on the windy side, for the fiend possessed a coolness which enabled him to seize upon every possible advantage. That he had combustibles about him was evident, for in less than fifteen minutes nearly one half of the house was enveloped in flames. On seeing this, the others rushed over to the spot where he and his gang were standing, and remonstrated earnestly, but in vain; the flames now burst forth with renewed violence, and as they flung their strong light upon the faces of the foremost group, I think hell itself could hardly present any thing more satanic than their countenances, now worked up into a paroxysm of infernal triumph, at their own revenge. The Captain's look had lost all its calmness, every feature started out into distinct malignity, the curve in his brow was deep, and ran up to the root of the hair, dividing his face into two segments, that did not seem to have been designed for each other. His lips were half open, and the corners of his mouth a little brought back on each side, like those of a man expressing intense hatred and triumph over an enemy who is in the death struggle under his grasp. His eyes blazed from beneath his knit eye-brows with a fire that seemed to be lighted up in the infernal pit itself. It is unnecessary, and only painful, to describe the rest of his gang; demons might have been proud of such horrible visages as they exhibited; for they worked under all the power of hatred, revenge, and joy; and these passions blended into one terrible scowl, enough almost to blast any human eye that would venture to look upon it.

When the others attempted to intercede for the lives of the inmates, there were at least fifteen guns and pistols levelled at them.

"Another word," said the Captain, "an' you're a corpse where you stand, or the first man who will dare to spake for them; no, no, it wasn't to spare them we came here. 'No mercy' is the pass word for the night, an' by the sacred oath I swore beyant in the chapel, any one among yees that will attempt to show it, will find none at my hand. Surround the house, boys, I tell ye, I hear them stirring. 'No quarther – no mercy,' is the ordher of the night."

Such was his command over these misguided creatures, that in an instant there was a ring round the house to prevent the escape of the unhappy inmates, should the raging element give them time to attempt it; for none present durst withdraw themselves from the scene, not only from an apprehension of the Captain's present vengeance, or that of his gang, but because they knew that even had they then escaped, an early and certain death awaited them from a quarter against which they had no means of defence. The hour now was about half-past two o'clock. Scarcely had the last words escaped from the Captain's lips, when one of the windows of the house was broken, and a human head, having the hair in a blaze, was descried, apparently a woman's, if one might judge by the profusion of burning tresses, and the softness of the tones, notwithstanding that it called, or rather shrieked, aloud, for help and mercy. The only reply to this was the whoop from the Captain and his gang, of "No mercy – no mercy!" and that instant the former, and one of the latter, rushed to the spot, and ere the action could be perceived, the head was transfixed with a bayonet and a pike, both having entered it together. The word mercy was divided in her mouth; a short silence ensued, the head hung down on the window, but was instantly tossed back into the flames!

This action occasioned a cry of horror from all present, except the *gang* and their leader, which startled and enraged the latter so much, that he ran towards one of them, and had his bayonet, now reeking with the blood of its innocent victim, raised to plunge it in his body, when, dropping the point, he said in a piercing whisper, that hissed in the ears of all: "It's no use *now*, you know; if one's to hang, all will hang; so our safest way, you persave, is to lave none of them to tell the story. Ye *may* go now, if you wish; but it won't save a hair of your heads. You cowardly set! I knew if I had tould yees the sport, that none of you, except my *own* boys, would come, so I jist played a thrick upon you; but remimber what you are sworn to, and stand to the oath ye tuck."

Unhappily, notwithstanding the wetness of the preceding weather, the materials of the house were extremely combustible; the whole dwelling was now one body of glowing flame, yet the shouts and shrieks within rose awfully above its crackling and the voice of the storm, for the wind once more blew in gusts, and with great violence. The doors and windows were all torn open, and such of those within as had escaped the flames rushed towards them, for the purpose of further escape, and of claiming mercy at the hands of their destroyers; but whenever they appeared, the unearthly cry of "NO MERCY" rang upon their ears for a moment, and for a moment only, for they were flung back at the points of the weapons which the demons had brought with them to make the work of vengeance more certain.

As yet there were many persons in the house, whose cry for life was strong as despair, and who clung to it with all the awakened powers of reason and instinct. The ear of man could hear nothing so strongly calculated to stifle the demon of cruelty and revenge within him, as the long and wailing shrieks which rose beyond the elements, in tones that were carried off rapidly upon the blast, until they died away in the darkness that lay behind the surrounding hills. Had not the house been in a solitary situation, and the hour the dead of night, any person sleeping within a moderate distance must have heard them, for such a cry of sorrow rising into a yell of despair, was almost sufficient to have awakened the dead. It was lost, however, upon the hearts and ears that heard it: to them, though in justice be it said, to only comparatively a few of them, it was as delightful as the tones of soft and entrancing music.

The claims of the surviving sufferers were now modified; they supplicated merely to suffer death *by the weapons of their enemies*; they were willing to bear that, provided they should be allowed to escape from the flames; but no, the horrors of the conflagration were calmly and malignantly gloried in by their merciless assassins, who deliberately flung them back into all their tortures. In the course of a few minutes a man appeared upon the side-wall of the house, nearly naked; his figure, as he stood against the sky in horrible relief, was so finished a picture of woebegone agony and supplication, that it is yet as distinct in my memory as if I were again present at the scene. Every muscle, now in motion by the powerful agitation of his sufferings, stood out upon his limbs and neck, giving him an appearance of desperate strength, to which by this time he must have been wrought up; the perspiration poured from his frame, and the veins and arteries of his neck were inflated to a surprising thickness. Every moment he looked down into the flames which were rising to where he stood; and as he looked, the indescribable horror which flitted over his features might have worked upon the devil himself to relent. His words were few: –

"My child," said he, "is still safe, she is an infant, a young crathur that never harmed you, or any one – she is still safe. Your mothers, your wives, have young innocent childhre like it. Oh, spare her, think for a moment that it's one of your own; spare it, as you hope to meet a just God, or if you don't, in mercy shoot me first – put an end to me, before I see her burned!"

The Captain approached him coolly and deliberately. "You'll prosecute no one now, you bloody informer," said he: "you'll convict no more boys for takin' an ould gun an' pistol from you, or for givin' you a neighbourly knock or two into the bargain."

Just then, from a window opposite him, proceeded the shrieks of a woman, who appeared at it, with the infant in her arms. She herself was almost scorched to death; but, with the presence of mind and humanity of her sex, she was about to put the little babe out of the window. The Captain noticed this, and, with characteristic atrocity, thrust, with a sharp bayonet, the little innocent, along with the person who endeavored to rescue it, into the red flames, where they both perished. This was the work of an instant. Again he approached the man: "Your child is a coal now," said he, with deliberate mockery; "I pitched it in myself, on the point of this," – showing the weapon – "an' now is your turn," – saying which, he clambered up, by the assistance of his gang, who stood with a front of pikes and bayonets bristling to receive the wretched man, should he attempt, in his despair, to throw himself from the wall. The Captain got up, and placing the point of his bayonet against his shoulder, flung him into the fiery element that raged behind him. He uttered one wild and terrific cry, as he fell back, and no more. After this nothing was heard but the crackling of the fire, and the rushing of the blast: all that had possessed life within were consumed, amounting either to eleven or fifteen persons.

When this was accomplished, those who took an active part in the murder, stood for some time about the conflagration; and as it threw its red light upon their fierce faces and rough persons, soiled as they now were with smoke and black streaks of ashes, the scene seemed to be changed to hell, the murderers to spirits of the damned, rejoicing over the arrival and the torture of some guilty soul. The faces of those who kept aloof from the slaughter were blanched to the whiteness of death: some of them fainted, and others were in such agitation that they were compelled to lean on their comrades. They became actually powerless with horror; yet to such a scene were they brought by the pernicious influence of Ribbonism.

It was only when the last victim went down, that the conflagration shot up into the air with most unbounded fury. The house was large, deeply thatched, and well furnished; and the broad red pyramid rose up with fearful magnificence towards the sky. Abstractedly it had sublimity, but now it was associated with nothing in my mind but blood and terror. It was not, however, without a purpose that the Captain and his gang stood to contemplate its effect. "Boys," said he, "we had betther be sartin that all's safe; who knows but there might be some of the sarpents crouchin' under a hape o' rubbish, to come out an' gibbet us to-morrow or next day: we had betther wait a while, anyhow, if it was only to see the blaze."

Just then the flames rose majestically to a surprising height. Our eyes followed their direction; and we perceived, for the first time, that the dark clouds above, together with the intermediate air, appeared to reflect back, or rather to have caught the red hue of the fire. The hills and country about us appeared with an alarming distinctness; but the most picturesque part of it was the effect or reflection of the blaze on the floods that spread over the surrounding plains. These, in fact, appeared to be one broad mass of liquid copper, for the motion of the breaking waters caught from the blaze of the high waving column, as reflected in them, a glaring light, which eddied, and rose, and fluctuated, as if the flood itself had been a lake of molten fire.

Fire, however, destroys rapidly. In a short time the flames sank – became weak and flickering – by and bye, they shot out only in fits – the crackling of the timbers died away – the surrounding darkness deepened – and, ere long, the faint light was overpowered by the thick volumes of smoke that rose from the ruins of the house, and its murdered inhabitants.

"Now, boys," said the Captain, "all is safe – we may go. Remember, every man of you, what you've sworn this night, on the book an' altar of God – not on a heretic Bible. If you perjure yourselves, you may hang us; but let me tell you, for your comfort, that if you do, there is them livin' that will take care the lase of your own lives will be but short."

After this we dispersed every man to his own home.

Reader, – not many months elapsed ere I saw the bodies of this Captain, whose name was Patrick Devann, and all those who were actively concerned in the perpetration of this deed of horror, withering in the wind, where they hung gibbeted, near the scene of their nefarious villany; and while I inwardly thanked heaven for my own narrow and almost undeserved escape, I thought in my heart how seldom, even in this world, justice fails to overtake the murder, and to enforce the righteous judgment of God – that "whoso sheddeth man's blood, by man shall his blood be shed."[8]

From *Auto-biographical Introduction*

From Traits and Stories of the Irish Peasantry (1843)

It will naturally be expected, upon a new issue of works which may be said to treat exclusively of a people who form such an important and interesting portion of the empire as the Irish peasantry do, that the author should endeavor to prepare the minds of his readers – especially those of the English and Scotch – for understanding more clearly their general character, habits of thought, and modes of feeling, as they exist and are depicted in the subsequent volumes. This is a task which the author undertakes more for the sake of his country than himself; and he rejoices that the demand for the present edition puts it in his power to aid in removing many absurd prejudices which have existed for time immemorial against his countrymen.

It is well known that the character of an Irishman has been hitherto uniformly associated with the idea of something unusually ridiculous, and that scarcely anything in the shape of language was supposed to proceed from his lips but an absurd *congeries* of brogue and blunder. The habit of looking upon him in a ludicrous light has been so strongly impressed upon the English mind, that no opportunity has ever been omitted of throwing him into an attitude of gross and overcharged caricature, from which you might as correctly estimate his intellectual strength and moral proportions, as you would the size of a man from his evening shadow. From the immortal bard of Avon down to the writers of the present day, neither play nor farce has ever been

Notes

[8] This tale of terror is, unfortunately, too true. The scene of hellish murder detailed in it, lies at Wildgoose Lodge, in the county of Louth, within about four miles of Carrickmacross, and nine of Dundalk. No such multitudinous murder has occurred, under similar circumstances, except the burning of the Sheas, in the county of Tipperary. The name of the family burned in Wildgoose Lodge was Lynch. One of them had, shortly before this fatal night, prosecuted and convicted some of the neighbouring Ribbonmen, who visited him with severe marks of their displeasure, in consequence of his having refused to enrol himself as a member of their body.

The Language of the story is partly fictitious; but the facts are pretty closely such as were developed during the trial of the murderers. Both parties were Roman Catholics. There were, if the author mistake not, either twenty-five or twenty-eight of those who took an active part in the burning, hanged and gibbeted in different parts of the county of Louth. Devann, the ringleader, hung for some months in chains, within about a hundred yards of his own house, and about half a mile from Wildgoose Lodge. His mother could neither go into nor out of her cabin without seeing his body swinging from the gibbet. Her usual exclamation on looking at him was – "God be good to the sowl of my poor marthyr!" The peasantry, too, frequently exclaimed, on seeing him, "Poor Paddy!" A gloomy fact that speaks volumes! (author).

presented to Englishmen, in which, when an Irishman is introduced, he is not drawn as a broad grotesque blunderer, every sentence he speaks involving a bull, and every act the result of headlong folly, or cool but unstudied effrontery. I do not remember an instance in which he acts upon the stage any other part than that of the buffoon of the piece, uttering language which, wherever it may have been found, was at all events never heard in Ireland, unless upon the boards of a theatre. As for the Captain O'Cutters, O'Blunders, and Dennis Bulgruderies of the English stage, they never had existence except in the imagination of those who were as ignorant of the Irish people as they were of their language and feelings. Even Sheridan himself was forced to pander to this erroneous estimate and distorted conception of our character; for, after all, Sir Lucius O'Trigger was *his* Irishman, but not Ireland's Irishman.[1] I know that several of my readers may remind me of Sir Boyle Roche, whose bulls have become not only notorious, but proverbial. It is well known now, however, and was when he made them, that they were studied bulls, resorted to principally for the purpose of putting government and opposition sides of the Irish House of Commons into good humour with each other, which they never failed to do – thereby, on more occasions than one, probably, preventing the effusion of blood, and the loss of life, among men who frequently decided even their political differences by the sword or pistol.

That the Irish either were or are a people remarkable for making bulls or blunders, is an imputation utterly unfounded, and in every sense untrue. The source of this error on the part of our neighbours is, however, readily traced. The language of our people has been for centuries, and is up to the present day, in a transition state. The English tongue is gradually superseding the Irish. In my own native place, for instance, there is not by any means so much Irish spoken now, as there was about twenty or five-and-twenty years ago. This fact, then, will easily account for the ridicule which is, and I fear ever will be, unjustly heaped upon those who are found to use a language which they do not properly understand. In the early periods of communication between the countries, when they stood in a hostile relation to each other, and even long afterwards, it was not surprising that "the wild Irishman" who expressed himself with difficulty, and often impressed the idiom of his own language upon one with which he was not familiar, should incur, in the opinion of those who were strongly prejudiced against him, the character of making the bulls and blunders attributed to him. Such was the fact, and such the origin of this national slander upon his intellect, – a slander which, every other, originates from the prejudice of those who were unacquainted with the quickness and clearness of thought that in general characterise the language of our people. At this moment there is no man acquainted with the inhabitants of the two countries, who does not know, that, where the English *is* vernacular in Ireland, it is spoken with far more purity and grammatical precision than is to be heard beyond the Channel. Those, then, who are in the habit of defending what are termed our bulls, or of apologising for them, do us injustice; and Miss Edgeworth herself, when writing an essay upon the subject, wrote an essay upon that which does not, and never did exist.[2] These observations, then, easily account for the view of us which has always been taken in the dramatic portion of English literature. There the Irishman was drawn in every instance as the object of ridicule, and consequently of contempt; for it is incontrovertibly true, that the man whom you laugh at, you will soon despise.

Notes

FROM AUTO-BIOGRAPHICAL INTRODUCTION
[1] R. B. Sheridan's *The Rivals* (1775).

[2] The Edgeworths' *Essay on Irish Bulls* (above, p. 180).

In every point of view this was wrong, but principally in a political one. At that time England and Englishmen knew very little of Ireland, and, consequently, the principal opportunities afforded them of appreciating our character were found on the stage. Of course, it was very natural that the erroneous estimate of us which they formed there should influence them everywhere else. We cannot sympathise with, and laugh at, the same object, at the same time; and if the Irishman found himself undeservedly the object of coarse and unjust ridicule, it was not very unnatural that he should requite it with a prejudice against the principles and feelings of Englishmen, quite as strong as that which was entertained against himself. Had this ridicule been confined to the stage, or directed at us in the presence of those who had other and better opportunities of knowing us, it would have been comparatively harmless. But this was not the case. It passed from the stage into the recesses of private life, wrought itself into the feelings until it became a prejudice, and the Irishman was consequently looked upon, and treated, as a being made up of absurdity and cunning, – a compound of knave and fool, fit only to be punished for his knavery or laughed at for his folly. So far, therefore, that portion of English literature which attempted to describe the language and habits of Irishmen, was unconsciously creating an unfriendly feeling between the two countries, – a feeling which, I am happy to say, is fast disappearing, and which only requires that we should have a full and fair acquaintance with each other in order to be removed for ever.

At present, indeed, their mutual positions, civil, commercial, and political, are very different from what they were half-a-century ago, or even at a more recent period. The progress of science, and the astonishing improvements in steam and machinery, have so completely removed the obstructions which impeded their intercourse, that the two nations can now scarcely be considered as divided. As a natural consequence, their knowledge of each other has improved; and, as will always happen with generous people, they begin to see that the one was neither knave nor fool, nor the other a churl or a boor. Thus has mutual respect arisen from mutual intercourse, and those who hitherto approached each other with distrust, are beginning to perceive, that in spite of political or religious prejudices, no matter how stimulated, the truthful experience of life will in the event create nothing but good-will and confidence between the countries.

Other causes, however, led to this; – causes which in every state of society exercise a quick and powerful influence over the minds of men: – I allude to literature.

When the Irishman was made to stand forth as the butt of ridicule to his neighbours, the first that undertook his vindication was Maria Edgeworth. During her day, the works of no writer made a more forcible impression upon the circles of fashionable life in England, if we except the touching and inimitable Melodies of my countryman, Thomas Moore.[3] After a lapse of some years, these two were followed by many others, who stood forth as lofty and powerful exponents of the national heart and intellect. Who can forget the melancholy but indignant reclamations of John Banim, – the dark and touching power of Gerald Griffin,[4] – or the unrivalled wit and irresistible drollery of Samuel Lover? Nor can I omit remarking, that amidst the array of great talents to which I allude, the genius of our female writers bore off, by the free award of public opinion, some of the brightest wreaths of Irish literature. It would be difficult indeed, in any country, to name three women who have done more in setting right the character of Ireland and her people, whilst exhibiting at the same time the manifestations of high genius, than Miss Edgeworth, Lady Morgan,

Notes

[3] Moore, *Irish Melodies*.

[4] Gerald Griffin (1803–40).

and Mrs. Hall.[5] About the female creations of the last-named lady, especially, there is a touching charm, blending the graceful and the pensive, which reminds us of a very general but peculiar style of Irish beauty, where the lineaments of the face combine at once both the melancholy and the mirthful in such a manner, that their harmony constitutes the unchangeable but ever-varying tenderness of the expression.

That national works like these, at once so healthful and so true, produced by those who knew the country, and exhibiting Irishmen not as the blundering buffoons of the English stage, but as men capable of thinking clearly and feeling deeply – that such works, I say, should enable a generous people, as the English undoubtedly are, to divest themselves of the prejudices which they had so long entertained against us, is both natural and gratifying. Those who achieved this great object, or aided in achieving it, have unquestionably rendered services of a most important nature to both the countries, as well as to literature in general.

Yet, whilst the highly gifted individuals whom I have named succeeded in making their countrymen respected, there was one circumstance which, notwithstanding every exhibition of their genius and love of country, still remained as a reproach against our character as a nation. For nearly a century we were completely at the mercy of our British neighbours, who probably amused themselves at our expense with the greater licence, and a more assured sense of impunity, inasmuch as they knew that we were utterly destitute of a national literature. Unfortunately the fact could not be disputed. For the last half century, to come down as far as we can, Ireland, to use a plain metaphor, instead of producing her native intellect for home consumption, was forced to subsist upon the scanty supplies which could be procured from the sister kingdom. This was a reproach which added great strength to the general prejudice against us.

A nation may produce one man or ten men of eminence, but if they cannot succeed in impressing their mind upon the spirit and intellect of their own country, so as to create *in her* a taste for literature or science, no matter how highly they may be appreciated by strangers, they have not reached the exalted purposes of genius. To make this more plain I shall extend the metaphor a little farther. During some of the years of Irish famine, such were the unhappy circumstances of the country, that she was exporting provisions of every description in the most prodigal abundance, which the generosity of England was sending back again for our support. So was it with literature. Our men and women of genius uniformly carried their talents to the English market, whilst we laboured at home under all the dark privations of a literary famine.

In truth until within the last ten or twelve years an Irish author never thought of publishing in his own country, and the consequence was that our literary men followed the example of our great landlords; they became absentees, and drained the country of its intellectual wealth precisely as the others exhausted it of its rents.

Thus did Ireland stand in the singular anomaly of adding some of her most distinguished names to the literature of Great Britain, whilst she herself remained incapable of presenting anything to the world beyond a school-book or a pamphlet; and even of the latter it is well known that if the subject of it were considered important, and its author a man of any talent or station in society, it was certain to be published in London.

Precisely in this state was the country when the two first volumes of the "Traits and Stories of the Irish Peasantry" were given to the public by the house of Messrs.

Notes ──────────────────────────────────────

[5] Mrs. S. C. Hall (Anna Maria Fielding, 1800–81).

Curry and Co., of Sackville-street. Before they appeared, their author, in consequence of their originating from an Irish press, entertained no expectation that they would be read, or excite any interest whatever in either England or Scotland. He was not, however, without a strong confidence that notwithstanding the wild and uncleared state of his own country at the time, so far as native literature was concerned, his two little pioneers would work their way with at least moderate success. He felt conscious that every thing depicted in them was true, and that by those who were acquainted with the manners, and language, and feelings of the people, they would sooner or later be recognised as faithful delineations of Irish life. In this confidence the event justified him; for not only were his volumes stamped with an immediate popularity at home, where they could be best appreciated, but awarded a very gratifying position in the literature of the day by the unanimous and not less generous verdict of the English and Scotch critics.

Thus it was that the publication of two unpretending volumes, written by a peasant's son, established an important and gratifying fact – that our native country, if without a literature at the time, was at least capable of appreciating, and willing to foster the humble exertions of such as endeavoured to create one. Nor was this all; for so far as resident authors were concerned, it was now clearly established that an Irish writer could be successful at home without the necessity of appearing under the name and sanction of the great London or Edinburgh booksellers.

The rapid sale and success of the first series encouraged the author to bring out a second, which he did, but with a different bookseller. The spirit of publishing was now beginning to extend, and the talent of the country to put itself in motion. The popularity of the second effort surpassed that of the first, and the author had the gratification of knowing that the generosity of public feeling and opinion accorded him a still higher position than before, as did the critics of the day, without a dissentient voice. Still, as in the case of his first effort, he saw with honest pride that his own country and his countrymen placed the highest value upon his works, because they best understood them.

About this time the literary taste of the metropolis began to feel the first symptoms of life. As yet, however, they were very faint. Two or three periodicals were attempted, and though of very considerable merit, and conducted by able men, none of them, I believe, reached a year's growth. The "Dublin Literary Gazette," the "National Magazine," the "Dublin Monthly Magazine," and the "Dublin University Review," all perished in their infancy – not, however, because they were unworthy of success, but because Ireland was not then what she is now fast becoming, a reading, and consequently a thinking, country. To every one of these the author contributed, and he has the satisfaction of being able to say that there has been no publication projected purely for the advancement of literature in his own country, to which he has not given the aid of his pen, such as it was, and this whether he received remuneration or not. Indeed, the consciousness that the success of his works had been the humble means of inciting others to similar exertion in their own country, and of thus giving the first impulse to our literature, is one which has on his part created an enthusiastic interest in it which will only die with him.

Notwithstanding the failure of the Periodicals just mentioned, it was clear that the intellect of the country was beginning to feel its strength, and put forth its power. A national spirit that rose above the narrow distinctions of creed and party began to form itself, and in the first impulses of its early enthusiasm a periodical was established, which it is only necessary to name – the "Dublin University Magazine" – a work unsurpassed by any magazine of the day; and which, moreover, without ever departing from its principles, has been as a bond of union for literary men of every class, who have from time to time enriched its pages by their contributions. It has been, and is, a neutral spot in a country where party feeling runs so high, on which the Roman Catholic Priest and the Protestant parson, the Whig, the Tory, and the Radical, divested of their respective prejudices, can meet in an amicable spirit. I mention these things with great satisfaction, for it is surely a gratification to know that literature, in a country which has been so much distracted as Ireland, is progressing in a spirit of noble candour and generosity, which is ere long likely to produce a most salutary effect among the educated classes of all parties, and consequently among those whom they influence. The number, ability, and importance of the works which have issued from the Dublin press within the last eight or ten years, if they could be enumerated here, would exhibit the rapid progress of the national mind, and satisfy the reader that Ireland in a few years will be able to sustain a native literature as lofty and generous, and beneficial to herself, as any other country in the world can boast of . . .

Of those whose physical state has been and is so deplorably wretched, it may not be supposed that the tone of morals can be either high or pure; and yet if we consider the circumstances in which he has been for such a lengthened period placed, it is undeniable that the Irishman is a remarkably moral man. Let us suppose, for instance, that in England and Scotland the great body of the people had for a couple or three centuries never received an adequate or proper education: in that case, let us ask, what the moral aspect of society in either country would be to-day? But this is not merely the thing to be considered. The Irishman was not only *not* educated, but actually punished for attempting to acquire knowledge in the first place, and in the second, punished also for the ignorance created by its absence. In other words, the penal laws rendered education criminal, and then caused the unhappy people to suffer for the crimes which proper knowledge would have prevented them from committing. It was just like depriving a man of his sight, and afterwards causing him to be punished for stumbling. It is beyond all question, that from the time of the wars of Elizabeth and the introduction of the Reformation, until very recently, there was no fixed system of wholesome education in the country. The people, possessed of strong political and religious prejudices, were left in a state of physical destitution and moral ignorance, such as were calculated to produce ten times the amount of crime which was committed. Is it any wonder, then, that in such a condition, social errors and dangerous theories should be generated, and that neglect, and poverty, and ignorance combined should give to the country a character for turbulence and outrage? The same causes will produce the same effects in any country, and were it not that the standard of personal and domestic comfort was so low in Ireland, there is no doubt that the historian would have a much darker catalogue of crime to record than he has. The Irishman, in fact, was mute and patient under circumstances which would have driven the better-fed and more comfortable Englishman into open outrage and contempt of all authority. God forbid that I for a moment should become the apologist of crime, much less the crimes of my countrymen! but it is beyond all question that the principles upon which the country was governed have been such as to leave down to the present day many of their evil consequences behind them. The penal code, to be sure, is now abolished, but so are not many of its political effects among the people.[6] Its

---

Notes

[6] Carleton refers here to the Penal Statutes which disadvantaged Catholics economically, politically, and educationally. Hedge schools proliferated to provide Catholic children with an education at a time when formal schools would pressure children to convert, if not require conversion, to the Anglican faith.

consequences have not yet departed from the country, nor has the hereditary hatred of the laws, which unconsciously descended from father to son, ceased to regulate their conduct and opinions. Thousands of them are ignorant that ever such a thing as a penal code existed; yet the feeling against law survives, although the source from which it has been transmitted may be forgotten. This will easily account for much of the political violence and crime which moments of great excitement produce among us, nor need we feel surprised that this state of things should be continued, to the manifest injury of the people themselves, by the baneful effects of agitation.

The period, therefore, for putting the character of our country fairly upon its trial has not yet arrived; although we are willing to take the Irishman as we find him; nor would we shrink even at the present moment from comparing him with any of his neighbours. His political sins and their consequences were left him as an heir-loom, and result from a state of things which he himself did not occasion. Setting these aside, where is the man to be found in any country who has carried with him through all his privations and penalties so many of the best virtues of our nature? In other countries the man who commits a great crime is always a great criminal, and the whole heart is hardened and debased, but it is not so in Ireland. The agrarian and political outrage is often perpetrated by men who possess the best virtues of humanity, and whose hearts as individuals actually abhor the crime. The moral standard here is no doubt dreadfully erroneous, and until a correct and Christian one, emanating from a better system of education, shall be substituted for it, it will, with a people who so think and feel, be impossible utterly to prevent the occurrence of these great evils. We must wait for thirty or forty years, that is, until the rising or perhaps the subsequent generation shall be educated out of these wild and destructive prejudices, before we can fully estimate the degree of excellence to which our national character may arrive. In my own youth, and I am now only forty-four years, I do not remember a single school under the immediate superintendence of either priest or parson, and that in a parish the extent of which is, I dare say, ten miles by eight. The instruction of the children was altogether a matter in which no clergy of any creed took an interest. This was left altogether to hedge schoolmasters, a class of men who, with few exceptions, bestowed such an education upon the people as is sufficient almost, in the absence of all other causes, to account for much of the agrarian violence and erroneous principles which regulate their movements and feelings on that and similar subjects. For further information on this matter the reader is referred to the "Hedge School."[7]

With respect to these darker shades of the Irish character, I feel that, consistently with that love of truth and impartiality which has guided, and I trust ever shall guide, my pen, I could not pass them over without further notice. I know that it is a very questionable defence to say that some, if not principally all, of their crimes originate in agrarian or political vengeance. Indeed, I believe that, so far from this circumstance being looked upon as a defence, it ought to be considered as an aggravation of the guilt; inasmuch as it is, beyond all doubt, at least a far more manly thing to inflict an injury upon an enemy face to face, and under the influence of immediate resentment, than to crouch like a cowardly assassin behind a hedge and coolly murder him without one moment's preparation, or any means whatsoever of defence. This is a description of crime which no man with one generous drop of blood in his veins can think of without shame and indignation. Unhappily, however, for the security of human life, every crime of the kind results more from the dark

Notes ——

[7] A tale in *Traits*.

tyranny of these secret confederacies, by which the lower classes are organised, than from any natural appetite for shedding blood. Individually, the Irish loathe murder as much as any people in the world; but in the circumstances before us, it often happens that the Irishman is not a free agent, – very far from it: on the contrary, he is frequently made the instrument of a system, to which he must become either an obedient slave or a victim.

Even here, however, although nothing can or ought to be said, to palliate the cowardly and unmanly crime of assassination, yet something can certainly be advanced to account for the state of feeling by which, from time to time, and by frequent occurrence, it came to be so habitual among the people, that by familiarity it became stripped of its criminality and horror.

Now it is idle, and it would be dishonest, to deny the fact, that the lower Irish, until a comparatively recent period, were treated with apathy and gross neglect by the only class to whom they could or ought to look up for sympathy or protection. The conferring of the elective franchise upon the forty shilling freeholders, or in other words upon paupers, added to the absence of proper education, or the means of acquiring it, generated, by the fraudulent sub-division of small holdings, by bribery, perjury, and corruption, a state of moral feeling among the poorer classes which could not but be productive of much crime. And yet, notwithstanding this shameful prostitution of their morals and comfort, for the purposes of political ambition or personal aggrandisement, they were in general a peaceable and enduring people; and it was only when some act of unjustifiable severity, or oppression in the person of a middleman, agent, or hardhearted landlord, drove them houseless upon the world, that they fell back upon the darker crimes of which I am speaking. But what, I ask, could be expected from such a state of things? And who generated it? It is not, indeed, to be wondered at that a set of men, who so completely neglected their duties as the old landlords of Ireland did, should have the very weapons turned against themselves which their own moral profligacy first put into the hands of those whom they corrupted. Up to this day the peasantry are charged with indiffer-ence to the obligation of an oath, and in those who still have anything to do in elections, I fear with too much truth. But then let us inquire who first trained and familiarised them to it? Why, the old landlords of Ireland; and now their descen-dants, and such of themselves as survive, may behold, in the crimes which disgrace the country, the disastrous effects of a bad system created by their forefathers or themselves.

In the mean time, I have no doubt that by the removal of the causes which produced this deplorable state of things, their disastrous effects will also soon disappear. That the present landlords of Ireland are, with the ordinary number of exceptions, a very different class of men from those who have gone before them, is a fact which will ultimately tell for the peace and prosperity of the country. Let the ignorance of the people, or rather the positive bad knowledge with which, as to a sense of civil duties, their minds are filled, be removed, and replaced with principles of a higher and more Christian tendency. Let the Irish landlords consider the interests of their tenantry as their own, and there is little doubt that with the aids of science, agricultural improvement, and the advantages of superior machinery, the Irish will become a prosperous, contented, and great people.

It is not just to the general character of our people, however, to speak of these crimes as national, for, in fact, they are not so. If Tipperary and some of the adjoining parts of Munster were blotted out of the moral map of the country, we would stand as a nation in a far higher position than that which we occupy in the opinion of our neighbours. This is a distinction which in justice to us ought to be made, for it is surely unfair to charge the whole kingdom with the crimes which disgrace only a single county of it, together with a few adjacent districts – allowing, of course, for some melancholy exceptions in other parts.

Having now discussed, with I think sufficient candour and impartiality, that portion of our national character which appears worst and weakest in the eyes of our neighbours, and attempted to show that pre-existing circumstances originating from an unwise policy had much to do in calling into existence and shaping its evil impulses, I come now to a more agreeable task – the consideration of our social and domestic virtues. And here it is where the Irishman immeasurably outstrips all competitors. His hospitality is not only a habit but a principle; and indeed of such a quick and generous temperament is he, that in ninety cases out of a hundred the feeling precedes the reflection, which in others prompts the virtue. To be a stranger and friendless, or suffering hunger and thirst, is at any time a sufficient passport to his heart and purse; but it is not merely the thing or virtue, but also his manner of doing it, that constitutes the charm which runs through his conduct. There is a natural politeness and sincerity in his manner which no man can mistake; and it is a fact, the truth of which I have felt a thousand times, that he will make you feel the acceptance of the favour or kindness he bestows to be a compliment to himself rather than to you. The delicate ingenuity with which he diminishes the nature or amount of his own kindness, proves that he is no common man either in heart or intellect; and when all fails he will lie like Lucifer himself, and absolutely seduce you into an acceptance of his hospitality or assistance. I speak now exclusively of the peasantry. Certainly in domestic life there is no man so exquisitely affectionate and humanized as the Irishman. The national imagination is active and the national heart warm, and it follows very naturally that he should be, and is, tender and strong in all his domestic relations. Unlike the people of other nations, his grief is loud but lasting, vehement but deep; and whilst its shadow has been chequered by the laughter and mirth of a cheerful disposition, still in the moments of seclusion, at his bedside prayer, or over the grave of those he loved, it will put itself forth after half a life with a vivid power of recollection which is sometimes almost beyond belief.

The Irish, however, are naturally a refined people; but by this I mean the refinement which appreciates and cherishes whatever there is in nature, as manifested through the influence of the softer arts of music and poetry. The effect of music upon the Irish heart I ought to know well, and no man need tell me that a barbarous or cruel people ever possessed national music that was beautiful and pathetic. The music of any nation is the manifestation of its general feeling, and not that which creates it; although there is no doubt but the one when formed perpetuates and reproduces the other. It is no wonder, then, that the domestic feelings of the Irish should be so singularly affectionate and strong, when we consider that they have been, in spite of every obstruction, kept under the softening influence of music and poetry. This music and poetry, too, essentially their own – and whether streaming of a summer evening along their pastoral fields, echoing through their still glens, or poured forth at the winter hearth, still, by its soft and melancholy spirit, stirring up a thousand tender associations that must necessarily touch and improve the heart. And it is for this reason that that heart becomes so remarkably eloquent, if not poetical, when moved by sorrow. Many a time I have seen a Keener commence her wail over the corpse of a near relative, and by degrees she has risen from the simple wail or cry to a high but mournful recitative, extemporized, under the excitement of the moment, into sentiments that were highly figurative and impressive. In this she was aided very much by the genius of the language, which possesses the finest and most copious vocabulary in the world for the expression of either sorrow or love.

It has been said that the Irish, notwithstanding a deep susceptibility of sorrow, are a light-hearted people; and this is strictly true. What, however, is the one fact but a natural consequence of the other? No man for instance ever possessed a high order of humour, whose temperament was not naturally melancholy, and no country in the world more clearly establishes that point than Ireland. Here the melancholy and mirth are not simply in a proximate state, but frequently flash together, and again separate so quickly, that the alternation or blending, as the case may be, whilst it is felt by the spectators, yet stands beyond all known rules of philosophy to solve it. Any one at all acquainted with Ireland, knows that in no country is mirth lighter, or sorrow deeper, or the smile and the tear seen more frequently on the face at the same moment. Their mirth, however, is not levity, nor their sorrow gloom; and for this reason none of those dreary and desponding reactions take place, which, as in France especially, so frequently terminate in suicide.

The recreations of the Irish were very varied, and some of them of a highly intellectual cast. These latter, however, have altogether disappeared from the country, or at all events are fast disappearing. The old Harper is now hardly seen; the Senachie, where he exists, is but a dim and faded representative of that very old Chronicler in his palmy days; and the Prophecy-man unfortunately has survived the failure of his best and most cherished predictions. The poor old Prophet's stock in trade is nearly exhausted, and little now remains but the slaughter which is to take place at the mill of Louth, when the mill is to be turned three times with human blood, and the miller to have six fingers and two thumbs on each hand, as a collateral prognostication of that bloody event.

The amusement derived from these persons was undoubtedly of a very imaginative character, and gives sufficient proof, that had the national intellect been duly cultivated, it is difficult to say in what position as a literary country Ireland might have stood at this day. At present the national recreations, though still sufficiently varied and numerous, are neither so strongly marked nor diversified as formerly. Fun, or the love of it, to be sure, is an essential principle in the Irish character; and nothing that can happen, no matter how solemn or how sorrowful it may be, is allowed to proceed without it. In Ireland the house of death is sure to be the merriest one in the neighbourhood; but here the mirth is kindly and considerately introduced, from motives of sympathy – in other words, for the alleviation of the mourners' sorrow. The same thing may be said of its association with religion. Whoever has witnessed a Station in Ireland made at some blessed lake or holy well, will understand this. At such places it is quite usual to see young men and women devoutly circumambulating the well or lake on their bare knees with all the marks of penitence and contrition strongly impressed upon their faces; whilst again, after an hour or two, the same individuals may be found in a tent dancing with ecstatic vehemence to the music of the bagpipe or fiddle.

All these things, however, will be found, I trust I may say faithfully, depicted in the following volumes – together with many other important features of our general character; which I would dwell on here, were it not that they are detailed very fully in other parts of my works, and I do not wish to deprive them of the force of novelty when they occur, nor to appear heavy by repetition.

In conclusion, I have endeavoured, with what success has been already determined by the voice of my own country, to give a panorama of Irish life among the people – comprising at one view all the strong points of their general character – their loves, sorrows, superstitions, piety, amusements, crimes and virtues; and in doing this, I can say with solemn truth that I painted them honestly, and without reference to the existence of any particular creed or party.

DUBLIN *August* 1842

Jeremiah John Callanan (1795–1829)

Jeremiah John Callanan was born in Co. Cork. He began training for the priesthood at St. Patrick's College at Maynooth, but instead of taking orders moved on to Trinity College Dublin, intending to study law. After a brief stint in the army and then as a private tutor, he returned to Cork and took up a position as a teacher in 1823. There, he joined a group of literati interested in the Irish past who called themselves the Anchorites – among them, Thomas Crofton Croker and William Maginn. His employment continued to be sporadic and focused largely on teaching, and he left Ireland to accompany a family as tutor to Lisbon, though he continued on a project to publish his collected poems in Ireland. He died in Lisbon in 1829, within weeks of his poems' publication in *The Recluse of Inchidony*.

Like his close contemporary, William Carleton, Callanan often writes of rural life. His earliest biographer in "Memoir of the Late Mr. Callanan" praises Callanan as a poet who ranks with Thomas Moore for poetic merits and links him with other translators such as Brooke and Morgan. The influence of Moore is traceable in Callanan's work, particularly in lyrics such as "Written to a Young Lady" and others dealing with the new figure of the emigrant as well as the more traditional one of the outlaw. He also incorporates details of daily life beyond the usual poetic subjects of love and religion, including an energetic view of hurling in "The Convict of Clonmel," prefaced by a comparison of hurling with golf and cricket that attends to the poem's first publication in a Scottish periodical. While he is best remembered as an Irish-language poet from rural Ireland, as recent scholars have noted, the Scottish publishing forum of *Blackwood's* exerted some pressure on Callanan to deal with subjects likely to appeal to British readers.

Further reading

Schirmer, Gregory A., *Out of What Began: A History of Irish Poetry in English*. Ithaca, NY: Cornell University Press, 1998.
— ed., *The Irish Poems of J. J. Callanan*. Gerrards Cross: Colin Smythe, 2005.
Welch, Robert, *A History of Irish Verse Translation from the Irish, 1789–1897*. Gerrards Cross: Colin Smythe, 1988.

The Convict of Clonmel: Is dubac é mo cás[1]

(trans. Callanan, *Blackwood's Edinburgh Magazine* 1823)

Who the hero of this song is, I know not; but convicts, from obvious reasons, have been peculiar objects of sympathy in Ireland.

Hurling, which is mentioned in one of the verses, is the principal national diversion, and is played with intense zeal, by parish against parish, barony against barony, county against county, or even province against province. It is played, not only by the peasant, but by the patrician students of the university, where it is an established pastime. Twiss, the most sweeping calumniator of Ireland, calls it, if I mistake not, the cricket of barbarians: but though fully prepared to pay every tribute to the elegance of the English game, I own that I think the Irish sport fully as civilized, and much better calculated for the display of vigour and activity. Perhaps I shall offend the Scottish

Notes —————————————————————

THE CONVICT OF CLONMEL
[1] The first line of the poem is a liberal translation of this Irish phrase.

nationality if I prefer either to golf, which is, I think, but trifling, compared with them. In the room belonging to the Golf Club, on the Links of Leith, there hangs a picture of an old Lord, (Rosslyn?) which I never could look at, without being struck with the disproportion between the gaunt figure of the peer, and the petty instrument in his hand. Strutt, in his Sports and Pastimes, (p. 78,) eulogizes the activity of some Irishmen, who played the game about 25 years before the publication of his work, (1801,) at the back of the British Museum, and deduces it from the Roman harpastum.[2] It was played in Cornwall formerly, he adds, but neither the Romans nor Cornishmen used a bat, or, as we call it in Ireland, a hurly. The description Strutt quotes from old Carew is quite graphic. The late Dr. Gregory, I am told, used to be loud in panegyric on the superiority of this game, when played by the Irish students, over that adopted by his young countrymen, north and south of the Tweed, particularly over golf, which he called "fiddling wi' a pick." But enough of this.

> How hard is my fortune,
>   And vain my repining!
> The strong rope of fate
>   For this young neck is twining.
> My strength is departed;   5
>   My cheek sunk and sallow;
> While I languish in chains,
>   In the gaol of Clonmala.[3]
>
> No boy in the village
>   Was ever yet milder,   10
> I'd play with a child,
>   And my sport would be wilder.
> I'd dance without tiring
>   From morning till even,
> And the goal-ball I'd strike   15
>   To the lightning of heaven.
>
> At my bed-foot decaying
>   My hurlbat is lying,
> Through the boys of the village,
>   My goal-ball is flying.   20
> My horse 'mong the neighbours
>   Neglected my fallow, –
> While I pine in my chains,
>   In the gaol of Clonmala.
>
> Next Sunday the patron[4]   25
>   At home will be keeping,
> And the young active hurlers
>   The field will be sweeping.
> With the dance of fair maidens
>   The evening they'll hallow,   30
> While this heart, once so gay,
>   Shall be cold in Clonmala.

Notes

[2] *Harpastum* was a team sport involving a small ball, a probable forerunner of football (soccer).

[3] Irish of Clonmell (author).

[4] Patron – Irish *Patruin* – a festive gathering of the people on tented ground. (This note was added in *The Recluse of Inchidony*.)

Jeremiah John Callanan

Written to a Young Lady, On entering a Convent

From The Recluse of Inchidony, and Other Poems (1830)

'Tis the rose of the desert,
 So lovely, so wild,
In the lap of the desert
 Its infancy smiled;
In the languish of beauty   5
 It droops o'er the thorn,
And its leaves are all wet
 With the bright tears of morn.

Yet 'tis better thou fair one,
 To dwell all alone,   10
Than recline on a bosom
 Less pure than thine own;
Thy form is too lovely
 To be torn from its stem,
And thy breath is too sweet   15
 For the children of men.

Bloom on thus in secret,
 Sweet child of the waste,
Where no lips of profaner,
 Thy fragrance shall taste;   20
Bloom on where no footsteps
 Unhallowed hath trod,
And give all thy blushes
 And sweets to thy God.

Lines, On the Death of an amiable and highly talented Young Man, who fell a victim to fever in the West Indies

From The Recluse of Inchidony, and Other Poems (1830)

All rack'd on his feverish bed he lay,
 And none but the stranger were near him;
No friend to console, in his last sad day;
 No look of affection to cheer him.

Frequent and deep were the groans he drew,   5
 On that couch of torture turning;
And often his hot, wild hand he threw
 O'er his brows, still wilder burning.

But, Oh! what anguish his bosom tore,
 How throbbed each strong pulse of emotion,   10
When he thought of the friends he should never see more,
 In his own green Isle of the Ocean.

When he thought of the distant maid of his heart, –
    Oh, must they thus darkly sever; –
No last farewell, ere his spirit depart; –   15
    Must he leave her unseen, and for ever!

One sigh for that maid his fond heart heaved,
    One pray'r for her weal he breathed;
And his eyes to that land for whose woes he had grieved
    Once looked, – and for ever were sheathed.   20

On a cliff that by footstep is seldom prest,
    Far sea-ward his dark head rearing,
A rude stone marks the place of his rest; –
    "Here lies a poor exile of Erin."

Yet think not, dear Youth, tho' far, far away   25
    From thy own native Isle thou art sleeping,
That no heart for thy slumber is aching to-day,
    That no eye for thy mem'ry is weeping.

Oh yes! – when the hearts that have wailed thy young blight,
    Some joy from forgetfulness borrow,   30
The thought of thy doom will come over their light,
    And shade them more deeply with sorrow.

And the maid who so long held her home in thy breast,
    As she strains her wet eye o'er the billow,
Will vainly embrace, as it comes from the west,   35
    Every breeze that has swept o'er thy pillow.

Hussa Tha Measg na Realtán More [1]

From The Recluse of Inchidony, and Other Poems (1830)

My love, my still unchanging love,
As fond, as true, as hope above;
Tho' many a year of pain passed by
Since last I heard thy farewell sigh,
This faithful heart doth still adore   5
Hussa tha measg na realtán more.

What once we hoped might then have been,
But fortune darkly frown'd between:
And tho' far distant is the ray
That lights me on my weary way,   10
I love, and shall 'till life is o'er,
Hussa tha measg na realtán more.

Tho' many a light of beauty shone
Along my path, and lured me on,

Notes ──────────────────────────

HUSSA THA MEASG NA REALTÁN MORE
[1] Thou who art amongst the greater Planets (author).

I better lov'd thy dark bright eye,   15
Thy witching smile, thy speaking sigh;
Shine on, – this heart shall still adore
Hussa tha measg na realtán more.

The Outlaw of Loch Lene (trans. Callanan)

From **The Recluse of Inchidony, and Other Poems** (1830)

O many a day have I made good ale in the glen,
That came not of stream, or malt; – like the brewing of men.
My bed was the ground; my roof, the greenwood above,
And the wealth that I sought one far kind glance from my love.

Alas! on that night when the horses I drove from the field,   5
That I was not near from terror my angel to shield.
She stretched forth her arms, – her mantle she flung to the wind,
And swam o'er Loch Lene, her outlawed lover to find.

O would that a freezing sleet-wing'd tempest did sweep,
And I and my love were alone, far off on the deep;   10
I'd ask not a ship, or a bark, or pinnace, to save, –
With her hand round my waist, I'd fear not the wind or the wave.

'Tis down by the lake where the wild tree fringes its sides,
The maid of my heart, my fair one of Heaven resides; –
I think as at eve she wanders its mazes along,   15
The birds go to sleep by the sweet wild twist of her song.

John Banim (1798–1842) and Michael Banim (1796–1874)

The brothers John and Michael Banim were born in Kilkenny and educated there, first at a local Catholic school. John was sent for a while to St. John's College in Kilkenny, and later to develop his talents as a painter in Dublin. Michael studied for a while to be a lawyer, but did not complete his studies for financial reasons. In his early twenties, John became a journalist and moved first to Dublin and then to London, where he lived for most of the 1820s, working as a playwright and a journalist. He returned to Ireland, seriously ill, in 1835 and later died in Kilkenny. Michael remained in Ireland, apart from occasional visits to his brother in England, taking over the family business.

The brothers, despite their separation, began to write collaboratively and published under the pseudonym "The O'Hara Family." The first series of *The Tales of the O'Hara Family* was published in 1825, and the second in 1827. They also published a number of novels, including Michael's *The Croppy, a Tale of 1798* (1828) and John's *The Anglo-Irish of the Nineteenth Century* (1828). Writing generally nationalist work with clear support for rural Catholics, but still appealing to their largely English-speaking audiences in Britain and Ireland, the Banims walked a fine line and bear comparison to Carleton, their contemporary from the north.

Some of their ballads endured throughout the nineteenth century, with "The Irish Peasant to His Priest" (or "Soggarth Aroon") in particular being praised by Katharine Tynan. "The Church-Yard Watch" is from one of their more successful volumes, *The Bit O' Writin' and Other Tales* (1838), and is part of the resurgence of the Irish gothic in the 1830s. Appearing soon after Mangan published his first translation of G. A. Bürger's "Leonore" (*Dublin University Magazine*, 1834), it repeats elements of Bürger's poem while critiquing serious social ills in a conventional English village.

Further reading

Ferris, Ina, *The Romantic National Tale and the Question of Ireland.* Cambridge: Cambridge University Press, 2002.

Gilligan, David, "Natural Indignation in the Native Voice: The Fiction of the Banim Brothers," in *Anglo-Irish and Irish Literature: Aspects of Language and Culture*, 2: 77–91. Uppsala: Uppsala University, 1988.

Hawthorne, Mark D., *John and Michael Banim (The "O'Hara Brothers"): A Study in the Early Development of the Anglo-Irish Novel.* Salzburg, Austria: Institut für Englische Sprache und Literatur, 1975.

Advertisement

From Chaunt of the Cholera, Songs for Ireland (1831)

Some of the following Songs were written before the passing of a great political measure;[1] perhaps those are indicated by the dates affixed to them. They were intended for publication previous to that event, but suppressed in consequence of its approach. Now, they can do no harm, and may help to remind us of feelings that have been, and also to call up curious speculation upon things which *might have* happened, growing out of those feelings, only for something else which *has* happened, in season.

The second portion of these Songs is a first attempt to throw into verse the peculiar phraseology, and occasionally the words, of the Irish peasantry, when they try to speak English.[2]

Should any of them ever reach the mountain hamlets of Ireland, and be caught up by the peasant in whose character they are written, it is hoped that no sentiment they contain can tend to make him worse than he is, in any respect. Nay, let the modesty of authorship permit the admission, that a contrary hope is entertained. Certainly, good has been intended. The Irish peasant has, at present, no songs which he can sing with much improvement, or even pleasure, to himself or others, and –

But the sentence may not be finished, lest it might provoke (and justly) a charge of something like anticipation, limited as is our subject.

Notes

ADVERTISEMENT

[1] Catholic Emancipation (1829).

[2] The Banims formally divided the *Songs* into two sections: "Songs for Ireland" (including "The Irish Mother to Her Child" and "Song," both dated 1828 in the text) and "Irish Peasants' Songs" (including "The Irish Peasant to His Priest," undated).

John and Michael Banim

The Irish Mother to Her Child

From **Chaunt of the Cholera, Songs for Ireland** (1831)

AIR – *The Song of Sorrow*

I

Now welcome, welcome, baby-boy, unto a mother's fears,
The pleasure of her sufferings, the rainbow of her tears,
The object of your father's hope, in all he hopes to do,
A future man of his own land, to live him o'er anew!

II

How fondly on thy little brow a mother's eye would trace,　　　　5
And in thy little limbs, and in each feature of thy face,
His beauty, worth, and manliness, and every thing that's his,
Except, my boy, the answering mark of where the fetter is!

III

Oh! many a weary hundred years his sires that fetter wore,
And he has worn it since the day that him his mother bore;　　　　10
And now, my son, it waits on you, the moment you are born,
The old hereditary badge of suffering and scorn!

IV

Alas, my boy so beautiful! – alas, my love so brave!
And must your gallant Irish limbs still drag it to the grave!
And you, my son, yet have a son, fore-doom'd a slave to be,　　　　15
Whose mother still must weep o'er him the tears I weep o'er thee!

Song

From **Chaunt of the Cholera, Songs for Ireland** (1831)

AIR – *The Moreen; or, The Minstrel Boy*

I

Yes! discord's hand to the last it was
　In every field of our story,
Which did our country's fortunes cross,
　And tear down all her glory –
And this we saw, and this we felt,　　　　5
　Yet still the warning slighted,
Till a clinging curse was to us dealt –
　The curse of the disunited!

II

But, warn'd at last, in our strength we stand
　Crying out, with one deep chorus,　　　　10

For requital to this outraged land –
    Land of our love, that bore us!
Millions shout, as a single man –
    "Now, now, thou shalt be righted,
For now thy sons thy future span,   15
    Because they are United!"

III

Ay! by the fate we shall weave for her,
    To atone for the fate we wove her!
By those, her name who hate and slur –
    By ourselves, who deeply love her!   20
By manhood's worth! by the sacred flame
    On her hearths and her altars lighted –
By her present shame – by her ancient fame –
    We are – we *are* United!

The Irish Peasant to His Priest[1]

From Chaunt of the Cholera, Songs for Ireland (1831)

Air – *Aileen aroon; or, Erin! the tear*

I

Am I the slave they say,
    Soggarth aroon?[2]
Since you did show the way,
    Soggarth aroon,
Their slave no more to be,   5
While they would work with me
Ould Ireland's slavery,
    Soggarth aroon?

II

Why not her poorest man,
    Soggarth aroon,   10
Try and do all he can,
    Soggarth aroon,
Her commands to fulfil
Of his own heart and will,
Side by side with you still,   15
    Soggarth aroon?

Notes

THE IRISH PEASANT TO HIS PRIEST   [2] Priest, dear (authors).
[1] This poem later became known as "Soggarth Aroon."

III

Loyal and brave to you,
   Soggarth aroon,
Yet be no slave to you,
   Soggarth aroon, –   20
Nor, out of fear to you,
Stand up so near to you –
Och! out of fear to you!
   Soggarth aroon!

IV

Who, in the winter's night,   25
   Soggarth aroon,
When the could blast did bite,
   Soggarth aroon,
Came to my cabin-dour,
And, on my earthen-flure,   30
Knelt by me, sick and poor,
   Soggarth aroon?

V

Who, on the marriage-day,
   Soggarth aroon,
Made the poor cabin gay,   35
   Soggarth aroon –
And did both laugh and sing,
Making our hearts to ring,
At the poor christening,
   Soggarth aroon?   40

VI

Who, as friend only met,
   Soggarth aroon,
Never did flout me yet,
   Soggarth aroon?
And when my hearth was dim,   45
Gave, while his eye did brim,
What I should give to him,
   Soggarth aroon?

VII

Och! you, and only you,
   Soggarth aroon! –   50
And for this I was true to you,
   Soggarth aroon;
In love they'll never shake,
When for ould Ireland's sake,
We a true part did take,   55
   Soggarth aroon!

The Church-Yard Watch

e Bit O' Writin' and Other Tales (1838)

the living should prey on them! – 'Tis a strange alliance – of the living with DEATH – that His kingdom and sovereignty may remain untrenched upon. In different parts of England, we have seen watch-houses, almost entirely composed of glass, built in lonesome church-yards, of which generally the parish sexton, and perhaps his dog (ill-fated among men and dogs!) are the appointed nightly tenants; with liberty, ceded or taken, to leave their dull lamp in the watch-box, and roam, here and there, at their pleasure, among the graves, until day light. What stern necessities man forces upon man! There can scarce be a more comfortless lot, or, making allowance for the almost in-born shudderings of the human heart, a more appalling one, than that of the poor grave scooper or bell-puller who is thus doomed to spend his night, summer and winter. Habit, indeed, may eventually blunt the first keenness of his aversion, if not terror: he may serve a due apprenticeship to horrors, and learn his trade. After a thousand secret and unowned struggles to seem brave and indifferent, he may at last grow callously courageous. His flesh may cease to creep as he strides on, in his accustomed round, over the abodes of the silent and mouldering, and hears his own dull footstep echoed through the frequent dreary hollowness beneath. But what has he gained, now, beyond the facility of earning his wretched crust for himself and his crying infants! – We have seen and spoken with such an unhappy being, who seemed to have lost, in the struggle which conquered nature's especial antipathy, (nature in a breast and mind like his, at least,) most of the other sympathies of his kind. He had a heavy, ox-like expression of face; he would scarce speak to his neighbours (although *we* contrived to make him eloquent) when they passed him at this door, or in the village street; his own children feared or disliked him, and did not smile nor whisper in his presence. We have watched him into the church-yard, at his usual hour, after night-fall; and as he began to stalk about there, the ghastly sentinel of the dead, he appeared to be in closer fellowship with them, than with the fair existence which he scarce more than nominally shared. It was said, indeed, that, upon his initiation, at a tender age and under peculiar circumstances, into his profession of church-yard watchman, temporary delirium prepared him for its regular and steady pursuit ever since; and that, although he showed no symptoms of distinct insanity, when we knew him, the early visitation had left a gloom on his mind, and a thick, nerveless insensibility in his heart, which then, at forty-five, formed his character. In fact, we learned a good deal about him, for every one talked of him – and, as has been hinted, much of that good deal from himself, to say nothing of his wife, in his absence; and if he did not deliberately invent fables of his past trials, for the purpose of gratifying a little spirit of mockery of our undisguised interest, as mad as the maddest bedlamite he must have been upon the occasion alluded to: nay, to recount, with a grave face (as he did) the particulars of the delusions of his time of delirium, did not argue him a very sound-minded man at the moment he gave us his confidence. We are about to tell his story, at length, in our own way, however; that is, we shall try to model into our own language (particularly the raving parts) what his neighbours, his spouse, and his own slow-moving and heavy lips have, from time to time, supplied us with.

He was the only child of an affectionate and gentle-mannered father, who died when he was little more than a boy, leaving him sickly and pining. His mother wept a month, mourned three months more, – and was no longer a widow. Her second husband proved a surly fellow, who married her little fortune, rather than herself, as the means of keeping his quart pot filled, almost from morning to night, at the village Tap, where he played good-fellow and politician to the expressed admiration of all his companions. He had long been the parish sexton, and took up his post, night after night, in the church-yard. Little fear had he of what he might see there; or, he had out-grown his fears; or, if he thought or felt of the matter, the lonely debauch which he was known to make in that strange banquet-place, served to drug him into obliviousness. He deemed his duty – or he said and swore he did – only a tiresome and slavish one, and hated it just as he hated daily labour. And – as he declared and harangued at the Tap – he had long ago forsworn it, only that it paid him well; but, now that his marriage made his circumstances easier, he was determined to drink alone in the church-yard no longer: and he fed an idle, useless lad at home, who with his dog – as idle as he – roamed and loitered about, here and there, and had never yet done a single thing to earn their bread. But it was full time that both were taught the blessings of industry; and he would teach them; – and – now that he thought of it – why should not Will take his place in the watchbox, and so keep the shillings in the family? His friends praised his views, one and all, and he grew thrice resolved.

Returned the next morning from his nocturnal charge, he reeled to bed in solemn, drunken determination. He arose, towards evening, only half reclaimed by sleep to ordinary sense, and set about his work of reformation. He ate his meal in silence, turned from the table to the fire without a word, looked at the blaze, grimly contemplative, then grumbling suddenly at his wife – "And where is that truant now?" he asked: "down by the marshes with his cur, I suppose; or gone a-nutting, or lying stretched in the sun, the two idlers together; what! – and must I work and work, and strive and strive – I, I, for ever – and will he never lend me a hand? – go where he likes, do what he likes, and laugh and fatten on my labour?"

"Master Hunks," said the wife, "Will is sickly, and won't fatten on either your labour or mine – not to talk of his own; – you know 'tis a puny lad, and wants some favour yet a-while; with God's help, and ours, he may be stronger soon."

Will and his dog here came in. From what followed, this evening, it will be seen, that the ill-fated lad promised, in early youth, to be of an open, kindly, intelligent character, very different indeed from that in which we found him husked up, at five-and-forty.

He saluted his step-father, and sat down quietly near the fire. His poor dumb companion – friend of his boyhood, and his father's gift – coiled himself up before the blaze, and prepared to surrender his senses to happy sleep, interspersed with dreams of all the sports he had enjoyed with his master that day. Hunks, his eye glancing from one object of dislike to the other, kicked the harmless brute, who jumped up, yelping in pain and bitter lamentation, and ran for shelter under Will's chair. Will's pale cheek broke out into colour, his weak eye sparkled, his feeble voice arose shrilly, and he asked – "Why is my poor dog beaten?"

"The lazy cur!" said Hunks – "he was in my way, and only got paid for his idleness."

" 'Twas ill done," resumed Will – "he was my father's dog, and my father gave him to me; and if my father were alive and well, he would not hurt him, nor see him hurt!" – Tears interrupted his sudden fit of spirit.

"Cur, as much as he is!" retorted Hunks – "do you put upon me, here at my own fireside? *You* are the idler – you – and he only learns of you – and I hadn't ought to have served him out, and you so near me."

"It has been God's will," said the boy, "to keep my strength from me."

"Be silent and hear me!" roared Hunks – "this is your life, I say – playing truant for ever – and what is mine, and your own good mother's here?"

"Master Hunks," pleaded the wife – "God knows I don't grudge nothing I can do for my poor Will's sake."

"And you – not a word from you either, Missis!" grunted Hunks – "I am put upon by one and t'other of you – ye sleep in comfort every night, and leave me to go a-watching, out o' doors, there, in all weathers; but stop a bit, my man, it shan't be this way much longer; I'll have my natural rest in my bed, some time or other, and soon; and you must earn it for me."

"How, father? how can I earn it?" asked Will – "I would if I could – but how? I hav'n't learnt no trade, and you know as well as any one knows it, I am not able to work in the fields or on the roads, or get my living any one way."

"Then you can sit still and watch – that's light work," muttered Hunks.

"Watch!" cried mother and son together – "watch what? and where? or whom?"

"The dead folk in the church-yard."

"Heaven defend me from it!" cried poor Will, clasping his hands and falling back in his chair.

"Ay, and this very night," continued the despot – "this very night you shall mount guard in my place, and I shall have my lawful sleep, that the whole parish cries shame on me for not having months ago."

"Master Hunks, 'twill kill the boy!" cried the mother.

"Missis – don't you go for to cross me so often!" – remonstrated her husband, with a fixed look, which, short as they had been one flesh, she had reason to understand and shrink at. – "Come, my man, stir yourself; 'tis time you were at the gate; the church clock has struck; *they will expect us*" – he interrupted himself in a great rage, and with a great oath – "but here I keep talking and the cur never minds a word I say! – Come along!"

"Don't lay hands on him!" screamed the mother as he strode towards the boy – "what I have often told you, has come to pass, Master Hunks – you have killed him!"

Hunks scoffed at the notion, although, indeed, Will's hands had fallen helplessly at his side, and his chin rested on his breast, while his eyes were closed, and his lips apart. But he had only become insensible from sheer terror acting on a weak frame. Sighs and groans soon gave notice of returning animation. His mother then earnestly besought their tyrant to go on his night's duty, and, at least till the following night, leave her son to her care. Half in fear of having to answer for a murder, incredulously as he pretended to speak, Hunks turned out of the house, growling and threatening.

"Is he gone?" asked Will, when he regained his senses – "gone not to come back?" – and having heard his mother's gentle assurances, he let his head fall on her shoulder, weeping, while he continued: –

"Mother, mother, it would destroy the little life I have! I could not bear it for an hour! The dread I am in of it was born with me! When I was a child of four years, I had dreams of it, and I remember them to this day; they used to come in such crowds round my cradle! As I grew up, you saw and you know my weakness. I could never sit still in the dark, nor even in the daylight out of doors in lonesome places. Now in my youth – a lad – almost a man – I am ashamed to speak of my inward troubles. Mother, you do not know me – I do not know myself! I walk out sometimes down by the river, and, listening to the noise of the water over the rocks, where it is shallow, and to the rustling of the trees as they nod in the twilight, voices and shrieks come round me – sometimes they break in my ears – and I have turned to see what thing it was that spoke, and thought some grey tree at my side had only just changed and become motionless, and seemed as if, a moment before, it had been something else, and had a tongue, and said the words that frightened me! – Oh, it was but yester evening I ran home from the banks of the river, and felt no heart within me till I had come in here to the fireside, and seen you moving near me!

"You know the lone house all in ruins upon the hill – I fear it, mother, more than my tongue can tell you! I have been taken through it, in my dreams, in terrible company, and here I could describe to you its bleak apartments, one by one – its vaults, pitch dark, and half-filled with stones and rubbish, and choked up with weeds – its winding, creeping staircases, and its flapping windows – I know them all, though my feet never yet crossed its threshold! – Never, mother – though I have gone near it, to enter it, and see if what I had dreamt of it was true – and I went in the first light of the morning; but when close by the old door-way, the rustle of the shrubs and weeds startled me, and I thought – but sure *that* was fancy – that some one called me in by name – and then I turned and raced down the hill, never looking back till I came to the meadow ground where cows and sheep are always grazing, and heard the dogs barking in the town, and voices of the children at play!"

"Will, my king," said his mother, soothingly, "this is all mere childishness at your years. God is above us and around us; and even if evil and strange things are allowed to be on earth, he will shield us from all harm. Arouse up like a man! for, indeed, your time of boyhood is passing – nay, it has passed with other lads not much older; only you have been poorly and weakly from your cradle, Will. Come, go to sleep; and before you lie down, pray for better health and strength to-morrow."

"To-morrow!" he repeated – "and did my step-father say anything of to-morrow?"

His mother answered him evasively, and he resumed, – "Oh, how I fear to-morrow! – oh, mother, you have loved me, and you do love me – for my weakness, my ill-health, and my dutifulness – and you loved my father – oh, for his sake as well as mine, mother, keep me from what I am threatened with! – keep me from it, if you would keep me alive another day?"

He went into his little sleeping-apartment, stricken to the very soul with supernatural fears.

After spending a miserable night, he stole out of the house next morning, and wandered about the private walks adjacent to the town, until he thought his step-father might have arisen and taken his usual walk to the Tap. But as the lad was about to re-enter the house, Hunks met him at the threshold. Will shrunk back; to his surprise and comfort, however, his fears now seemed ill-founded. The man bid him good morrow in as cheerful and kind a tone as he could command, shook his hand, tapped him on the head, and left the house. Delighted, though still agitated, Will sought his mother within doors, told her his good omens, and spent a happy day. At dinner, too, notwithstanding Hunks' presence, the mother and son enjoyed themselves, so amiable had the despot become, at least in appearance.

When their meal was over, Hunks, as if to attain the utmost civility, invited Will to go out with him for a walk by the river – "and let's have Barker (Will's dog) for company," continued Hunks; "he may show us sport with a rat, or such like, Will."

Accordingly, the three strolled out together, Will leading the way by many a well-known sedge or tuft of bushes, or undermined bank, the resorts of the water-rat, and sometimes of the outlaw otter; and Barker upheld his character, by starting, hunting down, and killing one of the first-mentioned animals. As twilight came on, they turned their faces towards the little town. They entered it. Its little hum of life was now hushed; its streets silent, and almost deserted; its doors and windows barred and bolted, and the sounds of the rushing river and the thumping mill were the only ones which filled the air. The clock pealed ten as they continued their way. Hunks had grown suddenly silent and reserved. They passed the old Gothic church, and now were passing the gate which led into its burial-ground. Hunks stopped short. His grey, bad eye fell on the lad – "Will," he said, "I be thinking we've walked enough for this time."

"Enough, indeed, – and thank you for your company – and good night, father," answered Will, trying to smile, though he began to tremble.

"Good night then, my man – and here be your watch-light" – and Hunks drew a dark lantern from his huge pocket.

"Nay, I want no light home," said Will; "I know the way so well; and 'tis not very dark; and you know you can't do without it on your post."

"My post!" Hunks laughed villainously – "your post you mean, Will; take it; I be thinking I shall sleep sound to-night without a dead-light – as if I were a corpse to need it. Come along."

"You cannot have the heart to ask me!" cried Will, stepping back.

"Pho, my man" – Hunks clutched him by the shoulder with one hand, with the other unlocked the gate and flung it open – "In with you; you'll like it so in a few nights, you'll wish no better post; the dead chaps be civil enough; only treat them well, and let them walk awhile, and they make very good company." He dragged Will closer to the gate.

"Have mercy!" shrieked the wretched lad, trying to kneel, "or kill me first, father, to make me company for them, if that will please you."

"Get in!" roared the savage – "get in! – ay, hollo out, and twist about, so, and I'll pitch your shivering carcass half way across the church-yard!" – he forced him in from the gate – "stop a bit, now – there be your lantern" – he set it down on a tomb-stone – "so, good night – yonder's your box – just another word – don't you be caught strolling too near the murderer's corner, over there, or you may trip and fall among the things that turn and twine on the ground, like roots of trees, to guard him."

With a new and piercing shriek, Will clung close to his fell tormentor. Hunks, partially carrying into effect a threat he had uttered, tore the lad's hands away, tossed him to some distance, strode out at the gate, locked it, and Will was alone with horror.

At first an anguish of fear kept him stupified and stationary. He had fallen on a freshly-piled grave, to which mechanically his fingers clung and his face joined, in avoidance of the scene around. But he soon recollected what clay it was he clung to, and at the thought, he started up, and, hushed as the sleepers around him, made some observations. High walls quite surrounded the churchyard, as if to part him from the habitable world. His lamp was burning upon the tombstone where Hunks had placed it – one dim red spot amid the thick darkness. The church clock now tolled eleven. It ceased; his ears ached in the resumed silence, and he listened and stared about him for what he feared. Whispers seemed to arise near him; he ran for his lamp, snatched it up, and instinctively hurried to the watch-box. Oh, he wished it made of solid rock! – it was chiefly framed of glass, useless as the common air to his terrors! He shut his eyes, and pressed his palms upon them – vain subterfuge! The fevered spirit within him brought before his mind's vision worse things than the church-yard could yawn up, were all that superstition has fancied of it true. He looked out from his watch-box in refuge from himself.

That evening a half-moon had risen early, and, at this moment, was sinking in gathering clouds behind distant hills. As he vaguely noticed the circumstance, he felt more and more desolate. Simultaneously with the disappearance of the planet, the near clock began again to strike – he knew what hour! Each stroke smote his ear as if it would crack the nerve; at the last sound, he shrieked out delirious! He had a pause from agony, then a struggle for departing reason, and then he was at rest.

At day-break his step-father found him asleep. He led him home. Will sat down to breakfast, smiling, but did not speak a word. Often, during the day, his now brilliant eye turned to the west; but why, his mother could not tell; until, as the evening made up her couch of clouds there, drawing around her the twilight for drapery, he left the house with an unusually vigorous step, and stood at the gate of the churchyard. Again he took up his post. Again the hour of twelve pealed from the old church, but now he did not fear it. When it had fully sounded, he clapped his hands, laughed and shouted.

The imaginary whispers he had heard the previous night – small, cautious whispers – came round him again; first, from a distance, then, nearer and nearer. At last he shaped them into words – "Let us walk," they said – "though he watches us, he fears us." *He*! – 'twas strange to hear the dim dead speak to a living man, of himself! the maniac laughed again at the fancy, and replied to them: –

"Ay, come! appear! I give leave for it. Ye are about in crowds, I know, not yet daring to take up your old bodies till I please; but up with them! – Graves, split on, and yield me my subjects! for am I not king of the church-yard? Obey me! ay, now your mouths gape – and what a yawning! – are ye musical, too? – a jubilee of groans! out with it, in the name of Death! – blast it about like giants carousing!

"Well blown! – and now a thousand heads popped up at once – their eyes fixed on mine, as if to ask my further leave for a resurrection; and they know I am good-humoured now, and grow upward, accordingly, like a grove of bare trees that have no sap in them. And now they move; passing along in rows, like trees, too, that glide by one on a bank, while one sails merrily down the river – and all is stark staring still: and others stand bolt upright against their own headstones to contemplate. I wonder what they think of! Move! move! young, old, boys, men, pale girls, and palsied grandmothers – my church-yard can never hold 'em! And yet how they pass each other from corner to corner! I think they make way through one another's bodies, as they do in the grave. They'll dance anon. Minuets, at least. Why they begin already! – and what partners! – a tall, genteel young officer takes out our village witch-of-the-wield – she that died at Christmas – and our last rector smirks to a girl of fifteen – ha! ha! yon tattered little fellow is a radical, making a leg to the old duchess! – music! music! – Go, some of you that look on there, and toll the dead bell! Well done! they tie the murderer to the bell-rope by the neck, (though he was hanged before,) and the bell swings out merrily! but what face is here?"

It was the vision of a child's face, which he believed he caught staring at him through the glass of his watch-box – the face of an only brother who had died young. The wretch's laughter changed into tears and low wailings. By the time that his mother came to seek him, just at day-break, he was, however, again laughing; but in such a state as to frighten mirth from her heart and lips till the day she died. As has been said, symptoms of positive insanity did not long continue to appear in his words or actions; yet, when he recovered, there was still a change in him – a dark and disagreeable change, under the inveterate confirmation of which, the curious student of human nature may, at this moment, observe him in his native village.

child both dead & alive

Samuel Lover (1797–1868)

Samuel Lover was born in Dublin, the son of a businessman. Little is known of his early education; it was interrupted by ill health, requiring him to spend time in Wicklow recovering. By his teenage years he was working in his father's office and, in 1814, moved to London for similar work. Lover was a talented composer and visual artist, especially as a miniaturist, and left the business world to support himself as a teacher and a painter. Much of his early musical and visual work was inspired by Moore's *Irish Melodies*, an influence visible in his short stories as well. He also completed several portraits of his mentor, Morgan, and commissioned portraits of several prominent contemporaries. Like Morgan, he moved to London and settled there in the 1830s, and earned a government pension for his contribution to the arts.

Most of his literary work is similar to that for which Carleton and the Banims were known: tales of rural Ireland. He was one of the co-founders of the *Dublin University Magazine* in 1833, a crucial forum for Irish writers from Carleton to Mangan and William Wilde, and then *Bentley's Miscellany* in London (1835). Lover published primarily tales in periodicals in the 1820s and collections of short fiction in the 1830s: *Legends and Stories of Ireland* (1832; second series, 1834) and *Popular Tales and Legends of the Irish Peasantry* (1834). Like Carleton, he came to novels late in his career: in 1837, he published his first novel, *Rory O'More*, quickly followed by his better-known novel, *Handy Andy* (1842).

He also began to publish plays at this time, beginning with a dramatization of *Rory O'More*, and to give public performances of his work, called "Irish Evenings," in England and during a tour of North America in the 1840s.

"King O'Toole and St. Kevin" exhibits one of the central concerns of *Legends and Stories of Ireland*, namely the capture of what Lover presents as an authentic, regional rural voice. In his Preface, he summarizes features of the Irish dialect and provides a key by which to translate his Irish dialect transcriptions into normative English. "King O'Toole and St. Kevin" is also an early instance of prose which purports to convey Irish oral traditions to an English-speaking audience, and a late instance of a longstanding Irish literary tradition of dialogues between an Irish bard or noble and a saint associated with early Christianity in Ireland. "The Chase," an example of such a dialogue between Oisin and St. Patrick, was among Brooke's translations in her *Reliques of Irish Poetry*, and Bram Stoker incorporated a dialogue much like Lover's in dialect as well as substance in his only Irish novel, *The Snake's Pass* (1890).

Further reading

Foster, Sally E., "Irish Wrong: Samuel Lover and the Stage-Irishman," *Éire–Ireland* 13 (1978): 34–44.

Waters, Maureen, "'no Divarshin': Samuel Lover's *Handy Andy*," *Éire–Ireland* 14 (1979): 53–64.

From Preface

From Legends and Stories of Ireland (1832)

... Most of the Stories are given in the manner of the peasantry; and this has led to some peculiarities that might be objected to, were not the cause explained – namely, frequent digressions in the course of the narrative, occasional adjurations, and certain words unusually spelt ... As for the orthographical dilemmas into which an attempt to spell their peculiar pronunciation has led me, I have ample and most successful precedent in Mr. Banim's works. Some general observations, however, it may not be irrelevant to introduce here, on the pronunciation of certain sounds in the English language by the Irish peasantry. – And here I wish to be distinctly understood, that I speak only of the midland and western districts of Ireland – and chiefly of the latter.

They are rather prone to curtailing their words; *of*, for instance, is very generally abbreviated into *o'* or *i'*, except when a succeeding vowel demands a consonant; and even in that case they would substitute *v*. The letters *d* and *t*, as finals, they scarcely ever sound; for example, pond, hand, slept, kept, are pronounced *pon, han, slep, kep*. These letters, when followed by a vowel, are sounded as if the aspirate *h* intervened, as tender, letter – *tindher, letther*. Some sounds they sharpen, and *vice versa*. The letter *e*, for instance, is mostly pronounced like *i* in the word litter, as *lind* for lend, *mind* for mend, &c.; but there are exceptions to this rule – Saint Kevin, for example, which they pronounce K*a*vin. The letter *o* they sound like *a* in some words, as off, *aff* or *av* – thus softening *f* into *v*; beyond, *beyant* – thus sharpening the final *d* to *t*, and making an exception to the custom of not sounding *d* as a final; in others they alter it to *ow* – as old *owld*. Sometimes *o* is even converted into *i* – as spoil, *spile*. In a strange spirit of contrariety, while they alter the sound of *e* to that of *i*, they substitute the latter for the former sometimes – as hinder, *hendher* – cinder, *cendher*: *s* they soften into *z* – as us, *uz*. There are other peculiarities which this is not an appropriate place to dilate upon. I have noticed the most obvious. Nevertheless, even these are liable to exceptions, as the peasantry are quite governed by ear – as in the word *of*, which is variously sounded *o', i', ov, av,* or *iv,* as best suits their pleasure ...

King O'Toole and St. Kevin: A Legend of Glendalough

From Legends and Stories of Ireland (1832)

> By that lake, whose gloomy shore
> Sky-lark never warbles o'er,
> Where the cliff hangs high and steep,
> Young Saint Kevin stole to sleep.
> (MOORE).[1]

Who has not read of St. Kevin, celebrated as he has been by MOORE in the melodies of his native land, with whose wild and impassioned music he has so intimately entwined his name? Through him, in the beautiful ballad whence the epigraph of this story is quoted, the world already knows that the sky-lark, through the intervention of the saint, never startles the morning with its joyous note, in the lonely valley of Glendalough. In the same ballad the unhappy passion which the saint inspired, and the "unholy blue" eyes of Kathleen, and the melancholy fate of the heroine by the saint's being "unused to the melting mood," are also celebrated; as well as the superstitious *finale* of the legend, in the spectral appearance of the love-lorn maiden.

> "And her ghost was seen to glide
> Gently o'er the fatal tide."

Notes _____

KING O'TOOLE AND ST. KEVIN
[1] Thomas Moore, "By That Lake Whose Gloomy Shore"
(above, p. 247), also quoted in the first paragraph of the tale.

Thus has Moore given, within the limits of a ballad, the spirit of two legends of Glendalough, which otherwise the reader might have been put to the trouble of reaching after a more round-about fashion. But luckily for those coming after him, one legend he has left to be

" — touched by a hand more unworthy" —[2]

and instead of a lyrical essence, the raw material in prose is offered, nearly *verbatim* as it was furnished to me by that celebrated guide and *bore*, Joe Irwin, who traces his descent in a direct line from the old Irish kings, and warns the public in general that "there's a power of them spalpeens sthravaigin' about, sthrivin' to put their *comether*[3] upon the quol'ty, (quality,)[4] and callin' themselves Irwin, (knowin', the thieves o' the world, how his name had gone far and near, as the rale guide,) for to deceave dacent people; but never for to b'lieve the likes – for it was only mulvatherin people they wor." For my part, I promised never to put faith in any but himself; and the old rogue's self-love being satisfied, we set out to explore the wonders of Glendalough. On arriving at a small ruin, situated on the south-eastern side of the lake, my guide assumed an air of importance, and led me into the ivy-covered remains, through a small square doorway, whose simple structure gave evidence of its early date: a lintel of stone lay across two upright supporters, after the fashion of such religious remains in Ireland.

"This, Sir," said my guide, putting himself in an attitude, "is the chapel of King O'Toole – av coorse y'iv often heerd o' King O'Toole, your honour?"

"Never," said I.

"Musha, thin, do you tell me so?" said he; "by Gor, I thought all the world, far and near, heerd o' King O'Toole – well! well!! but the darkness of mankind is ontellible. Well, Sir, you must know, as you didn't hear it afore, that there was wonst a king, called King O'Toole, who was a fine ould king in the ould ancient times, long ago; and it was him that ownded the churches in the airly days."

"Surely," said I, "the churches were not in King O'Toole's time?"

"Oh, by no manes, your honour – troth, it's yourself that's right enough there; but you know the place is called 'The Churches,' bekase they wor built *afther* by St. Kavin, and wint by the name o' the churches iver more; and therefore, av coorse, the place bein' so called, I say that the king ownded the churches – and why not Sir, seein' 'twas his birthright, time out o' mind, beyant the flood? Well, the king, you see, was the right sort – he was the *rale* boy, and loved sport as he loved his life, and huntin' in partic'lar; and from the risin' o' the sun, up he got, and away he wint over the mountains beyant afther the deer: and the fine times them wor; for the deer was as plinty thin, aye throth, far plintyer than the sheep is now; and that's the way it was with the king, from the crow o' the cock to the song o' the redbreast."

"In this counthry, Sir," added he, speaking parenthetically in an under tone, "we think it onlooky to kill the redbreast, for the robin is God's own bird."

Then, elevating his voice to its former pitch, he proceeded: –

"Well, it was all mighty good, as long as the king had his health; but, you see, in coorse o' time, the king grewn ould, by raison he was stiff in his limbs, and when he got sthricken in years, his heart failed him, and he was lost intirely for want o' divarshin, bekase he couldn't go a huntin' no longer; and, by dad, the poor king was obleeged at last for to get a goose to divart him."

Notes

[2] Lover revises a line from Moore's "Dear Harp of My Country": "touch'd by some hand less unworthy than mine."

[3] "Corruption of come hither" (Lover's Glossary).

[4] The Irish peasantry very generally call the higher orders "quality" (author).

Here an involuntary smile was produced by this regal mode of recreation, "the royal game of goose."[5]

"Oh, you may laugh, if you like," said he, half affronted, "but it's truth I'm tellin' you; and the way the goose diverted him was this-a-way: you see, the goose used for to swim acrass the lake, and go down divin' for throut, (and not finer throut in all Ireland than the same throut,) and cotch fish an a Friday for the king, and flew every other day round about the lake, divartin' the poor king, that you'd think he'd break his sides laughin' at the frolicksome tricks av his goose; so in coorse o' time the goose was the greatest pet in the counthry, and the biggest rogue, and diverted the king to no end, and the poor king was as happy as the day was long. So that's the way it was; and all went on mighty well, antil, by dad, the goose got sthricken in years, as well as the king, and grewn stiff in the limbs, like her masther, and couldn't divart him no longer; and then it was that the poor king was lost complate, and didn't know what in the wide world to do, seein' he was done out of all divarshin, by raison that the goose was no more in the flower of her blume.

"Well; the king was nigh hand broken-hearted, and melancholy intirely, and was walkin' one mornin' by the edge of the lake, lamentin' his cruel fate, an' thinkin' o' drownin' himself, that could get no divarshin in life, when all of a suddint, turnin' round the corner beyant, who should he meet but a mighty dacent young man comin' up to him.

" 'God save you,' says the king (for the king was a civil-spoken gintleman, by all accounts,) 'God save you,' says he to the young man.

" 'God save you, kindly,' says the young man to him back again, 'God save you,' says he, 'King O'Toole.'

" 'Thrue for you,' says the king, 'I am King O'Toole,' says he, 'prince and plenny-pennytinchery[6] o' these parts,' says he; 'but how kem you to know that?' says he.

" 'O, never mind,' says Saint Kavin.

"For you see," said old Joe, in his under tone again, and looking very knowingly, "it *was* Saint Kavin, sure enough – the saint himself in disguise, and no body else.' 'Oh, never mind,' says he, 'I know more than that,' says he, 'nor twice that.'

" 'And who are you?' said the king, 'that makes so bowld – who are you at all at all?'

" 'Oh, never you mind,' says Saint Kavin, 'who I am; you'll know more o' me before we part, King O'Toole,' says he.

" 'I'll be proud o' the knowledge o' your acquaintance, sir,' says the king, mighty p'lite.

" 'Troth, you may say that,' says Saint Kavin. 'And now, may I make bowld to ax, how is your goose, King O'Toole?' says he.

" 'Blur-an-agers, how kem you to know about my goose?' says the king.

" 'O, no matther; I was given to undherstand it,' says Saint Kavin.

" 'Oh, that's a folly to talk,' says the king; 'bekase myself and my goose is private frinds,' says he; 'and no one could tell you,' says he, 'barrin' the fairies.'

" 'Oh thin, it wasn't the fairies,' says Saint Kavin; 'for I'd have you to know,' says he, 'that I don't keep the likes of sitch company.'

" 'You might do worse then, my gay fellow,' says the king; 'for it's *they* could show you a crock o' money, as aisy as kiss hand; and that's not to be sneezed at,' says the king, 'by a poor man,' says he.

" 'Maybe I've a betther way of making money myself,' says the saint.

" 'By gor,' says the king, 'barrin' you're a coiner,' says he, 'that's impossible!'

" 'I'd scorn to be the like, my lord!' says Saint Kavin, mighty high, 'I'd scorn to be the like,' says he.

Notes ───

[5] a board game

[6] plenipotentiary

"'Then, what are you?' says the king, 'that makes money so aisy, by your own account.'

"'I'm an honest man,' says Saint Kavin.

"'Well, honest man,' says the king, 'and how is it you make your money so aisy?'

"'By makin' ould things as good as new,' says Saint Kavin.

"'Blur-an-ouns,[7] is it a tinker you are?' says the king.

"'No,' says the saint; 'I'm no tinker by thrade, King O'Toole; I've a betther thrade than a tinker,' says he – 'what would you say,' says he, 'if I made your old goose as good as new.'

"My dear, at the word o' makin' his goose as good as new, you'd think the poor ould king's eyes was ready to jump out iv his head, 'and,' says he – 'troth thin I'd give you more money nor you could count,' says he, 'if you did the like: and I'd be behoulden to you into the bargain.'

"'I scorn your dirty money,' says Saint Kavin.

"'Faith then, I'm thinkin' a thrifle o' change would do you no harm,' says the king, lookin' up sly at the ould *caubeen*[8] that Saint Kavin had an him.

"'I have a vow agin it,' says the Saint; 'and I am book sworn,' says he, 'never to have goold, silver, or brass in my company.'

"'Barrin' the thrifle you can't help,' says the king, mighty cute, and looking him straight in the face.

"'You just hot it,' says Saint Kavin; 'but though I can't take money,' says he, 'I could take a few acres o' land, if you'd give them to me.'

"'With all the veins o' my heart,' says the king, 'if you can do what you say.'

"'Thry me!' says Saint Kavin. 'Call down your goose here,' says he, 'and I'll see what I can do for her.'

"With that, the king whistled, and down kem the poor goose, all as one as a hound, waddlin' up to the poor ould cripple, her masther, and as like him as two *pays*. The minute the saint clapt his eyes an the goose, 'I'll do the job for you,' says he, 'King O'Toole!'

"'By *Jaminee*,' says King O'Toole, 'if you do, bud I'll say you're the cleverest fellow in the sivin parishes.'

"'Oh, by dad,' says Saint Kavin, 'you must say more nor that – my horn's not so soft all out,' says he, 'as to repair your ould goose for nothin'; what'll you gi' me, if I do the job for you? – that's the chat,' says Saint Kavin.

"'I'll give you whatever you ax,' says the king; 'isn't that fair?'

"'Divil a fairer,' says the saint; 'that's the way to do business. Now,' says he, 'this is the bargain I'll make with you, King O'Toole: will you gi' me all the ground the goose flies over, the first offer afther I make her as good as new?'

"'I will,' says the king.

"'You won't go back o' your word,' says Saint Kavin.

"'Honor bright!' says King O'Toole, howldin' out his fist."

Here old Joe, after applying his hand to his mouth, and making a sharp, blowing sound (something like "*thp*,") extended it to illustrate the action.[9]

Notes

[7] *Blur-an-ouns*, blood and wounds, i.e. of Christ.

[8] "An old hat" (Lover's Glossary).

[9] This royal mode of concluding a bargain has descended in its original purity, from the days of King O'Toole to the present time, and is constantly practised by the Irish peasantry. We believe something of *luck* is attributed to this same sharp blowing we have noticed, and which, for the sake of "ears polite," we have not ventured to call by its right name; for, to speak truly, a slight escapement of saliva takes place at that time. It is thus *hansel* is given and received; and many are the virtues attributed by the lower order of the Irish to "fasting spittle" (author).

" 'Honor bright,' says Saint Kavin, back agin, 'it's a bargain,' says he. 'Come here!' says he to the poor ould goose – 'come here you unfort'nate ould cripple,' says he, 'and it's *I* that 'ill make you the sportin' bird.'

"With that, my dear, he tuk up the goose by the two wings – 'criss o' my crass an you,' says he, markin' her to grace with the blessed sign at the same minute – and throwin' her up in the air, 'whew!' says he, jist givin' her a blast to help her; and with that, my jewel, she tuk to her heels, flyin' like one o' the aigles themselves, and cuttin' as many capers as a swallow before a shower of rain. Away she wint down there, right fornist you, along the side o' the clift, and flew over Saint Kavin's bed (that is where Saint Kavin's bed is *now*, but was not *thin*, by raison it wasn't made, but was conthrived afther by Saint Kavin himself, that the women might lave him alone,) and on with her undher Lugduff, and round the ind av the lake there, far beyant where you see the watherfall, (though indeed it's no watherfall at all now, but only a poor dhribble iv a thing; but if you seen it in the winther, it id do your heart good, and it roarin' like mad, and as white as the dhriven snow, and rowlin' down the big rocks before it, all as one as childher playin' marbles) – and on with her thin right over the lead mines o' Luganure, (that is where the lead mines is *now*, but was not *thin*, by raison they worn't discovered, *but was all goold in Saint Kavin's time*.) Well, over the ind o' Luganure she flew, stout and sturdy, and round the other ind av the *little* lake, by the churches, (that is, *av coorse*, where the churches is *now*, but was not *thin*, by raison they wor not built, but afterwards by St. Kavin,) and over the big hill here over your head, where you see the big clift – (and that clift in the mountain was made by *Fan Ma Cool*, where he cut it acrass with a big swoord, that he got made a purpose by a blacksmith out o' Rathdrum, a cousin av his own, for to fight a joyant [giant] that darr'd him an the Curragh o' Kildare; and he thried the swoord first an the mountain, and cut it down into a gap, as is plain to this day; and faith, sure enough, it's the same sauce he sarv'd the joyant, soon and suddent, and chopped him in two like a pratie, for the glory of his sowl and owld Ireland) – well, down she flew over the clift, and fluttherin' over the wood there at Poulanass, (where I showed you the purty wather-fall – and by the same token, last Thursday was a twelvemonth sence, a young lady, Miss Rafferty by name, fell into the same watherfall, and was nigh hand drownded – and indeed would be to this day, but for a young man that jumped in afther her; indeed a smart slip iv a young man he was – he was out o' Francis-street, I hear, and coorted her sence, and they wor married, I'm given to undherstand – and indeed a purty couple they wor.) Well – as I said – afther fluttherin' over the wood a little bit, to *plaze* herself, the goose flew down, and lit at the fut o' the king, as fresh as a daisy, afther flyin' roun' his dominions, just as if she hadn't flew three perch.

"Well, my dear, it was a beautiful sight to see the king standin' with his mouth open, lookin' at his poor ould goose flyin' as light as a lark, and betther nor ever she was: and when she lit at his fut, he patted her on the head, and *'ma vourneen,'*[10] says he, 'but you are the *darlint* o' the world.'

" 'And what do you say to me,' says Saint Kavin, 'for makin' her the like?'

" 'By gor,' says the king, 'I say nothin' bates the art o' man, barrin'[11] the bees.'

" 'And do you say no more nor that?' says Saint Kavin.

" 'And that I'm behoulden to you,' says the king.

" 'But will you gi'e me all the ground the goose flewn over?' says Saint Kavin.

Notes

[10] "My darling" (Lover's Glossary).

[11] *Barring* is constantly used by the Irish peasantry for *except* (author).

" 'I will,' says King O'Toole; 'and you're welkim to it,' says he, 'though it's the last acre I have to give.'

" 'But you'll keep your word thrue?' says the saint.

" 'As thrue as the sun,' says the king.

" 'It's well for you,' (says Saint Kevin, mighty sharp) – 'it's well for you, King O'Toole, that you said that word,' says he; 'for if you didn't say that word, *the divil receave the bit o' your goose id ever fly agin,*' says Saint Kavin.

"Oh, you needn't laugh" said old Joe, half offended at detecting the trace of a suppressed smile; "you needn't laugh, *for it's thruth I'm tellin' you.*

"Well, whin the king was as good as his word, Saint Kavin was *plazed* with him, and thin it was that he made himself known to the king. 'And,' says he, 'King O'Toole, you're a dacent man,' says he; 'for I only kem here to *thry you.* You don't know me,' says he, 'bekase I'm disguised.'[12]

" 'Troth, then, you're right enough,' says the king, 'I didn't perceave it,' says he; 'for indeed I never seen the sign o' sper'ts an you.'

" 'Oh! that's not what I mane,' says Saint Kavin; 'I mane I'm deceavin' you all out, and that I'm not myself at all.'

" 'Blur-an-agers! thin,' says the king, 'if you're not yourself, who are you?'

" 'I'm Saint Kavin,' said the saint, blessin' himself.

" 'Oh, queen iv heaven!' says the king, makin' the sign o' the crass betune his eyes, and fallin' down an his knees before the saint. 'Is it the great Saint Kavin,' says he, 'that I've been discoorsin' all this time, without knowin' it,' says he, 'all as one as if he was a lump iv a *gossoon*? – and so you're a saint,' says the king.

" 'I am,' says Saint Kavin.

" 'By gor, I thought I was only talking to a dacent boy,'[13] says the king.

" 'Well, you know the differ now,' says the saint. 'I'm Saint Kavin,' says he, 'the greatest of all the saints.'

"For Saint Kavin, you must know, Sir," added Joe, treating me to another parenthesis, "Saint Kavin is counted the greatest of all the saints, bekase he went to school with the prophet Jeremiah.

"Well, my dear, that's the way that the place kem, all at wanst, into the hands of Saint Kavin; for the goose flewn round every individyial acre o' King O'Toole's property you see, *bein' let into the saycret* by Saint Kavin, who was mighty *cute*;[14] and so, when he *done* the ould king out iv his property, for the glory o' God, he was *plazed* with him, and he and the king was the best o' friends iver more afther (for the poor ould king was *doatin'*, you see,) and the king had his goose good as new, to divart him as long as he lived: and the saint supported him afther he kem into his property, as I tould you, antil the day iv his death – and that was soon afther; for the poor goose thought he was ketchin' a throut one Friday; but my jewel, it was a mistake he made – and instead of a throut, it was a thievin' horse-eel;[15] and, by gor, instead iv the goose killin' a throut for the king's supper – by dad, the eel killed the king's

Notes

[12] A person in a state of drunkenness is said to be *disguised* (author).

[13] The English reader must not imagine the saint to have been very juvenile, from this expression of the king's. In Ireland, a man in the prime of life is called a "stout *boy*" (author).

[14] Cunning – an abbreviation of acute (author).

[15] Eels of uncommon size are said to exist in the upper lake of Glendalough: the guides invariably tell marvellous stories of them: they describe them of forbidding aspect, with manes as large as a horse's. One of these "slippery rogues" is said to have amused himself by entering a pasture on the borders of the lake, and eating a *cow* – maybe 'twas a *bull* (author). Lover is punning on the idea of a "bull" as a verbal blunder; see the Edgeworths' *Essay on Irish Bulls* (above).

goosc – and small blame to him; but he didn't ate her, bekase he darn't ate what Saint Kavin laid his blessed hands on.

"Howsumdever, the king never recovered the loss iv his goose, though he had her stuffed (I don't mane stuffed with pratees and inyans, but as a curiosity,) and presarved in a glass-case for his own divarshin; and the poor king died on the next Michaelmas-day, which was remarkable. – *Troth, it's thruth I'm tellin' you*; – and when he was gone, Saint Kavin gev him an iligant wake and a beautiful berrin'; and more betoken, he *said mass for his sowl, and tuk care av his goose.*"

O'Connell's Call and Pat's Reply

This political print, attributed to American artist Edward Williams Clay (1799–1857), is described in the Library of Congress catalogue as "A condemnation of Daniel O'Connell's agitation of Irish immigrants in the United States against slavery." Clay's prints often opposed attempts to ameliorate or end slavery. This cartoon is relatively unusual, however, for addressing foreign protests against US slavery, and for recognizing interest in Ireland and among the Irish diaspora about political issues not directly connected to Ireland.

O'Connell's Call and Pat's Reply (lithograph, 1843), Library of Congress, Prints and Photographs Division, LC USZ62-28072.

The Nation: The Early Years (1842–1844)

The nationalist, pro-repeal, and explicitly pan-sectarian newspaper *The Nation* was published weekly on Saturdays beginning October 15, 1842. The early years of the newspaper, under the editorship of Charles Gavan Duffy, were arguably its most influential, as *The Nation* helped to focus liberal nationalist sentiment, achieved wide circulation, and introduced to readers some of the leading poets of the mid-nineteenth century, including James Clarence Mangan, Denis Florence MacCarthy, Thomas D'Arcy McGee, and Lady Wilde. Occasionally, *The Nation* published supplements with, for instance, major speeches on the repeal of the Act of Union and collections of verse. One *Nation* supplement, *The Spirit of the Nation* (March 20, 1852), included Mangan's "The Warning Voice" and "The Lovely Land," MacCarthy's "The Voice in the Desert," and Lady Wilde's "The Supplication," all in the present anthology, in addition to verse by Duffy and McGee.

The newspaper was strongly associated with the Young Ireland movement and its secular, pan-sectarian support of repeal in particular and nationalist revival in general. From notices of new books to reports from the colonies of military action and colonial insurgency, from snippets of Irish history (often military history) to a "National Gallery" series which profiled leading Irish writers, and from accounts of diasporic Irish subjects (particularly in America) to information about support for repeal from

outside Ireland, with a regular section on poetry, *The Nation* offered its readers a diverse and yet directed course of reading: it placed Ireland on an international stage, with international connections and supporters, and within an extensive and proud history. The newspaper reproduced United Irishmen songs and published poems commemorating various Irish battles from previous centuries, both in Ireland and abroad. It also periodically criticized the more anglo-friendly *Dublin University Magazine*, and "How to Make an Irish Story" (see below) may in part be a critique of some of the fiction published in that magazine's pages.

The first issue of *The Nation* laid out its general agenda in an unsigned editorial entitled, "The Nation." "My Grave," by Thomas Davis, and "A Voice from America" demonstrate *The Nation*'s awareness of the literature associated with previous nationalist movements: "My Grave" echoes commemorations of national heroes in United Irishmen and Romantic-era texts, while "A Voice from America" continues the Irish celebration of the American Revolution evident not only in direct representations but also in the turning to the West which figures significantly in Porter's *Billy Bluff* and Drennan's "Erin." "Convicted Criminals" sheds some light on the political complexity of *The Nation*: defending Daniel O'Connell, from whom Young Ireland had split on ideological grounds, hailing both Catholic and anti-Catholic martyrs, depicting

Christ in largely secular terms, and closing with a racist slur, this *Nation* contributor is neither fully partisan nor fully liberal and pan-sectarian. Together, these pieces, all provided in their entirety, give some sense of the argumentation and range of subject in the pages of the early *Nation*.

Further reading

Davis, Richard, *The Young Ireland Movement*. Dublin: Gill and Macmillan, 1988.

Ryder, Seán, "Speaking of '98: Young Ireland and Republican Memory," *Éire–Ireland* 34 (1999): 51–69.

The Nation (October 15, 1842)[1]

With all the nicknames that serve to delude and divide us – with all their Orangemen and Ribbonmen, Torymen and Whigmen, Ultras and Moderados,[2] and Heaven knows what rubbish besides, there are, in truth, but two parties in Ireland: those who suffer from her National degradation, and those who profit by it. To a country like ours, all other distinctions are unimportant. This is the first article of our political creed; and as we desire to be known for what we are, we make it our earliest task to announce that the object of the writers of this journal is to organise the greater and better of those parties, and to strive, with all our soul and with all our strength, for the diffusion and establishment of its principles. This will be the beginning, middle, and end of our labours.

And we come to the task with a strong conviction that there never was a moment more favorable for such a purpose than the present. The old parties are broken, or breaking up, both in England and Ireland – Whiggery, which never had a soul, has now no body; and the simplest partisan, or the most selfish expectant – who is generally a creature quite as unreasonable – cannot ask us to fix the hopes of our country on the fortunes of a party so weak and fallen. Far less can we expect anything from Toryism, which could only serve us by ceasing to *be* Toryism; even in its new and modified form it means the identical reverse of all we require to make the masses in this country happier and better. But this shifting of parties – this loosening of belief in old distinctions and dogmas, has prepared men's minds for new and greater efforts. Out of the contempt for mere party politics will naturally grow a desire to throw aside small and temporary remedies – to refuse to listen any longer to those who would plaster a cut finger, or burn an old wart, and call this doctoring the body politic – and to combine for great and permanent changes. The point of honor which restrained multitudes from abandoning Whiggery, while their service could sustain it in its old accustomed place, can operate no more. The idiot hope, that Toryism might for once produce something good, has been pretty well disappointed; and, after an unexampled lull in politics, the popular party are ready, and willing, and anxious once again to be up and doing.

Notes

THE NATION

[1] This editorial appeared in the first issue of *The Nation*.

[2] The Orangemen (Protestant) and the Ribbonmen (Catholic) were both founded around the turn of the century and involved in violent sectarian clashes in the early decades of the nineteenth century. Tories and Whigs were the two leading political parties of the day; "Ultra" was the current term for an extreme conservative.

On this new spirit our hope for Ireland depends – and it will be our frequent duty hereafter to impress our views in detail on our readers, and to indicate all the ways and means of their accomplishment. We believe we will have the advice and co-operation of many of the wisest and best of our countrymen; and as our pages will be always open to fair discussion, we hope to reflect the popular mind, and gather the popular suffrage, within our columns upon this and all other questions of National politics.

But let us guard ourselves, from the very beginning, against being understood, when we speak of politics, to mean the thing which the phrase expresses in the vulgar tongue of journalism. By politics we mean the science of government, and all the facts and circumstances with which it must naturally deal. We do not mean, and never by any accident will mean, the calculation of chances on Mr. EDWARD LITTON's remaining for life a deputy in the Court of Chancery,[3] or the comparative merits or demerits of Messrs. BREWSTER and Sergeant GREENE, or any other matter or thing which has not some direct leaning on the condition of our country; not that we by any means debar ourselves from laughing with SYDNEY SMITH, or at TRESHAM GREGG,[4] upon all proper occasions; but we will call this badinage, or pleasantry, or anything but politics.

For this National party in Ireland we believe it indispensible to its usefulness to claim, now and always, the right to stand at the head of all combined movements of Reformers in this country. They have too long forgotten or mistaken their true position. Is it not a lamentable absurdity – a blunder almost too ludicrous for an English commander in Affghanistan – to have the officers of an army less resolute and courageous than the soldiers? NAPOLEON, we believe, did not choose the Generals who led his legions to victory from the most timid and hesitating of the aristocracy, but from bold and sagacious men, whether in the ranks or on the staff. Those who go farthest ought naturally to lead the way. "Come with us as far as we go together," says the Moderate or Non-National party. "Certainly," we are prepared on all occasions to reply; "but as we go farthest, just permit us, for convenience sake, to go foremost." This is the tone which naturally belongs to a National party, and wanting which they must always want the dignity and solidity necessary to accomplish great effects.

But the first duty of men who desire to foster Nationality, is to teach the People not only the elevating influence but the intrinsic advantage of the principle and the thing. You cannot kindle a fire with damp faggots; and every man in the country who has not an interest in the existing system ought to be shown, as clearly as an abstract truth can be demonstrated, that National feelings, National habits, and National government, are indispensable to individual prosperity. This will be our task; and we venture to think we will perform it indifferently well.

But no National feeling can co-exist with the mean and mendicant spirit which esteems everything English as greater and better than if it belonged to our own

Notes

[3] Edward Litton (1770–1870) was member of parliament for Coleraine.

[4] Among the publications of British clergyman Sydney Smith (1771–1845) is *Letters on the Subject of the Catholics to my Brother Abraham who Lives in the Country* (1807), published under the pseudonym Peter Plymley, which mocked opponents of Catholic emancipation; Smith made similar arguments in *The Edinburgh Review* (which he co-founded). Church of Ireland clergyman Tresham Gregg (1800–81) publicly and virulently opposed Catholicism.

country, and which looks at all the rest of the world through the spectacles of Anglican prejudice. There is no doubt at all that the chief source of the contempt with which we are treated by the English is our own sycophancy. We abandon our self-respect, and we are treated with contempt; nothing can be more natural – nothing, in fact, can be more just. But we must open our eyes and look our domineering neighbour in the face – we must inspect him, and endeavour to discover what kind of fellow he is. Not that we ought to do him injustice – not that we ought to run into opposite extremes – not, above all, that we ought to take universal England to be fairly represented by the disagreeable person who sometimes condescends to visit *Hireland*[5] – a fat man, with his head in the clouds and his brains in his belly, looking the incarnation of self-importance, and saying, as plainly as plumb-pudding countenance can speak – "I am a Great Briton." John Bull[6] is as much a better fellow than this animal, as he is worse than what our shameful sycophancy would make him. We must learn to think sensibly and candidly about him; and we do not doubt that The Nation will tend materially to this end.

We may be told that we expect to effect too much through the means of a newspaper, but nobody who knows this country thoroughly will say this. A newspaper is the only conductor to the mind of Ireland. Periodicals or books make no considerable impression, because they have no considerable circulation. Speeches are more effective; but we include them among the materials of journalism. O'Connell the orator, is as much the food of the Press as O'Connell the writer.[7] And it is undeniable that the journals, with all their means and appliances, were, and are, and are to be for many a day, the stimulating power in Ireland. Their work may not be apparent, but it is not the less sure; its slow and silent operation acts on the masses as the wind, which we do not see, moves the dust, which we do see – and in both cases the invisible giant is sometimes forgotten.

But, in addition to all that journalism has been, we shall add a new element to its strength. Men who have hitherto only written books, will now take this shorter and surer road to the popular mind. Already the ablest writers in the country are banded together to do this work; but we shall, besides, rally round us the young intellect of the country. Many a student, pent among books, has his mind full of benevolent and useful thoughts for his country, which the habits of a student's life would prevent him for ever from pouring out in the hot arena of politics. Such men will find a fitting vehicle in The Nation; and our kindred love of letters will often induce them to turn with us from the study of mankind in books, to the service of mankind in politics. Such a legion will be more formidable than "a thousand men all 'clad in steel;'" each of them may fairly represent the multitude whom his intellect can set in motion; and the weapons which they will lay to the root of corruption will not be less keen or trenchant because they may cover them with the flowers of literature.

Notes

[5] See Boucicault (below) for a similar depiction of English dialect.

[6] A stock figure depicting a stereotypical Englishman.

[7] Daniel O'Connell (1775–1847).

My Grave [by Thomas Davis] (October 29, 1842)

Shall they bury me in the deep,
Where wind-forgetting waters sleep?
Shall they dig a grave for me,
Under the green-wood tree?
Or on the wild heath,   5
Where the wilder breath
Of the storm doth blow?
Oh, no! oh, no!
Shall they bury me in the Palace Tombs,
Or under the shade of Cathedral domes?   10
Sweet 'twere to lie on Italy's shore;
Yet not there – nor in Greece, though I love it more.
In the wolf or the vulture my grave shall I find?
Shall my ashes career on the world-seeing wind?
Shall they fling my corpse in the battle mound,   15
Where coffinless thousands lie under the ground;
Just as they fall they are buried so?
Oh, no! oh, no!

No! on an Irish green hill-side,
On an opening lawn – but not too wide;   20
For I love the drip of the wetted trees –
On me blow no gales, but a gentle breeze –
To freshen the turf: But no tombstone there;
But green sods deck'd with daisies fair.
Nor sods too deep; but so that the dew,   25
The matted grass-roots may trickle through –
Be my epitaph writ on my country's mind,
"He scrv'd his country, and lov'd his kind."
Oh! 'twere merry unto the grave to go,
If one were sure to be buried so.   30

How to Make an Irish Story (January 14, 1843)

Lay your scene principally in Galway, and let your chief characters be the officers of a regiment of dragoons. Represent them as habitual drunkards, as duellists, and as practical jokers; but take care to exclude from their tricks everything like wit. Introduce as frequently as possible, with the necessary variation only of time, place, and circumstance, a tipsy brawl, with a table oversetting in the midst of it, and a ragamuffin, with a great stick in his hand, capering thereon. Do not omit to mention the bottles and glasses that whistle, during this performance, about his ears, nor the chairs and fire-irons which are used by the surrounding combatants; and under the table fail not to place your comic character; for instance, your priest. Upset mail-coaches, and make horses run away with their riders continually: and be careful, having bribed some clever artist to prostitute his talents, to have all these intellectually humorous scenes illustrated, in order that your readers may fully appreciate the only jokes they are likely to understand. Put an "affair of honor" into about every other chapter; and for the credit and renown of your country, you being an Irishman, exhibit it as conducted with the most insensate levity. Indeed, in furtherance of this object, depict your countrymen in general as a set of irrational, unfeeling, crazy blockheads; only not having sense enough to be selfish, as lavish and prodigal in the extreme. Never mind your plot, but string adventure upon adventure, without sequence or connexion; just remembering to wind up with a marriage. For example, your hero may shoot some old gentleman through the head, or hat, and run away with his niece an heiress. Whenever you are at a loss for fun – that is, when you find it impracticable to tumble or knock one another down – throw yourself on your brogue and introduce – "Arrah! now, honey, be aisy." "Long life to yer honor, sure, and didn't I?" "Is it praties ye mane?" "Sorrow a bit." *"Musha!"* *"Savourneen!"* and the like phrases (having the interjectional ones printed in italics, that their point may be the more obvious), which you will find excellent substitutes for wit. Your tale thus prepared, take it to some publisher, and let him serve it up monthly to the unintelligent portion of the public with puff sauce.

A Voice from America (May 6, 1843)

Air – *Grammachree*

I

A voice rolled o'er the western wave,
　From shore to shore it rushed –
It spoke of freedom to the slave –
　Of comfort to the crushed.

II

It told of hearts that burned to right　　　　　　　5
　Those wrongs the weak must bear –
Of hands to aid in freedom's fight –
　Then say, shall we despair?

III

What, though some dastards may be found
　Forgetful of their rights,　　　　　　　　　　　10
Who, crouching like a beaten hound,
　Still kiss the hand that smites –

IV

We heed them not, for they are few,
　While Ireland's camp contains
Millions of brave men, tried and true,　　　　　　15
　Who burn to break their chains.

Convicted Criminals (March 2, 1844)

He was astonished that members of that House should dare to cheer a convicted conspirator.
– Mr. Ferrand's speech[1]

History has some examples of convicted conspirators who were not altogether disreputable characters! Conspirators whose memory all good men revere, and whose conviction is the very thing that has advanced their principles and made their names immortal. By the verdict of a picked jury ("all staunch-royalists"), says HUME, and *then* to be a royalist was to be a slave, Lord WILLIAM RUSSELL was found guilty of a chimaera called the Rye-house Plot – was found guilty, and was executed.[2] And the name of that traverser, that convict, that executed criminal, is the proudest on my Lord JOHN RUSSELL's genealogical tree. Nay, posterity has reversed that jury's "finding," has called RUSSELL a martyr, and his enemies *unconvicted* conspirators – "So that it is impossible, says CHARLES JAMES FOX, "not to assent to the opinion of those who have ever stigmatised the condemnation and execution of RUSSELL as *a most flagrant violation of law and justice.*"[3]

And ALGERNON SIDNEY was a convicted conspirator. "The violent and inhuman JEFFRIES," says HUME, "was now Chief Justice, and by his direction a partial jury was easily prevailed upon to give verdict against SIDNEY." And so he died for that same Rye-house delusion.[4]

"Thus fell RUSSELL and SIDNEY," to quote Mr. Fox again, "two names that will, it is hoped, be for ever dear to every English heart. When their memory shall cease to be an object of respect and veneration, it requires no spirit of prophecy to foretell that English liberty will be fast approaching to its final consummation."

Ah! Mr. BUSFIELD FERRAND, these "partial juries" and violent "Chief Justices" are powerful indeed, but not all-powerful. They positively *cannot* turn innocence into guilt; and irrespective of all the Sheriffs, Judges, and Special panels in the world, "*Sunt certi denique fines,*"[5] the essence of crime and of virtue is absolutely out of the jurisdiction of the courts of law.

And what shall we say of Sir THOMAS MORE? What of the venerable STAFFORD? – of the good Lord COBHAM? – of the irreproachable Bishop OLIVER PLUNKETT?[6] Which

Notes

CONVICTED CRIMINALS

[1] English anti-Catholic campaigner, William (Busfield) Ferrand (1809–89), member of parliament for Knaresborough. Daniel O'Connell was convicted of conspiracy in early 1844; he was then a member of parliament and his conviction was overturned in late 1844.

[2] David Hume (1711–76), Scottish philosopher and historian. The Rye House plot included a number of conspirators who were supposedly planning to kill the English king, Charles II, and his brother (later James II) for their pro-Catholic inclinations.

[3] English politician Charles James Fox (1749–1806).

[4] English author Algernon Sidney (1623–83).

[5] This phrase is taken from a short passage in a poem by Roman author Horace (65–8 BCE); the passage was often used as a maxim on moderation. This particular phrase refers to staying within boundaries.

[6] Unlike the Rye House conspirators, all of these Renaissance plotters are pro-Catholic: Sir Thomas More (1478–1535), English Catholic martyr; Sir Edward Stafford (1552–1605), English diplomat, was accused of being a spy and supporting the Catholic Mary Queen of Scots's claims to the English throne; English courtier Henry Brooke (1564–1619), 11th Baron Cobham, was imprisoned for his apparent involvement in the Bye plot to force Catholic toleration by kidnapping James I of England; Oliver Plunket (1625–81) was a Catholic archbishop in Armagh, accused of being involved in the Popish Plot (a fiction born of sectarian fears) and executed on the charge of treason.

of all the noble army of martyrs was not convicted by a competent tribunal, and duly sentenced according to law? But if they could appear on earth again, this hon. member for Knaresboro' would be ashamed to recognise them – he would pass by on the other side, and be loud in his surprise if any one should dare to bid them welcome.

The wisest sage of Athens[7] was another convicted criminal: with enemies for his prosecutors and enemies for his judges, he was duly found guilty of corrupting the youth of Athens, of sedition and blasphemy, and he died the death of a felon and a traitor. It would almost seem that to complete the character of any great political or religious reformer, of any singular benefactor to his species, it needs that, before he dies, he be a convicted conspirator.

Jesus of Nazareth, was a convicted conspirator. "We found this fellow," said his accusers, "perverting the nation and forbidding to give tribute to CAESAR" – "He stirreth up the People, teaching throughout all Jewry, beginning from Galilee unto this place." Nay, that conspirator held *monster meetings*, 5,000 and 7,000 at a time, until the Scribes and Elders of the People exclaimed – "Perceive ye how we prevail nothing: behold the world is gone after him." And he sought *to bring the ordinary tribunals of the country into disrespect*, and to induce the People to adopt other modes of settling their disputes – "Agree with thine adversary whilst thou art in the way, lest he hale thee to the Judge, and the Judge deliver thee to the Magistrate." Such were the counts in that indictment, and before a court of Scribes and Pharisees, his chance of acquittal was slender. In that day, too, there were factious men who exasperated the People against their true benefactor, and so perverted their sense of justice, that when the Governor offered to release Jesus, the cry was – that the Arimathean thought it beneath him to bury the convict in his own tomb. And now, behold! that criminal is the SAVIOUR of the world, and those base Jews, and their children's children, have become an hissing and an abomination to the ends of the earth.[8]

Notes

[7] Socrates (469–399 BCE), Greek philosopher.
[8] *The Nation* here repeats a common racist slur, using it figuratively to close its attack on Ferrand. The newspaper's liberalism was explicitly extended to Catholics and Protestants alike, but clearly did not necessarily include non-Christian faiths. Quotations here are from the Bible (Luke, John, and Matthew).

James Clarence Mangan (1803–1849)

James Clarence Mangan was born in Dublin and educated there at a Jesuit school, with considerable emphasis on languages. Mangan never earned enough as an author to live on the proceeds, particularly since he helped to support his siblings and parents, and worked at various jobs after leaving school that involved other forms of writing: first as a scrivener, then as a clerk in a law office, then as a copyist on the Ordnance Survey, and finally as a library clerk at Trinity College. He died in 1849 during a cholera outbreak in Dublin. Despite his pre-eminence as a poet and his considerable presence in periodicals during the 1840s, as well as some notoriety in Dublin for his quirky behavior and clothing, his reputation to a large extent evolved after his death and little documented detail is available for his life, though it is clear that he struggled with alcoholism and drug use.

Despite his personal difficulties, Mangan was both active and prolific. In the early 1830s he became active in non-sectarian nationalist circles, beginning as a member of the pan-sectarian Comet Club; he contributed to its newspaper, *The Comet*, and was soon frequently contributing to other periodicals, especially the *Dublin University Magazine*. Much of this early work consisted of German translations, but by the late 1830s he was also translating verse from the languages of the Ottoman empire, especially Persian and Arabic. It was not until the 1840s that he began translating from Irish, and it was at about that time that he also became a regular contributor to *The Nation*. Only his German translations were published in book form during his lifetime, in his two-volume *German Anthology* (1845). His *Poets and Poetry of Munster* (1849) was edited and published posthumously by John O'Daly, and his full poetic corpus was collected by John Mitchel and published in 1859. His fragmentary *Autobiography* also appeared after his death.

Mangan's work is diverse, from the comic to the despondent, from nationalist lyrics to translations and idiosyncratic prose pieces, and from traditional verse forms to formally complex versification. "The Philosopher and the Child" (1833) appears to parody poetry by then-influential English author William Wordsworth, and much of his work is marked by a similar playfulness with language. In "Advice" (1846), for instance, the last word of each verse reverses the first word of the stanza. Arguably his work was at its best in the mid-1840s, when he published powerful famine poems such as "The Warning Voice" (1846).

Further reading

Campbell, Matthew, "Lyrical Unions: Mangan, O'Hussey and Ferguson," *Irish Studies Review* 8 (2000): 325–38.

Lloyd, David, *Nationalism and Minor Literature: James Clarence Mangan and the Emergence of Irish Cultural Nationalism*. Berkeley, CA: University of California Press, 1987.

Ryder, Seán, ed., *James Clarence Mangan: Selected Writings*. Dublin: University College Dublin Press, 2004.

The Philosopher and the Child[1]

From **The Comet (August 4, 1833)**

I met a venerable man, with looks
Of grand and meek benignity: he wore
Deep written on his brow the midnight lore
Accumulated from the wealth of books.
Wisdom and mildness from his features beamed   5
And by his side there moved a little child
With auburn locks, who pleasantly beguiled
The listening ear of that old man, who seemed
To be her sire, with playful words, which from
The heart of childhood, innocence, fresh fountain,   10
Spring brightly bubbling upward, till they come
To lose themselves on manhood's desert mountain.
So spake that lovely little child; and as
I gazed on her and on that aged man
With eye so thoughtful and with cheek so wan   15
I mused on Plato and Pythagoras,
But most I thought of Socrates, and of
The guardian-angel whose undying love
Never forsook the hoary sage of Greece
Until she closed his eyes in holy peace,   20
When tyrants, awed, acknowledged with a sigh
How nobly a philosopher can die!
And as these thoughts flashed flitting through my brain
I heard that venerable man so mild
Thus mutter to the sweet and blessed child,   25
"*Bad luck to dat owl' rap from Mary's lane,*
Dat come and axed me for to sky de copper!
Bad luck to him, de vagabone! to rob
An' swindle me wid pitch and toss, an' fob
De penny dat I wanted for de cropper!"   30

The Jacobite Relics of Ireland

From **The Irish Penny Journal (January 16, 1841)**

The Jacobite relics of England, and to a still greater extent those of Scotland, have
been given to the world, and are well deserving of such preservation; for they reflect
no small light on the character and temperament of the English and Scottish people

Notes ————————————————————————

THE PHILOSOPHER AND THE CHILD
[1] In *The Comet*, this poem was inserted into a list of somewhat comical comments on the business of publishing. Mangan's poem was framed by editorial suggestions that "*Clarence* was mad (*drunk*, dare we say) when he wrote" the poem and should "drive off to Sir Arthur Clarke's" for medical help. (Clarke was a well-known Dublin physician, married to Morgan's sister Olivia.)

during the last century. But until the appearance of Mr. Hardiman's Irish Minstrelsy[1] it was hardly known that in their political enthusiasm for the fate of a decaying family the Irish people participated with so large a portion of those of the sister islands, and that it gave birth to an equal number of poetical effusions in our own country – but with this difference, that their sentiments are usually veiled under an allegorical form, and always in the Irish language. To Mr. Hardiman we are indebted for the preservation of the originals of many of these productions, and also for translations of them. These translations are however too free to enable the English reader to form any very accurate idea of the Irish originals, and we are therefore tempted to present a series of these relics to our readers, with translations of a more literal and faithful description; not limiting ourselves to those which have already appeared in Mr. Hardiman's work – as in the specimen which we have selected to commence with, which is still popularly sung in Ireland to the old melody called "Kathaleen Ny-Houlahan."

We may observe, that the name of the author of this song, if ever known, is no longer remembered; but there seems to be no doubt that the song itself is of Munster origin.

Kathaleen Ny-Houlahan

Long they pine in weary woe, the nobles of our land,
Long they wander to and fro, proscribed, alas! and banned;
Feastless, houseless, altarless, they bear the exile's brand,
    But their hope is in the coming-to of Kathaleen Ny-Houlahan!

Think her not a ghastly hag, too hideous to be seen,   5
Call her not unseemly names, our matchless Kathaleen;
Young she is, and fair she is, and would be crowned a queen,
    Were the king's son at home here with Kathaleen Ny-Houlahan!

Sweet and mild would look her face, O none so sweet and mild,
Could she crush the foes by whom her beauty is reviled;   10
Woolen plaids would grace herself and robes of silk her child,
    If the king's son were living here with Kathaleen Ny-Houlahan!

Sore disgrace it is to see the Arbitress of thrones
Vassal to a *Saxoneen* of cold and sapless bones!
Bitter anguish wrings our souls – with heavy sighs and groans   15
    We wait the Young Deliverer of Kathaleen Ny-Houlahan!

Let us pray to Him who holds Life's issues in His hands –
Him who formed the mighty globe, with all its thousand lands;
Girding them with seas and mountains, rivers deep, and strands,
    To cast a look of pity upon Kathaleen Ny-Houlahan!   20

He, who over sands and waves led Israël along –
He, who fed, with heavenly bread, that chosen tribe and throng –
He, who stood by Moses, when his foes were fierce and strong –
    May He show forth His might in saving Kathaleen Ny-Houlahan!

Notes

THE JACOBITE RELICS OF IRELAND
[1] James Hardiman's *Irish Minstrelsy; Or, Bardic Remains of Ireland* was first published in 1831; sections of it later appeared serially in the *Dublin University Magazine* (1834).

An Irish Lamentation (by Johann Wolfgang von Goethe)

From German Anthology (1845)

O! raise the woeful *Pillalu*,
    And let your tears in streams be shed;
Och, orro, orro, ollalu!
    The Master's eldest hope is dead!

Ere broke the morning dim and pale   5
    The owlet flapped his heavy wing;
We heard the winds at evening wail,
    And now our dirge of death we sing,
        Och, orro, orro, ollalu!

Why wouldst thou go? How couldst thou die?   10
    Why hast thou left thy parents dear?
Thy friends, thy kindred far and nigh,
    Whose cries, *mo vrone!* thou dost not hear?
        Och, orro, orro, ollalu!

Thy mother, too! – how could she part   15
    From thee, her darling fair and sweet,
The heart that throbbed within her heart,
    The pulse, the blood that bade it beat?
        Och, orro, orro, ollalu!

Oh! lost to her and all thy race,   20
    Thou sleepest in the House of Death;
She sees no more thy cherub face,
    She drinks no more thy violet breath;
        Och, orro, orro, ollalu!

By strand and road, by field and fen,   25
    The sorrowing clans come thronging all;
From camp and dun, from hill and glen,
    They crowd around the castle wall.
        Och, orro, orro, ollalu!

From East and West, from South and North,   30
    To join the funeral train they hie;
And now the mourners issue forth,
    And far they spread the keening cry,
        Och, orro, orro, ollalu!

Then raise the woeful *Pillalu*,   35
    And let your tears in streams be shed,
Och, orro, orro, ollalu!
    The Chieftain's pride, his heir, is dead.

Advice

From **Dublin University Magazine (January 1846)**

Traverse not the globe for lore! The sternest
    But the surest teacher is the heart.
Studying that and that alone, thou learnest
    Best and soonest whence and what thou *art*.

Time, not travel, 'tis which gives us ready   5
    Speech, experience, prudence, tact, and wit.
Far more light the lamp that bideth steady
    Than the wandering lantern doth *emit*.

Moor, Chinese, Egyptian, Russian, Roman,
    Tread one common downhill path of doom: 10
Everywhere the names are Man and Woman,
    Everywhere the old sad sins find *room*.

Evil angels tempt us in all places.
    What but sands or snows hath Earth to give?
Dream not, friend, of deserts and oäses,   15
    But look inwards, and begin to *live*.

The Warning Voice

From **The Nation (February 21, 1846)**

Il me semble que nous sommes à la veille d'une grande bataille humaine. Les forces sont là;
mais je n'y vois pas de général.

(BALZAC: *Livre Mystique*)[1]

I

Ye Faithful! – ye Noble!
    A day is at hand
Of trial and trouble,
    And woe in the land!
O'er a once greenest path,   5
    Now blasted and sterile,
        Its dusk shadows loom –
It cometh with Wrath,
    With Conflict and Peril,
        With Judgment and Doom!   10

Notes

THE WARNING VOICE
[1] From *Louis Lambert* by French author Honoré de Balzac (1799–1850): "It seems to me that we are on the verge of a great human battle; the forces are there, but I do not see a general."

False bands shall be broken,
  Dead systems shall crumble,
    And the Haughty shall hear
Truths yet never spoken,
        Though smouldering like flame   15
      Through many a lost year
  In the hearts of the Humble;
For, Hope will expire
As the Terror draws nigher,
        And, with it, the Shame   20
Which so long overawed
  Men's minds by its might –
And the Powers abroad
  Will be Panic and Blight,
And phrenetic Sorrow –   25
  Black Pest all the night,
    And Death on the morrow!

Now, therefore, ye True,
Gird your loins up anew!
By the good you have wrought!   30
By all you have thought,
  And suffered, and done!
    By your souls! I implore you,
      Be leal to your mission–
Remembering that *one*   35
  Of the *two* paths before you
    Slopes down to Perdition!
To you have been given,
  Not granaries and gold,
But the Love that lives long,   40
  And waxes not cold;
And the Zeal that has striven
  Against Error and Wrong,
And in fragments hath riven
  The chains of the Strong!   45
Bide now, by your sternest
Conceptions of earnest
Endurance for others,
Your weaker-souled brothers!
Your true faith and worth   50
  Will be History soon,
And their stature stand forth
  In the unsparing Noon!

II

You have dreamed of an era
  Of Knowledge, and Truth,   55
    And Peace – the *true* glory!
Was this a chimera?
  Not so! – but the childhood and youth
    Of our days will grow hoary

Before such a marvel shall burst on their sight!   60
  On *you* its beams glow not –
  For *you* its flowers blow not!
You cannot rejoice in its light,
But in darkness and suffering instead
You go down to the place of the Dead!   65
To *this* generation
The sore tribulation,
The stormy commotion,
And foam of the Popular Ocean,
  The struggle of class against class;   70
The Dearth and the Sadness,
  The Sword and the War-Vest;
To the *next*, the Repose and the Gladness,
  "The sea of clear glass,"[2]
  And the rich Golden Harvest.   75

III

Know, then, your true lot,
  Ye Faithful, though Few!
    Understand your position,
    Remember your mission,
And vacillate not,   80
  Whatsoever ensue!
Alter not! Falter not!
  Palter not now with your own living souls,
  When each moment that rolls
    May see Death lay his hand   85
On some new victim's brow!
Oh! let not your vow
  Have been written in sand!
  Leave cold calculations
Of Danger and Plague   90
  To the slaves and the traitors
Who cannot dissemble
  The dastard sensations
That now make them tremble
  With phantasies vague! –   95
The men without ruth –
  The hypocrite haters
Of Goodness and Truth,
Who at heart curse the race
  Of the sun through the skies;   100
And would look in God's face
    With a lie in their eyes!
  To the last do your duty,
  Still mindful of this –

Notes ———————————————————————————

[2] Apoc., iv. 6 (author). See Revelation 4: 6 in the New
Testament of the Bible.

That Virtue is Beauty, 105
    And Wisdom, and Bliss;
So, howe'er, as frail men, you have erred on
    Your way through Life's throngèd road,
Shall your consciences prove a sure guerdon
    And tower of defence, 110
      Until Destiny summon you hence
To the Better Abode!

Dark Rosaleen (translated from the Irish)

From **The Nation** (**May 30, 1846**)

This impassioned song, entitled, in the original, *Roisin Duh*, or The Little Black Rose, was written in the reign of Elizabeth by one of the poets of the celebrated Tirconnellian chieftain, Hugh the Red O'Donnell. It purports to be an allegorical address from Hugh to Ireland on the subject of his love and struggles for her, and his resolve to raise her again to the glorious position she held as a nation before the irruption of the Saxon and Norman spoilers. The true character and meaning of the figurative allusions with which it abounds, and to two only of which I need to refer here – *viz.*, the "Roman wine" and "Spanish ale" mentioned in the first stanza – the intelligent reader will, of course, find no difficulty in understanding.

I

O, my Dark Rosaleen,
    Do not sigh, do not weep!
The priests are on the ocean green,
    They march along the Deep.
There's wine … from the royal Pope, 5
    Upon the ocean green;
And Spanish ale shall give you hope,
    My Dark Rosaleen!
    My own Rosaleen!
Shall glad your heart, shall give you hope, 10
Shall give you health, and help, and hope,
    My Dark Rosaleen!

II

Over hills, and through dales,
    Have I roamed for your sake;
All yesterday I sailed with sails 15
    On river and on lake.
The Erne, … at its highest flood,
    I dashed across unseen,
For there was lightning in my blood,
    My Dark Rosaleen! 20
    My own Rosaleen!
Oh! there was lightning in my blood,
Red lightning lightened through my blood.
    My Dark Rosaleen!

III

All day long, in unrest,   25
  To and fro, do I move.
The very soul within my breast
  Is wasted for you, love!
The heart ... in my bosom faints
  To think of you, my Queen,   30
My life of life, my saint of saints,
  My Dark Rosaleen!
  My own Rosaleen!
To hear your sweet and sad complaints,
My life, my love, my saint of saints,   35
  My Dark Rosaleen!

IV

Woe and pain, pain and woe,
  Are my lot, night and noon,
To see your bright face clouded so,
  Like to the mournful moon.   40
But yet ... will I rear your throne
  Again in golden sheen;
'Tis you shall reign, shall reign alone,
  My Dark Rosaleen!
  My own Rosaleen!   45
'Tis you shall have the golden throne,
'Tis you shall reign, and reign alone,
  My Dark Rosaleen!

V

Over dews, over sands,
  Will I fly, for your weal: 50
Your holy delicate white hands
  Shall girdle me with steel.
At home ... in your emerald bowers,
  From morning's dawn till e'en,
You'll pray for me, my flower of flowers,   55
  My Dark Rosaleen!
  My fond Rosaleen!
You'll think of me through Daylight's hours,
My virgin flower, my flower of flowers,
  My Dark Rosaleen!   60

VI

I could scale the blue air,
  I could plough the high hills,
Oh, I could kneel all night in prayer,
  To heal your many ills!
And one ... beamy smile from you   65
  Would float like light between
My toils and me, my own, my true,

My Dark Rosaleen!
My fond Rosaleen!
Would give me life and soul anew,   70
A second life, a soul anew,
    My Dark Rosaleen!

VII

O! the Erne shall run red,
    With redundance of blood,
The earth shall rock beneath our tread,   75
    And flames wrap hill and wood,
And gun-peal, and slogan-cry,
    Wake many a glen serene,
Ere you shall fade, ere you shall die,
    My Dark Rosaleen!   80
    My own Rosaleen!
The Judgement Hour must first be nigh,
Ere you can fade, ere you can die,
    My Dark Rosaleen!

A Vision of Connaught in the Thirteenth Century

From The Nation (**July 11, 1846**)

Et moi, j'ai été aussi en Arcadie – And I, I too have been a dreamer.
(Inscription on a Painting by Poussin)[1]

Kubla Khan

I

I walked entranced
    Through a land of Morn;
The sun, with wondrous excess of light,
    Shone down and glanced
        Over seas of corn   5
And lustrous gardens aleft and right
    Even in the clime
    Of resplendent Spain,
Beams no such sun upon such a land;
    But it was the time,   10
    'Twas in the reign,
Of Cáhal Mór of the Wine-red Hand.[2]

Notes ──────────────────────────────

A VISION OF CONNAUGHT
[1] French painter Nicolas Poussin (1594–1665) uses the phrase *"Et in Arcadia Ego"* in two paintings. Mangan's epigraph offers rather loose translations of this ambivalent Latin phrase (roughly, "I too am in Arcadia").

[2] The Irish and Oriental poets both agree in attributing favorable or unfavorable weather and abundant or deficient harvests to the good or bad qualities of the reigning monarch. What the character of Cáhal was will be seen below (author).

II

Anon stood nigh
    By my side a man
Of princely aspect and port sublime.   15
    Him queried I,
      "O, my Lord and Khan,[3]
What clime is this, and what golden time?"
    When he – "The clime
      Is a clime to praise,   20
The clime is Erin's, the green and bland;
    And it is the time,
      These be the days,
Of Cáhal Mór of the Wine-red Hand!"

III

Then saw I thrones,   25
    And circling fires,
And a Dome rose near me, as by a spell,
    Whence flowed the tones
      Of silver lyres,
And many voices in wreathèd swell;   30
    And their thrilling chime
      Fell on mine ears
As the heavenly hymn of an angel-band –
    "It is now the time,
      These be the years,   35
Of Cáhal Mór of the Wine-red Hand!"

IV

I sought the hall,
    And, behold! … a change
From light to darkness, from joy to woe!
    King, nobles, all,   40
      Looked aghast and strange;
The minstrel-groupe sate in dumbest show!
    Had some great crime
      Wrought this dread amaze,
This terror? None seemed to understand!   45
    'Twas then the time
      We were in the days,
Of Cáhal Mór of the Wine-red Hand.

V

I again walked forth,
    But lo! the sky   50

Notes

[3] Identical with the Irish *Ceann*, Head, or Chief; but I the
rather gave him the Oriental title, as really fancying myself
in one of the regions of Araby the Blest (author).

Showed fleckt with blood, and an alien sun
  Glared from the north,
    And there stood on high,
Amid his shorn beams, A SKELETON!⁴
  It was by the stream   55
    Of the castled Maine,
One Autumn eve, in the Teuton's land,
  That I dreamed this dream
    Of the time and reign
Of Cáhal Mór of the Wine-red Hand!   60

The Lovely Land

From The Nation (July 18, 1846)

(On a Landscape, painted by M******)[1]

I

Glorious birth of Mind and Color,
  Gazing on thy radiant face
  The most lorn of Adam's race
Might forget all dolour!

II

What divinest light is beaming   5
  Over mountain, mead and grove!
  That blue noontide sky above
Seems asleep and dreaming.

III

Rich Italia's wild-birds warble
  In the foliage of those trees,   10
  I can trace thee, Veronese,
In these rocks of marble!

IV

Yet no! Mark I not where quiver
  The sun's rays on yonder stream?
  Only a Poussin could dream   15
Such a sun and river!

Notes

⁴ "It was but natural that these portentous appearances should thus be exhibited on this occasion, for they were the heralds of a very great calamity that befel the Connacians in this year – namely, the death of Cathal of the Red Hand, son of Torlogh Mor of the Wine, and King of Connaught, a prince of most amiable qualities, and into whose heart GOD had infused more piety and goodness than into the hearts of any of his co[n]temporaries." – *Annals of the Four Masters*, A.D. 1224 (author).

THE LOVELY LAND
[1] Daniel Maclise (1806–70), leading Irish book illustrator and painter of literary and historical subjects.

V

What bold imaging! Stony valley,
   And fair bower of eglantine!
   Here I see the black ravine,
There the lilied alley!   20

VI

There is some rare clime so olden,
   Peopled, not by men, but fays;
   Some lone land of genii days,
Storyful and golden!

VII

Oh! for magic power to wander   25
   One bright year through such a land!
   Might I even one year stand
On the blest hills yonder!

VIII

But – what spy I? ... O, by noonlight!
   'Tis the same! – the pillar-tower   30
   I have oft passed thrice an hour,
Twilight, sunlight, moonlight!

IX

Shame to me, my own, my sire-land,
   Not to know thy soil and skies!
   Shame, that through Maclise's eyes   35
I first see thee, IRELAND!

X

No! no land doth rank above thee
   Or for loveliness or worth!
   So shall I, from this day forth,
Ever sing and love thee!   40

Leonora

From Dublin University Magazine (December 1846)[1]

I

Leonora rose at break of day,
   From dreams of gloomiest omen.
"How long, oh, Wilhelm, wilt thou stay?
   Art false, or slain by the foemen?"

Notes

LEONORA
[1] This is Mangan's second translation of the poem "Lenore" (1773) by German poet Gottfried Augustus Bürger (1748–94); the first, quite different, translation also appeared in the *Dublin University Magazine* (1834) and was republished in Mangan's *German Anthology* (1845).

He had gone to aid, on Prague's red plains,   5
King Frederick in his war-campaigns,
        And none had learned or listed
        News if he still existed.

II

The King, at length, grown weary of war,
  Withdrew his hosts from Russia,   10
And once again the blessèd star
  Of Peace shone over Prussia;
And the regiments all, in gallant array,
With drums and flutes, and standards gay,
        And wearing wreaths and blossoms,   15
        Marched home with joyous bosoms.

III

Green alley and valley, and hill and plain,
  Were thronged for this glad meeting;
The blithe blue air, as passed each train,
  Rang far with rapturous greeting;   20
Then many a mother, and wife, and son,
Bade welcome home the wandering one;
        But ah! none gave or bore a
        Kind word to Leonora!

IV

She roamed about, and called aloud   25
  For Wilhelm over and over,
But none in that gay glittering crowd
  Wist aught anent[2] her lover.
So, finding all her quest in vain,
She writhed and grovelled on the plain,   30
        And rent her hair and vesture,
        With many a frantic gesture.

V

There, as she lay in agony,
  Her anxious mother sought her. –
"Oh! GOD in Heaven look down on thee!   35
  GOD comfort thee, my daughter! –
"Oh, mother, mother, Gone is Gone!
Farewell the world and all thereon![3]
        Talk not of GOD in Heaven
        He leaveth me bereaven!"   40

Notes

[2] knew anything about

[3] *"O, Mutter, Mutter! Hin ist Hin!*
  Nun fahre welt und alles hin!"

  The peculiarly magnificent and dreary character of this couplet can scarcely be appreciated except by a very philosophical student of the original. Its repetition, also, in the ninth stanza, where Leonora, in the excess of her despair, takes no notice of the half-maddening suggestion of her mother, and can dwell only on the one miserable predominant idea, is a remarkable poetical beauty, and strikingly true to nature (author).

VI

"No, dearest child! – whate'er befall,
　　Thy GOD is ever near thee.
He pitieth all, He loveth all.
　　Pray, pray, and He will hear thee!"
"Oh, mother, hollow, hollow plea!　　　　　　　　　45
GOD loveth not nor pitieth me –
　　　　　　He recks not of mine anguish,
　　　　　　But lets me groan and languish." –

VII

"My dear, dear child, Heaven hath a cure
　　For every ill and dolor;　　　　　　　　　　　50
The Holy Sacrament, be sure,
　　Will prove thy best consoler!"
"Vah, mother, the asp that gnaws my heart –
No Sacrament can bid depart!
　　　　　　No Sacrament can quicken　　　　　55
　　　　　　Anew the once Death-stricken!" –

VIII

"My child, I fear thou art betrayed!
　　Thy lover may have plighted
His troth to some Hungarian maid,
　　And thus thy hopes are blighted.　　　　　　60
What then? Grieve not, but let him go!
His perfidy will work him woe,
　　　　　　And, ere his bad life ceases,
　　　　　　Will rend his heart in pieces!" –

IX

"Oh, mother, mother, Gone is Gone!　　　　　　65
　　Departed is Departed!
Woe, woe is me! – Alone, alone,
　　Alone and broken-hearted!
Die out, die out, my life's lost light!
Down, down in everlasting Night!　　　　　　　70
　　　　　　GOD spareth not nor careth,
　　　　　　Woe! woe! my soul despaireth!" –

X

"Oh, God of goodness, let not this
　　Provoke thy malediction! –
She doth but rave up from the abyss　　　　　　75
　　Of her profound affliction!
Ah, child! forget thine earthly love,
And lift thy heart to Heaven above.
　　　　　　The Spouse of Souls will take thee,
　　　　　　And HE will ne'er forsake thee!" –　　80

XI

"Oh, mother, what are Heaven and Hell?
    Where, where is Wilhelm, mother?
With him is Heaven, without him Hell;
    I want, I know, no other!
Die out, die out, my soul's lost light!   85
Down, down in everlasting Night!
        No Heaven for me without him!
        No Heaven if I must doubt him!"

XII

Thus dared this maiden, with a brain
    Made mad by tortured feelings,   90
In reckless impiousness arraign
    The All-Just GOD's wise dealings!
And smote her breast, and groaned and cried,
And wrung her hands till, at eventide,
        The pale-bright stars in millions,   95
        Bespangled Heaven's pavilions.

XIII

Then – hark! a horse's hoofs! – *Hopp, hopp!*
    They sound first farther, hoarser,
Then clearer, nearer; – then they stop,
    And a rider vaults from his courser,   100
With clank of spurs and ringing knoll;
Then – hark! – the portal bell – *Toll! toll!*
        Then stillness; then follow
        These words in accents hollow: –

XIV

"Ho-là, my love! I am here anew!   105
    Tell me what tides thou keepest; –
Art sad or gay? Art false or true?
    And wakest thou or sleepest?" –
"What, Wilhelm! Is it really thou?
Oh, I have watched and wept till now!   110
        But this drear midnight visit –
        What may it mean? Whence is it?"

XV

"I started from Bohemia late.
    We ride by midnight only.
Up! come with me, my faithful mate!   115
    Too long thou mournest lonely!"
"Ah, Wilhelm, here is somewhat wrong!
Hark! the wind bloweth strange and strong;
        Come in and warm thee, dearest,
        And here let thee and me rest!"   120

XVI

"So may the wind blow strange and strong,
  Blow stranger and blow stronger!
I must along! Thou must along!
  We linger here no longer!
Rise! Don thy attire and come with me,
My black barb snorts impatiently.   125
        We must leave leagues behind us
        Before the priest can bind us!"

XVII

"– Oh, Wilhelm, this but bodeth dole,
  Oh, tarry here till daylight!   130
Just now I heard 'Eleven' toll,
  And Heaven hath such a gray light!"
"– Look hither! Look thither! The moon shines bright,
The Dead and We ride fast by night!
        Ere Morning's red rays clamber   135
        The skies we'll reach our chamber."

XVIII

"– And where, say, is the young bride's room,
  Wherein her maids undress her?" –
– "Far hence! – cold, lone, and buried in gloom –
  Six large planks, and two lesser!"   140
– "But is there space?" – "Ay, space for both!
Come! no delay! Shake off thy sloth
        Lest Night perchance belate us.
        – The wedding-guests await us."

XIX

And Leonora, garbed and out,   145
  Sprang up behind the rider,
And flung her lily arms about
  Her lover and her guider.
Then, ho, ho! – hurry! – *hopp, hopp, hopp!*
Rode off the pair with never a stop;   150
        Until both gasped together,
        And flints and fire flashed nether!

XX

Aright, aleft, reeled, reft and cleft,
  Earth's globe around and under;
The sky swept by as a storm-blown weft;   155
  The bridges volleyed in thunder.
"Glance up! Queen Moon rides high and blue –
Hurrah! the Dead ride royally too!
        Dost fear the Dead, my best love?"
        – "Ah, leave the Dead at rest, love!"   160

XXI

But hark! – that dreary choral swell!
  Those night-birds' croak funereal!
Hark! knell of bell, and dirge as well –
  "Now, brethren, for the burial!"
And lo! a group who bear a bier,   165
A mourning group draw slowly near,
      With chant like some deep dismal
      Ghost-wail from realms abysmal.

XXII

"Halt, croakers, there! The corpse may bide
  Its funeral rites till dawning;   170
To-night I espouse my fair young bride,
  Lay down, then, bier and awning!
Come, sexton, come! – thy choir and thou
Shall troll us nuptial-songs enow!
      Come, priest, and bless the wedding!   175
      Then, ho for the feast and bedding!"

XXIII

Down went the bier; the dirge was hushed;
  And, light-limbed and unladen,
Tripp, tripp, trapp, trapp, the buriers rushed
  Behind the youth and maiden;   180
And, ho! ho! – hurry! – *hopp, hopp, hopp!*
Dashed forward all with never a stop,
      Until all gasped together,
      And flints and fire flashed nether!

XXIV

How twirled, how whirled, before, behind,   185
  The floods, the woods, the mountains!
Before, behind, like wind, like Mind,
  How flew dells, fells, and fountains!
"Glance up! The moon rides high and blue –
Hurrah! the Dead ride bravely too!   190
      Dost fear the Dead and Gone, love?"
      – "Ah! let the Dead sleep on, love!"

XXV

But look! Where yon high gibbet-wheels
  Wind-shaken, creak and wabble,
The moonlight suddenly reveals   195
  A dancing phantom-rabble!
"Ho, there, gay neighbours! – down to me!
We'll all ride home so merrily, we!
      And you shall dance before us,
      While these here lilt in chorus!"   200

XXVI

And down they came in eddying whirls,
  With whirr as when, the while Eve's
Clouds gather black, the night-blast swirls
  Through Autumn's birks of dry leaves.
And, ho, ho! – hurry! – *hopp, hopp, hopp!*   205
Away trooped all with never a stop,
        Till all gasped hard together,
        And flints and fire flashed nether!

XXVII

How sped, how fled, the sky, the stars,
  Like young steeds loosed from harness!   210
How danced the stars! how glanced their cars!
  How flew they through the Farness!
"Look up! The moon rides high and blue –
Hurrah! the Dead ride nobly too!
        Dost fear the Dead, my best love?"   215
        – "Ah, no! – but let them rest, love!"

XXVIII

"Enough! I scent the morning gale;
  My sands, I mark, are failing.[4]
Right well have we ridden o'er hill and dale.
  Behold yon grated railing   220
That shimmereth duskily! Inside
Its bars I hail thee as my bride!
        There shall we slumber sweetly.
        Hurrah! the Dead ride featly!"

XXIX

Anon they halt. The chancelled gate   225
  Swings o'er to the grey wall's border,
And that strange group, as urged by Fate,
  March through in solemn order.
The steed's reins trail along the ground,
While wild lamentings all around,   230
        Sad as the Trump of Doom's tones,
        Rise up from graves and tombstones!

XXX

But now, O, Horror! – see! As clay
  From some worn wall that moulders,
The horseman's garments fall away,   235
  Fall piecemeal from his shoulders!
With scythe and sand-glass high upraised,

Notes ————————————————————————————————

[4] See stanza XXX for the hourglass referred to here.

And grinning skull, now all ecrased[5]
    Of hair and flesh and feature,
    He stands, – DEATH, – or His Creature!   240

XXXI

High rears the steed, with mane upcurled,
  The earth yawns, rent asunder,
And down the hapless girl is hurled
  Into the dark pit under;
And, while drear howlings fill the air,   245
And cries of terror and despair,
    Behold her there, a-lying,
    Half living and half dying!

XXXII

And now the grisly spectre-band,
  As Night gives place to Morning,   250
Dance round their victim hand-in-hand,
  And sing and shriek this warning –
"Bear, – though thy proud heart break with pain,
Heaven's wrath is not invoked in vain!
    Thy body and thou must sever;   255
    GOD spare thy soul for ever!"*

The Nameless One

From **The Irishman (October 27, 1849)**

I

Roll forth, my song, like the rushing river,
  That sweeps along to the mighty sea;
God will inspire me while I deliver
  My soul of thee!

II

Tell thou the world, when my bones lie whitening   5
  Amid the last homes of youth and eld,
That there was once one whose veins ran lightning
  No eye beheld.

III

Tell how his boyhood was one drear night-hour,
  How shone for *him*, through his griefs and gloom,   10

Notes ──────────────────────────────────

[5] An *ecraseur* is a medical chainsaw for removing polypi and
other protuberances (*Oxford English Dictionary*).

No star of all Heaven sends to light our
    Path to the tomb.

IV

Roll on, my song, and to after-ages
    Tell how, disdaining all earth can give,
He would have taught Men, from Wisdom's pages,   15
    The way to live.

V

And tell how, trampled, derided, hated,
    And worn by Weakness, Disease, and Wrong,
He fled for shelter to GOD, who mated
    His soul with song –   20

VI

With song which alway, sublime or vapid,
    Flowed like a rill in the morning beam,
Perchance not deep, but intense and rapid –
    A mountain-stream.

VII

Tell how this Nameless, condemned for years long   25
    To herd with demons from Hell beneath,
Saw things that made him, with groans and tears, long
    For even Death.

VIII

Go on to tell how, with genius wasted,
    Betrayed in Friendship, befooled in Love,   30
With spirit shipwrecked, and young hopes blasted,
    He still, still strove –

IX

Till, spent with Toil, dreeing Death for others,
    And some whose hands should have wrought for *him*
(If children live not for sires and mothers),   35
    His mind grew dim;

X

And he fell far through that pit abysmal,
    The gulf and grave of Maginn and Burns,
And pawned his soul for the Devil's dismal
    Stock of returns –   40

XI

But yet redeemed it in days of darkness,
    And shapes and signs of the Final Wrath,

When Death, in hideous and ghastly starkness,
　　Stood on his path.

XII

And tell how now, amid Wreck and Sorrow,　　　　　　　　45
　　And Want, and Sickness, and houseless nights,
He bides in calmness the Silent Morrow,
　　That no ray lights.

XIII

And lives he still, then? Yes! Old and hoary
　　At thirty-nine, from Despair and Woe,　　　　　　　　50
He lives, enduring what future Story
　　Will never know.

XIV

Him grant a grave to, ye pitying Noble,
　　Deep in your bosoms! There let him dwell!
He, too, had tears for all souls in trouble,　　　　　　　55
　　Here and in Hell.

A Whack at the Whigs (by Andrew Magrath or the Mangaire Sugach)[1]

From The Poets and Poetry of Munster (1849)

AIR: Leather the Wig

O, heroes of ancient renown!
　　Good tidings we gladly bring to you –
Let not your high courage sink down,
　　For Eire has friends who'll cling to you.

Those insolent Sassenach bands,　　　　　　　　　　　5
　　Shall hold their white mansions transiently,
Ours shall again be those lands,
　　Long tilled by our fathers anciently!

We'll muster our clans, and their lords,
　　And with energy great and thunderous,　　　　　　　10
With lances, and axes, and swords,
　　We'll trample the Saxon under us!

We'll have masses, as always our wont,
　　And sweet hymns chanted melodiously;

A WHACK AT THE WHIGS
[1] According to John O'Daly, Magrath was "still living in
1790" and his sobriquet means "Merry Dealer."

'Twill go very hard if we don't
    Make the Minister look most odiously![2]   15

We'll have bonfires from Derry to Lene,
    And the foe shall in flames lie weltering –
All Limerick hasn't a green,
    Nor a ship that shall give them sheltering.[3]   20

See! Philip comes over the wave!
    O! Eire deserves abuse, if her
Bold heroes, and patriots brave
    Don't now drive their foes to Lucifer!

Up! arm now, young men, for our isle!   25
    We have here at hand the whole crew of 'em,
Let us charge them in haste and in style,
    And we'll dash out the brains of a few of 'em!

A tribe who can laugh at the jail,
    Have found on the banks of the Shannon aid –   30
O! how the blue Whigs will grow pale,
    When they hear our Limerick cannonade!

O! pity the vagabonds' case!
    We'll slaughter, and crush, and batter them –
They'll die of affright in the chase,   35
    When our valorous Prince shall scatter them!

Coming over the ocean to-day
    Is Charles, that hero dear to us –
His troops will not loiter or stay,
    Till to Inis Loire they come here to us!   40

Our camp is protected by Mars,
    And the mighty Fionn of the olden time,
These will prosper our troops in the wars,
    And bring back to our isle the golden time!

Our cowardly foes will drop dead,   45
    When the French only point their guns on 'em –
And Famine, and Slaughter, and Dread,
    Will together come down at once on 'em!

O, my two eyes might part with their fire,
    And palsying Age set my chin astir,   50
Could I once see those Whigs in the mire,
    And the blind old goat without Minister![4]

Notes

[2] Pitt, the Prime Minister of England (original). William Pitt the Younger (1759–1806).

[3] This is an allusion to the first siege of Limerick in 1690, when that town, although in an almost untenable condition, was held by 10,000 Irishmen against 38,500 of the finest troops in the world – Dutch, Huguenots, Danish, German, and British veterans, under William III … (original).

[4] *An sean-phoc dall, the old blind buck-goat*, i.e., George III., who became imbecile at the close of his life (original). George III of Britain was declared mentally incapacitated in 1810, and his son took power as Regent from 1811 to his father's death in 1820.

Edmund of the Hill

From The Poets and Poetry of Munster (1849)

"You, with voice shrill and sharp,
    Like the high tones of a harp,
Why knock you at my door like a warning?"
    "I am Ned of the Hill,
    I am wet, cold, and chill,   5
Toiling o'er hill and vale since morning" –
    "Ah, my love, is it you?
    What on earth can I do?
My gown cannot yield you a corner.
    Ah! they'll soon find you out –   10
    They'll shoot you, never doubt,
And it's I that will then be a mourner!"

"Long I'm wandering in woe,
    In frost and in snow,
No house can I enter boldly;   15
    My ploughs lie unyoked –
    My fields weeds have choked –
And my friends they look on me coldly!
    Forsaken of all,
    My heart is in thrall: 20
All-withered lies my life's garland,
    I must look afar
    For a brighter star,
Must seek my home in a far land!

"O! thou of neck fair,   25
    And curling hair,
With blue eyes flashing and sparkling!
    For a year and more
    Has my heart been sore,
And my soul for thee been darkling.   30
    O, could we but both, –
    You nothing loth, –
Escape to the wood and forest,
    What Light and Calm,
    What healing balm,   35
Should I have for my sorrows sorest!

My fond one and dear,
    The greenwood is near,
And the lake where the trout is springing –
    You will see the doe,   40
    The deer and the roe,
And will hear the sweet birds singing,
    The blackbird and thrush
    In the hawthorn bush,

And the lone cuckoo from his high nest,   45
   And you never need fear,
   That Death would be near,
In this bright scenery divinest!"

   O! could the sweet dove,
   The maiden of my love,   50
But know how fettered is her lover!
   The snows all the night
   Fell in valley and on height,[1]
Through our fated island over,
   But ere the sun's rays   55
   Glance over seven days,
She and I, as I hope, will renew love;
   And rather would I be
   Deep drowned in the sea,
Than be faithless to her, my true love!   60

From *Fragment of an Unpublished Autobiography*[1]

From The Irish Monthly (1882)

Chapter V

Farewell the tranquil mind! farewell content.[2]
         (Shakespeare)

On the south side of the city of Dublin, and about half-way down an avenue which breaks the continuity of that part of the Circular-road, extending from Harold's Cross to Dolphin's Barn, stands a house plain in appearance, and without any peculiarity of external structure to attract the passenger's notice. Adjoining the house is a garden, with a sort of turret-lodge at the extreme end, which looks forth on the high road. The situation is lone and picturesque; and he who should pause to dwell on it must be actuated by other and deeper and, possibly, sadder feelings than any that such a scene would be likely to excite in the breast of the poet or the artist. Perhaps he should be under the influence of such emotions as I recently experienced in passing the spot after an absence from it of seventeen years. Seventeen years! let me rather say seventeen centuries. For life upon life has followed and been multiplied on and within me during that long, long era of passion, trouble, and sin. The Pompeii and Herculaneum of my soul have been dug up from their ancient sepulchres. The few broken columns and solitary arches which form the present ruins of what was once Palmyra, present not a fainter or more imperfect picture of that great city as it

---

Notes

EDMUND OF THE HILL
[1] From this and the preceding line, it would appear that the song was composed in the year of the great frost, 1739 (original).

FROM FRAGMENT
[1] Chapter V is here included in full from the first printed version of Mangan's autobiography; the autobiography subsequently appeared, with minor changes, in a new edition of *The Poets and Poetry of Munster*. Kilroy's 1968 edition (see Bibliography), based on the original manuscript, is a more reliable version of the manuscript, if not of what nineteenth-century readers knew of it.
[2] *Othello*.

flourished in the days of its youth and glory than I, as I am now, of what I was before I entered on the career to which I was introduced by my first acquaintance with that lone house in 1831. Years of so much mingled pleasure and sorrow! whither have you departed? or rather, why were you allotted me? You delivered me from sufferings which, at least, were of a guiltless order, and would shortly, in a better world, have been exchanged for joys, to give me up to others, the bitter fruits of late repentance, and which await no recompense, and know no change, save change from severe to severer. But, alas! thus it was, is, and must be. My plaint is chorussed by millions. Generation preaches to generation in vain. It is ever and everywhere the same old immemorial tale. From the days of Adam in Eden to our own, we purchase knowledge at the price of innocence. Like Aladdin in the subterranean garden, we are permitted to heap together and gather up as much hard bright gold and diamonds as we will – but we are forever, therefore, entombed from the fresh natural green pastures and the healthy daylight.

In the course of my desultory rambles about the suburbs of the city it would sometimes happen that I should feel obliged to stop and rest, even though nothing better than a hedge-side or a field-hillock afforded me the means of a few moments' repose. The reader will, therefore, imagine me reclining, rather than seated, on a long knoll of grass by a stream-side beyond Rathfarnham, and closely adjacent to Round-town, while the sun is setting on an evening in June. I held in my hand a book, with the covers turned down; it was *Les Pensées de Pascal*.[3] As I lay revolving in my mind some of the sublime truths contained in this celebrated work, I was somewhat suddenly approached and accosted by a fashionably dressed and intelligent-looking young man, whom I had twice or thrice before observed sauntering about this neighbourhood.

"May I ask," he inquired, "the nature of your studies?"

I placed the book in his hand. He looked at it for a moment, and then returned it to me without speaking.

"You don't read French?" said I, interrogatively.

"Oh, yes, I do," he replied; "who does not now-a-days. But that is a very unhealthy work."

I perceived at once that there was a great gulf between us; and as I had even then learned enough of the nature of the human mind to know that disputation hardly ever converts or convinces, I contented myself with remarking, in an indifferent manner: "Everything in this world is unhealthy."

The stranger smiled. "And yet," said he, "you feel pleasure, I am sure, in the contemplation of this beautiful scenery; and you admire the glory of the setting sun."

"I have pleasure in nothing, and I admire nothing," answered I; "I hate scenery and suns. I see nothing in creation but what is fallen and ruined."

My companion made no immediate remark upon this, but after a pause took the book out of my hand, and turning over the leaves, read aloud that passage in which Pascal compares the world to a dungeon, and its inhabitants to condemned criminals, awaiting the summons to execution.

"Can you believe, my friend," the stranger asked, "for short as our acquaintance has been, I venture to call you such, can you believe this to be true?"

"Why not?" I replied. "My own experiences, feelings, life, sufferings, all testify to my soul of its truth. But before I add anything further, will you allow me to ask what religion you profess?"

Notes ───

[3] *Pensées* (1660), by French scientist Blaise Pascal (1623–62), is a somewhat unorthodox defense of Christian faith.

"A good one, I hope," he answered; "I have been reared a Catholic Christian."

"Then," said I, "you know that it is the belief of the holiest and most learned theologians of your Church that the majority of mankind will be irrevocably consigned to eternal misery."

"Really I know no such thing," he replied.

"Have you never read Massillon,"[4] I asked, "on the small number of the saved?"

"I take the judgment of no one individual, even in my own Church," he answered, "as my guide. The goodness, the justice of God — "

I interrupted him. "Stop," said I, "What do you —"[5]

Samuel Ferguson (1810–1886)

Samuel Ferguson was born in Belfast, the descendant of seventeenth-century Scottish immigrants to Ireland. His interest in the Irish language began at an early age, and he took classes in the subject at the Belfast Academical Institution. He practiced law for a while after being called to the Irish bar in 1838, but his law career, as well as his early studies, were interrupted by illness. He was briefly involved in the repeal movement, and other nationalist activities in the late 1840s as well. He married in 1848 and soon thereafter settled permanently in Dublin. He often traveled to study antiquarian sites in Europe and Ireland, and was a member of the Royal Irish Academy – a prestigious group that elected him president in 1881. His antiquarian scholarship perhaps prepared him for the government position he would occupy from 1867, first deputy keeper of the records in Ireland. He was knighted for his work as a civil servant on St. Patrick's Day, 1878.

Like many poets of his generation, he published much of his early work in periodicals, including the *Ulster Magazine*, *Blackwood's*, and the *Dublin University Magazine*. He was also a contributor to key works such as Duffy's *Ballad Poetry of Ireland* (1845). After thirty years of contributing to various periodicals, he finally published a volume of his own, *Cromlech on Howth* (1864), soon followed by *Lays of the Western Gael, and Other Poems* (1865) and later *Congal* (1872), *Poems* (1880), the rather odd but utterly Victorian *Shakespearian Breviates* (1882), and a volume publication of his early poem, *The Forging of the Anchor* (1883). Ferguson was distinctive in his day as an Ulster poet – raised as a Presbyterian, but generally Church of Ireland as an adult – who hesitated over some branches of Irish nationalism while supporting both repeal and Irish-language studies, a continuation of the United Irishmen's pan-sectarian project of the previous century and its support for the study of the Irish language and pre-colonial history. While "Willy Gilliland" is reminiscent of Orr's poetry, "The Burial of King Cormac" bears comparison to Corry's *Patriot* as well as Dublin-centered antiquarian work of the nineteenth century by Mangan and others. While best remembered as an Ulster poet and an antiquarian who contributed extensively to the translation of Irish-language material, his corpus is strikingly diverse, including religious poems, powerful elegies, and the celebration of maritime masculinity in "The Forging of the Anchor."

His poem on the death of Thomas Davis is perhaps his most important nationalist work.

Notes

[4] Jean-Baptiste Massillon (1663–1742), French bishop and author.

[5] This line is followed with the note "*Here the Manuscript comes suddenly to an end.*"

The poem has since become known as "Lament for Thomas Davis," but it was first published anonymously and untitled in an article on Davis in the *Dublin University Magazine*. Ferguson did not include it in his volumes of verse, and his widow titled it "Thomas Davis: an Elegy – 1845" in her memoir of the poet. The anonymous author of the article on Davis apologizes for the poem's style, suggesting that Ferguson "adopted the peculiar Irish taste in his composition, which it was poor Davis's delight to inculcate, and which, although it invites to a composition that may seem rugged to English eyes, possesses a regular melody for Irish ears, and, we believe, comes home to the Irish heart." The form of the "Lament" bears closer comparison to Mangan's translations than earlier ones such as Brooke's. The other elegiac poem by Ferguson included here, on the death of William Wilde, is in heroic couplets, a more conventionally English form for serious verse, if not elegy, although there are precedents for Ferguson's choice.

Further reading

Campbell, Matthew, "Lyrical Unions: Mangan, O'Hussey and Ferguson," *Irish Studies Review* 8 (2000): 325–38.

Denman, Peter, *Samuel Ferguson: The Literary Achievement.* Gerrards Cross: Colin Smythe, 1990.

Graham, Colin, *Ideologies of Epic: Nation, Empire and Victorian Epic Poetry.* Manchester: Manchester University Press, 1998.

The Forging of the Anchor

From Blackwood's Edinburgh Magazine (1832)

Come, see the Dolphin's Anchor forg'd; 'tis at a white heat now:
The bellows ceased, the flames decreased; though on the forge's brow,
The little flames still fitfully play through the sable mound;
And fitfully you still may see the grim smiths ranking round,
All clad in leathern panoply, their broad hands only bare;   5
Some rest upon their sledges here, some work the windlass there.

The windlass strains the tackle chains, the black mound heaves below;
And red and deep, a hundred veins burst out at every throe:
It rises, roars, rends all outright – O, Vulcan,[1] what a glow!
'Tis blinding white, 'tis blasting bright; the high sun shines not so!   10
The high sun sees not, on the earth, such fiery fearful show,
The roof-ribs swarth, the candent hearth, the ruddy lurid row
Of smiths, that stand, an ardent band, like men before the foe;
As, quivering through his fleece of flame, the sailing monster, slow
Sinks on the anvil – all about the faces fiery grow –   15
"Hurrah!" they shout, "leap out – leap out;" bang, bang the sledges go:
Hurrah! the jetted lightnings are hissing high and low;
A hailing fount of fire is struck at every squashing blow;
The leathern mail rebounds the hail; the rattling cinders strow
The ground around; at every bound the sweltering fountains flow;   20
And thick and loud the swinking[2] crowd, at every stroke, pant "ho!"

Leap out, leap out, my masters; leap out and lay on load!
Let's forge a goodly Anchor; a Bower,[3] thick and broad:

Notes _____

THE FORGING OF THE ANCHOR
[1] Roman god of the forge.

[2] toiling
[3] Anchor placed at the bow of a ship.

For a heart of oak is hanging on every blow, I bode;
And I see the good Ship riding, all in a perilous road,   25
The low reef roaring on her lee; the roll of ocean pour'd
From stem to stern, sea after sea; the mainmast by the board;
The bulwarks down; the rudder gone; the boats stove at the chains;
But courage still, brave mariners – the Bower yet remains,
And not an inch to flinch he deigns save when ye pitch sky high,   30
Then moves his head, as though he said, "Fear nothing – here am I!"

Swing in your strokes in order; let foot and hand keep time;
Your blows make music sweeter far than any steeple's chime:
But, while you sling your sledges, sing; and let the burthen[4] be,
The Anchor is the Anvil King, and royal craftsmen we!   35
Strike in, strike in – the sparks begin to dull their rustling red;
Our hammers ring with sharper din, our work will soon be sped:
Our Anchor soon must change his bed of fiery rich array,
For a hammock at the roaring bows, or an oozy couch of clay;
Our Anchor soon must change the lay of merry craftsmen here,   40
For the Yeo-heave-o', and the Heave-away, and the sighing seaman's cheer;
When, weighing slow, at eve they go, far, far from love and home;
And sobbing sweethearts, in a row, wail o'er the ocean foam.

In livid and obdurate gloom he darkens down at last;
A shapely one he is, and strong, as e'er from cat[5] was cast. –   45
O trusted and trustworthy guard, if thou hadst life like me,
What pleasures would thy toils reward beneath the deep green sea!
O deep Sea-diver, who might then behold such sights as thou?
The hoary monster's palaces! methinks what joy 'twere now
To go plumb plunging down amid the assembly of the whales,   50
And feel the churn'd sea round me boil beneath their scourging tails!
Then deep in tangle-woods to fight the fierce sea unicorn,
And send him foiled and bellowing back, for all his ivory horn;
To leave the subtle sworder-fish of bony blade forlorn;
And for the ghastly-grinning shark to laugh his jaws to scorn: 55
To leap down on the kraken's[6] back, where 'mid Norwegian isles
He lies, a lubber anchorage for sudden shallow'd miles;
Till snorting, like an under-sea volcano, off he rolls;
Meanwhile to swing, a-buffeting the far astonished shoals
Of his back-browsing ocean-calves; or, haply in a cove,   60
Shell-strown, and consecrate of old to some Undiné's[7] love,
To find the long-hair'd mermaidens; or, hard by icy lands,
To wrestle with the Sea-serpent, upon cerulean sands.

O broad-armed Fisher of the Deep, whose sports can equal thine?
The Dolphin weighs a thousand tons, that tugs thy cable line;   65
And night by night, 'tis thy delight, thy glory day by day,
Through sable sea and breaker white, the giant game to play –
But shamer of our little sports! forgive the name I gave –

Notes

[4] chorus
[5] A kind of large and sturdy ship often used to transport coal.

[6] A mythical sea monster; see English poet Tennyson's "The Kraken" (1830).
[7] A water nymph.

A fisher's joy is to destroy – thine office is to save.
O lodger in the sea-kings' halls, couldst thou but understand   70
Whose be the white bones by thy side, or who that dripping band,
Slow swaying in the heaving wave, that round about thee bend,
With sounds like breakers in a dream blessing their ancient friend –
Oh, couldst thou know what heroes glide with larger steps round thee,
Thine iron side would swell with pride; thou'dst leap within the sea!   75

Give honour to their memories who left the pleasant strand,
To shed their blood so freely for the love of Father-land –
Who left their chance of quiet age and grassy churchyard grave,
So freely, for a restless bed amid the tossing wave –
Oh, though our Anchor may not be all I have fondly sung,   80
Honour him for their memory, whose bones he goes among!

[*Thomas Davis: An Elegy*]¹

From Dublin University Magazine (1847)

I walked through Ballinderry in the spring-time,
    When the bud was on the tree;
And I said, in every fresh-ploughed field beholding
    The sowers striding free,
Scattering broad-cast forth the corn in golden plenty,   5
    On the quick seed-clasping soil,
Even such this day, among the fresh-stirred hearts of Erin,
    Thomas Davis, is thy toil!

I sat by Ballyshannon in the Summer,
    And saw the salmon leap;   10
And I said, as I beheld the gallant creatures
    Spring glittering from the deep,
Through the spray, and through the prone heaps striving onward
    To the calm, clear streams above,
So seekest thou thy native founts of freedom, Thomas Davis,   15
    In thy brightness of strength and love!

I stood on Derrybawn in the Autumn,
    And I heard the Eagle call,
With a clangorous cry of wrath and lamentation,
    That filled the wide mountain-hall,   20
O'er the bare, deserted place of his plundered eyrie;
    And I said, as he screamed and soared,
So callest thou, thou wrathful-soaring Thomas Davis,
    For a nation's rights restored!

Notes ──────────────────────────────────

[THOMAS DAVIS: AN ELEGY]
¹ Thomas Davis (1814–45), leading thinker in Young Ireland
and co-founder of *The Nation*.

And, alas! to think but now, and thou art lying   25
  Dear Davis, dead at thy mother's knee;
And I, no mother near, on my own sick bed,
  That face on earth shall never see;
I may lie and try to feel that I am not dreaming,
  I may lie and try to say "Thy will be done" –   30
But a hundred such as I will never comfort Erin
  For the loss of the noble son!

Young husbandman of Erin's fruitful seed-time,
  In the fresh track of danger's plough!
Who will walk the heavy, toilsome, perilous furrow,   35
  Girt with Freedom's seed-sheets, now?
Who will banish with the wholesome crop of knowledge
  The flaunting weed and the bitter thorn,
Now that thou thyself art but a seed for hopeful planting
  Against the resurrection morn?   40

Young salmon of the flood-tide of Freedom
  That swells round Erin's shore!
Thou wilt leap against their loud oppressive torrent
  Of bigotry and hate no more: –
Drawn downward by their prone material instinct   45
  Let them thunder on their rocks and foam –
Thou hast leapt, aspiring soul, to founts beyond their raging,
  Where troubled waters never come!

But I grieve not, eagle of the empty eyrie,
  That thy wrathful cry is still;   50
And that the songs alone of peaceful mourners
  Are heard to-day on Erin's hill;
Better far, if brothers war be destined for us
  (God avert that horrid day I pray!)
That ere our hands be stained with slaughter fratricidal,   55
  Thy warm hand should be cold in clay.

But my trust is strong in God, who made us brothers,
  That he will not suffer those right hands,
Which thou hast joined in holier rites than wedlock,
  To draw opposing brands.   60
Oh, many a tuneful tongue that thou mad'st vocal
  Would lie cold and silent then; –
And songless long once more, should often-widowed Erin
  Mourn the loss of her brave young men.

Oh, brave young men, my love, my pride, and promise,   65
  'Tis on you my hopes are set,
In manliness, in kindliness, in justice
  To make Erin a nation yet:
Self-respecting, self-relying, self-advancing,
  In union or in severance, free and strong –   70
And if God grant this, then, under God, to Thomas Davis
  Let the greater praise belong!

The Burial of King Cormac

From Lays of the Western Gael, and Other Poems (1865)

Introductory Note

Cormac, son of Art, son of Con Cead-Catha,[1] enjoyed the sovereignty of Ireland through the prolonged period of forty years, commencing from A.D. 213. During the latter part of his reign, he resided at Sletty on the Boyne, being, it is said, disqualified for the occupation of Tara by the personal blemish he had sustained in the loss of an eye, by the hand of Angus "Dread-Spear," chief of the Desi, a tribe whose original seats were in the barony of Deece, in the county of Meath. It was in the time of Cormac and his son Carbre, if we are to credit the Irish annals, that Fin, son of Comhal, and the Fenian heroes, celebrated by Ossian, flourished. Cormac has obtained the reputation of wisdom and learning, and appears justly entitled to the honour of having provoked the enmity of the Pagan priesthood, by declaring his faith in a God not made by hands of men.

The Burial of King Cormac

"Crom Cruach and his sub-gods twelve,"
    Said Cormac, "are but carven treene;
The axe that made them, haft or helve,
    Had worthier our worship been.

"But He who made the tree to grow,   5
    And hid in earth the iron-stone,
And made the man with mind to know
    The axe's use, is God alone."

Anon to priests of Crom was brought –
    Where, girded in their service dread,   10
They minister'd on red Moy Slought –
    Word of the words King Cormac said.

They loosed their curse against the king;
    They cursed him in his flesh and bones;
And daily in their mystic ring   15
    They turn'd the maledictive stones,[2]

Till, where at meat the monarch sate,
    Amid the revel and the wine,

Notes

THE BURIAL OF KING CORMAC
[1] *i.e.* Hundred-Battle (author).
[2] A pagan practice in use among the Lusitanian as well as the Insular Celts, and of which Dr. O'Donovan records an instance, among the latter, as late as the year 1836, in the island of Inishmurray, off the coast of Sligo. Among the places and objects of reverence included within the pre-christian stone *Cashel*, or cyclopean citadel of the island, he mentions the *clocha breca*, i.e., the *speckled stones*. "They are round stones of various sizes, and arranged in such order as that they cannot be easily reckoned, and, if you believe the natives, they cannot be reckoned at all. These stones are turned, and, if I understand them rightly, their order changed by the inhabitants on certain occasions, when thy visit this shrine to *wish* good or evil to their neighbours." – *MS. Collections for Ordnance Survey, Lib. R. I. A.* (author). "R.I.A." refers to the Royal Irish Academy.

He choked upon the food he ate,
   At Sletty, southward of the Boyne.   20

High vaunted then the priestly throng,
   And far and wide they noised abroad
With trump and loud liturgic song
   The praise of their avenging God.

But ere the voice was wholly spent   25
   That priest and prince should still obey,
To awed attendants o'er him bent
   Great Cormac gather'd breath to say, –

"Spread not the beds of Brugh for me[3]
   When restless death-bed's use is done: 30
But bury me at Rossnaree
   And face me to the rising sun.

For all the kings who lie in Brugh
   Put trust in gods of wood and stone;
And 'twas at Ross that first I knew   35
   One, Unseen, who is God alone.

His glory lightens from the east;
   His message soon shall reach our shore;
And idol-god, and cursing priest
   Shall plague us from Moy-Slaught no more."   40

Dead Cormac on his bier they laid: –
   "He reign'd a king for forty years,
And shame it were," his captains said,
   "He lay not with his royal peers.

His grandsire, Hundred-Battle, sleeps   45
   Serene in Brugh: and, all around,
Dead kings in stone sepulchral keeps
   Protect the sacred burial ground.

What though a dying man should rave
   Of changes o'er the eastern sea?   50
In Brugh of Boyne shall be his grave,
   And not in noteless Rossnaree."

Then northward forth they bore the bier,
   And down from Sletty side they drew,
With horseman and with charioteer,   55
   To cross the fords of Boyne to Brugh.

Notes

[3] The principal cemetery of the pagan Irish kings was at Brugh, which seems to have been situated on the northern bank of the Boyne. A series of tumuli and sepulchral *cairns* extends from the neighbourhood of Slane towards Drogheda, beginning ... with the *imdae in Dagda*, or "Bed of the Dagda," a king of the Tuath de Danaan, supposed, with apparently good reason, to be the well-known tumulus now called New Grange. This and the neighbouring cairn of Dowth appear to be the only Megalithic sepulchres in the west of Europe distinctly referable to persons whose names are historically preserved (author).

There came a breath of finer air
    That touch'd the Boyne with ruffling wings,
It stirr'd him in his sedgy lair
    And in his mossy moorland springs.   60

And as the burial train came down
    With dirge and savage dolorous shows,
Across their pathway, broad and brown
    The deep, full-hearted river rose;

From bank to bank through all his fords,   65
    'Neath blackening squalls he swell'd and boil'd;
And thrice the wondering gentile lords
    Essay'd to cross, and thrice recoil'd.

Then forth stepp'd grey-hair'd warriors four:
    They said, "Through angrier floods than these,   70
On link'd shields once our king we bore
    From Dread-Spear and the hosts of Deece.

And long as loyal will holds good,
    And limbs respond with helpful thews,
Nor flood, nor fiend within the flood,   75
    Shall bar him of his burial dues."

With slanted necks they stoop'd to lift;
    They heaved him up to neck and chin;
And, pair and pair, with footsteps swift,
    Lock'd arm and shoulder, bore him in.   80

'Twas brave to see them leave the shore;
    To mark the deep'ning surges rise,
And fall subdued in foam before
    The tension of their striding thighs.

'Twas brave, when now a spear-cast out,   85
    Breast-high the battling surges ran;
For weight was great, and limbs were stout,
    And loyal man put trust in man.

But ere they reach'd the middle deep,
    Nor steadying weight of clay they bore,   90
Nor strain of sinewy limbs could keep
    Their feet beneath the swerving four.

And now they slide, and now they swim,
    And now, amid the blackening squall,
Grey locks afloat, with clutchings grim,   95
    They plunge around the floating pall.

While, as a youth with practised spear
    Through justling crowds bears off the ring,
Boyne from their shoulders caught the bier
    And proudly bore away their king.   100

At morning, on the grassy marge
    Of Rossnaree, the corpse was found,

And shepherds at their early charge
    Entomb'd it in the peaceful ground.

A tranquil spot: a hopeful sound   105
    Comes from the ever youthful stream,
And still on daisied mead and mound
    The dawn delays with tenderer beam.

Round Cormac Spring renews her buds:
    In march perpetual by his side,   110
Down come the earth-fresh April floods,
    And up the sea-fresh salmon glide;

And life and time rejoicing run
    From age to age their wonted way;
But still he waits the risen Sun,   115
    For still 'tis only dawning Day.

Willy Gilliland: An Ulster Ballad

From Lays of the Western Gael, and Other Poems (1865)

Up in the mountain solitudes, and in a rebel ring,
He has worshipp'd God upon the hill, in spite of church and king;
And seal'd his treason with his blood on Bothwell bridge he hath;
So he must fly his father's land, or he must die the death;
For comely Claverhouse has come along with grim Dalzell,   5
And his smoking rooftree testifies they've done their errand well.[1]

In vain to fly his enemies he fled his native land;
Hot persecution waited him upon the Carrick strand;
His name was on the Carrick cross, a price was on his head,
A fortune to the man that brings him in alive or dead!   10
And so on moor and mountain, from the Lagan to the Bann,
From house to house, and hill to hill, he lurk'd an outlaw'd man.

At last, when in false company he might no longer bide,
He stay'd his houseless wanderings upon the Collon side,
There in a cave all underground he lair'd his heathy den,   15
Ah, many a gentleman was fain to earth like hill fox then!
With hound and fishing-rod he lived on hill and stream by day;
At night, betwixt his fleet greyhound and his bonny mare he lay.

It was a summer evening, and, mellowing and still,
Glenwhirry to the setting sun lay bare from hill to hill;   20
For all that valley pastoral held neither house nor tree,

Notes

WILLY GILLILAND
[1] In the Battle of Bothwell Bridge (1679), in Scotland, Covenanters (Presbyterians) were defeated by the British military, led by the Duke of Monmouth with the assistance of John Graham of Claverhouse and Thomas Dalzell. The battle is the subject of popular ballads as well as Scottish novelist Sir Walter Scott's *Old Mortality* (1816); the central issue was religious freedom. "Willy Gilliland" is set in Argyll, Scotland.

But spread abroad and open all, a full fair sight to see,
From Slemish foot to Collon top lay one unbroken green,
Save where in many a silver coil the river glanced between.

And on the river's grassy bank, even from the morning grey, 25
He at the angler's pleasant sport had spent the summer day:
Ah! many a time and oft I've spent the summer day from dawn,
And wonder'd, when the sunset came, where time and care had gone,
Along the reaches curling fresh, the wimpling pools and streams,
Where he that day his cares forgot in those delightful dreams. 30

His blithe work done, upon a bank the outlaw rested now,
And laid the basket from his back, the bonnet from his brow;
And there, his hand upon the Book, his knee upon the sod,
He fill'd the lonely valley with the gladsome word of God;
And for a persecuted kirk, and for her martyrs dear, 35
And against a godless church and king he spoke up loud and clear.

And now, upon his homeward way, he cross'd the Collon high,
And over bush and bank and brae he sent abroad his eye;
But all was darkening peacefully in grey and purple haze,
The thrush was silent in the banks, the lark upon the braes – 40
When suddenly shot up a blaze, from the cave's mouth it came;
And troopers' steeds and troopers' caps are glancing in the same!

He couch'd among the heather, and he saw them, as he lay,
With three long yells at parting, ride lightly east away:
Then down with heavy heart he came, to sorry cheer came he, 45
For ashes black were crackling where the green whins used to be,
And stretch'd among the prickly coomb, his heart's blood smoking round,
From slender nose to breast-bone cleft, lay dead his good greyhound!

"They've slain my dog, the Philistines! they've ta'en my bonny mare!" –
He plung'd into the smoky hole; no bonny beast was there – 50
He groped beneath the burning bed, (it burn'd him to the bone,)
Where his good weapon used to be, but broadsword there was none;
He reel'd out of the stifling den, and sat down on a stone,
And in the shadows of the night 'twas thus he made his moan –

"I am a houseless outcast; I have neither bed nor board, 55
Nor living thing to look upon, nor comfort save the Lord:
Yet many a time were better men in worse extremity;
Who succour'd them in their distress, He now will succour me, –
He now will succour me, I know; and, by His holy Name,
I'll make the doers of this deed right dearly rue the same! 60

"My bonny mare! I've ridden you when Claver'se rode behind,
And from the thumbscrew and the boot[2] you bore me like the wind;
And, while I have the life you saved, on your sleek flank, I swear,
Episcopalian rowel[3] shall never ruffle hair!

Notes ─────────────────────────────────────

[2] Instruments of torture.

[3] "Episcopalian" here means Anglican, the established
Church from which the Covenanters were Dissenters;
"rowel" is part of a spur.

Though sword to wield they've left me none – yet Wallace wight, I wis,　　　65
Good battle did on Irvine side wi' waur weapon than this."[4] –

His fishing-rod with both his hands he griped it as he spoke,
And, where the butt and top were spliced, in pieces twain he broke;
The limber top he cast away, with all its gear abroad,
But, grasping the tough hickory butt, with spike of iron shod,　　　70
He ground the sharp spear to a point; then pull'd his bonnet down,
And, meditating black revenge, set forth for Carrick town.

The sun shines bright on Carrick wall and Carrick Castle grey,
And up thine aisle, St. Nicholas, has ta'en his morning way,
And to the North-Gate sentinel displayeth far and near　　　75
Sea, hill, and tower, and all thereon, in dewy freshness clear,
Save where, behind a ruin'd wall, himself alone to view,
Is peering from the ivy green a bonnet of the blue.

The sun shines red on Carrick wall and Carrick Castle old,
And all the western buttresses have changed their grey for gold;　　　80
And from thy shrine, Saint Nicholas, the pilgrim of the sky
Has gone in rich farewell, as fits such royal votary;
But, as his last red glance he takes down past black Slieve-a-true,
He leaveth where he found it first, the bonnet of the blue.

Again he makes the turrets grey stand out before the hill;　　　85
Constant as their foundation rock, there is the bonnet still!
And now the gates are open'd, and forth in gallant show
Prick jeering grooms and burghers blythe, and troopers in a row;
But one has little care for jest, so hard bested is he,
To ride the outlaw's bonny mare, for this at last is she!　　　90

Down comes her master with a roar, her rider with a groan,
The iron and the hickory are through and through him gone!
He lies a corpse; and where he sat, the outlaw sits again,
And once more to his bonny mare he gives the spur and rein;
Then some with sword, and some with gun, they ride and run amain;　　　95
But sword and gun, and whip and spur, that day they plied in vain!

Ah! little thought Willy Gilliland, when he on Skerry side
Drew bridle first, and wiped his brow after that weary ride,
That where he lay like hunted brute, a cavern'd outlaw lone,
Broad lands and yeoman tenantry should yet be there his own:　　　100
Yet so it was; and still from him descendants not a few
Draw birth and lands, and, let me trust, draw love of Freedom too.

Notes

[4] William Wallace (?–1305), Scottish national hero. According to a 1488 account available in nineteenth-century editions, Wallace became an outlaw after fighting a group of English soldiers who demanded the fish he had just caught in the Irvine; he killed some of his assailants and took one of their horses, using it to flee arrest. *wight*, valiant; *waur*, worse.

From Versions from the Irish

From Lays of the Western Gael, and Other Poems (1865)

Lament over the Ruins of the Abbey of Timoleague (by John Collins, d. 1816)

Lone and weary as I wander'd
   By the bleak shore of the sea,
Meditating and reflecting
   On the world's hard destiny;

Forth the moon and stars 'gan glimmer,   5
   In the quiet tide beneath, –
For on slumbering spray and blossom
   Breathed not out of heaven a breath.

On I went in sad dejection,
   Careless where my footsteps bore,   10
Till a ruin'd church before me
   Open'd wide its ancient door, –

Till I stood before the portals,
   Where of old were wont to be,
For the blind, the halt, and leper,   15
   Alms and hospitality.

Still the ancient seat was standing,
   Built against the buttress grey,
Where the clergy used to welcome
   Weary travellers on their way.   20

There I sat me down in sadness,
   'Neath my cheek I placed my hand,
Till the tears fell hot and briny
   Down upon the grassy land.

There, I said in woeful sorrow,   25
   Weeping bitterly the while,
Was a time when joy and gladness
   Reign'd within this ruin'd pile; –

Was a time when bells were tinkling,
   Clergy preaching peace abroad,   30
Psalms a-singing, music ringing
   Praises to the mighty God.

Empty aisle, deserted chancel,
   Tower tottering to your fall,
Many a storm since then has beaten   35
   On the grey head of your wall!

Many a bitter storm and tempest
   Has your roof-tree turn'd away,
Since you first were form'd a temple
   To the Lord of night and day.   40

Holy house of ivied gables,
    That wert once the country's pride,
Houseless now in weary wandering
    Roam your inmates far and wide.

Lone you are to-day, and dismal, –   45
    Joyful psalms no more are heard
Where, within your choir, her vesper
    Screeches the cat-headed bird.

Ivy from your eaves is growing,
    Nettles round your green hearth-stone,   50
Foxes howl, where, in your corners,
    Dropping waters make their moan.

Where the lark to early matins
    Used your clergy forth to call,
There, alas! no tongue is stirring,   55
    Save the daw's upon the wall.

Refectory cold and empty,
    Dormitory bleak and bare,
Where are now your pious uses,
    Simple bed and frugal fare?   60

Gone your abbot, rule and order,
    Broken down your altar stones;
Nought see I beneath your shelter,
    Save a heap of clayey bones.

Oh! the hardship, oh! the hatred,   65
    Tyranny, and cruel war,
Persecution and oppression,
    That have left you as you are!

I myself once also prosper'd; –
    Mine is, too, an alter'd plight;   70
Trouble, care, and age have left me
    Good for nought but grief to-night.

Gone, my motion and my vigour, –
    Gone, the use of eye and ear;
At my feet lie friends and children,   75
    Powerless and corrupting here:

Woe is written on my visage,
    In a nut my heart would lie –
Death's deliverance were welcome –
    Father, let the old man die.   80

Grace Nugent (by Carolan)

Brightest blossom of the Spring,
Grace, the sprightly girl I sing:
Grace, who bore the palm of mind
From all the rest of womankind.

Whomso'er the fates decree,   5
Happy fate! for life to be
Day and night my Coolun near,
Ache or pain need never fear!

Her neck outdoes the stately swan,
Her radiant face the summer dawn: 10
Ah, happy thrice the youth for whom
The fates design that branch of bloom!
Pleasant are your words benign,
Rich those azure eyes of thine:
Ye who see my queen, beware   15
Those twisted links of golden hair!

This is what I fain would say
To the bird-voiced lady gay, –
Never yet conceived the heart
Joy which Grace cannot impart: 20
Fold of jewels! case of pearls!
Coolun of the circling curls!
More I say not, but no less
Drink you health and happiness!

The Morning's Hinges

From Poems (1880)

A solis ortûs cardine.[1]
(SEDULIUS)

I

Where the Morning's hinges turn,
Where the fires of sunset burn,
Where the Pole its burthen weighty
Whirls around the starry hall;
Beings, whereso'er ye are,   5
Ether, vapour, comet, star,
There art Thou, Lord God Almighty,
Thou that mad'st and keep'st them all.

II

Where, on earth, battalioned foes
In the deadly combat close;   10
Where the plagues have made their stations,
Dropped from Heaven's distempered air;

THE MORNING'S HINGES
[1] A fifth-century Latin hymn by Caelius Sedulius, translated
by English clergyman John Mason Neale (1818–66) as "Lands
that See the Sun Arise."

Where, within the human breast,
Rising hints of thought suggest
Sin's insane hallucinations,   15
Dread One, Thou art also there.

III

O most Mighty, O most High,
Past Thought's compass, what am I
That should dare Thy comprehending
In this narrow, shallow brain?   20
Yea, but Thou hast given a Soul
Well capacious of the whole,
And a Conscience ever tending
Right-ward, surely not in vain.

IV

Yea, I'd hinder, if I could,   25
Wrath and pain and spilling blood;
I would tell the cannon loaded
"Fire not"! and the sabre stay
Mid-cut: but the matter brute
Owns its own law absolute;   30
And the grains will be exploded,
And the driven iron slay.

V

Deaf the nitre; deaf the steel:
And, if I the Man appeal,
Answer Soldier and Commander,   35
"We, blind engines, even as these,
Do but execute His plan,
Working since the world began,
Towards some consummation grander
Than your little mind can seize."   40

VI

What! does all, then, end in this,
That, amid a world amiss,
Man must ever be but parcel-
Imperfection? and the soul
Ever thus in poise between   45
Things contrarient, rest, a mean
Averaged of the universal
Good and ill that make the whole?

VII

No, a something cries within;
No; I am not of your kin   50
Broods of evil! all the forces

Of my nature answer No!
Though the world be overspread
With the riddle still unread
Of your being, of your sources,　　　　　　　　55
This with sense supreme I know;

VIII

That, behoves me, and I can,
Work within the inner man
Such a weeding, such a cleansing
Of this moss-grown home-plot here,　　　　　60
As shall make its herbage meet
For the soles of angels' feet,
And its blooms for eyes dispensing
Light of Heaven's own atmosphere.

IX

"Yea, what thou hast last advanced,　　　　　65
Creature, verily thou canst."
(Hark, the Master!) "Up. Bestir thee;
And, that thou may'st find the way,
Things inscrutable laid by,
Be content to know that I,　　　　　　　　70
Hoping, longing, waiting for thee,
Stand beside thee, every day."

X

Lord, and is it Thou, indeed,
Takest pity on my need,
Who nor symbol show nor token　　　　　　75
Vouching aught of right in me?
"I, dear soul," the Master said,
"Come to some through broken bread;
Come to some through message spoken;
Come in pure, free grace to thee."　　　　　80

Dear Wilde: An Elegy

From **Poems (1880)**

INTRODUCTORY NOTE

THE late Sir William Wilde[1] will be best known by the noble collection of Celtic antiquities which he was the chief instrument in assembling, and has the sole credit of

Notes ————————————————

DEAR WILDE: AN ELEGY
[1] William Wilde (1815–76), husband of Lady Wilde and father of Oscar Wilde, and one of the leading experts of his generation on Irish antiquities. Ferguson, a friend of the Wilde family, dated the poem 1876, the year of Wilde's death.

having so far catalogued, at the Royal Irish Academy House. The Government Department of Science and Art has now, after long resistance by the Academy, acquired the property in this collection for future exhibition in a State Museum, where it is to be hoped that a bust of Wilde will be placed near that of its other founder, Petrie. Wilde had a sweet poetic sentiment, largely influenced by the pastoral scenery and pursuits of his native county, Roscommon.

Dear Wilde, the deeps close o'er thee; and no more
Greet we or mingle on the hither shore,
Where other footsteps now must print the sand,
And other waiters by the margin stand.
Gone; and, alas! too late it wrings my breast,   5
The word unspoken, and the hand unpress'd;
Yet will affection follow, and believe
The sentient spirit may the thought receive,
Though neither eye to eye the soul impart
Nor answering hand confess the unburthen'd heart.   10
Gone; and alone rests for me that I strive
In song sincere to keep thy name alive,
Though nothing needing of the aids of rhyme,
While they who knew thee tread the ways of time,
And cherish, ere their race be also run,   15
Their memories of many a kindness done –
Of the quick look that caught the unspoken need
And back returned the hand's benignant deed
In help and healing, or with ardour high
Infused the might of patriot-sympathy.   20
And when we all have followed, and the last
Who loved thee living shall have also passed, –
This crumbling castle, from its basement swerved,
Thy pious under-pinning skill preserved;
That carven porch from ruined heaps anew   25
Dug out and dedicate by thee to view
Of wond'ring modern men who stand amazed,
To think their Irish fathers ever raised
Works worthy such a care; this sculptured cross
Thou gathered'st piecemeal, every knop and boss   30
And dragon-twisted symbol, side by side
Laid, and to holy teachings re-applied;
Those noble jewels of the days gone by
The goldsmith's and the penman's art supply,
With rarest products of progressive man   35
Since civil life in Erin first began,
Described by thee, wheree'er their destined place,
Whether, still sharing Academic grace
And Cyclopaediac union, they retain
Their portion in the high clear-aired domain   40
Of arc and sine and critic-judgment heard
Alternate with the searcher's symbol-word,
Historic aids, to little arts unknown,
Heirlooms of all our Past, and all our own,
Or whether, at despotic power's command,   45

They bow their beauty to a stranger's hand,
Mid various wares in halls remote display'd
To swell a programme or promote a trade; –
These all will speak thee: and, dear Wilde, when these,
In course of time, by swift or slow degrees, 50
Are also perished from the world, and gone,
The green grass of Roscommon will grow on;
And, though our several works of hand and pen
Our names and memories be forgotten then,
Oft as the cattle in the dewy ray 55
Of tender morn, by Tulsk or Castlerea,
Crop the sweet herbage, or adown the vale
The ruddy milkmaid bears her evening pail;
Oft as the youth to meet his fair one flies
At labour's close, where sheltering hawthorns rise 60
By Suck's smooth margin; or the merry round
Of dancers foot it to the planxty's sound,
And some warm heart, matched with a mind serene,
Shall drink its full refreshment from the scene,
With thanks to God whose bounty brings to pass 65
That maids their sweethearts, and that kine their grass
Find by His care provided, and there rise
Soft and sweet thoughts for all beneath the skies; –
Then, though unknown, thy spirit shall partake
Refreshment, too, for old communion's sake. 70

Aubrey Thomas De Vere (1814–1902)

Aubrey Thomas De Vere was born in Co. Limerick, a younger son of the poet and baronet Sir Aubrey De Vere. (Much of Aubrey Thomas De Vere's work appeared under the name "Aubrey De Vere"; "Thomas" is used to distinguish him from his father.) Sir Aubrey De Vere, though a member of the Anglo-Irish elite, was also a strong supporter of Catholic Emancipation and, like his son, often took religion as his poetic subject. The younger Aubrey De Vere was educated privately as a child and then formally at Trinity College Dublin. He did not train for the Church of Ireland, but was clearly interested in theology, meeting with leading English Catholic thinker John Henry Newman (later Cardinal Newman) during a visit to Oxford and the Apostles debating group at Cambridge in the late 1830s. He converted to Catholicism in 1851. When Newman became the first rector of the Catholic University of Ireland in 1854, De Vere was appointed to the faculty, but his central work continued to be writing and he published dozens of volumes in his lifetime. Many of his volumes, as befits a professor of politics, are treatises on Irish affairs, including *English Misrule and Irish Misdeeds* (1848) and *Ireland's Church Question* (1868). Recognized in his day as an Irish Catholic poet and a participant in the English Catholic revival, De Vere, like his father, traversed some of the lines which nominally divided Ireland.

De Vere's first volume of poetry, *The Waldenses, or the Fall of Rora* (1842), dwells largely on religious subjects. His third volume of verse, *Poems* (1855), however, to a significant degree

383

Aubrey Thomas De Vere

established the De Vere canon. Other important volumes include *Inisfail, A Lyrical Chronicle of Ireland* (1863) and *The Fall of Rora, the Search After Proserpine, and Other Poems* (1877). De Vere's essays on literature are suggestive, well-executed, Victorian-era examples of the form, appearing in *Essays, Chiefly on Poetry* (1887) and *Essays, Chiefly Literary and Ethical* (1889). He also made attempts at verse drama, in works such as *Alexander the Great* (1874), and published the autobiographical *Recollections* (1897) toward the end of his life. His religious poetry, in particular, was important in establishing his literary reputation, and he was cited in key Modernist assessments of nineteenth-century Irish literature (see, for instance, the prefaces by Tynan and Yeats, below).

Like many of his contemporaries, De Vere included the same poems in different collections across decades, often revising them. His *Irish Odes and Other Poems* (1869), for instance, explicitly directed at the Irish diaspora in the US, gathers together new and old poems for an American readership. Changes were often minor, as in the retitling of "St. Mary Magdalene" (1842) as "Magdalene in the Desert" (1855) with a couple of minor variations In wording. Sometimes, however, revisions were substantial: for instance, in comparison to the 1855 versions given here, the *Irish Odes* edition of "To Burns's 'Highland Mary'" omits a number of verses, and later editions of "The Year of Sorrow" omit a stanza, leaving "Autumn" with just twelve stanzas and so breaking the pattern of four

sections of thirteen stanzas each to follow the four seasons of thirteen weeks each.

De Vere's literary debts were wide-ranging, from that Ulster staple, the Scottish poet Robert Burns, to such English poets as John Milton and William Wordsworth. "To Burns's 'Highland Mary' " is, like Orr's "Elegy" on Burns, peppered with references to Burns's poems, including "To a Mouse," "Highland Mary," and "To a Mountain Daisy." In "The Year of Sorrow," De Vere contributes to mid-century famine literature on terms that bear comparison to such works as Lady Wilde's "The Famine Year," though recent critics have lamented his relatively complacent acceptance of others' suffering – a stance that arguably aligns him with the English Catholic revival, particularly the verse of English poet Gerard Manley Hopkins. His preface to *Irish Odes* pursues an argument found in his literary essays, namely the liberal identification of literature with civic progress, while both condemning sectarianism and encouraging (as in "An Irish 'God Save the Queen'") acceptance of the existing state structure – implicitly arguing against US Fenianism.

Further reading

Morash, Christopher, *Writing the Irish Famine.* Oxford: Clarendon Press, 1995.
Ridden, Jennifer, "The Forgotten History of the Protestant Crusade: Religious Liberalism in Ireland," *Journal of Religious History* 31 (2007): 78–102.
Schirmer, Gregory A., *Out of What Began: A History of Irish Poetry in English.* Ithaca, NY: Cornell University Press, 1998.

To Burns's "Highland Mary"[1]

From Poems (1855)

I

O loved by him whom Scotland loves,
Long loved, and honoured duly

Notes

To Burns's "Highland Mary"
[1] "Highland Mary" by Scottish poet, Robert Burns (1759–96).

By all who love the bard who sang
   So sweetly and so truly!
In cultured dales his song prevails;   5
   Thrills o'er the eagle's aëry, –
Ah! who that strain has caught, nor sighed
   For Burns's "Highland Mary?"

2

I wandered on from hill to hill,
   I feared nor wind nor weather;   10
For Burns beside me trode the moor,
   Beside me pressed the heather.
I read his verse: – his life – alas!
   O'er that dark shades extended: –
With thee at last, and him in thee,   15
   My thoughts their wanderings ended.

3

His golden hours of youth were thine;
   Those hours whose flight is fleetest:
Of all his songs to thee he gave
   The freshest and the sweetest.   20
Ere ripe the fruit, one branch he brake,
   All rich with bloom and blossom;
And shook its dews, its incense shook,
   Above thy brow and bosom.

4

And when his Spring, alas, how soon!   25
   Had been by care subverted,
His Summer, like a god repulsed,
   Had from his gates departed;
Beneath the evening star, once more,
   Star of his morn and even!   30
To thee his suppliant hands he spread,
   And hailed his love "in heaven."

5

And if his spirit in "a waste
   Of shame" too oft was squandered,
And if too oft his feet ill-starred   35
   In ways erroneous wandered;
Ah! still his spirit's spirit bathed
   In purity eternal;
And all fair things through thee retained
   For him their aspect vernal!   40

6

Nor less that tenderness remained
   Thy favouring love implanted;

Compunctious pity, yearnings vague
  For love to earth not granted;
Reserve with freedom, female grace   45
  Well matched with manly vigour,
In songs where fancy twined her wreaths
  Round judgment's stalwart rigour.

7

A mute but strong appeal was made
  To him by feeblest creatures: 50
In his large heart had each a part
  That part had found in Nature's.
The wildered sheep, sagacious dog,
  Old horse reduced and crazy;
The field-mouse by the plough upturned,   55
  And violated daisy.

8

In him there burned that passionate glow,
  All Nature's soul and savour,
Which gives its hue to every flower,
  To every fruit its flavour.   60
Nor less the kindred power he felt; –
  That love of all things human,
Whereof the fiery centre is
  The love man bears to woman.

9

He sang the dignity of man,   65
  Sang woman's grace and goodness;
Passed by the world's half-truths, her lies
  Pierced through with lance-like shrewdness.
Upon life's broad highways he stood,
  And aped nor Greek nor Roman;   70
But snatched from heaven Promethean fire
  To glorify things common.

10

He sang of youth, he sang of age,
  Their joys, their griefs, their labours;
Felt with, not for, the people; hailed   75
  All Scotland's sons his neighbours:
And therefore all repeat his verse –
  Hot youth, or greybeard steady,
The boatman on Loch Etive's wave,
  The shepherd on Ben Ledi.[2]   80

Notes ──────────────────────────────

[2] A lake and mountain, respectively, in Scotland.

Aubrey Thomas De Vere

11

He sang from love of song; his name
    Dunedin's[3] cliff resounded: –
He left her, faithful to a fame
    On truth and nature founded.
He sought true fame, not loud acclaim;   85
    Himself and Time he trusted:
For laurels crackling in the flame
    His fine ear never lusted.

12

He loved, and reason had to love,
    The illustrious land that bore him: 90
Where'er he went, like heaven's broad tent
    A star-bright Past hung o'er him.
Each isle had fenced a saint recluse,
    Each tower a hero dying;
Down every mountain-gorge had rolled   95
    The flood of foemen flying.

13

From age to age that land had paid
    No alien throne submission;
For feudal faith had been her Law,
    And freedom her Tradition.   100
Where frowned the rocks had Freedom smiled,
    Sung, mid the shrill wind's whistle –
So England prized her garden Rose,
    But Scotland loved her Thistle.

14

The land thus pure from foreign foot,   105
    Her growing powers thus centred
Around her heart, with other lands
    The race historic entered.
Her struggling dawn, convulsed or bright,
    Worked on through storms and troubles,   110
Whilst a heroic line of kings
    Strove with heroic nobles.

15

Fair field alone the brave demand,
    And Scotland ne'er had lost it:
And honest prove the hate and love   115
    To objects meet adjusted.
Intelligible course was hers

Notes ─────────────────────────────

[3] Dunedin is an alternative name for Edinburgh.

By safety tried or danger:
The native was for native known –
   The stranger known for stranger.   120

16

Honour in her a sphere had found,
   Nobility a station,
The patriots' thought the task it sought,
   And virtue – toleration.
Her will and way had ne'er been crossed   125
   In fatal contradiction;
Nor loyalty to treason soured,
   Nor faith abused with fiction.

17

Can song be false where hearts are sound?
   Weak doubts – away we fling them!   130
The land that breeds great men, great deeds,
   Shall ne'er lack bards to sing them.
That vigour, sense, and mutual truth
   Which baffled each invader,
Shall fill her marts, and feed her arts,   135
   While peaceful olives shade her.

18

Honour to Scotland and to Burns!
   In him she stands collected.
A thousand streams one river make –
   Thus Genius, heaven-directed,   140
Conjoins all separate veins of power
   In one great soul-creation;
Thus blends a million men to make
   The Poet of the nation.

19

Honour to Burns! and her who first   145
   Let loose the abounding river
Of music from the Poet's heart,
   Borne through all lands for ever!
How much to her mankind has owed
   Of song's selected treasures!   150
Unsweetened by her kiss, his lips
   Had sung far other measures.

20

Be green for aye, green bank and brae
   Around Montgomery's Castle!
Blow there, ye earliest flowers, and there,   155
   Ye sweetest song-birds, nestle!

For there was ta'en that last farewell
    In hope, indulged how blindly;
And there was given that long last gaze
    "That dwelt" on him "sae kindly."[4]   160

21

No word of thine recorded stands;
    Few words that hour were spoken:
Two Bibles there were interchanged,
    And some slight love-gift broken.
And there thy cold faint hands he pressed,   165
    Thy head, by dewdrops misted;
And kisses, ill-resisted first,
    At last were unresisted.

22

Ah cease! – she died. He too is dead.
    Of all her girlish graces   170
Perhaps one nameless lock remains:
    The rest stern Time effaces –
Dust lost in dust. Not so: a bloom
    Is hers that ne'er can wither;
And in that lay which lives for aye   175
    The twain live on together.

The Year of Sorrow – Ireland – 1849

From **Poems** (1855)

Spring

1

Once more, through God's high will and grace,
    Of hours that each its task fulfils,
Heart-healing Spring resumes its place; –
    The valley throngs and scales the hills,

2

In vain. From earth's deep heart o'ercharged,   5
    The exulting life runs o'er in flowers; –
The slave unfed is unenlarged:
    In darkness sleep a Nation's powers.

Notes ───────────────────────────────

[4] The phrases in quotation marks, and various other words
in this verse (including the setting of Montgomery's castle),
are from Burns' "Highland Mary."

3

Who knows not Spring! Who doubts, when blows
   Her breath, that Spring is come indeed?   10
The swallow doubts not; nor the rose
   That stirs, but wakes not; nor the weed.

4

I feel her near, but see her not;
   For these with pain uplifted eyes
Fall back repulsed; and vapours blot   15
   The vision of the earth and skies.

5

I see her not – I feel her near,
   As, charioted in mildest airs,
She sails through yon empyreal sphere,
   And in her arms and bosom bears   20

6

That urn of flowers and lustral dews
   Whose sacred balm, o'er all things shed,
Revives the weak, the old renews,
   And crowns with votive wreaths the dead.

7

Once more the cuckoo's call I hear;   25
   I know, in many a glen profound,
The earliest violets of the year
   Rise up like water from the ground.

8

The thorn I know once more is white;
   And, far down many a forest dale,   30
The anemones in dubious light
   Are trembling like a bridal veil.

9

By streams released that singing flow
   From craggy shelf through sylvan glades,
The pale narcissus, well I know,   35
   Smiles hour by hour on greener shades.

10

The honeyed cowslip tufts once more
   The golden slopes; – with gradual ray
The primrose stars the rock, and o'er
   The wood-path strews its milky way.   40

11

From ruined huts and holes come forth
　　Old men, and look upon the sky!
The Power Divine is on the earth:
　　Give thanks to God before ye die!

12

And ye, O children worn and weak,　　　　　　　45
　　Who care no more with flowers to play,
Lean on the grass your cold, thin cheek,
　　And those slight hands, and whispering, say,

13

"Stern Mother of a race unblest,
　　In promise kindly, cold in deed; –　　　　　50
Take back, O Earth, into thy breast,
　　The children whom thou wilt not feed."

Summer

1

Approved by works of love and might,
　　The Year, consummated and crowned,
Has scaled the zenith's purple height,　　　　　55
　　And flings his robe the earth around.

2

Impassioned stillness – fervours calm –
　　Brood, vast and bright, o'er land and deep:
The warrior sleeps beneath the palm;
　　The dark-eyed captive guards his sleep.　　　60

3

The Iberian labourer rests from toil;
　　Sicilian virgins twine the dance;
Laugh Tuscan vales in wine and oil;
　　Fresh laurels flash from brows of France.

4

Far off, in regions of the North,　　　　　　　65
　　The hunter drops his winter fur;
Sun-stricken babes their feet stretch forth;
　　And nested dormice feebly stir.

5

But thou, O land of many woes!
　　What cheer is thine? Again the breath　　　　70

Of proved Destruction o'er thee blows,
   And sentenced fields grow black in death.

6

In horror of a new despair
   His blood-shot eyes the peasant strains,
With hands clenched fast, and lifted hair,   75
   Along the daily-darkening plains.

7

"Why trusted he to them his store?
   Why feared he not the scourge to come?"
Fool! turn the page of History o'er, –
   The roll of Statutes – and be dumb!   80

8

Behold, O People! thou shalt die!
   What art thou better than thy sires?
The hunted deer a weeping eye
   Turns on his birthplace, and expires.

9

Lo! as the closing of a book,   85
   Or statue from its base o'erthrown,
Or blasted wood, or dried-up brook,
   Name, race, and nation, thou art gone.

10

The stranger shall thy hearth possess;
   The stranger build upon thy grave: 90
But know this also – he, not less,
   His limit and his term shall have.

11

Once more thy volume, open cast,
   In thunder forth shall sound thy name;
Thy forest, hot at heart, at last   95
   God's breath shall kindle into flame.

12

Thy brook dried up a cloud shall rise,
   And stretch an hourly widening hand,
In God's good vengeance, through the skies,
   And onward o'er the Invader's land.   100

13

Of thine, one day, a remnant left
   Shall raise o'er earth a Prophet's rod,

And teach the coasts of Faith bereft
    The names of Ireland, and of God.

Autumn

1

Then die, thou Year – thy work is done: 105
    The work ill done is done at last.
Far off, beyond that sinking sun
    Which sets in blood, I hear the blast

2

That sings thy dirge, and says – "Ascend,
    And answer make amid thy peers,   110
(Since all things here must have an end,)
    Thou latest of the famine years!"

3

I join that voice. No joy have I
    In all thy purple and thy gold;
Nor in the nine-fold harmony   115
    From forest on to forest rolled:

4

Nor in that stormy western fire,
    Which burns on ocean's gloomy bed,
And hurls, as from a funeral pyre,
    A glare that strikes the mountain's head;   120

5

And writes on low-hung clouds its lines
    Of cyphered flame, with hurrying hand;
And flings amid the topmost pines
    That crown the steep, a burning brand.

6

Make answer, Year, for all thy dead,   125
    Who found not rest in hallowed earth;
The widowed wife, the father fled,
    The babe age-stricken from his birth.

7

Make answer, Year, for virtue lost;
    For courage proof 'gainst fraud and force .   130
Now waning like a noontide ghost;
    Affections poisoned at their source.

8

The labourer spurned his lying spade;
  The yeoman spurned his useless plough;
The pauper spurned the unwholesome aid,   135
  Obtruded once, exhausted now.

9

The weaver wove till all was dark,
  And, long ere morning, bent and bowed
Above his work with fingers stark;
  And made, nor knew he made, a shroud.   140

10

The roof-trees fall of hut and hall,
  I hear them fall, and falling cry –
"One fate for each, one fate for all;
  So wills the Law that willed a lie."

11

Dread power of Man! what spread the waste   145
  In circles, hour by hour more wide,
And would not let the past be past? –
  That Law that promised much, and lied.

12

Dread power of God! whom mortal years
  Nor touch, nor tempt; who sitt'st sublime   150
In night of night, – O bid thy spheres
  Resound at last a funeral chime.

13

Call up at last the afflicted race,
  Whom man, not God, abolished. – Sore,
For centuries, their strife: the place   155
  That knew them once shall know no more!

Winter

1

Fall, snow, and cease not! Flake by flake
  The decent winding-sheet compose.
Thy task is just and pious; make
  An end of blasphemies and woes.   160

2

Fall flake by flake! by thee alone,
  Last friend, the sleeping draught is given:
Kind nurse, by thee the couch is strewn –
  The couch whose covering is from heaven.

3

Descend and clasp the mountain's crest;   165
  Inherit plain and valley deep:
This night, in thy maternal breast,
  A vanquished nation dies in sleep.

4

Lo! from the starry Temple gates
  Death rides, and bears the flag of peace: 170
The combatants he separates;
  He bids the wrath of ages cease.

5

Descend, benignant Power! But O,
  Ye torrents, shake no more the vale:
Dark streams, in silence seaward flow: 175
  Thou rising storm, remit thy wail.

6

Shake not, to-night, the cliffs of Moher,
  Nor Brandon's base, rough sea! Thou Isle,
The Rite proceeds! From shore to shore,
  Hold in thy gathered breath the while.   180

7

Fall, snow! in stillness fall, like dew,
  On temple's roof and cedar's fan;
And mould thyself on pine and yew;
  And on the awful face of man.

8

Without a sound, without a stir,   185
  In streets and wolds, on rock and mound,
O, omnipresent Comforter,
  By thee, this night, the lost are found!

9

On quaking moor and mountain moss,
  With eyes upstaring at the sky,   190
And arms extended like a cross,
  The long-expectant sufferers lie.

10

Bend o'er them, white-robed Acolyte!
  Put forth thine hand from cloud and mist,
And minister the last sad Rite,   195
  Where altar there is none, nor priest.

11

Touch thou the gates of soul and sense;
  Touch darkening eyes and dying ears;
Touch stiffening hands and feet, and thence
  Remove the trace of sin and tears.   200

12

And ere thou seal those filmèd eyes,
  Into God's urn thy fingers dip,
And lay, 'mid eucharistic sighs,
  The sacred wafer on the lip.

13

This night the Absolver issues forth: 205
  This night the Eternal Victim bleeds:
O winds and woods – O heaven and earth!
  Be still this night. The Rite proceeds!

From *Preface*

From Irish Odes and Other Poems (1869)

A wish has sometimes been expressed by my American friends that an edition of my poems should be published in their country. No one who has written in the English language, whether with the lower or the higher aims of literature, can fail to desire that his work should have a circulation in America. That country must ere long contain far the larger number of those who speak English; in it, despite those material interests which imperiously demand the attention of a young country, poetry has already been produced with an abundance, and read with an eagerness, rare in the old world; and it cannot be doubted that every liberal art must achieve new triumphs amid a race dowered with all that can develop moral and social energies, and naught that can depress intellect or divide brethren. The Liberal Arts are the children of a virtuous, unboastful Liberty, frank-hearted, and not self-respecting alone, but full of respect for all that is human. Their larger growths are quickened from the soil of sympathies wide as the earth, and are freshened by aspirations not restrained to the earth. Like the spontaneous growths of Nature, they are also in part, it is true, Traditions; but the allegation that America must wait long for a past, is an error. She has only to *remember*, as well as look forward, and the Past of all those nations from which her race is derived is her Past also.

For me the question is not merely one of Literature. There now exist in America more of my Irish fellow-countrymen than remain in their native country; and I cannot but wish that my Poetry, much of which illustrates their History and Religion, should reach those Irish "of the dispersion" in that land which has extended to them its hospitality. Whoever loves that people must follow it in its wanderings with an earnest desire that, upon whatever shore the storms may have cast it, and by whatever institutions it may be cherished or proved, it may retain with vigilant fidelity, and be valued for retaining, those among its characteristics which most belong to the Ireland of History and Religion. The Irish character is one easily mistaken by the "rough and ready" philosophy of the caricaturist. "A little part, and that the worst, he sees." To the rest he has not the key.[1] Broad farce, and broad romance, have familiarized men with its coarser traits. Its finer reveal themselves to poetry. She deals with what lies beneath the surface. She makes her study, not of the tavern, but of the hill-side chapel, and of the cottage-hearth without stain and faithful to the departed. She ponders the tear-blotted letter, and the lip-worn rosary. In a face seldom joyless, but not seldom overcast, she finds something which makes her tread the wanderer's native land, and share with him the recollections of the Past. Those recollections, dear to all deep-hearted Races, but dearest to the saddest, have to the Irish been a reality in times when the present seemed a dream. But hitherto they have also been vindictive. Now that a Sectarian Ascendancy is on the point of ceasing, they will lose their bitterness wherever the old and true Irish character remains. That character is generous where love is not curdled into hate by wrong. To attain Civil Freedom and Religious Equality was long the task which nature and duty imposed upon Ireland. To develop, and rightly to direct the energies, moral, intellectual, and industrial, of a People set free, must ere long become the task of a thoughtful patriotism. These convictions will be traced in the poems which give the present volume its name, and occupy its earlier portion – poems written at various periods, but, like those in the latter part of the volume, not included in the writer's previous publications. The intermediate poems are a selection from his works.

It is sometimes said that the poetry of a Catholic, even when its subjects are, as in the present instance, mainly secular, should not expect an impartial audience in a country predominantly Protestant. The remark can hardly be one of universal application. Religious jealousies, now in most countries happily on the wane, are not produced by diversities of Faith; they are but social passions or panics – an after-swell bequeathed by the political tempests of past times. America, since she became a nation, has never persecuted, and therefore can afford to be just. Let it be for her to teach the world that true liberty – the liberty which accords all that it demands – has no better friend than true Catholicity. The age is one of progress; Catholicity has much that is in direct harmony with its furthest and hardiest aspirations, and as much that is indirectly supplemental to them. It fears no progress that is not downward. It loves the people; it sojourned with them in the Catacombs; it delivered them from Pagan Imperialism, protected them from the Mahometan yoke, and struck from them the chains of Feudal serfdom. It rejoices in the expansion of their justly-regulated rights and powers, in which, as in a dilated breast, its free spirit respires with ease. But it also hallows Authority. It asserts Equality, not in the form of a surly and barren independence, but in that of a reciprocal dependence fruitful in mutual good. It emancipates us first from lawless passions, and next from those lawless tyrannies which are at once their offspring and their punishment; but it works these marvellous works only because it pays and demands an allegiance based neither on a servile nor

Notes

FROM PREFACE
[1] De Vere invokes a work by English poet William Wordsworth, "Stanzas Suggested in a Steamboat off Saint Bees' Heads," which deals at some length with Catholic religious life: "A little part, and that the worst, he sees / Who thinks that priestly cunning holds the keys."

a selfish motive, and therefore unaggrieved and unashamed. It generates a reverential good-will which, as by an inner law, subdues the aggressions of selfishness, and gives to each a protector in his neighbour; but it at the same time takes from external laws its sting by creating the virtue of a proud and generous loyalty. That loyalty looks on the State not as a mere aggregate, the administrator of Society's material interests, but as the sacred unity of the nation, the majestic inheritor of its duties, the vindicator of a Divine Justice – nay, as, in its vastness and its permanence, a shadow of the Universal Church. Yet it remembers that to a loyal People the loyalty of the State is also due. We are made up of habits. Man requires both obedience and liberty: and it is where the priceless freedom of the heart is sustained by a willing and reasonable obedience in the spiritual sphere, that liberty, civil and social, can walk securely while steadied by the lightest yoke ...

Ode X, An Irish "God Save the Queen"[1]

From Irish Odes and Other Poems (1869)

I

God save the Queen! A widowed land
   May bless a Widow keeping[2]
Beside a grave her faithful stand,
   Long watching, and late weeping:
Well versed in woes, that land may pray,   5
   "While the great night draws nearer,
Lady, may stars unseen by day
   For thee grow clear and clearer!"

II

God save the Queen, and drive far off
   Each whisperer – clown or noble –   10
That dares her People's Faith to scoff,
   Her People's peace to trouble;
Rebuke bad laws that bar with gloom
   Her empire's rifted centre,
And freeze its Eden to a tomb –   15
   A many-centuried winter.

III

God save the Queen! His Strength, His Right
   Keep well: – they long have kept her!
All majesties of Love and Might
   Like eaglets haunt her sceptre!   20
Be hers a Realm for virtue praised,
   Not wealth alone; a Nation

Notes

ODE X
[1] The unofficial British anthem, "God Save the King [Queen],"
was penned around 1740 and exists in various versions.

[2] The British Queen Victoria was widowed in 1861.

Aloft in all its Orders raised,
   With just and wise gradation.

IV

God save the Queen! Let flatterers run   25
   To hail the rising splendor:
To *her* more dear the sinking sun,
   That Island true and tender!
She that fought last for Charles – for James – [3]
   Will yield more generous duty   30
To Virtue's grace, and Sorrow's claims
   Than all thy new-crowned beauty!

V

God save the Queen! The land that weeps
   Her children fled or flying,
That, age by age, on carnage heaps   35
   Beheld her princes lying,
That land, O royal Mother, prays,
   Thy children round thee pressing,
May crown thy dimmed, autumnal days,
   With glory and with blessing.   40

VI

God save the Queen! From Chiefs of yore
   Who left for Alba's mountains
Dalriad Ireland's northern shore,[4]
   Her life-blood tracks its fountains: –
Ring out, strong voices, and be glad!   45
   Make answer, tower and steeple!
God save the Queen! But let her add
   Her prayer, "God save my People!"

On a Recent Volume of Poems[1]

From Irish Odes and Other Poems (1869)

Hid in each cord there winds one central strand:
Hid in each breast a panting heart doth lie:
Hid in the lines that map the infant's hand

Notes

[3] British monarchs who had Irish military support: Charles I against Cromwell in the 1640s and James II against William of Orange in the 1680s.

[4] See Sir Walter Scott's History of Scotland (author). In the first chapter of his *History of Scotland* (1830), this Scottish author refers to the Irish settlement of Scotland (Alba) "about the year 503" by "Dalriads," "natives of Ulster."

ON A RECENT VOLUME OF POEMS
[1] By Dr. Newman (author). English theologian John Henry Newman (1801–90). The "recent volume" may be Newman's *Verses on Various Occasions* (1867).

There lurks, men say, a life-long destiny:
Through the dropt leaf 'gainst wintry sunset scanned   5
Shines that fine net whose strong geometry
Sustained the nascent shape, and each new dye
Fed by Spring dews, by pensive Autumn fanned.
Hid in this Book what note we? One Decree
Writ by God's finger on a destined soul,   10
That stamped each thought an act, and leaving free
The spirit, shaped the life into a whole.
What was that great behest – that mastering vow?
England, when Christ hath conquered, answer thou!

Joseph Sheridan LeFanu (1814–1873)

Joseph Thomas Sheridan LeFanu was born in Dublin, the great-grandson of Thomas and Frances Sheridan. He was also the father of Eleanor Frances LeFanu, who published novels under the pseudonym "Russell Gray." His family had strong ties to the Church of Ireland as well as the literary world: LeFanu's father, two paternal great-uncles, and maternal grandfather were all clergymen in the Church of Ireland. In 1826, his father moved the family to Limerick to assume his post as rector in Abington as well as Dean of Emly. LeFanu scholars, particularly those interested in LeFanu's gothic writing, have made much of these early years in Limerick, where insurgency leading up to the Tithe War of the 1830s created a climate of fear. From 1832 to 1836, he studied law at Trinity College Dublin, but he was never a serious lawyer. At university, he became involved with the College Historical Society (through which he met *The Nation*'s Thomas Davis) and, more significantly, the *Dublin University Magazine*, a periodical central in Irish letters for much of the nineteenth century.

LeFanu began publishing anonymously in the *Dublin University Magazine* in the late 1830s. His first two novels soon followed: *The Cock and Anchor* (1845) and *The Fortunes of Colonel Turlogh O'Brien* (1847). Both were historical novels, but LeFanu continued his work on shorter

fiction in the overlapping gothic and sensation traditions. His first collection of stories, *Ghost Stories and Tales of Mystery*, appeared in 1851 and included "The Murdered Cousin," an early rehearsal of the plot that would structure his best-known novel, *Uncle Silas* (1864). *Uncle Silas*, along with other LeFanu novels such as *The House by the Church-Yard* (1863), were published serially first in the *Dublin University Magazine* and then in book form. LeFanu was simultaneously working in the managerial and proprietorial side of the Dublin publishing world, first for *The Statesman* and *The Warder*, then becoming co-editor of the *Dublin Evening Mail* and then the *Dublin University Magazine* itself, which he owned and edited from 1861 to 1870. LeFanu continued to publish his work serially, though in a wider array of periodicals. His influential vampire tale, "Carmilla," which influenced Bram Stoker's *Dracula*, was serialized in *Dark Blue* (1871–2) and then collected in *In a Glass Darkly* (1872). He also published poetry, collected in Alfred Perceval Graves's *Poems of Joseph Sheridan LeFanu* (1896).

"A Chapter in the History of a Tyrone Family" was published in the *Dublin University Magazine* as part of what LeFanu framed as the "Purcell Papers" (1838–40), a series of tales purportedly collected by a fictional priest, Father Francis Purcell. It is, moreover, an early engagement with LeFanu's recurring themes of men guilty of past and still-hidden crimes, isolated young women whose parents are either absent or emotionally remote, and gothically depicted domestic dangers. "A Chapter in the History of a Tyrone Family" is also well known as a possible source for British author Charlotte Brontë's *Jane Eyre* (1847). The two texts share a significant number of plot and character elements, and LeFanu's story may have been available to Brontë, the daughter of Irish author Patrick Brontë. The issue of the *Dublin University Magazine* in which LeFanu's tale appeared included on its title page the claim: "Sold by all booksellers in the United Kingdom."

Further reading

Harris, Sally, "Spiritual Warnings: The Ghost Stories of Joseph Sheridan LeFanu," *Victorians Institute Journal* 31 (2003): 9–39.
McCormack, W. J., *Sheridan LeFanu and Victorian Ireland*. New York: Oxford University Press, 1990.
Milbank, Alison, *Daughters of the House: Modes of the Gothic in Victorian Fiction*. New York: Palgrave Macmillan, 1992.

A Chapter in the History of a Tyrone Family

From Dublin University Magazine (1839)

[In the following narrative, I have endeavoured to give as nearly as possible the *"ipsissima verba"*[1] of the valued friend from whom I received it, conscious that any aberration from *her* mode of telling the tale of her own life, would at once impair its accuracy and its effect. Would that, with her words, I could also bring before you her animated gesture, her expressive countenance, the solemn and thrilling air and accent with which she related the dark passages in her strange story; and, above all, that I could communicate the impressive consciousness that the narrator had seen with her own eyes, and personally acted in the scenes which she described; these accompaniments, taken with the additional circumstance, that she who told the tale was one far too deeply and sadly impressed with religious principle, to misrepresent or fabricate what she repeated as fact, gave to the tale a depth of interest which the events recorded could hardly, themselves, have produced. I became acquainted with the lady from whose lips I heard this narrative, nearly twenty years since, and the story struck my fancy so much that I committed it to paper while it was still fresh in my mind, and should its perusal afford you entertainment for a listless half hour, my labour shall not have been bestowed in vain. I find that I have taken the story down as she told it, in the first person, and, perhaps, this is as it should be. She began as follows.]

My maiden name was Richardson,[2] the designation of a family of some distinction in the county of Tyrone. I was the younger of two daughters, and we were the only children. There was a difference in our ages of nearly six years, so that I did not, in my childhood, enjoy that close companionship which sisterhood, in other circumstances, necessarily involves; and while I was still a child, my sister was married. The person upon whom she bestowed her hand, was a Mr. Carew, a gentleman of property and consideration in the north of England. I remember well the eventful day of the

Notes
_____

A CHAPTER IN THE HISTORY
[1] The very words (Latin).
[2] I have carefully altered the names as they appear in the original MSS., for the reader will see that some of the circumstances recorded are not of a kind to reflect honour upon those involved in them; and, as many are still living, in every way honoured and honourable, who stand in close relation to the principal actors in this drama, the reader will see the necessity of the course which we have adopted (author).

wedding; the thronging carriages, the noisy menials, the loud laughter, the merry faces, and the gay dresses. Such sights were then new to me, and harmonised ill with the sorrowful feelings with which I regarded the event which was to separate me, as it turned out, for ever, from a sister whose tenderness alone had hitherto more than supplied all that I wanted in my mother's affection. The day soon arrived which was to remove the happy couple from Ashtown-house. The carriage stood at the hall-door, and my poor sister kissed me again, and again, telling me that I should see her soon. The carriage drove away, and I gazed after it until my eyes filled with tears, and, returning slowly to my chamber, I wept more bitterly and so, to speak more desolately, than ever I had done before. My father had never seemed to love, or to take an interest in me. He had desired a son, and I think he never thoroughly forgave me my unfortunate sex. My having come into the world at all as his child, he regarded as a kind of fraudulent intrusion, and, as his antipathy to me had its origin in an imperfection of mine, too radical for removal, I never even hoped to stand high in his good graces. My mother was, I dare say, as fond of me as she was of any one; but she was a woman of a masculine and a worldly cast of mind. She had no tenderness or sympathy for the weaknesses, or even for the affections of woman's nature, and her demeanour towards me was peremptory, and often even harsh. It is not to be supposed, then, that I found in the society of my parents much to supply the loss of my sister. About a year after her marriage, we received letters from Mr. Carew, containing accounts of my sister's health, which, though not actually alarming, were calculated to make us seriously uneasy. The symptoms most dwelt upon, were, loss of appetite and cough. The letters concluded by intimating that he would avail himself of my father and mother's repeated invitation to spend some time at Ashtown, particularly as the physician who had been consulted as to my sister's health had strongly advised a removal to her native air. There were added repeated assurances that nothing serious was apprehended, as it was supposed that a deranged state of the liver was the only source of the symptoms which at first had seemed to intimate consumption. In accordance with this announcement, my sister and Mr. Carew arrived in Dublin, where one of my father's carriages awaited them, in readiness to start upon whatever day or hour they might choose for their departure. It was arranged that Mr. Carew was, as soon as the day upon which they were to leave Dublin was definitely fixed, to write to my father, who intended that the two last stages should be performed by his own horses, upon whose speed and safety far more reliance might be placed than upon those of the ordinary *post-horses*, which were at that time, almost without exception, of the very worst order. The journey, one of about ninety miles, was to be divided; the larger portion being reserved for the second day. On Sunday a letter reached us, stating that the party would leave Dublin on Monday, and, in due course, reach Ashtown upon Tuesday evening. Tuesday came: the evening closed in, and yet no carriage appeared; darkness came on, and still no sign of our expected visitors. Hour after hour passed away, and it was now past twelve; the night was remarkably calm, scarce a breath stirring, so that any sound, such as that produced by the rapid movement of a vehicle, would have been audible at a considerable distance. For some such sound I was feverishly listening. It was, however, my father's rule to close the house at nightfall, and the window-shutters being fastened, I was unable to reconnoitre the avenue as I would have wished. It was nearly one o'clock, and we began almost to despair of seeing them upon that night, when I thought I distinguished the sound of wheels, but so remote and faint as to make me at first very uncertain. The noise approached; it became louder and clearer; it stopped for a moment. I now heard the shrill screaking of the rusty iron, as the avenue gate revolved on its hinges; again came the sound of wheels in rapid motion.

"It is they," said I, starting up; "the carriage is in the avenue." We all stood for a few moments, breathlessly listening. On thundered the vehicle with the speed of a whirlwind; crack went the whip, and clatter went the wheels, as it rattled over the uneven pavement of the court; a general and furious barking from all the dogs about the house, hailed its arrival. We hurried to the hall in time to hear the steps let down with the sharp clanging noise peculiar to the operation, and the hum of voices exerted in the bustle of arrival. The hall-door was now thrown open, and we all stepped forth to greet our visitors. The court was perfectly empty; the moon was shining broadly and brightly upon all around; nothing was to be seen but the tall trees with their long spectral shadows, now wet with the dews of midnight. We stood gazing from right to left, as if suddenly awakened from a dream; the dogs walked suspiciously, growling and snuffing about the court, and by totally and suddenly ceasing their former loud barking, as also by carrying their tails between their legs, expressing the predominance of fear. We looked one upon the other in perplexity and dismay, and I think I never beheld more pale faces assembled. By my father's direction, we looked about to find anything which might indicate or account for the noise which we had heard; but no such thing was to be seen – even the mire which lay upon the avenue was undisturbed. We returned to the house, more panic struck than I can describe. On the next day, we learned by a messenger, who had ridden hard the greater part of the night, that my sister was dead. On Sunday evening, she had retired to bed rather unwell, and, on Monday, her indisposition declared itself unequivocally to be malignant fever. She became hourly worse and, on Tuesday night, a little after midnight, she expired.[3] I mention this circumstance, because it was one upon which a thousand wild and fantastical reports were founded, though one would have thought that the truth scarcely required to be improved upon; and again, because it produced a strong and lasting effect upon my spirits, and indeed, I am inclined to think, upon my character. I was, for several years after this occurrence, long after the violence of my grief subsided, so wretchedly low-spirited and nervous, that I could scarcely be said to live; and during this time, habits of indecision, arising out of a listless acquiescence in the will of others, a fear of encountering even the slightest opposition, and a disposition to shrink from what are commonly called amusements, grew upon

Notes

[3] The residuary legatee of the late Francis Purcell, who has the honour of selecting such of his lamented old friend's manuscripts as may appear fit for publication, in order that the lore which they contain may reach the world before scepticism and utility have robbed our species of the precious gift of credulity, and scornfully kicked before them, or trampled into annihilation, those harmless fragments of picturesque superstition, which it is our object to preserve, has been subjected to the charge of dealing too largely in the marvellous; and it has been half insinuated that such is his love for *diablerie*, that he is content to wander a mile out of his way, in order to meet a fiend or a goblin, and thus to sacrifice all regard for truth and accuracy to the idle hope of affrighting the imagination, and thus pandering to the bad taste of his reader. He begs leave, then, to take this opportunity of asserting his perfect innocence of all the crimes laid to his charge, and to assure his reader that he never *pandered to his bad taste*, nor went one inch out of his way to introduce witch, fairy, devil, ghost, or any other of the grim fraternity of the redoubted Raw-head and bloody-bones. His province, touching these tales, has been attended with no difficulty and little responsibility; indeed, he is accountable for nothing more than an alteration in the names of persons mentioned therein, when such a step seemed necessary, and for an occasional note, whenever he conceived it possible, innocently, to edge in a word. These tales have been *written down*, as the heading of each announces, by the Rev. Francis Purcell, P. P. of Drumcoolagh; and in all the instances, which are many, in which the present writer has had an opportunity of comparing the manuscript of his departed friend with the actual traditions which are current amongst the families whose fortunes they pretend to illustrate, he has uniformly found that whatever of supernatural occurred in the story, so far from having been exaggerated by him, had been rather softened down, and, wherever it could be attempted, accounted for (author). "Raw-head and bloody-bones" is a supernatural figure associated with water and identified in the nineteenth century as part of Irish folklore; the creature is invoked from Lover's *Legends and Stories of Ireland* to James Joyce's *Ulysses*.

me so strongly, that I have scarcely even yet, altogether overcome them. We saw nothing more of Mr. Carew. He returned to England as soon as the melancholy rites attendant upon the event which I have just mentioned were performed; and not being altogether inconsolable, he married again within two years; after which, owing to the remoteness of our relative situations, and other circumstances, we gradually lost sight of him. I was now an only child; and, as my elder sister had died without issue, it was evident that, in the ordinary course of things, my father's property, which was altogether in his power, would go to me; and the consequence was, that before I was fourteen, Ashtown-house was besieged by a host of suitors. However, whether it was that *I* was too young, or that none of the aspirants to my hand stood sufficiently high in rank or wealth, I was suffered by both parents to do exactly as I pleased; and well was it for me, as I afterwards found that fortune, or, rather Providence, had so ordained it, that I had not suffered my affections to become in any degree engaged, for my mother would never have suffered any *silly fancy* of mine, as she was in the habit of styling an attachment, to stand in the way of her ambitious views; views which she was determined to carry into effect, in defiance of every obstacle, and in order to accomplish which, she would not have hesitated to sacrifice anything so unreasonable and contemptible as a girlish passion.

When I reached the age of sixteen, my mother's plans began to develope themselves, and, at her suggestion, we moved to Dublin to sojourn for the winter, in order that no time might be lost in disposing of me to the best advantage. I had been too long accustomed to consider myself as of no importance whatever, to believe for a moment that I was in reality the cause of all the bustle and preparation which surrounded me, and being thus relieved from the pain which a consciousness of my real situation would have inflicted, I journeyed towards the capital with a feeling of total indifference.

My father's wealth and connection had established him in the best society, and, consequently, upon our arrival in the metropolis, we commanded whatever enjoyment or advantages its gaieties afforded. The tumult and novelty of the scenes in which I was involved did not fail considerably to amuse me, and my mind gradually recovered its tone, which was naturally cheerful. It was almost immediately known and reported that I was an heiress, and of course my attractions were pretty generally acknowledged. Among the many gentlemen whom it was my fortune to please, one, ere long, established himself in my mother's good graces, to the exclusion of all less important aspirants. However, I had not understood or even remarked his attentions, nor, in the slightest degree suspected his or my mother's plans respecting me, when I was made aware of them rather abruptly by my mother herself. We had attended a splendid ball, given by Lord M—— , at his residence in Stephen's-green, and I was, with the assistance of my waiting-maid, employed in rapidly divesting myself of the rich ornaments which, in profuseness and value, could scarcely have found their equals in any private family in Ireland. I had thrown myself into a lounging chair beside the fire, listless and exhausted, after the fatigues of the evening, when I was aroused from the reverie into which I had fallen by the sound of footsteps approaching my chamber, and my mother entered.

"Fanny, my dear," said she, in her softest tone, "I wish to say a word or two with you before I go to rest. You are not fatigued, love, I hope?"

"No, no, madam, I thank you," said I, rising at the same time from my seat with the formal respect so little practised now.

"Sit down, my dear," said she, placing herself upon a chair beside me; "I must chat with you for a quarter of an hour or so. Saunders, (to the maid) you may leave the room; do not close the room-door, but shut that of the lobby."

This precaution against curious ears having been taken as directed, my mother proceeded.

"You have observed, I should suppose, my dearest Fanny – indeed, you *must* have observed Lord Glenfallen's marked attentions to you?"

"I assure you, madam," I began.

"Well, well, that is all right," interrupted my mother; "of course you must be modest upon the matter; but listen to me for a few moments, my love, and I will prove to your satisfaction that your modesty is quite unnecessary in this case. You have done better than we could have hoped, at least, so very soon. Lord Glenfallen is in love with you. I give you joy of your conquest," and saying this, my mother kissed my forehead.

"In love with me!" I exclaimed, in unfeigned astonishment.

"Yes, in love with you," repeated my mother; "devotedly, distractedly in love with you. Why, my dear, what is there wonderful in it; look in the glass, and look at these," she continued, pointing with a smile to the jewels which I had just removed from my person, and which now lay a glittering heap upon the table.

"May there not," said I, hesitating between confusion and real alarm; "is it not possible that some mistake may be at the bottom of all this?"

"Mistake! dearest; none," said my mother. "None; none in the world; judge for yourself; read this, my love." And she placed in my hand a letter, addressed to herself, the seal of which was broken. I read it through with no small surprise. After some very fine complimentary flourishes upon my beauty and perfections, as, also, upon the antiquity and high reputation of our family, it went on to make a formal proposal of marriage, to be communicated or not to me at present, as my mother should deem expedient; and the letter wound up by a request that the writer might be permitted, upon our return to Ashtown-house, which was soon to take place, as the spring was now tolerably advanced, to visit us for a few days, in case his suit was approved.

"Well, well, my dear," said my mother, impatiently; "do you know who Lord Glenfallen is?"

"I do, madam," said I rather timidly, for I dreaded an altercation with my mother.

"Well, dear, and what frightens you?" continued she; "are you afraid of a title? What has he done to alarm you? he is neither old nor ugly."

I was silent, though I might have said, "He is neither young nor handsome."

"My dear Fanny," continued my mother, "in sober seriousness you have been most fortunate in engaging the affections of a nobleman such as Lord Glenfallen, young and wealthy, with first-rate – yes, acknowledged *first-rate* abilities, and of a family whose influence is not exceeded by that of any in Ireland – of course you see the offer in the same light that I do – indeed I think you *must*."

This was uttered in no very dubious tone. I was so much astonished by the suddenness of the whole communication that I literally did not know what to say.

"You are not in love?" said my mother, turning sharply, and fixing her dark eyes upon me, with severe scrutiny.

"No, madam," said I, promptly; horrified, as what young lady would not have been, at such a query.

"I'm glad to hear it," said my mother, drily. "Once, nearly twenty years ago, a friend of mine consulted me how he should deal with a daughter who had made what they call a love match, beggared herself, and disgraced her family; and I said, without hesitation, take no care for her, but cast her off; such punishment I awarded for an offence committed against the reputation of a family not my own; and what I advised respecting the child of another, with full as small compunction I would *do* with mine. I cannot conceive anything more unreasonable or intolerable than that the fortune and the character of a family should be marred by the idle caprices of a girl."

She spoke this with great severity, and paused as if she expected some observation from me. I, however, said nothing.

"But I need not explain to you, my dear Fanny," she continued, "my views upon this subject; you have always known them well, and I have never yet had reason to believe you likely, voluntarily, to offend me, or to abuse or neglect any of those advantages which reason and duty tell you should be improved – come hither, my dear; kiss me, and do not look so frightened. Well, now, about this letter, you need not answer it yet; of course you must be allowed time to make up your mind. In the meantime I will write to his lordship to give him my permission to visit us at Ashtown – good night, my love."

And thus ended one of the most disagreeable, not to say astounding, conversations I had ever had; it would not be easy to describe exactly what were my feelings towards Lord Glenfallen; – whatever might have been my mother's suspicions, my heart was perfectly disengaged; and hitherto, although I had not been made in the slightest degree acquainted with his real views, I had liked him very much, as an agreeable, well informed man, whom I was always glad to meet in society; he had served in the navy in early life, and the polish which his manners received in his after intercourse with courts and cities had not served to obliterate that frankness of *manner* which belongs proverbially to the sailor. Whether this apparent candour went deeper than the outward bearing I was yet to learn; however, there was no doubt that as far as I had seen of Lord Glenfallen, he was, though perhaps not so young as might have been desired in a lover, a singularly pleasing man, and whatever feeling un-favourable to him had found its way into my mind, arose altogether from the dread, not an unreasonable one, that constraint might be practised upon my inclinations. I reflected, however, that Lord Glenfallen was a wealthy man, and one highly thought of; and although I could never expect to love him in the romantic sense of the term, yet I had no doubt but that, all things considered, I might be more happy with him than I could hope to be at home. When next I met him it was with no small embarrassment, his tact and good breeding, however, soon reassured me, and effec-tually prevented my awkwardness being remarked upon; and I had the satisfaction of leaving Dublin for the country with the full conviction that nobody, not even those most intimate with me, even suspected the fact of Lord Glenfallen's having made me a formal proposal. This was to me a very serious subject of self gratulation, for, besides my instinctive dread of becoming the topic of the speculations of gossip, I felt that if the situation which I occupied in relation to him were made publicly known, I should stand committed in a manner which would scarcely leave me the power of retraction. The period at which Lord Glenfallen had arranged to visit Ashtown-house was now fast approaching, and it became my mother's wish to form me thoroughly to her will, and to obtain my consent to the proposed marriage before his arrival, so that all things might proceed smoothly, without apparent opposition or objection upon my part; whatever objections, therefore, I had entertained were to be subdued; whatever disposition to resistance I had exhibited or had been supposed to feel, were to be completely eradicated before he made his appearance; and my mother addressed herself to the task with a decision and energy against which even the barriers, which her imagination had created, could hardly have stood. If she had, however, expected any determined opposition from me, she was agreeably disappointed; my heart was perfectly free, and all my feelings of liking and preference were in favour of Lord Glenfallen, and I well knew that in case I refused to dispose of myself as I was desired, my mother had alike the power and the will to render my existence as utterly miserable as any, even the most ill-assorted marriage could possibly have done. You will remember, my good friend, that I was very young and very completely under the controul of my parents, both of whom, my mother particularly, were unscrupulously determined in matters of this kind, and willing, when voluntary obedience on the part of those within their power was withheld, to compel a forced acquiescence by an unsparing use of all the engines of the most stern and rigorous domestic discipline. All these combined, not unnaturally, induced me to resolve upon yielding at once, and without useless opposition, to what appeared almost to be my fate. The appointed time was come, and my now accepted suitor arrived; he was in high spirits, and, if possible, more entertaining than ever. I was not, however, quite in the mood to enjoy his sprightliness; but whatever I wanted in gaiety was amply made up in the triumphant and gracious good-humour of my mother, whose smiles of benevolence and exultation were showered around as bountifully as the summer sunshine. I will not weary you with unnecessary prolixity. Let it suffice to say, that I was married to Lord Glenfallen with all the attendant pomp and circumstance of wealth, rank, and grandeur. According to the usage of the times, now humanely reformed, the ceremony was made, until long past midnight, the season of wild, uproarious, and promiscuous feasting and revelry. Of all this I have a painfully vivid recollection, and particularly of the little annoyances inflicted upon me by the dull and coarse jokes of the wits and wags who abound in all such places, and upon all such occasions. I was not sorry, when, after a few days, Lord Glenfallen's carriage appeared at the door to convey us both from Ashtown; for any change would have been a relief from the irksomeness of ceremonial and formality which the visits received in honour of my newly acquired titles hourly entailed upon me. It was arranged that we were to proceed to Cahergillagh, one of the Glenfallen estates, lying, however, in a southern county, so that a tedious journey (then owing to the impracticability of the roads,) of three days intervened. I set forth with my noble companion, followed by the regrets of some, and by the envy of many; though God knows I little deserved the latter; the three days of travel were now almost spent, when passing the brow of a wild heathy hill, the domain of Cahergillagh opened suddenly upon our view. It formed a striking and a beautiful scene. A lake of considerable extent stretching away towards the west, and reflecting from its broad, smooth waters, the rich glow of the setting sun, was overhung by steep hills, covered by a rich mantle of velvet sward, broken here and there by the grey front of some old rock, and exhibiting on their shelving sides, their slopes and hollows, every variety of light and shade; a thick wood of dwarf oak, birch, and hazel skirted these hills, and clothed the shores of the lake, running out in rich luxuriance upon every promontory, and spreading upward considerably upon the side of the hills.

"There lies the enchanted castle," said Lord Glenfallen, pointing towards a considerable level space intervening between two of the picturesque hills, which rose dimly around the lake. This little plain was chiefly occupied by the same low, wild wood which covered the other parts of the domain; but towards the centre a mass of taller and statelier forest trees stood darkly grouped together, and among them stood an ancient square tower, with many buildings of an humbler character, forming together the manor-house, or, as it was more usually called, the court of Cahergillagh. As we approached the level upon which the mansion stood, the winding road gave us many glimpses of the time-worn castle and its surrounding buildings; and seen as it was through the long vistas of the fine old trees, and with the rich glow of evening upon it, I have seldom beheld an object more picturesquely striking. I was glad to perceive, too, that here and there the blue curling smoke ascended from stacks of chimneys now hidden by the rich, dark ivy which, in a great measure, covered the building; other indications of comfort made themselves manifest as we approached; and indeed, though the place was evidently one of considerable antiquity, it had nothing whatever of the gloom of decay about it.

"You must not, my love," said Lord Glenfallen, "imagine this place worse than it is. I have no taste for antiquity – at least I should not choose a house to reside in because it is old. Indeed I do not recollect that I was even so romantic as to overcome my aversion to rats and rheumatism, those faithful attendants upon your noble relics of feudalism; and I much prefer a snug, modern, unmysterious bedroom, with well-aired sheets, to the waving tapestry, mildewed cushions, and all the other interesting appliances of romance; however, though I cannot promise you all the discomfort generally pertaining to an old castle, you will find legends and ghostly lore enough to claim your respect; and if old Martha be still to the fore, as I trust she is, you will soon have a supernatural and appropriate anecdote for every closet and corner of the mansion; but here we are – so, without more ado, welcome to Cahergillagh."

We now entered the hall of the castle, and while the domestics were employed in conveying our trunks and other luggage which we had brought with us for immediate use to the apartments which Lord Glenfallen had selected for himself and me, I went with him into a spacious sitting room, wainscoted with finely polished black oak, and hung round with the portraits of various worthies of the Glenfallen family. This room looked out upon an extensive level covered with the softest green sward, and irregularly bounded by the wild wood I have before mentioned, through the leafy arcade formed by whose boughs and trunks the level beams of the setting sun were pouring; in the distance a group of dairy maids were plying their task, which they accompanied throughout with snatches of Irish songs which, mellowed by the distance, floated not unpleasingly to the ear; and beside them sat or lay, with all the grave importance of conscious protection, six or seven large dogs of various kinds; farther in the distance, and through the cloisters of the arching wood, two or three ragged urchins were employed in driving such stray kine as had wandered farther than the rest to join their fellows. As I looked upon this scene which I have described, a feeling of tranquillity and happiness came upon me, which I have never experienced in so strong a degree; and so strange to me was the sensation that my eyes filled with tears. Lord Glenfallen mistook the cause of my emotion, and taking me kindly and tenderly by the hand, he said, "Do not suppose, my love, that it is my intention to *scttle* here, whenever you desire to leave this, you have only to let me know your wish, and it shall be complied with; so I must entreat of you not to suffer any circumstances which I can control to give you one moment's uneasiness; but here is old Martha; you must be introduced to her, one of the heir-looms of our family."

A hale, good-humoured, erect, old woman was Martha, and an agreeable contrast to the grim, decrepid hag, which my fancy had conjured up, as the depository of all the horrible tales in which I doubted not this old place was most fruitful. She welcomed me and her master with a profusion of gratulations, alternately kissing our hands and apologising for the liberty, until at length Lord Glenfallen put an end to this somewhat fatiguing ceremonial, by requesting her to conduct me to my chamber if it were prepared for my reception. I followed Martha up an old-fashioned oak stair-case into a long, dim passage at the end of which lay the door which communicated with the apartments which had been selected for our use; here the old woman stopped, and respectfully requested me to proceed. I accordingly opened the door and was about to enter, when something like a mass of black tapestry, as it appeared disturbed by my sudden approach, fell from above the door, so as completely to screen the aperture; the startling unexpectedness of the occurrence, and the rustling noise which the drapery made in its descent, caused me involuntarily to step two or three paces backwards, I turned, smiling and half ashamed, to the old servant, and said, "You see what a coward I am." The woman looked puzzled, and without saying any more, I was about to draw aside the curtain and enter the room, when upon turning to do so, I was surprised to find that nothing whatever interposed to obstruct the passage. I went into the room, followed by the servant woman, and was amazed to find that it, like the one below, was wainscoted, and that nothing like drapery was to be found near the door.

"Where is it?" said I; "what has become of it?"

"What does your ladyship wish to know?" said the old woman.

"Where is the black curtain that fell across the door, when I attempted first to come to my chamber?" answered I.

"The cross of Christ about us!" said the old woman, turning suddenly pale.

"What is the matter, my good friend?" said I; "you seem frightened."

"Oh, no, no, your ladyship," said the old woman, endeavouring to conceal her agitation; but in vain, for tottering towards a chair, she sunk into it, looking so deadly pale and horror-struck that I thought every moment she would faint.

"Merciful God, keep us from harm and danger!" muttered she at length.

"What can have terrified you so?" said I, beginning to fear that she had seen something more than had met my eye, "you appear ill, my poor woman!"

"Nothing, nothing, my lady," said she, rising; "I beg your ladyship's pardon for making so bold; may the great God defend us from misfortune!"

"Martha," said I, "something *has* frightened you very much, and I insist on knowing what it is; your keeping me in the dark upon the subject will make me much more uneasy than anything you could tell me; I desire you, therefore, to let me know what agitates you; I command you to tell me."

"Your ladyship said you saw a black curtain falling across the door when you were coming into the room," said the old woman.

"I did," said I; "but though the whole thing appears somewhat strange, I cannot see anything in the matter to agitate you so excessively."

"It's for no good you saw that, my lady," said the Crone; "something terrible is coming; it's a sign, my lady – a sign that never fails."

"Explain, explain what you mean, my good woman," said I, in spite of myself, catching more than I could account for, of her superstitious terror.

"Whenever something – something *bad* is going to happen to the Glenfallen family, some one that belongs to them sees a black handkerchief or curtain just waved or falling before their faces; I saw it myself," continued she, lowering her voice, "when I was only a little girl, and I'll never forget it; I often heard of it before, though I never saw it till then, nor since, praised be God; but I was going into Lady Jane's room to waken her in the morning; and sure enough when I got first to the bed and began to draw the curtain, something dark was waved across the division, but only for a moment; and when I saw rightly into the bed, there was she lying cold and dead, God be merciful to me; so, my lady, there is small blame to me to be daunted when any one of the family sees it, for it's many's the story I heard of it, though I saw it but once."

I was not of a superstitious turn of mind; yet I could not resist a feeling of awe very nearly allied to the fear which my companion had so unreservedly expressed; and when you consider my situation, the loneliness, antiquity, and gloom of the place, you will allow that the weakness was not without excuse. In spite of old Martha's boding predictions, however, time flowed on in an unruffled course; one little incident however, though trifling in itself, I must relate as it serves to make what follows more intelligible. Upon the day after my arrival, Lord Glenfallen of course desired to make me acquainted with the house and domain; and accordingly we set forth upon our ramble; when returning, he became for some time silent and moody, a state so unusual with him as considerably to excite my surprise. I endeavoured by observations and questions to arouse him – but in vain; at length, as we approached the house, he said, as if speaking to himself, "'Twere madness – madness – madness," repeating the word bitterly – "sure and speedy ruin." There was here a long pause; and at length turning sharply towards me in a tone very unlike that in which he had hitherto addressed me, he said, "do you think it possible that a woman can keep a secret?"

"I am sure," said I, "that women are very much belied upon the score of talkativeness, and that I may answer your question with the same directness with which you put it; I reply that I *do* think a woman can keep a secret."

"But I do not," said he, drily.

We walked on in silence for a time; I was much astonished at his unwonted abruptness; I had almost said rudeness. After a considerable pause he seemed to recollect himself, and with an effort resuming his sprightly manner, he said, "well, well, the next thing to keeping a secret well is, not to desire to possess one – talkativeness and curiosity generally go together; now I shall make test of you in the first place, respecting the latter of these qualities. I shall be your *Bluebeard*[4] – tush, why do I trifle thus; listen to me, my dear Fanny, I speak now in solemn earnest; what I desire is, intimately, inseparably, connected with your happiness and honour as well as my own; and your compliance with my request will not be difficult; it will impose upon you a very trifling restraint during your sojourn here, which certain events which have occurred since our arrival, have determined me shall not be a long one. You must promise me, upon your sacred honour, that you will visit *only* that part of the castle which can be reached from the front entrance, leaving the back entrance and the part of the building commanded immediately by it, to the menials, as also the small garden whose high wall you see yonder; and never at any time seek to pry or peep into them, nor to open the door which communicates from the front part of the house through the corridor with the back. I do not urge this in jest or in caprice, but from a solemn conviction that danger and misery will be the certain consequences of your not observing what I prescribe. I cannot explain myself further at present – promise me, then, these things as you hope for peace here and for mercy hereafter."

I did make the promise as desired, and he appeared relicved; his manner recovered all its gaiety and elasticity, but the recollection of the strange scene which I have just described dwelt painfully upon my mind. More than a month passed away without any occurrence worth recording; but I was not destined to leave Cahergillagh without further adventure; one day intending to enjoy the pleasant sunshine in a ramble through the woods, I ran up to my room to procure my bonnet and shawl; upon entering the chamber, I was surprised and somewhat startled to find it occupied; beside the fireplace and nearly opposite the door, seated in a large, old-fashioned elbow-chair, was placed the figure of a lady; she appeared to be nearer fifty than forty, and was dressed suitably to her age, in a handsome suit of flowered silk; she had a profusion of trinkets and jewellery about her person, and many rings upon her fingers; but although very rich, her dress was not gaudy or in ill taste; but what was remarkable in the lady was, that although her features were handsome, and upon the whole pleasing; the pupil of each eye was dimmed with the whiteness of cataract, and she was evidently stone blind. I was for some seconds so surprised at this unaccountable apparition, that I could not find words to address her.

"Madam," said I, "there must be some mistake here – this is my bed-chamber."

"Marry come up," said the lady, sharply; "*your* chamber! Where is Lord Glenfallen?"

Notes ——————————————————————————————————

[4] A fairytale character who marries and then murders his wives in succession.

"He is below, madam," replied I; "and I am convinced he will be not a little surprised to find you here."

"I do not think he will," said she; "with your good leave, talk of what you know something about; tell him I want him; why does the minx dilly dally so?"

In spite of the awe which this grim lady inspired, there was something in her air of confident superiority which, when I considered our relative situations, was not a little irritating.

"Do you know, madam to whom you speak?" said I.

"I neither know nor care," said she; "but I presume that you are some one about the house, so, again, I desire you, if you wish to continue here, to bring your master hither forthwith."

"I must tell you madam," said I, "that I am Lady Glenfallen."

"What's that?" said the stranger, rapidly.

"I say, madam," I repeated, approaching her, that I might be more distinctly heard, "that I am Lady Glenfallen."

"It's a lie, you trull!"[5] cried she, in an accent which made me start, and, at the same time, springing forward, she seized me in her grasp and shook me violently, repeating, "it's a lie, it's a lie!" with a rapidity and vehemence which swelled every vein of her face; the violence of her action, and the fury which convulsed her face, effectually terrified me, and disengaging myself from her grasp, I screamed as loud as I could for help; the blind woman continued to pour out a torrent of abuse upon me, foaming at the mouth with rage, and impotently shaking her clenched fists towards me. I heard Lord Glenfallen's step upon the stairs, and I instantly ran out; as I past him I perceived that he was deadly pale, and just caught the words, "I hope that demon has not hurt you?" I made some answer, I forget what, and he entered the chamber, the door of which he locked upon the inside; what passed within I know not; but I heard the voices of the two speakers raised in loud and angry altercation. I thought I heard the shrill accents of the woman repeat the words, "let her look to herself;" but I could not be quite sure. This short sentence, however, was, to my alarmed imagination, pregnant with fearful meaning; the storm at length subsided, though not until after a conference of more than two long hours. Lord Glenfallen then returned, pale and agitated, "that unfortunate woman," said he, "is out of her mind. I dare say she treated you to some of her ravings; but you need not dread any further interruption from her, I have brought her so far to reason. She did not hurt you I trust."

"No, no," said I; "but she terrified me beyond measure."

"Well," said he, "she is likely to behave better for the future; and I dare swear that neither you nor she would desire after what has passed to meet again."

This occurrence, so startling and unpleasant, so involved in mystery, and giving rise to so many painful surmises, afforded me no very agreeable food for rumination. All attempts on my part to arrive at the truth were baffled; Lord Glenfallen evaded all my inquiries, and at length peremptorily forbid any further allusion to the matter. I was thus obliged to rest satisfied with what I had actually seen, and to trust to time to resolve the perplexities in which the whole transaction had involved me. Lord Glenfallen's temper and spirits gradually underwent a complete and most painful change; he became silent and abstracted, his manner to me was abrupt and often harsh, some grievous anxiety seemed ever present to his mind; and under its influence his spirits sunk and his temper became soured. I soon perceived that his gaiety was rather that which the stir and excitement of society produces, than the result of

Notes ———————————————————————————————————————

[5] prostitute

a healthy habit of mind; and every day confirmed me in the opinion, that the considerate good-nature which I had so much admired in him was little more than a mere manner; and to my infinite grief and surprise, the gay, kind, open-hearted nobleman who had for months followed and flattered me, was rapidly assuming the form of a gloomy, morose, and singularly selfish man; this was a bitter discovery, and I strove to conceal it from myself as long as I could, but the truth was not to be denied, and I was forced to believe that Lord Glenfallen no longer loved me, and that he was at little pains to conceal the alteration in his sentiments. One morning after breakfast, Lord Glenfallen had been for some time walking silently up and down the room, buried in his moody reflections, when pausing suddenly, and turning towards me, he exclaimed,

"I have it – I have it! We must go abroad and stay there, too, and if that does not answer, why – why we must try some more effectual expedient. Lady Glenfallen, I have become involved in heavy embarrassments, a wife you know must share the fortunes of her husband, for better for worse, but I will waive my right if you prefer remaining here – here at Cahergillagh; for I would not have you seen elsewhere without the state to which your rank entitles you; besides, it would break your poor mother's heart," he added, with sneering gravity, "so make up your mind – Cahergillagh or France. I will start if possible in a week, so determine between this and then."

He left the room, and in a few moments I saw him ride past the window, followed by a mounted servant; he had directed a domestic to inform me that he should not be back until the next day. I was in very great doubt as to what course of conduct I should pursue, as to accompanying him in the continental tour so suddenly determined upon, I felt that it would be a hazard too great to encounter; for at Cahergillagh I had always the consciousness to sustain me, that if his temper at any time led him into violent or unwarrantable treatment of me, I had a remedy within reach, in the protection and support of my own family, from all useful and effective communication with whom, if once in France, I should be entirely debarred. As to remaining at Cahergillagh in solitude, and for aught I knew, exposed to hidden dangers, it appeared to me scarcely less objectionable than the former proposition; and yet I feared that with one or other I must comply, unless I was prepared to come to an actual breach with Lord Glenfallen; full of these unpleasing doubts and perplexities, I retired to rest. I was wakened, after having slept uneasily for some hours, by some person shaking me rudely by the shoulder; a small lamp burned in my room, and by its light, to my horror and amazement, I discovered that my visitant was the self-same blind, old lady who had so terrified me a few weeks before. I started up in the bed, with a view to ring the bell, and alarm the domestics, but she instantly anticipated me by saying, "do not be frightened, silly girl; if I had wished to harm you I could have done it while you were sleeping, I need not have wakened you; listen to me, now, attentively and fearlessly, for what I have to say, interests you to the full as much as it does me; tell me, here, in the presence of God, did Lord Glenfallen marry you, *actually marry* you – speak the truth, woman."

"As surely as I live and speak," I replied, "did Lord Glenfallen marry me in presence of more than a hundred witnesses."

"Well," continued she, "he should have told you *then*, before you married him, that he had a wife living, which wife I am; I feel you tremble – tush! do not be frightened. I do not mean to harm you – mark me now – you are *not* his wife. When I make my story known you will be so, neither in the eye of God nor of man; you must leave this house upon to-morrow; let the world know that your husband has another wife living; go, you, into retirement, and leave him to justice, which will surely overtake him. If you remain in this house after to-morrow you will reap the bitter fruits of your sin," so saying, she quitted the room, leaving me very little disposed to sleep.

Here was food for my very worst and most terrible suspicions; still there was not enough to remove all doubt. I had no proof of the truth of this woman's statement. Taken by itself there was nothing to induce me to attach weight to it; but when I viewed it in connection with the extraordinary mystery of some of Lord Glenfallen's proceedings, his strange anxiety to exclude me from certain portions of the mansion, doubtless, lest I should encounter this person – the strong influence, nay, command, which she possessed over him, a circumstance clearly established by the very fact of her residing in the very place, where, of all others, he should least have desired to find her – her thus acting, and continuing to act in direct contradiction to his wishes; when, I say, I viewed her disclosure in connection with all these circumstances, I could not help feeling that there was at least a fearful veri-similitude in the allegations which she had made. Still I was not satisfied, nor nearly so; young minds have a reluctance almost insurmountable to believing upon any thing short of unquestionable proof, the existence of premeditated guilt in any one whom they have ever trusted; and in support of this feeling I was assured that if the assertion of Lord Glenfallen, which nothing in this woman's manner had led me to disbelieve, were true, namely, that her mind was unsound, the whole fabric of my doubts and fears must fall to the ground. I determined to state to Lord Glenfallen freely and accurately the substance of the communication which I had just heard, and in his words and looks to seek for its proof or refutation; full of these thoughts, I remained wakeful and excited all night, every moment fancying that I heard the step, or saw the figure of my recent visitor towards whom I felt a species of horror and dread which I can hardly describe. There was something in her face, though her features had evidently been handsome, and were not, at first sight, unpleasing, which, upon a nearer inspection, seemed to indicate the habitual prevalence and indulgence of evil passions, and a power of expressing mere animal anger, with an intenseness that I have seldom seen equalled, and to which an almost unearthly effect was given by the convulsive quivering of the sightless eyes. You may easily suppose that it was no very pleasing reflection to me to consider, that whenever caprice might induce her to return, I was within the reach of this violent and, for aught I knew, insane woman, who had, upon that very night, spoken to me in a tone of menace, of which her mere words, divested of the manner and look with which she uttered them, can convey but a faint idea. Will you believe me when I tell you that I was actually afraid to leave my bed in order to secure the door, lest I should again encounter the dreadful object lurking in some corner or peeping from behind the window curtains, so very a child was I in my fears.

The morning came, and with it Lord Glenfallen. I knew not, and indeed I cared not, where he might have been; my thoughts were wholly engrossed by the terrible fears and suspicions which my last night's conference had suggested to me; he was, as usual, gloomy and abstracted, and I feared in no very fitting mood to hear what I had to say with patience, whether the charges were true or false. I was, however, determined not to suffer the opportunity to pass, or Lord Glenfallen to leave the room, until, at all hazards, I had unburdened my mind.

"My Lord," said I, after a long silence, summoning up all my firmness – "my lord, I wish to say a few words to you upon a matter of very great importance, of very deep concernment to you and to me." I fixed my eyes upon him to discern, if possible, whether the announcement caused him any uneasiness; but no symptom of any such feeling was perceptible.

"Well, my dear," said he, "this is, no doubt, a very grave preface, and portends, I have no doubt, something extraordinary – pray let us have it without more ado."

He took a chair, and seated himself nearly opposite to me.

"My lord," said I, "I have seen the person who alarmed me so much a short time since, the blind lady, again, upon last night;" his face upon which my eyes were fixed, turned pale, he hesitated for a moment, and then said –

"And did you, pray madam, so totally forget or spurn my express command, as to enter that portion of the house from which your promise, I might say, your oath, excluded you – answer me that?" he added, fiercely.

"My lord," said I, "I have neither forgotten your *commands*, since such they were, nor disobeyed them. I was, last night, wakened from my sleep, as I lay in my own chamber, and accosted by the person whom I have mentioned – how she found access to the room I cannot pretend to say."

"Ha! this must be looked to," said he, half reflectively; "and pray," added he, quickly, while in turn he fixed his eyes upon me, "what did this person say? since some comment upon her communication forms, no doubt, the sequel to your preface."

"Your lordship is not mistaken," said I; "her statement was so extraordinary that I could not think of withholding it from you; she told me, my lord, that you had a wife living at the time you married me, and that she was that wife."

Lord Glenfallen became ashy pale, almost livid; he made two or three efforts to clear his voice to speak, but in vain, and turning suddenly from me, he walked to the window; the horror and dismay, which, in the olden time, overwhelmed the woman of Endor, when her spells unexpectedly conjured the dead into her presence, were but types of what I felt, when thus presented with what appeared to be almost unequivocal evidence of the guilt, whose existence I had before so strongly doubted. There was a silence of some moments, during which it were hard to conjecture whether I or my companion suffered most. Lord Glenfallen soon recovered his self-command; he returned to the table, again sat down and said –

"What you have told me has so astonished me, has unfolded such a tissue of motiveless guilt, and in a quarter from which I had so little reason to look for ingratitude or treachery, that your announcement almost deprived me of speech; the person in question, however, has one excuse, her mind is, as I told you before, unsettled. You should have remembered that, and hesitated to receive as unexceptionable evidence against the honour of your husband, the ravings of a lunatic. I now tell you that this is the last time I shall speak to you upon this subject, and, in the presence of the God who is to judge me, and as I hope for mercy in the day of judgment, I swear that the charge thus brought against me, is utterly false, unfounded, and ridiculous; I defy the world in any point to taint my honour; and, as I have never taken the opinion of madmen touching your character or morals, I think it but fair to require that you will evince a like tenderness for me; and now, once for all, never again dare to repeat to me your insulting suspicions, or the clumsy and infamous calumnies of fools. I shall instantly let the worthy lady who contrived this somewhat original device, understand fully my opinion upon the matter – good morning;" and with these words he left me again in doubt, and involved in all horrors of the most agonising suspense. I had reason to think that Lord Glenfallen wreaked his vengeance upon the author of the strange story which I had heard, with a violence which was not satisfied with mere words, for old Martha, with whom I was a great favourite, while attending me in my room, told me that she feared her master had ill used the poor, blind Dutch woman, for that she had heard her scream as if the very life were leaving her, but added a request that I should not speak of what she had told me to any one, particularly to the master.

"How do you know that she is a Dutch woman?" inquired I, anxious to learn anything whatever that might throw a light upon the history of this person, who seemed to have resolved to mix herself up in my fortunes.

"Why, my lady," answered Martha, "the master often calls her the Dutch hag, and other names you would not like to hear, and I am sure she is neither English nor Irish; for, whenever they talk together, they speak some queer foreign lingo, and fast enough, I'll be bound. But I ought not to talk about her at all; it might be as much as my place is worth to mention her – only you saw her first yourself, so there can be no great harm in speaking of her now."

"How long has this lady been here?" continued I.

"She came early on the morning after your ladyship's arrival," answered she; "but do not ask me any more, for the master would think nothing of turning me out of doors for daring to speak of her at all, much less to *you*, my lady."

I did not like to press the poor woman further, for her reluctance to speak on this topic was evident and strong.

You will readily believe that upon the very slight grounds which my information afforded, contradicted as it was by the solemn oath of my husband, and derived from what was, at best, a very questionable source, I could not take any very decisive measure whatever; and as to the menace of the strange woman who had thus unaccountably twice intruded herself into my chamber, although, at the moment, it occasioned me some uneasiness, it was not, even in my eyes, sufficiently formidable to induce my departure from Cahergillagh.

A few nights after the scene which I have just mentioned, Lord Glenfallen having, as usual, early retired to his study, I was left alone in the parlour to amuse myself as best I might. It was not strange that my thoughts should often recur to the agitating scenes in which I had recently taken a part; the subject of my reflections, the solitude, the silence, and the lateness of the hour, as also the depression of spirits to which I had of late been a constant prey, tended to produce that nervous excitement which places us wholly at the mercy of the imagination. In order to calm my spirits I was endeavouring to direct my thoughts into some more pleasing channel, when I heard, or thought I heard, uttered, within a few yards of me, in an odd, half-sneering tone, the words, "There is blood upon your ladyship's throat." So vivid was the impression, that I started to my feet, and involuntarily placed my hand upon my neck. I looked around the room for the speaker, but in vain. I went then to the room-door, which I opened, and peered into the passage, nearly faint with horror, lest some leering, shapeless thing should greet me upon the threshold. When I had gazed long enough to assure myself that no strange object was within sight,

"I have been too much of a rake lately; I am racking out my nerves," said I, speaking aloud, with a view to re-assure myself. I rang the bell, and, attended by old Martha, I retired to settle for the night. While the servant was, as was her custom, arranging the lamp which I have already stated always burned during the night in my chamber, I was employed in undressing, and, in doing so, I had recourse to a large looking-glass which occupied a considerable portion of the wall in which it was fixed, rising from the ground to a height of about six feet; this mirror filled the space of a large panel in the wainscoting opposite the foot of the bed. I had hardly been before it for the lapse of a minute, when something like a black pall was slowly waved between me and it.

"Oh, God! there it is," I exclaimed, wildly. "I have seen it again, Martha – the black cloth."

"God be merciful to us, then!" answered she, tremulously crossing herself. "Some misfortune is over us."

"No, no, Martha," said I, almost instantly recovering my collectedness; for, although of a nervous temperament, I had never been superstitious. "I do not believe in omens. You know, I saw, or fancied I saw, this thing before, and nothing followed."

"The Dutch lady came the next morning," replied she.

"Methinks, such an occurrence scarcely deserved a supernatural announcement," I replied.

"She is a strange woman, my lady," said Martha; "and she is not *gone* yet – mark my words."

"Well, well, Martha," said I, "I have not wit enough to change your opinions, nor inclination to alter mine; so I will talk no more of the matter. Good-night," and so I was left to my reflections. After lying for about an hour awake, I at length fell into a kind of doze; but my imagination was still busy, for I was startled from this unrefreshing sleep by fancying that I heard a voice close to my face exclaim as before, "There is blood upon your ladyship's throat." The words were instantly followed by a loud burst of laughter. Quaking with horror, I awakened, and heard my husband enter the room. Even this was [a] relief. Scared as I was, however, by the tricks which my imagination had played me, I preferred remaining silent, and pretending to sleep, to attempting to engage my husband in conversation, for I well knew that his mood was such, that his words would not, in all probability, convey anything that had not better be unsaid and unheard.

Lord Glenfallen went into his dressing-room, which lay upon the right-hand side of the bed. The door lying open, I could see him by himself, at full length upon a sofa, and, in about half an hour, I became aware, by his deep and regularly drawn respiration, that he was fast asleep. When slumber refuses to visit one, there is something peculiarly irritating, not to the temper, but to the nerves, in the consciousness that some one is in your immediate presence, actually enjoying the boon which you are seeking in vain; at least, I have always found it so, and never more than upon the present occasion. A thousand annoying imaginations harassed and excited me, every object which I looked upon, though ever so familiar, seemed to have acquired a strange phantom-like character, the varying shadows thrown by the flickering of the lamplight, seemed shaping themselves into grotesque and unearthly forms, and whenever my eyes wandered to the sleeping figure of my husband, his features appeared to undergo the strangest and most demoniacal contortions. Hour after hour was told by the old clock, and each succeeding one found me, if possible, less inclined to sleep than its predecessor. It was now considerably past three; my eyes, in their involuntary wanderings, happened to alight upon the large mirror which was, as I have said, fixed in the wall opposite the foot of the bed. A view of it was commanded from where I lay, through the curtains, as I gazed fixedly upon it, I thought I perceived the broad sheet of glass shifting its position in relation to the bed; I riveted my eyes upon it with intense scrutiny; it was no deception, the mirror, as if acting of its own impulse, moved slowly aside, and disclosed a dark aperture in the wall, nearly as large as an ordinary door; a figure evidently stood in this; but the light was too dim to define it accurately. It stepped cautiously into the chamber, and with so little noise, that had I not actually seen it, I do not think I should have been aware of its presence. It was arrayed in a kind of woollen night-dress, and a white handkerchief or cloth was bound tightly about the head; I had no difficulty spite of the strangeness of the attire in recognising the blind woman whom I so much dreaded. She stooped down, bringing her head nearly to the ground, and in that attitude she remained motionless for some moments, no doubt in order to ascertain if any suspicious sound were stirring. She was apparently satisfied by her observations, for she immediately recommenced her silent progress towards a ponderous mahogany dressing-table of my husband's; when she had reached it, she paused again, and appeared to listen attentively for some minutes; she then noiselessly opened one of the drawers, from which, having groped for some time, she took something which I soon perceived to be a case of razors; she opened it and tried the edge of each of the two instruments upon the skin of her hand; she quickly selected one, which she fixed firmly in her grasp; she now stooped down as before, and having listened for a time, she, with the hand that was disengaged, groped her way into the dressing-room where Lord Glenfallen lay fast asleep. I was fixed as if in the tremendous spell of a nightmare. I could not stir even a finger; I could not lift my voice; I could not even breathe; and though I expected every moment to see the sleeping man murdered, I could not even close my eyes to shut out the horrible spectacle, which I had not the power to avert. I saw the woman approach the sleeping figure, she laid the unoccupied hand lightly along his clothes, and having thus ascertained his identity, she, after a brief interval, turned back and again entered my chamber; here she bent down again to listen. I had now not a doubt but that the razor was intended for my throat; yet the terrific fascination which had locked all my powers so long, still continued to bind me fast. I felt that my life depended upon the slightest ordinary exertion, and yet I could not stir one joint from the position in which I lay, nor even make noise enough to waken Lord Glenfallen. The murderous woman now, with long, silent steps, approached the bed; my very heart seemed turning to ice; her left hand, that which was disengaged, was upon the pillow; she gradually slid it forward towards my head, and in an instant, with the speed of lightning, it was clutched in my hair, while, with the other hand, she dashed the razor at my throat. A slight inaccuracy saved me from instant death; the blow fell short, the point of the razor grazing my throat; in a moment I know not how, I found myself at the other side of the bed uttering shriek after shriek; the wretch was, however, determined if possible to murder me, scrambling along by the curtains; she rushed round the bed towards me; I seized the handle of the door to make my escape; it was, however, fastened; at all events I could not open it, from the mere instinct of recoiling terror, I shrunk back into a corner – she was now within a yard of me – her hand was upon my face – I closed my eyes fast, expecting never to open them again, when a blow, inflicted from behind by a strong arm, stretched the monster senseless at my feet; at the same moment the door opened, and several domestics, alarmed by my cries, entered the apartment. I do not recollect what followed, for I fainted. One swoon succeeded another so long and death-like, that my life was considered very doubtful. At about ten o'clock, however, I sunk into a deep and refreshing sleep, from which I was awakened at about two, that I might swear my deposition before a magistrate, who attended for that purpose. I, accordingly, did so, as did also Lord Glenfallen; and the woman was fully committed to stand her trial at the ensuing assizes. I shall never forget the scene which the examination of the blind woman and of the other parties afforded. She was brought into the room in the custody of two servants; she wore a kind of flannel wrapper which had not been changed since the night before; it was torn and soiled, and here and there smeared with blood, which had flowed in large quantities from a wound in her head; the white handkerchief had fallen off in the scuffle; and her grizzled hair fell in masses about her wild and deadly pale countenance. She appeared perfectly composed, however, and the only regret she expressed throughout, was at not having succeeded in her attempt, the object of which she did not pretend to conceal. On being asked her name, she called herself the Countess Glenfallen, and refused to give any other title.

"The woman's name is Flora Van-Kemp," said Lord Glenfallen.

"It *was*, it *was*, you perjured traitor and cheat!" screamed the woman; and then there followed a volley of words in some foreign language. "Is there a magistrate here," she resumed; "I am Lord Glenfallen's wife – I'll prove it – write down my words. I am willing to be hanged or burned, so *he* meets his deserts. I did try to kill that doll of his; but it was he who put it into my head to do it – two wives were too many – I was to murder her, or she was to hang me – listen to all I have to say."

Here Lord Glenfallen interrupted.

"I think, sir," said he, addressing the magistrate, "that we had better proceed to business; this unhappy woman's furious recriminations but waste our time; if she refuses to answer your questions, you had better, I presume, take my depositions."

"And are you going to swear away my life, you black perjured murderer?" shrieked the woman. "Sir, sir, sir, you must hear me," she continued, addressing the magistrate; "I can convict him – he bid me murder that girl, and then when I failed, he came behind me, and struck me down, and now he wants to swear away my life – take down all I say."

"If it is your intention," said the magistrate, "to confess the crime with which you stand charged, you may, upon producing sufficient evidence, criminate whom you please."

"Evidence! – I have no evidence but myself," said the woman. "I will swear it all – write down my testimony – write it down, I say – we shall hang side by side, my brave Lord – all your own handy-work, my gentle husband." This was followed by a low, insolent, and sneering laugh, which, from one in her situation, was sufficiently horrible.

"I will not at present hear anything," replied he, "but distinct answers to the questions which I shall put to you upon this matter."

"Then you shall hear nothing," replied she sullenly, and no inducement or intimidation could bring her to speak again.

Lord Glenfallen's deposition and mine were then given, as also those of the servants who had entered the room at the moment of my rescue; the magistrate then intimated that she was committed, and must proceed directly to gaol, whither she was brought in a carriage of Lord Glenfallen's, for his lordship was naturally by no means indifferent to the effect which her vehement accusations against himself might produce, if uttered before every chance hearer whom she might meet with between Cahergillagh and the place of confinement whither she was despatched.

During the time which intervened between the committal and the trial of the prisoner, Lord Glenfallen seemed to suffer agonies of mind which baffle all description, he hardly ever slept, and when he did, his slumbers seemed but the instruments of new tortures, and his waking hours were, if possible, exceeded in intensity of terrors by the dreams which disturbed his sleep. Lord Glenfallen rested, if to lie in the mere attitude of repose were to do so, in his dressing-room, and thus I had an opportunity of witnessing, far oftener than I wished it, the fearful workings of his mind; his agony often broke out into such fearful paroxysms that delirium and total loss of reason appeared to be impending; he frequently spoke of flying from the country, and bringing with him all the witnesses of the appalling scene upon which the prosecution was founded; then again he would fiercely lament that the blow which he had inflicted had not ended all.

The assizes arrived, however, and upon the day appointed, Lord Glenfallen and I attended in order to give our evidence. The cause was called on, and the prisoner appeared at the bar. Great curiosity and interest were felt respecting the trial, so that the court was crowded to excess. The prisoner, however, without appearing to take the trouble of listening to the indictment, pleaded guilty, and no representations on the part of the court, availed to induce her to retract her plea. After much time had been wasted in a fruitless attempt to prevail upon her to reconsider her words, the court proceeded, according to the usual form, to pass sentence. This having been done, the prisoner was about to be removed, when she said, in a low, distinct voice –

"A word – a word, my Lord: – Is Lord Glenfallen here in the court?" On being told that he was, she raised her voice to a tone of loud menace, and continued –

"Hardress, Earl of Glenfallen, I accuse you here in this court of justice of two crimes, – first, that you married a second wife, while the first was living; and again, that you prompted me to the murder, for attempting which I am to die; secure him – chain him – bring him here."

There was a laugh through the court at these words, which were naturally treated by the judge as a violent extemporary recrimination, and the woman was desired to be silent.

"You won't take him, then?" she said; "you won't try him? You'll let him go free?"

It was intimated by the court that he would certainly be allowed "to go free," and she was ordered again to be removed. Before, however, the mandate was executed, she threw her arms wildly into the air, and uttered one piercing shriek so full of preternatural rage and despair, that it might fitly have ushered a soul into those realms where hope can come no more. The sound still rang in my ears, months after the voice that had uttered it was for ever silent. The wretched woman was executed in accordance with the sentence which had been pronounced.

For some time after this event, Lord Glenfallen appeared, if possible, to suffer more than he had done before, and altogether, his language, which often amounted to half confessions of the guilt imputed to him, and all the circumstances connected with the late occurrences, formed a mass of evidence so convincing that I wrote to my father, detailing the grounds of my fears, and imploring him to come to Cahergillagh without delay, in order to remove me from my husband's control, previously to taking legal steps for a final separation. Circumstanced as I was, my existence was little short of intolerable, for, besides the fearful suspicions which attached to my husband, I plainly perceived that if Lord Glenfallen were not relieved, and that speedily, insanity must supervene. I therefore expected my father's arrival, or at least a letter to announce it, with indescribable impatience.

About a week after the execution had taken place, Lord Glenfallen one morning met me with an unusually sprightly air –

"Fanny," said he, "I have it now for the first time, in my power to explain to your satisfaction every thing which has hitherto appeared suspicious or mysterious in my conduct. After breakfast come with me to my study, and I shall, I hope, make all things clear."

This invitation afforded me more real pleasure than I had experienced for months; something had certainly occurred to tranquillize my husband's mind in no ordinary degree, and I thought it by no means impossible that he would, in the proposed interview, prove himself the most injured and innocent of men. Full of this hope I repaired to his study at the appointed hour; he was writing busily when I entered the room, and just raising his eyes, he requested me to be seated. I took a chair as he desired, and remained silently awaiting his leisure, while he finished, folded, directed, and sealed his letter; laying it then upon the table with the address downward, he said –

"My dearest Fanny, I know I must have appeared very strange to you and very unkind – often even cruel; before the end of this week I will show you the necessity of my conduct; how impossible it was that I should have seemed otherwise. I am conscious that many acts of mine must have inevitably given rise to painful suspicions – suspicions, which indeed, upon one occasion you very properly communicated to me. I have gotten two letters from a quarter which commands respect, containing information as to the course by which I may be enabled to prove the negative of all the crimes which even the most credulous suspicion could lay to my charge. I expected a third by this morning's post, containing documents which will set the matter for ever at rest, but owing, no doubt, to some neglect, or, perhaps, to some difficulty in collecting the papers, some inevitable delay, it has not come to hand this morning, according to my expectation. I was finishing one to the very same quarter when you came in, and if a sound rousing be worth any thing, I think I shall have a special messenger before two days have passed. I have been thinking over the matter within myself, whether I had better imperfectly clear up your doubts by submitting to your inspection the two letters which I have already received, or wait till I can triumphantly vindicate myself by the production of the documents which I have already mentioned, and I have, I think, not unnaturally decided upon the latter course; however, there is a person in the next room, whose testimony is not without its value – excuse me for one moment."

So saying, he arose and went to the door of a closet which opened from the study, this he unlocked, and half opening the door, he said, "it is only I," and then slipped into the room, and carefully closed and locked the door behind him. I immediately heard his voice in animated conversation; my curiosity upon the subject of the letter was naturally great, so smothering any little scruples which I might have felt, I resolved to look at the address of the letter which lay as my husband had left it, with its face upon the table. I accordingly drew it over to me and turned up the direction. For two or three moments I could scarce believe my eyes, but there could be no mistake – in large characters were traced the words, "To the Archangel Gabriel in heaven." I had scarcely returned the letter to its original position, and in some degree recovered the shock which this unequivocal proof of insanity produced, when the closet door was unlocked, and Lord Glenfallen re-entered the study, carefully closing and locking the door again upon the outside.

"Whom have you there?" inquired I, making a strong effort to appear calm.

"Perhaps," said he, musingly, "you might have some objection to seeing her, at least for a time."

"Who is it?" repeated I.

"Why," said he, "I see no use in hiding it – the blind Dutchwoman; I have been with her the whole morning. She is very anxious to get out of that closet, but you know she is odd, she is scarcely to be trusted."

A heavy gust of wind shook the door at this moment with a sound as if something more substantial were pushing against it.

"Ha, ha, ha! – do you hear her?" said he, with an obstreperous burst of laughter. The wind died away in a long howl, and Lord Glenfallen, suddenly checking his merriment, shrugged his shoulders, and muttered –

"Poor devil, she has been hardly used."

"We had better not tease her at present with questions," said I, in as unconcerned a tone as I could assume, although I felt every moment as if I should faint.

"Humph! may be so," said he, "well, come back in an hour or two, or when you please, and you will find us here."

He again unlocked the door, and entered with the same precautions which he had adopted before, locking the door upon the inside, and as I hurried from the room, I heard his voice again exerted as if in eager parley. I can hardly describe my emotions; my hopes had been raised to the highest, and now in an instant, all was gone – the dreadful consummation was accomplished – the fearful retribution had fallen upon the guilty man – the mind was destroyed – the power to repent was gone. The agony of the hours which followed what I would still call my *awful* interview with Lord Glenfallen, I cannot describe; my solitude was, however, broken in upon by Martha, who came to inform me of the arrival of a gentleman, who expected me in the parlour. I accordingly descended, and to my great joy, found my father seated by the fire. This expedition upon his part was easily accounted for: my communications had touched the honor of the family. I speedily informed him of the dreadful malady which had fallen upon the wretched man. My father suggested the necessity of placing some person to watch him, to prevent his injuring himself or others. I rang the bell, and desired that one Edward Cooke, an attached servant of the family, should be sent to me. I told him distinctly and briefly, the nature of the service required of him, and, attended by him, my father and I proceeded at once to the study; the door of the inner room was still closed, and everything in the outer chamber remained in the same order in which I had left it. We then advanced to the closet-door, at which we knocked, but without receiving any answer. We next tried to open the door, but in vain – it was locked upon the inside; we knocked more loudly, but in vain. Seriously alarmed, I desired the servant to force the door, which was, after several violent efforts, accomplished, and we entered the closet. Lord Glenfallen was lying on his face upon a sofa.

"Hush!" said I, "he is asleep;" we paused for a moment.

"He is too still for that," said my father; we all of us felt a strong reluctance to approach the figure.

"Edward," said I, "try whether your master sleeps."

The servant approached the sofa where Lord Glenfallen lay; he leant his ear towards the head of the recumbent figure, to ascertain whether the sound of breathing was audible; he turned towards us, and said –

"My Lady, you had better not wait here, I am sure he is dead!"

"Let me see the face," said I, terribly agitated, "you *may* be mistaken."

The man then, in obedience to my command, turned the body round, and, gracious God! what a sight met my view; – he was, indeed, perfectly dead. The whole breast of the shirt, with its lace frill, was drenched with gore, as was the couch underneath the spot where he lay. The head hung back, as it seemed almost severed from the body by a frightful gash, which yawned across the throat. The instrument which had inflicted it, was found under his body. All, then, was over; I was never to learn the history in whose termination I had been so deeply and so tragically involved.

The severe discipline which my mind had undergone was not bestowed in vain. I directed my thoughts and my hopes to that place where there is no more sin, nor danger, nor sorrow.

Thus ends a brief tale, whose prominent incidents many will recognise as having marked the history of a distinguished family; and though it refers to a somewhat distant date, we shall be found not to have taken, upon that account, any liberties with the facts, but in our statement of all the incidents to have rigorously and faithfully adhered to the truth.

Denis Florence MacCarthy (1817–1882)

Denis Florence MacCarthy (or M'Carthy) was born in Dublin. As a young man he trained for two years at Maynooth for the priesthood, but then switched to law at Trinity College Dublin and was called to the bar in 1846. In 1853, he became a professor of English literature at Catholic University, Dublin, but resigned after less than a year. He married and had nine children, including the poet Sister Mary Stanislaus MacCarthy. Politically, he was involved in various movements to repeal the Act of Union, including Daniel O'Connell's Repeal Association, the Young Ireland movement, and a related association that he founded in 1845, the '82 Club.

MacCarthy was heralded in his lifetime as the heir to Thomas Moore as Ireland's national poet, and he commemorated Moore in two poems, an elegy in 1857 and an ode in 1880. He was also a frequent contributor to *The Nation*. While publishing much of his work in periodicals, often under pseudonyms, he produced a number of volumes of his verse, including *Ballads, Poems, and Lyrics* (1850), *The Bell-Founder, and Other Poems* (1857), *Underglimpses, and Other Poems* (1857), and *The Centenary of Moore* (1880). He also edited *The Book of Irish Ballads* (1846), wrote a biography of English poet Percy Bysshe Shelley, and published important translations of dramas by the Spanish playwright, Pedro Calderón de la Barca, in a number of volumes between 1848 and 1873. MacCarthy's reputation was perhaps longest sustained in the nineteenth century by the latter, and Lady Wilde discusses his translations in her own essay on Calderón.

"The Pillar Towers of Ireland" is perhaps MacCarthy's most remembered poem, depicting the distinctive towers that Mangan uses in "The Lovely Land" (see above) to shock his speaker into an awareness that a landscape is Irish. It is similar to a number of the poems that MacCarthy wrote for *The Nation*, texts which owe much to the ballad form and deal with specifically Irish subjects, such as "A Voice in the Desert" (reprinted in an 1852 supplement to *The Nation*). His elegy for Thomas Davis, "The Living Land," should be considered in the line of Irish nationalist elegy from Drennan forward, but is distinctive for its refusal of the pathetic fallacy. The hero has died, but the land is not wintry with grief; it is a "living land" and its very vitality calls patriots to unite in Ireland's defense. "Afghanistan" is a topical tour de force, a compelling engagement with the British defeat in the first Anglo-Afghan war; MacCarthy not only paints a benign and beautiful Afghanistan in orientalist colors, but situates British imperial expansion within a world history of empires. The topographical "A Walk by the Bay of Dublin" addresses similar themes, representing the scene as the site of both aesthetic power and defeated invasions which thus renews the patriot.

Further reading

Leerssen, Joep, *Remembrance and Imagination: Patterns in the Historical and Literary Representation of Ireland in the Nineteenth Century*. Notre Dame, IN: University of Notre Dame Press, 1997.

Schirmer, Gregory A., *Out of What Began: A History of Irish Poetry in English*. Ithaca, NY: Cornell University Press, 1998.

Wright, Julia M., *Ireland, India, and Nationalism in Nineteenth-century Literature*. Cambridge: Cambridge University Press, 2007.

The Pillar Towers of Ireland

From **Ballads, Poems, and Lyrics** (1850)

I

The pillar towers of Ireland, how wondrously they stand
By the lakes and rushing rivers through the valleys of our land;
In mystic file, through the isle, they lift their heads sublime,
These grey old pillar temples – these conquerors of time!

II

Beside these grey old pillars, how perishing and weak   5
The Roman's arch of triumph, and the temple of the Greek,
And the gold domes of Byzantium, and the pointed Gothic spires,
All are gone, one by one, but the temples of our sires!

III

The column, with its capital, is level with the dust,
And the proud halls of the mighty and the calm homes of the just;   10
For the proudest works of man, as certainly, but slower,
Pass like the grass at the sharp scythe of the mower!

IV

But the grass grows again when in majesty and mirth,
On the wing of the Spring comes the Goddess of the Earth;
But for man in this world no springtide e'er returns   15
To the labours of his hands or the ashes of his urns!

V

Two favourites hath Time – the pyramids of Nile,
And the old mystic temples of our own dear isle;
As the breeze o'er the seas, where the halcyon has its nest,
Thus Time o'er Egypt's tombs and the temples of the West!   20

VI

The names of their founders have vanished in the gloom,
Like the dry branch in the fire or the body in the tomb;
But to-day, in the ray, their shadows still they cast –
These temples of forgotten Gods – these relics of the past!

VII

Around these walls have wandered the Briton and the Dane –   25
The captives of Armorica, the cavaliers of Spain –
Phoenician and Milesian, and the plundering Norman Peers –
And the swordsmen of brave Brian, and the chiefs of later years!

VIII

How many different rites have these grey old temples known?
To the mind what dreams are written in these chronicles of stone!   30
What terror and what error, what gleams of love and truth,
Have flashed from these walls since the world was in its youth?

IX

Here blazed the sacred fire, and, when the sun was gone,
As a star from afar to the traveller it shone;
And the warm blood of the victim have these grey old temples drunk,   35
And the death-song of the Druid and the matin of the Monk.

X

Here was placed the holy chalice that held the sacred wine,
And the gold cross from the altar, and the relics from the shrine,
And the mitre shining brighter with its diamonds than the East,
And the crozier of the Pontiff and the vestments of the Priest!   40

XI

Where blazed the sacred fire, rung out the vesper bell –
Where the fugitive found shelter, became the hermit's cell;
And hope hung out its symbol to the innocent and good,
For the Cross o'er the moss of the pointed summit stood!

XII

There may it stand for ever, while this symbol doth impart   45
To the mind one glorious vision, or one proud throb to the heart;
While the breast needeth rest may these grey old temples last,
Bright prophets of the future, as preachers of the past!

The Living Land

From Ballads, Poems, and Lyrics (1850)

We have mourned and sighed for our buried pride,
    We have given what Nature gives,
A manly tear o'er a brother's bier,
    But now for the Land that lives!
He who passed too soon, in his glowing noon,   5
    The hope of our youthful band
From heaven's blue wall doth seem to call
    "Think! think of your Living Land!
I dwell serene in a happier scene –
    Ye dwell in a Living Land!"   10

Yes! yes! dear shade, thou shalt be obeyed,
    We must spend the hour that flies,
In no vain regret for the sun that has set,
    But in hope for another to rise;
And though it delay with its guiding ray,   15
    We must each, with his little brand,
Like sentinels light through the dark, dark night,
    The steps of our Living Land.
She needeth our care in the chilling air –
    Our old, dear Living Land!   20

Yet our breasts will throb, and the tears will throng
    To our eyes for many a day,
For an eagle in strength and a lark in song
    Was the spirit that's pass'd away.
Though his heart be still as a frozen rill,   25
    And pulseless his glowing hand,
We must struggle the more for that old green shore
    He was making a Living Land.
By him we have lost, at whatever the cost,
    She must be a Living Land!   30

A Living Land such as Nature plann'd,
    When she hollowed our harbours deep,
When she bade the grain wave over the plain,
    And the oak wave over the steep:
When she bade the tide roll deep and wide   35
    From its source to the ocean strand,
Oh! it was not to slaves she gave these waves,
    But to sons of a Living Land!
Sons who have eyes and hearts to prize
    The worth of a Living Land!   40

Oh! when shall we lose the hostile hues,
    That have kept us so long apart?
Or cease from the strife, that is crushing the life
    From out of our mother's heart?
Could we lay aside our doubts and our pride   45
    And join in a common band,
One hour would see our country free,
    A young and a Living Land!
With a nation's heart and a nation's part,
    A free and a Living Land![1]   50

The Voice in the Desert

From **Ballads, Poems, and Lyrics (1850)**

Oh! my country. Oh! my Erin,
    Once so gladsome, once so gay,
Must thou, slowly disappearing,
    Vanish from the face of day?
Will the angry Godhead grant us   5
    Nought from thee except a grave?
Thou, alas! a true Atlantis
    Sinking down in ruin's wave!

He enslaveth – who delivers,
    And the hand doth smite, that shields –   10
Erin of the fishful rivers –
    Erin of the golden fields –
Strange her destiny, but stranger,
    If the just God could forgive
Her, who gave unto the stranger   15
    What should make her children live!

But why use this nomenclature?
    Why the frank avowal shun?

Notes

THE LIVING LAND
[1] This poem was written a few months after the death of Thomas Davis, when the first outburst of grief for his premature and unexpected loss had commenced a little to subside (author). See Samuel Ferguson, "[Thomas Davis: An Elegy]" (1847) above, p. 368.

Dare to blame not God or Nature,
    For what we ourselves have done.   20
Blame not God's benign intentions,
    Nor the wily statesman's snares;
Let us blame our mad dissensions,
    Boasts and brawls and braggart airs!

Let us make the sad confession   25
    And the bitter fruit bewail,
It was partly indiscretion,
    Partly caution, made us fail:[1]
Some too slow, and some too rapid,
    Some too timid, some too bold,   30
Some too volatile or vapid, –
    And the tragic tale is told!

But whate'er the cause, 'tis over,
    And the sad result remains;
Desolation's wing doth hover   35
    Daily darklier o'er our plains;
Save the buried and the banished,
    Nought to ponder proudly o'er;
What was Ireland hath vanished,
    What was Irish is no more!   40

Who shall guide us? – who shall save us? –
    Break our chains? – unbind our cords?
Cold the burning heart of Davis,
    Hush'd O'Connell's thunder-words;
Gone the Nobly-rash, Bold-spoken –   45
    He, with danger first to cope;
Ah! "our ranks *are* thinn'd and broken" –
    Who remains to give us hope?

Oh! Ierne, oh! ill-omened
    Mother, rend thy tresses grey,   50
Wail the noblest heir of Thomond,
    Wifeless, childless, borne away!
Look athwart the watery Lybian
    Waste, and yonder captives wail,
There the golden-tongued young Tribune   55
    And his brave companions sail!

Oh! our sad, our painful story,
    What can equal? what can rival?
Gone the Island's ancient glory,
    Gone the dreams of its revival.   60
Mute the clairseach that had woken
    Hopes and tears and throbs and sighs;

Notes

THE VOICE IN THE DESERT
[1] The failure of those expectations which the strength, enthusiasm, and intellectual propagandism of the national party in Ireland some few years ago, had led even the coldest among us to form, is here alluded to (author).

For with heart and harp-strings broken,
    The Prince of all the Minstrels lies![2]

Still the old material Island   65
    Looks as fertile, smiles as fair,
As when Baal-fires[3] lit the highland,
    And the bell-towers tolled to prayer.
'Mid the upland meads expanding,
    See the hopeful peasant walks,   70
See the girdled sheaves are standing
    Grain-filled 'mid the golden stalks.

The Isle's vitality astounds us,
    As smiles upon a death-face traced –
For, ah! the desert that surrounds us   75
    Spreads darkly round – a moral waste.
The faith, the hope, the trust that lighted
    Our footsteps on for many a day –
These, with our very hearts, are blighted,
    And, withering, waste and fade away.   80

From out that desert, where the Gifted
    Dreamed verdurous isle and halls of gold;
Still from that desert, is uplifted,
    A Warning Voice, like that of old:
"God hath this punishment permitted   85
    For what we've done, and left undone: –
Repent ye, of the sins committed,
    And freedom's kingdom may be won!"

Afghanistan[1]

From Ballads, Poems, and Lyrics (1850)

On Fancy's wing when favoured poets rise,
Burst from the earth, and soar amid the skies,
Attending spirits through the realms of light
Nerve their strong wings, and guide their daring flight;
A thousand zephyrs fan the favouring airs,   5
Venus her doves and pearly chariot shares:

Notes ────────────────────────────

[2] This allusion to THOMAS MOORE was written under an impression, very general in Ireland, that the health of our illustrious countryman and greatest poet had become seriously affected. It has given me, as I am sure it has given thousands, heartfelt pleasure to learn, from a recent statement in the newspapers, that he is in the enjoyment of good health, physically and mentally. Long may he continue so! (author).

[3] Baal is a deity associated with fire (see Jeremiah, Bible).

AFGHANISTAN
[1] MacCarthy dated this poem 1842. The first issue of *The Nation* included a lengthy report on British military difficulties in Afghanistan during June and July 1842 as well as an editorial on the subject, particularly the holding of English prisoners in Cabul (Kabul). Subsequent issues returned to the subject, and an article in the fifth issue begins, "The English are becoming humble! Their press is in hysterics of delight because one mail has arrived unladen with defeat" ("The English Army in India").

But when a feebler bard essays to fly,
No friendly goddess wafts him through the sky.
Born of the earth, along the earth he creeps,
Knows his own sphere, and shuns the azure deeps.   10
'Tis thus, alas! with humbly-breathing lay,
Down the dim vales I wend my lowly way.
In vain the timid throbbings of my breast
Prompt me to rise and flutter with the rest.
What dewy Dryad of the greenwood shade,   15
What sportive sylph, in rainbow hues arrayed,
What shepherd-queen of pastoral vale or hill,
Nymph of the fount, or Naiad of the rill,
Would from their grottos heed my trembling sighs,
Tune my rude harp, and lift me to the skies?   20
What classic Muse would deign to deck the page
That tells of blood-stained crimes, and war's barbaric rage?
One, one alone, omnipotent and fair,
Bends her sweet brow, and listens to my prayer.
That power benign, beneath whose shadowing wings   25
Bursts the bright germ of all created things;
Who, grasping gently the revolving poles,
Turns the green earth, and gilds it as it rolls;
To whom the barbarous feuds of Shah or Khan
Merge in the wise economy of man;   30
And to whose heart the insect is as dear
As the bright planet glistening in its sphere.
Yes! wondrous Nature, on thy name I call,
Queen of this glorious world, and parent of us all!

Of all the lovely lands to Nature dear,   35
And to the Sun – "The Painter of the Year"[2] –
One favoured spot appears more blest than all
Its rival wonders o'er this earthly ball;
'Tis where CABUL her flowery meads expand,
The pride and boast of all the Asian land.   40
Who has not felt his boyish bosom beat,
When Fancy half revealed this bright retreat? –
When young Imagination, lingering o'er
The magic page of Oriental lore,
The gorgeous scenes by Inatulla made,   45
And all the thousand tales of Scheherzade,[3]
Dreamed of some dazzling region far away,
Lit by the earliest beams of opening day;
Where all the earth was strewed with gem-like flowers,
And flower-like gems illumed the crystal bowers.   50
This is the land – 'twas here our fancy strayed,

Notes

[2] In the Persian tales of Inatulla, the sun is called "The Painter of the Year" (author). Alexander Dow, *Tales from the Persian of Inatulla* (1768).

[3] *1001 Arabian Nights*, available in translation to Europeans from the early eighteenth century.

Here are the valleys where in dreams we played,
When Bagdad rivalled Rome's imperial name,
And Caesar dwindled in Alraschid's fame;[4]
When, in the wonders Sinbad brought to light,   55
Thy name, Columbus, faded from our sight;[5]
And when more bright than golden Istamboul,
Spread the delicious gardens of Cabul.

Though now we view the land with calmer glance,
Still 'tis the land of beauty and romance: 60
A mingled maze of sunshine and of snows,
Rocks for the pine, and valleys for the rose.
Thunder in its torrents, music in its rills,
Lambs on its plains, and lions on its hills;
A neutral land, where every flower is known   65
That loves the torrid or the temperate zone.
Where Indian palm-trees spread their feathery hands
Above the tender flowers of chillier lands!
Here every clime presents its fragrant store,
Here every flower recalls some distant shore;   70
From simple plants that love the western ray,
To white and yellow roses of Cathay.

Oh! words are weak, description is but mean,
To paint the glories of this brilliant scene.
Here the cool groves rich mulberry fruits adorn,   75
Pale as the moon, or purple as the morn;
Here giant planes with fan-like branches rise
And shield the cistus from the burning skies;
Here the pomegranate spreads its scarlet flowers,
And tapering dates enrich the palm-tree bowers;   80
The silvery plantain rises on our view,
The same as when in Eden's bowers it grew;[6]
The guava hangs its claret-coloured fruit,
While the narcissus nestles at its foot!
Its blushing fruits the wild pistachio yields,   85
And the tall tamarisk towers among the fields.

'Twere vain to tell of all the countless flowers
That o'er this land indulgent Nature showers:
The fragrant thyme – the Prophet rose's bloom –
The jessamine's breath – the violet's perfume.   90
The tulip here in matchless beauty glows,
And steals a fragrance from its neighbouring rose.
The humble poppy here the sight deceives,
And waves "the tulip of a hundred leaves."

Notes

[4] Julius Caesar (100–44 BCE), general and ruler of Rome and its empire; Harun Al-Rashid (766–809), ruler of most of what is now called the Middle East.

[5] Sinbad's voyages are recounted in *Arabian Nights*; Christopher Columbus (1451–1506), Italian explorer.

[6] The Plantain Tree. Gerard calls this plant "Adam's apple-tree," from a notion that it was the forbidden fruit of Eden. Others suppose it to have been the grape brought out of the promised land to Moses. – *Loudon's Encyclopaedia of Gardening* (author).

The simple daisy – lovelier, dearer far   95
Than Ghuzni's plums or figs of Candahar –
Sports in the meads, and climbs each mossy cliff,
Among the purple vines of Istalif.
Through every vale, where'er we chance to roam,
Crowd the sweet sights that glad our eyes at home.   100
The pink-white blossoms of the apple there
Mix with the pearly clusters of the pear.
The cherry hangs its coral balls on high,
And the soft peach swells tempting to the eye.
The magpie chatters in the golden vales,   105
Where sings the "Bulbul of a thousand tales,"
Whose silvery notes can imitate the strain
Of every bird in Nature's wide domain!
Oh! if 'twere true, as Eastern fables tell,[7]
That 'mid these groves the first-arch rebel fell,   110
When the lost seraph, hurled from on high,
Flashed like a burning star along the flaming sky!
Recovering slowly from his dreadful trance,
And casting round his wonder-waking glance,
He must have thought – so fair each vale and hill –   115
His fall a dream, and Heaven around him still!

If ever land were made to be the seat
Of happy homes, and pleasure's calm retreat,
'Twere surely this. Here Peace should have its birth,
High on the topmost regions of the Earth,   120
Far, far removed from tumult and from strife,
And all the crimson crimes of human life.
These mountain Tempes – smiling, verdant, gay –
Shining like emeralds o'er the Himalay,
Should not, in faintest echoes, even repeat   125
The murderous din that thunders at their feet.
But ah! how different the truth has been:
This sunny land is discord's favourite scene,
Made, both by foreign and domestic crime,
One field of ruin since the birth of Time.   130
When native treachery ceased but for an hour,
Then surely came the scourge of foreign power;
And all the ills that crowd the conqueror's train,
From Alexander down to Tamarlane,[8]
Whose fitting titles, on their flags unfurled,   135
Like Jehansoz', were "burners of the world."[9]
Those vulgar victors, whose ill-omened names
The dotard Fame, with babbling tongue, proclaims;

Notes

[7] It is a popular belief that when the Devil was cast out of heaven he fell in Cabul (author).

[8] Alexander the Great (356–323 BCE) and Tamarlane (1336–1405), both conquerors in Asia, including Afghanistan.

[9] *Jehansoz*, the burner or desolator of the world. He is said to have got that name from his horrible massacre at Ghuzni (author). The massacre took place during an attack on the city in the twelfth century.

Whose conquests form, in every clime and age,
The blood-red rubric of the historic page;   140
Whose fatal path, the trampled nations o'er,
On the world's map is traced in lines of gore.
Like to those insects of a summer hour
Which float with gaudy wing from flower to flower,
And leave (as oft the startled swain perceives)   145
A shower of blood upon the rifled leaves.[10]
Pity that fairest lands should have their charms,
But as attractions for the conqueror's arms;
When War's dread vulture wings its screaming flight
O'er the doomed earth, which shudders at the sight,   150
No hideous desert tempts its blood-shot eye,
No useless waste allures it from the sky;
But should it chance to view a smiling scene,
Where the blithe bee floats humming o'er the green,
Where flocks and herds repose beneath the trees,   155
And the rich harvest bends before the breeze,
Then, then, alas! he checks his fatal wing,
And, like the bolt of Heaven's avenging King,
With frightful ruin burns along the air,
And of a garden makes a desert there.   160
Like to that wonder of a thousand dyes,
The famed Chameleon Bird[11] of eastern skies,
Which high in air wings wildly to and fro,
Save when a tempting vineyard smiles below,
Then, only then, his soaring pinion fails,   165
And down he falls amid the purple vales.
But while we brand these regal robbers' lust,
Let the indignant muse at least be just;
Let one be singled from the gory crowd,
Of whom his sect and nation may be proud.   170
Yes, Baber[12], yes, to thee the praise is due,
Praise that, alas! is merited by few,
Who, having power to injure and destroy,
Feel, in restoring, more ecstatic joy.

Notes

[10] The showers of blood which caused so much terror formerly were caused by the excrements of insects. Sleidan relates that, "In the year 1553, a vast multitude of butterflies swarmed through a great part of Germany, and sprinkled plants, leaves, buildings, clothes, and men, with bloody drops, as if it had rained blood" (author).

[11] "In these mountains (N. E. of Cabul) is found the bird *Lokeh*, which is also termed *Bukelemun*, or *Chameleon bird*, and which has, between its head and its tail, five or six different colours, like the neck of a dove …" (author). MacCarthy gives his source only as *Baber*.

[12] "We delight to see him describe his success in rearing a new plant, in introducing a new fruit-tree, or in repairing a decayed aqueduct, with the same pride and complacency that he relates the most splendid victories. He had cultivated the art of poetry from his early years, and his Diwan of Turki poems is mentioned as giving him a high rank among the poets of his country. He was skilful in the science of music, on which he wrote a treatise." The translator of his "Memoirs" (written by himself), concludes his character of Baber in these words: "In activity of mind, in the gay equanimity and unbroken spirit with which he bore the extremes of good or bad fortune, in the possession of manly and social virtues, so seldom the portion of princes, in his love of letters, and his successful cultivation of them, we shall probably find no other Asiatic prince who can fairly be placed beside him." – *Memoirs of the Emperor Baber* (author). Baber (or Babur, 1483–1530), descended from Tamarlane, made Kabul the capital of Afghanistan.

Oft have I thought, when wandering fancy ran 175
To that small marble mosque of Shah Jehan,[13]
Which lifts its polished dome unto the sky
In that sweet garden where your ashes lie,
Of all your simple tastes, in quiet hours,
For hills, and trees, and fountains, and sweet flowers, – 180
Your love of nature, gently gilding all
Those stains which even on souls like thine may fall.
For ah! how few upon this earth are found,
Who, like the Huma,[14] never touch the ground!

But to return to this distracted land – 185
These snow-clad mountains, which so proudly stand,
And to whose peaks the privilege is given
To turn aside the clouds and winds of heaven,
Were powerless all to save these smiling vales
From man's attacks and war's destructive gales. 190
Alas! that England should conclude the page
That bears the spoilers' names of every age.
A rumour spreads – it flies from mouth to mouth –
"The Russian Eagle flieth to the south;
With daring wing he wanders wild and free 195
From the cold Baltic to the Indian Sea."
When lo! forgetful of her fame and might,
England, forsooth, must stop the Eagle's flight.
With hurried pace her veteran legions rush
Up the steep summits of the Hindoo Cush,[15] 200
To raise a shout, and threaten from afar
The imperial bird of conquest and the Czar?
Must England ever play this selfish game?
Must England's fears obscure even England's fame?
Must England's policy in every land, 205
So coldly great, so miserably grand,
Like Bamean's monstrous deity be known,[16] –
Vast, yet deformed – a god, and yet a stone?
What though her banners floated for an hour
From the high top of Balla Hissar's tower;[17] 210

Notes

[13] The tomb of the Emperor Baber is situated about a mile from the city of Cabul, in the sweetest spot of the neighbourhood. He had directed his body to be interred in this place, to him the choicest in his dominions. These are his own words regarding Cabul: "The climate is extremely delightful, and there is no such place in the known world." The grave is marked by two erect slabs of white marble. Many of his wives and children have been interred around him. A running clear stream yet waters the fragrant flowers of this cemetery, which is the great holiday resort of the people of Cabul. In front of the grave there is a small but chaste mosque of white marble, built in the year 1640, by order of the Emperor *Shah Jehan*, "that poor Mohamedans might here offer up their prayers" (author). Shah Jehan (1592–1666), Indian emperor and builder of the Taj Mahal.

[14] "*The Huma* is a bird much celebrated in Oriental poetry; it never alights on the ground; and it is believed that every head which it overshadows will one day wear a crown." – *Notes to Baber* (author).

[15] The Hindu Kush is a mountain chain in the region, and includes the famous Khyber Pass.

[16] The excavated city of Bamean. The gigantic idols of Bamean are cut in alto-relievo on the face of the hill, one about 120 feet high (author). The Buddhas of Bamiyan, destroyed in 2001.

[17] A citadel in Cabul (Kabul).

What though her bullets scared the peaceful bee
From the red blossoms of the argwhan tree;
What though her arms in dreadful vengeance rang
Through the fair city where Ferdusi sang,[18]
And every dome, and every glistening spire,   215
Fell in the flames of her avenging fire;
What though she bore, as trophies of its doom,
Those gates of sandal-wood from Mahmoud's tomb,
Perhaps once more in Indian groves to shine,
The dazzling portals of some idol's shrine; – [19]   220
Do these repay the blood and treasure lost?
Do these restore to life her slaughtered host,
Whose shroudless corses – that Soojah might rule –
Glut the fierce vultures of the Khoord Cabul.[20]

Oh, may we learn experience from the past,   225
And peace and love possess the world at last.
Instead of frowning forts, let altars rise,
To bless the nations under distant skies;
O'er towering hills and vales of purple moss,
Let peaceful armies bear the saving cross!   230
And let those fleets that made the whole world weep,
With useful arts go bounding o'er the deep,
To every clime and every ocean isle,
Like to those fragrant navies of the Nile,
Which bear the bee and its ambrosial store,   235
A blessing and a joy to every peaceful shore.[21]

Notes

[18] Ghuzni, the most celebrated of the cities of Cabul, where Mahmoud reigned and Ferdusi sang (author). Mahmud (971–1030) established his capital at Ghuzni and was a patron of the important Persian poet Ferdusi (or Firdausi, 935–1020).

[19] The sandal-wood gates at the shrine of the Emperor Mahmoud were brought, 800 years ago, from Sommat in India, where Mahmoud smote the idol, and the precious stones fell from his body. – Burnes. In the capture and destruction of Ghuzni in 1842, these celebrated gates were carried off in triumph by the British forces (author).

[20] The scene of Akhbar Khan's treachery, and the destruction of the 1600 British soldiers, in the disastrous retreat from Cabul to Jellalabad, on the 6th of January, 1842 (author). Soojah (Shah Shujah) ruled Afghanistan from 1803 until he was deposed in 1809; restoring him to power was the nominal excuse for the British invasion of Afghanistan which initiated the first Anglo-Afghan War. Akbar Khan was the son of Afghanistan's current ruler, Dost Mohammed; he guaranteed retreating British troops safe passage in January 1842 but did not honor the commitment and British forces were all but annihilated.

[21] "In Lower Egypt, where the flower harvest is not so early by several weeks as in the upper district of that country, the practice of transportation is carried on to a considerable extent. About the end of October the hives, after being collected together from the different villages, and conveyed up the Nile, marked and numbered by the individuals to whom they belong, are heaped pyramidically upon the boats prepared to receive them, which floating gradually down the river, and stopping at certain stages of their passage, remain there a longer or shorter time, according to the produce which is afforded by the surrounding country. After travelling three months in this manner, the bees having culled the perfumes of the orange flowers of the Said, the essence of the roses of the Faicum, the treasures of the Arabian jessamine, and a variety of flowers, are brought back, about the beginning of February, to the places from which they have been carried. The productiveness of the flowers, at each respective stage, is ascertained by the gradual descent of the boats in the water, and which is probably noted by a scale of measurement. This industry produces for the Egyptians delicious honey, and abundance of bees' wax." – Dr. Bevan, p. 233, quoted in an article in the Quarterly Review (author).

A Walk by the Bay of Dublin

From **Ballads, Poems, and Lyrics** (1850)

Denis Florence MacCarthy

While travelled poets pen their polished rhymes
In praise of distant lands and southern climes, –
While tourists tell of gorgeous realms afar,
How bless'd by heaven – how beautiful thcy are! –
While every scene but moderately fair,   5
Shines on their page, as if all heaven were there! –
Scenes which, if viewed by their discerning eyes
Within the circle of their native skies,
Tho' decked with all that Nature's hands bestow,
Were passed unheeded as too mean and low! –   10
While thus are praised, in learned rhyme and prose,
Italia's sun and wild Helvetia's snows,[1]
The trackless forest and the teeming mine,
Ice at the Poles and earthquakes at the Line, –
One who, yet free from fashion's freezing zone,   15
Admires not every country but – his own! –
Whose heart unchill'd and whose impartial eye
Dare to be just to scenes which round him lie! –
With skilless hand he ventures to portray
A sketch, Eblana, of thy beauteous bay, –   20
Rival and twin of bright Parthenope![2]
'Tis that sweet hour when morning melts away
In the full splendours of the golden day,
When sea and sky, when mountain, vale, and stream,
Bask in the glories of the noontide beam!   25
Oh! what a vision bursts upon my sight! –
Offspring of heaven and parent of delight.
This scene, which now my raptured eyes survey,
Those purple mountains and this silvery bay,
Those verdant heights, with tall trees waving o'er,   30
Those fearful crags which guard the crescent shore,
Those dazzling villas, crowding every steep,
Those snow-white sails which skim along the deep,
Those pointed hills which pierce the cloudless sky,
Those ruined towers which tell of days gone by, –   35
Form such a picture both for eye and heart,
As puts to shame the poet's – painter's art!
What words can tell – what pencil here can trace
The mingled magic of this matchless place?
On either shore what glorious views expand!   40
What varying wonders crowd on either hand!

Notes

A WALK BY THE BAY OF DUBLIN
[1] Helvetia is a poetic name for Switzerland.

[2] Eblana is an early name for Dublin; Parthenope was a Greek colony in what is now Naples.

Oft have I paced and traversed o'er and o'er
Marino's woods and Moynealta's[3] shore, –
Both classic spots, both worthy of the bay, –
The one of old, the other of to-day.   45
Here aged Brian taught the Danish horde
The offended justice of a patriot's sword.[4]
Here too, when nigh a thousand years had roll'd
Their blood-stained waves to mix with those of old, –
When peace and freedom bless'd again our shore,   50
And Brian lived in Charlemont once more! –
Mid those fair groves, with taste and virtue bless'd,
Here did the patriot take his well-earned rest.
But not alone the lore of vanish'd days
Gilds this sweet spot with its reflected rays.   55
Here nature sports in most indulgent mood,
Laughs on the lawn and wantons in the wood!
The pansy opes its gold and violet wings,
The soaring sky-lark in the sun-light sings;
The red valerian and the ivy green,   60
With fragrant wild-flowers, weave their tangled screen
Round ancient trees and rocks and aged walls,
Where the thrush whistles and the cuckoo calls!

Now passing o'er, but not with careless haste,
Ratheny's strand and wild Kilbarrock's waste,   65
By rushy fields whose herbage oft disclose
The green-winged orchis and the pale primrose,
Let us ascend to scenes more wildly fair,
Up the brown slopes of lofty Bennadair![5]
That lonely mountain which above the tide   70
Lifts its long back and swells its dusky side!
As some dread monster from its ocean lair
Bursts o'er the wave to breathe the upper air,
Then, fixed by magic in eternal sleep,
Spreads its huge length along the shuddering deep!   75
What tho' no giant oaks adorn the scene,
As fond tradition tells there once had been;
What tho' its groveless heights no more prolong
The cheerful chirpings of the wild bird's song;
Still is it rich in many a charm and grace,   80
Which age revives and time cannot efface;
Rich in the relics which its glens retain,
The druid altar and the ruined fane.

Notes

[3] One of the ancient names of Clontarf was Moynealta
(author).

[4] Brian Boru (c.941–1014), king of Ireland often invoked as a
national hero for unifying Ireland under one ruler and for
repelling Viking settlement.

[5] The Hill of Howth. There seems to be some doubt as to
the meaning of this word. D'Alton, in his History of the
County of Dublin, says, "it was anciently called Ben-na-dair,
as it is supposed from the quantity of venerable oaks that
then waved o'er its fertile declivities;" – while Moore, in his
History of Ireland, vol. ii., p. 105, spells it Benadar, and
explains it "the mountain of birds." Ben Háder, however, is
the more correct way of spelling and pronouncing the name
(author).

The samphire gatherer on each mossy glade,
Here may pursue his wild and "dreadful trade."[6]   85
Here those who love to view a noble scene,
Tho' vast, distinct, – sublime, but still serene, –
Here may they rest, and feast their dazzled sight
With all the glories circling round this height.
From Edria's Isle[7] to where Three Sisters[8] stand,   90
Like giant Graces o'er the southern land,
The waveless sea like one vast mirror shines,
Bright as the treasures of ten thousand mines!
Here, lovely bay! above thy tranquil sea,
Here let me take my fond farewell of thee.   95
When grief or pain, despondency or care,
Fell on my heart, and worked their ruin there,
One quiet walk along thy silent shore,
One look at thee, and all my grief was o'er!
When friends and brothers quickly pass'd away,   100
The fond companions of my earlier day,
When disappointment came to dwell with me,
Still, still I clung to nature and to thee!
Like a fond mother watching o'er her child,
Thus has thou ever on my footsteps smiled,   105
Oh! shame if then I acted not my part,
And gave not back to thee my ever-grateful heart!

Spirit Voices

From Underglimpses, and Other Poems (1857)

I

There are voices, spirit voices, sweetly sounding everywhere,
At whose coming earth rejoices, and the echoing realms of air,
And their joy and jubilation pierce the near and reach the far –
From the rapid world's gyration to the twinkling of the star.

2

One, a potent voice uplifting, stops the white cloud on its way,   5
As it drives with driftless drifting o'er the vacant vault of day,
And in sounds of soft upbraiding calls it down the void inane
To the gilding and the shading of the mountain and the plain.

3

Airy offspring of the fountains, to thy destined duty sail –
Seek it on the proudest mountains, seek it in the humblest vale;   10

Notes

[6] On the sides of the hill grows *the samphire* celebrated by Shakespeare: "Half way down / Hangs one that gathers samphire, – dreadful trade." LEAR, *Act* IV. *Sc.* 6 (author). *King Lear* IV. vi. 14–15.

[7] Ireland's Eye (author).

[8] The three hills, of which Killiney forms the centre, that so beautifully terminate the southern shore of the Bay of Dublin, have been called "The Three Sisters," from the extraordinary resemblance they bear to each other (author).

Howsoever high thou fliest, how so deep it bids thee go,
Be a beacon to the highest and a blessing to the low.

4

When the sad earth, broken-hearted, hath not even a tear to shed,
And her very soul seems parted for her children lying dead,
Send the streams with warmer pulses through that frozen fount of fears, 15
And the sorrow that convulses, soothe and soften down to tears.

5

Bear the sunshine and the shadow, bear the rain-drop and the snow,
Bear the night-dew to the meadow, and to hope the promised bow,[1]
Bear the moon, a moving mirror for her angel face and form,
And to guilt and wilful error bear the lightning and the storm. 20

6

When thou thus hast done thy duty on the earth and o'er the sea,
Bearing many a beam of beauty, ever bettering what must be,
Thus reflecting heaven's pure splendour and concealing ruined clay,
Up to God thy spirit render, and dissolving pass away.

7

And with fond solicitation, speaks another to the streams – 25
Leave your airy isolation, quit the cloudy land of dreams,
Break the lonely peak's attraction, burst the solemn, silent glen,
Seek the living world of action and the busy haunts of men.

8

Turn the mill-wheel with thy fingers, turn the steam-wheel with thy breath,
With thy tide that never lingers save the dying fields from death; 30
Let the swiftness of thy currents bear to man the freight-fill'd ship,
And the crystal of thy torrents bring refreshment to his lip.

9

And when thou, O rapid river, thy eternal home dost seek –
When no more the willows quiver but to touch thy passing cheek –
When the groves no longer greet thee and the shore no longer kiss – 35
Let infinitude come meet thee on the verge of the abyss.

10

Other voices seek to win us – low, suggestive, like the rest –
But the sweetest is within us in the stillness of the breast;
Be it ours, with fond desiring, the same harvest to produce
As the cloud in its aspiring and the river in its use. 40

Notes ———————————————————————————

Spirit Voices
[1] rainbow

Dion Boucicault (1820–1890)

Dion Boucicault was born Dionysius Lardner Boursiquot in Dublin. His mentor, and possibly biological father, was Dionysius Lardner. When Lardner was appointed a professor of natural philosophy at University College London, Boucicault, as well as his mother and most of his siblings, moved to London with him. In the 1830s, Boucicault was educated at various schools in England as well as Dublin, and began acting on the stage in 1838. His career as a playwright began in 1841 and produced (depending on how you count revised and reissued plays) over a hundred dramas. Many were not published in volume form, but were successful on the stage and survive as copies used in the theater. Some of his plays, including *Arrah-na-Pogue*, were even transformed into short fiction for US publication. Boucicault traveled a great deal, living in Paris for a while in the 1840s and taking his touring company to New Zealand and Australia in the 1880s, but it was the US to which he repeatedly returned to stage plays.

His first play, *London Assurance*, was staged in 1841, and was followed by *The Irish Heiress* in 1842. Boucicault began with fairly conventional comedies, but by the 1850s was working with melodrama, the theatrical counterpart of the sensation fiction at which his contemporary and fellow-Dubliner J. Sheridan LeFanu excelled. This proved suitable for plays on social themes, including American plays such as *The Poor of New York* (1857) and *The Octoroon* (1859), and *Jessie Brown: Or the Relief of Lucknow* (1858), which appeared in the year that the British government regained control after the so-called Indian Mutiny. Boucicault's better-known Irish plays include *The Colleen Bawn* (1860), *Arrah-na-Pogue* (1864), and *The Shaughraun* (1874). He also published a pamphlet critical of colonial rule in Ireland, *The Story of Ireland* (1881).

Arrah-na-Pogue deals with the Uprising of 1798, the forced exile of nationalists, linguistic difference, and tensions between the ruled and the military administrators of rule. While *Arrah-na-Pogue* can be charged with using the figure of the "stage Irishman," condemned from Thomas Sheridan's *Brave Irishman* to Carleton's "Auto-biographical Introduction" nearly a century later, Boucicault (like Sheridan) also plays with other national stereotypes. As Elizabeth Butler Cullingford has argued (see Further reading below), Boucicault, alluding to the 1798 Uprising in the midst of Fenian unrest in the 1860s, offers a "stage Englishman" to counter the "stage Irishman"; while Cullingford stresses Coffin and the English soldier who acts as prison warden, we can add Winterbottom to the list of the play's "stage Englishmen." His accent, confusion about time zones, and excessive servility make him much like the stage Irishman, even as his stiffness and the specifics of his prejudices distinguish him from the Irish stereotype.

The copy-text of this edition was a printed version for the use of theater-workers; technical stage directions have been silently deleted. The Irish phrases here are sometimes English–Irish hybrids, and are phonetically spelled at best in the original.

Further reading

Boltwood, Scott, " 'The Ineffaceable Curse of Cain': Race, Miscegenation, and the Victorian Staging of Irishness," *Victorian Literature and Culture* 29 (2001): 383–96.

Cullingford, Elizabeth Butler, "National Identities in Performance: The Stage Englishman of Boucicault's Irish Drama," *Theatre Journal* 49 (1997): 287–300.

Arrah-na-Pogue; Or, the Wicklow Wedding (1864)

Dramatis Personae

Shaun the Post, *Driver of the Mail Car between Hollywood and Rathdrum*
Colonel Bagenal O'Grady, *The O'Grady*
Beamish Mac Coul, *The Mac Coul*
Major Coffin, *An English Officer*
Michael Feeny, *A Process Server*
Secretary
Winterbottom
Sergeant
Oiny Farrell
Lanigan
Patsey
Andy Regan
Lanty
Moran
Tim Cogan
Arrah Meelish, *Nick-named by the Peasantry Arrah-na-Pogue, or Arrah of the Kiss*
Fanny Power, *of Cabinteely*
Katty Walsh
Soldiers and Peasants

ACT I

SCENE 1 – *Glendalough; Moonlight. The Ruins of St. Kevin's Abbey; the Round Tower; the Ruined Cemetery; the Lake and Mountains beyond; Music;* BEAMISH MAC COUL *discovered.*

Enter OINY.

OINY. All right, sir; the car from Hollywood is in sight.
BEAM. How many passengers?
OINY. There's only one, sir.
BEAM. That is our man. Hark ye, boys! [*Enter* LANTY, LANIGAN, REGAN, *and* MORAN] take your stations so that you may give me timely warning of any alarm in the barracks yonder, or the approach of the patrol.
REGAN. More power, sir.
OINY. We'll be as 'cute as crows, yer honour.
ALL. Never fear, sir.
BEAM. Away with you! [*They retire;* BEAMISH *stands behind a part of the ruin.*]

Enter FEENY.

FEENY. When a man thravels wid a big lump of money in his pocket, he is offering a reward for his own murdher. Why am I afeard? Sure this district is proclaimed; so divil a one dare set fut outside his cabin dure afther night-fall widout a pass.

And there below is the barrack full of soldiers, widin the cast of my voice. [*Beamish appears.*] I'd like to see the skulkin' rebel that would show his nose on Derrybawn. [*Going as he speaks, finds Beamish opposed to him.*] Oh, Lord!

BEAM. It is a fine night, Mr. Michael Feeny.

FEENY. So – o it is, long li – life to it; good night, sir.

BEAM. Stop. You have just come from Hollywood, where you have collected the rents of an estate.

FEENY. Is it me? I'd be on me oath –

BEAM. Silence. The estates of the rebel Beamish Mac Coul were confiscated – your employer collects the rent for the Government, now I collect for the Mac Coul; so, hand over the amount.

FEENY. Is this robbery? and widin call of the barracks!

BEAM. If you lift your voice over a whisper to alarm the patrol, it will be murder as well as robbery. Not a word.

FEENY [*whispering*]. I wouldn't wake a weazel.

BEAM. Quick, the money.

FEENY. Whisht, you'll rise the soldiers, an I'll be kilt. [*Drops on his knees.*] There's the money.

BEAM. Right. A bag of gold, and a roll of notes. [*Receives the money from Feeny.*]

FEENY [*while Beamish examines it, aside*]. Oh, wait a bit me fine fellow, you can't move very far widout a pass, and only let me get safe out of this, and widin half an hour I will set a pack of redcoats on yer scent that will scour these hills and hunt the life out of ye.

BEAM. Good. Now your pass.

FEENY. Me what?

BEAM. Your pass – out with it – I want it to secure my free passage across the mountains.

FEENY [*giving Beamish papers*]. But how am I to get home widout it?

BEAM. There's your road. At every fifty paces there's a man stationed behind either a rock or a bush, he will see you straight to your door; and take a friendly advice, don't turn from the path, nor speak a word till you are safe in bed. Now be off.

FEENY. Oh, tare an' ages. Captain, dear, don't ax me to go alone. Oh, murdher, is it pass them file of divils. Are they armed, Colonel?

BEAM. Each man has two blunderbusses on full cock, and a bayonet pointed straight at you.

FEENY. I'm a corpse! Two blunderbushes lookin at me. Oh, Captain, Colonel, darlin', don't lave me! and a bagginet on full cock. How will I get home at all? I've got a canal running down the middle of my back. I'm as wake[1] as a wet rag this minit.

BEAM. Come, off with you.

FEENY. I'm goin', sir. Where's my legs at all? Captain, jewel, may I run?

BEAM. No, that would alarm the patrols and seal your fate.

FEENY. Oh, murdher, don't sale[2] my fate, sir, and I'll creep on my hands and knees; pass the word, Colonel, to kape them quiet. Oh do, sir, give them the office. Oh, blessed day, my inside is all fiddle strings, and my blood is turnin' into butther milk. [*Exit.*]

BEAM. Hush! [*Re-enter the men as before.*] There he goes, we need fear no alarm from him, I have turned every stone and every bush on his road into a sentinel, ha! ha! Now, boys, divide this gold among ye. [*Throws them the gold.*] You need not hesitate

Notes ───────────────────────────────────────

ARRAH-NA-POGUE   [2] seal

[1] weak

to take it, for the money is my own – I leave Ireland to-morrow, and for ever. I could not part from you without giving you some token of my gratitude for the fidelity and love you have shown towards me.

OINY. Ah, sir, wouldn't we pour out our blood dhrop by dhrop any day for the Mac Coul.

BEAM. I know it. For six weeks past I have found shelter on these hills under the noses of the military, while a reward of £500 offered for the capture of the rebel Beamish Mac Coul has not tempted your starvation to betray me.

ALL. Long life t'ye, sir; bless you always!

BEAM. See, the morning is beginning to tip the heights of Mullacor; we must part. In a few hours I shall be on the sea, bound for a foreign land; perhaps never again shall I hear your voices nor see my native hills. Oh, my own land! my own land! Bless every blade of grass upon your green cheeks! The clouds that hang over ye are the sighs of your exiled children, and your face is always wet with their tears. *Eirne meelish, Shlawn loth!*[3] Fare ye well! And you, dear Abbey of St. Kevin, around which the bones of my forefathers are laid.

OINY. Long life to them!

ALL. The Mac Coul! the Mac Coul! [*They crowd round him.*]

BEAM. Easy, boys, for your own sakes. No noise, no cries – let us part in silence. God bless you all.

REGAN. Heaven keep you.

ALL. Blessins on you! May heaven be your bed! The good angels follow and surround ye always. [*He shakes hands with them.*]

REGAN. Hoult! the red-coats are on us.

ALL. Where? [*They crowd up.*]

REGAN. There! It's the dragoons, for I hear the horse peltin' up the boryeen.[4]

BEAM. Do not be alarmed; the person who approaches is one who loves me so well, that she leaves home, fortune, and friends to accompany the poor exile across the seas. So, whenever you remember Beamish Mac Coul in your prayers, don't forget to invoke a blessing also on the name of Fanny Power, of Cabinteely. [*Exit* BEAMISH.]

ALL. Long life to ye both, sir!

OINY. Now, boys, let us kape watch over the young masther while he is to the fore, and until we see him safe off.

REGAN. I will hould the hill here below, and watch the barracks.

MORAN. Lanigan and meself will watch the road to Laragh.

OINY. The rest of us will be off to the cabin of Arrah-na-Pogue, where he finds shelther every night – and blessins on the brave girl that does not fear to face the gallows for his sake. Oh, it's small mercy they would show Arrah Meelish if it was known that she gave aid and protection to the outlaw, although he is her own foster-brother.

REGAN. Bedad, if he was her own father and mother, too, she'd hang for givin' them a God bless ye, if they wor what Beamish Mac Coul is this day.

OINY. Here comes the masther – hurry now. [*Exeunt.*]

Re-enter BEAMISH *with* FANNY.

BEAM. Dearest Fanny! is all prepared for our flight?

FANNY. Oh, Beamish, what will the world say of me? What will they think of me after I am gone?

Notes ──────────────────────────────

[3] Sweet Ireland, farewell.   [4] road

BEAM. They will say that Beamish Mac Coul returned from his exile in France to claim the hand of the woman he loved; for the fairest woman in Wicklow had remained faithful to him during his four long years of absence.

FANNY. Can he say as much? Was he faithful to her during those four long years?

BEAM. Do you doubt me?

FANNY. I wish I did not! for now you are going to take me goodness knows where – and if you grew weary of me – or fell in love with some foreign beauty, with big eyes and a voice like silk velvet, what would become of me? Oh, Beamish, last night I took up a book to read, and there I found between the leaves an old love-letter of yours I had placed as a marker there long ago, and I thought – Ah, maybe one day Beamish will leave me as I have left that letter, as a mark in the middle of a love story, and shut me up with the tale only half read.

BEAM. Oh, very well; I see how it is. You have not sufficient confidence in me to entrust your fate in my keeping.

FANNY. No; it is not that.

BEAM. You wish me to remain here until you have made up your mind. You are not sure that you love me to the extent of the sacrifice of fortune, friends.

FANNY. Oh!

BEAM. Admirers. Yes; of course it is a great denial to relinquish the admiration – the worship of half the county.

FANNY. Oh. Hear this.

BEAM. Very well. I will remain here until you love me better. I shall spend my days in the hollows of these rocks, or concealed in some tree; I pass my nights in some cave – cold, miserable, and alone.

FANNY. Oh! Beamish. I will go anywhere, do anything – my poor love. What a dreadful life you endure. Do you indeed sleep in a cave or up a tree? I wonder you are not frozen to death.

BEAM. I think of you, dearest; and that image is warmth, joy, and company.

FANNY. Don't! don't! I deserve all your reproaches for doubting you; tell me what I am to do.

BEAM. To-night, at an hour before midnight, meet me at the Chapel near Tullabogue. There the ceremony of marriage will be performed, and before daylight we shall be on board a French craft, now lying off Bray Head, waiting my signal to assist in our escape.

FANNY. Well, I suppose I am in for it; but it feels very dreadful.

BEAM. Did you expect the banns would be published at St. Patrick's Cathedral, between Beamish Mac Coul, rebel, and Fanny Power, spinster?

FANNY. How cruel you are to laugh at my fears.

BEAM. When I ought to kiss them away.

FANNY. Hush! What noise was that?

Enter REGAN.

REGAN. Sir, sir, the pathrol is coming.

FANNY. The patrol. Fly, fly, Beamish!

BEAM. Not I. Regan, away with you; I will keep these fellows in check while you escape.

REGAN. More power, sir. [*Exit.*]

FANNY. Are you mad?

Enter the SERGEANT *and file of* SOLDIERS. *One* SOLDIER *bears a lantern.*

SERGEANT. Halt [*advancing*]. Ho, my friend, what business have you abroad at this hour?

BEAM. Oh, Sergeant, have I not a beautiful excuse by my side? look.

SERGEANT. I don't want to see your excuse; I want to see your pass.

BEAM. Charmed to oblige you; there it is.

FANNY [*aside*]. I am dying of fright.

BEAM. Hold your tongue.

SERGEANT. Quite correct, sir; sorry to be obliged to make these inquiries.

BEAM. I admire the precaution. Will you allow your men to drink this crown piece to my health?

SERGEANT. Sir, we are greatly obliged to you.

BEAM. I see you are going towards Laragh. Would you mind seeing me safe on my road? I am afraid these mountains are not at all secure for persons like me travelling with a large sum of money.

SERGEANT. You will be quite safe with us. This way.

BEAM. And, Sergeant, if ever you meet me again, not a word of this little affair. You understand?

SERGEANT. All right, sir! Mum's the word! Forward. March.

Scene closes in.

SCENE 2 – ARRAH*'s Cottage at Laragh.* SHAUN *is heard singing outside.*

Enter SHAUN.

SHAUN. This is my weddin' mornin'; sure my breast is so big wid my heart this minit, that I feel like a fowl wid her first egg. Egorra, and this same love brings a man out in a fine perspiration, long life to it. And there's Arrah's cabin; the oysther shell that's got the pearl of my heart in it. I wonder is she awake. [*Knocks.*] Arrah, suilis! Arrah, mo millia stooreen![5] If you are slapin' don't answer me; but, if you are up, open the dure softly. [*He sings through the keyhole:*] –

> Open the dure softly,
> Somebody wants ye, dear;
> Give me a chink no wider than
>   You'll fill up wid your ear.
> Or, if you're hard of hearing, dear,
>   Your mouth will do as well;

Notes ————————————————————————————

[5] Arrah, light! Arrah, my thousand treasures!

Just put your lips agan the crack,
    And hear what I've to tell.
    Open the dure softly,
    Somebody wants you, dear. [ARRAH *opens the window.*]

ARRAH. Hur-roosh! hoo! that porkawn has got loose again, the marauder.

SHAUN. Is it the pig she takes me for?

ARRAH [*aside*]. It's that thief o' the world, Shaun. [*Aloud.*] Or is it the ould cow that's broke her sugaun.[6] [*Calls.*] Coop, coop, coop.

SHAUN. Another baste! Have I been singin' to the ould mare till I've got a quadruped voice.

ARRAH [*aside*]. Where is he hidin'? I'll take a peep. [*She puts out her head; he catches her round the neck.*] Oh, murther! who's that?

SHAUN. It's the pig that's got loose.

ARRAH. Let me go, Shaun! D'ye hear me, sir? let me go.

SHAUN. First I'll give ye the coward's blow. Come here, ye vagabone, till I hit ye undher the nose wid my mouth.

ARRAH. I'll sthrike back, ye villin! [*He kisses her; she pushes him away.*] Isn't this purty thratement for a lone woman?

SHAUN. Ye'll get no betther, now, I warn ye; so don't go marryin' me this blessed day wid sthravagin[7] expectations; ye'll have to live from hand to mouth, and whin you're out of timper I'll set my face agin you; mind that.

ARRAH. You're back mighty early, Shaun; didn't you say that you had to dhrive Michael Feeny over from Hollywood last night?

SHAUN. Sure enough; but he got down at Glendalough to walk across the hill.

ARRAH. What brings ye up here at all, at all. Did ye think anybody was wantin' ye?

SHAUN. Iss, indeed, ses I, there's that Colleen Dhas all alone, wid the cow to milk, and the pigs to feed, an chickeens; and the big barn beyant to get clane and swate by the evenin', for the weddin' to-night, an' not a ha'porth of help she'll take from mortial. I'll go and give her a lift.

ARRAH. Is it afther bein' up all night on the road betune Hollywood and Rathdrum; sure you have had no rest at all?

SHAUN. Rest, darlin! what would I want wid rest for the next six months to come. Wid the love in my heart that makes every minit a fortune, sure rest is only a waste of time, and to shut my eyes on the sight of your face before me is sinful exthravagance, my darlin'.

ARRAH. Won't you rest sometimes, anyway?

SHAUN. I'll look at you slapin', jewel, and that will do as well.

ARRAH. Go on, now, ye comedtherin'[8] schamer. Is it robbin' the beehives, or ating the honey clover, you have been, for you've the smell of it on your tongue? Go on, I tell ye. Dhrive the cow up from the field below, and maybe when you are back I'll lave a hot whatemale cake on the griddle to stop your mouth wid.

SHAUN. Ah! there's a griddle in the middle of your own face, Arrah, that has a cake on it always warm and ready to stop a boy's mouth.

ARRAH. D'ye want me to bate ye, ye provoker. [*Beats him off.*] Oh, Shaun, cuishla agus machree,[9] my heart goes wid ye and keeps stip beside you for ever and ever.

Notes

[6] rope
[7] extravagant

[8] "come-hithering" or enticing
[9] My pulse and my heart.

Song – ARRAH.

"Oh, I love him dearly."

Enter BEAMISH.

BEAM. Has he gone?

ARRAH. Oh, Masther Beamish, it goes sore agin me to be decavin' the poor boy this
way. Isn't it better to let him know that it's yourself that's in it?

BEAM. My dear Arrah, if I were discovered in your cabin you know the penalty you
would pay for the shelter and protection you have afforded the rebel.

ARRAH. Ah, sir; but sure Shaun would lay down his life for you.

BEAM. Is it not enough that you should live with the halter round your neck, without
including Shaun's foolish head in the same rope?

ARRAH. And would they hang him for only knowing that you were here to the fore?

BEAM. Ay, would they – both you and he together – and although this day is your
wedding day, that's not the sort of noose you expect to get into.

ARRAH. Bedad it's not!

BEAM. Then don't deceive yourself. While I remain here you and I are standing under
the same gibbet.

ARRAH. I'm proud to stand anywhere beside yourself, Master Beamish; and sure isn't
the cabin there your own, anyway? 'Twas your gift to my mother that nursed you.
You were fostered under that ould thatch itself; and if they tuk and hung me to the
durepost beyant, sure my life 'ud be the only rint we ever paid the Mac Coul for all
the blessins we owe the ould family.

BEAM. Hold out your hands. [*Places money in them.*] There.

ARRAH. What's this?

BEAM. It is my wedding gift; the marriage portion you will bestow on Shaun this day.

ARRAH. Bank notes! But oh, sir, why would I take this from yourself, and you so poor!

BEAM. That is precisely the reason you cannot refuse it. Sure, if I was rich, there would
be less pleasure to me in giving it you, goose.

ARRAH. But how will I tell Shaun that I came by so much money?

BEAM. In three days I shall be in France; till then answer no questions. Then you may
tell him all.

ARRAH. Well, I promise; but he'll never forgive me. It'll be a sore place wid him agin me.

BEAM. I'll engage you will find a way of drawing out the pain.

ARRAH. Faith, I've a notion I will.

BEAM. Now, I must return till dark to my nook in the barn, where I roost under the
thatch, where my only companion is the cat.

ARRAH. Ah! sir, why have I not as many lives as they say she has? I'd give the whole
nine of them for your sake.

BEAM. I know it. [*Exit* BEAMISH.]

ARRAH. He's goin' away to the wild wars, wid death and danger by the wayside. Shall
I ever see him agin after this night? Oh! my brother! May the sweet angels of heaven
put out the fire of the guns, and turn away the bagginets foreninst ye!

Enter FEENY.

FEENY. Where is Shaun?

ARRAH. How would I know.

FEENY. Aisy now, Arrah. As I come over the top of the hill beyant, sure I saw ye both on this spot, colloquin[10] togithir.

ARRAH. Did ye? I hope the sight was plazin' to ye, sir.

FEENY. And as I turned the corner there, I saw the tail of his coat as he went into the cabin.

ARRAH [*aside*]. 'Twas Master Beamish.

FEENY. Ah! Arrah, it's the bad luck that is over me entirely this day. There's yourself that I love, wid all my heart!

ARRAH. That's not sayin' much.

FEENY. And this blessed day I'm goin' to be robbed of you!

ARRAH. Whisht! he'll hear ye.

FEENY. Shaun, is it? D'ye think I'm ashamed of my love for you?

ARRAH. No; but I am. I wouldn't like him to think so manely of me as to feel that you loved me.

FEENY. Well, I'm a poor thing entirely. Bedad! one would think I was a disorder that was catchin'; but maybe you'll repint the hour you made little of me, for I can wait, my darlin'; and to them that waits their time comes round, and when mine comes I'll make you feel a little of what I feel now.

ARRAH. If Shaun heard them words he'd have to answer for your life.

FEENY. Let him answer first for my money! This mornin' on Derrybawnn, not five minutes after I left his car, I was waylaid and robbed by twenty blackguards that lay ready for me. Who but Shaun knew that I had the rents of Hollywood in my pocket? Who but he knew the hour and the place where I could be caught?

ARRAH. Robbed! and by Shaun! What could he want wid your dirty money?

FEENY. He'd want it for you.

ARRAH. Be all that's mane, I believe the crature thinks that sweethearts pay one another, and ye can buy a ha'porth of love at the hucksther's shop. Look here, man! d'ye see that? [*Shows him the money she received from Beamish.*] It isn't money we want.

FEENY. Oh! what's that?

ARRAH. Look! – 10 and 5, and 10 agin, and 3 and 5 once more. Look! that's right; I know the sight warms your heart.

FEENY. Can I believe my eyes?

ARRAH. I thought I'd astonish you.

FEENY [*aside*]. They are the same that a few hours ago I was robbed of on Derrybawn. [*Aloud.*] Let me look agin.

ARRAH. Oh! look and feel. Don't you long that they were yours?

FEENY [*examining a note*]. Yes; here's my own name upon the back. [*Returns it to her.*]

ARRAH. Now, you see we don't want your money, nor your company aither. There's your road [*points off*]; it is waitin' for ye. Good mornin'! [*Exit into cottage.*]

FEENY. Shaun is one of the gang that robbed me – divil a doubt of it. I'll swear to them notes; and there he is inside wid her this minute! Stop! I'll take a peep, that I may make oath I saw himself. [*Goes to cabin.*] Oh! tare alive! but this is too good to be thrue. I don't desarve it. [*Looks through keyhole into cabin.*]

SHAUN [*entering*]. Well, bad luck to her for a cow! Ah! you're the only famale of your sex I never could make any hand of at all.

FEENY. Divil a thing I see but the dark.

SHAUN. What's that? [*Sees Feeny.*]

Notes ——————————————————————————————

[10] conversing

FEENY. Yes; there he is! Now I see him!

SHAUN. Do ye? [*Seizing him.*] Well, and d'ye feel him, you spyin' vagabone? [*shaking him.*]

FEENY. What's this, Shaun? I thought – I mean – I – aint you inside the cabin?

SHAUN. No! I don't find it convanient to be in two places at onst.

FEENY. And it wasn't you that was here, and it is somebody else that – phew. [*Aside.*] What's all this at all. Oh, tare and ages, I smell a rat.

SHAUN. Now, Michael Feeny, listen hether, and take a friendly warnin'. This day will make me masther of that cabin and all that's in it, and if I find your nose in my kayhole, be the tongs of the divil I'll lave ye nothin' to blow for the rest of your dirty life.

Enter ARRAH.

ARRAH. Shaun!

FEENY [*aside*]. She is bothered.

ARRAH. What is the matter?

FEENY. It's only a mistake; I thought Shaun was inside there wid yerself – didn't ye tell me he was?

ARRAH. No! I didn't.

FEENY [*aside*]. She's tremblin'. [*Aloud.*] I was thinkin' you said 'twas he gave you all the money you showed me.

SHAUN. What money is he talkin' about?

ARRAH. Ah, never mind him.

FEENY [*aside*]. She's frightened; there's a man hidin' widin there, that Shaun knows nothing about. 'Twas he, not Shaun, that gav' her the money – 'twas he that robbed me. Oh, Arrah Meelish, I have ye now. Ye despise me, do you – well, I'll bring you down to my feet, low as I am. I'll show you to all the neighbours, wid your fine lover hidin' in your cabin, and we'll see which you like best round your purty neck – my arms or the felon's rope, my jewel.

SHAUN. When you and the divil have done colloguin together, I'd like to see the full front of your back.

FEENY. The top of the mornin' t'ye both. [*Exit.*]

SHAUN. Well, sweet bad luck go wid ye, and that's my blessin' on ye.

ARRAH. Ah, never mind him, dear! it's thrue what he said about the money, and here it is, Shaun. It is a present I got on my weddin' day.

SHAUN. What's this? Oh, Biddy Mulligan! Bank notes; and have you found a crock o' goold full of bank notes, or did ye catch a leprichaun, an' squeeze this out of him between your finger and thumb?

ARRAH. Yes, indeed, it was one of the good people that gav' it to me, and he tould me not to tell you a word about it for three days – them's the conditions I recaved wid it. [*Going.*]

SHAUN. Well, that's an asy way ov risin' money: three days! Can ye get any more of it on the same conditions. Make it six, dear, and divil a word I'll ax, but open my mouth and shut my eyes, and let it roll down widout a wink. Powdhers of war; Arrah! what am I marryin' at all? Beauty and wealth, no less. It's my belief you are a fairy, born and bred. Your mother was sweet Vanus[11] herself, and your father was the Bank of Ireland. [*Exit.*]

Notes

[11] Venus, Roman goddess of beauty.

SCENE 3 – *The Armoury in* O'GRADY*'s House.*

Enter FANNY POWER.

FANNY. I have managed to regain my room without discovery. Well! this is nice behaviour for a young lady! The inmate of a respectable house to be scampering over the country by moonlight. I wonder I'm not ashamed of myself! And this is my wedding day! I must spend it in deceit and fear! not daring to look in the face of those that love and trust me. After dark, dressed in an old cloak, I must creep away like a thief to be married by rushlight in an old ruin; then I'll be hurried on board a dirty smuggler, among fifty strange men, who will know all I've been at. That is a nice programme.

O'GRADY. Congratulate me, my dear Fanny. This is the happiest day of my life.

FANNY. Then you are not going to be married?

O'GRADY. You must let me hope that I am. D'ye remember about six months ago – I mean the last time you refused me –

FANNY. Haven't I refused you since then? Well.

O'GRADY. You said to me: "O'Grady! never pronounce the word love to me again until you bring me the royal pardon of Beamish Mac Coul."

FANNY. And did not my anxiety awake any jealous feelings in your breast?

O'GRADY. Not in the least. Sure I knew that your interest sprang from the romantic sympathy of your little seditious heart for the rebel, and not from any love for a man you never saw; so I set to work, and mighty hard work it was!

FANNY. Do you mean to tell me that you have succeeded? Oh, dear Bagenal, are there hopes?

O'GRADY. Fanny! if you talk and look at me like that I'll ring for help.

FANNY. Speak, you dearest of injured mortals!

O'GRADY. I have accomplished the task you imposed upon me, and you are free to reward me. Don't be overcome, Fanny; I am yours.

FANNY. I am bewildered with joy.

O'GRADY. Here is the letter from the Secretary of State – [*reads*]: "My dear Colonel, – In consideration of your eminent services –

FANNY. Oh, never mind that: to the point.

O'GRADY. That *is* the point. "In considera – [*she snatches the letter*].

FANNY [*reads*]. Um – um! Ah! "The matter was brought before the Council." So. "A free pardon is granted to young Mac Coul provided he is not implicated in the fresh disturbances which once more threaten to agitate your neighbourhood."

O'GRADY. Fortunately, Beamish is in France; so that proviso cannot apply to him. There's the pardon – the life of your hero. What's to be the next step?

FANNY. Throw it into the fire.

O'GRADY. Upon my conscience, Fanny, I believe you are not a woman at all, but a book of Euclid; for there's no understanding you.

FANNY. Is there not? Well, to-night you will understand me, and then you will know upon what a deceitful, unworthy baggage you have thrown away your generous heart.

O'GRADY. By the love that's in me, what makes you most perfect in my eyes are your faults; and it's the weak points of your character that are the most irresistible. [*Chorus outside and shouts.*] What is that agreeable uproar?

PATSEY. Plase your honor, it's the weddin' party from Laragh – Shaun the Post and Arrah Meelish, wid all their followin', are on their way to the Chapel, sir.

O'GRADY. Show them in, Patsey. [*Exit* SERVANT.] I suppose the young couple want my
    license to keep open house to-night to regale their friends.

FANNY. Are they followers of the O'Grady?

O'GRADY. No; they belong to the sept of the Mac Coul.

FANNY. Ah.

Re-enter PATSEY, *and enter* SHAUN, ARRAH, *and* VILLAGE GIRLS *and* MEN.

ALL. Long life to you, sir.

ARRAH. It is the smile of fortune we bring, your honour. May the grass never grow on
    your dure-step, nor fail on your hills. May your hearthstone be always as warm as
    your heart; and when you die may the wail of the poor be the only sorrow of your life.

O'GRADY. Now, Shaun, what's the good word from you?

SHAUN. Well, your honor, seein' the sweet lady that's by your side, I can think of
    nothin' else to say but "More power t'ye, and long life to enjoy it."

ALL. Hurroo!

O'GRADY. Thank ye, Shaun; and may this day that will change the name of your bride,
    never change the heart of Arrah-na-Pogue.

FANNY. Arrah-na-Pogue, that means Arrah-of-the-Kiss.

O'GRADY. Don't you know why she is called so? Tell her, Arrah.

ARRAH. Sure I do be ashamed, sir.

SHAUN. Ah! what for? It's proud I am of the kiss you gave, though it wasn't meself that
    got the profit of it.

FANNY. Indeed; and who was the favoured one?

SHAUN. Beamish Mac Coul, miss; her comdaltha. I mane her foster-brother that is.
    It was four years ago. He was lyin' in Wicklow Gaol, the day before he was to be
    hung, wid the rest of us in regard of the risin'.

FANNY. He escaped from prison the day before his execution.

SHAUN. Thrue for ye, miss. The boys had planned the manes of it, but couldn't schame
    any way to give him the office, because no one was let in to see the masther, barrin'
    they wor sarched, and then they could only see his face at a peep-hole in the dure of
    his cell.

FANNY. Did Arrah succeed in conveying to him the necessary intelligence?

SHAUN. She did. Bein' only a dawny little crature that time, they didn't suspect the
    cunnin' that was in her; so she gave him the paper in spite of them, and before
    their faces.

FANNY. How so? You say they searched her. Did they not find it?

SHAUN. No. She had rowled it up and put it in her mouth, and when she saw her foster-
    brother she gave it to him in a kiss.

ARRAH. And that's why they call me Arrah-na-Pogue.

FANNY. No one but a woman would have thought of such a post-office.

ARRAH. It's a poor thing I did for him that has done so much for Shaun and me.
    We owe him every feet of land that gives us bread, and the roof that covers us.
    There isn't a ha'porth we have but belongs to him.

FANNY [*aside*]. How her face blushes, and her eyes fill as she speaks of him.

O'GRADY. Well, Shaun, I suppose you want a magistrate's permission to keep open
    house to-night? You shall have it. Patsey, put a keg or two of liquor on the car;
    if I can't attend in person at your feast I will be there in spirit, anyway.

ALL. Long life t'ye, sir. The O'Grady for ever. Hurroo! [*Exeunt.*]

O'GRADY. Here's another woman infatuated with the Mac Coul. It is wonderful.

FANNY. I'm uneasy about myself. I thought I was his only case; I hope he is not an
    epidemic.

Re-enter PATSEY.

PATSEY. Major Coffin, sir.
O'GRADY. I am delighted to see him.

Enter MAJOR COFFIN.

No bad news from the disturbed districts I hope, Major.
MAJOR [*bowing*]. Miss Power, I'm yours. Colonel, my news is excellent. The French emissary, whose presence in this neighbourhood we have for six weeks suspected, but who has eluded our efforts to trace –
O'GRADY. Because no such person is to be found.
FANNY [*aside*]. 'Tis Beamish!
O'GRADY. Well, Major, is there any news of your wild goose?[12]
MAJOR. The most precise. We have discovered his nest. A thousand pardons, Miss Power, for entering on a such a matter in your presence.
FANNY. Not at all. I beg you to proceed. I – I am more deeply interested in your success than you can imagine. You have not – caught the – the rebel?
MAJOR. Had we done so, I beg to assure you, the first tree would have settled his business, without occupying your attention with such a vagabond. [*To the O'Grady.*] Do you know the collecting clerk of the Government Agent, one Mr. Michael Feeny?
O'GRADY. I do well; he's the biggest thief in the County Wicklow, and that's the best I know of him.
MAJOR [*calls*]. Step this way, Mr. Feeny.
O'GRADY. Oh! Mr. Feeny, I think we are acquainted; when last we met I introduced myself.
FEENY. Yes, Colonel; I think – I – that is – you –
O'GRADY. I kicked you from the hall door to the lodge gate, for serving a process on a guest of mine.
FEENY. I am afraid, Colonel, that I left an unfavourable impression on you.
O'GRADY. I am sure, sir, I left a number of unfavourable impressions on you. What does this fellow want?
MAJOR. He alleges that last night he was robbed by fifty armed men on Derrybawn Hill. His description of their leader tallies with that of the man of whom we are in search. By accident he has traced part of the plunder, and discovered, at the same time, the rebel's nest.
O'GRADY. Poor devil! Well, I suppose you want me to hear this fellow's depositions? If you will step into the justice-room I am sure Miss Power will excuse us. This way, Major. [*Exeunt.*]
FANNY [*alone*]. It is Beamish they seek! He was on Derrybawn last night, and that wretch has tracked him, and marked him down, in some cave or up a tree, where he lies now, little expecting the fate that awaits him. Can I hear what they say? [*Listens at the door.*] Yes! – hush! – he speaks! he recognised the notes to be the same

Notes ―――

[12] "Wild Geese" referred generally to Irish soldiers forced into exile.

of which he was robbed! Eh? What does he say? In the possession of Arrah Meelish? – Arrah, the girl that was here just now! Hush! The rebel chief is her lover, and he is concealed in her cabin, at Laragh! Oh! what have I heard? Beamish there! No! it is not possible. Yet how the girl's face beamed when she spoke of him. Ah! they return.

Re-enter O'GRADY, MAJOR COFFIN, *and* FEENY.

MAJOR. I propose to make a descent on this girl's cabin tonight.

O'GRADY. To-night! and this is her wedding day, poor thing! Couldn't you put it off till to-morrow?

MAJOR. And risk the escape of our man?

FEENY. Oh! divil a fear o' that, your honour; the cabin is well watched this minute by them that won't let a mouse stir out of it widout givin' the alarm. We've got him safe enough.

FANNY [*aside*]. How, then, can I warn him of his danger!

O'GRADY. Major, speaking from experience, I believe that fellow is lying. The truth would be ashamed to be seen coming out of him. I know the girl he has denounced, and I'll pledge my honour for hers.

FANNY. And I'll pledge mine for the man. No! I mean, I don't think it possible any woman could be so base.

O'GRADY. What do you know about it?

FANNY. I am only saying what you say, and you are not going to turn round now, and say otherwise because I say so too.

MAJOR. If this innocent investigation can only confirm your good opinion in which I am resolved to share.

O'GRADY. Then I will go with you!

FANNY. So will I.

O'GRADY. You, Fanny!

FANNY. Yes; I cannot restrain the interest I feel in this investigation. I will not believe that a man can be so base to maintain a love affair up to his very wedding day; and with such a secret in his breast abuse the honest heart of one who loves him.

O'GRADY. But it isn't a man; it is a woman.

FANNY. Well, it is all the same thing. Don't annoy with your fine distinctions. Come, Major, let me hear the particulars from yourself; for the O'Grady gets so confused when he attempts to explain anything, that my understanding becomes as muddled as his own. [*Exit with* MAJOR.]

O'GRADY. Tender-hearted angel! See how she stands up for one of her own sex in trouble!

FEENY. I hope, Colonel, dear, you will disremember the little matter betune us, sir, and not hould it agin me; I'm only a tool, sir, in my employer's hands, and sixteen shillins a week is all I get for the dirty work.

O'GRADY. Then you get more kicks than ha'pence. Stand outside the gate, my man, and don't let the dogs smell ye. [*Exit.*]

FEENY. Aha! oho! Arrah-na-Pogue. I tould ye that I'd take down that purty nose of your own, that ye turned up at me, when I axed ye to say the word. It's a grand weddin' ye'll have, my lady; but it is in Wicklow Gaol ye'll pass this night! I tould you my time would come, and that I would bring ye to my fut, and when ye rise from that it shall be into my arms.

SCENE 4 – *A Barn attached to* ARRAH*'s Cabin at Laragh. Through the wide-open door the Village is seen, dotted with lights, and straggling up the Valley towards Glendalough, which is visible in the distance. The Ruins and Round Tower are also seen beyond the Village.*

BEAM. [*descends staircase*]. This place is watched. Has my retreat been discovered? When the wedding party returns, I can mix unnoticed with the crowd, and escape in the dark. [*Music and shouts outside.*] Here they come. [*He ascends to the loft.*]

Enter a PROCESSION, *preceded by* BEGGARS *and* CHILDREN *then, a* PIPER *and* FIDDLERS; *then the* BRIDESMAIDS *and* MEN; *then* SHAUN *and* ARRAH *in a car, with the* PRIEST; *then a* CROWD.

SHAUN. A kind welcome to every mother's son of ye, and a warmer one agin to every petticoat. Bad luck to the first that laves the house, barrin' he doesn't know any better.

ALL. Hurroo!

SHAUN. There's lashins of mate inside, and good liquor galore, and him that spares what's there, I look upon as my inimy. [*He jumps on a barrel. Music again. Exeunt all into inner room,* ARRAH *first with the Priest as they go in.*] Pat Ryan, lave that girl alone till the grace is said; in wid ye, you are welkim as the flowers in May. Nora Kavinagh, don't be provokin' that boy before he's able for ye. Ah! Tim Conolly, is it cologuin wid two girls at a time you are: I'm lookin' at ye. Walk in, my darlin's, and cead mille failtha.[13] [*He leaps down and follows them.*]

Re-enter ARRAH; *she looks round cautiously.*

ARRAH. Are ye gone, sir?

BEAM. [*appearing on the stairs, and leaning over*]. No, from my trap door, in the roof above, I can see men on the road below, who seem to be watching this place. Surely they cannot suspect my retreat here. Who could have betrayed me?

ARRAH. From the roof of the barn you can rache a tree, and by its branches climb to the rock above.

BEAM. I won't try that except as a last expedient. Oh! Arrah, if I were caught here, what would become of you?

ARRAH. Never mind me, save yourself.

BEAM. Come what may, I must be at Tullabogue in two hours from this time – [*cries and laughter within*], – but don't let me detain you from the feast. Good bye, Arrah, we may not see each other again, so, heaven bless and preserve you. Good bye, dear Arrah, good bye.

ARRAH. Good bye, sir. [*He disappears.*] He is gone! and while they are hunting the life out of him, here I am dancing and marryin', and laffin', wid no more feeling in me than if I wor a wet sod of turf that hasn't a ha'porth of warmth in its heart, although ye stick it in the middle of the fire.

Enter SHAUN.

SHAUN. Where are ye at all? Oh! is it alone we are for a blessed minute itself; and I have you all to myself, my darlin'; my own that ye are, now. Oh, murther! when I luk at

Notes ————————————————————————

[13] A hundred thousand welcomes.

you, so clane and nate, and purty, it's fit you are for a bit of chaney on the chimbley-piece[14] of the quality in a drawing-room, not for my dirty cabin. And how did you come to love a poor ignorant crature like meself, at all, at all.

ARRAH. Poor and ignorant! How dar' ye say that of my husband.

SHAUN. Iss poor, I am; I never knew it till I saw you inside my dure. Ignorant, I am; I never felt it till I thried to tell ye what was in my heart, and found I hadn't larnin' to do it, anyway. No! I can't make it out at all, unless you are a fairy that has stooped to make fun of a poor boy. I'm expectin' every minute to see your wings breakin' out behind upon ye; and may be you'll rise up like a butterfly, and be off to the skies above, where you belong.

ARRAH. Ah, Shaun, my darlin', don't spake to me that way – don't make so much of me.

SHAUN. Oh, my threasure! Oh, mo storreen bheg![15] If there was a diamond as big as yourself, it would be a poor thing beside you, my darlin'. But what's the matter, dear? Is it cryin' you are? Oh, is it anything I've said, bad luck to me, that's made ye cry, my darlin.'

ARRAH. No! no! don't ax me.

SHAUN. I won't, dear – av coorse – why would I? Ye see, I'm not used to the tindher and soft ways of women, an' if I'm rough or wrong any way, wont ye tell me till I larn how to behave for oh, acuishla, I do be afraid to go near some girls, for fear of spoilin' their new and beautiful clothes; but I'm afraid of touchin' you for fear of spoilin' the bloom on your fresh and beautiful sowl.

ARRAH. Oh, Shaun! when I listen to you talkin' of me that way, you make me feel ashamed of myself, beside you. [*He kisses her.*]

Enter CROWD.

ALL. Oh! we caught ye – ha! ha! ha! [ARRAH *pushes* SHAUN *away.*]

SHAUN. Is a good example to be thrown away upon ye? Boys, when the bride gets her first kiss, sure, it's a kiss all round. [*A scramble among the girls and boys.*]

OINY. More power, yer souls, here's ould Tim Cogan, of Ballimore, says he'll take the flure agin any famale ov his age and sex in the company.

SHAUN. Whoo! d'ye hear that! For the honor of the County Wicklow, isn't there a pair of brogues undher a petticoat that will stand up agin the County Kildare?

KATTY. Come out o' that, Tim Cogan, till I take the consate out of yiz.

ALL. Hurroo, for Katty! Katty Walsh, aboo!

SHAUN. Aisy, now, ye rapparees. Katty, darlin', let me lade ye out. It's yourself that'll stretch Tim Cogan like a dead fowl this blessed evenin', if you'll put it to him sthrong before he gits his second wind. What shall be the time of it, avourneen?

KATTY. Fatther Jack Welsh agin the world.

SHAUN. That's the daisy; and it's yirself will tatther Tim Cogan, I'll go bail. Would ye take a sup first, or will ye dance dhry? There's a one-pound note among the fiddlers if the lady is plazed wid the tune of it.

ALL. Hurroo!

SHAUN. Now, ye scrapin' thieves, pull out the plug and run it sthrong. [*Dance. A jig by Katty and Tim Cogan.*] Whoo! that's iligant! Welt the flure, Katty.

OINY. Hould up to her, Tim.

SHAUN. Cover the buckle fair, ye ould schamer.

Notes
_____

[14] china on the chimney-piece (mantle-piece).   [15] Oh, my little treasure!

REGAN. Kildare for a tinpenny.

SHAUN. Ah, don't decave yerselves; Katty is only jokin'. Wait till she offers her fut to him. Whoo! that's the sthroke!

REGAN. Hould up the credit of the county, Tim.

SHAUN. Put your back into it Katty; his off leg is a Quaker. Stick to him, my jewel, he's goin'; he's goin'. [*Tim falls exhausted. A shout from all the crowd.*]

KATTY. Whoo! [*Dances round him amidst general applause, and is led ceremoniously by Shaun to a seat. He hands her a jug of punch.*]

SHAUN. Now, boys, one glass all round, and then I'll call upon Paddy Finch for a song.

ALL. Whoo! Where's Pat? Pat, ye schamer, clare yer pipes. Paddy, yer wantin'.

LANIGAN. If ye plaze, here he is; but not a note ye'll get out of him this night, barrin' its a snore. He's overtaken.

SHAUN. Is he salted down intirely?

KATTY. He is contint.

ARRAH. Come, Shaun, for want of a betther, we'll take a song from yourself.

ALL. Hurroo. Rise it, Shaun, avich.

SHAUN. Will, ladies, its for you to choose the time of it. What shall it be?

REGAN. The "Wearing of the green."

ALL. Hurroo! The "Wearing of the green."

SHAUN. Whist, boys, are ye mad; is it sing that song and the soldiers widin gunshot? Sure there's sudden death in every note of it.

OINY. Niver fear; we'll put a watch outside and sing it quiet.

SHAUN. It is the "Twistin' of the rope" ye are axin' for.

REGAN. Divil an informer is to the fore – so out wid it.

SHAUN. Is it all right, outside there?

OINY [*advancing*]. Not a sowl can hear ye, barrin' ourselves.

SHAUN. Murdher alive! kape lookin' out.

SONG.

ARRAH. Well, this is purty goings on at my weddin' Boys, I am spoilin' for a dance, and not one among ye has axed me the time I'd like, nor offered to provoke my fut to the flure. Oiny Farrell, stand out and face me if ye dar. Come, girls, the fiddlers are ashamed of ye.

ALL. Hurroo!

[*They take their places for a jig, the fiddlers commence playing. A drum heard outside; general consternation. Enter a* FILE OF SOLDIERS, *led by the* SERGEANT; *he disposes the men so as to surround the cabin.* BEAMISH, *who has been visible during the previous scenes in the loft formed by the rafters of the barn, now is seen to throw off his coat, and to open the trap door in the roof; he disappears through it.*]

Enter MAJOR COFFIN, THE O'GRADY, FANNY POWER, *and* FEENY.

MAJOR. Guard the doors; let no one pass.

O'GRADY. We are sorry to spoil your diversion, boys, but a robbery was committed last night on Derrybawn Hill, and we have received information that some of the plunder has been traced to this spot.

SHAUN. Is it a thief you are afther, sir? Ah, thin, if any such a one is undher this roof ye are welcome to him.

MAJOR. Now, Mr. Feeny, whom do you charge with having possession of the plunder?

FEENY. That woman, Arrah Meelish.

ALL. Arrah!

FEENY [*advancing*]. Oh, never fear; we'll find the money in her pocket. Let her be sarched.

SHAUN [*springing before her*]. Lay a finger on her and I'll brain ye.

MAJOR. Arrest that fellow.

O'GRADY. 'Asy, Major; what would you do if a man offered to lay a hand on the woman you loved? Be the powers, I'd have brained him first and warned him afthewards. Shaun, my man, the thing is settled in a moment. We don't believe a word this fellow has deposed, but if Arrah has any money – Bank notes about her –

SHAUN. She has, sir.

O'GRADY. See that; then let us just look at them.

SHAUN. Wid all the pleasure in life. Arrah, dear, gi' me them notes you showed me a while ago. Don't be frightened, darlin'. Come.

ARRAH gives SHAUN the notes, with trembling reluctance.

O'Grady [*receiving the notes from Shaun*]. The Bank of Naas.

FEENY. And they are part of them that I was robbed of last night on Derrybawn. I'll swear to them. Luk, and you'll find my name on the back of one o' them. There, that's the one. See, d'ye believe me now?

O'GRADY. Where and from whom did you receive this money. [*A pause.*]

SHAUN [*aside*]. Why doesn't she spake.

O'GRADY. I'm sure you won't refuse to tell us how you became possessed of these notes. [*A pause.*] Afther what you have heard, if you are innocent, as I am sure you are, you won't help to screen the thief!

The MAJOR advances.

MAJOR. You are silent. Well, then, perhaps you will answer another question. Where is the young man who has been concealed in your cabin for the last six weeks. [ARRAH *clasps her hands over her face. A murmur amongst the crowd*]. Do you hear me. I want the young man, your lover – the secret leader of the rebel movement in this neighbourhood – who committed this robbery last night, and then shared with you the proceeds of his crime.

SHAUN. Arrah!

ARRAH. Shaun, let me spake to ye.

MAJOR. No; you are my prisoner. This girl must hold no communication with any here. [*Two soldiers arrest her, while a third unlocks a pair of handcuffs*]. Search this place.

FEENY. I know every hole and corner in it. Folly me. [*Some soldiers go out. A party led by Feeny ascend the staircase, and are seen in the loft above, thrusting their bayonets into the sacks and trusses of straw, &c.*]

FANNY. Arrah Meelish! for the sake of that loving heart that is bleeding yonder, for the sake of those honest girls, who stand bewildered at this charge against you, oh! for your own sake speak out, say that no one has been concealed here. Raise up your face, girl, and say it is a lie. [*A pause.*]

ALL [*murmuring*]. She doesn't spake! She doesn't spake!

FANNY. You desire, then, that all here should believe you guilty. You wish that Shaun should accept your silence as a confession of your shame.

ARRAH. Fanny Power, if all Ireland thought me guilty; Ay! if I said the word myself, and swore to it, he would not believe it agin' his own heart, that knows mine too well to doubt me.

Re-enter FEENY *and* SOLDIERS.

FEENY. He has escapcd; but here is his coat he left behind him; and look, here in the pocket, is my pass that he stole.

MAJOR. This evidence, Colonel, is pretty conclusive.

O'GRADY. You see this, Arrah. Reflect, my good girl, that a cruel and painful death is the penalty of this crime; I believe that you are screening some unworthy villain, at the cost of your own life. Speak, Arrah!

ARRAH. Take me away; don't I offer my hands to the irons; why don't ye take me away?

SHAUN [*rising*]. Stop! if she wont spake, I will. That coat there belongs to me; I robbed Feeny of his money, and gave the notes to Arrah.

ARRAH. Shaun! Shaun! what are you saying? [ARRAH *bursts from the Soldiers and embraces Shaun.*]

SHAUN. Hould up your head, my darlin' – [*looks round.*] Who dar say a word agin ye now? Yes, O'Grady, put it all down to me, if ye plaze, sir. Don't cry, acuishla, sure they can't harm a hair of your head now.

ARRAH. Oh, Shaun! what have you done! [*They handcuff Shaun between two Soldiers.*]

SHAUN. Ye see how wrong ye all wor to be so hard upon her, and she as innocent as a child. Take her, Colonel dear, quick – 'asy! She has fainted, the crature. There, now, get me away handy before she's sinsible, the poor thing! Major, dear, is it agin the regulations for me to take one kiss from her before I lave her may be for ever? [*He stoops over Arrah and embraces her. As they take him off the Curtain falls.*]

ACT II

SCENE 1 – *The Devil's Glen.*

Enter BEAMISH.

BEAM. What a night of adventure! I had a narrow escape from the barn, but favoured by the darkness I scaled the cliff, and stole away like a fox over the hills. What can detain Fanny? The hour appointed for our meeting has passed. Hark! some one comes down the glen. No, those are the footsteps of a man. 'Tis surely Oiny Farrell.

Enter OINY.

OINY. Himself yer honour, and it's the bad luck that's in it, sir, entirely.

BEAM. What has happened?

OINY. Oh the devil and all, sir – rade that while I get my breath. [*Hands him a letter.*]

BEAM. It is from Fanny! Something has occurred to frustrate our plans. [*Reads.*] "When I inform you that I have become acquainted with the relations subsisting between yourself and the person whose cabin you have lately inhabited, it will scarcely be necessary to add that we can never meet again!" Great heavens, what does this mean? [*Reads.*] "I shudder when I think of you, so do not expose yourself to peril by attempting to see me. If any gentle feeling be awakened in your breast by the sad result of your crime, I appeal to that feeling to protect me from the insult of your presence. FANNY POWER."

OINY. It's thrue, indeed, sir! They found signs of yourself in Arrah's cabin. The girl wouldn't spake a word to let on who was in it, and when all the people was down upon her for the shame of the thing, sure Shaun stud up, and ses he "I am the man," ses he, and so he wos tuk.

BEAM. What horrible porridge are you talking? Shaun arrested, for what?

OINY. For robbing Feeny! Sure the notes was found in Arrah's pocket, and she wouldn't say how she come by them. Oh, but she stud it well.

BEAM. And this occurred after I left the barn?

OINY. It did, sir.

BEAM. And was Miss Power present?

OINY. Indeed she was, and she was mighty hard on Arrah, small blame to her! and all the neighbours was agin her, in regard to her desavin' Shaun.

BEAM. But why did you not tell the truth at once, and rescue the poor girl?

OINY. Is it bethray her honour.

BEAM. Do you mean that Shaun, to save me, has acknowledged to crimes that he never committed?

OINY. Devil a ha'porth, sir; it was to save Arrah.

BEAM. He is ignorant, then, that I was the person concealed in the barn; for she promised me to keep my presence here a secret from him. He must believe the poor girl guilty.

OINY. Well, it won't trouble him long, for they say the court-martial will be held on him to-day, and he'll be hung before mornin'.

BEAM. No. I will give myself up, and confess all.

OINY. Confess that Arrah gave shelter to the outlaw. You would only shift the rope from his neck to hers.

BEAM. No – I think – at least, I hope no such unjust and inhuman sacrifice will be demanded. I will go at once to the Secretary of State at Dublin, and lay the whole history of my folly before him. Surely he will spare Arrah's life if I surrender mine.

OINY. Ah! sure, sir, you wouldn't give yourself up?

BEAM. What object have I now in life? This cruel letter deprives me of defence and appeal. I know too well the promptitude of martial law. I have but a few hours to reach Dublin, obtain an audience, and to despatch the order from the authorities to suspend Shaun's execution. Meanwhile, return at once to Arrah, and tell her she has my leave to speak.

OINY. She'd never do it, sir.

BEAM. Then let Shaun know the truth, and out with it.

OINY. How can he, when it will convict his own girl.

BEAM. Then stand out yourself and proclaim these poor people to be innocent.

OINY. Oh, iss! and how would I look; faith I'd put myself in for it entirely. Sure I'd have to confess that I was through it all wid your honour.

BEAM. Then Fanny shall make the avowal. Yes, my confession will serve as the best answer to this letter, and she will understand my truth when I seal its utterance with my life. This evidence produced at the trial will save Shaun.

OINY. But, sure I'll never be able to get back to Ballybetagh before the court-martial comes on.

BEAM. Follow me then, quickly. Oh could I have foreseen that my wild adventure on Derrybawn would have had so unhappy a termination. [*Exit.*]

SCENE 2 – *The Armoury in* O'GRADY's *House.*

THE O'GRADY *and* MAJOR COFFIN.

MAJOR. Really, Colonel, I cannot understand the grounds on which you profess to believe in the innocence of this fellow.

O'GRADY. Sir, I have known him to be an honest man ever since he was a child.

MAJOR. But he has confessed his guilt.

O'GRADY. That is the only bad feature in his case.

MAJOR. Bad feature! What evidence can be more conclusive? Don't you believe his word?

O'GRADY. Egad, Major, if you think that he is capable of picking a pocket, won't you let me think him capable of telling a lie?

MAJOR. The court-martial will decide that question. I am anxious to despatch this fellow's case at once, for the country is agitated, and prompt measures are required to restore order. It is my firm conviction that an example is particularly required at this moment to check a popular disturbance. This man's case admits of no doubt, and his execution will, I hope, prove a salutary public lesson. That being my firm conviction, Colonel, I trust you will excuse my prolonging any discussion upon the point. Good morning. [*Exit* MAJOR.]

O'GRADY. There goes a kind-hearted gentleman, who would cut more throats on principle and firm conviction than another blackguard would sacrifice to the worst passions of his nature. If there be one thing that mislades a man more than another thing it is having a firm conviction about anything.

Enter FANNY POWER.

FANNY. You are quite right, I had a firm conviction; but if ever I have another – if ever I trust one of your sex again may I be deceived, as I shall deserve to be!

O'GRADY. What has happened?

FANNY. A change has come over me since last night. I am no longer the fool I was. I have learned a bitter lesson. Oh may you never know what it is to be deceived by the being you love!

O'GRADY. That will depend a good deal on yourself, my dear.

FANNY. May you never find the idol of your heart to be a worthless, treacherous, unfeeling thing, whose life is one long falsehood.

O'GRADY. What is the matter with her?

FANNY. Oh! When I compare you with other men, how noble, how good you appear.

O'GRADY [*aside*]. I wonder what I've been doing.

FANNY. And how base I feel when I reflect on the past.

O'GRADY. Then don't reflect on it. Why should you remember it? Upon my word I'll forget it, with all my heart, whatever it is.

FANNY. Will you forgive me?

O'GRADY. The man who hesitates to forgive a woman, under any circumstances, even when he hasn't the smallest notion of what she is talking about, deserves –

FANNY. That's enough – I ask no protestations – I have had over enough of them. Now to business, do you love me?

O'GRADY. Ah Fanny!

FANNY. You do. Oh yes. I know too well that I have inspired you, and you only, with a true and faithful devotion – fool, fool that I have been.

O'GRADY. I can't quite follow the process of reasoning by which you get to that result.

FANNY. There is my hand – you desire to make it yours. Well, it is yours on one condition.

O'GRADY. I accept it whatever it is.

FANNY. You must save the life of this poor fellow – Shaun the Post – for I am in some measure the cause of his misfortunes.

O'GRADY. You! What in the name of wonder can you have to do with his affairs?

FANNY. Don't seek to learn more than is good for you to know. I was an accomplice in all this mischief, and the same bad influence, from which I have barely escaped with my life, has ruined Arrah Meelish.

O'GRADY. But I would like to understand –

FANNY. Listen, then, for this much I may at least tell you. If I had not been deceiving you for the last two months; if I did not feel that I was unworthy of your love, and that I owe you some reparation for the sufferings which I intended to inflict upon you, I would not say to you as I do now, "O'Grady, I am yours." [*Aside.*] Now, Beamish, farewell for ever. I have placed an impassable barrier between us, and I am miserable for ever. [*Exit.*]

O'GRADY. I am bothered! She said "I am yours." But something within me, that feels like the conscience of my heart, refuses to send through every vein in my body those congratulations of delight that make a man feel conscious he is beloved. Woman! you were always the disturbing influence in the peaceful realms of human nature! Oh, father Adam! why didn't ye die with all your ribs in your body? [*Exit.*]

SCENE 3 – *The Prison.* SHAUN *discovered.*

SHAUN. Well, this is a sorry place for a man to spend his weddin' day in. It is not wid the iron cuffs on me, and wid a jug of could water for a companion, I expected to find myself this blessed night. [SERGEANT *and* FEENY *appear at door.*]

SERGEANT. The prisoner all right?

SENTRY. All right, sir.

SHAUN. Who's that? It is Feeny, the dirty spalpeen,[16] come to crow over my throuble. He shan't see that I am onaisy in my mind, any way. [SHAUN *sings.*]

FEENY. So it is singing ye are! as gay as a lark, eh? kapin up your sperits? That's right, my man, by and bye you will be put on yer thrial, before the court-martial.

SHAUN. Well, to be sure! a court-martial itself. Is it in full jerrimentals[17] they'll be?

SERGEANT. Certainly.

SHAUN. And they won't charge me anything for seeing the show?

FEENY. They'll charge you with rebellion and robbery.

SHAUN. And what'll they do to me for all that?

FEENY. You will be hung free of all expense – hung before to-morrow mornin' – that's the weddin' night you'll have. It's a wooden bride that is waiting for you, my jewel. It's only one arm she's got, and one leg, ho! ho! but, once she takes you round the neck, she's your's till death, ha! ha!

SHAUN. And is hanging all they'll do to me?

FEENY. Nothing else, my dear.

Notes ————————————————————————————————

[16] rascal

[17] *regimentals* or full military uniform

SHAUN. It's well it's no worse.

FEENY. Worse! What could be worse?

SHAUN [*rising*]. They could make me a process-server, a polis spy, and a coward!

FEENY. Ho! you think to decave me wid your high sperits, but you don't! I know how you feel, wid the canker that's atin' your heart out. Sure, I loved Arrah, but I knew the bad dhrop wos in her.

SHAUN. It is well for you that I am tied. Go on! go on!

FEENY. So don't be onaisy, she'll have somebody to comfort her afther you arc gone, and that will be myself.

SHAUN. Folly on! folly on!

FEENY. D'ye think I was decaved wid the cloak you threw over her shame – not a ha'porth! She is guilty, and you know it as well as I do. You thought to save her by this schame; but, will I tell you what you have done? You have made her over to me as clane as if you had left her by will. To-morrow, when you are over your throuble, I will show her the proofs I hould agin her, and she will be mine rather than face the disgrace of your death and the fear of her own.

SHAUN [*breaks his chains with a cry of rage*]. Not when I can make sure of you first [*seizes him*]. Now, since the divil won't fetch ye, I'll send ye home.

FEENY. Help, Sergeant! he's loose! he is loose! [*The* SERGEANT, *who has been speaking with the* SENTRY, *seizes* SHAUN, *and forces him off* FEENY.] Hould him fast! have ye got him? Call the guard, till they skewer him agin the wall. Isn't this purty tratement for an officer of the law in purshoot of his jooty? Oh, it is cryin' ye are, at last, Mr. Shaun. I thought your bright sperits would not last, ho! ho! [*The* SERGEANT *takes him by the collar, and swings him to the door.*] Hollo!

SERGT. Clear out! you mistake the place. This is a man in trouble, and not a badger in a hole to be baited by curs like you.

FEENY. I'll tell you what it is.

SERGT. Sentry.

FEENY. I've got an ordther from your shupariors to visit the prisoner.

SERGT. Put that man out. [*The* SENTRY *takes him by the collar, and swings him out in a formal manner, recovers, salutes, faces about, and exit.*]

FEENY [*returning at door*]. What am I going out for? I've got an ord – [*meets the bayonet of the* SENTRY, *and disappears.*]

SERGT. Come, prisoner, keep up your pluck, don't give way like a girl. This will never do – come, come, heads up, eyes right, you are not at the foot of the ladder yet.

SHAUN. Oh! It's not what they can do to me that hurts me, but it is her sorrow that breaks my heart entirely.

Enter FANNY POWER.

FANNY. There is an order from Major Coffin to admit me to see your prisoner. [*Hands* SERGEANT *a paper.*] Tell me, Sergeant, as I entered I saw a girl sitting outside the prison gate, how long has she been there?

SERGEANT. Well, miss, she has been lying there all night; the sentry warned her off, and I told her that dogs and women was agin the regulations in barracks, but we didn't like to drive the poor thing away, as she promised to be quiet: so there she is.

FANNY. Leave us. [*Exit* SERGEANT.] Shaun, you did not commit the crime of which you are self-accused, and rather than you shall suffer for the guilt of another, I will denounce the man I have loved, for 'twas he, my affianced husband, who was concealed in Arrah's cabin.

SHAUN. And you believe he is false to you.

FANNY. Alas! I know it.

SHAUN. Thank ye kindly, miss; but I'd rather you'd hould your tongue about me, and let me die my own way.

FANNY. You believe, then, in Arrah's honesty.

SHAUN. I never doubted her love.

FANNY. Poor, weak, blind, infatuated fool, you shall not sacrifice so truthful a heart to so bad an object. Shaun, the girl is outside now; will you see her?

SHAUN. Will I see her? Would you ax a man dyin' of drooth if he'd have a drop of water?

FANNY. It is a cruel kindness to undeceive him, but I will have out this truth, cost what it may. [*Exit* FANNY.]

SHAUN. She's comin'! I'll see her again before I die. Now, Shaun, mind me. Don't be showin' the sorrow in your breast, but comfort the poor crature you're going to leave behind ye. Tuck in your sowl, ye poor, mane bodagh,[18] and don't be showin' her the rags of your heart. [ARRAH *enters, and the door is closed behind her: he does not see her approaching him.*]

ARRAH. Shaun!

SHAUN. Ar – Arrah!

ARRAH. Shaun, don't ye – don't ye know your own wife?

SHAUN [*embracing her*]. My wi – my own wife. Ah! say it again, for I darn't.

Enter FANNY POWER, *softly: she listens.*

ARRAH. No, I won't; I did not mane to call myself by that name until you'd let me – until I had tould ye –

SHAUN. Whisht, dear, what talk is that? There, now, your eyes are heavy wid the tears in them, and your poor mouth it thrembles all over; don't spake about anything you don't like, acuishla.

ARRAH. Oh, don't talk so softly to me, Shaun, for that hurts me. I have been decavin' you – I couldn't help it; but it's truth what they said. There was a young man concealed in the barn, and I am come to tell you who it was, an – an all about it. [*Sobs.*]

SHAUN. Don't cry, darlin'; sure, I won't put any questions to you at all!

ARRAH. Oh, but you must hear me, dear, for d'ye think if I had not sworn to kape his sacret, that I would have held my tongue last night, when, foreninst all the neighbours, your own wife was accused of bein' onthrue to ye? But I can't bear it any longer, Shaun, and sure he'd never hold me to a promise that made me look in your eyes the mane and guilty thing they call me.

SHAUN. It would be a great comfort entirely to myself, darlin', to feel that you had no sacrets from me, but you have made a promise, and you must kape your word, Arrah. You never broke it yet, and I won't ax you to begin now. Sure when I'm dead I'll know all about it, but plaze God I'll die wid my faith in you entire, and no patches in it.

FANNY [*advancing*]. But no promise restrains me. The man concealed in your cabin was Beamish Mac Coul!

ARRAH. Oh.

Notes —————————————————————————————————————

[18] lout

SHAUN. The Mac Coul! Oh, daylight to my sowl! The Mac Coul himself! Oh! bad luck to me for an omadhaun,[19] and I never guessed it. Oh, Arrah, Arrah, don't think poorly of me for the joy that fills my heart; but wid the gallows before me, and not six hours maybe to live, I would not change that little ha'porth of time for any other hundred years of life, knowin' now as I know, and feelin' as I feel, that you are my own, that you love me, and me alone, always, now and for ever and ever. Amen.

FANNY [aside]. I begin to feel very uncomfortable; have I made a fool of myself, after all?

SHAUN. The Mac Coul himself! and he never let on to me that he was here in this place.

ARRAH. It was for my sake, Shaun; he would not get ye in throuble.

SHAUN. Oh, what did I do to deserve this of him, me that would go from the devil to Upper Canada to plaze the smallest hair of his head. Oh, wurrah, deelish,[20] see this!

FANNY. Fool! aint you going to die for him?

SHAUN. Thrue for ye, miss. Well, that's some consolation, any way. It's a proud man I'll be this day when I stand in the dock, and Arrah to the fore looking at me, and saying: It is Master Beamish himself would have been there if Shaun hadn't stud up in his place.

FANNY. Why did he not confess to me that he had found shelter in your cabin?

ARRAH. Maybe he knew that you did not love him well enough to trust him, and how could he put my life into the power of one in whom he had so little faith?

FANNY. Oh, what have I done! My word is passed to O'Grady. I feel as if I had committed suicide in a moment of temporary insanity. [A drum is heard outside.] Hark! they are coming to take Shaun before the court-martial. What is to be done? Shaun, come what may, you must not die.

SHAUN. Well, miss, to be sure. Life and Arrah is mighty sweet when taken together.

ARRAH. Maybe he'll get off after all. They say the law is mighty unsartin.

FANNY. Unfortunately, Shaun has confessed he is guilty.

SHAUN. Well, sure, now; if I confess I'm innocent, won't one go agin the other?

ARRAH. No. I believe that they always take a man's word that he is a thief, but it's not worth a thrawneen[21] to prove him an honest man.

FANNY. If we could have got up an *alibi*.

SHAUN. I've heern till that's a mighty fine thing entirely.

FANNY. But that is not to be thought of in your case.

ARRAH [aside to SHAUN]. What is it she is axin' for?

SHAUN. I don't know rightly, jewil, but it's what lawyers always want when a man's in throuble. Have ye got ere an *alibi*, ses the judge. I have, ses the lawyer. That's enough, ses the court; discharge the prisoner.

FANNY. Listen; you must deny your guilt.

ARRAH. D'ye hear, Shaun?

SHAUN. But I won't be makin' out anything agin the masther that way, will I, miss?

ARRAH. Hould yer whist, and mind what you're bid.

FANNY. If they put any questions to you, avoid betraying yourself.

SHAUN. Oh, never fear, I'm aquil to botherin' a regiment of the likes of them. [A drum outside.]

SERGT. [outside]. Halt. [Exit FANNY.]

Notes ————————————————————————————

[19] idiot

[21] straw

[20] Loosely, "Oh, darling!"

[*Enter* SERGEANT, *and File of* MEN. *They unlock* SHAUN's *handcuffs.*]

Sorry to interrupt you, but we must conduct the prisoner before the court-martial.

ARRAH. Never fear, darlin', I will get as near to you as they will let me.

SHAUN. Oh, Arrah, the sight of your face, and the sound of your voice, is the mate and dhrink of me soul. Good bye, darlin', my heart goes wid you.

ARRAH. If they put ye out of the world, dear, I'll soon be afther ye; for Heaven has joined us together, and no law shall put us asundher. [*Exit.*]

SERGEANT. She gives a man a desire to be executed. She puts me in mind of a glass of brandy. Eh, prisoner, how's the courage, eh? Can I get you anything to keep your heart up before the trial?

SHAUN. Well, Sergeant, dear, have ye such a thing about you as an *alibi*? or could ye borry it of a friend?

SERGEANT. A halibi! Is it anything in the way of a furrin[22] liquor?

SHAUN. I don't know, but I thought you might.

SERGEANT. I am afraid it's agin the regulations, for I never saw one in barracks. What quantity do you want?

SHAUN. Egorra, that's a puzzler. Get me a whole one.

SERGEANT. If it costs a month's pay you shall have it. Now, then, forward. [*Exeunt.*]

SCENE 4 – *Ballbybetagh.*

Enter FANNY.

FANNY. I would like to know what I could be guilty of now to add to my folly and to my iniquity. By this time Beamish must have received my letter. What will he do? Why he will come here at once, and deliver himself up. He will never permit Shaun to suffer in his place. Then what will become of me?

Enter OINY.

OINY. Long life t'ye, miss. Here's a bit of writin' that's in a hurry.

FANNY. 'Tis from Beamish! [*Opens and reads.*] "When you receive this, I shall have surrendered to the authorities. My avowal will exonerate Shaun, and my death will allay all fear in your breast that you will ever again be insulted with the presence of Beamish Mac Coul." I knew it; I have driven him to this. Where is he?

OINY. He's gone to inform on himself, miss. Sure, ses he, my life is worth Shaun's and Arrah's put together. I'm off, ses he.

FANNY. Where to?

OINY. Well, to some grand man that dales in them things, I believe, miss.

FANNY. Oiny, go at once and order my horse to be harnessed to the lightest vehicle in the O'Grady's stables.

OINY. That's the buggy, miss.

FANNY. Give the horse a big feed, for a man's life is on his speed to-night.

OINY. Then I'll wet his oats with a glass of whisky, and he'll fly, miss, never fear. [*Exit.*]

Notes ———————————————————————————————

22 foreign

FANNY. I have but one hope left. I must throw myself on the generosity of the only man who can avert this terrible catastrophe. He has granted a pardon to Beamish already; but to be effective it must be unconditional. I must avow my folly to him. I will appeal to his mercy – not for Beamish – but for my wretched self. He can't refuse me; he won't; he shan't. [*Exit.*]

SCENE 5 – *The Justice Hall at Ballybetagh. A row of seats slightly raised and oblique; a table opposite them; a barrier across the back; a crowd of peasants,* OINY, REGAN, LANIGAN, KATTY, &c.; FEENY *at the table; two clerks also at the table; the* SERGEANT; *two or three non-commissioned officers; soldiers on guard and officers; a drum on table; open doors at back;* COLONEL O'GRADY, MAJOR COFFIN, *and three officers.*

OINY. Ah, d'ye see where you are scroogin' to?
KATTY. D'ye think there's nobody here but yourself?
LANIGAN [*behind her*]. Mrs. Cooley, ma'am, would ye mind takin' the back of your nightcap out of my mouth?
SERGEANT. Order in the Court. Order!
KATTY. Sergeant, dear, which is the Court, av ye plaze?
REGAN. It's thim beyant in the goold lace.
LANIGAN. Ah! go an – where's the wigs! [*Roll of the drum.*]
SERGEANT. Attention! [*The Court sits.*]
MAJOR. Sergeant, is everything prepared? Are we ready to try the prisoner?
O'GRADY. Let the prisoner be brought into Court.

Enter SHAUN *between two* SOLDIERS. *Movement in the Court.*

REGAN. Get out o' that, boys, and make room there for Arrah.
LANIGAN. Stand back, Katty.
SERGEANT. Less noise there.
KATTY. Then hold your own whisht.

Enter ARRAH.

MAJOR. Has the article of your constituting this court-martial been duly read? [*Sergeant bows.*] I think then, Colonel, we may proceed.
ARRAH. Now mind what you are sayin' darlin'.
MAJOR. Your name?
SHAUN. Is it my name, sir. Ah, you're jokin'! Sure there's his honour beside ye can answer for me, long life to him.
MAJOR. Will you give the Court your name, fellow.
SHAUN. Well, I'm not ashamed of it.
O'GRADY. Come, Shaun, my man.
SHAUN. There, didn't I tell ye! he knows me well enough.
MAJOR. Shaun [*writing*], that's the Irish for John I suppose?
SHAUN. No, sir; but John is the English for Shaun.
MAJOR. What is your other name?

SHAUN. My other name? Sure I never did anything I wanted to hide under any other. Did ye ever know me, boys, only as Shaun?

ALL. That's thrue. Ye may put that down agin him, Major.

SERGEANT. Order.

O'GRADY. He is called Shaun the Post.

SHAUN. In regard of me carrying the letter bag by the car, yer honour.

MAJOR. Now, prisoner, are you guilty or not guilty?

SHAUN. Sure, Major, that's what your going to find out.

ARRAH. Don't confess, Shaun.

SHAUN. Never fear; I'm not such a fool as they think.

O'GRADY. Well, Shaun, you have pleaded guilty to this charge of robbery and rebellion.

SHAUN. Well, O'Grady –

MAJOR. Prisoner, you must not presume to address the Court with curt insolence, calling this gentleman "O'Grady" in that familiar manner.

O'GRADY. Your pardon, Major. You are not aware of our Irish ways. I am the O'Grady, the head of the sept. This man belongs to the sept of the Mac Coul; and as your kings are called without offence by their Christian names, "George," or "William," our chiefs are called "O'Grady," or "Mac Coul." Pardon the digression – but the man gives me my title and no more. [*Major bows.*] Go on, my good man.

SHAUN. I did plade guilty last night, and so I was thin, your worship; but I want to say, that I am as innocent as a fish this morning.

MAJOR. You wish to withdraw your plea?

SHAUN. I don't know, sir, but I want to do whatever will get me off.

MAJOR. Withdraw his plea. The prisoner pleads "Not guilty."

SHAUN. Thank ye kindly, Major. It is all over, Arrah. [*Is going down.*]

MAJOR. What is the fellow doing!

SHAUN. Oh, Major, sure ye wouldn't go back of your word. Didn't his honour say fair and plain – "He is not guilty," ses he.

ALL. Oh, Major, ye did. Long life to the Major, boys.

SERGT. Order there.

MAJOR. Really this must be stopped; the dignity of the Court must be preserved.

SHAUN [*to the crowd*]. D'ye hear that, boys. Preserve your dignity, you blackguards, till ye get outside.

MAJOR. Now, Mr. Feeny, state your charge.

FEENY [*rising*]. Plase your worships.

O'GRADY. Stop. What's your name?

FEENY. Michael Feeny.

O'GRADY. Your business?

FEENY. Well, your worship –

O'GRADY. Don't worship me, man, and confound me in your mind with the devil. Speak straight, if you can. What's your dirty trade?

FEENY. Sure ye know well enough, sir. I am an officer of the law, sir.

O'GRADY. I *do* know you well enough, but these gentlemen do not, and I mean they shall. Are you a process-server?

FEENY. Well?

O'GRADY. Yes or no?

FEENY. Y – e – e – es.

O'GRADY. An informer on occasions?

FEENY. I did –

O'GRADY. Out with it; yes or no?

FEENY. Y – yes.

O'GRADY. How many times have you been committed to gaol?

FEENY. Is it me that's on my thrial, Colonel, or Shaun the Post?

O'GRADY. Don't question me, sir. I want an answer. Come, how often were you in prison?

FEENY. I disremember.

O'GRADY. No doubt, but I don't [*takes up a paper and reads*]. Three times for perjury, once for theft, and six times for petty offences. [*Looks up.*] Will I name the prisons and the length of your periods of incarceration?

FEENY. I wouldn't ax –

O'GRADY. Yes or no?

FEENY. No. [*A laugh in the Court.*]

O'GRADY. Now, go on; the Court has your name and trade; you may proceed.

FEENY [*whimpering*]. It's mighty hard, so it is, to be put upon this way, and me only doing my duty. Sure your worships knows well all I've got to say. It's tuk down in the impositions agin the prisoner. Is it my faut if Shaun confessed to the robbery? did I put the idaya in his head or the notes in his pocket? Then why am I to be schraped down to bethray my misfortunes underneath? It's mighty hard upon me entirely, so it is.

O'GRADY. You come here to accuse the prisoner; stop snivelling over yourself, and thry your hand on him.

FEENY. Sure, Colonel, dear, Shaun has accused himself.

MAJOR. Do you swear that the notes produced were part of the property of which you were robbed?

FEENY. I do, sir.

MAJOR. Prisoner, do you wish to ask this witness any questions?

SHAUN. I wouldn't bemane myself by bein' seen talkin' to him.

MAJOR. Stand down. [*Feeny retires.*] Now we are ready to hear what defence you may have to this charge.

O'GRADY. And recollect, Shaun, you are talking for your life.

ARRAH. Mind what you're sayin', now.

SHAUN. Well, your honours, I cannot say much; but if I am to be found guilty on that chap's swearin', it will be a wrong bill. The Recordher knows him well, and wouldn't sintence a flay for backbitin' on that fellow's oath. Come out of that, Michael Feeny, and hear me. When St. Pathrick drove all the crapin' things out of Ireland, he left one sarpint behind, and that was your great grandfather.

MAJOR. This is not to the point.

O'GRADY. It is a mighty fine outburst of natural eloquence; go on, my man, crush that reptile if you can.

SHAUN. Crush him. I'd ax no betther. I've had him under my fist; but he is like some vermin ye can't crush, they stick so flat in the dirt.

MAJOR. This is very irrelevant.

O'GRADY. That's prejudice, Major. I never listened to anything more compact in the way of vituperation.

MAJOR. But abuse is not evidence. [*To SHAUN.*] Have you any witnesses to call?

SHAUN. Devil a one, Major, barrin' you'd like to stand up for a poor boy in throuble yourself, and say a good word for me.

MAJOR. Then this case is closed. I think, gentlemen, the facts are plain. We have but one duty to perform.

O'GRADY. I'm for letting him off.

MAJOR. On what grounds?

O'GRADY. The eloquence of the defence.

MAJOR. I regret to say that we cannot admit so Irish a consideration.

O'GRADY. Well, gentlemen, I have private reasons for believing this man to be innocent, and you will oblige me in a particular manner if you will believe so too.

MAJOR. In defiance of your convictions, Colonel?

O'GRADY. That will only add to obligation, Major. I have given my word to a lady that I would get this fellow off.

MAJOR. Do you consider, sir, the debt of duty we owe your sovereign?

O'GRADY. I do, sir; but a promise made to a lady is a debt of honour, and that is always paid before taxes.

MAJOR. Gentlemen, your voices.

ARRAH. Oh, the pain that is in my heart. [*A pause, after which the Court reseats.*]

MAJOR. Prisoner; the Court having considered the evidence against you, and having duly weighed the matters alleged by you in defence, declares the charge made against you of associating and conspiring with rebels in arms against the peace of His Majesty and the realm; and also of robbery with violence, done on the person of Michael Feeny, to be fully proven, and of the felonies aforesaid you are found guilty.

ALL. Guilty! Poor Shaun! Oh, blessed day! Oh, murdher! what'll be done to him?

ARRAH. Shaun. [*Throws herself into his arms.*]

O'GRADY. I'm sorry for you, Shaun. I would have let you off if a minority of one against four would have done it; but you see we are unanimous against you, my poor boy, so whether you committed the crimes or not, you are guilty. It's mighty hard upon you to say so.

MAJOR. Colonel, permit me to remark that these observations coming from the Court are subversive of its dignity.

O'GRADY. Ah, Major, look at that poor girl that lies broken-hearted on the body of the man she loves, knowing that there's not a day's life in the breast she's clinging to. It is a hard duty that obliges a gentleman to put a rope round that boy's neck, while dignity forbids him to say that he's mighty sorry for it. [*Rises and quits the room, the Officers rise and bow, and reseat themselves.*]

MAJOR. Prisoner; we deeply regret the sentence which it is incumbent upon us to pass upon you, but the Court knows only its duty, and the penalty ascribed to your crime. The sentence of the Court is [*the Officers remove their hats*] that you be taken hence to your prison from whence you came, and to-morrow at daylight you suffer death, and Heaven have mercy upon you. [*The Officers replace their hats.*]

SHAUN. Well, yer honour, I don't blame ye, for you have done your jooty, I suppose, by the King that made ye what ye are. Long life to him, and that jooty is now to hang me; and I have done my duty by the man that made me and mine what we are, and that's to die for him. I could do no more, and you could do no less. I dare say you would have let me off if you could, so God bless ye, all the same.

MAJOR. Remove the prisoner.

ALL. Oh, poor Arrah! Heaven help the poor thing. Ah, it's hard upon her entirely. [*Scene closes in.*]

ACT III

SCENE 1 – *A room in Dublin Castle; a fire place with screen; a table, with papers and shaded light, chairs, &c.; a bay window, curtained; a door in flat.*

WINTERBOTTOM, *asleep in chair before fire.* [*A knock*].

WINTERBOTTOM [*awaking*]. Hi was hunder the happreension I 'erd a knoek.[23] His Lordship is werry late. They're a keepin' of it hup at the Lord Chief Justices, has husual, I persume. [*A knock.*] That's him. [*Rises.*] That lazy Hirish 'allporter was asleep.

Notes ───

[23] Winterbottom adds 'h's before some vowels and regularly drops 'h's that are properly pronounced.

Enter THE SEC.

THE SEC. A little late, I think, Winterbottom so. My dressing gown? [*throws off his coat.*] You are an invaluable fellow [*puts on his dressing gown*]. Now for work. You will come to me as usual at four o'clock, and rouse me to go to bed. [*Sits at table examining letters, and writes.*]

WINTER. Four o'clock, hay, hem! I hawakes him hat height. Four hours sleep, its calkilated to kill an oss.

SEC. [*writing.*] You forget. I go to bed by the Dublin clock, but you awake me by your watch, and that keeps London time.

WINTER. Greenwich, my lord; its a good Hinglish watch, and wouldn't bemean itself to keep no hother.

SEC. Well, don't you see I get half an hour now by that means. Irish time being late.

WINTER. Hindeed, my lord; I wasn't aware, but hime no ways surprised, for they har be'ind 'and in heverything 'ere.

SEC. The sun rises you know in London half an hour before it rises in Ireland.

WINTER. And a very proper mark of respect it is, my lord, and doo likewise to the country and constituotion, to sarve up stairs first, afore the day is sent down here to the servants' hall, as a body may say. Can I do hanything helse for your lordship.

SEC. Nothing, my good Winterbottom, I thank you. Good night!

WINTER. Good night, my lord. Ho! I forgot, there's a young gentleman, a perfect gentleman, 'as been a waiting below since six o'clock. Whether he's gone or not I won't take on me to say, but he said has his business was life and death, and so he'd wait.

SEC. Who is he? did he give you his name?

WINTER. No, my lord.

SEC. Then how did you know he was a perfect gentleman?

WINTER. He give' me a fi' 'pun' note, my lord.

SEC. I beg your pardoon. Show that perfect gentleman here. [*Exit* WINTERBOTTOM, *carrying the* SECRETARY's *coat.*] These disturbances in Wicklow threaten to involve us once more in endless trouble. Could we discover the ringleaders of the movement, we might arrest its progress, but all our efforts to detect them seem fruitless.

Re-enter WINTERBOTTOM, *ushering in* BEAMISH MAC COUL;
the SECRETARY *rises; they bow.*

WINTER. Shall I wait my lord, or –

SEC. No, you can go to bed.

WINTER. Werry good, my lord. [*Bows, and exit.*]

SEC. I regret, sir, to have kept you so long in waiting. Will you favour me with your name, and in what manner I can be of service to you; I pray you to be seated. [*Sits.*]

BEAM. My name, my lord, is Beamish Mac Coul, and I come to place my person at the disposition of the crown.

SEC. You select a strange time for such a proceeding.

BEAM. It is true, and I rely on your forbearance to listen kindly to my apology. For six weeks past, I have been organising an insurrection in the mountain districts of Wicklow; I saw enough to prove that our designs would be a useless waste of life, therefore, our plans were abandoned, and I had resolved to return to France this day.

SEC. A very prudent resolution: I regret you have not adhered to it.

BEAM. Here, my lord, is a confession of my participation in this affair. One of my former tenants has been arrested, tried, and by this time has, doubtless, been found guilty, on his own confession, of the acts which I committed, and of which he is totally innocent.

SEC. Wherefore has this fellow confessed?

BEAM. That he might bear the penalty of my crime, while I escaped.

SEC. And you come here to claim his release and your own execution?

BEAM. If you please, my lord.

SEC. I presume, then, that you and this fellow are disputing which of the two shall die?

BEAM. And I rely on your lordship's sense of justice to give me the preference.

SEC. [*rises and walks to the fire*]. Shall I ever be able to understand this extraordinary people? [*A knock.*] What new disturbance comes at this untimely hour? My poor Winterbottom can scarcely have gained his bed.

WINTER. [*half undressed*]. A gentleman on horseback, my lord.

THE SEC. Is he a perfect gentleman?

WINTER. I can't say, my lord. He only give me his card [*handing it in*]. Hexcuse me, my lord, but in my 'aiste I haint quite in the condition I should wish to appear.

SEC. [*takes card and reads*]. Ha, indeed, show the gentleman here at once. [WINTER-BOTTOM *at once disappears.*] Will you withdraw into the recess of yonder window, for this interview I think concerns you.

BEAM. I consider myself a crown prisoner, and am at your lordship's disposal. [*Retires behind curtain of window.*]

SEC. So, Colonel O'Grady, you applied for and obtained this young gentleman's pardon at the very moment when he was provoking a sedition, and for which you were about to bestow upon him the hand of your ward.

[*Enter* WINTERBOTTOM, *showing in the* O'GRADY.]

SEC. Your servant, colonel.

WINTER. Shall I wait hup, my lord?

SEC. By no means. You will get no rest at all.

WINTER. No Hinghlishman hexpects hanny, my lord, in this country. It keeps us hall hup, and continiually deprives Hingland of her natural rest. [*Aside.*] I 'ope the gentleman will take the 'int. [*Exit.*]

SEC. Now, colonel, I am at your service.

O'GRADY. I know your lordship will pardon this untimely intrusion when you learn, that the sentence of death will in a few hours be executed on a man, who is –

SEC. As innocent as you are of the acts of which he is accused. [*Reading.*] Let me see. His name is Shaun the Post, residing at Rathdrum.

O'GRADY. You astonish me; how could this intelligence have reached you? I left the court martial a few hours ago, and spurred across the country as fast as my horse could carry me.

SEC. My dear, colonel, the government sources of information are much more extraordinary than we care to acknowledge. Here you see we have all the particulars of the matter.

O'GRADY. I am glad to see you share my conviction that this fellow is not guilty.

SEC. Because I share your motives for that conviction I know the real culprit.

O'GRADY. The devil you do!

SEC. Allow me to enjoy your confusion.

O'GRADY. Will you allow me to enjoy a little of it also, for hang me if I know who you mean.

SEC. Beamish Mac Coul.

O'GRADY. The devil! A thousand pardons; but would you say that again?

SEC. Come, colonel, your surprise is admirably assumed! but since you carry it so far I must inform you that the Government sources of information even extend to occurrences in your own household. [*Looking over paper.*] Six weeks ago Beamish Mac Coul landed in Wicklow, coming from France, with the design of marrying your ward, Miss Fanny Power of Cabinteely, to whom he has for many years been ardently attached. You see, colonel, disguise is useless. Your little family matters are well known to the Privy Council.

O'GRADY. By the Lord Harry! the council then is privy to more of my family matters than I am at all acquainted with. [*A knock.*]

SEC. Another attack on poor Winterbottom. Who can this be?

O'GRADY. I don't know, my lord, what your sources of information may be; but when I inform you, that the lady in question is my affianced wife, I hope you will excuse me if I accord more confidence to my sources of information on this point than to any in which your Government may rely.

SEC. [*aside*]. His affianced wife! [*Aloud.*] Then why, colonel, have you so ardently besought this young man's pardon?

O'GRADY. Because Fanny demanded it.

WINTER. [*in a night cap*]. A lady in a buggy, my lord.

SEC. Are you sure, Winterbottom, that it is a lady?

WINTER. Quite sure, my lord. She wouldn't take no for a hanswer. She was wery 'igh indeed with the 'all porter, and she 'anded him this note. [*Gives in a letter.*]

SEC. [*reads it*]. Oh, indeed. I will see the lady immediately.

WINTER. Yes, my lord.

SEC. I regret, colonel, to defer your business for a few moments. Would you take this chair by the fire, while I give audience to that fair intruder; and I hope to be able to convince you sooner perhaps than you suspect how perfect is our detective system of police. [*O'Grady sits behind screen.*]

Re-enter WINTERBOTTOM, *dressed, and bearing the* SECRETARY's *coat, which he assists him to put on.*

SEC. [*reads card*]. Miss Fanny Power of Cabinteely. So now I perceive the drift of this business. Young Mac Coul was evidently an old sweetheart of this girl. In his absence she found another swain. He returns to claim her hand, and the crafty mind obtains through lover No. 2, the pardon of her old flame, with which she pays off his prior claim. A very neat female transaction! [WINTERBOTTOM *bows in* FANNY POWER. *Exit with dressing gown, concealing it from Fanny's sight as he bows himself out, handing her to a seat.*] To what good fortune may I attribute this favour?

FANNY [*throwing back her mantle*]. Oh, my lord, it is ill-fortune brings me to your feet.

BEAM. [*looking out*]. Fanny!

O'GRADY [*turning to listen*]. Powdhers of war! what's that?

FANNY. Pardon my agitation, but now that I find myself in your presence I have lost the courage that sustained me, and perceive only the shame of my proceeding.

SEC. Compose your feelings while I assist you to put in due order the favours you have resolved to obtain from me. First. You will ask me for a remission of the sentence of Shaun the Post, now left for execution for a felony committed by Beamish Mac Coul.

FANNY. By what power can you read my thoughts?

SEC. Ahem! My dear young lady, the sources of information at the command of His Majesty's Government are extraordinary.

FANNY. Then you know that for many a happy year I have corresponded with the Outlaw: that he returned from his exile, invited by and relying upon my love.

SEC. But meanwhile a certain gallant colonel had won your affections away from the absentee, and as you have lately become the affianced wife of this gentleman, you desired, in lieu of your hand, to recompense your discarded lover with a full pardon.

FANNY. I am afraid the sources of information of His Majesty's Government fail when they try to investigate a woman's heart, or to account for her motives. I love Beamish with a deeper passion since I wronged him by suspicion, and I became irrevocably his from the moment I gave myself to another.

O'GRADY [*falling back in his chair*]. Oh, Fanny!

SEC. [*aside*]. Ahem! What an awkward disclosure! I am not distinguishing myself in this business.

FANNY. I have deceived these two gentlemen, who love me with all their honest hearts, and how have I requited them? I enticed Beamish to return to this country, to the foot of the scaffold, and then in a moment of anger I cast him off and bestowed my worthless self on the O'Grady.

SEC. Whereupon, the young rebel surrendered himself, and is now a Crown prisoner. Under the circumstances you allege, you must pardon me if I speak in the language your future husband would employ, if he were here and could exercise the powers I hold. The surrender of this hot-headed young man is only known to me. Let him return at once to his exile, and pledge his word never again to set foot in this country. On these conditions he is free to depart.

FANNY. He will do so; he will. He is not so cruel as I am. He will not sacrifice his life as I have done to be revenged upon his love.

SEC. [*withdrawing the curtain*]. Let him answer for himself.

FANNY. Beamish.

BEAM. I have heard your confession, and [*to* SECRETARY] I understand the motives which prompt your lordship's generous offer; for your sake, Miss Power, I accept it. I yield to one who loves you sincerely, and who deserves you far better than I do. You have wronged him; tell him so. He is generous enough to love you none the less for it.

FANNY. Can you, will you ever forgive me?

BEAM. My exile, which hitherto has been my sole regret, now becomes my only consolation; for when thus separated from you I shall feel entitled to indulge that love which absence never has enfeebled and time can never efface.

FANNY. Oh, Beamish, do not part from me in this cruel manner. Will you not give me your hand? What! not even a look? Do you think O'Grady would blame you if at such a moment you bestowed on me one poor embrace?

O'GRADY [*kicking over the screen*]. No! I'll be hanged if he would. Look you, my lord, what d'ye take me for? You would make me serve a writ of ejectment on my rival that I may enjoy his property in this lady. Dam'me, my lord, I'll fight him for it, if you like; but when you ask me to take legal means of righting myself, you forget I am an Irish gentleman, and not a process server!

FANNY. Oh, now I'm ruined entirely.

SEC. I seem to have conducted this affair to a successful eruption.

O'GRADY. What harm did I ever do you that you should contemplate making a tombstone of me to remind you of that young gentleman? Don't you know that the woman that marries one man when she loves another commits bigamy with malice prepense.

FANNY. I am a mass of iniquity. I don't know what is to be done with me.

O'GRADY. Yes you do; you know well enough you will become Mrs. Beamish Mac Coul, if his lordship will only give you the chance! and if the Government feels, as he says, under any slight obligations to me, they will requite them if they will enable you to make that gentleman as miserable as you have made me.

THE SEC. Can he find two securities for his future good behaviour?

O'GRADY. I'll be one.

FANNY. I'll be the other. I'll secure him.

BEAM. How shall I express my acknowledgments in language –

O'GRADY. Oh!!! [*striking his forehead, and then running to look for his hat and whip*]. The divil admire me – I forgot Shaun. Here we are exchanging the height of politeness while we left him beside the door of death, and it only on a jar.

FANNY. Here's your hat.

O'GRADY. It's not that I want so much as me whip.

SEC. Shall I despatch a courier to arrest proceedings? [*Rings bell and writes at table.*]

O'GRADY. Give it to me. I know what Government speed is. If any animal can get over the ground in time to save the boy [*receives paper*], I am that individual. So, my lord, pardon the disordher of my leavetaking, and the hasty expression of my acknowledgments.

Enter WINTERBOTTOM.

Now, Mr. Summerbottom, show me the door. [*The Scene closes in as* O'GRADY *goes out and* FANNY *and* BEAMISH *are taking leave of the* THE SEC.]

SCENE 2 – *Ballybetagh – moonlight.*

Enter REGAN, OINY, MORAN, LANIGAN.

REGAN. Not a sign of anybody comin' from Dublin.

OINY. And them military would'nt sthretch an hour though they knew a minute itself would save them.

Enter PATSEY.

Well, Patsey, is there a good word in your mouth?

PATSEY. Oh, murdther, boys, but it's no use; his place is tuk be the car that never comes back. He is lyin' beyant in the cell there, where ye see the light. Divil a soul is let near him, only the priest.

OINY. Isn't Arrah wid him?

PATSEY. Not a bit of her; she's keenin round the place like a bewildered sheep, and they keepin' her off wid their bagginets.

LAN. *and* REGAN. Ah! the poor creature.

OINY. That's the way of it. Divil a consolation they'll let him have, only bread and wather for tay, and the sound of the clock for company.

PATSEY. I'd give half of my life to save Shaun.

OINY. The half you're done wid, I suppose.

PATSEY. Couldn't some one get up by some manes to his windy outside there?

OINY. Ah, Baithershin, is it up the face of the cliff! D'ye think you're a fly, and can walk on nothin'?

REGAN. Not a human crature could rache that, barrin' he was a saygull.

PATSEY. Well, then, sure I know where the gunpowdher is stoored in the vaults below the Castle. Wouldn't it be easy to blow the place to smithereens?

REGAN, LAN., and MORAN. Oh that's fine! that ud astonish them.

OINY. Iss! and it would take a rise out of Shaun, be the same token.

PATSEY. Oh be japers! I never thought o' that.

OINY. Don't decave yourselves, boys. Shaun is bespoke. The spade is ready for him; and if help doesn't come from Dublin in time, he is past prayin' for. Let us go, and say a soft word to Arrah. Where will we find the poor thing?

PATSEY. I saw her just now climbin' the Castle hill there, to get on the battlements above Shaun's cell, to be as near him as she cud.

OINY. Ah then let her alone. Her sorrow is as wide and deep as the salt say. It would be only foolish for ourselves to thry and dhraw it off wid a bucket. [*Exeunt.*]

SCENE 3 – *The Prison.* SHAUN *discovered with the* PRIEST *at a table.*

SHAUN. It's thrue for your rivarence. I know, sir, that I have only a couple of hours to live, and I ought to be listenin' and mindin' what you say, and turnin' my sowl to its prospects. But my heart is too sthrong for me, and I can't hould it back from thinkin' of the poor darlin' girl I'm lavin' behind me. But go on, sir; I'll thry to – to attend, an' make meself fit to die. Iss, sir, now I'm listenin'. I won't think of her for ten whole minutes. [*The Priest draws the candle to him, and is about to read.* SHAUN *looks up.*] Didn't ye say you saw her standin' outside the prison gate, as you come in? Poor crature – outside – iss – think o' that. I think I see her hungry eyes lookin' through the bars. Bless her. Ah! I forgot, sir; I ax your pardon, sir; I won't do it agin'. Now I'm – I'm – not thinkin' of her. [*The Priest is going to recommence.*]

Enter the SERGEANT. [SHAUN *runs to him.*]

Ah! Sergeant did you see her? Where is she.

SERGT. Yes; I saw her.

SHAUN. Oh! Sergeant, dear. What a happy man you are. Ah! if I could have given you my eyes. You saw her, and where is she at all!

SERGT. She is sitting on the Watch Tower, just above here.

SHAUN. Above our heads! Is it my darlin' is up there, or may be she'd be more this way to the corner. Eh! Sergeant. Ah! tell me – tell me where she is, that I may look to the spot, and fix the lips of my heart upon it.

SERGT. If that window were not closed with iron bars you might see her; for her eyes are fixed on it. She's just over that corner of your cell.

SHAUN. High up; on the top of the Castle, where it joins the cliff. I know the place. And did you spake to her?

SERGT. I did, as well as I could. Her tears fell faster than I could wipe them away with my handkercher – [*draws it out*] – and I'd enough to do to cry halt to my own.

SHAUN [*taking his handkerchief away, as he was going to dry his eyes with it*]. Are her tears in this? [*Kisses it.*] Sergeant, when I die you'll put this round my eyes, won't ye. [*Puts it in his breast.*] And did she spake t'ye?

SERGT. Yes; she said Sergeant would you ordher a fire to be lighted in Shaun's cell.

SHAUN. A fire! Sure it is not cowld.

SERGT. So I replied; but she only repeated the same words, and I promised I would have it done.

Enter two SOLDIERS, *with fuel. They go to the open hearth, and make a fire.*

SHAUN. Ah, my poor Arrah! I know what she wants. Sure won't she see the smoke comin' from the chimbly above, and she will know it comes from where I am. Ah, your riverance, don't ax me to think of anything else for a while. In another hour will ye see me again, and thin my heart will be broken entirely, and ye can do wid me what ye will. [*Sits down.*] [*Exit the Priest.*]

SERGT. There now I will leave you for half an hour; but if you feel lonely I shall be in the guardroom. Kick at the door yonder, and the sentry will pass the word for me.

SHAUN. Ah, Sergeant, but the milk of a good nature is as new in your heart this minute as when you first dhrew a woman's kindness from your mother's breast.

SERGT [*shaking his hand*]. If I am obliged to refuse your girl admission to see you, don't blame me, Shaun. It is my duty, and the reg'lation, you know.

SHAUN. Av coorse it's your jooty: you can't help it. I would do the same if I was in your place. [*Exit* SERGT.] That's a lie; but no matther; it will be a comfort to him to think so. Ah! now I can look at her: there she is this minute. I can hear the bating of her heart. No; it's my own, I hear. Well, it's all the same thing. Oh, Arrah, jewel if you could hear me; if – [*a stone falls down the chimney.*] What's that? [*runs and picks it up.*] A stone, and a bit of paper rowld round it—'tis from her – from herself – there's writin' on it. Oh, that's why she wanted me to have a fire – ho! ho! he! God bless her! think o' that. Ah, the cunnin' of the crature [*kisses the paper*]. Oh, murdher, what am I about; may be I'd rub it out. Now let me read. What the divil's got in my eye [*he cries, and wipes his eyes with the Sergeant's handkerchief*]. There, now there, hav'nt your tears done kissin' one another yet? [*reads*] "My darlin', I am near by you. Oh, but my eyes is hungry for you, Shaun. I'm lookin' down to where you are now radin this. I'm stretchin' my arms towards ye. Oh! Shaun, God bless ye, and may he help you to find the heaven that I have lost in this world." Oh, Arrah! me heart is brakin' entirely. [*Arrah is heard above, and at a distance singing.*] Whisht – 'tis herself – she's thryin' to let me know that she is there. [*He draws the table to the window, and clings to the bars as he listens.*] She's there – she's there – she calls to me, and I'm caged. Arrah! Arrah! I can't rache ye; I can't kiss away your tears, and howld ye to my heart. Oh! the curse of Crumwell on these stones. Eh, the iron moves under my hand: the bars are loose in their sockut. Whisht – no – it's the stone itself that's split. Oh, murther, could I push it out. It's goin'; by jakers it's gone. Whisht! I hear it thundering down the wall. Splash – it's in the waves below – it is a hundred feet clane fall. [*Arrah repeats her song.*] She's callin' me agin. I'll go to her [*throws off his coat*]. The wall is ould and full of cracks; the ivy grows agin it. It is death may be, but I'll die in sthrivin to rache my girl, and chate the gallows that's waitin' for me. She's on the road to heaven, any way; and if I fall, may the kind angels that lift up my sowl, stop for one minute as they pass the place where she is waitin' for me, till I see her once agin. [*He escapes through the window.*]

The Scene changes to the exterior of the same tower; the outside of the cell is seen, and the window by which he has just escaped. Shaun is seen clinging to the face of the wall; he climbs the ivy. The tower sinks as he climbs; the guard-room windows lighted within are seen descending, and above them a rampart, and sentry on guard. – Chorus of soldiers inside guard-room. – As Shaun climbs past the window, the ivy above his head gives way, and a large mass falls carrying him with it, the leaves and matted branches cover him. His descent is checked by some roots of the ivy which hold fast. An alarm. The sentry advances and looks over rampart into the abyss; the curtains of the guard-room window are withdrawn; the Sergeant, with candle, and five soldiers put out their heads.

SENTRY. Who goes there? [*Distant alarms – a pause. Arrah's song – repeats above.*]

SERGT. It's all right. 'Tis only that girl above there – has displaced some of the masonry [*withdraws with the Soldiers; the curtains are replaced.*]

SENTRY. All's well.

Several SENTRIES *in the distance.* All's well. All's well. [*Arrah's song continues. The ivy moves, and Shaun's head appears amongst it; he emerges, and continues his ascent; he eludes* the SENTRY, *and disappears round the corner of the tower, still ascending. The Scene still descends, showing the several stages of the keep, until it sinks to the platform, in which Arrah is discovered seated and leaning over the abyss, still singing the song. Beyond, there is seen the lake and the tops of the Castle.*]

Enter FEENY.

FEENY. There she is! I thought I heern her keenin' an howlin. Arrah! jewel, listen to me. It is all over wid Shaun. Salt pether[24] wouldn't save him. And the whole country is up in arms agin you and me.

ARRAH [*rocking herself*]. What is the whole country, or the whole world to me now? Oh! ochone!

FEENY. They say that Shaun is dying to save your character, and you have let him do it. The place will be too hot to howld ye, or me aither. Let us lave it entirely, and if you'll put up wid me, I'll help ye to forget Shaun.

ARRAH. Michael Feeny, I'd rather take the man that puts my boy to death this comin' mornin', than have you, if you were rowlin in goold and dimins. Is that enough for you?

FEENY. Will nothin' bend your heart? [*Goes up to her.*]

ARRAH. Nothin! it will break first.

FEENY. What's that noise there? [*Advances, looks over.*] Whisht. Something is moovin' over the face of the wall – there below. It's a man climbin' to this – Oh! Arrah, come here – come quick. Oh your heart will break rather than bend or stoop to me! then it shall break: look down there. D'ye see that form below clingin' to the ivy, and crawlin' slowly towards this spot? does your heart tell ye who it is?

ARRAH. Ah!!

FEENY. 'Tis Shaun! Shaun, that your voice is drawin' up to your side – crawlin' through the jaws of death.

ARRAH [*falling on her knees as she looks*]. Oh, my darlin'. Oh, my dear.

FEENY. Will I give the alarm? A bullet from the senthry would send him to glory wid one plunge, or this stone would pick him off.

ARRAH. No [*clings to him*].

FEENY. I tould ye my time would come when I'd make you feel the sorro ye haped on me.

ARRAH. Let me, let me spake t'ye.

FEENY. Not a word but one. Will ye be mine? [*Seizes the stone.*]

ARRAH. Would ye murther him?

FEENY. It's no murther; but anybody's right to kill the condemned felon escaping from his sentence. Spake out, and answer.

ARRAH. Must I take ye, or see him killed under my eyes?

FEENY. Will you have me?

ARRAH. No.

FEENY. Then to the divil wid him, ye have spoke his doom [*he raises the stone,* ARRAH *flies at him; they struggle.* SHAUN'*s arm is seen over the edge of the battlement; it seizes* FEENY'*s ankle, who utters a cry, as he is dragged to the edge of the precipice, he throws up his arms, and falls over with a cry.* SHAUN *throws himself on the platform breathless. An alarm, drums, cries outside,* ARRAH *throws herself on her knees beside* SHAUN. *They embrace*].

Notes ————————————————————————————

[24] Saltpetre is a component in gunpowder.

Enter the SERGEANT, SOLDIERS *with torches,* O'GRADY, BEAMISH, FANNY, *the* MAJOR, *omnes except* OINY.

[*An Alarm without. Cries.* SHAUN *leaps up and runs; he hides himself in a corner of the ruin.* Arrah *conceals him by standing before the nook in which he has taken refuge. Drums.*]

Enter SOLDIERS, *with torches, the* MAJOR.

MAJOR. A man has fallen from the battlements into the lake below.

Enter O'GRADY *and the* SERGEANT *bearing* SHAUN's *clothes.*

O'GRADY. It was Shaun. The poor fellow was trying to escape; he had broken through the bars of his prison window. We found the cell empty, and these clothes the evidence of his desperate adventure.

Enter FANNY *and* BEAMISH.

BEAM. He may be rescued yet. The boys had seen his attempt at evasion, and they put off in their boats to assist him if he fell.

FANNY. Heaven grant they may succeed.

O'GRADY. A hundred pounds to the man that saves him! Ah! has he perished after all? It's a poor consolation for this unfortunate girl to know that here is Shaun's pardon. It has just come in time to be too late.

Enter OINY.

OINY. They've got him. I saw him pulled out of the wather lukin' like a dhrowned kitten.

O'GRADY. Is he alive?

FANNY. It is impossible he can have survived a fall from so fearful a height.

SHAUN. Spake up, ye thief, and tell me am I dead?

ALL. Shaun!

O'GRADY. Shaun himself!

BEAM. And alive?

FANNY. Oh how glad I am to see you. [*They bring him forward.*]

ALL. Hurroo!

OINY. Then who was it was fished up below there?

REGAN [*entering*]. It was Feeny.

O'GRADY. Feeny! I withdraw the reward.

MAJOR. Feeny! What induced the fellow to commit suicide?

SHAUN. I did, sir. He wanted me to go wid him, but I hadn't time, seein' I'm not half through my weddin' yet.

PATSEY [*entering*]. He's recovered; but his washing is done for the rest of his life.

O'GRADY. Hang him out to dhry.

BEAM. Shaun, can you forgive the sorrow I have caused you?

SHAUN. Bless you for it, sir, for widout it I'd never have known how Arrah loved me. Ye think, maybe now, that she was in a bad way about you awhile ago. But, oh, if you'd seen her afther me, I'd consint to be thried, convicted, and executed once a week to feel myself loved as I have been loved all this blessed day.

ARRAH. Oh, I can hardly understand my sinses – it comes on me all of a suddint. Is there nothin' agin Shaun?

BEAM. Nothing, Arrah! he is free.

ALL. Hurroo!

ARRAH. And he won't be tuk from me agin. Will he, sir?

O'GRADY. No – the law has no further call to him, nor to Beamish either; there's a free pardon to both.

ARRAH. D'ye hear that, Shaun?

SHAUN. I do, dear; but it's a mistake; it isn't a pardon I've got. Instead of death, I'm to be transported for life – and it's yourself that's to see the sintence rightly carried out, my darlin'.

ARRAH. Ah, sure, I've done nothin' but what any woman in my place would have done. It is when a man is in throuble that the breast of his girl grows bowld agin misfortune. When *he's* wake, *she's* sthrong, and if he can purtect her wid his arm, she can cover him wid her heart. It's then she is full of sinse an' cuteness – for her heart gets into her head, and makes a man of her entirely. It's to the famales of my own sex I appale in this case. Had any of ye been in my place would ye have done a ha'porth less for the man you loved than was done by ARRAH-NA-POGUE.

Lady Jane Wilde (1821–1896)

Lady Jane Wilde, also known because of her pseudonym in *The Nation* as "Speranza," was born in Wexford as Jane Frances Agnes Elgee to a family from the professional classes. When *The Nation* began publishing, Wilde became a prominent contributor; one piece she wrote during the politically tense summer of 1848 called for an uprising, and contributed to the newspaper being shut down briefly. Many of her poetic contributions were more plaintive, lamenting in particular the ravages of the Famine. In 1851, she married William Wilde, a ground-breaking eye surgeon and leading scholar on ancient Ireland (see Samuel Ferguson's elegy, "Dear Wilde," above), who published on both medical and historical subjects and was knighted for his medical work in 1864. The Wildes had three children, including author Oscar Wilde, and played a significant role in the Dublin literary scene, hosting salons as well as publishing widely. Jane Wilde left Dublin after her husband's death, but continued her close connections to Dublin literary circles, including such notables of the next generation as W. B. Yeats and Katharine Tynan.

In addition to her important contributions to *The Nation* and the *Dublin University Magazine*, Wilde published a number of volumes, beginning with her translation, *Sidonia the Sorceress* (1849), a work influential on the British Pre-Raphaelites[1] and her son Oscar, as well as a long poem on the Italian nationalist movement, *Ugo Bassi: A Tale of the Italian Revolution* (1857). She collected her shorter verse, much of it from *The Nation*, in *Poems by Speranza* (1864). She later turned to non-fiction work that continued her and her husband's shared interest in early Ireland, publishing *Ancient Legends, Mystic Charms, and Superstitions of Ireland* (1887) and *Ancient Cures, Charms, and Usages of Ireland: Contributions to Irish Lore* (1890). She also wrote as a critic and social commentator, publishing essays later collected

Notes

[1] The Pre-Raphaelite Brotherhood founded in the late 1840s by a group of English artists, including Dante Gabriel Rossetti.

in *Notes on Men, Women, and Books* (1891) and *Social Studies* (1893).

If MacCarthy is Moore's heir, Wilde is arguably Morgan's: both interweaved feminism and nationalism in their writing, developed a public persona that attained near-iconic status – "Speranza" (Wilde) and "Glorvina" (Morgan) – were coy about their ages and hosted vibrant literary salons, and focused the latter part of their careers on politically instructive non-fiction. Famously, when Oscar Wilde first toured the United States he was welcomed by Irish Americans as the son of Speranza. While largely discussed until recently only as a literary influence on her son, the power of her famine verse, particularly "The Famine Year," and the interest of her non-fiction writing remain. Her substantial

essay on Thomas Moore, here included in full, not only offers some insight on Moore's late-nineteenth-century reputation but also a sophisticated reading of *Lalla Rookh*'s "The Fire-Worshippers" as a national allegory, anticipating critical analyses of Moore's work a century later.

Further reading

Horan, Patrick M., *The Importance of Being Paradoxical: Maternal Presence in the Works of Oscar Wilde*. London: Associated University Presses, 1997.

Howes, Marjorie, "Tears and Blood: Lady Wilde and the Emergence of Irish Cultural Nationalism," *Journal* × 1 (1997): 203–23.

Morash, Christopher, *Writing the Irish Famine*. Oxford: Clarendon Press, 1995.

The Famine Year

From Poems (1864)

I

Weary men, what reap ye? – Golden corn for the stranger.
What sow ye? – Human corses that wait for the avenger.
Fainting forms, hunger-stricken, what see you in the offing?
Stately ships to bear our food away, amid the stranger's scoffing.
There's a proud array of soldiers – what do they round your door?   5
They guard our masters' granaries from the thin hands of the poor.
Pale mothers, wherefore weeping? – Would to God that we were dead –
Our children swoon before us, and we cannot give them bread.

II

Little children, tears are strange upon your infant faces,
God meant you but to smile within your mother's soft embraces.   10
Oh! we know not what is smiling, and we know not what is dying;
But we're hungry, very hungry, and we cannot stop our crying.
And some of us grow cold and white – we know not what it means;
But, as they lie beside us, we tremble in our dreams.
There's a gaunt crowd on the highway – are ye come to pray to man,   15
With hollow eyes that cannot weep, and for words your faces wan?

III

No; the blood is dead within our veins – we care not now for life;
Let us die hid in the ditches, far from children and from wife;
We cannot stay and listen to their raving, famished cries –
Bread! Bread! Bread! and none to still their agonies.   20

We left our infants playing with their dead mother's hand:
We left our maidens maddened by the fever's scorching brand:
Better, maiden, thou were strangled in thy own dark-twisted tresses –
Better, infant, thou wert smothered in thy mother's first caresses.

IV

We are fainting in our misery, but God will hear our groan;   25
Yet, if fellow-men desert us, will He hearken from His Throne?
Accursed are we in our own land, yet toil we still and toil;
But the stranger reaps our harvest – the alien owns our soil.
O Christ! how have we sinned, that on our native plains
We perish houseless, naked, starved, with branded brow, like Cain's?[1]   30
Dying, dying wearily, with a torture sure and slow –
Dying, as a dog would die, by the wayside as we go.

V

One by one they're falling round us, their pale faces to the sky;
We've no strength left to dig them graves – there let them lie.
The wild bird, if he's stricken, is mourned by the others,   35
But we – we die in Christian land – we die amid our brothers,
In the land which God has given, like a wild beast in his cave,
Without a tear, a prayer, a shroud, a coffin, or a grave.
Ha! but think ye the contortions on each livid face ye see,
Will not be read on judgment-day by eyes of Deity?   40

VI

We are wretches, famished, scorned, human tools to build your pride,
But God will yet take vengeance for the souls for whom Christ died.
Now is your hour of pleasure – bask ye in the world's caress;
But our whitening bones against ye will arise as witnesses,
From the cabins and the ditches, in their charred, uncoffin'd masses,   45
For the Angel of the Trumpet[2] will know them as he passes.
A ghastly, spectral army, before the great God we'll stand,
And arraign ye as our murderers, the spoilers of our land.

A Supplication

From Poems (1864)

De profundis clamavi ad te domine.[1]

By our looks of mute despair,
By the sighs that rend the air,
From lips too faint to utter prayer,
        Kyrie Eleison.[2]

Notes ───────────────────────────────────

THE FAMINE YEAR
[1] See Genesis 4 (Bible).
[2] In Revelation (Bible), the sixth angel holds the trumpet and releases the four angels who destroy one-third of humanity.

A SUPPLICATION
[1] From Psalm 129 in the Latin Bible, translated in the Authorized Version of King James as Psalm 130: "Out of the depths have I cried unto thee, O Lord."
[2] Lord have mercy.

By the last groans of our dying,
Echoed by the cold wind's sighing,
On the wayside as they're lying,
      Kyrie Eleison.   5

By our fever-stricken bands,
Lifting up their wasted hands,
For bread throughout the far-off lands,
      Kyrie Eleison.

Miserable outcasts we,   10
Pariahs of humanity,
Shunned by all where'er we flee,
      Kyrie Eleison.

For our dead no bell is ringing,
Round their forms no shroud is clinging,
Save the rank grass newly springing,   15
      Kyrie Eleison.

Golden harvests we are reaping,
With golden grain our barns heaping,
But for us our bread is weeping,
      Kyrie Eleison.

Death-devoted in our home,
Sad we cross the salt sea's foam,   20
But death we bring where'er we roam,
      Kyrie Eleison.[3]

Whereso'er our steps are led,
They can track us by our dead,
Lying on their cold earth bed,
      Kyrie Eleison.

We have sinned – in vain each warning –   25
Brother lived his brother scorning,
Now in ashes see us mourning,
      Kyrie Eleison.

Heeding not our country's state,
Trodden down and desolate,
While we strove in senseless hate,   30
      Kyrie Eleison.

We have sinned but holier zeal
May we Christian patriots feel,
Oh! for our dear country's weal,
      Kyrie Eleison.

Notes

[3] Typhus compounded the suffering of those fleeing the Famine. Those who survived the transatlantic voyage in crowded, unsanitary conditions were often quarantined on arriving in North America in conditions that were little better. Thousands died in quarantine at Grosse-Île in Canada in 1847 alone.

Let us lift our streaming eyes
To God's throne above the skies,   35
He will hear our anguish cries,
    Kyrie Eleison.

Kneel beside me, oh! my brother,
Let us pray each with the other,
For Ireland, our mourning mother,
    Kyrie Eleison.

Ruins

From Poems (1864)

I

Shall we tread the dust of ages,
 Musing, dreamlike, on the past,
Seeking on the broad earth's pages
 For the shadows Time hath cast;
Waking up some ancient story,   5
 From each prostrate shrine or hall,
Old traditions of a glory
 Earth may never more recall?

II

Poet thoughts of sadness breathing,
 For the temples overthrown;   10
Where no incense now is wreathing,
 And the gods are turned to stone.
Wandering by the graves of heroes,
 Shrouded deep in classic gloom,
Or the tombs where Egypt's Pharaohs   15
 Wait the trumpet and the doom.

III

By the city, desert-hidden,[1]
 Which Judea's mighty king
Made the Genii, at his bidding,
 Raise by magic of his ring;   20
By the Lake Asphaltian wander,
 While the crimson sunset glow
Flings its radiance, as we ponder
 On the buried towns below.

Notes

RUINS
[1] Palmyra, or Tadmor (author). Ancient ruins in what is
now Syria.

IV

By the Cromleach,[2] sloping downward,   25
   Where the Druid's victim bled;
By those Towers, pointing sunward,
   Hieroglyphics none have read:
In their mystic symbols seeking,
   Of past creeds and rites o'erthrown,   30
If the truths they shrined are speaking
   Yet in Litanies of Stone.

V

By the Temple of the Muses,
   Where the climbers of the mount
Learned the soul's diviner uses   35
   From the Heliconian fount.[3]
By the banks of dark Illysus,
   Where the Parae[4] walked of old,
In their crowns of white narcissus,
   And their garments starred with gold.   40

VI

By the tomb of queenly Isis,
   Where her fallen prophets wail,
Yet no hand has dared the crisis
   Of the lifting of the vail.
By the altar which the Grecian   45
   Raised to God without a name;
By the stately shrine Ephesian,
   Erostratus burned for fame.[5]

VII

By the Libyan shrine of Ammon,
   Where the sands are trod with care,   50
Lest we, bending to examine,
   Start the lion from his lair.
Shall we tread the halls Assyrian,
   Where the Arab tents are set;
Seek the glory of the Tyrian,   55
   Where the fisher spreads his net?

VIII

Shall we seek the "Mene, mene,"
   Wrote by God upon the wall,[6]

Notes ——————————————————————————————

[2] prehistoric stone arch

[3] Helicon, a mountain, was sacred to the muses and had on its summit the Hippocrene fountain, associated with inspiration.

[4] The Fates.

[5] Erostratus attempted to achieve fame by burning a temple of Diana.

[6] See Daniel 5 (Bible).

While the proud son of Mandane[7]
    Strode across the fated hall?   60
Shall we mourn the Loxian's lyre,
    Or the Pythian priestess mute?
Shall we seek the Delphic fire,
    Though we've lost Apollo's lute?[8]

IX

Ah! the world has sadder ruins   65
    Than these wrecks of things sublime;
For the touch of man's misdoings
    Leaves more blighted tracks than Time.
Ancient lore gives no examples
    Of the ruins here we find –   70
Prostrate souls for fallen temples,
    Mighty ruins of the mind.

X

We had hopes that rose as proudly
    As each sculptured marble shrine;
And our prophets spake as loudly   75
    As their oracles divine.
Grand resolves of giant daring,
    Such as Titans breathed of old;
Brilliant aims their front uprearing,
    Like a temple roofed with gold.   80

XI

Souls of fire, like columns pointing,
    Flamelike, upward to the skies;
Glorious brows, which God's anointing
    Consecrated altar-wise.
Stainless hearts, like temples olden,   85
    None but priest hath ever trod;
Hands as pure as were the golden
    Staves which bore the ark of God.[9]

XII

Oh! they built up radiant visions,
    Like an iris after rain;   90
How all paradise traditions
    Might be made to live again.
Of Humanity's sad story,
    How their hand should turn the page,

Notes ──

[7] Mother of Cyrus the Great, a Persian ruler.
[8] The Pythian priestess delivered oracles at Apollo's temple at Delphi.

[9] The Ark of the Covenant held in Solomon's Temple (Bible).

And the ancient primal glory,   95
    Fling upon this latter age.

XIII

How with Godlike aspirations,
    Up the souls of men would climb,
Till the fallen, enslavéd nations
    Trod in rhythmic march sublime;   100
Reaching heights the people knew not,
    Till their Prophet Leaders led –
Bathed in light that mortals view not,
    While the spirit life lies dead.

XIV

How the pallid sons of labour,   105
    They should toil, and toil to raise,
Till a glory, like to Tabor,[10]
    Once again should meet earth's gaze.
How the poor, no longer keeping
    Count of life alone by groans,   110
With the strong cry of their weeping,
    Start the angels on their thrones.

XV

Ah! that vision's bright ideal,
    Must it fade and perish thus?
Must its fall alone be real?   115
    Are its ruins trod by us?
Ah! they dreamed an Eldorado,[11]
    Given not to mortal sight;
Yet the souls that walk in shadow,
    Still bend forward to its light.   120

XVI

Earnest dreamers, sooth we blame not
    If ye failed to reach the goal –
If the glorious real came not
    At the strong prayer of each soul.
By the path ye've trod to duty,   125
    Blessings yet to man may flow,
Though the proud and stately beauty
    Of your structure lieth low.

Notes

[10] Mountain mentioned in the Old Testament (Bible).

[11] Legendary city of gold in South America, imagined in the wake of the Spanish conquest.

XVII

Low as that which Salem mourneth,
  On Moriah's holy hill;   130
While the heathen proudly scorneth,
  Yet the wrecks are glorious still:
Like the seven columns frowning,
  On the desert city down;[12]
Or the seven cedars crowning   135
  Lofty Lebanon.

XVIII

Poet wanderer, hast thou bent thee
  O'er such ruins of the soul?
Pray to God that some Nepenthe[13]
  May efface that hour of dole.   140
We may lift the shrine and column,
  From the dust which Time hath cast;
Choral chants may mingle solemn,
  Once again where silence passed;

XIX

But the stately, radiant palace,   145
  We had built up in our dreams,
With Hope's rainbow-woven trellis,
  And Truth's glorious sunrise beams;
Our aims of towering stature,
  Our aspirations vain,   150
And our prostrate human nature –
  Who will raise them up again?

La Via Dolorosa

From Poems (1864)

I wander here, I wander there,
  Through the desert of life, all wearily;
No joy on earth for the pilgrim soul –
  On, on for ever, drearily;
    O'er the mountain height,   5
    In the tempest night,
    Through the mist and gloom,
    We press on to the tomb
While the death-like pall of a midnight sky
Hangs over past and futurity.   10

And the echo of wandering feet I hear,
And human voices and hearts are near;

Notes

[12] Likely to be Palmyra.

[13] Drink that causes forgetfulness of grief.

But lonely, lonely each one goeth
On his dark path, and little knoweth
Of love, kind words, or sympathy. 15
Oh! fain would I lay me down and die;
For the upward glance of a tearful eye,
Is all I have known of humanity.

Yet must I on, tho' darker and drearer
    And lonelier ever the pathway seems, 20
And the spectral shadow of death draws nearer,
    And rare and faint are the sun-light gleams;
An unseen power impelleth us on –
No pause, no rest for the weary one,
Till we reach the shores of that fathomless sea 25
Where Time poureth down to Eternity.

The Midnight Ride: A Peasant's Tale

From Ancient Legends, Mystic Charms, and Superstitions of Ireland (1887)

One evening a man called Shawn Ruadh was out looking for a red cow that had strayed away, when he heard voices round him, and one said "Get me a horse," and another cried "Get me a horse."

"And get me a horse, too," said Shawn, "since they seem so plenty, for I'd like a ride along with you," and with that he found himself on the instant mounted on a fine grey horse beside another man who rode a black horse. And they rode away and away till they came to a great city.

"Now, do you know where you are?" said the black horseman. "You are in London, and whatever you want you can have."

"Thank you kindly, my friend," said the other, "so, with your leave, I'll just have a good suit of clothes, for I'm much in want of that same. Can I have them?"

"By all means," said the black horseman; "there, go into that merchant's shop and ask for what you like, and if he refuses just throw the stone I give you on the floor and the whole place will seem on fire. But don't be frightened; only wait your good luck."

So Shawn went into the biggest shop there, and he spoke to the merchant quite stiff and proud.

"Show me the best suit of clothes you have," said he. "Never mind the price, that's of no consequence, only be very particular as to the fit."

But the shopman laughed aloud.

"We don't make clothes for beggars like you," he said. "Be off out of this."

Then Shawn threw down the stone on the floor, and immediately the whole place seemed on fire, and the merchant ran out himself and all the shopmen after him to get pails of water, and Shawn laughed when he saw them all drenched.

"Now what will you give me," said he, "if I put out the fire for you?"

"You shall have the price of the best suit of clothes in the shop," answered the merchant, "all paid down in gold; only help me to put out the fire."

So Shawn stooped down and picked up the stone, and put it quietly into his pocket, and instantly all the flames disappeared: and the merchant was so grateful that he paid him down all the gold for the clothes and more. And Shawn bid him good night, and mounted the grey steed again quite happy in himself.

"Now," said the black horseman, "is there anything else you desire? for it is near ten o'clock, and we must be back by midnight; so just say what you would like to do."

"Well," said Shawn Ruadh, "I would like of all things to see the Pope of Rome, for two of our priests are disputing as to who is to get the parish, and I want Father M'Grath to have it, for I have a great opinion of him, and if I ask his Holiness he'll settle it all in no time and for ever."

"Come then," said the black horseman; "it is a long way to Rome, certainly, but I think we'll manage it in the two hours, and be back before twelve o'clock."

So away they rode like the wind, and in no time Shawn found himself before the great palace of the Pope; and all the grand servants with gold sticks in their hand stared at him, and asked him what he wanted.

"Just go in," said he, "and tell his Holiness that Shawn Ruadh, all the way from Ireland, is here and wants to see him very particularly."

But the servants laughed, and struck him with their gold sticks and hunted him away from the gate. Now the Pope hearing the rout looked out of the windows, and seeing Shawn Ruadh he came down and asked him what he wanted.

"Just this, your Holiness," answered Shawn, "I want a letter on behalf of Father M'Grath bidding the Bishop give him the parish, and I'll wait till your Holiness writes it; and meanwhile let me have a little supper, for it's hungry I am after my long ride."

Then the Pope laughed, and told the servants to drive the fellow away, for he was evidently out of his wits.

So Shawn grew angry, and flung down the stone on the floor, and instantly all the palace seemed on fire, and the Pope ordered the grand servants to go for water; and they had to run about like mad getting pails and jugs of water, whatever they could lay hands on; and all their fine clothes were spoiled, and the beautiful gold sticks were flung away in their fright, while they took the jugs and splashed and dashed the water over each other.

Now it was Shawn's turn to laugh till his sides ached, but his Holiness looked very grave.

"Well," said Shawn, "if I put out the fire what will you do for me? Will you write that letter?"

"Ay, I will," said the Pope, "and you shall have your supper also; only help us to put out the fire, my fine fellow."

So Shawn quietly put the stone back in his pocket, and instantly all the flames disappeared.

"Now," said the Pope, "you shall have supper of the best in the palace; and I'll write a letter to the Bishop ordering him to give Father M'Grath the parish. And here, besides, is a purse of gold for yourself, and take it with my blessing."

Then he ordered all the grand servants to get supper for the excellent young man from Ireland, and to make him comfortable. So Shawn was mightily pleased, and ate and drank like a prince. Then he mounted his grey steed again, and just as midnight struck he found himself at his own door, but all alone; for the grey steed and the black horseman had both vanished. But there stood his wife crying her eyes out and in great trouble.

"Oh Shawn, Agra! I thought you were dead, or that evil had fallen on you."

"Not a bit of it," said Shawn, "I've been supping with the Pope of Rome, and look here at all the gold I've brought home for you, my darlint."

And he put his hand in his pocket to get the purse; but lo! there was nothing there except a rough, grey stone. And from that hour to this his wife believes that he dreamed the whole story as he lay under the hay-rick, on his way home from a carouse with the boys.

However, Father M'Grath got the parish, and Shawn took good care to tell him how he had spoken up boldly for him to the Pope of Rome, and made his Holiness write the letter to the Bishop about him. And Father M'Grath was a nice gentleman, and he smiled and told Shawn he thanked him kindly for his good word.

The Bards

From Ancient Legends, Mystic Charms, and Superstitions of Ireland (1887)

The Irish kings in ancient times kept up splendid hospitality at their respective courts, and never sat down to an entertainment, it was said, without a hundred nobles at least being present. Next in rank and superb living to the royal race came the learned men, the ollamhs and poets; they were placed next the king, and above the nobles at the festivals, and very gorgeous was the appearance of the Ard-Filé on these occasions, in his white robes clasped with golden brooches, and a circlet of gold upon his head; while by his side lay the golden harp, which he seized when the poetic frenzy came upon him, and swept the chords to songs of love, or in praise of immortal heroes. The queen alone had the privilege to ask the poet to recite at the royal banquets, and while he declaimed, no man dared to interrupt him by a single word.

A train of fifty minor bards always attended the chief poet, and they were all entertained free of cost wherever they visited, throughout Ireland, while the Ard-Filé was borne on men's shoulders to the palace of the king, and there presented with a rich robe, a chain, and a girdle of gold. Of one bard, it is recorded that the king gave him, in addition, his horse and armour, fifty rings to his hand, one thousand ounces of pure gold, and his chess-board.

The game of chess is frequently referred to in the old bardic tales; and chess seems to have been a favourite pastime with the Irish from the most remote antiquity. The pieces must have been of great size, for it is narrated that the great Cuchullen killed a messenger who had told him a lie, by merely flinging a chessman at him, which pierced his brain. The royal chess-board was very costly and richly decorated. One is described in a manuscript of the twelfth century: "It was a board of silver and pure gold, and every angle was illuminated with precious stones. And there was a man-bag of woven brass wire." But the ancestors of the same king had in their hall a chess-board with the pieces formed of the *bones of their hereditary enemies*.

The dress of the bards added to their splendour, for the Brehon laws enacted that the value of the robes of the chief poet should be five milch cows, and that of the poetess three cows; the queen's robes being of the value of seven cows, including a diadem and golden veil, and a robe of scarlet silk, embroidered in divers colours. The scions of the royal house had also the right to seven colours in their mantle; while the poet was allowed six, and the poetess five – the number of colours being a sign of dignity and rank.

Learning was always highly esteemed in Ireland, and in ancient Erin the *literati* ranked next to the kings.

The great and wise *Ollamh-Fodla*, king of Ireland in Druidic times, built and endowed a college at Tara, near the royal palace, which was called *Mur-Ollamh*, "the Wall of the Learned." All the arts and sciences were represented there by eminent professors, the great ollaves of music, history, poetry, and oratory; and they lived and feasted together, and formed the great Bardic Association, ruled over by their own president, styled the Ard-Filé, or chief poet of Ireland, from *Filidecht* (philosophy or the highest wisdom); for the poets, above all men, were required to be pure and free from all sin that could be a reproach to learning. From them was demanded –

> "Purity of hand,
> Purity of mouth,
> Purity of learning,
> Purity of marriage;"

and any ollamh that did not preserve these four purities, lost half his income and his dignity, the poet being esteemed not only the highest of all men for his learning and intellect, but also as being the true revealer of the supreme wisdom.

Music was sedulously taught and cultivated at the college of the ollamhs; for all the ancient life of Ireland moved to music.

The Brehons seated on a hill intoned the laws to the listening people; the Senachies chanted the genealogies of the kings; and the Poets recited the deeds of the heroes, or sang to their gold harps those exquisite airs that still enchant the world, and which have been wafted down along the centuries, an echo, according to tradition, of the soft, pathetic, fairy music, that haunted the hills and glens of ancient Ireland.

The chief poet was required to know by heart four hundred poems, and the minor bards two hundred. And they were bound to recite any poem called for by the kings at the festivals. On one occasion a recitation was demanded of the legend of the *Taine-bo-Cualgnia*, or The Great Cattle Raid, of which Maeve, queen of Connaught, was the heroine, but none of the bards knew it. This was felt to be a great disgrace, and Seanchan and the bards set forth to traverse Ireland in search of the story of the Taine, under *Geasa*, or a solemn oath, not to sleep twice in the same place till it was found.

At length it was revealed to them that only the dead Fergus-Roy knew the poem, and forthwith they proceeded to his grave, and fasted and prayed for three days, while they invoked him to appear. And on their invocation Fergus-Roy uprose in awful majesty, and stood in his grave clothes before them, and recited the Taine from beginning to end, to the circle of listening bards. Then, having finished, he descended again into the grave, and the earth closed over him.

During this expedition, Guaire the Generous took charge of all the wives and the poetesses of the Bardic Association, so as they should not trouble the bards while on their wanderings in search of the ballad of the Taine. Yet they do not seem to have been great feeders, these learned ladies; for it is related of one of them, Brigit the poetess, that although she ate only one hen's egg at a meal, yet she was called "Brigit of the great appetite."

It was on their return from the search for the Taine that the bards decreed a vote of thanks to Guaire the king.

In order to keep up the dignity of the great bardic clan, an income was paid by the State to each of the professors and poets according to his eminence; that of the chief poet being estimated by antiquarians at about five thousand a year of our money, for the lofty and learned Bardic Association disdained commerce and toil. The Fileas lived only on inspiration and the hospitality of their royal and noble patrons, which they amply repaid by laudatory odes and sonnets. But, if due homage were denied them, they denounced the ungenerous and niggard defaulter in the most scathing and bitter satires. Of one chief it is recorded that he absolutely went mad and died in consequence of the malignant poems that were made on him by a clever satirical bard.

At last the Brehons found it necessary to take cognizance of this cruel and terrible implement of social torture, and enactments were framed against it, with strict regulations regarding the quality and justice of the satires poured out by the poets on those who had the courage to resist their exactions and resent their insolence.

Finally, however, the ollamhs, poets, and poetesses became so intolerable, that the reigning king of Ireland about the seventh century made a great effort to extirpate the whole bardic race, but failed; they were too strong for him, though he succeeded in, at least, materially abridging their privileges, lessening their revenues, and reducing their numbers; and though they still continued to exist as the Bardic Association, yet they never afterwards regained the power and dignity which they once held in the land, before their pride and insolent contempt of all classes who were not numbered amongst the ollamhs and fileas, had aroused such violent animosity. The Brehon laws also decreed, as to the distraint of a poet, that his horsewhip be taken from him, "as a warning that he is not to make use of it until he renders justice." Perhaps by the horsewhip was meant the wand or staff which the poets carried, made of wood, on which it is conjectured they may have inscribed their verses in the Ogham character.

The Brehons seem to have made the most minute regulations as to the life of the people, even concerning the domestic cats. In the *Senchas Mor* (The Great Antiquity), it is enacted that the cat is exempt from liability for eating the food which he finds in the kitchen, "owing to negligence in taking care of it." But if it were taken from the security of a vessel, then the cat is in fault, and he may safely be killed. The cat, also, is exempt from liability for injuring an idler in catching mice while mousing; but *half-fines* are due from him for the profitable worker he may injure, and the excitement of his mousing takes the other half. For the distraint of a dog, a stick was placed over his trough, in order that he be not fed. And there was a distress of two days for a black and white cat if descended from the great champion, which was taken from the ship of Breasal Breac, in which were white-breasted black cats; the same for the lapdog of a queen.

From St. Patrick

From Ancient Legends, Mystic Charms, and Superstitions of Ireland (1887)

Many saints in old time used to come and take up their abode on these wild desolate islands for the rest and sanctity of solitude, and innumerable evidences of their presence still remain in the ancient ruins of the so-called cells or churches built in the rudest form, but always placed in a picturesque locality beside a well, which ever since has been held sacred, and no woman is allowed to wash her feet in the water.

In one of these islands is a stone bed called "The Bed of the Holy Ghost," and many people go from the mainland to lie a night in this bed, though the sea is always rough and dangerous, believing that it heals all diseases, and it brings good luck to all, and to women the blessing of children.

If the lark sings on St. Bridget's Day it is a good omen, and a sign of fine weather. And whoever hears it the first thing in the morning will have good luck in all he does for that whole day. St. Bridget was granted by the Lord to have every second Sunday fine so that she might preach to the converts that came to her.

Then St. Patrick greatly desired that his day should also be fine so that the people might gather in remembrance of him, and this also was granted. So from that time forth the Saints' Day, the 17th of March, is always fine, for so it was decreed from the ancient times when he was upon earth.

On St. Patrick's Day it is the usage in the islands to affix large crosses made of straw and flowers on the door-posts, and a black cock is sacrificed in honour of the saint, though no one can tell why it is considered necessary that blood should be spilt, except that the idea of sacrifice is found in all religions and rituals of worship. At first the object most loved or most prized was sacrificed – a child, or a costly jewel. Then the human sacrifice began to be replaced by the offering of an animal, who was made the medium of expiation. And the god was satisfied so that blood was spilled to purify from sin.

It is remarkable that relics of this ancient ritual of sacrifice can still be found even in the enlightened households of this advanced nineteenth century. An ox is still slaughtered at Christmas, though Baal is forgotten; and a lamb is sacrificed at Easter, as the Druids offered the firstlings of the flock to the Sun-god; while a goose is slain on St. Michael's Day as a burnt-offering to the saint.

The Well of the Book

When St. Patrick was one time amongst the Pagan Irish they grew very fierce and seemed eager to kill him. Then, his life being in great danger, he kneeled down before them and prayed to God for help and for the conversion of their souls. And the fervour of the prayer was so great that as the saint rose up the mark of his knees was left deep on the stone, and when the people saw the miracle they believed.

Now when he came to the next village the people said if he performed some wonder for them they also would believe and pray to his God. So St. Patrick drew a great circle on the ground and bade them stand outside it; and then he prayed, and lo! the water rushed up from the earth, and a well pure and bright as crystal filled the circle. And the people believed and were baptized.

The well can be seen to this day, and is called *Tober-na-Lauer* (The Well of the Book), because St. Patrick placed his own prayer-book in the centre of the circle before the water rose.

St. Patrick and the Serpent

There is a lake in one of the Galtee mountains where there is a great serpent chained to a rock, and he may be heard constantly crying out, "O Patrick, is the *Luan*, or Monday, long from us?" For when St. Patrick cast this serpent in the lake he bade him be chained to the rock till *La-an-Luan* (The Day of Judgment). But the serpent mistook the word, and thought the saint meant *Luan*, Monday.

So he still expects to be freed from one Monday to another, and the clanking of chains on that day is awful to hear as he strives to break them and get free.

In another lake there is a huge winged creature, it is said, which escaped the power of St. Patrick, and when he gambols in the water such storms arise that no boat can withstand the tumult of the waves.

St. Bridget

From Ancient Legends, Mystic Charms, and Superstitions of Ireland (1887)

At one time a certain leper came to St. Bridget to beg a cow from her.

"Which would you prefer?" said the holy Bridget, "to be healed of your disease or to have the cow?"

"I would be healed," he answered.

Then she touched him, and he became whole and went away rejoicing.

After this Bridget's fame spread all over Ireland; and a man of the Britons, and his son, came to be healed; but she was at Mass, and sent to them to wait till Mass was over.

Now the Britons are a hasty people, and the man said, "You healed your own people yesterday and you shall heal us to-day."

Then Bridget came forth and prayed over them, and they were healed.

Another time, two lepers came to beg, and Bridget said, "I have but this one cow – take it between you and go in peace."

But one leper was proud, and made answer: "I shall divide my goods with no man. Give me the cow and I shall go."

And she gave it to him.

Then the other leper said, "Give me your prayers, holy Bridget, I ask no more."

And she gave him her blessing. And as he turned to depart a man came in, and offered a cow as a present to the holy woman.

"Now the Lord has blessed you," she said to the humble leper. "Take this cow and depart to your home."

So the man drove the cow before him, and presently came up with the proud leper just at the ford of the river. "Cross you first," said the proud leper, "there is not room for two," and the humble leper crossed in safety with his cow; but when the other entered the ford, the river rose, and he and his cow were carried away and drowned, for the blessing of St. Bridget was not on him.

Another time, two lepers came to be healed, and Bridget ordered one of them to wash the other; which he did, and the man was healed.

"Now," she said, "do to your comrade as he has done to you; wash him with water that he may be made clean of his leprosy."

"Oh, veiled woman," he answered, "why should I, that am clean now in body and limb, touch this filthy leper of the blue-grey skin? Ask me not to do this thing."

Then Bridget took water and washed the leper herself. Immediately the other who had been healed, cried out, "A fire is raging under my skin;" and the disease came again on him worse than ever. Thus was he punished for his pride.

The lark is sacred to St. Bridget because its song woke her every morning to prayers, when she had service for the women who were her converts.

The influence of St. Bridget remains a permanent power in Ireland even to this day, and she is much feared by the enemy of souls and the ill-doer. When Earl Strongbow was dying, he affirmed that he saw St. Bridget approaching his bed, and she struck him on the foot, and the wound she gave him mortified, and of this he died. This happened six hundred years after Bridget's death.

St. Bridget, throughout her long life, held the highest position and dignity in the Irish Church. She erected a temple in Kildare, ordained bishops, and was head and chief of all the sacred virgins.

She also held equal rank with the archbishop; if he had an episcopal chair (*cathedra episcopalis*), so St. Bridget had a virginal chair (*cathedra puellaris*), and was pre-eminent above all the abbesses of Ireland, or of the Scots, for sanctity and power.

St. Kevin

From Ancient Legends, Mystic Charms, and Superstitions of Ireland (1887)

It is related of St. Kevin that after he had been seven years at Glendalough, a weariness of life came over him, and a longing to hear the voice of man once more. Then Satan came to him in the form of an angel, bright and beautiful, and persuaded him that he should quit the valley and travel abroad and see the world, while yet his youth was left to him. And St. Kevin was near yielding to the words of the tempter, when fortunately St. Munna came by that way, and he at once saw through the trick, and showed to St. Kevin that the advice was from the devil, and not from God. And St. Kevin promised St. Munna that he would never leave the valley till his death. However, God, not wishing that the saint should eat his heart away in idleness, bade him build a monastery on the east of the lake, the place where the resurrection was to be; and he sent his angel to show him the exact spot.

But St. Kevin, when he saw the place so wild and rude, could not help telling the friendly angel that it was very rugged and difficult to build on; and the stones were heavy and hard to be moved. Then the angel, to prevent any difficulty in the building, rendered the stones light and easy to move, and so the work of building went on to the glory of God; and St. Kevin rejoiced in the task set before him.

And the monk who tells the story adds, that from that day in all the place which the angel appointed for the building, there is now no stone that cannot be lightly moved and easily worked all through the valley of Glendalough.

Thomas Moore

From Notes on Men, Women, and Books (1891)

Strong nations fight, oppressed nations sing; and thus, not with armies and fleets, but with the passionate storm of lyric words have the Irish people kept up for centuries their ceaseless war against alien rule. For words have a mystic power over men, and with the word Liberty on their lips, and the ideal of Nationhood in their hearts, the Irish have been preserved by their poets and orators from degenerating into the coarse vulgarisms of music and song so popular amongst a people who have no aspirations, no ideal beyond the greed of gain and the plenitude of all the sensuous enjoyments of life.

It is Ruskin[1] who says "all that is best in a nation comes from the spirit of revolt," and it is this spirit, transmitted through successive generations, that has kept Ireland from much that is debasing and degrading in the ordinary life and amusements of more prosperous nations. All honour, then, to the chief of Irish poets, "the sweetest lyrist of her saddest wrong," as Shelley has so beautifully designated Moore.[2] Love of country was the source of all his highest utterances, the divine fire that kindled his genius, and has given enduring vitality to his words; for the Irish melodies will live for ever in the heart of the Irish race, though everything else he wrote must be forgotten. Through Moore's lyrics, set to the pathetic Irish music, the wrongs of Ireland were first made known to Europe, and the sympathy excited by them for a people so gifted and so unfortunate materially helped to break the terrible and insulting bondage of the penal laws.

Moore was born in 1780, the same year as Béranger,[3] the national poet of France, and both sprang from the people. But while Béranger's genius was nourished by the revolution that established the rights of man, the young Irish poet found himself a degraded serf in his own land, the crushed and helpless victim of a foreign tyranny.

Notes

THOMAS MOORE
[1] John Ruskin (1819–1900), English author.
[2] The phrase is from *Adonais* (1821) by English poet Percy Bysshe Shelley (1792–1822).

[3] Pierre Jean de Béranger (1780–1857).

All progress, all distinctions, all means of education were forbidden to Catholics. They were not allowed the common rights of citizens, and were even denied the exercise of the franchise. It was not till 1793, when Moore was old enough to be conscious of the degradation of his race and creed, that Catholics were allowed to enter Trinity College, though all university honours and emoluments were still withheld from them. Moore was one of the first of the young helots who accepted the privilege of entering the university, and in time he stood for a scholarship, to which he was entitled by his answering, but was refused on account of his religion.

What wonder if he felt bitterly, and expressed openly his detestation of English rule? The college authorities grew alarmed; a spirit of nationality, which in Ireland is supposed to mean rebellion, was suspected amongst the students, and the most daring and fiery and gifted of the young alumni were arraigned before the Board, and subjected to the ordeal of a trial for sedition and sympathy with revolution. Moore behaved nobly on this occasion, denying nothing he had said or done, but refusing by a word to implicate others with his own expressed opinions. The authorities were awed, and he was permitted to continue his college course without further molestation. His time then was devoted to literature and study. Buried amongst the old books of Marsh's Library, the Psyche wings began to unfold themselves, and before he was twenty the "Anacreon," which first made him celebrated, was finished.

He went to London with the manuscript, and fortune and fame quickly followed on its publication. The first red-rose dawn of a new and true poet-soul appearing above the literary horizon was at once recognised and welcomed. From the Regent down, society seized on the young poet, and nearly strangled all that was good in him, Armida-like, with chains of roses.[4]

The "Anacreon" suited the taste of a luxurious, sensualised age, and in his next work, "Little's Poems," Moore unhappily degraded his genius to the level of the society that worshipped him.[5] The "Anacreon" had not the immortal element in it, still it lives, and is sometimes read; but "Little's Poems" had the seeds of death in them, and they died. The true fount of eternal song had not yet opened in Moore's soul. He was himself unconscious where his great strength lay, and wasted in the sentimentalities of frivolous and affected feeling the power that was made to move the world's great heart.

The magic influence that at last unsealed the fount, and revealed to the poet the riches of his own genius, came from the divinely beautiful spirit of Irish music. At once, when it touched his soul, the hidden stream of inspiration rushed up to heaven, clear and pure and sparkling, and fell to earth again in showers of many coloured splendours, strengthening and refreshing not only his own loved land, but stimulating amongst the far-off nations the growth of Freedom's goodly tree.

Moore himself describes the effect which Irish music had on him when he first began to study it for the purpose of writing words suitable to the airs – this mournful music, so sad and so expressive, that made Beethoven exclaim, when he first heard it, "That must be the music of an oppressed and suffering people."[6] The whole history and genius and temperament of the nation can be traced in its fluctuations of mirth and sadness, its transient discords, and triumphant marches mingled with wailing, pathetic minors, the alternate languor and turbulence, the despondency and defiance, so characteristic of the vain but ceaseless efforts of a nation to throw off an intolerable yoke.

Notes

[4] Armida is a sorceress and seductress from *Jerusalem Delivered* (1581) by Italian poet Torquato Tasso (1544–95).

[5] *Odes of Anacreon* (1800); *The Poetical Works of the Late Thomas Little* (1801).

[6] European composer Ludwig van Beethoven (1770–1827).

All this Moore found in our national music, whose origin is lost in the night of time, but whose sweetest and saddest airs date from the cruel era of the Tudors; and his genius flowed rapidly in a divine harmony with its blended gaiety and gloom. It was no effort to him to write then; the thoughts came with tears, and crystallised into imperishable gems of song. He had felt and he had suffered, that was sufficient; he was one of the helots, with the penal brand on him, and he appealed to a whole people who burned with the same indignant sense of wrong. It was not the voice of one heart, but the cry of a nation that went up from his verses, and startled the world into sympathy and pity for Ireland.

Translations of the "Melodies" were rapidly made into all the tongues of Europe. Wherever oppression existed, they helped to give resistance utterance. They passed from nation to nation, as a burning torch passes from hand to hand, the signal of the uprising of a people against tyranny; and so they exist an enduring portion of the world's heritage, graven with a diamond pen upon the rocks for ever.

The enthusiasm kindled by them in Ireland alarmed the Government. Their tendency was pronounced "mischievous," and the idea was entertained of forcibly suppressing their publication. Moore had to defend himself against the charge of "stirring up the passions of a turbulent mob." "To those," he says, "who can identify nationality with treason, I shall not deign to offer an apology for the political sentiments expressed;" "besides," he adds sarcastically, "this volume is for the pianofortes of the rich, for those who can afford to have their national zeal a little stimulated, without exciting much dread of the excesses into which it may lead them; and whose nerves may be alarmed with advantage, since more may be expected from their fears than could be gained from their justice."[7]

Moore was then but twenty-seven, in the full flush of youth and genius, and that inspiration which fame gives to the poet while she crowns him. Whatever was best and truest in his nature he enshrined in these national songs, and by them he lives; all else he has written, rich as they are in fancy, beauty, and exquisite diction, are almost unheeded by the people; the "Melodies" form the true pedestal of his glory. He has been made immortal by a hundred songs. His principles, also triumphed at last over the petty factions of the hour, and what was pronounced "sedition" when he wrote, soon, by the overwhelming power of public opinion, was forced to become law. The strong arm of O'Connell guided the passions, and directed those mighty energies evoked by the divine gift of song, and the fetters lifted from a nation by the Act of Emancipation fell as a trophy at the poet's feet.[8] Moore's verses were the inspiration of "the Liberator," and even Wellington may have been touched by this noble appeal: –

> Yet, still the last crown of thy toils is remaining,
>   The grandest, the purest even thou hast yet known,
> Tho' proud was thy task other nations unchaining,
>   Far prouder to heal the deep wounds of thy own.
> At the foot of that throne for whose weal thou hast stood,
>   Go! plead for the Land that first cradled thy fame,
> And bright o'er the flood of her tears and her blood
>   Let the rainbow of hope be her Wellington's name.[9]

Notes

[7] Wilde slightly misquotes Moore's "Letter to the Marchioness Dowager of Donegal" (above, p. 244).
[8] Daniel O'Connell, "the Liberator."
[9] "While History's Muse." The Duke of Wellington, born in Dublin, was prime minister of Britain when Catholic Emancipation passed (1829).

The history of Ireland repeats itself from age to age with such a mournful rhythm, that Moore's poems find as quick a response in the hearts of the people now as when first published. Each generation goes through the same phases – resistance, defeat, despair. The new generation follows with hopes as brilliant and resolves as bold, again to try, again to fail. And so the sad trilogy is acted from age to age, while the nation can only helplessly mourn, as victim after victim falls dead in the dust of the arena.

Moore was the truest interpreter of these successive moods of aspiration and gloom; and his verse so simple, yet so passionate and powerful, has become almost the national idiom for the expression of national feeling. No poet is so often quoted. His lyrics are in the hearts and on the lips of our people, and our orators still wing their arrows against oppression with a line from Moore to make the aim more fatal.

A very perfect and beautiful translation of the "Melodies" into Irish was made by Dr. M'Hale, the learned and patriotic Archbishop of Tuam; and as the impetuous peasantry of the West listen with tears, or wild applause to Moore's verses, sung to their national music in their native tongue, one feels that love of freedom and dreams of independence can never die out amongst a people so sensitive to all that is noble, tender, and heroic. Moore knew that his glory was linked with these songs: for all poets that have once touched the nation's heart live evermore with the nation's life. It was the passionate wail of an oppressed people he uttered, and all nations adopted it. It was the cry of humanity against wrong, and found a universal echo. The prophetic words have been fulfilled which he wrote with prescience of his own world-wide fame –

> The stranger shall hear thy lament on his plains,
> The sigh of thy harp shall be sent o'er the deep,
> Till thy masters themselves as they rivet our chains,
> Shall pause at the song of their captives and weep.[10]

When his "Melodies" were completed, Moore was at the summit of his glory. The world and its publishers were at his feet. At once he received an offer of £3,000 for any poem he would choose to write on an Eastern subject. Moore describes his own anxieties after the acceptance of this splendid offer. No inspiration came; for he had none, he says, unconnected with country; no strength unless he lay on the breast of his mother earth; and the very magnitude of the offer seemed to weigh down and deaden all thought and fancy in him. "At length," he adds, "the thought occurred to me of founding a story on the fierce struggle between the Ghebers, the ancient fire-worshippers of Persia, and their haughty Moslem masters. From this moment a new and deep interest took possession of me, and the spirit that had spoken in the 'Melodies' of Ireland soon found itself a home in the East."[11]

Thus, the true inspiration came, and the poem flowed on rapidly.

"The Fire Worshippers," though the scene is laid in Persia, is, in fact, an episode of '98, and the portrait of Hafed, the young dauntless hero, is drawn from Lord Edward Fitzgerald. Though Moore sang of Iran, his thoughts were of Erin; and underlying every page of the poem is an allusion to the wrongs which Ireland has suffered from her conquerors; while all the smouldering indignation of his own feelings is expressed in the lines: –[12]

Notes

[10] "Oh! Blame Not the Bard" (above, p. 244).
[11] Wilde quotes from the Preface that Moore added to Lalla Rookh on the occasion of its twentieth edition.

[12] Except for the lines beginning "Iran's Song" and depicting death, all of Wilde's quotations appear in the excerpt above from Lalla Rookh. See lines 367–72, 609–14, 498–500, 935–46, and 20–35.

> Yes, *I* am of that outcast few,
> To Iran and vengeance true;
> Who curse the hour your Arabs came
> To desolate our shrines of flame;
> And swear, before God's burning eye,
> To break our country's chains, or die.

While the passionate but vain efforts of the Ghebers to throw off the yoke of the intolerant invader recall the story of the fated Geraldine, who is described as

> One of the ancient hero line,
> Along whose glorious currents shine
> Names that have sanctified their blood,
> As Lebanon's small mountain flood
> Is rendered holy by the ranks
> Of sainted cedars on its banks.

And our own people may find their likeness drawn in –

> Iran's sons that never, never
> Will stoop to be the victor's slaves,
> While heaven has light or earth has graves!
> Spirits of fire, that brood not long,
> But flash resentment back for wrong;
> And hearts where slow, but deep, the seeds
> Of vengeance ripen into deeds.
> Who tho' they know the riven chain
> Snaps but to enter in the heart
> Of him who rends its links apart,
> Yet dare the issue, blest to be,
> Even for one bleeding moment free,
> And die in pangs of liberty!

The allusions, also, to the desecrated altars of the people are numerous: –

> The fierce invaders pluck the gem
> From Iran's broken diadem,
>   And bind her ancient faith in chains.

In the fall of the young chief, who fought for freedom "on the green sea brink," we recognise the fate of Lord Edward: – [13]

> 'Tis come, his hour of martyrdom
> In Iran's sacred cause, is come;
> And tho' his life hath passed away,

Notes ───────────────────────────────────

[13] See "Edward" from *Paddy's Resource* (above, p. 133) for an account of the death of Lord Edward Fitzgerald, including the role of Sirr, who Wilde condemns below as "the captor of Lord Edward."

Like lightning on a stormy day,
Yet, shall his death-hour leave a track
  Of glory, permanent and bright,
To which the brave shall long look back
  With fond regret, and by its light
Watch through the hours of slavery's night.

So dies the Gheber chief:

His glories lost, his cause betrayed,
Iran, his own loved country, made
A land of carcases and slaves;
One dreary waste of chains and graves!

But he and his band meet death heroically, as many an Irish patriot has done, and call

For God and Iran! as they fall.

Then the informers are denounced, as they might often be in Irish history before and since:

Oh! for a tongue to curse the slave
  Whose treason, like a deadly blight,
Comes o'er the councils of the brave,
  And blasts them in their hour of might.
His country's curse, his children's shame,
Outcast of virtue, peace, and fame.

Even the captor of Lord Edward, the exceedingly unpopular gentleman who was generally believed to be both sanctimonious and cruel, is drawn with the characteristics attributed to him by the Irish people, who detested his name: –

He sleeps
Calm while a nation round him weeps;
While curses load the air he breathes,
And falchions from unnumbered sheaths
Are starting to avenge the shame
His race hath brought on Iran's name,
Hard, heartless chief, unmoved alike
Mid eyes that weep and swords that strike,
One of that saintly murderous brood,
Who think through unbeliever's blood,
Lies their directest path to heaven –
One who will pause, and kneel unshod
In the warm blood his hand hath pour'd,
To mutter o'er some text of God,
Engraven on his reeking sword.

The perfect and beautiful poem of ''Lalla Rookh'' was received by the public with the most intense enthusiasm, and ''The Fire Worshippers'' was pronounced the best of all the tales, probably because it was vital with true feeling. Lord Jeffrey, in the

"Edinburgh,"[14] gave it the palm for excellence, though he entirely overlooked its cryptic political signification. Moore was engaged for two years on this work; for he says of himself that he worked slowly, and was a far more *painstaking workman* than people imagined.

For his next poem, "The Loves of the Angels," he received £1,000. And his charming prose tale followed, "The Epicurean," which, though closely imitated from the French Romance of "Sethos," is yet full of Moore's peculiar beauties.[15] Then he worked for years at his history of Ireland, which, if somewhat imperfect for want of adequate knowledge, is yet a model of style in eloquence and diction. When the first glow of youth was over, Moore led a retired life in his English home, far from the brilliant world, in the soul's quiet that genius loves. Sometimes he visited his native country, and was always received with triumphs and ovations. When he entered the theatre at Dublin the whole audience rose up to welcome him as if he were a king; and he was a king over the hearts of the nation, and this spontaneous homage was the sacred symbol of the poet's coronation.

His last years were made sad and desolate by home sorrows; all his children died before him. His family became extinct; the race culminated and ended with him. But that which is best in the utterance of a great human soul can never die; the children of the poet's brain are immortal –

> And the hearts and the voices of Erin prolong
> Through the answering future his name and his song.[16]

His library and his harp, that Irish harp which gave him inspiration, have been placed in the keeping of the Royal Irish Academy, as heirlooms of the nation, and a room has been set apart for their reception, which is now called "The Moore Library;" while his statue, the first ever publicly erected in Ireland to an Irishman, has, by a kind of poetical justice, been placed in sight of the college that tried to have him expelled for his nationality; and was inaugurated by the Viceroy of the Government that would willingly have stopped the publication of the "Irish Melodies" and had the poet prosecuted for sedition.

But Moore lies in his death-sleep in English earth. Is this right? Should not the poet's sacred dust be laid in holy Ireland, amidst the people to whom his genius was consecrated? Let us hope that a day will come when his mortal remains will be brought back to the land he loved so well, with the reverent homage of a nation, and then a fitting monument will be raised in the Irish capital to the great national poet of Ireland, and the most perfect lyrist of the age.

William Allingham (1824–1889)

William Allingham was born in Ballyshannon, the son of a merchant. His early education was local, but in 1837 he was briefly sent to a boarding school in Co. Cavan before returning to Ballyshannon to work in a bank. After seven years of banking, he took up a post in Customs at Donegal, and took advantage of the light workload to fill his days with reading. By the late 1840s he was beginning to make literary contacts, corresponding with American poet Ralph Waldo Emerson, and by the early 1850s he was acquainted as well with English authors Leigh

Notes —————————————————————————————

[14] *The Edinburgh Review.*

[15] *The Loves of the Angels* (1823); *The Epicurean* (1827).

[16] ""Twas One of those Dreams."

Hunt, Tennyson and Coventry Patmore. In 1854 he resigned from Customs and moved to London and began writing for the leading periodicals of the day, including *Household Words* and the *Athenaeum*, but soon returned to his old job in Irish Customs. He returned to London frequently, however, and eventually moved to England permanently in the early 1860s. While visiting London, he became close to Dante Gabriel Rossetti and other members of the Pre-Raphaelite group in England; William Makepeace Thackeray, Thomas Carlyle, and the Brownings were also among Allingham's English literary circle.

His most important work is the verse novel *Laurence Bloomfield in Ireland*, first published serially in *Fraser's Magazine* and then in volume form (1864). He also published numerous volumes of verse, including *Poems* (1850), *The Music-Master* (1855), and *Evil May-Day* (1882), and compiled *The Ballad Book*, a collection of British ballads, for the Golden Treasury Series (1864) – a work that was reprinted for over a hundred years. Allingham became the editor of the prominent *Fraser's Magazine* in 1874, and W. B. Yeats published a selection of Allingham's poems in 1905. His "Winding Banks of Erne" participates in the lengthy tradition of Irish exilic literature, while "Sleepy" captures a more universal mood. The other selections here stress an emerging association of Ireland with the supernatural (see the section on Bridget and Julia Kavanagh, below, on Irish fairy literature).

Further reading

Cowan, Yuri, "William Allingham's Ballad Book and its Victorian Readers," *University of Toronto Quarterly* 73 (2004): 1003–10.

Life, Allan R., "The Art of Not 'Going Halfway': Rossetti's Illustration for 'The Maids of Elfen-Mere,'" *Victorian Poetry* 20 (1982): 65–87.

Warner, Alan, *William Allingham*. Lewisburg: Bucknell University Press, 1975.

The Fairies: A Nursery Song

From The Music-Master, A Love Story, and Two Series of Night and Day Songs (1855)

Up the airy mountain,
  Down the rushy glen,
We daren't go a hunting
  For fear of little men;
Wee folk, good folk,   5
  Trooping all together;
Green jacket, red cap,
  And white owl's feather!

Down along the rocky shore
  Some make their home,   10
They live on crispy pancakes
  Of yellow tide-foam;
Some in the reeds
  Of the black mountain-lake,
With frogs for their watch-dogs,   15
  All night awake.

High on the hill-top
  The old King sits;
He is now so old and grey
  He's nigh lost his wits.   20

With a bridge of white mist
   Columbkill he crosses,
On his stately journeys
   From Slieveleague to Rosses;
Or going up with music   25
   On cold starry nights,
To sup with the Queen
   Of the gay Northern Lights.

They stole little Bridget
   For seven years long;   30
When she came down again
   Her friends were all gone.
They took her lightly back,
   Between the night and morrow,
They thought that she was fast asleep,   35
   But she was dead with sorrow.
They have kept her ever since
   Deep within the lakes,
On a bed of flag-leaves,
   Watching till she wakes.   40

By the craggy hill-side,
   Through the mosses bare,
They have planted thorn-trees
   For pleasure here and there.
Is any man so daring   45
   To dig one up in spite,
He shall find the thornies set
   In his bed at night.

Up the airy mountain,
   Down the rushy glen,   50
We daren't go a hunting
   For fear of little men;
Wee folk, good folk,
   Trooping all together;
Green jacket, red cap,   55
   And white owl's feather!

The Maids of Elfen-Mere

From The Music-Master, A Love Story, and Two Series of Night and Day Songs (1855)

'Twas when the spinning-room was here,
There came Three Damsels clothed in white,
With their spindles every night;
Two and one, and Three fair Maidens,
Spinning to a pulsing cadence,   5
Singing songs of Elfen-Mere;

Till the eleventh hour was toll'd,
Then departed through the wold.
  Years ago, and years ago;
  And the tall reeds sigh as the wind doth blow. 10

Three white Lilies, calm and clear,
And they were loved by every one;
Most of all, the Pastor's Son,
Listening to their gentle singing,
Felt his heart go from him, clinging 15
Round these Maids of Elfen-Mere;
Sued each night to make them stay,
Sadden'd when they went away.
  Years ago, and years ago;
  And the tall reeds sigh as the wind doth blow. 20

Hands that shook with love and fear
Dared put back the village clock, –
Flew the spindle, turn'd the rock,
Flow'd the song with subtle rounding,
Till the false "eleven" was sounding; 25
Then these Maids of Elfen-Mere
Swiftly, softly, left the room,
Like three doves on snowy plume.
  Years ago, and years ago;
  And the tall reeds sigh as the wind doth blow. 30

One that night who wander'd near
Heard lamentings by the shore,
Saw at dawn three stains of gore
In the waters fade and dwindle.
Nevermore with song and spindle 35
Saw we Maids of Elfen-Mere.
The Pastor's Son did pine and die;
Because true love should never lie.
  Years ago, and years ago;
  And the tall reeds sigh as the wind doth blow. 40

The Winding Banks of Erne: Or, the Emigrant's Adieu to Ballyshanny[1]

From Songs, Ballads, and Stories (1877)

(A Local Ballad)

Adieu to Ballyshanny! where I was bred and born;
Go where I may, I'll think of you, as sure as night and morn,
The kindly spot, the friendly town, where every one is known,

THE WINDING BANKS OF ERNE

[1] The vernacular, and more correct, form of the name (author).

And not a face in all the place but partly seems my own;
There's not a house or window, there's not a field or hill,   5
But, east or west, in foreign lands, I'll recollect them still.
I leave my warm heart with you, though my back I'm forced to turn –
So adieu to Ballyshanny, and the winding banks of Erne.

No more on pleasant evenings we'll saunter down the Mall,
When the trout is rising to the fly, the salmon to the fall.   10
The boat comes straining on her net, and heavily she creeps,
Cast off, cast off! – she feels the oars, and to her berth she sweeps;
Now fore and aft keep hauling, and gathering up the clew,
Till a silver wave of salmon rolls in among the crew.
Then they may sit, with pipes a-lit, and many a joke and "yarn"; –   15
Adieu to Ballyshanny, and the winding banks of Erne!

The music of the waterfall, the mirror of the tide,
When all the green-hill'd harbour is full from side to side –
From Portnasun to Bulliebawns, and round the Abbey Bay,
From rocky Inis Saimer to Coolnargit sandhills grey;   20
While far upon the southern line, to guard it like a wall,
The Leitrim mountains clothed in blue gaze calmly over all,
And watch the ship sail up or down, the red flag at her stern; –
Adieu to these, adieu to all the winding banks of Erne!

Farewell to you, Kildoney lads, and them that pull an oar,   25
A lug-sail set, or haul a net, from the Point to Mullaghmore;
From Killybegs to bold Slieve-League, that ocean-mountain steep,
Six hundred yards in air aloft, six hundred in the deep;
From Dooran to the Fairy Bridge, and round by Tullen strand,
Level and long, and white with waves, where gull and curlew stand;   30
Head out to sea when on your lee the breakers you discern! –
Adieu to all the billowy coast, and winding banks of Erne!

Farewell, Coolmore, – Bundoran! and your summer crowds that run
From inland homes to see with joy th' Atlantic-setting sun;
To breathe the buoyant salted air, and sport among the waves;   35
To gather shells on sandy beach, and tempt the gloomy caves;
To watch the flowing, ebbing tide, the boats, the crabs, the fish;
Young men and maids to meet and smile, and form a tender wish;
The sick and old in search of health, for all things have their turn –
And I must quit my native shore, and the winding banks of Erne!   40

Farewell to every white cascade from the Harbour to Belleek,
And every pool where fins may rest, and ivy-shaded creek;
The sloping fields, the lofty rocks, where ash and holly grow,
The one split yew-tree gazing on the curving flood below;
The Lough, that winds through islands under Turaw mountain green;   45
And Castle Caldwell's stretching woods, with tranquil bays between;
And Breesie Hill, and many a pond among the heath and fern, –
For I must say adieu – adieu to the winding banks of Erne!

The thrush will call through Camlin groves the live-long summer day;
The waters run by mossy cliff, and banks with wild flowers gay;   50
The girls will bring their work and sing beneath a twisted thorn,

Or stray with sweethearts down the path among the growing corn;
Along the river side they go, where I have often been, –
O, never shall I see again the days that I have seen!
A thousand chances are to one I never may return, –   55
Adieu to Ballyshanny, and the winding banks of Erne!

Adieu to evening dances, when merry neighbours meet,
And the fiddle says to boys and girls, "Get up and shake your feet!"
To "shanachus"[2] and wise old talk of Erin's days gone by –
Who trench'd the rath on such a hill, and where the bones may lie   60
Of saint, or king, or warrior chief; with tales of fairy power,
And tender ditties sweetly sung to pass the twilight hour.
The mournful song of exile is now for me to learn –
Adieu, my dear companions on the winding banks of Erne!

Now measure from the Commons down to each end of the Purt,   65
Round the Abbey, Moy and Knather, – I wish no one any hurt;
The Main Street, Back Street, College Lane, the Mall, and Portnasun,
If any foes of mine are there, I pardon every one.
I hope that man and womankind will do the same by me;
For my heart is sore and heavy at voyaging the sea.   70
My loving friends I'll bear in mind, and often fondly turn
To think of Ballyshanny, and the winding banks of Erne.

If ever I'm a money'd man, I mean, please God, to cast
My golden anchor in the place where youthful years were pass'd;
Though heads that now are black and brown must meanwhile gather gray,   75
New faces rise by every hearth, and old ones drop away –
Yet dearer still that Irish hill than all the world beside;
It's home, sweet home, where'er I roam, through lands and waters wide.
And if the Lord allows me, I surely will return
To my native Ballyshanny, and the winding banks of Erne.   80

Sleepy

From Evil May-Day (1882)

O leave me quiet for a thousand years!
No duties, troubles, pleasures, hopes or fears,
No sun or moon with sad returning beam,
Only a faintly glimmering world, half dream,
To faintly touch my senses: rest I would,   5
Forget the tangled life, the bad and good,
And everything that has been,– drinking deep
The freshness of regenerating sleep,
Ages and aeons of celestial rest;
To wake – I know not when, – sleep now were best.   10

Notes

2 "Shanachus," old stories, – histories, genealogies (author).

Bridget Kavanagh (c.1800–1887) and Julia Kavanagh (1824–1877)

Bridget Fitzpatrick Kavanagh and her daughter Julia Kavanagh were from Co. Tipperary. Julia's father, Morgan Kavanagh, was a writer of little note who abandoned the family in the 1840s. Before that, the family traveled to London and Paris, with Bridget and Julia returning to London in the mid-1840s and settling there while Julia Kavanagh began her literary career. Eventually, mother and daughter moved to Italy, where Julia Kavanagh died in 1877.

Apart from her collaboration with her daughter on short fiction, *The Pearl Fountain and Other Fairy Tales* (1876), Bridget Kavanagh is not known to have published any literary work. Julia Kavanagh, however, published children's literature, as well as novels, biographies, and travel writing. Much of her work was published or republished by Tauchnitz, an important German publisher at the time whose mammoth book series of "British and American authors" included works by many of the leading writers of the day. Kavanagh's novels were generally titled after female protagonists, and include *Madeleine* (1848), *Nathalie* (1850), *Daisy Burns* (1853), *Rachel Gray* (1856), *Beatrice* (1862), and nearly a dozen others. Her work as a biographer of leading women is also notable: *Woman in France during the Eighteenth Century* (1850), for instance, stresses women with political power and influence, while *English Women of Letters* and *French Women of Letters* (1862) aim "to show how far, for the last two centuries and more, women have contributed to the formation of the modern novel." She also wrote on her travels in *A Summer and Winter in the Two Sicilies* (1858), and she published another collection of shorter fiction, *Seven Years, and Other*

Tales (1860). Her reputation as a successful author was such that her estranged father tried to capitalize on it by naming her as the editor of his 1857 novel, *The Hobbies*; Julia Kavanagh vigorously denied her involvement in the periodical *The Athenaeum*.

In *The Pearl Fountain and Other Fairy Tales*, the Kavanaghs return to Julia's early work on children's literature, as well as pick up on the growing fashion for fairytales after the publication of Hans Christian Andersen's and the Grimm Brothers' tales in English during the first half of the nineteenth century. In Ireland, a number of writers published work in this vein, including Thomas Crofton Croker (*Fairy Legends and Traditions of the South of Ireland*, 1825), Allingham ("The Fairies" and "The Maids of Elfen-Mere"), Lady Wilde (*Ancient Legends, Mystic Charms, and Superstitions of Ireland*, 1887), Oscar Wilde (*The Happy Prince and Other Tales*, 1888), and W. B. Yeats (*Fairy and Folk Tales of the Irish Peasantry*, 1888). Despite wide interest in Irish literary fairytales and women's fiction in this period, and her significant reputation in her own day, Julia Kavanagh remains a much-neglected writer, and none of the Further reading suggested here, uniquely in this anthology, addresses Kavanagh's work directly.

Further reading

Bourke, Angela, "Reading a Woman's Death: Colonial Text and Oral Tradition in Nineteenth-century Ireland," *Feminist Studies* 21 (1995): 553–86.

Vejvoda, Kathleen, " 'Too Much Knowledge of the Other World': Women and Nineteenth-century Irish Folktales," *Victorian Literature and Culture* 32 (2004): 41–61.

The Pearl Fountain

From **The Pearl Fountain and Other Fairy Tales (1876)**

A long time ago the Fairy Queen thought she would go about to see how all the fairies who live in floods, rivers, streams, and fountains were getting on since the last hundred years, for it is only once a century that her Majesty can take such a survey of her subjects. After travelling a long time, scolding some fairies who had got into mischief, and praising others who had behaved well, the Queen came at length to an old, old forest which grew on the very top of a rocky mountain, and where the trees were so large and the shade was so thick that it was all green within. Indeed it was so green a place, so dark and so cool, that people were afraid of it, and kept aloof. But the Fairy Queen was afraid of nothing; moreover she had particular business in that forest. She wanted to see a little fairy who was only three days old, and to whom the fountain of the forest had been given by her mother. The Queen found the little Fairy all alone by her fountain. It was a beautiful fountain; the water was as clear as clear could be; it came sparkling out of a rock, leaped down other rocks, then ran away and hid itself in the moss. It looked quite a merry sort of fountain, and the little Fairy to whom it belonged looked every bit as merry; for when the Queen came upon her, she was dancing in the shade and singing to herself in a sweet clear voice, because you see fairies can talk, just as they can run about, as soon as they are born.

The Queen of the Fairies has no children of her own, but she is very fond of little children, and she always thinks the last baby she sees the prettiest. She thought so of this young Fairy, who was really a pretty creature, for she had golden hair, blue eyes, and rosy cheeks, and her mother, knowing the Queen was coming, had dressed her out in a little frock of silver tissue, shot with green and blue.

"Well, my dear," graciously said the Queen of the Fairies to this young thing, "do you know who I am?"

"Oh, yes," answered the little Fairy, "you are her Majesty."

"What a clever child you are," said the Queen, quite pleased; "and who are you?"

"Please your Majesty, I am the little Fairy of the little Fountain."

"My dear, you could not have answered me better; and now what gift will you have from me, my love?"

"Pearls," answered the little Fairy.

"Then pearls you shall have," said the Queen, "as many as ever you can wish for. Your fountain shall be all pearls, and you may do what you like with them; but you will have to count them, every one."

"I shall like that," answered the little Fairy, "for no one must ever take so much as one of my pearls."

"Well," said the Queen, "if you mean to keep your pearls to yourself, you must live here all alone, and never go out."

"I shall like that, too," said the little Fairy, "for I shall sing to myself, and play with my pearls; and, please your Majesty, may I be called the Fairy of the Pearl Fountain."

The Queen let her have that also, then went her way. The Fairy of the Pearl Fountain remained in the forest, and lived there till she grew up to be the loveliest young Fairy that had ever been seen. She had a white marble basin, made for the water of her fountain to fall into, and the most beautiful wild flowers set in the green moss around it. The water sprang up in a jet from the centre of the basin, and the delight of the Fairy was to stand in the very middle of it, clothed in her robe of silver tissue, shot with green and blue, for it was not a frock now that she was grown up, and to throw the water up ever so high, till it reached the sunshine; and every drop of water she threw up was a pearl when it came down again – a beautiful white pearl. Some were big pearls and some were little ones, and the bottom of the marble basin was covered with them. Indeed, there were so many that the Fairy was obliged to let the smallest trickle away every night through a little slit in the basin; for if she had not done so, it would have overflowed. So the pearls slipped away, and rolled down the rocks on the mountain-side, but no one minded them, or if some passer-by did see them by chance, why he thought he saw drops of water and no more. Though she had so many pearls the young Fairy never thought she had too many, and all her delight was to adorn herself with them. She strung the largest and the clearest on a thread of gold, and mixed it up in her hair, and she made a necklace of more, and bracelets for her wrists, and a waist-band, and the hem of her silver tissue robe was all studded with pearls; and there was not a fairy who had so many. She counted them every one as the Queen had ordered her, and when she laid herself down on the moss at night she still counted them in her sleep. Indeed, she was so fond of her pearls, and so jealous of them, that she never left her fountain lest any one should come and steal them whilst she was away.

This lasted a long time; till one day the Fairy, finding that no one ever came near the place, and wishing to go and see her sister, who lived outside the forest in a crystal turret on a rock, and was indeed no less than the Fairy of the Waterfall, put on her best pearls and left her fountain for the first time. Being a fairy, she could go on counting the pearls of her fountain all the same. Well, the Fairy was glad to see her sister, and pleased to climb up to the very top of the crystal turret, and look down at the world below, for she had never been out before, and she was enjoying herself very much, when all of a sudden she cried out: "I must go; I miss a pearl; no, it is not one, but two. I declare three pearls are gone."

"What matter about three pearls," said her sister; "have you not got enough?"

But the Fairy of the Pearl Fountain declared that there was no misfortune like that of losing one's pearls, and went away in a great hurry. She missed two more pearls as she walked through the forest, for she was not one of those fairies who have only to wish themselves in a place to be in it; and on reaching the fountain, she looked at once for the thief; but she only saw a little wren, perched on the edge of the marble basin, and catching a drop of the spray in her bill as it fell.

"You little robber," cried the Fairy in a rage; "is it you who have been stealing my pearls?"

"Please, ma'am," replied the Wren, quite frightened at seeing her so angry, "I am only drinking a drop of water."

"A drop of water! don't you know, you dishonest bird, that what was only a drop of water when you drank it, would have turned into a beautiful pearl if it had fallen into the basin. Look down at the bottom and see. All these pearls were drops of water once."

"I protest, ma'am, I knew nothing of the kind," answered the little Wren, speaking very humbly, for she had never seen so grand a lady as the Fairy of the Pearl Fountain, with her beautiful hair and her pearls; "I saw water," continued the Wren, "I was very thirsty, and I made bold to drink. Surely, I thought, the good Fairy who owns this lovely fountain will never be angry with me for taking a drop of water; and I can assure you, ma'am," added the Wren, dropping the Fairy a curtsey, "that it was the very sweetest water I ever tasted, and I do hope you will forgive me." The Fairy of the Pearl Fountain had a hasty temper, but she was not hard-hearted; she looked kindly down on the little Wren, and said, "You are a silly bird, and I daresay did not know pearls from water. I suppose I must forgive you this once, but mind you never do such a thing again."

"Oh no, ma'am, never," answered the Wren very earnestly. "And please, ma'am, may I go home to the palace now?"

"Home to the palace?" repeated the Fairy. "What do you mean?"

Now every one, big or little, has a story; and the story of the Wren was this: – She had built her nest in the garden of the King's palace, and was making herself comfortable there, when the young Prince found her out, caught her, and would have killed her, if his sister had not come up in time to save her life. The Princess did more; for she took the poor little Wren, who was frightened to death, to her own room, and gave her a beautiful cage to live in, and keep her out of danger; but as the Wren is fond of going about, she let her have a fly every day, and kept a window in her room always open, so that she might have no trouble in getting in or out. All this the Wren told the Fairy, not in a few words, but in a good many; for she is a chatterbox if ever there was one, and can talk by the hour. The Fairy, however, did not mind letting her have her say; for she had got into the fountain again, and was throwing up the water ever so high, and trying to catch the beautiful pearls as they fell back. She missed a good many, for some rolled down her neck and shoulders, and others got in her hair and stayed there; and others, again, slipped through her fingers and fell into the basin.

"Oh! ma'am, how beautiful you are!" the Wren could not help saying; "and how pretty it is to see you playing with those lovely pearls."

"You have a great deal of sense," said the Fairy. "By the way, what is your name?"

"Jenny, ma'am," answered the Wren, dropping her another curtsey. "The Princess always calls me Jenny."

"Never mind the Princess," said the Fairy a little tartly; "but mind what I say. Well, then, Jenny, suppose that you and I have a game together with my pearls. I shall throw them, and you shall catch them again and drop them into the basin; and when we have done, I do not mind letting you have a drop of water to drink. You are a very little bird, and a little drop of water will do you."

The Wren asked no better than to play with the Fairy; so the game began. The Fairy caught the drops of water as they fell, and threw them to the Wren, who caught them in her bill – one after another, of course – then dropped them into the basin. The Wren was a clever bird, and played so well that she only missed three times. The Fairy was delighted and declared she had never had such fun. In short, they played till they were both tired, when the Fairy said, "There, Jenny; that will do for to-day. Drink your drop of water, and go home to the palace. You may come again to-morrow and have another game with me, but mind that you tell no one about my Pearl Fountain."

"May I not tell the Princess?" asked the Wren.

"Certainly not," said the Fairy; "if you do, I shall never forgive you; besides, I am a fairy, and I shall find it out and punish you at once."

The Wren promised not to say a word, and flew home to her cage in the palace. She was afraid lest the Princess should ask her where she had been, as she often did; but she had just been told by her father that he had promised her in marriage to the King of the Diamond Isles, and she was so full of that, and of all the diamonds she was to have, that she never even saw when the Wren flew in through the window. The Wren made as little noise as she could, and pecked her supper quietly, though she had never been so hungry in her life. Water may turn into pearls, but it is not the thing to satisfy one's appetite.

Well the next day the Wren flew to the Pearl Fountain, and the Fairy threw the pearls at her, and the Wren caught them in her bill and dropped them into the basin. When she was tired she had her drop of water, but though she asked to be allowed to bathe in the fountain, the Fairy would not hear of it, and was very cross with her for so much as thinking of such a thing. The Princess was not in her room when the Wren flew back to her cage that day, and when she came in the Wren had her head under her wing and was fast asleep.

Matters went on so for a good while. Every day the Wren flew to the Pearl Fountain, and played at catching the pearls with the Fairy, and every evening she flew home to her cage in the room of the Princess, who was so taken up with her wedding clothes that she never thought of asking her where she had been.

The Fairy became so fond of the Wren that she thought she would leave her in charge of the fountain, whilst she went to see her sister again. The Wren did not like being left alone, but the Fairy promised not to be long away. "I shall be back before sunset," she said, "and you can play as much as you like with my pearls, and even drink three drops of water, and all I want you to do is to stay and watch by the fountain, and if any one should come nigh it to call me three times. I shall hear you and come at once."

The Wren agreed to this, and stayed by the fountain whilst the Fairy went to see her sister. She played with the pearls till she was tired, then she drank three drops of water, then she stood on the edge of the basin, and thought how nice and cool a bath would be. The day was a hot one, the Fairy was away. "She will never know anything about it," said the Wren to herself. She spread out her wings, fluttered over the water, and had the most delightful bath she had ever had in her life. She was enjoying herself to her heart's content, and had just begun drying herself in the sun, when there came a great rushing noise which filled the whole forest. It was the King of the Fairies driving by, but the Wren knew nothing about that. She was frightened out of her wits. Indeed she lost her head entirely, and instead of calling the Fairy as she had promised to do in case of danger, she flew home to the palace as fast as ever her wings would take her, and never thought herself safe till she lay panting in the bottom of her cage. It unluckily happened that the Princess was in her room just then, trying on her wedding-dress.

"Why, Jenny," she cried, "what is the matter with you?"

"I was bathing in the forest," answered the Wren, "when there came a great noise that frightened me, so I flew home. See, I am not dry yet." She shook her wings and a beautiful pearl rolled down on the bottom of the cage.

"I declare that is a pearl," said the Princess, all amazed. "Why, Jenny, where have you been bathing, and where did you get that lovely pearl?"

"A pearl!" repeated the Wren, who did not know what to say.

"Yes, a pearl," said the Princess, who had picked it up and was looking at it, "the biggest, whitest, loveliest pearl I ever saw. Where did you get it?"

The Wren tried not to answer this, but the Princess insisted upon knowing how she had got the pearl, and the Wren did not dare to deny her. So having first made her promise that she would not mention it again, she told her all about the Fairy and the Pearl Fountain. When the Princess heard about a fountain in which every drop of water became a pearl she nearly went crazy, so eager was she to get at it. She wanted the Wren to take her to it at once, but that the Wren would not do; then she tried to coax her into stealing some of the pearls and bringing them home to her, but the Wren would not hear of such a thing.

"Well, at least I shall keep that pearl," said the Princess, and the Wren, who could not take it from her, said, yes, she might. When the Wren flew to the Pearl Fountain the next day, the Fairy gave her an angry look.

"Why did you leave my fountain yesterday before I came home?" she asked.

"I heard a great noise and I got frightened," answered the Wren.

"Why did you not call me?" asked the Fairy.

"I forgot it," replied the Wren.

"I miss a pearl," said the Fairy; "what have you done with it?"

The Wren was afraid to say the truth, so she answered, "I was playing with the pearls, when one rolled out and fell in the grass, and I could not find it again."

The Fairy could have known the truth by looking in her book, but she kept it under a stone in the bottom of her basin, and there were so many pearls on the top of it that she did not like to disturb them.

"Well," she said to the Wren, "you have behaved very badly, and I am very angry with you; but if I forgive you this time will you do it again?"

"Oh no, indeed!" answered the Wren. So they made it up, and had a game, and were as happy together as they had ever been.

As soon as she took the pearl from the Wren, the Princess sent for the Court jeweller, and gave it to him to set, for she meant to wear it on her wedding-day. The jeweller declared that the pearl was the finest he had ever seen, upon which the Princess, instead of being glad that she had it, only thought of all the pearls in the fountain which she had not. She lay awake the whole of that night, thinking of them still; and one thing she was resolved upon when she got up in the morning, and that was to find out the Pearl Fountain, and to take some of the Fairy's pearls. "She has so many of them," thought the Princess, "that she ought not to mind my having a few; and then what a fine thing it will be for me to be spoken of as the Princess who had so many pearls, and who married the King of the Diamond Isles!"

The Wren was in no hurry to meet the Fairy that day. She took her fly rather late; but the Princess, who had been watching her since the morning, followed her at a distance, entered the forest after her, and stealing behind the trees, soon found out the Pearl Fountain, and saw the Fairy and the Wren playing together. At last the Wren flew away, and the Fairy, who was tired, laid herself down on the moss to sleep. The Princess waited a while, then she stole softly on tip-toe to the edge of the marble basin, and holding up both her hands, she caught the pearls as fast as they fell. When her hands were full, she dropped the pearls down on the moss, and thought to begin again and have quite a heap of them. But the Fairy, who had been counting them in her sleep all the time, now missed them, and starting up, said angrily, "Who steals my pearls?"

The Princess was so frightened that she had not a word to say for herself, and the Fairy said again in the same angry voice:

"What brought you here?"

"I wanted some pearls from the Pearl Fountain," replied the Princess.

"And who told you about the Pearl Fountain?" asked the Fairy.

"The Wren told me," answered the Princess.

"And who are you?" inquired the Fairy.

"I am the King's daughter," said the Princess, "and I am going to marry the King of the Diamond Isles, and as your fountain is in my father's kingdom, I think you might give me some pearls for a wedding present."

"You shall not have one pearl from my fountain," said the Fairy; "I keep all these for myself, but go back the way you came, and stand at the foot of the rock on your right hand as you leave the forest. You will see pearls rolling down its sides. These you may pick up. They are small, and I do not mind letting you have them."

"May I have them all?" asked the Princess.

"Every one," replied the Fairy, "but mind it is only for this once; and though you may stay as long as you please, and take away as many pearls as you can pick up, you need never come again, for not another pearl of mine shall you get."

Though the Princess thought the Fairy very stingy not to let her have a few big pearls, she also thought that little pearls were better than none, so she thanked her, and went back the way she had come. She found the rock to her right just outside the forest, and, sure enough, there were the beautiful pearls rolling down its sides, and looking so white and clear in the moonlight. The Princess began picking them up as fast as she could. "I must have a necklace," she thought, "and as the pearls are small it will take a good many." Then when she really had enough for a necklace she wanted some for a tiara, after that she wanted bracelets, and after bracelets a waistband like the fairy's, then a trimming for her wedding dress, then pearls for rings, ear-rings, and brooches, then more pearls for double-sets of everything, then pearls to give away to her ladies, then pearls for herself to keep; in short, though she spent the night gathering pearls, she had not got half enough by day-break. She was very tired, but since she could have pearls only this once, she thought it would be the greatest pity in the world to go away without taking as many as she could. So the pearls rolled down the rocks, and the Princess picked them up, and the more she had, the more she wished to have.

When the King heard that the Princess was missing he was in a sad way. He asked the Wren about her, but all the Wren knew was, that the Princess was in her room when she went out to have her fly, and that she was no longer there when she came back. No one else knew anything, and only one thing was certain, that the Princess had not spent the night in the palace. The King, her father, was distracted with grief, and the King of the Diamond Isles, who had just arrived in order to marry the Princess, lost his appetite at once, he felt in such trouble. The King sent messengers to look for his daughter in every direction. They scoured the country, and found her at length very tired and rather hungry, but still picking up pearls. When they wanted to take her back to the palace, she said it was out of the question, and they were to tell the King that she had still ever so many pearls to gather before she could leave the spot. The King was very much amazed when the messengers came back without the Princess, and told him where they had found her, what she was doing, and what she had said.

"Pearls," said the King; "and what can she want with pearls when she is going to marry the King of the Diamond Isles to-morrow! I must go and see about all that myself."

But when the King went and found the Princess, and saw all the pearls she had gathered, and those she was gathering still, and when she told him that if she once left this spot she could never have any pearls again, he began to think what a pity it would be not to let her get as many as she could.

"Well, my dear," he said to his daughter, "I shall ask the King of the Diamond Isles to wait a day or two, and in the meanwhile you may go on gathering pearls. And suppose that for fear of accidents I should take away these and keep them for you under lock and key."

The Princess agreed to this. The King took away all the pearls she had picked up, and there was quite a heap of them, and stowed them away in great chests in the palace. He also asked the King of the Diamond Isles, who recovered his appetite directly on learning that the Princess was safe, to wait a few days for her. The King of the Diamond Isles grumbled a little, but to please his father-in-law that was to be, he said he would wait seven days for the Princess.

But when the seven days were out, the Princess said she had not yet got pearls enough, and her father persuaded the King of the Diamond Isles to wait seven days more. And so matters went on from one seven days to another, the Princess still gathering pearls, and the King her father taking them away, and locking them up, and neither thinking they had enough, till the King of the Diamond Isles got tired waiting, and went off one morning without so much as ever saying good-bye. Indeed he went straight off to the Queen of Emeralds, whose daughter he married that afternoon.

The King was vexed and the Princess felt rather sorry, but she thought she must only gather more pearls to make up for all the diamonds she had missed. So she went on picking them up, and when she had a heap her father took it away in a great sack, and locked it up, till at length all his chests were full, and he thought one day he must see how many thousand pearls he had got. He unlocked one chest and opened a sack, and out came ever so many drops of water, that rolled all over the floor.

"My goodness!" cried the King, "there's some mistake."

He opened the next sack; out came more drops of water. Then the next and the next again, and all the sacks, and all the chests were full of drops of water, and in the whole of them there was not so much as one pearl. For the pearls were pearls for the Princess only, and for nobody else. When the King saw this, and what a mistake he had made, he got into such a rage that he had a fit, of which he died the next day. The Princess was very sorry for her father's death, but she said the pearls were pearls indeed, and she went on gathering them at the foot of the rock. There she stands to this day picking them up as fast as she can, and never thinking she has enough.

When the Wren flew to the forest again, the Fairy was ever so angry with her for having told the Princess about the Pearl Fountain, but the Wren begged so hard for forgiveness, and fluttered so prettily about her feet, that the Fairy said:

"Well, I shall forgive you once more, but lest you should tell tales again, you shall stay for ever in the forest with me."

So whilst the Princess is gathering pearls at the foot of the rock, the Fairy and the Wren are playing their game with the pearls of the Pearl Fountain; and no one has ever found out in what forest that fountain is, nor on what mountain that forest grows, nor in what part of the world that mountain lies.

Thomas D'Arcy McGee (1825–1868)

Thomas D'Arcy McGee was born in Co. Louth; his father's family was from the north of Ireland and his mother's from Dublin, and his maternal grandfather had been a participant in the 1798 Uprising. McGee's father worked for the Coast Guard and moved the family to Wexford where McGee received his only formal education in a hedge school. In 1842, McGee emigrated to the United States, where he was soon working for the *Boston Pilot*, a leading Catholic newspaper; by 1844, he was an editor of the periodical, but in 1845 he returned to Ireland to take a job with the *Freeman's Journal* in Dublin. Within months, McGee was part of Young Ireland and publishing in *The Nation*. In 1848, McGee was involved in plans for an Irish uprising; arrested and then released, McGee left again for the United States. He started his own *Nation* newspaper in New York,

but was so controversial in his political positions that he left the city in 1850. He returned to Boston and started up new periodicals, moving between Boston and New York and working in publishing over the next few years.

In 1857, he moved to Montreal, and was soon elected to the Legislative Assembly; he quickly rose through the governmental ranks, becoming a minister in 1863. He then became a leading figure in the discussions which unified most of the British-controlled territories north of the United States into the Dominion of Canada under the British North America Act (1867), and is remembered in Canada as a "Father of Confederation." As an expatriate Irish nationalist, McGee took the position that Catholics were treated, by and large, liberally in British North America. His public pronouncements on this subject caused considerable friction between him and the Fenians in the 1860s. When he was murdered in Ottawa in 1868, his assassination was quickly attributed to the Fenians, even though it is not clear that Patrick Whelan, the man executed as his assassin, actually was a Fenian – and considerable doubt remains whether Whelan was even the killer.

Most of McGee's publishing was in non-fiction prose, including *Historical Sketches of O'Connell and his Friends* (1845), *The Catholic History of North America* (1855), *A Popular History of Ireland, from the Earliest Period to the Emancipation of the Catholics* (1863), and *The Irish Position in British and in Republican North America: A Letter to the Editors of the Irish Press Irrespective of Party* (1866). He also published some fiction, including *Eva Macdonald, a Tale of the United Irishmen and their Times* (1844).

McGee's poetry was collected by Mary Sadlier and published in 1869, but the provenance of some of the poems in her collection is unclear; much of the poetry McGee published during his lifetime appeared in periodicals under pseudonyms, including the generic "An Irish Exile," making some difficult to identify definitively. But a lot of his poetry appeared under his name, including his only volume of verse published during his lifetime, *Canadian Ballads and Occasional Verses* (1858). McGee's contributions to *The Nation*, like those of Lady Wilde, Mangan, MacCarthy, and others, draw broadly on a ballad style and diction. His poems "Experience" and "St. Patrick's of the Woods" deal with the experiences of the Irish diaspora, the latter, in particular, viewing North America as a place where Irish Catholics can celebrate their religious and cultural traditions in safety, including the words of Daniel O'Connell and Thomas Moore. "Hail to the Land" is a nationalist rallying cry, while "Freedom's Journey" repeats a theme McGee frequently addressed in his non-fiction after he moved to Montreal, namely that British North America was a haven of religious tolerance and freedom, even in comparison to the United States.

Further reading

Böss, Michael, "Exiles No More: Ethnic Leadership and the Construction of the Myth of Thomas D'Arcy McGee," in *Re-mapping Exile: Realities and Metaphors in Irish Literature and History*, ed. Michael Böss, Irene Gilsenan Nordin, and Britta Olinder, 64–88. Aarhus, Denmark: Aarhus University Press, 2005.

Shanahan, David, "Young Ireland in a Young Canada: Thomas D'Arcy McGee and the New Nationality," *British Journal of Canadian Studies* 12 (1997): 1–8.

Hail to the Land

From Poems by Thomas D'Arcy McGee, Chiefly Written in America (1854)

I

Hail to the land where freedom first,
Through all the feudal fetters burst,
And planting men upon their feet,
Cried, "Onward, never more retreat,
Be it yours to plant your starry flag,   5
On royal roof and castle crag,
Be it yours to climb Earth's eastern slope
In championship of human hope,
Your war-cry – Truth – immortal word!
Your weapon – Justice – glorious sword!   10

Your fame far-travelled, as the Cirn,
And lasting as the Arch of Heaven.
     Hail to the Happy Land!"

II

Hail to the land where Franklin lies
At peace beneath disarmed skies,   15
Where Jefferson, and Jackson rest,
Like valiant men on victory's breast,
Where, his benignant day task done,
The clouds have closed round Washington –
The star amid the luminous host   20
Which guides mankind to freedom's coast.
I feel my heart beat fast and high,
As to the coast our ship draws nigh,
I burn the fresh foot-prints to see
Of the heroes of humanity.   25
     Hail to the Happy Land.

III

Hail to the land whose wide domain
Rejoices under Freedom's reign,
Where neither right nor race is bann'd,
Where more is done e'en than is plann'd –   30
Where a lie liveth not in stone,
Nor truth in bible leaves alone:
Where filial lives are monuments
To noble names and high intents –
Oh! where the living still can tread   35
Unblushingly amid the dead!
     Hail to that Happy Land.

IV

What can I lay on Freedom's shrine
Meet offering to the power divine.
I have nor coronet, nor crown,   40
Nor wealth, nor fame can I lay down;
But I have hated tyrants still
And struggled with their wrathful will,
And when through Europe's length they lied
For thee I feebly testified,   45
And oft, in better champion's stead,
In thy behoof I've striven and said,
"Ah, be the offering meet to thee,
My life, my all, dread Liberty.
     Hail to thy Happy Land."   50

V

The land is worthy of its place
The vanguard of the human race –

Its rivers still refresh the sea,
As Truth does Time, unceasingly;
Its volum'd plains as open lie   55
As a saint's soul before God's eye;
Its broad based mountains firmly stand
Like Faith and Hope in their own land.
Heaven keep this soil, and may it bear
New worth and wealth to every year,   60
And may men never here bend knee
To any Lord – oh Lord! but Thee.
     Hail to the Happy Land.

Experience

From **Poems by Thomas D'Arcy McGee, Chiefly Written in America (1854)**

I

Twice have I sailed the Atlantic o'er,
 Twice dwelt an exile in the west;
Twice did kind nature's skill restore,
 The quiet of my troubled breast –
As moss upon a rifted tree,   5
 So time its gentle cloaking did,
But though the wound no eye could see,
 Deep in my heart the barb was hid.

II

I felt a weight where'er I went –
 I felt a void within my brain: 10
My day hopes and my dreams were blent,
 With sable threads of mental pain;
My eye delighted not to look,
 On forest old or rapids grand;
The stranger's joy I scarce could brook,   15
 My heart was in my own dear land.

III

Where'er I turned some emblem still,
 Rousced consciousness upon my track;
Some hill was like an Irish hill,
 Some wild bird's whistle called me back;   20
A sea-bound ship bore off my peace,
 Between its white, cold wings of woe;
Oh if I had but wings like these,
 Where my peace went I too would go.

St. Patrick's of the Woods

From Poems by Thomas D'Arcy McGee, Chiefly Written in America (1854)

I

"Sir, my Guest, it is Sunday morning,
   And we are ready to Mass to go;
For the Sexton sent us word of warning,
   That the Priest would be in the glen below."

II

Quickly I rose, in mind delighted   5
   To find the old faith held so fast;
That even in western wilds benighted
   My people still to the Cross were claspt.

III

We trod the forest's broken byeway,
   We burst through brush and forded floods,   10
Until we came to the valley's highway,
   Where stood St. Patrick's of the Woods.

IV

A simple shed it was, but spacious,
   With ample entrance open wide;
Where forest veterans, green and gracious,   15
   Stood sentinels at either side.

V

And there, old friends with friends were meeting,
   And the last new-comer told his tale;
And kindred, kindred there were greeting,
   In the loving speech of the Island Gael.   20

VI

And here a group of anxious faces,
   Were drawn around a bowering tree,
While one – a reader – with sage grimaces
   Read from a record spread on his knee.

VII

Betimes I heard loud bursts of laughter   25
   At O'Connell's wit, from the eager throng;

And then, deep sighs would follow after
    Some verse of Moore's melodious song.[1]

VIII

Till at length the bell of the lowly altar
    Summoned to prayer, the scattered flock,   30
And they moved with steps that would not falter,
    If that summons led to the martyr's block.

IX

I've knelt in churches, new, and ancient,
    In grand cathedrals betimes I've stood,
But never felt my soul such transport,   35
    As in thine – St. Patrick's of the Wood.

Freedom's Journey

From Canadian Ballads and Occasional Verses (1858)

I

Freedom! a nursling of the North,
    Rock'd in the arms of stormy pines,
On fond adventure wander'd forth
    Where south the sun superbly shines;
        The prospect shone so bright and fair,   5
        She dream't her home was there, was there.

II

She lodged 'neath many a gilded roof,
    They gave her praise in many a hall,
Their kindness check'd the free reproof,
    Her heart dictated to let fall;   10
        She heard the Negro's helpless prayer,
        And felt her home could not be there.

III

She sought thro' rich Savannah's green
    And in the proud Palmetto grove,[1]
And where her Altar should have been   15
    She found nor liberty nor love;
        A cloud came o'er her forehead fair,
        She found no shrine to freedom there.

Notes

St. Patrick's of the Woods
[1] Daniel O'Connell; Thomas Moore.

Freedom's Journey
[1] Locations in Georgia, USA.

IV

Back to her native scenes she turn'd,
Back to the hardy, kindly North,
Where bright aloft the Pole-star burned,
Where stood her shrine by every hearth;
"Back to the North I will repair,"
The Goddess cried, "my home is there."

20

Oscar Wilde (1854–1900)

Oscar Fingal O'Flahertie Wills Wilde was born in Dublin, the son of authors Lady Jane Wilde and Sir William Wilde. When Oscar was young, his parents' literary social circle including many of the leading writers of mid-century Dublin, such as LeFanu, Carleton, and Ferguson, as well as political figures such as Isaac Butt, instrumental in the emergence of the Home Rule movement. Educated first at home and then at a school in Fermanagh, while paying regular visits to family homes in Wexford and Mayo, Wilde stayed in Dublin for university, studying at Trinity College Dublin from 1870 to 1874. He won a scholarship to Oxford, where he studied until 1878, became involved in the British Aesthetic movement, and published his first volume of verse, *Ravenna* (1878). He also counted among his friends a number of the leading Irish writers of his generation and earlier, including Boucicault (who assisted him in the theater) and Bram Stoker.

In 1879, after completing his university studies, he moved to London, where he moved in elite circles. He also went on a lecture tour in North America, spending much of 1882 lecturing across the continent on the subjects of art and poetry, earning a considerable sum of money. Shortly after his tour was over, he proposed to Constance Lloyd; they married in 1884. (Wilde had earlier proposed marriage to Florence Balcome, who married Wilde's friend Bram Stoker instead.) The couple had two children but were separated a decade later by scandal and Victorian homophobia. Wilde had a number of relationships and liaisons with men, but homosexuality was still illegal in Britain. He sued the Marquess of Queensberry, the father of one of his lovers, for slandering him after the Marquess left a note for Wilde at his club openly referring to Wilde's homosexuality (and misspelling the key word), leading to a series of trials and court actions in which Wilde was ultimately convicted of "gross indecency" in 1895 and sentenced to two years' hard labor, a brutal sentence at the time that involved back-breaking labor, spartan living conditions, and inadequate food. His pleas for consideration on medical grounds were unanswered, and he never recovered his health. After his release in 1897, he moved to Paris and assumed the name "Sebastian Melmoth," the surname taken from the title character of his great-uncle Maturin's gothic novel, *Melmoth the Wanderer* (1820). He died just three years later.

While at Oxford, Wilde began publishing in Irish periodicals, including some of the same forums as his parents, including the *Dublin University Magazine* and *The Nation*. His *Poems* (1881) was followed by a number of still-popular plays, including *The Importance of Being Earnest* (1895), as well as the haunting *Salomé* (1893), written in French. His success on the stage is legendary, but he also continued working for the periodical press, contributing to the *Pall Mall Gazette* after 1885, editing *The Woman's World* from 1887 to 1889, and serializing his only novel, *The Picture of Dorian Gray*, in *Lippincott's Magazine* (1890). He also published collections of short stories, such as *The Happy Prince and Other Tales* (1888), that critics suggest draw on his mother's work on Irish fairytales.

"The Selfish Giant," a mix of folklore and Christian belief, is part of this group, bearing comparison both to such works as the Kavanaghs' "The Pearl Fountain" and to religious verse such as De Vere's "Year of Sorrow." Like his mother in the same period, he also published essays on art and life, including "The Decay of Lying," a critique of realism in general and its literary dominance in France and England in particular. The text here of "The Decay of Lying" is taken from its first publication in a periodical, where it differs from the version in *Intentions* (1891) mostly in the framing dialogue rather than in Vivian's essay, but there are changes both minor and substantive throughout. Wilde draws on a wide canon of English authors, from William Shakespeare to John Ruskin and Rider Haggard, as well as American and French writers, to suggest that art should not be constrained by realism's narrow dictates and range of interests – celebrating instead a wide array of literature that includes the fantastic and romance. Wilde also critiques the interpretation of literature as a credible record of the past: "To pass from the art of a time to the time itself is the great fallacy of all historians."

Despite his connection to English writers of the Aesthetic movement, including Walter Pater, and such poems as "Requiescat" and "In the Gold Room," his early verse does not always fall within that framework. Writing on British and European politics as well, his early verse perhaps betrays his debts to his mother more than his fairytales. He organized some of the poems in his first volume under subheadings, such as *Eleutheria* and *Rosa Mystica*, preserved here, linking works into tighter clusters and sequences than the usual miscellany format allows. After his release from prison, he wrote on the harsh conditions there in letters to the *Daily Chronicle*. After his release, he also published *The Ballad of Reading Gaol* (1898), a gothic exploration of prison conditions with echoes of other gothic ballads, including English poet S. T. Coleridge's "Rime of the Ancient Mariner." *The Ballad* was first published anonymously under Wilde's designation as a prisoner, "C. 3. 3." (subsequent editions included minor changes, and a first edition is the copy-text here). In his short but incredibly prolific career, Wilde published nearly twenty volumes and countless pieces for various periodicals.

Further reading

Alkalay-Gut, Karen, "The Thing He Loves: Murder as Aesthetic Experience in *The Ballad of Reading Gaol*," *Victorian Poetry* 35 (1997): 349–66.

Frankel, Nick, " 'Ave Imperatrix': Oscar Wilde and the Poetry of Englishness," *Victorian Poetry* 35 (1997): 117–37.

Pine, Richard, *The Thief of Reason: Oscar Wilde and Modern Ireland*. Dublin: Gill and Macmillan, 1995.

Sonnet to Liberty

From Eleutheria[1] (Poems, 1881)

Not that I love thy children, whose dull eyes
See nothing save their own unlovely woe,
Whose minds know nothing, nothing care to know,–

Notes ——————————————————

SONNET TO LIBERTY

[1] The title of this group of poems is the Greek word for liberty. Wilde may also be alluding to a motto popular during the Greek struggle for independence in the early nineteenth century, *Eleutheria i thanatos* (liberty or death).

But that the roar of thy Democracies,
Thy reigns of Terror, thy great Anarchies,   5
Mirror my wildest passions like the sea
And give my rage a brother–! Liberty!
For this sake only do thy dissonant cries
Delight my discreet soul, else might all kings
By bloody knout or treacherous cannonades   10
Rob nations of their rights inviolate
And I remain unmoved – and yet, and yet,
These Christs that die upon the barricades,
God knows it I am with them, in some things.

Ave Imperatrix[1]

From Eleutheria (Poems, 1881)

Set in this stormy Northern sea,
    Queen of these restless fields of tide,
England! what shall men say of thee,
    Before whose feet the worlds divide?

The earth, a brittle globe of glass,   5
    Lies in the hollow of thy hand,
And through its heart of crystal pass,
    Like shadows through a twilight land,

The spears of crimson-suited war,
    The long white-crested waves of fight,   10
And all the deadly fires which are
    The torches of the lords of Night.

The yellow leopards, strained and lean,
    The treacherous Russian knows so well,
With gaping blackened jaws are seen   15
    Leap through the hail of screaming shell.

The strong sea-lion of England's wars
    Hath left his sapphire cave of sea,
To battle with the storm that mars
    The star of England's chivalry.   20

The brazen-throated clarion blows
    Across the Pathan's reedy fen,
And the high steps of Indian snows
    Shake to the tread of armèd men.

Notes

AVE IMPERATRIX
[1] The second Anglo-Afghan war had only recently ended when this poem was published. The Russian empire, bordering Afghanistan on the northern side while British India was the country's southern neighbor, was Britain's main competitor for control of the region. Most of the geographical references here are to the larger region: for instance, Cabool (Kabul) is in Afghanistan, Ispahan is in modern-day Iran, and Samarcand is in modern-day Uzbekistan but was under Russian control when Wilde was writing.

And many an Afghan chief, who lies 25
    Beneath his cool pomegranate-trees,
Clutches his sword in fierce surmise
    When on the mountain-side he sees

The fleet-foot Marri scout, who comes
    To tell how he hath heard afar 30
The measured roll of English drums
    Beat at the gates of Kandahar.

For southern wind and east wind meet
    Where, girt and crowned by sword and fire,
England with bare and bloody feet 35
    Climbs the steep road of wide empire.

O lonely Himalayan height,
    Grey pillar of the Indian sky,
Where saw'st thou last in clanging flight
    Our wingèd dogs of Victory? 40

The almond-groves of Samarcand,
    Bokhara, where red lilies blow,
And Oxus, by whose yellow sand
    The grave white-turbaned merchants go:

And on from thence to Ispahan, 45
    The gilded garden of the sun,
Whence the long dusty caravan
    Brings cedar and vermilion;

And that dread city of Cabool
    Set at the mountain's scarpèd feet, 50
Whose marble tanks are ever full
    With water for the noonday heat:

Where through the narrow straight Bazaar
    A little maid Circassian
Is led, a present from the Czar 55
    Unto some old and bearded khan, –

Here have our wild war-eagles flown,
    And flapped wide wings in fiery fight;
But the sad dove, that sits alone
    In England – she hath no delight. 60

In vain the laughing girl will lean
    To greet her love with love-lit eyes:
Down in some treacherous black ravine,
    Clutching his flag, the dead boy lies.

And many a moon and sun will see 65
    The lingering wistful children wait
To climb upon their father's knee;
    And in each house made desolate

Pale women who have lost their lord
    Will kiss the relics of the slain – 70

Some tarnished epaulette – some sword –
    Poor toys to soothe such anguished pain.

For not in quiet English fields
    Are these, our brothers, lain to rest,
Where we might deck their broken shields   75
    With all the flowers the dead love best.

For some are by the Delhi walls,
    And many in the Afghan land,
And many where the Ganges falls
    Through seven mouths of shifting sand.   80

And some in Russian waters lie,
    And others in the seas which are
The portals to the East, or by
    The wind-swept heights of Trafalgar.

O wandering graves! O restless sleep!   85
    O silence of the sunless day!
O still ravine! O stormy deep!
    Give up your prey! give up your prey!

And thou whose wounds are never healed,
    Whose weary race is never won,   90
O Cromwell's England! must thou yield
    For every inch of ground a son?

Go! crown with thorns thy gold-crowned head,
    Change thy glad song to song of pain;
Wind and wild wave have got thy dead,   95
    And will not yield them back again.

Wave and wild wind and foreign shore
    Possess the flower of English land –
Lips that thy lips shall kiss no more,
    Hands that shall never clasp thy hand.   100

What profit now that we have bound
    The whole round world with nets of gold,
If hidden in our heart is found
    The care that groweth never old?

What profit that our galleys ride,   105
    Pine-forest-like, on every main?
Ruin and wreck are at our side,
    Grim warders of the House of pain.

Where are the brave, the strong, the fleet?
    Where is our English chivalry?   110
Wild grasses are their burial-sheet,
    And sobbing waves their threnody.[2]

Notes ————————————————————————————

[2] dirge

O loved ones lying far away,
    What word of love can dead lips send!
O wasted dust! O senseless clay!   115
    Is this the end! Is this the end!

Peace, peace! we wrong the noble dead
    To vex their solemn slumber so;
Though childless, and with thorn-crowned head,
    Up the steep road must England go,   120

Yet when this fiery web is spun,
    Her watchmen shall descry from far
The young Republic like a sun
    Rise from these crimson seas of war.

To Milton

From Eleutheria (Poems, 1881)

Milton! I think thy spirit hath passed away
    From these white cliffs, and high-embattled towers;
    This gorgeous fiery-coloured world of ours
Seems fallen into ashes dull and grey,
And the age turned unto a mimic play   5
    Wherein we waste our else too-crowded hours:
    For all our pomp and pageantry and powers
We are but fit to delve the common clay,
Seeing this little isle on which we stand,
    This England, this sea-lion of the sea,   10
    By ignorant demagogues is held in fee,
Who love her not: Dear God! is this the land
    Which bare a triple empire in her hand
    When Cromwell spake the word Democracy!

Theoretikos

From Eleutheria (Poems, 1881)

This mighty empire hath but feet of clay:
    Of all its ancient chivalry and might
    Our little island is forsaken quite:
Some enemy hath stolen its crown of bay,
And from its hills that voice hath passed away   5
    Which spake of Freedom: O come out of it,
    Come out of it, my Soul, thou are not fit
For this vile traffic-house, where day by day
    Wisdom and reverence are sold at mart,
    And the rude people rage with ignorant cries   10
Against an heritage of centuries.

It mars my calm: wherefore in dreams of Art
And loftiest culture I would stand apart,
Neither for God, nor for his enemies.

Resquiescat

From **Rosa Mystica (Poems, 1881)**

Tread lightly, she is near
   Under the snow,
Speak gently, she can hear
   The daisies grow.

All her bright golden hair   5
   Tarnished with rust,
She that was young and fair
   Fallen to dust.

Lily-like, white as snow,
   She hardly knew   10
She was a woman, so
   Sweetly she grew.

Coffin-board, heavy stone,
   Lie on her breast,
I vex my heart alone   15
   She is at rest.

Peace, Peace, she cannot hear
   Lyre or sonnet,
All my life's buried here,
   Heap earth upon it.   20

In the Gold Room: A Harmony

From Poems (**1881**)

Her ivory hands on the ivory keys
   Strayed in fitful fantasy,
Like the silver gleam when the poplar trees
   Rustle their pale leaves listlessly,
Or the drifting foam of a restless sea   5
When the waves show their teeth in the flying breeze.

Her gold hair fell on the wall of gold
   Like the delicate gossamer tangles spun
On the burnished disk of the marigold,
   Or the sun-flower turning to meet the sun   10
   When the gloom of the jealous night is done,
And the spear of the lily is aureoled.

And her sweet red lips on these lips of mine
   Burned like the ruby fire set
In the swinging lamp of a crimson shrine,   15
   Or the bleeding wounds of the pomegranate,
   Or the heart of the lotus drenched and wet
With the spilt-out blood of the rose-red wine.

The Selfish Giant

From The Happy Prince and Other Tales (1888)

Every afternoon, as they were coming from school, the children used to go and play in the Giant's garden.

It was a large lovely garden, with soft green grass. Here and there over the grass stood beautiful flowers like stars, and there were twelve peach-trees that in the spring-time broke out into delicate blossoms of pink and pearl, and in the autumn bore rich fruit. The birds sat on the trees and sang so sweetly that the children used to stop their games in order to listen to them. "How happy we are here!" they cried to each other.

One day the Giant came back. He had been to visit his friend the Cornish ogre, and had stayed with him for seven years. After the seven years were over he had said all that he had to say, for his conversation was limited, and he determined to return to his own castle. When he arrived he saw the children playing in the garden.

"What are you doing here?" he cried in a very gruff voice, and the children ran away.

"My own garden is my own garden," said the Giant; "any one can understand that, and I will allow nobody to play in it but myself." So he built a high wall all round it, and put up a notice-board.

> TRESPASSERS
>
> WILL BE
>
> PROSECUTED

He was a very selfish Giant.

The poor children had now nowhere to play. They tried to play on the road, but the road was very dusty and full of hard stones, and they did not like it. They used to wander round the high wall when their lessons were over, and talk about the beautiful garden inside. "How happy we were there," they said to each other.

Then the Spring came, and all over the country there were little blossoms and little birds. Only in the garden of the Selfish Giant it was still winter. The birds did not care to sing in it as there were no children, and the trees forgot to blossom. Once a beautiful flower put its head out from the grass, but when it saw the notice-board it was so sorry for the children that it slipped back into the ground again, and went off to sleep. The only people who were pleased were the Snow and the Frost. "Spring has forgotten this garden," they cried, "so we will live here all the year round." The Snow covered up the grass with her great white cloak, and the Frost painted all the trees silver. Then they invited the North Wind to stay with them, and he came. He was wrapped in furs, and he roared all day about the garden, and blew the chimney-pots down. "This is a delightful spot," he said, "we must ask the Hail on a visit." So the Hail came. Every day for three hours he rattled on the roof of the castle till he broke most of the slates, and then he ran round and round the garden as fast as he could go. He was dressed in grey, and his breath was like ice.

"I cannot understand why the Spring is so late in coming," said the Selfish Giant, as he sat at the window and looked out at his cold white garden; "I hope there will be a change in the weather."

But the Spring never came, nor the Summer. The Autumn gave golden fruit to every garden, but to the Giant's garden she gave none. "He is too selfish," she said. So it was always Winter there, and the North Wind, and the Hail, and the Frost, and the Snow danced about through the trees.

One morning the Giant was lying awake in bed when he heard some lovely music. It sounded so sweet to his ears that he thought it must be the King's musicians passing by. It was really only a little linnet singing outside his window, but it was so long since he had heard a bird sing in his garden that it seemed to him to be the most beautiful music in the world. Then the Hail stopped dancing over his head, and the North Wind ceased roaring, and a delicious perfume came to him through the open casement. "I believe the Spring has come at last," said the Giant; and he jumped out of bed and looked out.

What did he see?

He saw a most wonderful sight. Through a little hole in the wall the children had crept in, and they were sitting in the branches of the trees. In every tree that he could see there was a little child. And the trees were so glad to have the children back again that they had covered themselves with blossoms, and were waving their arms gently above the children's heads. The birds were flying about and twittering with delight, and the flowers were looking up through the green grass and laughing. It was a lovely scene, only in one corner it was still winter. It was the farthest corner of the garden, and in it was standing a little boy. He was so small that he could not reach up to the branches of the tree, and he was wandering all round it, crying bitterly. The poor tree was still quite covered with frost and snow, and the North Wind was blowing and roaring above it. "Climb up! little boy," said the Tree, and it bent its branches down as low as it could; but the boy was too tiny.

And the Giant's heart melted as he looked out. "How selfish I have been!" he said; "now I know why the Spring would not come here. I will put that poor little boy on the top of the tree, and then I will knock down the wall, and my garden shall be the children's playground for ever and ever." He was really very sorry for what he had done.

So he crept downstairs and opened the front door quite softly, and went out into the garden. But when the children saw him they were so frightened that they all ran away, and the garden became winter again. Only the little boy did not run, for his eyes were so full of tears that he did not see the Giant coming. And the Giant stole up behind him and took him gently in his hand, and put him up into the tree. And the tree broke at once into blossom, and the birds came and sang on it, and the little boy stretched out his two arms and flung them round the Giant's neck, and kissed him. And the other children, when they saw that the Giant was not wicked any longer, came running back, and with them came the Spring. "It is your garden now, little children," said the Giant, and he took a great axe and knocked down the wall. And when the people were going to market at twelve o'clock they found the Giant playing with the children in the most beautiful garden they had ever seen.

All day long they played, and in the evening they came to the Giant to bid him good-bye.

"But where is your little companion?" he said: "the boy I put into the tree." The Giant loved him the best because he had kissed him.

"We don't know," answered the children; "he has gone away."

"You must tell him to be sure and come here to-morrow," said the Giant. But the children said that they did not know where he lived, and had never seen him before; and the Giant felt very sad.

Every afternoon, when school was over, the children came and played with the Giant. But the little boy whom the Giant loved was never seen again. The Giant was very kind to all the children, yet he longed for his first little friend, and often spoke of him. "How I would like to see him!" he used to say.

Years went over, and the Giant grew very old and feeble. He could not play about any more, so he sat in a huge armchair, and watched the children at their games, and admired his garden. "I have many beautiful flowers," he said; "but the children are the most beautiful flowers of all."

One winter morning he looked out of his window as he was dressing. He did not hate the Winter now, for he knew that it was merely the Spring asleep, and that the flowers were resting.

Suddenly he rubbed his eyes in wonder, and looked and looked. It certainly was a marvellous sight. In the farthest corner of the garden was a tree quite covered with lovely white blossoms. Its branches were all golden, and silver fruit hung down from them, and underneath it stood the little boy he had loved.

Downstairs ran the Giant in great joy, and out into the garden. He hastened across the grass, and came near to the child. And when he came quite close his face grew red with anger, and he said, "Who hath dared to wound thee?" For on the palms of the child's hands were the prints of two nails, and the prints of two nails were on the little feet.

"Who hath dared to wound thee?" cried the Giant; "tell me, that I may take my big sword and slay him."

"Nay!" answered the child; "but these are the wounds of Love."

"Who art thou?" said the Giant, and a strange awe fell on him, and he knelt before the little child.

And the child smiled on the Giant, and said to him, "You let me play once in your garden, to-day you shall come with me to my garden, which is Paradise."

And when the children ran in that afternoon, they found the Giant lying dead under the tree, all covered with white blossoms.

From *The Decay of Lying: A Dialogue*

From The Nineteenth Century (1889)

SCENE – *The Library of a Country House in England.*

PERSONS – CYRIL *and* VIVIAN.

CYRIL [*coming in through the open window from the terrace*]. My dear Vivian, don't coop yourself up all day in the library. It is a perfectly lovely afternoon. Let us go and lie on the grass and smoke cigarettes and enjoy nature.

VIVIAN. Enjoy nature! I am glad to say that I have entirely lost that faculty. People tell us that art makes us love nature more than we loved her before; that it reveals her secrets to us; and that after a careful study of Corot and Constable[1] we see things in

Notes ————————————————————

FROM THE DECAY OF LYING
[1] French realist painter Jean-Baptiste-Camille Corot (1796–1875) and English landscape painter John Constable (1776–1837).

her that had escaped us. My own experience is that the more we study art, the less we care for nature. What art really reveals to us is nature's lack of design, her curious crudities, her extraordinary monotony, her absolutely unfinished condition. When I look at a landscape I cannot help seeing all its defects. It is fortunate for us, however, that nature is so imperfect, as otherwise we should have had no art at all. Art is our spirited protest, our gallant attempt to teach Nature her proper place. As for the infinite variety of Nature, that is a pure myth. It is not to be found in Nature herself, but in the imagination, or fancy, or cultivated blindness, of the man who looks at her.

c. Well, you need not look at the landscape. You can lie on the grass and smoke and talk.

v. But nature is so uncomfortable. Grass is hard and lumpy and damp, and full of horrid little black insects. Why, even Maple[2] can make you a more comfortable seat than nature can. Nature pales before the Tottenham Court Road. I don't complain. If nature had been comfortable, mankind would never have invented architecture, and I prefer houses to the open air. In a house we all feel of the proper proportions. Everything is subordinated to us, fashioned for our use and our pleasure. Egotism itself, which is so necessary to a proper sense of human dignity, is absolutely the result of indoor life. Out of doors one becomes abstract and impersonal. One's individuality absolutely leaves one. And then nature is so indifferent, so unappreciative. Whenever I am walking in the park here, I always feel that I am no more to nature than the cattle that browse on the slope, or the burdock that blooms in the ditch. Nothing is clearer than that Nature hates Mind. Thinking is the most unhealthy thing in the world, and people die of it just as of any other disease. Fortunately, in England at least, it is not catching. Our splendid physique as a people is entirely due to our national stupidity. I only hope we shall be able to keep this great historic bulwark of our happiness for many years to come; but I am afraid that we are beginning to be over-educated; at least everybody who is incapable of learning has taken to teaching – that is really what our enthusiasm for education has come to. In the meantime you had better go back to your wearisome uncomfortable Nature, and leave me to correct my proofs.

c. Writing an article! That is not very consistent after what you have just said.

v. Who wants to be consistent? The dullard and the doctrinaire, the tedious people who carry out their principles to the bitter end of action, to the *reductio ad absurdum* of practice? Not I. Like Emerson,[3] I write over the door of my library the word "Whim." Besides, my article is really a most salutary and valuable warning. If it is attended to, there may be a new Renaissance of Art.

c. What is the subject?

v. I intend to call it "The Decay of Lying: A Protest."

c. Lying! I should have thought our politicians kept up that habit.

v. I assure you that they do not. They never rise beyond the level of misrepresentation, and actually condescend to prove, to discuss, to argue. How different from the temper of the true liar, with his frank, fearless statements, his superb irresponsibility, his healthy, natural disdain of proof of any kind! After all, what is a fine lie? Simply that which is its own evidence. If a man is sufficiently unimaginative to produce evidence in support of a lie, he might just as well speak the truth at once. No, the politicians won't do, and besides, what I am pleading for is lying in art. Shall I read you what I have written? It might do you a great deal of good.

Notes ——————————————————————————————————————

[2] A furniture business on Tottenham Court Road, run by the Maple family.

[3] American poet Ralph Waldo Emerson (1803–82).

c. Certainly, if you give me a cigarette. Thanks. By the way, what magazine do you intend it for?

v. For the *Retrospective Review*. I think I told you that we had revived it.

c. Whom do you mean by "we"?

v. Oh, the Tired Hedonists of course. It is a club to which I belong. We are supposed to wear faded roses in our button-holes when we meet, and to have a sort of cult for Domitian.[4] I am afraid you are not eligible. You are too fond of simple pleasures.

c. I should be black-balled on the ground of animal spirits, I suppose?

v. Probably. Besides, you are a little too old. We don't admit anyone who is of the usual age.

c. Well, I should fancy you are all a good deal bored with each other.

v. We are. That is one of the objects of the club. Now, if you promise not to interrupt too often, I will read you my article.

c. [*flinging himself down on the sofa*]. All right.

v. [*reading in a very clear, musical voice*]. "THE DECAY OF LYING: A PROTEST. – One of the chief causes of the curiously commonplace character of most of the literature of our age is undoubtedly the decay of lying as an art, a science, and a social pleasure. The ancient historians gave us delightful fiction in the form of fact; the modern novelist presents us with dull facts under the guise of fiction. The blue-book[5] is rapidly becoming his ideal both for method and manner. He has his tedious '*document humain*,' his miserable little '*coin de la création*,'[6] into which he peers with his microscope. He is to be found at the Librairie Nationale, or at the British Museum, shamelessly reading up his subject. He has not even the courage of other people's ideas, but insists on going directly to life for everything, and ultimately, between encyclopaedias and personal experience, he comes to the ground, having drawn his types from the family circle or from the weekly washerwoman, and having acquired an amount of useful information from which he never, even in his most thoughtful moments, can thoroughly free himself.

"The loss that results to literature in general from this false ideal of our time can hardly be overestimated. People have a careless way of talking about a 'born liar,' just as they talk about a 'born poet.' But in both cases they are wrong. Lying and poetry are arts – arts, as Plato saw,[7] not unconnected with each other – and they require the most careful study, the most disinterested devotion. Indeed, they have their technique, just as the more material arts of painting and sculpture have, their subtle secrets of form and colour, their craft-mysteries, their deliberate artistic methods. As one knows the poet by his fine music, so one can recognise the liar by his rich rhythmic utterance, and in neither case will the casual inspiration of the moment suffice. Here, as elsewhere, practice must precede perfection. But in modern days while the fashion of writing poetry has become far too common, and should, if possible, be discouraged, the fashion of lying has almost fallen into disrepute. Many a young man starts in life with a natural gift for exaggeration which, if nurtured in congenial and sympathetic surroundings, or by the imitation of the best models, might grow into something really great and wonderful. But, as a rule, he comes to nothing. He either falls into careless habits of accuracy –"

Notes

[4] Domitian (51–96), Roman emperor, who insisted he be addressed as Lord and God.

[5] Published government reports, often bought in large numbers by the public in this era; soon after "Decay of Lying" appeared, Wilde published an essay on a blue-book on Ireland.

[6] *Document humain* (a record of human experience) is a term related to realism, particularly naturalism as a branch of French realism; *coin de la création*, corner of the world. Wilde may be alluding specifically to writing on naturalism by French novelist Emile Zola (1840–1902).

[7] See Plato's *The Republic*.

c. My dear Vivian!

v. Please don't interrupt in the middle of a sentence. "He either falls into careless habits of accuracy, or takes to frequenting the society of the aged and the well-informed. Both things are equally fatal to his imagination, as indeed they would be fatal to the imagination of anybody, and in a short time he develops a morbid and unhealthy faculty of truth-telling, begins to verify all statements made in his presence, has no hesitation in contradicting people who are younger than himself, and often ends by writing novels which are so like life that no one can possibly believe them. This is no isolated instance that we are giving. It is simply one example out of many; and if something cannot be done to check, or at least to modify, our monstrous worship of facts, art will become sterile, and beauty will pass away from the land.

"Even Mr. Robert Louis Stevenson, that delightful master of delicate and fanciful prose, is tainted with this modern vice, for we positively know no other name for it. There is such a thing as robbing a story of its reality by trying to make it too true, and *The Black Arrow* is so inartistic that it does not contain a single anachronism to boast of, while the transformation of Dr. Jekyll reads dangerously like an experiment out of the *Lancet*. As for Mr. Rider Haggard, who really has, or had once, the makings of a perfectly magnificent liar, he is now so afraid of being suspected of genius that when he does tell us anything marvellous, he feels bound to invent a personal reminiscence, and to put it into a footnote as a kind of cowardly corroboration.[8] Nor are our other novelists much better. Mr. Henry James[9] writes fiction as if it was a painful duty, and wastes upon mean motives and imperceptible 'points of view' his neat literary style, his felicitous phrases, his swift and caustic satire. Mrs. Oliphant[10] prattles pleasantly about curates, lawn-tennis parties, domesticity, and other wearisome things. Mr. Marion Crawford has immolated himself upon the altar of local colour. He is like the lady in the French comedy who is always talking about 'le beau ciel d'Italie.'[11] Besides, he has fallen into a bad habit of uttering moral platitudes. At times he is almost edifying. *Robert Elsmere* is of course a masterpiece – a masterpiece of the 'genre ennuyeux,'[12] the one form of literature that the English people seem to thoroughly enjoy. Indeed it is only in England that such a novel could be possible. As for that great and daily increasing school of novelists for whom the sun always rises in the East-End, the only thing that can be said about them is that they find life crude, and leave it raw.

"... M. Ruskin once described the characters in George Eliot's novels as being like the sweepings of a Pentonville omnibus,[13] but M. Zola's characters are much worse. They have their dreary vices, and their drearier virtues. The record of their lives is absolutely without interest ... It is a humiliating confession, but we are all of us made out of the same stuff. In Falstaff there is something of Hamlet, in Hamlet there is not a little of Falstaff. The fat knight has his moods of melancholy, and the young prince his moments of coarse humour.[14] Where we differ from each

Notes

[8] Stevenson (1850–94) and Haggard (1856–1924) are British authors of adventure and gothic fiction; both *Black Arrow* (1883) and *The Strange Case of Dr. Jekyll and Mr. Hyde* (1886) are by Stevenson. *The Lancet* was the leading British medical journal.

[9] American writer Henry James (1843–1916).

[10] British novelist Margaret Oliphant (1828–97).

[11] "The beautiful sky of Italy." American novelist Francis Marion Crawford (1854–1909).

[12] English novelist Mary Augusta Ward's *Robert Elsmere* (1888); the novel had been reviewed in *The Nineteenth Century*. *Genre ennuyeux* means broadly "wearisome kind."

[13] English writers John Ruskin (1819–1900) and George Eliot (1819–80).

[14] See Shakespeare's *Hamlet* and, for Falstaff, *The Merry Wives of Windsor*, the source of the epithet "fat knight" (Falstaff also appears in both parts of Shakespeare's *Henry IV*).

other is purely in accidentals: in dress, in manner, tone of voice, personal appearance, tricks of habit, and the like. The more one analyses people, the more all reasons for analysis disappear. Sooner or later one comes to that dreadful universal thing called human nature. Indeed, as any one who has ever worked among the poor knows only too well, the brotherhood of man is no mere poet's dream, it is a terrible reality; and if a writer insists upon analysing the upper classes, he might just as well write of match-girls and costermongers at once." However, my dear Cyril, I will not detain you any further on this point. I quite admit that modern novels have many good points. All I say is that, as a class, they are quite unreadable.

c. That is certainly a very grave qualification, but I must say that I think you are rather unfair in some of your strictures. I like *Robert Elsmere* for instance. Not that I can look upon it as a serious work. As a statement of the problems that confront the earnest Christian it is ridiculous and antiquated. It is simply Arnold's *Literature and Dogma*[15] with the literature left out ... I also cannot help expressing my surprise that you have said nothing about the two novelists whom you are always reading, Balzac and George Meredith.[16] Surely they are realists, both of them?

v. Ah! Meredith! Who can define him? His style is chaos illumined by flashes of lightning. As a writer he has mastered everything, except language: as a novelist he can do everything, except tell a story: as an artist he is everything, except articulate. Somebody in Shakespeare – Touchstone, I think – talks about a man who is always breaking his shins over his own wit,[17] and it seems to me that this might serve as the basis of a criticism of Meredith's style. But whatever he is, he is not a realist. Or rather I would say that he is a child of realism who is not on speaking terms with his father. By deliberate choice he has made himself a romanticist ...

c. There is something in what you say, and there is no doubt that whatever amusement we may find in reading an absolutely modern novel, we have rarely any artistic pleasure in re-reading it. And this is perhaps the best rough test of what is literature and what is not. If one cannot enjoy reading a book over and over again, there is no good reading it at all. But what do you say about the return to Life and Nature? This is the panacea that is always being recommended to us.

v. [*taking up his proofs*]. I will read you what I say on that subject. The passage comes later on in the article, but I may as well read it now: –

"The popular cry of our time is 'Let us return to Life and Nature; they will recreate Art for us, and send the red blood coursing through her veins; they will give her feet swiftness and make her hand strong.' But, alas! we are mistaken in our amiable and well-meaning efforts. Nature is always behind the age; and as for Life, she is the solvent that breaks up Art, the enemy that lays waste her house."

c. What do you mean by saying that nature is always behind the age?

v. Well, perhaps that is rather obscure. What I mean is this. If we take nature to mean natural simple instinct as opposed to self-conscious culture, the work produced under this influence is always old-fashioned, antiquated, and out of date. If, on the other hand, we regard Nature as the collection of phenomena external to man, people only discover in her what they bring to her. She has no suggestions of her own. Wordsworth went to the lakes, but he was never a lake poet. He found in stones the sermons he had already hidden there. He went moralising about the district, but his good work was produced when he returned, not to nature

Notes

[15] *Literature and Dogma: An Essay Towards the Better Apprehension of the Bible* (1873) by English author Matthew Arnold (1822–88).

[16] French author Honoré de Balzac (1799–1850) and English writer George Meredith (1828–1909).

[17] See Shakespeare's *As You Like It*, Act II, scene iv.

but to poetry. Poetry gave him "Laodamia," and the fine sonnets, and the "Ode to Immortality," and nature gave him "Martha Ray" and "Peter Bell."[18]

c. I think that view might be questioned. I am rather inclined to believe in the "impulse from a vernal wood,"[19] though of course the artistic value of such an impulse depends entirely on the kind of temperament that receives it. However, proceed with your article.

v. [*reading*]. "Art begins with abstract decoration, with purely imaginative and pleasurable work dealing with what is unreal and non-existent. This is the first stage. Then Life becomes fascinated with this new wonder, and asks to be admitted into the charmed circle. Art takes Life as part of her rough material, recreates it, and refashions it in fresh forms, is absolutely indifferent to fact, invents, imagines, dreams, and keeps between herself and reality the impenetrable barrier of beautiful style, of decorative or ideal treatment. The third stage is when Life gets the upper hand, and drives Art out into the wilderness. That is the decadence, and it is from this that we are now suffering.

"Take the case of the English drama. At first in the hands of the monks dramatic art was abstract, decorative, and mythological. Then she enlisted life in her service, and using some of life's external forms, she created an entirely new race of beings, whose sorrows were more terrible than any sorrow man has ever felt, whose joys were keener than lover's joys, who had the rage of the Titans and the calm of the gods, who had monstrous and marvellous sins, monstrous and marvellous virtues. To them she gave a language different from that of actual life, a language full of resonant music and sweet rhythm, made stately by solemn cadence, or made delicate by fanciful rhyme, jewelled with wonderful words, and enriched with lofty diction. She clothed her children in strange raiment and gave them masks, and at her bidding the antique world rose from its marble tomb. A new Caesar stalked through the streets of risen Rome, and with purple sail and flute-led oars another Cleopatra passed up the river to Antioch.[20] Old myth and legend and dream took form and substance. History was entirely re-written, and there was hardly one of the dramatists who did not recognise that *the object of art is not simple truth but complex beauty.* In this they were perfectly right. Art herself is simply a form of exaggeration; and selection, which is the very spirit of art, is nothing more than an intensified mode of over-emphasis.

"But life soon shattered the perfection of the form. Even in Shakespeare we can see the beginning of the end. It shows itself by the gradual breaking up of the blank verse in the later plays, by the predominance given to prose, and by the over-importance assigned to characterisation. The passages in Shakespeare – and they are many – where the language is uncouth, vulgar, exaggerated, fantastic, obscene even, are due entirely to life calling for an echo of its own voice, and rejecting the intervention of beautiful style, through which alone it should be allowed to find expression. Shakespeare is not by any means a flawless artist. He is too fond of going directly to life, and borrowing life's natural utterance. He forgets that when *art surrenders her imaginative medium she surrenders everything* ..."

And now let me read you a passage which deals with the commonplace character of our literature: –

Notes

[18] English poet William Wordsworth (1770–1850). Two titles are incorrect: "Martha Ray" is the name of a character in "The Thorn" and the Ode is "Ode: Intimations of Immortality."

[19] Wordsworth's "The Tables Turned" (1798).

[20] See Shakespeare's *Antony and Cleopatra*, esp. Act II, scene ii for this description of Cleopatra's barge.

"It was not always thus. We need not say anything about the poets, for they, with the unfortunate exception of Mr. Wordsworth, have always been faithful to their high mission, and are universally recognised as being absolutely unreliable. But in the works of Herodotus, who, in spite of the shallow and ungenerous attempts of modern sciolists to verify his history, may be justly called the 'Father of Lies'; in the published speeches of Cicero and the biographies of Suetonius; in Tacitus at his best; in Pliny's *Natural History*; in Hanno's *Periplus*; in all the early chronicles; in the Lives of the Saints; in Froissart and Sir Thomas Mallory; in the travels of Marco Polo; in Olaus Magnus, and Aldrovandus, and Conrad Lycosthenes, with his magnificent *Prodigiorum et Ostentorum Chronicon*; in the autobiography of Benvenuto Cellini; in the memoirs of Casanuova; in Defoe's *History of the Plague*; in Boswell's *Life of Johnson*; in Napoleon's despatches, and in the works of our own Carlyle, whose *French Revolution* is one of the most fascinating historical romances ever written, facts are either kept in their proper subordinate position, or else entirely excluded on the general ground of dulness.[21] Now everything is changed. Facts are not merely finding a footing in history, but they are usurping the domain of Fancy, and have invaded the kingdom of Romance. Their chilling touch is over everything. They are vulgarising mankind. The crude commercialism of America, its materialising spirit, its indifference to the poetical side of things, and its lack of imagination and of high, unattainable ideals, are entirely due to that country having adopted for its national hero, a man, who according to his own confession, was incapable of telling a lie, and it is not too much to say that the story of George Washington and the cherry-tree has done more harm, and in a shorter space of time, than any other moral tale in the whole of literature."[22]

c. My dear boy!

v. I assure you it is quite true, and the amusing part of the whole thing is that the story of the cherry-tree is an absolute myth. However, you must not think that I am too despondent about the artistic future of America or of our own country. Listen to this: –

"That some change will take place before this century has drawn to its close, we have no doubt whatsoever. Bored by the tedious and improving conversation of those who have neither the wit to exaggerate nor the genius to romance, tired of the intelligent person whose reminiscences are always based upon memory, whose statements are invariably limited by probability, and who is at any time liable to be corroborated by the merest Philistine who happens to be present, society sooner or later must return to its lost leader, the cultured and fascinating liar . . .

"No doubt there will always be critics who, like a recent writer in the *Saturday Review*,[23] will gravely censure the teller of fairy tales for his defective knowledge of natural history, who will measure imaginative work by their own lack of any imaginative faculty, and who will hold up their inkstained hands in horror if some honest gentleman, who has never been farther than the yew trees of his own garden, pens a fascinating book of travels like Sir John Mandeville, or, like great Raleigh, writes a whole history of the world, in prison, and without knowing anything about the past.[24] To excuse themselves they will try and shelter under the shield of him who made Prospero the magician, and gave him Caliban and Ariel as

[21] This long list surveys an international array of history writing and biography from the classical period forward to the nineteenth century.

[22] George Washington (1732–99), first US president. In legend, if not in fact, Washington as a young boy illicitly chopped down a cherry tree; when asked who destroyed the tree, the child answered, "I cannot tell a lie" and confessed.

[23] An English literary journal.

[24] The fourteenth-century *Travels of John Mandeville* – for which the author is not definitively identified – is a notoriously fantastic travelogue; English courtier and imperial traveler Sir Walter Ralegh (1544–1618), author of *History of the World* (1614).

his servants, who heard the Tritons blowing their horns round the coral-reefs of the Enchanted Isle, and the fairies singing to each other in a wood near Athens, who led the phantom kings in dim procession across the misty Scottish heath, and hid Hecate in a cave with the weird sisters.[25] They will call upon Shakespeare – they always do – and will quote that hackneyed passage about Art holding up the mirror to Nature, forgetting that this unfortunate aphorism is deliberately said by Hamlet in order to convince the bystanders of his absolute insanity in art-matters."[26]

c. Ahem! Ahem! Another cigarette, please.

v. My dear fellow, whatever you may say, it is merely a dramatic utterance, and no more represents Shakespeare's real views upon art than the speeches of Iago[27] represent his real views upon morals. But let me get to the end of the passage: –

"Art finds her own perfection within, and not outside, herself. She is not to be judged by any external standard of resemblance. She is a veil, rather than a mirror. She has flowers that no botanist knows of, birds that no museum possesses. She makes and unmakes many worlds, and can draw the moon from heaven with a scarlet thread. Hers are the 'forms more real than living man,' and hers the great archetypes of which things that have existence are but unfinished copies. Nature has, in her eyes, no laws, no uniformity. She can work miracles at her will, and when she calls monsters from the deep they come. She can bid the almond tree blossom in winter, and send the snow upon the ripe cornfield. At her word the frost lays its silver finger on the burning mouth of June, and the winged lions creep out from the hollows of the Lydian hills. The dryads peer from the thicket as she passes by, and the brown fauns smile strangely at her when she comes near them. She has hawk-faced gods that worship her, and the centaurs gallop at her side."

c. Is that the end of this dangerous article?

v. No. There is one more passage, but it is purely practical. It simply suggests some methods by which we could revive this lost art of lying.

c. Well, before you read me that, I should like to ask you a question. What do you mean by saying that life, "poor, probable, uninteresting human life," will try to reproduce the marvels of art? I can quite understand your objection to art being treated as a mirror. You think it would reduce genius to the position of a cracked looking-glass. But you don't mean to say that you seriously believe that life imitates art, that life in fact is the mirror, and art the reality?

v. Certainly I do. Paradox though it may seem – and paradoxes are always dangerous things – it is none the less true that *life imitates art far more than art imitates life*. We have all seen in our own day in England how a certain curious and fascinating type of beauty, invented and emphasised by two imaginative painters,[28] has so influenced life that whenever one goes to a private view or to an artistic salon one sees here the mystic eyes of Rossetti's dream, the long ivory throat, the strange square-cut jaw, the loosened shadowy hair that he so ardently loved, there the sweet maidenhood of "The Golden Stair," the blossom-like mouth and weary loveliness of the "Laus Amoris," the passion-pale face of Andromeda, the thin hands and lithe beauty of the Vivien in "Merlin's Dream."[29] And it has always been so. A great artist invents

Notes

[25] See Shakespeare's *The Tempest* and *Macbeth*.
[26] Shakespeare, *Hamlet*, Act III, scene ii.
[27] See Shakespeare's *Othello*.
[28] English Pre-Raphaelite artists Dante Gabriel Rossetti (1828–82) and Sir Edward Coley Burne-Jones (1833–98).
[29] Paintings by Burne-Jones. Paintings were sometimes retitled or known by their subject matter, making identification less

certain, but these are likely to be *The Golden Stairs* (1872–80), *Laus Veneris* (1870–5), *Perseus and Andromeda* (1888, sometimes titled *The Doom Fulfilled*, from the eight-painting *Perseus Cycle*), and *The Beguiling of Merlin* (1870–4, also known as *Merlin and Vivien*). "Rossetti's dream" may refer to Rossetti's painting, *Dante's Dream* (1871).

a type, and Life tries to copy it, to reproduce it in a popular form, like an enterprising publisher ... Shortly after Mr. Stevenson published his curious psychological story of transformation,[30] a friend of mine, called Mr. Hyde, was in the north of London, and being anxious to get to a railway station, he took what he thought was a short cut, lost his way, and found himself in a network of mean, evil-looking streets. Feeling rather nervous he was walking extremely fast, when suddenly out of an archway ran a child right between his legs. The child fell on the pavement, he tripped over it, and trampled upon it. Being of course very much frightened and not a little hurt, it began to scream, and in a few seconds the whole street was full of rough people who kept pouring out of the houses like ants. They surrounded him, and asked him his name. He was just about to give it when he suddenly remembered the opening incident in Mr. Stevenson's story. He was so filled with horror at having realised in his own person that terrible scene, and at having done accidentally what the Mr. Hyde of fiction had done with deliberate intent, that he ran away as hard as he could go. He was, however, very closely followed, and he finally took refuge in a surgery, the door of which happened to be open, where he explained to a young man, apparently an assistant, who happened to be there, exactly what had occurred. The crowd was induced to go away on his giving them a small sum of money, and as soon as the coast was clear he left. As he passed out, the name on the brass door-plate of the surgery caught his eye. It was "Jekyll." ...

However, I do not wish to dwell any further upon individual instances. Personal experience is a most vicious and limited circle ... Scientifically speaking, the basis of life – the energy of life, as Aristotle would call it – is simply the desire for expression, and art is always presenting various forms through which this expression can be attained. Life seizes on them and uses them, even if they be to her own hurt. Young men have committed suicide because Rolla did so, have died by their own hand because by his own hand Werther died.[31] Think of what we owe to the imitation of Christ, of what we owe to the imitation of Caesar.

c. The theory is certainly a very curious one. But even admitting this strange imitative instinct in life, surely you would acknowledge that art expresses the temper of its age, the spirit of its time, the moral and social conditions that surround it, and under whose influence it is produced.

v. Certainly not! *Art never expresses anything but itself.* This is the principle of my new aesthetics; and it is this, and not any vital connection between form and substance, as Mr. Pater fancies,[32] that makes music the type of all the arts. Of course, nations and individuals, with that healthy natural vanity which is the secret of life, are always under the impression that it is of them that the Muses are talking, always trying to find in the calm dignity of imaginative art some mirror of their own turbid passions, always forgetting that the singer of life is not Apollo, but Marsyas.[33] Remote from reality, and with her eyes turned away from the shadows of the cave, Art reveals her own perfection,[34] and the wondering crowd that watches the opening of the marvellous, many-petalled rose fancies that it is its own history that is being told to it, its own spirit that is finding expression in a new form. But it is not

Notes

[30] Robert Louis Stevenson, *The Strange Case of Dr. Jekyll and Mr. Hyde* (1886).

[31] Aristotle (384–322 BCE), Greek philosopher. See "Rolla" (1833) by French poet Alfred de Musset (1810–57) and *The Sorrows of Young Werther* (1774) by the German poet Johann Wolfgang von Goethe (1749–1832).

[32] English writer on aesthetics Walter Pater (1839–94), influential on Wilde and the Aesthetic movement in general.

[33] Apollo, the Greek god of the sun and of poetry; Marsyas, a satyr in Greek mythology, was flayed alive after being defeated in a contest with Apollo in which Marsyas played the flute and Apollo the lyre.

[34] See Plato's *Republic* (Book VII).

so. The highest art rejects the burden of the human spirit, and gains more from a new medium or a fresh material than she does from any enthusiasm for art, or from any lofty passion, or from any great awakening of the human consciousness. She develops purely on her own lines. She is not symbolic of any age. It is the ages that are her symbols, her reflections, her echoes ...

C. Well, after that I think I should like to hear the end of your article.

V. With pleasure. Whether it will do any good I really cannot say ... "What we have to do, what at any rate it is our duty to do, is to revive this old art of lying. Much of course may be done, in the way of educating the public, by amateurs in the domestic circle, at literary lunches, and at afternoon teas. But this is merely the light and graceful side of lying, such as was probably heard at Cretan dinner parties. There are many other forms. Lying for the sake of gaining some immediate personal advantage, for instance – lying for a moral purpose, as it is usually called – though of late it has been rather looked down upon, was extremely popular with the antique world. Athena laughs when Odysseus tells her what a Cambridge professor once elegantly termed a 'whopper,' and the glory of mendacity illumines the pale brow of the stainless hero of Euripidean tragedy, and sets among the noble women of the world the young bride of one of Horace's most exquisite odes.[35] Later on what at first had been merely a natural instinct was elevated into a self-conscious science. Elaborate rules were laid down for the guidance of mankind, and an important school of literature grew up round the subject. Indeed, when one remembers the excellent philosophical treatise of Sanchez[36] on the whole question, one cannot help regretting that no one has ever thought of publishing a cheap and condensed edition of the works of that great casuist. A short primer, 'When to Lie and how,' if brought out in an attractive and not too expensive form, would no doubt command a large sale, and would prove of real practical service to many earnest and deep-thinking people. Lying for the sake of the improvement of the young, which is the basis of home education, still lingers amongst us, and its advantages are so admirably set forth in the early books of the *Republic* that it is unnecessary to dwell upon them here. It is a form of lying for which all good mothers have peculiar capabilities, but it is capable of still further development, and has been sadly overlooked by the School Board. Lying for the sake of a monthly salary is of course well known in Fleet Street,[37] and the profession of a political leader-writer is not without its advantages. But it is said to be a somewhat dull occupation, and it certainly does not lead to much beyond a kind of ostentatious obscurity. The only form of lying that is absolutely beyond reproach is lying for its own sake, and the highest development of this is, as we have already pointed out, lying in Art. Just as those who do not love Plato more than truth cannot pass beyond the threshold of the Academe, so those who do not love beauty more than truth never know the inmost shrine of Art. The solid stolid British intellect lies in the desert sands like the Sphinx in Flaubert's marvellous tale, and fantasy, *La Chimère*, dances round it, and calls to it with her false, flute-toned voice.[38] It may not hear her now, but surely some day, when we are all bored to death with the commonplace character of modern fiction, it will hearken to her and try to borrow her wings.

"And when that day dawns, or sunset reddens, how joyous we shall all be! Facts will be regarded as discreditable, Truth will be found mourning over her fetters, and

Notes

[35] Homer's classical Greek epic *Odyssey*; Greek classical dramatist, Euripides (c.480–406 BCE); and Roman poet Horace (65–8 BCE).

[36] Portuguese writer Francisco Sanches (c.1550–1623).

[37] London street associated with newspaper publishing.

[38] See *La Tentation de St. Antoine* (1874) by the French author Gustave Flaubert (1821–80).

Romance, with her temper of wonder, will return to the land. The very aspect of the world will change to our startled eyes. Out of the sea will rise Behemoth and Leviathan, and sail round the high-pooped galleys, as they do on the delightful maps of those ages when books on geography were actually readable. Dragons will wander about the waste places, and the phoenix will soar from her nest of fire into the air. We shall lay our hands upon the basilisk, and see the jewel in the toad's head. The hippogriff will stand in our stalls, champing his gilded oats, and over our heads will float the Blue Bird singing of beautiful and impossible things, of things that are lovely and that never happen, of things that are not and that should be.[39] But before this comes to pass we must cultivate the lost art of lying."

c. Then we must certainly cultivate it at once. But in order to avoid making any error I want you to briefly tell me the doctrines of the new aesthetics.

v. Briefly, then, they are these. Art never expresses anything but itself. It has an independent life, just as Thought has, and develops purely on its own lines. It is not necessarily realistic in an age of realism, nor spiritual in an age of faith. So far from being the creation of its time, it is usually in direct opposition to it, and the only history that it preserves for us is the history of its own progress. Sometimes it returns on its own footsteps, and revives some old form, as happened in the archaistic movement of late Greek art, and in the pre-Raphaelite movement of our own day.[40] At other times it entirely anticipates its age, and produces in one century work that it takes another century to understand, to appreciate, and to enjoy. In no case does it reproduce its age. To pass from the art of a time to the time itself is the great fallacy of all historians.

The second doctrine is this. All bad art comes from returning to life and nature, and elevating them into ideals. Life and nature may sometimes be used as part of art's rough material, but before they are of any real service to art they must be translated into artistic conventions. The moment art surrenders its imaginative medium it surrenders everything. As a method Realism is a complete failure, and the two things that every artist should avoid are modernity of form and modernity of subject-matter. To us, who live in the nineteenth century, any century is a suitable subject for art except our own. The only beautiful things are things that do not concern us. It is, to have the pleasure of quoting myself, exactly because Hecuba is nothing to us that her sorrows are so suitable a motive for a tragedy.[41]

The third doctrine is that Life imitates Art far more than Art imitates Life. This results not merely from Life's imitative instinct, but from the fact that the desire of Life is simply to find expression, and that Art offers it certain beautiful forms through which it may realise that energy. It is a theory that has never been formularised before, but it is extremely fruitful, and throws an entirely new light on the history of Art.

The last doctrine is that Lying, the telling of beautiful untrue things, is the proper aim of Art. But of this I think I have spoken at sufficient length. And now let us go out on the terrace, where "the milk-white peacock glimmers like a ghost," while the evening star "washes the dusk with silver."[42] At twilight nature becomes a wonderfully suggestive effect and is not without loveliness, though perhaps its chief use is to illustrate quotations from the poets. Come! We have talked long enough.

Notes

[39] Wilde invokes a number of fantastic creatures, mostly from the Bible and medieval folklore.

[40] The Pre-Raphaelite Brotherhood was founded in the late 1840s by a group of English artists, including Dante Gabriel Rossetti; they rejected various elements of modern aesthetics (from the sixteenth-century Italian painter Raphael forward), often in favor of overtly medieval aesthetics and subjects.

[41] See Euripedes' *Hecuba*.

[42] The quotations are from English poets: *The Princess* (1847) (VII.165) by Alfred, Lord Tennyson (1809–92) and "To the Evening Star" (1782) by William Blake (1757–1827).

The Ballad of Reading Gaol (1898)

In Memoriam
C. T. W.
Sometime Trooper of the Royal Horse Guards.
Obiit[1] H. M. Prison, Reading, Berkshire, July 7th, 1896

I

He did not wear his scarlet coat,
    For blood and wine are red,
And blood and wine were on his hands
    When they found him with the dead,
The poor dead woman whom he loved,   5
    And murdered in her bed.

He walked amongst the Trial Men
    In a suit of shabby gray;
A cricket cap was on his head,
    And his step seemed light and gay;   10
But I never saw a man who looked
    So wistfully at the day.

I never saw a man who looked
    With such a wistful eye
Upon that little tent of blue   15
    Which prisoners call the sky,
And at every drifting cloud that went
    With sails of silver by.

I walked, with other souls in pain,
    Within another ring,   20
And was wondering if the man had done
    A great or little thing,
When a voice behind me whispered low,
    "That fellow's got to swing."

Dear Christ! the very prison walls   25
    Suddenly seemed to reel,
And the sky above my head became
    Like a casque of scorching steel;
And, though I was a soul in pain,
    My pain I could not feel.   30

I only knew what hunted thought
    Quickened his step, and why
He looked upon the garish day
    With such a wistful eye;

Notes ———————————————————————

THE BALLAD OF READING GAOL
[1] He died (Latin).

The man had killed the thing he loved,　　　　　　　35
　　And so he had to die.

***

Yet each man kills the thing he loves,
　　By each let this be heard,
Some do it with a bitter look,
　　Some with a flattering word,　　　　　　　　40
The coward does it with a kiss,
　　The brave man with a sword!

Some kill their love when they are young,
　　And some when they are old;
Some strangle with the hands of Lust,　　　　　45
　　Some with the hands of Gold:
The kindest use a knife, because
　　The dead so soon grow cold.

Some love too little, some too long,
　　Some sell, and others buy;　　　　　　　　　50
Some do the deed with many tears,
　　And some without a sigh:
For each man kills the thing he loves,
　　Yet each man does not die.

***

He does not die a death of shame　　　　　　　55
　　On a day of dark disgrace,
Nor have a noose about his neck,
　　Nor a cloth upon his face,
Nor drop feet foremost through the floor
　　Into an empty space.　　　　　　　　　　　60

He does not sit with silent men
　　Who watch him night and day;
Who watch him when he tries to weep,
　　And when he tries to pray;
Who watch him lest himself should rob　　　　65
　　The prison of its prey.

He does not wake at dawn to see
　　Dread figures throng his room,
The shivering Chaplain robed in white,
　　The Sheriff stern with gloom,　　　　　　　70
And the Governor all in shiny black,
　　With the yellow face of Doom.

He does not rise in piteous haste
　　To put on convict-clothes,
While some coarse-mouthed Doctor gloats, and notes　　75
　　Each new and nerve-twitched pose,
Fingering a watch whose little ticks
　　Are like horrible hammer-blows.

He does not know that sickening thirst
    That sands one's throat, before   80
The hangman with his gardener's gloves
    Comes through the padded door,
And binds one with three leathern thongs,
    That the throat may thirst no more.

He does not bend his head to hear   85
    The Burial Office read,
Nor, while the terror of his soul
    Tells him he is not dead,
Cross his own coffin, as he moves
    Into the hideous shed.   90

He does not stare upon the air
    Through a little roof of glass:
He does not pray with lips of clay
    For his agony to pass;
Nor feel upon his shuddering cheek   95
    The kiss of Caiaphas.

II

Six weeks our guardsman walked the yard,
    In the suit of shabby gray:
His cricket cap was on his head,
    And his step seemed light and gay,   100
But I never saw a man who looked
    So wistfully at the day.

I never saw a man who looked
    With such a wistful eye
Upon that little tent of blue   105
    Which prisoners call the sky,
And at every wandering cloud that trailed
    Its ravelled fleeces by.

He did not wring his hands, as do
    Those witless men who dare   110
To try to rear the changeling Hope
    In the cave of black Despair:
He only looked upon the sun,
    And drank the morning air.

He did not wring his hands nor weep,   115
    Nor did he peek or pine,
But he drank the air as though it held
    Some healthful anodyne;
With open mouth he drank the sun
    As though it had been wine!   120

And I and all the souls in pain,
    Who tramped the other ring,
Forgot if we ourselves had done
    A great or little thing,

And watched with gaze of dull amaze   125
   The man who had to swing.

For strange it was to see him pass
   With a step so light and gay,
And strange it was to see him look
   So wistfully at the day,   130
And strange it was to think that he
   Had such a debt to pay.

              ***

For oak and elm have pleasant leaves
   That in the spring-time shoot:
But grim to see is the gallows-tree,   135
   With its adder-bitten root,
And, green or dry, a man must die
   Before it bears its fruit!

The loftiest place is that seat of grace
   For which all worldlings try: 140
But who would stand in hempen band
   Upon a scaffold high,
And through a murderer's collar take
   His last look at the sky?

It is sweet to dance to violins   145
   When Love and Life are fair:
To dance to flutes, to dance to lutes
   Is delicate and rare:
But it is not sweet with nimble feet
   To dance upon the air!   150

So with curious eyes and sick surmise
   We watched him day by day,
And wondered if each one of us
   Would end the self-same way,
For none can tell to what red Hell   155
   His sightless soul may stray.

              ***

At last the dead man walked no more
   Amongst the Trial Men,
And I knew that he was standing up
   In the black dock's dreadful pen,   160
And that never would I see his face
   In God's sweet world again.

Like two doomed ships that pass in storm
   We had crossed each other's way:
But we made no sign, we said no word,   165
   We had no word to say;
For we did not meet in the holy night,
   But in the shameful day.

A prison wall was round us both,
   Two outcast men we were: 170
The world had thrust us from its heart,
   And God from out His care:
And the iron gin that waits for Sin
   Had caught us in its snare.

III

In Debtors' Yard the stones are hard,   175
   And the dripping wall is high,
So it was there he took the air
   Beneath the leaden sky,
And by each side a Warder walked,
   For fear the man might die.   180

Or else he sat with those who watched
   His anguish night and day;
Who watched him when he rose to weep,
   And when he crouched to pray;
Who watched him lest himself should rob   185
   Their scaffold of its prey.

The Governor was strong upon
   The Regulations Act:
The Doctor said that Death was but
   A scientific fact: 190
And twice a day the Chaplain called,
   And left a little tract.

And twice a day he smoked his pipe,
   And drank his quart of beer:
His soul was resolute, and held   195
   No hiding-place for fear;
He often said that he was glad
   The hangman's hands were near.

But why he said so strange a thing
   No Warder dared to ask: 200
For he to whom a watcher's doom
   Is given as his task,
Must set a lock upon his lips,
   And make his face a mask.

Or else he might be moved, and try   205
   To comfort or console:
And what should Human Pity do
   Pent up in Murderers' Hole?
What word of grace in such a place
   Could help a brother's soul?   210

***

With slouch and swing around the ring
   We trod the Fools' Parade!

We did not care: we knew we were
    The Devil's Own Brigade:
And shaven head and feet of lead   215
    Make a merry masquerade.

We tore the tarry rope to shreds
    With blunt and bleeding nails;
We rubbed the doors, and scrubbed the floors,
    And cleaned the shining rails: 220
And, rank by rank, we soaped the plank,
    And clattered with the pails.

We sewed the sacks, we broke the stones,
    We turned the dusty drill:
We banged the tins, and bawled the hymns,   225
    And sweated on the mill:
But in the heart of every man
    Terror was lying still.

So still it lay that every day
    Crawled like a weed-clogged wave: 230
And we forgot the bitter lot
    That waits for fool and knave,
Till once, as we tramped in from work,
    We passed an open grave.

With yawning mouth the yellow hole   235
    Gaped for a living thing;
The very mud cried out for blood
    To the thirsty asphalte ring:
And we knew that ere one dawn grew fair
    Some prisoner had to swing.   240

Right in we went, with soul intent
    On Death and Dread and Doom:
The hangman, with his little bag,
    Went shuffling through the gloom:
And each man trembled as he crept   245
    Into his numbered tomb.

             ★★★

That night the empty corridors
    Were full of forms of Fear,
And up and down the iron town
    Stole feet we could not hear,   250
And through the bars that hide the stars
    White faces seemed to peer.

He lay as one who lies and dreams
    In a pleasant meadow-land,
The watchers watched him as he slept,   255
    And could not understand
How one could sleep so sweet a sleep
    With a hangman close at hand.

But there is no sleep when men must weep
   Who never yet have wept: 260
So we – the fool, the fraud, the knave –
   That endless vigil kept,
And through each brain on hands of pain
   Another's terror crept.

★★★

Alas! it is a fearful thing   265
   To feel another's guilt!
For, right within, the sword of Sin
   Pierced to its poisoned hilt,
And as molten lead were the tears we shed
   For the blood we had not spilt.   270

The Warders with their shoes of felt
   Crept by each padlocked door,
And peeped and saw, with eyes of awe,
   Gray figures on the floor,
And wondered why men knelt to pray   275
   Who never prayed before.

All through the night we knelt and prayed,
   Mad mourners of a corse!
The troubled plumes of midnight were
   The plumes upon a hearse: 280
And bitter wine upon a sponge
   Was the savour of Remorse.

★★★

The grey cock crew, the red cock crew,
   But never came the day:
And crooked shapes of Terror crouched,   285
   In the corners where we lay:
And each evil sprite that walks by night
   Before us seemed to play.

They glided past, they glided fast,
   Like travellers through a mist: 290
They mocked the moon in a rigadoon
   Of delicate turn and twist,
And with formal pace and loathsome grace
   The phantoms kept their tryst.

With mop and mow, we saw them go,   295
   Slim shadows hand in hand:
About, about, in ghostly rout
   They trod a saraband:
And the damned grotesques made arabesques,
   Like the wind upon the sand!   300

With the pirouettes of marionettes,
   They tripped on pointed tread:

But with flutes of Fear they filled the ear,
    As their grisly masque they led,
And loud they sang, and long they sang,   305
    For they sang to wake the dead.

"Oho!" they cried, *"The world is wide*
    But fettered limbs go lame!
And once, or twice, to throw the dice
    Is a gentlemanly game,   310
But he does not win who plays with Sin
    In the secret House of Shame."

No things of air these antics were,
    That frolicked with such glee:
To men whose lives were held in gyves,   315
    And whose feet might not go free,
Ah! wounds of Christ! they were living things
    Most terrible to see.

Around, around, they waltzed and wound;
    Some wheeled in smirking pairs;   320
With the mincing step of a demirep
    Some sidled up the stairs:
And with subtle sneer, and fawning leer,
    Each helped us at our prayers.

***

The morning wind began to moan,   325
    But still the night went on:
Through its giant loom the web of gloom
    Crept till each thread was spun:
And, as we prayed, we grew afraid
    Of the Justice of the Sun.   330

The moaning wind went wandering round
    The weeping prison-wall:
Till like a wheel of turning steel
    We felt the minutes crawl:
O moaning wind! what had we done   335
    To have such a seneschal?

At last I saw the shadowed bars,
    Like a lattice wrought in lead,
Move right across the whitewashed wall
    That faced my three-plank bed,   340
And I knew that somewhere in the world
    God's dreadful dawn was red.

***

At six o'clock we cleaned our cells,
    At seven all was still,
But the sough and swing of a mighty wing   345
    The prison seemed to fill,

For the Lord of Death with icy breath
　　Had entered in to kill.

He did not pass in purple pomp,
　　Nor ride a moon-white steed.　　　　　　　　　　350
Three yards of cord and a sliding board
　　Are all the gallows' need:
So with rope of shame the Herald came
　　To do the secret deed.

***

We were as men who through a fen　　　　　　　　355
　　Of filthy darkness grope:
We did not dare to breathe a prayer,
　　Or to give our anguish scope:
Something was dead in each of us,
　　And what was dead was Hope.　　　　　　　　　　360

For Man's grim Justice goes its way,
　　And will not swerve aside:
It slays the weak, it slays the strong,
　　It has a deadly stride:
With iron heel it slays the strong,　　　　　　　　365
　　The monstrous parricide!

***

We waited for the stroke of eight:
　　Each tongue was thick with thirst:
For the stroke of eight is the stroke of Fate
　　That makes a man accursed,　　　　　　　　　　370
And Fate will use a running noose
　　For the best man and the worst.

We had no other thing to do,
　　Save to wait for the sign to come:
So, like things of stone in a valley lone,　　　　　375
　　Quiet we sat and dumb:
But each man's heart beat thick and quick,
　　Like a madman on a drum!

***

With sudden shock the prison-clock
　　Smote on the shivering air,　　　　　　　　　　380
And from all the gaol rose up a wail
　　Of impotent despair,
Like the sound that frightened marshes hear
　　From some leper in his lair.

And as one sees most fearful things　　　　　　　385
　　In the crystal of a dream,
We saw the greasy hempen rope
　　Hooked to the blackened beam,

And heard the prayer the hangman's snare
  Strangled into a scream.   390

And all the woe that moved him so
  That he gave that bitter cry,
And the wild regrets, and the bloody sweats,
  None knew so well as I:
For he who lives more lives than one   395
  More deaths than one must die.

IV

There is no chapel on the day
  On which they hang a man:
The Chaplain's heart is far too sick,
  Or his face is far too wan,   400
Or there is that written in his eyes
  Which none should look upon.

So they kept us close till nigh on noon,
  And then they rang the bell,
And the Warders with their jingling keys   405
  Opened each listening cell,
And down the iron stair we tramped,
  Each from his separate Hell.

Out into God's sweet air we went,
  But not in wonted way,   410
For this man's face was white with fear,
  And that man's face was gray,
And I never saw sad men who looked
  So wistfully at the day.

I never saw sad men who looked   415
  With such a wistful eye
Upon that little tent of blue
  We prisoners called the sky,
And at every careless cloud that passed
  In happy freedom by.   420

But there were those amongst us all
  Who walked with downcast head,
And knew that, had each got his due,
  They should have died instead:
He had but killed a thing that lived,   425
  Whilst they had killed the dead.

For he who sins a second time
  Wakes a dead soul to pain,
And draws it from its spotted shroud,
  And makes it bleed again,   430
And makes it bleed great gouts of blood,
  And makes it bleed in vain!

★★★

Like ape or clown, in monstrous garb
   With crooked arrows starred,
Silently we went round and round
   The slippery asphalte yard;   435
Silently we went round and round,
   And no man spoke a word.

Silently we went round and round,
   And through each hollow mind   440
The Memory of dreadful things
   Rushed like a dreadful wind,
And Horror stalked before each man,
   And Terror crept behind.

        ★★★

The Warders strutted up and down,   445
   And kept their herd of brutes,
Their uniforms were spick and span,
   And they wore their Sunday suits,
But we knew the work they had been at,
   By the quicklime on their boots.   450

For where a grave had opened wide,
   There was no grave at all:
Only a stretch of mud and sand
   By the hideous prison-wall,
And a little heap of burning lime,   455
   That the man should have his pall.[2]

For he has a pall, this wretched man,
   Such as few men can claim:
Deep down below a prison-yard,
   Naked for greater shame,   460
He lies, with fetters on each foot,
   Wrapt in a sheet of flame!

And all the while the burning lime
   Eats flesh and bone away,
It eats the brittle bone by night,   465
   And the soft flesh by day,
It eats the flesh and bone by turns,
   But it eats the heart alway.

        ★★★

For three long years they will not sow
   Or root or seedling there: 470

Notes

[2] Bodies buried within prison walls were covered in quick lime to speed up decomposition. The practice fell out of use in the early twentieth century, and so it was highly controversial that Roger Casement, executed in 1916 for treason after the Easter Rising, was buried naked and without a coffin in quick lime, like Wilde's protagonist.

For three long years the unblessed spot
    Will sterile be and bare,
And look upon the wondering sky
    With unreproachful stare.

They think a murderer's heart would taint   475
    Each simple seed they sow.
It is not true! God's kindly earth
    Is kindlier than men know,
And the red rose would but blow more red,
    The white rose whiter blow.   480

Out of his mouth a red, red rose!
    Out of his heart a white!
For who can say by what strange way,
    Christ brings His will to light,
Since the barren staff the pilgrim bore   485
    Bloomed in the great Pope's sight?[3]

***

But neither milk-white rose nor red
    May bloom in prison air;
The shard, the pebble, and the flint,
    Are what they give us there: 490
For flowers have been known to heal
    A common man's despair.

So never will wine-red rose or white,
    Petal by petal, fall
On that stretch of mud and sand that lies   495
    By the hideous prison-wall,
To tell the men who tramp the yard
    That God's Son died for all.

***

Yet though the hideous prison-wall
    Still hems him round and round,   500
And a spirit may not walk by night
    That is with fetters bound,
And a spirit may but weep that lies
    In such unholy ground,

He is at peace – this wretched man –   505
    At peace, or will be soon:
There is no thing to make him mad,
    Nor does Terror walk at noon,

Notes ─────────────────────────────

[3] Likely to be a reference to the medieval story of the knight Tannhäuser who goes on a pilgrimage to Rome to ask forgiveness from the Pope for his sins; he is denied, but his staff then blooms as a sign of divine forgiveness. German composer Richard Wagner (1813–83) adapted the story for an opera frequently staged in the nineteenth century, *Tannhäuser* (1845).

For the lampless Earth in which he lies
   Has neither Sun nor Moon. 510

          ***

They hanged him as a beast is hanged:
   They did not even toll
A requiem that might have brought
   Rest to his startled soul,
But hurriedly they took him out, 515
   And hid him in a hole.

They stripped him of his canvas clothes,
   And gave him to the flies:
They mocked the swollen purple throat,
   And the stark and staring eyes: 520
And with laughter loud they heaped the shroud
   In which their convict lies.

The Chaplain would not kneel to pray
   By his dishonoured grave:
Nor mark it with that blessed Cross 525
   That Christ for sinners gave,
Because the man was one of those
   Whom Christ came down to save.

Yet all is well; he has but passed
   To Life's appointed bourne: 530
And alien tears will fill for him
   Pity's long-broken urn,
For his mourners will be outcast men,
   And outcasts always mourn.

          V

I know not whether Laws be right, 535
   Or whether Laws be wrong;
All that we know who lie in gaol
   Is that the wall is strong;
And that each day is like a year,
   A year whose days are long. 540

But this I know, that every Law
   That men have made for Man,
Since first Man took his brother's life,
   And the sad world began,
But straws the wheat and saves the chaff 545
   With a most evil fan.

This too I know – and wise it were
   If each could know the same –
That every prison that men build
   Is built with bricks of shame, 550
And bound with bars lest Christ should see
   How men their brothers maim.

With bars they blur the gracious moon,
    And blind the goodly sun:
And they do well to hide their Hell,
    For in it things are done 555
That Son of God nor son of Man
    Ever should look upon!

***

The vilest deeds like poison weeds
    Bloom well in prison-air: 560
It is only what is good in Man
    That wastes and withers there:
Pale Anguish keeps the heavy gate,
    And the Warder is Despair.

For they starve the little frightened child 565
    Till it weeps both night and day:
And they scourge the weak, and flog the fool,
    And gibe the old and gray,
And some grow mad, and all grow bad,
    And none a word may say. 570

Each narrow cell in which we dwell
    Is a foul and dark latrine,
And the fetid breath of living Death
    Chokes up each grated screen,
And all, but Lust, is turned to dust 575
    In Humanity's machine.

The brackish water that we drink
    Creeps with a loathsome slime,
And the bitter bread they weigh in scales
    Is full of chalk and lime, 580
And Sleep will not lie down, but walks
    Wild-eyed, and cries to Time.

***

But though lean Hunger and green Thirst
    Like asp with adder fight,
We have little care of prison fare, 585
    For what chills and kills outright
Is that every stone one lifts by day
    Becomes one's heart by night.

With midnight always in one's heart,
    And twilight in one's cell,
We turn the crank, or tear the rope, 590
    Each in his separate Hell,
And the silence is more awful far
    Than the sound of a brazen bell.

And never a human voice comes near 595
    To speak a gentle word:

And the eye that watches through the door
　　Is pitiless and hard:
And by all forgot, we rot and rot,
　　With soul and body marred.　　　　　　　　　　　　600

And thus we rust Life's iron chain
　　Degraded and alone:
And some men curse, and some men weep,
　　And some men make no moan:
But God's eternal Laws are kind　　　　　　　　　　　605
　　And break the heart of stone.

　　　　　　　　★★★

And every human heart that breaks,
　　In prison-cell or yard,
Is as that broken box that gave
　　Its treasure to the Lord,　　　　　　　　　　　　610
And filled the unclean leper's house
　　With the scent of costliest nard.[4]

Ah! happy they whose hearts can break
　　And peace of pardon win!
How else may man make straight his plan　　　　　　615
　　And cleanse his soul from Sin?
How else but through a broken heart
　　May Lord Christ enter in?

　　　　　　　　★★★

And he of the swollen purple throat,
　　And the stark and staring eyes,　　　　　　　　　620
Waits for the holy hands that took
　　The Thief to Paradise;
And a broken and a contrite heart
　　The Lord will not despise.

The man in red who reads the Law　　　　　　　　　625
　　Gave him three weeks of life,
Three little weeks in which to heal
　　His soul of his soul's strife,
And cleanse from every blot of blood
　　The hand that held the knife.　　　　　　　　　　630

And with tears of blood he cleansed the hand,
　　The hand that held the steel:
For only blood can wipe out blood,
　　And only tears can heal:
And the crimson stain that was of Cain　　　　　　　635
　　Became Christ's snow-white seal.

Notes ————————————————————————————

[4] An ointment (spikenard) mentioned in the Bible.

VI

In Reading gaol by Reading town
   There is a pit of shame,
And in it lies a wretched man
   Eaten by teeth of flame,   640
In a burning winding-sheet he lies,
   And his grave has got no name.

And there, till Christ call forth the dead,
   In silence let him lie:
No need to waste the foolish tear,   645
   Or heave the windy sigh:
The man had killed the thing he loved,
   And so he had to die.

And all men kill the thing they love,
   By all let this be heard,   650
Some do it with a bitter look,
   Some with a flattering word,
The coward does it with a kiss,
   The brave man with a sword!

Katharine Tynan (1861–1931)

Katharine Tynan was born in Dublin. Her father was first a farmer and dairy owner, and then a cattle trader. She had formal schooling from the age of five, completing her studies at the school of Drogheda's Dominican convent. She had limited vision because of a childhood illness, but was a voracious reader and became literary editor of the *Irish Daily Independent*; she also joined the Ladies' Land League. W. B. Yeats famously proposed to her in 1891, but she was already engaged to Henry Albert Hinkson and married him in 1893. They settled first in London, then in Co. Mayo; Tynan returned to Dublin after her husband's death in 1919, but spent her last years in Britain and the Continent. Her daughter, Pamela Hinkson, also became a successful author, publishing a number of novels.

Tynan published her first poem in 1878, and thereafter followed a number of volumes of poetry, beginning with *Louise de la Vallière and other Poems* (1885). She was soon moving in Irish literary circles, and collaborated with Yeats on *Poems and Ballads of Young Ireland* (1888). She supported her family through her prodigious production of literary volumes, including dozens of novels as well as volumes of poetry and short fiction. In the 1890s, she published a number of short-story collections, including *A Cluster of Nuts, Being Sketches Among My Own People* (1894) and *An Isle in the Water* (1895), and volumes of verse, including *Ballads and Lyrics* (1891) and *The Wind in the Trees* (1898). Much of her writing in this period focuses on rural life, but her early nationalist roots as a Parnellite and member of the Ladies' Land League emerge in some of her verse as well as the major project of expanding Charles A. Read's *Cabinet of Irish Literature* (1879) for a new edition in 1902.

Further reading

Kelleher, Margaret, "The Cabinet of Irish Literature: A Historical Perspective on Irish Anthologies," *Éire–Ireland* 38 (2003): 68–89.

Potts, Donna L., "Irish Poetry and the Modernist Canon: A Reappraisal of Katharine Tynan," in *Border Crossings: Irish Women Writers and National Identities*, ed. Kathryn Kirkpatrick, 79–99. Tuscaloosa, AL: University of Alabama Press, 2000.

The Wild Geese[1] (A Lament for the Irish Jacobites)

From **Ballads and Lyrics** (1891)

I have heard the curlew crying
  On a lonely moor and mere;
And the sea-gull's shriek in the gloaming
  Is a lonely sound in the ear:
And I've heard the brown thrush mourning   5
  For her children stolen away; –
But it's O for the homeless Wild Geese
  That sailed ere the dawn of day!

For the curlew out on the moorland
  Hath five fine eggs in the nest;   10
And the thrush will get her a new love
  And sing her song with the best.
As the swallow flies to the Summer
  Will the gull return to the sea:
But never the wings of the Wild Geese   15
  Will flash over seas to me.

And 'tis ill to be roaming, roaming
  With the homesick heart in the breast!
And how long I've looked for your coming,
  And my heart is the empty nest!   20
O sore in the land of the stranger
  They'll pine for the land far away!
But Day of Aughrim, my sorrow,
  It was you was the bitter day!

The Unlawful Mother

From **An Isle in the Water** (1895)

In the Island the standard of purity is an extraordinarily high one, and it is almost unheard of that a woman should fall away from it. Purity is the unquestioned prerogative of every Island girl or woman, and it only comes to them as a vague

Notes

THE WILD GEESE
[1] The term "Wild Geese" generally refers to Irish men working as soldiers in continental Europe, including the Irish Jacobites who went into exile after the Battle of Aughrim and the Treaty of Limerick (1691) and those who left after the Uprising of 1798.

far-off horror in an unknown world that there are places under the sun and the stars where such is not the case. The punishment is appalling in the very few cases where sin has lifted its head amongst these austere people. The lepers' hut of old was no such living death of isolation as surrounds an Island girl who has smirched her good name. Henceforth there is an atmosphere about her that never lifts – of horror for some, of tragedy for others, according to their temperament. There she stands lonely for all her days, with the seal set upon her that can never be broken, the consecration of an awful and tragic destiny.

I knew of such an one who was little more than a child when this horror befell her. She has dark blue eyes and thick black lashes, and very white skin. The soft dark hair comes low on her white forehead. With gaily-coloured shawl covering her head, and drawn across her chin, as they wear it in the Island, she looks, or looked when I last saw her, a hidden, gliding image of modesty. And despite that sin of the past she is modest. It was the ignorant sin of a child, and out of the days of horror and wrath that followed – her purging – she brought only the maternity that burns like a white flame in her. The virtuous were more wroth against her in old days that she carried her maternity so proudly. Why, not the most honourable and cherished of the young Island mothers dandled her child with such pride. No mother of a young earl could have stepped lighter, and held her head higher, than Maggie when she came down the fishing street, spurning the very stones, as it seemed, so lightly she went with the baby wrapped in her shawl. She did not seem to notice that some of the kindly neighbours stepped aside, or that here and there a woman pulled her little daughter within doors, out of the path of the unlawful mother. Those little pink fingers pushed away shame and contempt. The child was her world.

She was the daughter of a fisherman who died of a chest complaint soon after she was born. Her mother still lives, a hard-featured honest old woman, with a network of fine lines about her puckered eyes. Her hair went quite white the year her daughter's child was born, but I remember it dark and abundant with only a silver thread glistening here and there. She has grown taciturn too; she was talkative enough in the old days when I was a child in the Island, and, often and often, came clattering in by the half-door to shelter from a shower, and sat till fine weather on a stool by the turf ashes, gravely discussing the fishing and the prospects of pigs and young fowl that season.

There are three sons, but Jim was married and doing for himself before the trouble befell the family. Tom and Larry were at home, Tom, gentle and slow-spoken, employed about the Hall gardens. Larry, a fisherman like his father before him. Both were deeply attached to their young sister, and had been used to pet and care for her from her cradle.

There is yet a tradition in the island of that terrible time when Maggie's mother realised the disgrace her daughter had brought on an honest name. There had been a horrified whisper in the Island for some time before, a surmise daily growing more certain, an awe-stricken compassion for the honest people who never suspected the ghastly shadow about to cross their threshold. People had been slow to accept this solution of Maggie's pining and weakness. This one had suggested herb-tea, and that one had offered to accompany Maggie to see the dispensary doctor who came over from Breagh every Tuesday. But Maggie accepted none of their offices, only withdrew herself more and more in a sick horror of herself and life, and roamed about the cliffs where but the gulls and the little wild Island cattle looked on at her restless misery.

Her mother was half-fretted and half impatient of her daughter's ailing. She was a very strong woman herself, and except for a pain in the side which had troubled her of late, she had never known a day of megrims. She listened chafing to the neighbours' advice – and every one of them had their nostrum – and heeded none of them. She had an idea herself that the girl's sickness was imaginary and could be thrown off if she willed it. When the neighbours all at once ceased offering her advice and sympathy she felt it a distinct relief. She had not the remotest idea that she was become the centre of an awe-stricken sympathy, that her little world had fallen back and stood gaping at her and hers as they might at one abnormally stricken: if their gabble ceased very suddenly and no more idlers came in for a chat by the fireside she was not the one to fret; she had always plenty to do without idle women hindering her, and, now the girl had her sick fit on her, all the work fell to the mother's share.

The girl's time was upon her before the mother guessed at the blinding and awful truth. She was a proud, stern, old woman, come of a race strong in rectitude, and she would scarcely have believed an angel if one had come to testify to her daughter's dishonour. But the time came when it could no longer be hidden, when the birth-pains were on the wretched girl, and in the quietness of the winter night, her sin stood forth revealed.

Some merciful paralysis stiffened the mother's lips when she would have cursed her daughter. She lifted up her voice indeed to curse, but it went from her; her lips jabbered helplessly; over her face came a bluish-gray shade, and she fell in a chair huddled with one hand pressed against her side.

The two men came in on this ghastly scene. The girl was crouched on the floor with her face hidden, shrinking to the earth from the terrible words she expected to hear. The men lifted the sister to her bed in the little room. They forced some spirit between their mother's lips, and in a few minutes the livid dark shade began to pass from her face. Her lips moved. "Take her," she panted, "take that girl and her shame from my honest house, lest I curse her."

The two men looked at each other. They turned pale through their hardy brown-ness, and then flushed darkly red. It flashed on them in an instant. This was the meaning of the girl's sickness, of a thousand hints they had not understood. Tom, with characteristic patience, was the first to bend his back to the burden.

"Whisht, mother," he said, "whisht. Don't talk about cursing. If there's one black sin under our roof-tree, we won't open the door to another." He put his arm around her in a tender way. "Come, achora," he said, as if he were humouring a child, "come and lie down. You're not well, you creature."

"Oh Tom," said the mother, softening all at once, "the black shame's on me, and I'll never be well again in this world."

She let him lift her to her bed in one of the little rooms that went off the kitchen. Then he came back to where Larry stood, with an acute misery on his young face, looking restlessly from the turf sods he was kicking now and again to the door behind which their young sister lay in agony.

"There's no help for it, Larry," said Tom, touching him on the shoulder. "We can't trust her and the mother under one roof. We must take her to the hospital. It's low water to-night, and you can get the ass-cart across the sand. You'll take her, Larry, an' I'll stay an' see to the mother."

They wrapped the girl in all the bed-clothes they could find and lifted her into the little cart full of straw. The Island lay quiet under the moon, all white with snow except where a black patch showed a ravine or cleft in the rocks. In the fishing village the doors were shut and the bits of curtains drawn. It was bitterly cold, and not a night for any one to be abroad. The ass-cart went quietly over the snow. The two men walked by it, never speaking; a low moaning came from the woman in the cart. They did not meet a soul on their way to the shore.

At that point the Island sends out a long tongue of rock and sand towards the mainland. At very low water there is but a shallow pool between the two shores; over this they crossed. Sometimes the ass-cart stuck fast in the sand. Then the men lifted the wheels gently, so as not to jerk the cart, and then encouraging the little ass, they went on again. When they had climbed the rocky shore to the mainland, and the cart was on the level road, they parted. Before Tom turned his face homewards he bent down to Maggie. "You're goin' where you'll be taken care of, acushla. Don't fret; Larry'll fetch you home as soon as you can travel," he said. And then, as if he could scarcely bear the sight of her drawn face in the moonlight, he turned abruptly, and went striding down the rocky shore to the strand.

Because Tom and Larry had forgiven out of their great love, it did not therefore follow that the shame did not lie heavily on them. Tom went with so sad a face and so lagging a step that people's hearts ached for him; while young Larry, who was always bright and merry, avoided all the old friends, and when suddenly accosted turned a deep painful red and refused to meet the eyes that looked their sympathy at him.

A few weeks passed and it was time for the girl to leave the hospital. There had been long and bitter wrangles – bitter at least on one side – between the mother and sons. She had sworn at first that she would never live under the roof with the girl, but the lads returned her always the same answer, "If she goes we go too." And by degrees their dogged persistence dulled the old woman's fierce anger. Maggie came home, and the cradle was established beside the hearth. At first the brothers had whispered together of righting her, but when she had answered them a question – a dull welt of shame tingling on their cheek and hers as though some one had cut them with a whip – they knew it was useless. The man had gone to America some months before, and was beyond the reach of their justice.

But the child throve as if it had the fairest right to be in the world, and was no little nameless waif whose very existence was a shame. He was a beautiful boy, round and tender, with his mother's dark-blue eyes, and the exquisite baby skin which is softer than any rose-leaf. From very early days he crowed and chuckled and was a most cheerful baby. Left alone in his cradle he would be quietly happy for hours; he slept a great deal, and only announced his waking from sleep by a series of delighted chuckles, which brought his mother running to his side to hoist him in her arms.

He must have been about a year old when I first saw him. Maggie intruded him on no one, though people said that if any one admired her baby it made her their lover for life. I happened to be in the Island for a while, and one evening on a solitary ramble round the cliffs I came face to face with Maggie, – Maggie stepping high, and prettier than ever with that rapt glory of maternity in her face which made ordinary prettiness common beside her.

I saw by the way she wisped the shawl round her full white chin that I was welcome to pass her if I would. But I did not pass her. I stopped and spoke a little on indifferent topics, and then I asked for the baby. A radiant glow of pleasure swept over the young mother's healthily pale face. She untwisted the shawl and lifted a fold of it, and stood looking down at the sleeping child with a brooding tenderness, almost divine. He was indeed lovely, with the flush of sleep upon him and one little dimpled hand thrust against her breast. "What a great boy!" I said. "But you must be half killed carrying him." She laughed out joyfully, a sweet ringing laughter like the music of the bells. "Deed then," she said, "'tis the great load he is entirely, an' any wan but meself 'ud be droppin' under the weight of him. But it 'ud be the quare day I'd complain of my jewel. Sure it's the light heart he gives me makes him lie light in my arms."

But Maggie's mother remained untouched by the child's beauty and winsomeness. Mother and daughter lived in the same house absolutely without speech of each other. The girl was gentleness and humility itself. For her own part she never forgot she was a sinner, though she would let no one visit it on the child. I have been told that it was most pathetic to see how she strove to win forgiveness from her mother, how she watched and waited on her month after month with never a sign from the old woman, who was not as strong as she had been. The pain in her side took her occasionally, and since any exertion brought it on she was fain at last to sit quietly in the chimney-corner a good deal more than she had been used to. She had seen the doctor, very much against her will, and he had said her heart was affected, but with care and avoiding great excitement, it might last her to a good old age.

Maggie was glad of the hard work put upon her. She washed and swept and scrubbed and polished all day long, with a touching little air of cheerfulness which never ceased to be sad unless when she was crooning love-songs to the baby. She made no effort to take up her old friends again, though she was so grateful when any one stopped and admired the baby. She quite realised that her sin had set her apart, that nothing in all the world could give her back what she had lost, and set her again by the side of those happy companions of her childhood.

As the time passed she never seemed to feel that her mother was hard and unrelenting. She bore her dark looks and her silence with amazing patience. Usually the old woman seemed never to notice the child; but once Maggie came in and saw her gazing at the sleeping face in the cradle with what seemed to her a look of scorn and dislike. She gave a great cry, like the cry of a wounded thing, and snatching the child, ran out with him bareheaded, carrying him away to the high cliffs covered with flowers full of honey, and there she crooned and cried over him till the soothing of the sweet wind and the sunshine eased her heart, and the blighting gaze that had fallen upon her darling had left no shadow.

For her two brothers she felt and displayed a doglike devotion and gratitude. The big fellows were sometimes almost uneasy under the love of her eyes, and the thousand and one offices she was always doing for them to try to make up to them for her past. They had come to take an intense interest, at first half shamefaced, in the baby. But as he grew older and full of winning ways, one could not always remember that he was a child of shame, and he made just as much sunshine as any lawful child makes in a house. More indeed, for in all the Island was never so beautiful a child. The sun seemed to shed all its rays on his head; his eyes were blue as the sea; his limbs were sturdy and beautiful, and from the time he began to take notice he sent out little tendrils that gathered round the hearts of all those who looked upon him. So kind is God sometimes to a little nameless child.

But to see Maggie while her brothers played with the boy, tossing him in their arms, and letting him spring from one to the other, was indeed a pretty sight. You know the proud confidence with which an animal that loves you looks on at your handling of her little ones – her anxiety quite swallowed up in her pride and confidence and her benevolent satisfaction in the pleasure she is giving you. That is how Maggie watched those delightful romps. But the old woman in the chimney-corner turned away her head; and never forgot that Maggie had stolen God's gift, and that the scarlet letter was on the boy's white forehead.

As the years passed and the boy throve and grew tall, I heard of Maggie becoming very devout. "A true penitent," said Father Tiernay to me, "and I believe that in return for the patience and gentleness with which she has striven to expiate her sin God has given her a very unusual degree of sanctity." In the intervals of her work she was permitted as a great privilege to help about the altar linen, and keep the church clean. She used to carry the boy with her when she went to the church, and I have come upon him fast asleep in a sheltered corner, while his mother was sweeping and dusting, with a radiant and sanctified look on a face that had grown very spiritual.

But still the old mother remained inexorable. I am sure in her own mind she resented as a profanation her daughter's work about the church. She herself had never entered that familiar holy place since her daughter's disgrace. Sunday and holiday all these years she had trudged to Breagh, a long way round by the coast, for mass. All expostulations have been vain, even Father Tiernay's own. Whatever other people may forget, the sin has lost nothing of its scarlet for her.

It was the last time I was on the Island that I was told of Maggie's marriage. Not to an Island man: oh no, no Island man would marry a girl with a stain on her character, not though she came to be as high in God's favour as the blessed Magdalen herself. He was the mate of a Scotch vessel, a grave, steady, strong-faced Highlander. He had come to the Island trading for years, and knew Maggie's story as well as any Islander. But he had seen beyond the mirk of the sin the woman's soul pure as a pearl.

Maggie could not believe that any man, least of all a man like Alister, wanted to marry her. "I am a wicked woman," she said with hot blushes, "and you must marry a good woman."

"I mean to marry a good woman, my lass," he said, "the best woman I know. And that is your bonny self." Maggie hesitated. He smoothed back her hair with a fond proprietary touch. "We'll give the boy a name," he said, "and before God, none will ever know he's not my own boy."

That settled it. Jack was a big lad of six now, and would soon begin to understand things, and perhaps ask for his father. It opened before her like an incredible exquisite happiness that perhaps he need never know her sin. She put her hand into Alister's and accepted him in a passion of sobbing that was half joy, half sorrow.

The brothers were all in favour of the marriage. They loved her too much not to want her to have a fair chance in a new life. Here on the Island, though she were a saint, she would still be a penitent. It came hardest on Tom, – for Larry was soon to bring home a wife of his own, but neither man talked much of what he felt. They put aside their personal sorrow and were glad for Maggie and her boy.

But Maggie's mother was consistent to the last. No brazen and flaunting sinner could have seemed to her more a lost creature than the girl who had been so dutiful a daughter, so loving a sister, so perfect a mother, all those years. Tom told her the news. "I wash my hands of her," she said. "Let her take her shame under an honest man's roof if she will. I wish her neither joy nor sorrow of it." And more gentle words than these Tom could not bring her to say.

So Maggie was married, the old woman preserving her stony silence and apparent unconcern. She only spoke once, – the day the girl was made a wife. It was one of her bad days, and she had to lie down after an attack of her heart. Maggie dressed to go to the church and meet her bridegroom. She was not to return to the cottage, and her modest little luggage and little Jack's were already aboard the Glasgow brig. At the last, hoping for some sign of softening, the girl went into the dim room where her mother lay, ashen-cheeked. The mother turned round on her her dim eyes. "What do you want of me?" she asked, breaking the silence of years. The girl helplessly covered her eyes with her hands. "Did you come for my blessing?" gasped the old woman. "It is liker my curse you'd take with you. But I promised Tom long ago that I would not curse you. Go then. And I praise God that Larry will soon give me an honest daughter instead of you, my shame this many a year."

That was the last meeting of mother and daughter. They say Alister is a devoted husband, but he comes no more to the Island. He has changed out of his old boat, and his late shipmates say vaguely that he has removed somewhere Sunderland or

Cardiff way, and trades to the North Sea. Tom is very reticent about Maggie, though Miss Bell, the postmistress, might tell, if she were not a superior person, and as used to keeping a secret at a pinch as Father Tiernay himself, how many letters he receives with the post-mark of a well-known seaport town.

Poor Maggie! Said I not that in the Island the way of transgressors is hard?

From *Introduction*

From The Cabinet of Irish Literature (1902)

Anglo-Irish [literature] was having its beginnings, though it is long till the writings of the Anglo-Irish bear any trace that their makers were born on Irish soil. Sir John Denham, Richard Stanihurst, Sir James Ware, Usher, Congreve, Farquhar, were only Irish by accident of birth; and the same may be said of practically the whole Anglo-Irish school down to Swift and Goldsmith.[1] It may have been to Swift that his Irish birth and connection with Ireland seemed his inalienable misfortune; but whether that is so or not, his whole character and genius derived from the place of his birth. The profound and hopeless melancholy of the Celt was his bitter inheritance. His *soeva indignatio*, his pity and love and rage, were for his people whom he would break to make nearer his heart's desire … Goldsmith, with his sunny temperament, was of course very Irish; and from Swift and Goldsmith on, the Irish influence begins to show in the Anglo-Irish literature …

Meanwhile, interest in the ancient Irish poetry had awakened. Walker's *Historical Memoirs of the Irish Bards* was the first sign. To this Miss Charlotte Brooke contributed her first translations. Her *Reliques of Irish Poetry* was the next noteworthy event; and later came Hardiman's *Irish Minstrelsy*, with the contributions of Furlong and others.[2] This was all excellent scholarship; but the translators who were capable of thinking in Irish and writing in English were yet to come. Moore's advent makes a little blaze of glory in those end-of-century days. He had the excellent good fortune to marry a pretty gift of song-writing to the beautiful old Irish airs. Without the music it is doubtful whether even his own countrymen would persist in thinking Moore a great poet. Anyhow, he overshadowed everyone else in his day. He had a great opportunity, and took it, and he remains the idol of his country-people while other poets languish in cold neglect. Among English people he made Ireland and her woes fashionable; and he is even yet singing in many English homes where Ireland and the Irish sentiment are in little favour … However, real sincerity in Irish literary work was on its way. Davis was perhaps too determined to be Irish, and poetically Irish, and he was a spendthrift of his gift. Both in his own case and that of others he insisted upon the Muse being the handmaid of politics, frequently with disastrous results to the poetry. He had no time himself to be anything but fluent and careless; he had bigger things to do than the making of literature, and he insisted rather on quantity than quality in the poets of the *Nation* … With Davis, oratory, history, and poetry were the drums and fifes of his movement; and he himself showed them how the playing should be done. So there is plenty of fine and even splendid rhetoric in the poetry of those days; nobly

Notes

From Introduction

[1] Poet Sir John Denham (1614/15–69), translator Richard Stanihurst (1547–1618), historian Sir James Ware (1594–1666), theological writer and historian James Ussher (1581–1656), playwrights William Congreve (1670–1729) and George Farquhar (1677–1707), poet and satirist Jonathan Swift (1667–1745), and Oliver Goldsmith. Congreve moved to Ireland as a child and is the only author here not born in Ireland.

[2] James Hardiman (1782–1855) published his *Irish Minstrelsy* in 1831 and parts were subsequently reprinted in the *Dublin University Magazine* (1834); Thomas Furlong (1794–1827) was one of its most significant contributors.

inspiriting as it is, it crashes and cries against the ear, is heard, not overheard, as someone says poetry should be.[3] Poetry is not to be pressed into causes however ideal, and the spirit not seldom fled from the exaltations and energies of the *Nation* to quieter places ... Of the essentially political poets of the time D'Arcy M'Gee seems to me the best. Of course there were men on the fringe of the movement who were poets first – nay, poets altogether. There was Mangan, whose inspiration only failed him when he became political or ceased to be Irish. There was Walsh, who must have felt as his brothers of a century earlier had felt if they had seen "the Blackbird" come home at last. And there was Ferguson, quite alien in politics, whose "Lament for the Death of Thomas Davis" is perhaps the truest poetry Davis ever inspired.[4] It comes very easy to the Irishman to write. Give him a Cause, and he is as much a ready writer as a ready speaker. '98 had its scores of poets as it had its scores of historians. '48 had Davis to fuse it all, to set it a thousand paths, though but one way, for its energy ...

But now the names of Banim and Griffin remind me that I have been writing as if the Irish literature were but the Irish poetry. As a matter of fact, the art of romance and story-telling had become natural to the Irish people in the English tongue much sooner than the art of poetry. Of course Miss Edgeworth, our one acknowledged name of the first magnitude, came of a stock originally "planted." But like some Irish writers of to-day, the Edgeworths had become strongly Irish, and no doubt the extraordinary wit and observation of the great Maria owed something to that aloofness of race and blood which enabled her to see and to interpret dispassionately. Carleton, however, was altogether Irish; and while Miss Edgeworth displayed to the world the topsy-turvy life of the gentry in *Castle Rackrent* and *The Absentee*, Carleton showed us the Irish peasant from within as no one else has done. He was no gentle idealist. He was a big, coarse peasant of a genius; and while the genius in him enabled him at times to paint the soft and beautiful side of the Irish peasant character, especially as it is sometimes seen in a peasant mother, soft as Ireland itself, yet the very genius of the man was for something grinding and melancholy ... John Banim had something of Carleton's gloomy power, but was a *bourgeois*, not a peasant, and had a lighter, sweeter side to his character. Like Carleton with "The Churchyard Bride," John Banim produced one beautiful poem, "Soggarth Aroon,"[5] with others less beautiful. Michael Banim, working in the same *genre* as his brother, is less powerful and more pleasing. *Father Connell* is a charming book; and both brothers had a gift of humour, which one needs in describing a life so often concerned with things melancholy and tragic. Griffin, with *The Collegians*, is another memorable novelist; and one cannot but be sorry that he did not produce more novels instead of training the young mind of Ireland as a Christian Brother. Lever and Lover were also excellent in their kind. To my mind it is a good kind. The high spirits of *Charles O'Malley*, *Harry Larroquer*, *Jack Hinton*, and all that gay company, seem to me genius; and while *Luttrell of Arran* has perhaps more serious literary qualities, Lever seems destined to immortality by reason of his roisterers ... Lover is frankly farcical, the professional humorist, and very successful at his trade ...[6]

Notes

[3] English writer John Stuart Mill (1806–73), "Thoughts on Poetry and its Varieties" (1859).

[4] For Brooke, Walker, Moore, McGee, Mangan, and Ferguson, see above; for Davis, see *The Nation*, above. John Walsh (1830–98), like Hardiman and Furlong, was known as a translator.

[5] Originally titled "The Irish Peasant to His Priest" (see above, p. 315).

[6] For Edgeworth, Carleton, the Banims, and Lover, see above. Gerald Griffin (1803–40) is best known for *The Collegians* (1829), and Charles Lever (1806–72) is the author of the four novels mentioned here: *Confessions of Harry Lorrequer* (1839), *Charles O'Malley* (1841), *Jack Hinton: The Guardsman* (1842), and *Luttrell of Arran* (1865).

As for drama, the Anglo-Irish mind seems to have always run to that; and the *Cabinet* has more than its share of dramatists, though their number is fewer in our own day.

Since '48 Irish and English have fused rapidly. Even our scholars and antiquaries are oftener than not of English extraction ... In the years between '48 and '78 there was not much doing in general literature in Ireland. The Fenian time produced no one more interesting than Kickham,[7] whose peasant ballads are faultless, and who has written in *Knocknagow* a beautiful if too gentle novel of Irish life. Aubrey de Vere of course was working in poetry, and so was Allingham. Ferguson also produced his Epics, so that in poetry the time was memorable enough. Indeed, if one had to make a selection, instead of a collection, of Irish poems, and of the choicest kind, one would certainly draw largely on the work of those years, in which Ferguson wrote so much that was virile and romantic, De Vere that was beautiful and dignified, and Allingham that was exquisite and perfectly right ...

To be an Irish writer nowadays has its advantages, though they are not those of pelf.[8] Even a humble writer may hope for a little and sweet remembrance because of his accidental prominence as among the first drops in a shower. By-and-by, when the ranks of Irish writers are thronged as the ranks of English writers are, many more deserving than some of us will be trodden down, crushed out and clean forgotten. It is our compensation for being little read in our lifetime; for the race of Irish readers of Irish books is not yet: and the more Irish we are the less likely we are to find favour with English readers. That is to say, that with the best will in the world the two people are widely different.

William Butler Yeats (1865–1939)

William Butler Yeats was born in Dublin. The Yeats family moved in Dublin's artistic circles, and knew, for instance, the Wildes quite well. Yeats's family was remarkably artistic, and his father, sisters, and brother were all artists in various media. He is, of course, a leading Modernist poet and member of the Irish Literary Revival. He published numerous volumes of verse and prose, and was enormously influential on twentieth-century literature in English, winning the Nobel Prize for Literature in 1923. Much of his most important work was published after 1900, and so is beyond the scope of this anthology, but he edited *A Book of Irish Verse* quite early in his literary career, and the volume offers an interesting glimpse of Yeats's late-nineteenth-century views of Irish literary history.

Further reading

Chaudhry, Yug Mohit, *Yeats: The Irish Literary Revival and the Politics of Print.* Cork: Cork University Press, 2001.

Gould, Warwick, ed., *Yeats and the Nineties.* New York: Palgrave, 2001.

Howes, Marjorie and John Kelly, eds., *The Cambridge Companion to Yeats.* Cambridge: Cambridge University Press, 2006.

Notes ————————————————————————————————

[7] Charles Kickham (1826–82).

[8] money

From *Introduction*

From **A Book of Irish Verse (1895)**

The Irish Celt is sociable, as may be known from his proverb, "Contention is better than loneliness," and the Irish poets of the nineteenth century have sung their loudest when a company of rebels or revelers has been at hand to applaud. The Irish ballad-makers of the eighteenth found both at a hostelry in Limerick, above whose door was written in Gaelic –

> "Poor poet, do not pass me by,
> For though your tongue is always dry,
> And not a thraneen in your purse,
> O'Toomey welcomes you no worse."

Its owner was a ballad-maker himself,[1] and as long as his money lasted entertained them bountifully, and then took to minding the hens and chickens of an old peasant woman for a living, and ended his days in tatters, but not, one imagines, wholly without content. Among his friends and guests had been the most famous ballad-makers of his time, – O'Sullivan the Red, O'Sullivan the Gaelic, O'Heffernan the Blind, and many another,[2] – and their songs had made the people, crushed by the disasters of the Boyne and the Aughrim, remember their ancient greatness. The powers that history commemorates are but the coarse effects of influences delicate and vague as the beginning of twilight, and in those days these influences were woven like a web about the hearts of men by farm-labourers, peddlers, potato-diggers, hedge-schoolmasters, and grinders at the quern, poor wastrels who put the troubles of their native land, or their own happy or unhappy loves, into songs of an extreme beauty. But in the midst of this beauty is a flitting incoherence, a fitful dying out of the sense, as though the passion had become too great for words, as must needs be when life is the master and not the slave of the singer. The great bardic order, with its perfect artifice and imperfect art, had gone down in the wars of the seventeenth century, and poetry had found shelter amid the turf-smoke of the cabins.

English-speaking Ireland had meanwhile no poetic voice, for Goldsmith had chosen to celebrate English scenery and manners; and Swift was but an Irishman by what Mr. Balfour has called the visitation of God, and sore against his will; and Congreve by education and early association; while Parnell, Denham, and Roscommon were poets but to their own time.[3] Nor did the coming with the new century of the fame of Moore change matters for the better, for his Irish Melodies are to most cultivated ears but excellent drawing-room songs, pretty with a prettiness which is contraband of Parnassus; and all he had of high poetry is probably in "The light of other days," and in the exquisite lines beginning "At the mid hour of night." In England his power is over, but in Ireland numbers think him the first of lyric poets, and no persuasion can make them believe that poetry has cast him out because he had not distinction of style; his conventional phrases are too closely interwoven with their patriotism, his mechanical cadences too firmly married to the ancient music of their country. It was

Notes

From Introduction
[1] Seán Ó Tuama (1706–75).
[2] Eoghan Ruadh Ó Súilleabháin (1748–84), Tadhg Gaedhealach Ó Súlliobháin (1715–95), and Liam Dall O hIfearnáin (1720–60).

[3] Goldsmith (above), poet and satirist Jonathan Swift (1667–1745), playwright William Congreve (1670–1729), and poets Thomas Parnell (1679–1718), Sir John Denham (1615–69), and Wentworth Dillon, fourth earl of Roscommon (1637–85).

not indeed until Callanan wrote his naïve and haunting translations from the Gaelic, that anything of an honest style came into use.[4] "Shule Aroon" and the immortal "Kathleen O'More" had indeed been written for a good while, but had passed without notice and influence. Now, however, the lead of Callanan was followed by a host of translators, and they in turn by the poets of "Young Ireland," who mingled a little learned from the Gaelic ballad-writers with a great deal learned from Scott, Macaulay, and Campbell, and turned poetry once again into a principal means for spreading ideas of nationality and patriotism.[5] They were full of earnestness, but never understood that though a poet may govern his life by his enthusiasms, he must, when he sits down at his desk, but use them as the potter the clay. Their thoughts were a little insincere, because they lived in the half illusions of their admirable ideals; and their rhythms not seldom mechanical, because their purpose was served when they had satisfied the dull ears of the common man. They had no time to listen to the voice of the insatiable artist, who stands erect, or lies asleep waiting until a breath arouses him, in the heart of every craftsman. Life was their master, as it had been the master of the poets who gathered about O'Toomey's hearth, though it conquered them not by unreasoned love for a woman, or for native land, but by reasoned enthusiasm, and practical energy. No man was more sincere, no man had a less mechanical mind than Thomas Davis,[6] and yet he is often a little insincere and mechanical in his verse. When he sat down to write he had so great a desire to make the peasantry courageous and powerful that he half believed them already "the finest peasantry upon the earth," and wrote not a few such verses as –

> "Lead him to fight for native land,
>   His is no courage cold and wary;
> The troops live not that could withstand
>   The headlong charge of Tipperary," –

and to-day we are paying the reckoning with much bombast ... His contemporary, Clarence Mangan,[7] kept out of public life by a passion for opium and rum, wrought many powerful lyrics. He translated largely from the German, and imitated Oriental poetry, but only his Irish work is permanently interesting. He is usually classed with the Young Ireland poets, because he contributed to their periodicals and shared their political views; but his style was formed before their movement began, and for this reason perhaps he was always able to give sincere expression to the mood which he had chosen, the only sincerity literature knows of; and with happiness and cultivation might have displaced Moore. But as it was, whenever he had no fine ancient song to inspire him, he fell into rhetoric which was only lifted out of commonplace by an arid intensity. In his "Irish National Hymn," "Soul and Country," and the like, we look into a mind full of parched sands where the sweet dews have never fallen. A miserable man may think well and express himself with great vehemence, but he cannot make beautiful things, for Aphrodite never rises from any but a tide of joy. Mangan knew nothing of the happiness of the outer man, and it was only when prolonging the tragic exultation of some dead bard, that he knew the unearthly happiness which clouds the outer man with sorrow, and is the foundation of the

Notes ───────────────────────────────

[4] Moore and Callanan (above).
[5] For "Young Ireland," see *The Nation*, Mangan, MacCarthy, Lady Wilde, and McGee (above). Scottish authors Sir Walter Scott (1771–1832), Thomas Babington Macaulay (1800–59) (who is better known for his prose, but penned such

poems as "Epitaph on a Jacobite"), and Thomas Campbell (1777–1844).
[6] Thomas Davis (1814–45), "Tipperary."
[7] See Mangan (above).

impassioned art. Like those who had gone before him, he was the slave of life, for he had nothing of the self-knowledge, the power of selection, the harmony of mind, which enables the poet to be its master, and to mould the phantasmagoria of the world as he pleases ...

Meanwhile Samuel Ferguson, William Allingham, and Mr. Aubrey de Vere[8] were working quietly as men of letters, Ferguson selecting his subjects from the traditions of the Bardic age, and Allingham from those of his native Ballyshannon, and Mr. Aubrey de Vere wavering between English, Irish, and Catholic tradition. They were wiser than Young Ireland in the choice of their models, for, while drawing not less from purely Irish sources, they turned to the great poets of the world, Mr. de Vere owing something of his gravity to Wordsworth, Ferguson much of his simplicity to Homer, while Allingham had trained an ear, too delicate to catch the tune of but a single master, upon the lyric poetry of many lands. Allingham was the best artist, but Ferguson had the more ample imagination, the more epic aim. His "Vengeance of the Welshmen of Tirawley" is the best Irish ballad, and his "Conary," a long battle tale in blank verse, the best Irish poem of any kind. He had not the subtlety of feeling, the variety of cadence of a great lyric poet, but he has touched, here and there, an epic vastness and naïvety, as in the description in "Congal" of the mire-stiffened mantle of the giant spectre Mananan macLir, striking against his calves with as loud a noise as the mainsail of a ship makes, "when with the coil of all its ropes it beats the sounding mast." He is frequently dull, for he often lacked the "minutely appropriate words" necessary to embody those fine changes of feeling which enthral the attention; but his sense of weight and size, of action and tumult, has set him apart and solitary, an epic figure in a lyric age. Allingham, whose pleasant destiny has made him the poet of his native town, and put "The Winding Banks of the Erne" into the mouths of the ballad-singers of Ballyshannon, is, on the other hand, a master of "minutely appropriate words," and can wring from the luxurious sadness of the lover, from the austere sadness of old age, the last golden drop of beauty; but amid action and tumult he can but fold his hands. He is the poet of the melancholy peasantry of the West, and, as years go on, and voluminous histories and copious romances drop under the horizon, will take his place among those minor immortals who have put their souls into little songs to humble the proud.

Dora Sigerson (1866–1918)

Dora Sigerson was born in Dublin to the authors Hester and George Sigerson. Her parents were closely connected to Dublin literary circles, counting a young W. B. Yeats among their house guests, and Dora Sigerson was able to join literary groups in Dublin during the resurgence of literary nationalism, including the National Literary Society, in the late 1880s and early 1890s. Her first volume of poetry, *Verses* (1893), was published with the support of the then-editor of the *Irish Monthly*, a periodical to which she was a contributor. In 1896 she married the English journalist Clement King Shorter, and moved to England. This effectively separated

Notes

[8] See Ferguson, Allingham, and De Vere above.

her from the core of the Irish Modernist and Literary Revival movements, despite her social connections to authors such as Yeats, Katharine Tynan, and Alice Furlong, but she remained engaged with the nationalist literary project as well as Irish nationalism more generally, participating in efforts, for instance, to save Roger Casement from execution after the 1916 Rising.

Only her early poetry is included here, but after her marriage Sigerson continued to publish regularly, including *The Fairy Changeling, and Other Poems* (1897), *Ballads and Poems* (1899), *The Woman Who Went to Hell, and Other Ballads and Lyrics* (1902), and material on contemporary events in *Comfort the Women: A Prayer in Time of War* (1915) and *Love of Ireland, with which is incorporated Poems of the Irish Rebellion, 1916* (1916). *A Legend of Glendalough, and Other Ballads* (1919) was published posthumously. Despite early twentieth-century celebrations of her work by contemporary authors from Tynan to Douglas Hyde and by British authors from

George Meredith to Thomas Hardy, Sigerson's place in Irish literary history, and the emergence of Irish Modernism in particular, has yet to be fully assessed. The devastating poem "Man's Discontent" can be read in light of the British Pre-Raphaelites' representation of women in poetry and painting, while "What We Must Do" is a more direct challenge to Victorian constraints. Her poem "The Flight of the Wild Geese" is one of her early engagements with nationalist literature – the "Wild Geese" had been a theme of nationalist poetry for decades, from the pages of *The Nation* to the verse of Sigerson's friend Tynan (see Tynan's "The Wild Geese" above).

Further reading

Hanley, Evelyn A., "Dora Sigerson Shorter: Late Victorian Romantic," *Victorian Poetry* 3 (1965): 223–34.

Logan, Deborah A., "Kathleen's Legacy: Dora Sigerson Shorter's Vagrant Heart," *Victorian Newsletter* 97 (2000): 14–21.

Man's Discontent

From Verses (1893)

White feet half hid in violets, small hands in a burden fair,
A burden of Spring's first blossoms she wove for her neck and hair
Into wreaths, as she paused a moment on the threshold of maidenhood.
O my child love! hesitating, there I met her as she stood.
So I stayed till I grew weary – man's discontent, I ween –   5
Then I thought I longed for Summer, with trees for ever green.
I tired of primrose blossoms and the budding boughs of spring,
And the chirp! chirp! of this year's birds that had not learned to sing.
I thought her soft arms too slender, and the smooth young cheek too clear,
And the April eyes that loved me too ready with smile or tear,   10
Too ready to read my wishes in mine that she might obey
Ere I spoke; so in the springtime I went from her arms away.

I sought my love and I found her, when Summer days were long,
All the hedges bright with blossoms and musical with song,
But the eyes that saw me coming no answer to mine would speak;   15
The lids drooped till the lashes lay dark on her crimson cheek,
The hands I clasped for a moment would but struggle to be free,
As I tried to win her to speak of love, of herself, of me.

"Hark! the young birds," she only said; "dost hear them sing in the wood?"
Love's rosy wings had brushed her eyes as she passed to maidenhood.   20
So I stayed, but soon grew weary – man's discontent, I ween –
And I longed for Autumn colours, not trees for ever green.
Cried I: "Its sky at sunset is far more fair than this."
Then I thought, my love's cheek flushes too ready 'neath my kiss,
That the gentle voice replying spoke love too timidly,   25
And the shy hands culling blossoms had no caress for me.
I tired of roses' perfume and the song the wild-birds sung,
So I left her in the noon-time, when Summer yet was young.
'Neath the sunset skies of Autumn, all the heath-clad hills flushed red;
Sweet the lark his matins singing in the blue sky overhead,   30
And the languid breeze was perfumed by a rose's stolen breath;
'Twas the last white bud of Summer that escaped the hand of death,
And my sweet, I feared to meet her for my yesterday of scorn;
Then I flung myself beside her as she knelt amid the corn.
She only said: "To red and gold grew the green young leaf of Spring.   35
The rose filled the dead cowslip's throne; now poppy reigns a king."
Then she sighed, with blue eyes tearful and quivering lips that smiled,
"And to woman's perfection came the promise of the child.
But the rose and cowslip withered, and the poppy's death is nigh,
For the changing leaf that lingers there remains nought but to die.   40
Through the bitter winds of Winter let me shelter by thy side;
Prithee, stray not with the Autumn, O my love! unsatisfied."

So I stayed, but soon grew weary – man's discontent, I ween –
Of the woods all clad in splendour, rarest red, and gold, and green;
Of the hands that toiling for me pressed the red juice from the vine,   45
And brought the fragrant peaches that I might not trouble mine;
Of the fawn-like eyes that watched me, ever speaking of their love;
Of the neck I once thought softer than the white breast of a dove.
So I rose up from my resting ere the Autumn days were dead,
And the oak, and beech, and chestnut had not yet their bright leaves shed;   50
While the birds were singing gaily from their shelter in the thorn,
Still the sleep-bestowing poppies lit their red lamps in the corn.

I sought my love in the Winter, for I sorrowed for the past,
And in the long nights of thinking I knew my own heart at last;
That mine were the imperfections that I seemed in her to find,   55
That happiness ever beside me made me to sorrow grow blind,
How I of God's gifts grew weary – man's discontent, I ween –
That to-day sighs for to-morrow, then to weep for what had been.
She was sleeping when I found her, O my love! in one hand lay
Spring's young buds and Summer roses with their fair bloom passed away;   60
But the poison-breathing poppy on her lip was lying red,
Ah! the sleep-bestowing poppy had left me but the dead;
The calm eyes gazing heavenwards could not see the love mine bore,
And the pale brow 'neath my kisses still its marble colour wore;
Till the snow that was not whiter hid the silent face from me –   65
Hid the lips that could not answer and the eyes that could not see.
Flake by flake came down and hid her from the cold sky overhead.
Thus, having all, I lost all, ere the Winter days had fled.

Spring Song – To Ireland

From Verses (1893)

Weep no more, heart of my heart, no more!
    The night has passed and the dawn is here,
The cuckoo calls from the budding trees,
    And tells us that Spring is near.

Sorrow no more, beloved, no more;   5
    For see, sweet emblem of hope untold!
The tears that soft on the shamrocks fall
    There turn to blossoms of gold.

Winter has gone with his blighting breath,
    No more to chill thee with cold or fear,   10
The brook laughs loud in its liberty,
    Green buds on the hedge appear.

Weep no more, life of my heart, no more!
    The birds are carolling sweet and clear;
The warmth of Summer is in the breeze,   15
    And the Spring – the Spring is here.

The Flight of the Wild Geese

From Verses (1893)

Wrapt in the darkness of the night,
Gathering in silence on the shore,
Wild geese flown from hiding on the hills
(Hark! the wolf-hound; thrice he howled before),
Wild geese with forest leaves tangled in their hair.   5
Is that blood on the heaving breasts of some,
Or dull red clay from fox-deserted lair?
Why thus so stealthy do they come?
Wild geese, women's arms round you in the darkness;
Women's hearts forbid you to cry though they break;   10
Little children must not sob in their kissing;
"Brother, forever? O hush thee, for God's sake!"
Wild geese with fierce eyes, deathless hope in your hearts,
Stretching your strong white wings eager for your flight.
These women's eyes will watch your swift returning.   15
(Thrice the banshee cried in the stormy night.)
Flinging the salt from their wings, and despair from their hearts,
They arise on the breast of the storm with a cry and are gone.
When will you come home, wild geese, with your thousand strong?
(The wolf-dog loud in the silence of night howls on.)   20
Not the fierce wind can stay your return or tumultuous sea,

Nor the freedom France gives to your feet on her luxuriant shore.
No smiles for your love like the tears of your sorrowing land,
Only Death in his reaping could make you return no more.
White birds, white birds, I dream of that glad homecoming;   25
Though human eyes could not mark your silent flight,
Women lie face down with clenchèd hands in the sea.
(Thrice the banshee cries in the stormy night.)

What We Must Do

From Verses (1893)

What we must do and may not do.
  This is the World's whole refrain,
  Till beating on the wearied brain,
We wonder what is true.

My love! my love! who passes by,   5
  As Fate hath willed ere we were born,
  Could I but face the people's scorn,
And tell my love, or die.

But this is not a woman's part,
  A careless brow you dare to show;   10
  She smiles upon you as you go,
To hide a breaking heart.

My friend did take my hand to-day,
  Light kisses laid upon my face;
  My sad reproach was in its place –   15
She could not tell me Nay!

How poor we are with all our laws
  Of ever-changing form and dress!
  The world becomes a weariness,
Life's current choked with straws.   20

I sometimes think the brain more wise
  Where madness reason hath out-thrown,
  And gave the fool a life his own,
That had no guilt in lies –

Than we, who claim to Reason's rule   25
  And chain our freedom ruthlessly,
  Not to what is, but what must be –
Forever in a school.

The ox, the ass, 'neath Nature's dome,
  Follow his teachings without strife;   30
  And yet they reach the heights of life,
And bring their harvest home.

I ask, O World, a wider sight
    For men, that they to see be strong –
    Your little wrongs that are not wrong,   35
Your little rights that are not right.

There's not so much sin here below
    As petty fashions make believe;
    Yet so the world's sad eyes deceive –
Sin is much greater than they know.   40

Bibliography

Sources for Copy-texts

Allingham, William, *The Music-Master, A Love Story, and Two Series of Night and Day Songs*. London: G. Routledge and Co., 1855.

—— *Songs, Ballads, and Stories, including many now first collected and the rest revised and rearranged*. London: George Bell and Sons, 1877.

—— *Evil May-Day*. London: David Stott, 1882.

Banim, Michael and Banim, John, *Chaunt of the Cholera, Songs for Ireland*. London: James Cochrane and Co., 1831.

—— *The Bit O'Writin' and Other Tales*, 3 vols. London: Saunders and Otley, 1838.

Bickerstaffe, Isaac, *The Captive: A Comic Opera, as it is perform'd at the Theatre-Royal in the Hay-Market*. London, 1769.

Boucicault, Dion, *Arrah-na-Pogue*. London, 1864.

Brooke, Charlotte, *Reliques of Irish Poetry*. Dublin: George Bonham, 1789.

Burke, Edmund, *A Philosophical Enquiry Into the Origin of Our Ideas of the Sublime and Beautiful*. London, 1757.

—— *Thoughts on the Cause of the Present Discontents*. London: J. Dodsley, 1770.

Callanan, J. J., "The Convict of Clonmel," *Blackwood's Edinburgh Magazine*, 13 (1823): 211–12.

—— *The Recluse of Inchidony, and Other Poems*. London: Hurst, Chance and Company, 1830.

Carleton, William, *Traits and Stories of the Irish Peasantry*, second series, 3 vols. Dublin: William Frederick Wakeman, 1833.

—— *Traits and Stories of the Irish Peasantry*. Dublin: William Curry, Jr., and Co., 1843.

Corry, John, *Odes and Elegies, Descriptive and Sentimental, with The Patriot: A Poem*. Newry: R. Moffet, 1797.

—— *The Detector of Quackery; Or, Analyser of Medical, Philosophical, Political, Dramatic, and Literary Imposture*. London: T. Hurst et al., 1802.

[Davis, Thomas], "My Grave," *The Nation* (October 29, 1842): 42.

Dermody, Thomas, *Poems*. Dublin: Chambers, 1789.

—— *Poems, Consisting of Essays, Lyric, Elegaic, &c*. Dublin: J. Jones, 1792.

—— *Poems, Moral and Descriptive*. London: Vernor and Hood, 1800.

De Vere, Aubrey [Thomas], *Poems*. London: Burns and Lambert, 1855.

—— *Irish Odes and Other Poems*. New York: Catholic Publication Society, 1869.

Drennan, William, *Fugitive Pieces in Verse and Prose*. Belfast: F. D. Finlay, 1815.

Edgeworth, Maria, *Popular Tales*, 3 vols. London: J. Johnson, 1804.

—— and Richard Lovell Edgeworth, *Essay on Irish Bulls*. London: J. Johnson, 1802.

Ferguson, Samuel, "The Forging of the Anchor," *Blackwood's Edinburgh Magazine* 31 (February 1832): 281–3.

—— ["Lament for Thomas Davis,"] *Dublin University Magazine* 29 (February 1847): 198–9.

—— *Lays of the Western Gael, and Other Poems*. London: Bell and Daldy, 1865.

—— *Poems*. Dublin: William McGee, 1880.

Goldsmith, Oliver, *The Citizen of the World; Or, Letters from a Chinese Philosopher Residing in London, to his Friends in the East*, 2 vols. Dublin: George and Alex. Ewing, 1762.

—— *The Deserted Village, a Poem*, 2nd edn. Dublin, 1770.

—— *Poems, by the Late Dr. Oliver Goldsmith*. Belfast, 1775.

Kavanagh, Bridget and Kavanagh, Julia, *The Pearl Fountain and Other Fairy Tales*. London: Chatto and Windus, 1876.

Leadbeater, Mary, *Extracts and Original Anecdotes; For the Improvement of Youth*. Dublin: R. M. Jackson, 1794.

—— *Poems, by Mary Leadbeater (Late Shackleton) to Which Is Prefixed Her Translation of the Thirteenth Book of the Aeneid*. London: Longman, Hurst, Rees and Orme, 1808.

—— *Cottage Dialogues among the Irish Peasantry*, part I, 4th edn. Dublin: J. Cumming, 1813.

Lefanu, Joseph Sheridan, "A Chapter in the History of a Tyrone Family, being a Tenth Extract from the Legacy of the late Francis Purcell, P. P. of Drumcoolagh," *Dublin University Magazine* 14 (October 1839): 398–415.

Leslie, John, *Killarney: A Poem*. London: George Robinson, 1772.

Lover, Samuel, *Legends and Stories of Ireland*, 2nd edn. Dublin: W. F. Wakeman, 1832.

MacCarthy, Denis Florence, *Ballads, Poems, and Lyrics, Original and Translated*. Dublin: James M'Glashan, 1850.

—— *Underglimpses, and Other Poems*. London: David Bogue, 1857.

McGee, Thomas D'Arcy, *Poems by Thomas D'Arcy McGee, Chiefly Written in America. Supplement to the "Nation."* Dublin, 1854.

—— *Canadian Ballads and Occasional Verses*. Montreal: J. Lovell, 1858.

Mangan, James Clarence, "The Philosopher and the Child," *The Comet* (August 4, 1833): 532.

—— "The Jacobite Relics of Ireland," *The Irish Penny Journal* 1.29 (January 16, 1841): 228–9.

—— *German Anthology: A Series of Translations from the Most Popular of the German Poets*, 2 vols. Dublin: William Curry, Jr. and Co., 1845.

—— "Advice," *Dublin University Magazine* 27 (January 1846): 57–8.

—— "The Warning Voice," *The Nation* (February 21, 1846): 297.

—— "Dark Rosaleen," *The Nation* (May 30, 1846): 521.

—— "A Vision of Connaught in the Thirteenth Century," *The Nation* (July 11, 1846): 619.

—— "The Lovely Land," *The Nation* (July 18, 1846): 633.

—— "Leonora," *Dublin University Magazine* 28 (December 1846): 656–62.

—— "The Nameless One," *The Irishman* (October 27, 1849): 683.

—— *The Poets and Poetry of Munster: A Selection of Irish Songs by the Poets of the Last Century, With Poetical Translations by the Late James Clarence Mangan*. With the Original Music, and Biographical Sketches of the Authors, by John O'Daly. Dublin: John O'Daly, 1849.

—— "Fragment of an Unpublished Autobiography," *The Irish Monthly: A Magazine of General Literature* 10 (1882): 675–89.

Moore, Thomas, *Epistles, Odes, and Other Poems*. London: James Carpenter, 1806.

—— *Intercepted Letters; Or, the Two-Penny Post-Bag. To Which are Added, Trifles Reprinted*, by Thomas Brown, the Younger, 2nd edn. London: J. Carr, 1813.

—— *Lalla Rookh, An Oriental Romance*. London: Longman, Hurst, Rees, Orme, and Brown, 1817.

—— *Irish Melodies*. With an Appendix, Containing the Original Advertisements, and the Prefatory Letter on Music. London: J. Power and Longman, Hurst, Rees, Orme, and Brown, 1821.

—— *Fables for the Holy Alliance, Rhymes on the Road, &c. &c.*, by Thomas Brown, the Younger, Secretary of the Pocu-curante Society, and Author of the Fudge Family, and the Two-Penny Post-Bag. London: Longman, Hurst, Rees, Orme, and Brown, 1823.

The Nation, "The Nation," *The Nation* (October 15, 1842): 8.

—— "How to Make an Irish Story," *The Nation* (January 14, 1843): 218.

—— "A Voice from America," *The Nation* (May 6, 1843): 474.

—— "Convicted Criminals," *The Nation* (March 2, 1844): 329.

—— *The Spirit of the Nation*. Supplement to *The Nation* (March 20, 1852).

O'Brien, Mary, *The Political Monitor; Or Regent's Friend*. Dublin, 1790.

Orr, James, *Poems, on Various Subjects*. Belfast: Smyth and Lyons, 1804.

Owenson, Sydney (Lady Morgan), *Twelve Original Hibernian Melodies, with English Words, imitated and translated, from the Works of the Ancient Irish Bards*. London: Preston [1805].

—— *The Lay of an Irish Harp; Or Metrical Fragments*. London: Richard Phillips, 1807.

—— "Absenteeism," Part I. *New Monthly Magazine* 10 (1824): 481–95.

Paddy's Resource, Being a Select Collection of Original Patriotic Songs for the Use of the People of Ireland. No place or publisher identified, c.1800.

Porter, James, *Billy Bluff and 'Squire Firebrand: Or, A Sample of the Times, as it Periodically Appeared in the Northern Star.* Belfast, 1812.

Ryves, Elizabeth, *Poems on Several Occasions.* London, 1777.

Sheridan, Frances, *The Discovery: A Comedy, As it is Performed at the Theatres-Royal in Dublin and London.* Dublin, 1763.

—— "Ode to Patience" in a Letter to Samuel Whyte (May 12, 1764). *A Miscellany*, by Samuel Whyte and Edward Athenry Whyte, 113–16. Dublin, 1799.

Sheridan, Richard Brinsley, *St. Patrick's Day; Or, the Scheming Lieutenant. A Comic Opera. As it is Acted at the Theatre-Royal, Smoke-Alley.* Dublin, 1788.

—— *Speeches of the Late Right Honourable Richard Brinsley Sheridan*, ed. "A Constitutional Friend," 5 vols. London: Patrick Martin, 1816.

Sheridan, Thomas, *An Humble Appeal to the Publick, Together with Some Considerations on the Present Critical and Dangerous State of the Stage in Ireland.* Dublin, 1758.

—— *The Brave Irishman: Or, Captain O'Blunder. A Farce.* Dublin, 1759.

Sigerson, Dora, *Verses.* London: Elliot Stock, 1893.

Tighe, Mary, *Psyche, With Other Poems*, 3rd edn. London: Longman, Hurst, Rees, Orme, and Brown, 1811.

Tynan, Katharine (Hinkson), *Ballads and Lyrics.* London: Kegan Paul, Trench, Trübner and Co., 1891.

—— *An Isle in the Water.* London: Adam and Charles Black, 1895.

—— Introduction. *The Cabinet of Irish Literature*, ed. Charles A. Read, rev. and extended by Katharine Tynan Hinkson, xi–xxiv. London: Gresham Publishing, 1902.

Walker, Joseph C., *Historical Memoirs of the Irish Bards.* London, 1786.

Wilde, Jane, *Poems.* Dublin: James Duffy, 1864.

—— *Ancient Legends, Mystic Charms, and Superstitions of Ireland*, 2 vols. London: Ward and Downey, 1887.

—— *Notes on Men, Women, and Books.* London: Ward and Downey, 1891.

Wilde, Oscar, *Poems.* London: David Bogue, 1881.

—— *The Happy Prince and Other Tales.* London: D. Nutt, 1888.

—— "The Decay of Lying: A Dialogue," *The Nineteenth Century: A Monthly Review* 25 (1889): 35–56.

—— *The Ballad of Reading Gaol* by C. 3. 3. London: Leonard Smithers, 1898.

Yeats, W. B., *A Book of Irish Verse, Selected from Modern Writers.* London: Methuen, 1895.

Selected Sources for Notes

Augustine, Saint, *Confessions*, trans. Henry Chadwick. Oxford: Oxford University Press, 1991.

Babcock, R. W., "Benevolence, Sensibility and Sentiment in Some Eighteenth-century Periodicals," *Modern Language Notes* 62 (1947): 394–7.

Bolg an Tsolair: Or, Gælic Magazine. Containing Laoi na Sealga: Or, the Famous Fenian Poem, called The Chase, with a Collection of Choice Irish Songs, Translated by Miss Brooke, To which is Prefixed an Abridgment of Irish Grammar, with A Vocabulary, and Familiar Dialogues. Belfast, 1795.

Cleeve, Brian, *Dictionary of Irish Writers*, 3 vols. Cork: Mercier Press, 1969.

Davis, Richard, *The Young Ireland Movement.* Dublin: Gill and Macmillan, 1988.

Dictionary of Canadian Biography Online, Library and Archives Canada (http://www.biographi.ca/EN/index.html).

Dictionary of National Biography, ed. Lawrence Goldman. Oxford: Oxford University Press, 2004–6.

Dixon, W. Hepworth, ed., *Lady Morgan's Memoirs, Autobiography, Diaries, and Correspondence.* London: William H. Allen, 1863.

Ellman, Richard, *Oscar Wilde.* London: Viking, 1987.

Ferguson, [Lady], *Sir Samuel Ferguson in Ireland of his Day*, 2 vols. London: William Blackwood, 1896.

Grove Music Online. Oxford: Oxford University Press, 2006.

Henry the Minstrel, *Wallace; Or, the Life and Acts of Sir William Wallace, of Ellerslie.* 1488. Vol. II of *The Bruce; and Wallace; Published from Two Ancient Manuscripts*, 2 vols, ed. John Jamieson. Edinburgh: James Ballantyne, 1820.

Hogan, Robert, *Dictionary of Irish Literature*, rev. edn., 2 vols. London: Greenwood, 1996.

Homer, *The Iliad of Homer*, trans. Richmond Lattimore. Chicago: University of Chicago Press, 1951.

Houghton, Walter Edwards, ed., *The Wellesley Index to Victorian Periodicals 1824–1900*. London: Routledge and Kegan Paul, 1966–89.

Kavanagh, Julia, *English Women of Letters: Biographical Sketches*. Leipzig: Bernhard Tauchnitz, 1862.

Kilroy, James, *The Autobiography of James Clarence Mangan*. Dublin: Dolmen Press, 1968.

Lemprière, John, *Lemprière's Classical Dictionary of Proper Names Mentioned in Ancient Authors*. 1788. London: Routledge and Kegan Paul, 1984.

Lover, Samuel, "Glossary," *Legends and Stories of Ireland*, 2nd edn. Dublin: W. F. Wakeman, 1832.

"Memoir of the Late Mr. Callanan," *Bolster's Quarterly Magazine* (1831): 280–97.

Mill, John Stuart, *Collected Works of John Stuart Mill*, vol. 1, ed. John M. Robson and Jack Stillinger. Toronto: University of Toronto Press, 1981.

Muir, Percy H., "Thomas Moore's Irish Melodies, 1808–1834," *The Colophon: A Book Collector's Quarterly*, pt. 15 (1933): unpaginated.

Murray, Christopher, ed., "Drama, 1690–1800," *The Field Day Anthology of Irish Writing*, gen. ed. Seamus Deane, 1: 500–657. Derry: Field Day, 1991.

Murray, Isobel, "*Sidonia the Sorceress*: Pre-Raphaelite Cult Book," *Durham University Journal* 75 (1982): 53–7.

The Nation, "The Overland Mail: India, Affghanistan, and China," *The Nation* (October 15, 1842): 6.

—— "The English Army in Affghanistan, and the 'Notions' of the English Press Thereupon," *The Nation* (October 15, 1842): 8.

—— "National Gallery: No. 1 – Thomas Moore," *The Nation* (October 29, 1842): 44.

—— "The English Army in India," *The Nation* (November 12, 1842): 73.

—— " 'The Wake of William Orr' by Dr. Drennan," *The Nation* (March 25, 1843): 378.

—— "National Gallery: No. V – the Late John Banim," *The Nation* (September 23, 1843): 794.

O'Donoghue, D. J., *The Poets of Ireland: A Biographical and Bibliographical Dictionary of Irish Writers of English Verse*. London: Oxford University Press, 1912.

Ovid, *The Metamorphoses*, trans. Horace Gregory. New York: Mentor, 1958.

Robinson, Mairi, ed., *The Concise Scots Dictionary*. Aberdeen: Aberdeen University Press, 1985.

Ryves, Elizabeth, *Dialogue in the Elysian Fields, between Caesar and Cato*. London: J. Davis, 1784.

—— *The Hastiniad; An Heroic Poem, in Three Cantos*. London: J. Debrett, 1785.

Shakespeare, William, *The Riverside Shakespeare*, ed. G. Blakemore Evans. Boston: Houghton Mifflin Company, 1974.

Virgil, *The Aeneid*, trans. W. F. Jackson Knight. New York: Penguin, 1956.

Webb, Alfred, *A Compendium of Irish Biography: Comprising Sketches of Distinguished Irishmen, and of Eminent Persons Connected with Ireland by Office or by Their Writings*. Dublin: M. H. Gill, 1878.

Welch, Robert, ed., *The Oxford Companion to Irish Literature*. Oxford: Clarendon Press, 1996.

White, Terence de Vere, *The Parents of Oscar Wilde: Sir William and Lady Wilde*. London: Hodder and Stoughton, 1967.

—— *Tom Moore: The Irish Poet*. London: Hamish Hamilton, 1977.

Selected Further Reading: Irish Literature

Backus, Margot Gayle, *The Gothic Family Romance: Heterosexuality, Child Sacrifice, and the Anglo-Irish Colonial Order*. Durham, NC: Duke University Press, 1999.

Boulton, James T., *The Language of Politics in the Age of Wilkes and Burke*. London: Routledge and Kegan Paul, 1963.

Brogan, Howard O., "Thomas Moore, Irish Satirist and Keeper of the English Conscience," *Philological Quarterly* 24 (1945): 255–76.

Butler, Marilyn, *Maria Edgeworth: A Literary Biography*. Oxford: Clarendon Press, 1972.

Connolly, Claire, ed., *Theorizing Ireland*. London: Palgrave Macmillan, 2003.

Corbett, Mary Jean, *Allegories of Union in Irish and English Writing, 1790–1870: Politics, History, and the Family from Edgeworth to Arnold*. Cambridge: Cambridge University Press, 2000.

Deane, Seamus, "Maria Edgeworth, Romanticism and Utilitarianism," *Gaeliana* 8 (1986): 9–15.

—— *A Short History of Irish Literature*. Notre Dame, IN: University of Notre Dame Press, 1986.

—— "Fiction and Politics: Irish Nineteenth-century National Character 1790–1900," in *The Writer as Witness: Literature as Historical Evidence*, 90–113. Cork: Cork University Press, 1987.

—— "The Production of Cultural Space in Irish Writing," *boundary 2* 21:3 (1994): 117–44.

Bibliography

—— *Strange Country: Modernity and Nationhood in Irish Writing since 1790*. Oxford: Oxford University Press, 1997.

Dickson, David, Keogh, Dáire, and Whelan, Kevin, eds., *The United Irishmen: Republicanism, Radicalism and Rebellion*. Dublin: Lilliput Press, 1993.

Dunne, Tom, *Maria Edgeworth and the Colonial Mind*. Cork: University College (Cork), 1984.

—— "Haunted by History: Irish Romantic Writing 1800–50," in *Romanticism in National Context*, ed. Roy Porter and Mikuláš Teich, 68–91. New York: Cambridge University Press, 1988.

Eagleton, Terry, *Heathcliff and the Great Hunger: Studies in Irish Culture*. New York: Verso, 1996.

—— *Crazy John and the Bishop and Other Essays on Irish Culture*. Notre Dame, IN: University of Notre Dame Press, 1998.

—— *Scholars and Rebels in Nineteenth-century Ireland*. Oxford: Blackwell, 1999.

Gibbons, Luke, *Transformations in Irish Culture*. Notre Dame, IN: Notre Dame University Press, 1996.

—— "Between Captain Rock and a Hard Place: Art and Agrarian Insurgency," in *Ideology and Ireland in the Nineteenth Century*, ed. Tadhg Foley and Seán Ryder, 23–44. Dublin: Four Courts Press, 1998.

Hall, Wayne E., *Dialogues in the Margins: A Study of the Dublin University Magazine*. Washington, DC: The Catholic University of America Press, 1999.

Kelleher, Margaret, *The Feminization of Famine: Expressions of the Inexpressible?* Durham, NC: Duke University Press, 1997.

—— and O'Leary, Philip, eds., *The Cambridge History of Irish Literature*, 2 vols. Cambridge: Cambridge University Press, 2006.

Keogh, Dáire and Furlong, Nicholas, eds., *The Women of 1798*. Dublin: Four Courts Press, 1998.

Kiberd, Declan, "The Fall of the Stage Irishman," *Genre* 12 (1979): 451–72.

—— *Inventing Ireland*. Cambridge, MA: Harvard University Press, 1995.

—— *Irish Classics*. London: Granta, 2000.

—— *The Irish Writer and the World*. Cambridge: Cambridge University Press, 2005.

Kirkpatrick, Kathryn J., *Border Crossings: Irish Women Writers and National Identities*. Tuscaloosa, AL: University of Alabama Press, 2000.

Leerssen, J. Th., *Mere Irish and Fíor-Gael: Studies in the Idea of Irish Nationality, its Development and Literary Expression Prior to the Nineteenth Century*. Philadelphia: John Benjamins, 1986.

—— "On the Edge of Europe: Ireland in Search of Oriental Roots, 1650–1850," *Comparative Criticism* 8 (1986): 91–112.

—— "On the Treatment of Irishness in Romantic Anglo-Irish Fiction," *Irish University Review* 20 (1990): 251–63.

Lloyd, David, "Race under Representation," *Oxford Literary Review* 13 (1991): 62–94.

—— *Anomalous States: Irish Writing and the Post-Colonial Moment*. Durham, NC: Duke University Press, 1993.

—— *Ireland after History*. Notre Dame, IN: University of Notre Dame Press, 1999.

McCormack, W. J., "The Genesis of Protestant Ascendancy," in *1789: Reading Writing Revolution*, ed. Francis Barker et al., 303–23. Colchester: University of Essex, 1982.

—— *Ascendancy and Tradition in Anglo-Irish Literary History, 1789–1939*. Oxford: Clarendon Press, 1985.

—— *The Pamphlet Debate on the Union between Great Britain and Ireland, 1797–1800*. Dublin: Irish Academic Press, 1996.

Morash, Christopher, *A History of Irish Theatre, 1601–2000*. Cambridge: Cambridge University Press, 2002.

Moynahan, Julian T., *Anglo-Irish: The Literary Imagination in a Hyphenated Culture*. Princeton, NJ: Princeton University Press, 1995.

Paulin, Tom, "English Political Writers on Ireland: Robert Southey to Douglas Hurd," in *Critical Approaches to Anglo-Irish Literature*, ed. Michael Allen and Angela Wilcox, 132–145. Gerrards Cross: Colin Smythe, 1989.

Pittock, Murray G. H., *Poetry and Jacobite Politics in Eighteenth-century Britain and Ireland*. Cambridge: Cambridge University Press, 1994.

Ryder, Seán, "Literature in English," in *Nineteenth-century Ireland: A Guide to Recent Research*, ed. Laurence M. Geary and Margaret Kelleher, 118–35. Dublin: University College Dublin Press, 2005.

Tracy, Robert, *The Unappeasable Host: Studies in Irish Identities*. Dublin: University College Dublin Press, 1998.

Trumpener, Katie, *Bardic Nationalism: The Romantic Novel and the British Empire*. Princeton, NJ: Princeton University Press, 1997.

Vance, Norman, *Irish Literature: A Social History: Tradition, Identity, and Difference*. Oxford: Blackwell, 1990.

Wright, Julia M., ed., *Reconsidering the Nineteenth Century*. Special issue of *Canadian Journal of Irish Studies* 30.1 (Spring 2004).

—— " 'National Feeling' and the Colonial Prison: Teeling's *Personal Narrative*," in *Captivating Subjects: Writing Confinement, Citizenship and Nationhood in the Nineteenth Century*, ed. Jason Haslam and Julia M. Wright, 175–98. Toronto: University of Toronto Press, 2005.

—— " 'All the Fire-side Circle': Irish Women Writers and the Sheridan–Lefanu Coterie," *Keats–Shelley Journal* 55 (2006): 63–72.

Selected Further Reading: Some Literary and Historical Contexts

Barnard, F. M., "National Culture and Political Legitimacy: Herder and Rousseau," *Journal of the History of Ideas* 44 (1983): 231–53.

Bhabha, Homi K., *The Location of Culture*. New York: Routledge, 1994.

Canuel, Mark, *Religion, Toleration, and British Writing, 1790–1830*. Cambridge: Cambridge University Press, 2002.

Colley, Linda, *Britons: Forging the Nation, 1707–1837*. New Haven, CT: Yale University Press, 1992.

—— *Captives*. New York: Pantheon Books, 2002.

Crawford, Rachel, *Poetry, Enclosure and the Vernacular Landscape, 1700–1830*. Cambridge: Cambridge University Press, 2002.

Fulford, Tim, *Landscape, Liberty and Authority: Poetry, Criticism and Politics from Thomson to Wordsworth*. Cambridge: Cambridge University Press, 1996.

Gikandi, Simon, *Maps of Englishness: Writing Identity in the Culture of Colonialism*. New York: Columbia University Press, 1996.

Gould, Eliga H. and Onuf, Peter S., eds., *Empire and Nation: The American Revolution in the Atlantic World*. Baltimore, MD: The Johns Hopkins University Press, 2005.

Hooper, Glenn, "The Wasteland: Writing and Resettlement in Post-Famine Ireland," *Canadian Journal of Irish Studies* 23 (1997): 55–76.

Ignatiev, Noel, *How the Irish Became White*. New York: Routledge, 1995.

McClintock, Anne, *Imperial Leather: Race, Gender and Sexuality in the Colonial Contest*. New York: Routledge, 1995.

McGann, Jerome J., *The Poetics of Sensibility: A Revolution in Poetic Style*. Oxford: Clarendon Press, 1996.

Mancke, Elizabeth and Shammas, Carole, eds., *The Creation of the British Atlantic World*. Baltimore, MD: The Johns Hopkins University Press, 2006.

Mansergh, Nicholas, *The Irish Question, 1840–1921*, 3rd edn. Toronto: University of Toronto Press, 1975.

Moran, Gerard P., *Sending Out Ireland's Poor: Assisted Emigration to North America in the Nineteenth Century*. Dublin: Four Courts Press, 2004.

de Nie, Michael, *The Eternal Paddy: Irish Identity and the British Press, 1798–1882*. Madison: University of Wisconsin Press, 2004.

Nixon, Jude V., ed., *Victorian Religious Discourse: New Directions in Criticism*. New York: Palgrave Macmillan, 2004.

Pratt, Mary Louise, *Imperial Eyes: Travel Writing and Transculturation*. New York: Routledge, 1992.

Punter, David, ed., *A Companion to the Gothic*. Oxford: Blackwell, 2000.

Smith, Anthony D., "Neo-Classicist and Romantic Elements in the Emergence of Nationalist Conceptions," in *Nationalist Movements*, ed. Anthony D. Smith, 74–87. London: Macmillan Press, 1976.

Smyth, Jim, ed., *Revolution, Counter-revolution and Union: Ireland in the 1790s*. Cambridge: Cambridge University Press, 2000.

Spivak, Gayatri Chakravorty, "Can the Subaltern Speak?," in *Marxism and the Interpretation of Culture*, ed. Cary Nelson and Larry Grossberg, 271–313. Chicago: University of Illinois Press, 1988.

Summerhill, Thomas and Scott, James C., eds., *Transatlantic Rebels: Agrarian Radicalism in Comparative Context*. East Lansing: Michigan State University Press, 2004.

Todd, Janet, *Sensibility: An Introduction*. New York: Methuen, 1986.

Van Dussen, D. Gregory, "Methodism and Cultural Imperialism in Eighteenth-century Ireland," *Éire–Ireland* 23 (1988): 19–37.

Bibliography

Viswanathan, Gauri, *Outside the Fold: Conversion, Modernity, and Belief.* Princeton, NJ: Princeton University Press, 1998.

Whelan, Kevin, *The Tree of Liberty: Radicalism, Catholicism and the Construction of Irish Identity, 1760–1830.* Notre Dame, IN: Notre Dame University Press, 1996.

White, Hayden, *Metahistory: The Historical Imagination in Nineteenth-century Europe.* Baltimore, MD: The Johns Hopkins University Press, 1973.

Williams, Anne, *Art of Darkness: A Poetics of Gothic.* Chicago: University of Chicago Press, 1995.

Index of Titles and First Lines of Verse

Index to Headnotes and Notes

CPSIA information can be obtained
at www.ICGtesting.com
Printed in the USA
BVHW012210050622
638533BV00011B/2